A·N·N·U·A·L E·D·I·T·I·O·N·S

Early Childhood and Elementary Literacy *05/06*

First Edition

EDITOR

Glenda Moss

Indiana University Purdue University Fort Wayne

Glenda Moss, Assistant Professor of Secondary Education at Indiana University Purdue University Fort Wayne (IPFW) and Associate Director of the Appleseed Writing Project—Indiana, attended East Texas State University (now Texas A & M at commerce, Texas) to earn a B.A. in English and History in 1972 and served as a teaching assistant for three semesters while taking graduate classes in History. In 1974, she received her Texas Teacher Certification from Abilene Christian University. She received her M.Ed. from The University of Texas at Tyler in 1983 and her Professional Administrative Certification in 1996. She taught on the middle school level from 1985 until 1998 at which time she began her doctoral studies in educational leadership. She received her Ed.D. from Stephen F. Austin State University in the summer of 2001 and began teaching at IPFW in the fall of 2001. Glenda has transitioned her pre-service English and Social Studies methods courses to a field-based high school site, where students learn to implement critical reading and content instruction theory into practice.

Terri Jo Swim

Indiana University Purdue University Fort Wayne

Terri Jo Swim, Early Childhood Education Program Coordinator at IPFW, received her B.S. in Early Childhood Education at Purdue University and her doctorate in Child Development and Family Relations from the University of Texas-Austin. She has worked with toddlers through 8th graders in a variety of educational settings, including for-profit childcare centers, university-based laboratory schools, and summer camps for gifted and talented young adolescents. She has over 12 years of experience teaching child development and early childhood education at the undergraduate and graduate levels. Terri received a grant for providing Head Start teachers and administrators with education about emergent literacy when she worked in Ohio.

Denise Jean Cross

Whitney Young Early Childhood Center
Fort Wayne Community Schools

Denise Cross earned her B.S. and M.S. in Elementary Education from IPFW in 1993 and 1997. She holds endorsements in kindergarten and early childhood education. Denise has taught in the Fort Wayne Community School district for the past 12 years in grades preschool to 2nd grade. For the past four years she has helped develop a preschool and kindergarten program at Whitney Young Early Childhood Center. This Reggio Emilia inspired program focuses on the child, parent, and teacher as equal partners with the students leading the curriculum and teachers as action researchers. Active in her district she has written district curriculum, served as her building's Technology Coordinator, Intervention Assistant Team Leader, Quality Improvement Team Member, and mentored first year teachers, student teachers, and practicum students. She has received 3 Reading Is Fundamental grants, which have provided 3000 free books for young children.

Penny Sholl

Hendry Park Elementary
Metropolitan School District of Steuban County

Penny Sholl, a fourth-grade teacher and Teacher Consultant for the Appleseed Writing Project—Indiana, received her B.S. and M.S. in Elementary Education from IPFW. She began her teaching career in Fort Wayne, teaching elementary students with learning disabilities. She then taught pre-schoolers with physical disabilities, and later worked with children who were developmentally delayed. Penny took a ten-year leave from the formal classroom setting to devote time to her own children. She reentered the classroom in Metropolitan School District of Steuben County, where she taught at the kindergarten level nine years and is currently in her fourth year as a fourth-grade teacher. Throughout her career she has specialized in early childhood education and Writer's Workshop. Penny has provided leadership for her school by serving as grade-level chair, writing district curriculum, supervising pre-service teachers, and is a member of the School Improvement Plan Steering Committee and Differentiation Committee.

Ingrid Laidroo

Fort Wayne Community Schools

Ingrid Laidroo, Language Arts Instructional Facilitator at Fort Wayne Community Schools and Technology Liason for the Appleseed Writing Project—Indiana, graduated from IPFW in 1990 with a B.S. in Elementary Education. She has taught fifth grade—English as a Second Language, Reading Recovery—and 1st grade. Ingrid has provided leadership for teachers in her district in the areas of balanced literacy instruction, technology, diversity, and building professional leaning communities.

McGraw-Hill/Dushkin

2460 Kerper Blvd, Dubuque, IA 52001

Visit us on the Internet
http://www.dushkin.com

Credits

1. **Literacy Foundations**
   Unit photo—© Getty Images/Jim Arbogast
2. **Creating a Literacy Culture**
   Unit photo—© Getty Images/David Buffington
3. **Current Theory Guiding Best Practices**
   Unit photo—© Getty Images/Ryan McVay
4. **Implementing Best Practices in the Field**
   Unit photo—© Getty Images/Geostock
5. **Integrated Curriculum**
   Unit photo—© CORBIS/Royalty Free
6. **Critical Teacher Leadership in Literacy Development**
   Unit photo—© Getty Images/SW Productions

Copyright

Cataloging in Publication Data
Main entry under title: Annual Editions: Early Childhood and Elementary Literacy. 2005/2006.
1. Early Childhood and Elementary Literacy—Periodicals. I. Moss, Glenda., comp. II. Title: Early Childhood and Elementary Literacy.
ISBN 0–07–319900–1   658'.05   ISSN 1554–2548

First Edition

Cover image Corbis/Royalty Free/David Buffington/Getty Images.
Printed in the United States of America   1234567890QPDQPD987654   Printed on Recycled Paper

Editors/Advisory Board

Members of the Advisory Board are instrumental in the final selection of articles for each edition of ANNUAL EDITIONS. Their review of articles for content, level, currentness, and appropriateness provides critical direction to the editor and staff. We think that you will find their careful consideration well reflected in this volume.

Preface

In publishing ANNUAL EDITIONS we recognize the enormous role played by the magazines, newspapers, and journals of the public press in providing current, first-rate educational information in a broad spectrum of interest areas. Many of these articles are appropriate for students, researchers, and professionals seeking accurate, current material to help bridge the gap between principles and theories and the real world. These articles, however, become more useful for study when those of lasting value are carefully collected, organized, indexed, and reproduced in a low-cost format, which provides easy and permanent access when the material is needed. That is the role played by ANNUAL EDITIONS.

Literacy development has always been central to early childhood and elementary programs. In 1998 the International Reading Association (IRA) and the National Association for the Education of Young Children (NAEYC) delivered a joint position statement concerning literacy development practices for young children. This position statement is reprinted with permission from the NAEYC and appears as the first article in this annual edition. Stated here are the five reasons given for the joint statement:

- It is essential and urgent to teach children to read and write competently, enabling them to achieve today's high standards of literacy.
- With the increasing variation among young children in our programs and schools, teaching today has become more challenging.
- Among many early childhood teachers, a maturationist view of young children's development persists despite much evidence to the contrary.
- Recognizing the early beginnings of literacy acquisition too often has resulted in use of inappropriate teaching practices suited to older children or adults perhaps, but ineffective with children in preschool, kindergarten, and early grades.
- Current policies and resources are inadequate in ensuring that preschool and primary teachers are qualified to support the literacy development of all children, a task requiring strong pre-service preparation and ongoing professional development.

In 2001 the No Child Left Behind Act (NCLB) outlined a narrow focus of literacy development to five components: phonemic awareness, phonics, vocabulary, fluency, and comprehension. The second article in this annual edition examines the requirements of NCLB, considers how educators can address the requirements, and frames the complexity of literacy development under the restrictions created by federally approved reading programs. While the five components outlined in the NCLB are addressed in multiple articles in this annual edition, educators will find many more articles will go far beyond basic reading skills and address the development of children as individuals contextualized by home language and culture, local community norms, school policies and practices, state standards and accountability testing, as well as social and economic conditions that advantage some and disadvantage others.

I am all too familiar with the continuing complexity of literacy development for every generation. I remember my early experiences learning to read nearly a half a century ago. After two years in second-grade, I was promoted even though I was below level and close to the bottom of my class. I remember parenting children as they learned to read at home and school nearly a quarter of a century ago. Determined to not let them get behind and experience the frustration and embarrassment that I experienced throughout elementary and middle school, I made some of the same mistakes my parents and teachers made of using "inappropriate teaching practices suited to older children or adults perhaps but ineffective with children in preschool, kindergarten, and early grades." I simply started earlier and did more of what had not worked with me.

I was not sure how to answer my son, a fourth-grade teacher in a large urban school, when he called during his first week of teaching two years ago and asked, "Mom, I can teach children to read even if I have to use a packaged program, can't I?" His teacher educator in an alternative certification program had stated to his class that none of them should accept jobs in schools where they were required to use federally mandated reading programs. My son had transitioned to teaching because he specifically wanted to work in an urban school setting following 9-11. I responded to my son, "Yes, you can teach your children to read using whatever curriculum your district mandates," and he did. He learned as most teachers do, to use strategies that promote a love for reading and to supplement the adopted program with a classroom full of literature. Hitting every used bookstore and thrift shop in town, and garage sales on the weekend, my son had 1000 books in his classroom by Christmas. Before his second year, he had built a reading loft with shelves for books and a fish tank. He is still learning how to teach reading, but just as important if not more so, he reads to his children regularly, makes sure they are never lacking in a book to read at home, reads professional literature, and attends professional development in the area of reading.

In approaching the preparation of this annual edition, I sought the expertise of four other professional educators: early childhood teacher educator, early childhood classroom teacher, fourth-grade teacher, and a language arts instructional facilitator. The editors of this annual edition are committed to upholding and supporting the joint statement of the IRA and NAEYC by pulling together a collection of articles from current research that addresses developmentally appropriate practices for teaching young children to read and write within the social setting we call "school." Keeping in mind the very reasons that prompted the two organizations to issue a joint statement, we hope that the articles in this annual edition will contribute to the professional development of classroom teachers and pre-service teachers.

Glenda Moss

Editor

Contents

UNIT 1
Literacy Foundations

The concepts in bold italics are developed in the article. For further expansion, please refer to the Topic Guide and the Index.

UNIT 2
Creating a Literacy Culture

The concepts in bold italics are developed in the article. For further expansion, please refer to the Topic Guide and the Index.

UNIT 3
Current Theory Guiding Best Practices

The concepts in bold italics are developed in the article. For further expansion, please refer to the Topic Guide and the Index.

UNIT 4
Implementing Best Practices in the Field

The concepts in bold italics are developed in the article. For further expansion, please refer to the Topic Guide and the Index.

UNIT 5
Integrated Curriculum

The concepts in bold italics are developed in the article. For further expansion, please refer to the Topic Guide and the Index.

The concepts in bold italics are developed in the article. For further expansion, please refer to the Topic Guide and the Index.

UNIT 6
Critical Teacher Leadership in Literacy Development

The concepts in bold italics are developed in the article. For further expansion, please refer to the Topic Guide and the Index.

The concepts in bold italics are developed in the article. For further expansion, please refer to the Topic Guide and the Index.

Topic Guide

This topic guide suggests how the selections in this book relate to the subjects covered in your course. You may want to use the topics listed on these pages to search the Web more easily.

On the following pages a number of Web sites have been gathered specifically for this book. They are arranged to reflect the units of this *Annual Edition.* You can link to these sites by going to the DUSHKIN ONLINE support site at *http://www.dushkin.com/online/.*

ALL THE ARTICLES THAT RELATE TO EACH TOPIC ARE LISTED BELOW THE BOLD-FACED TERM.

World Wide Web Sites

The following World Wide Web sites have been carefully researched and selected to support the articles found in this reader. The easiest way to access these selected sites is to go to our DUSHKIN ONLINE support site at *http://www.dushkin.com/online/*.

AE: Early Childhood and Elementary Literacy 05/06

The following sites were available at the time of publication. Visit our Web site—we update DUSHKIN ONLINE regularly to reflect any changes.

General Sources

Children's Defense Fund (CDF)
http://www.childrensdefense.org
At this site of the CDF, an organization that seeks to ensure that every child is treated fairly, there are reports and resources regarding current issues facing today's youth, along with national statistics on various subjects.

National Association for the Education of Young Children
http://www.naeyc.org
The NAEYC Web site is a valuable tool for anyone working with young children. Also see the National Education Association site: *http://www.nea.org.*

U.S. Department of Education
http://www.ed.gov/pubs/TeachersGuide/
Government goals, projects, grants, and other educational programs are listed here as well as many links to teacher services and resources.

UNIT 1: Literacy Foundations

The National Center for Family Literacy
http://www.famlit.org/index.cfm
This site provides resources for parents and educators to help provide students with the literacy support they need.

The National Association of State Boards of Education
http://www.nasbe.org/
Included on this site is an extensive overview of the No Child Left Behind Act. There are links to specific state's plans.

UNIT 2: Creating a Literacy Culture

National Literacy Trust
http://www.literacytrust.org.uk/index.html
This site provides current ideas and practices as well as many other resources to building a literate nation.

UNIT 3: Current Theory Guiding Best Practices

Center for Academic and Reading Skills
http://cars.uth.tmc.edu/debate/understand.shtml
This site brings some light to the debate over phonics versus whole language.

UNIT 4: Implementing Best Practices in the Field

Teaching Strategies
http://www.teachingstrategies.com
Teaching Strategies is a site which provides practical, innovative, and developmentally appropriate curriculum materials, training services, training material, and parenting resources.

UNIT 5: Integrated Curriculum

California Reading Initiative
http://www.sdcoe.k12.ca.us/score/promising/prreading/prreadin.html
The California Reading Initiative site provides valuable insight into topics related to emergent literacy. Many resources for teachers and staff developers are provided.

Early Childhood Education Online
http://www.umaine.edu/eceol/
This site gives information on developmental guidelines and issues in the field, presents tips for observation and assessment, and gives information on advocacy.

International Reading Association
http://www.reading.org
This organization for professionals who are interested in literacy contains information about the reading process and assists teachers in dealing with literacy issues.

Reggio Emilia
http://www.ericdigests.org/2001-3/reggio.htm
Through ERIC, link to publications related to the Reggio Emilia approach and to resources, videos, and contact information.

UNIT 6: Critical Teacher Leadership in Literacy Development

Teacher Quick Source
http://www.teacherquicksource.com
Originally designed to help Head Start teachers meet the child outcomes, this site can be useful to all preschool teachers. Domains can be linked to developmentally appropriate activities for classroom use.

Teachers Helping Teachers
http://www.pacificnet.net/~mandel/
Basic teaching tips, new teaching methodologies, and forums for teachers to share experiences are provided on this site. Download software and participate in chats. It features educational resources on the Web, with new ones added each week.

www.dushkin.com/online/

Awesome Library for Teachers
http://www.neat-schoolhouse.org/teacher.html
   Open this page for links and access to teacher information on
   everything from educational assessment to general child
   development topics.

**Prospects: The Congressionally Mandated Study of
Educational Growth and Opportunity**
http://www.ed.gov/pubs/Prospects/index.html
   This report analyzes cross-sectional data on language-minority
   and LEP students and outlines what actions are needed to
   improve their educational performance. Family and economic
   situations are addressed plus information on related reports and
   sites.

We highly recommend that you review our Web site for expanded information and our
other product lines. We are continually updating and adding links to our Web site in order
to offer you the most usable and useful information that will support and expand the value
of your Annual Editions. You can reach us at: *http://www.dushkin.com/annualeditions/*.

UNIT 1
Literacy Foundations

Unit Selections

1. **Learning to Read and Write: Developmentally Appropriate Practices for Young Children**, National Association for the Education of Young Children
2. **Early Literacy Instruction in the Climate of No Child Left Behind**, Margaret Taylor Stewart
3. **Literacy, Learning, and Libraries: Common Issues and Common Concerns**, Ken Haycock
4. **Public Libraries and Early Literacy: Raising a Reader**, Renea Arnold
5. **"The Best Way is Always Through the Children": The Impact of Family Reading**, Sarah J. McNicol and Pete Dalton
6. **Enhancing Phonological Awareness, Print Awareness, and Oral Language Skills in Preschool Children**, Paige C. Pullen and Laura M. Justice
7. **Parent Involvement in Children's Acquisition of Reading**, Sharon Darling and Laura Westberg
8. **Beyond Shared Book Reading: Dimensions of Home Literacy and Low-Income African American Preschoolers' Skills**, Pia Rebello Britto and Jeanne Brooks-Gunn

Key Points to Consider

- What environmental factors impact acquisition of emergent and conventional literacy skills?

- Should families be expected to "prepare" children for school by intentionally teaching their children how to read and write?

- What assistance should be provided to families to create home environments where literacy is a salient feature?

- How should early childhood and elementary programs develop meaningful partnerships with families to promote literacy?

- What role should libraries and librarians play in promoting and supporting literacy development for members of their communities?

 **Links: www.dushkin.com/online/**
These sites are annotated in the World Wide Web pages.

The National Center for Family Literacy
http://www.famlit.org/index.cfm

The National Association of State Boards of Education
http://www.nasbe.org/

Even before birth, the first seeds of literacy are planted as a growing fetus hears the sounds of its uterine environment and those of the outside world—the rhythm of its mother's heartbeat, her voice and conversations, music, and a myriad of other sensory stimuli. When a baby is born, she will turn her head when she hears her mother's voice and look at her with knowing eyes, that yes, this is my mother, I have heard her voice many times.

As the infant grows and develops his/her repertoire of sounds and noises, communication begins. Consider the following examples of how very young children use language and literacy to make sense of their world.

- Penny listens to her eight-month-old niece jawing away with a rather angry edge to her voice as she sits in her highchair. A couple of minutes of that irritating tone is all it takes for Penny to lift Faith from the chair. Immediately, Faith begins bouncing and laughing and smiling delightedly.
- A fourteen-month-old toddler, Adriana, is sitting on the floor in front of a bookshelf with books scattered all around her. She picks up a chunky book, smiles, opens the first page, and begins to babble. She vocalizes as she looks at each page, turning from the front to the back of the book.
- A preschooler, Randy, is sitting at the kitchen table crying. He wants an ice cream sandwich for a snack, but he has already eaten one today. His father, Danny, is trying to explain the reason behind saying no, when the child says, "Let's write a note." Danny asks "What should we write?" while locating paper and pencil. Randy replies, "Tell Mom

that I can have an ice cream sandwich for a snack after lunch tomorrow." The note is posted on the freezer and Randy wipes away his tears.
- Terri observes a small group of children enjoying story hour at the library. They are making up a silly rhyming song. The librarian sings different phrases then pauses for the children to add rhyming words. As the song is finished, the librarian asks the children to remember their song so they can compare it to the upcoming story.

Clearly these children possess a vast array of knowledge about literacy. As infants and toddlers, they already know that communication is pleasurable; when you read, you say words; and pages are turned from front to back. As preschoolers, they are aware of the power of words to inform another of a personal need and how to play with sounds to make rhyming words. How might they have acquired this knowledge at such a young age? What should a classroom teacher do for these children and others like them to assist in the further development of literacy skills and knowledge? This Unit contains information about how families, schools, libraries and national standards impact children's movement along the literacy pathway.

The progression to conventional reading and writing is a long and bumpy road with steps forward and backwards. In the past, it was naively believed by many teachers and researchers that learning to read and write began when children received formal instruction in kindergarten. Current research, included in this section, provides evidence that very young children acquire important language and literacy skills that assist with the construction and reconstruction of conventional literacy skills. The first article in this section refers to the joint position statement created by IRA and NAEYC (1998) which describes the typical paths towards literacy and environmental influences on that development for young children.

Taking an ecological theory perspective (i.e., Bronfenbrenner, 1979, 1989) on literacy development assists with understanding how adults, peers, and institutions effect literacy development. This theory proposes that a child's development is influenced by the natural environments—such as immediate and extended families, childcare centers, community services, and political practices—experienced by the child. These nested spheres influence all areas of development, including language and literacy.

As observed, literacy development begins at birth as infants engage in relationships with those around them. Through these relationships, infants acquire speaking skills that begin them on the road to literacy. However, children are by no means passive recipients of their environments. Of course, a critical question to examine is how much should families *intentionally teach* about literacy? Research clearly demonstrates that families differ in how *salient* literacy is in the environment (see, for example, Rebello Britto & Brooks-Gunn, 2001). Some families, like Randy's, read frequently to their child and engage in literacy activities to accomplish daily tasks, such as writing messages. Children whose families do not demonstrate this importance may become at-risk for language, literacy, and academic difficulties when they enter school.

Accordingly, children arrive at educational settings with very different skill levels and experiences from which to build future skills. How does a teacher respond to these variations in a way that respects and honors the children's prior knowledge? Following guidelines for best practices, early childhood educators know the importance of continuously and carefully observing, assessing, and planning responsive, individualized curriculum that supports each child's home environment. Pullen and Justice (2003) and others are included because they provide important information about how teachers can assume an active role in children's literacy development. Effective teachers also realize that they must create partnerships with community agencies and families to support literacy development.

Moving beyond the school walls to another sphere of influence demonstrates how community resources can provide a context for literacy development. Libraries, via librarians, assist children with learning about rhyming words, concepts about print, and a love of reading. Currently, the national focus on literacy has called into question the specific role of libraries and librarians in facilitating literacy development. Should librarians be responsible for teaching childcare providers more effective ways for creating quality literacy experiences (Arnold, 2003)? According to the article, "Literacy, Learning, and Libraries: Common Issues and Common Concerns," a transformation of the role of libraries is warranted because stronger partnerships are related to greater student achievement.

The current political climate in the United States, fueled by No Child Left Behind, provides evidence of how national policies, designed to raise student achievement, can directly impact the daily lives of children, and, thus, the development of young children. Bronfenbrenner proposed that spheres of influence which are farther removed from the child typically have less impact than those more proximal. Nonetheless, we are currently experiencing the reverse.

No Child Left Behind is drastically changing the literacy climates in classrooms and thus the literacy experiences of young children. This law was based on the report produced by the National Reading Panel who closely examined experimental studies. Their conclusions stand in stark contrast to the vast array of "scientifically based, rigorous, and pertinent" (Taylor Stewart, 2004) research on the roles families, teachers, and communities play in literacy development. Teachers now face a complex challenge of resolving the contradictions in the literature. Narrowing instruction to a limited number of isolated skills may address the law's requirements, but it is arguable whether this will facilitate optimal literacy development.

While this overview was written to reflect the theoretical influence of the various spheres of influence, the articles are arranged according to the current context in which teachers find themselves.

Terri Jo Swim and Penny Sholl

References

Bronfenbrenner, U. (1989). Ecological systems theory. In R. Vasta (Ed.), *Annals of child development* (Vol. 6, pp.187-251). Greenwich, CT: JAI Press.

Bronfenbrenner, U. (1979). *The ecology of human development: Experiments by nature and design.* Cambridge, MA: Harvard University Press.

Learning to Read and Write: Developmentally Appropriate Practices for Young Children

A joint position of the International Reading Association *and the National Association for the Education of Young Children*

Adopted May 1998

This joint NAEYC/IRA position statement is endorsed by the following organizations: American Speech-Language-Hearing Association, Association for Childhood Education International, Association of Teacher Educators, Council for Early Childhood Professional Recognition, Division for Early Childhood/Council for Exceptional Children, National Association of Early Childhood Specialists in State Departments of Education, National Association of Early Childhood Teacher Educators, National Association of Elementary School Principals, National Association of State Directors of Special Education, National Council of Teachers of English, Zero to Three/National Center for Infants, Toddlers, & Families.

The concepts in this joint position statement are supported by the following organizations: American Academy of Pediatrics, American Association of School Administrators, American Educational Research Association, and the National Head Start Association.

Learning to read and write is critical to a child's success in school and later in life. One of the best predictors of whether a child will function competently in school and go on to contribute actively in our increasingly literate society is the level to which the child progresses in reading and writing. Although reading and writing abilities continue to develop throughout the life span, the early childhood years—from birth through age eight—are the most important period for literacy development. It is for this reason that the International Reading Association (IRA) and the National Association for the Education of Young Children (NAEYC) joined together to formulate a position statement regarding early literacy development. The statement consists of a set of principles and recommendations for teaching practices and public policy.

The primary purpose of this position statement is to provide guidance to teachers of young children in schools and early childhood programs (including child care centers, preschools, and family child care homes) serving children from birth through age eight. By and large, the principles and practices suggested here also will be of interest to any adults who are in a position to influence a young child's learning and development—parents, grandparents, older siblings, tutors, and other community members.

Teachers work in schools or programs regulated by administrative policies as well as available resources. Therefore secondary audiences for this position statement are school principals and program administrators whose roles are critical in establishing a supportive climate for sound, developmentally appropriate teaching practices; and policymakers whose decisions determine whether adequate resources are available for high-quality early childhood education.

A great deal is known about how young children learn to read and write and how they can be helped toward literacy during the first five years of life. A great deal is known also about how to help children once compulsory schooling begins, whether in kindergarten or the primary grades. Based on a thorough review of the research, this document reflects the commitment of two major professional organizations to the goal of helping children learn to read well enough by the end of third grade so that they can read to learn in all curriculum areas. IRA and NAEYC are committed not only to helping young children learn to read and write but also to fostering and sustaining their interest and disposition to read and write for their own enjoyment, information, and communication.

First, the statement summarizes the current issues that are the impetus for this position; then it reviews what is known from research on young children's literacy development. This review of research as well as the collective wisdom and experience of IRA and NAEYC members provides the basis for a position statement about what constitutes developmentally appropriate practice in early literacy over the period of birth through age eight. The position concludes with recommendations for teaching practices and policies.

Statement of the issues

Why take a position on something as obviously important as children's learning to read and write? The IRA and NAEYC believe that this position statement will contribute significantly to an improvement in practice and the development of supportive educational policies. The two associations saw that a clear, concise position statement was needed at this time for several reasons.

- **It is essential and urgent to teach children to read and write competently, enabling them to achieve today's high standards of literacy.**

Although the United States enjoys the highest literacy rate in its history, society now expects virtually everyone in the population to function beyond the minimum standards of literacy. Today the definition of *basic proficiency* in literacy calls for a fairly high standard of reading comprehension and analysis. The main reason is that literacy requirements of most jobs have increased significantly and are expected to increase further in the future. Communications that in the past were verbal (by phone or in person) now demand reading and writing—messages sent by electronic mail, Internet, or facsimile as well as print documents.

- **With the increasing variation among young children in our programs and schools, teaching today has become more challenging.**

Experienced teachers throughout the United States report that the children they teach today are more diverse in their backgrounds, experiences, and abilities than were those they taught in the past. Kindergarten classes now include children who have been in group settings for three or four years as well as children who are participating for the first time in an organized early childhood program. Classes include both children with identified disabilities and children with exceptional abilities, children who are already independent readers and children who are just beginning to acquire some basic literacy knowledge and skills. Children in the group may speak different languages at varying levels of proficiency. Because of these individual and experiential variations, it is common to find within a kindergarten classroom a five-year range in children's literacy-related skills and functioning (Riley 1996). What this means is that some kindergartners may have skills characteristic of the typical three-year-old, while others might be functioning at the level of the typical eight-year-old. Diversity is to be expected and embraced, but it can be overwhelming when teachers are expected to produce uniform outcomes for all, with no account taken of the initial range in abilities, experiences, interests, and personalities of individual children.

- **Among many early childhood teachers, a maturationist view of young children's development persists despite much evidence to the contrary.**

A readiness view of reading development assumes that there is a specific time in the early childhood years when the teaching of reading should begin. It also assumes that physical and neurological maturation alone prepare the child to take advantage of instruction in reading and writing. The readiness perspective implies that until children reach a certain stage of maturity all

exposure to reading and writing, except perhaps being read stories, is a waste of time or even potentially harmful. Experiences throughout the early childhood years, birth through age eight, affect the development of literacy. These experiences constantly interact with characteristics of individual children to determine the level of literacy skills a child ultimately achieves. Failing to give children literacy experiences until they are school age can severely limit the reading and writing levels they ultimately attain.

- **Recognizing the early beginnings of literacy acquisition too often has resulted in use of inappropriate teaching practices suited to older children or adults perhaps but ineffective with children in preschool, kindergarten, and the early grades.**

Teaching practices associated with outdated views of literacy development and/or learning theories are still prevalent in many classrooms. Such practices include extensive whole-group instruction and intensive drill and practice on isolated skills for groups or individuals. These practices, not particularly effective for primary-grade children, are even less suitable and effective with preschool and kindergarten children. Young children especially need to be engaged in experiences that make academic content meaningful and build on prior learning. It is vital for all children to have literacy experiences in schools and early childhood programs. Such access is even more critical for children with limited home experiences in literacy. However, these school experiences must teach the broad range of language and literacy knowledge and skills to provide the solid foundation on which high levels of reading and writing ultimately depend.

- **Current policies and resources are inadequate in ensuring that preschool and primary teachers are qualified to support the literacy development of all children, a task requiring strong preservice preparation and ongoing professional development.**

For teachers of children younger than kindergarten age in the United States, no uniform preparation requirements or licensure standards exist. In fact, a high school diploma is the highest level of education required to be a child care teacher in most states. Moreover, salaries in child care and preschool programs are too low to attract or retain better qualified staff. Even in the primary grades, for which certified teachers are required, many states do not offer specialized early childhood certification, which means many teachers are not adequately prepared to teach reading and writing to young children. All teachers of young children need good, foundational knowledge in language acquisition, including second-language learning, the processes of reading and writing, early literacy development, and experiences and teaching practices contributing to optimal development. Resources also are insufficient to ensure teachers continuing access to professional education so they can remain current in the field or can prepare to teach a different age group if they are reassigned.

What research reveals: Rationale for the position statement

Children take their first critical steps toward learning to read and write very early in life. Long before they can exhibit reading and writing production skills, they begin to acquire some basic understandings of the concepts about literacy and its functions. Children learn to use symbols, combining their oral language, pictures, print, and play into a coherent mixed medium and creating and communicating meanings in a variety of ways. From their initial experiences and interactions with adults, children begin to read words, processing letter-sound relations and acquiring substantial knowledge of the alphabetic system. As they continue to learn, children increasingly consolidate this information into patterns that allow for automaticity and fluency in reading and writing. Consequently reading and writing acquisition is conceptualized better as a developmental continuum than as an all-or-nothing phenomenon (see part 4).

But the ability to read and write does not develop naturally, without careful planning and instruction. Children need regular and active interactions with print. Specific abilities required for reading and writing come from immediate experiences with oral and written language. Experiences in these early years begin to define the assumptions and expectations about becoming literate and give children the motivation to work toward learning to read and write. From these experiences children learn that reading and writing are valuable tools that will help them do many things in life.

The beginning years (birth through preschool)

Even in the first few months of life, children begin to experiment with language. Young babies make sounds that imitate the tones and rhythms of adult talk; they "read" gestures and facial expressions, and they begin to associate sound sequences frequently heard—words—with their referents (Berk 1996). They delight in listening to familiar jingles and rhymes, play along in games such as peek-a-boo and pat-a-cake, and manipulate objects such as board books and alphabet blocks in their play. From these remarkable beginnings children learn to use a variety of symbols.

In the midst of gaining facility with these symbol systems, children acquire through interactions with others the insight that specific kinds of marks—print—also can represent meanings. At first children will use the physical and visual cues surrounding print to determine what something says. But as they develop an understanding of the alphabetic principle, children begin to process letters, translate them into sounds, and connect this information with a known meaning. Although it may seem as though some children acquire these understandings magically or on their own, studies suggest that they are the beneficiaries of considerable, though playful and informal, adult guidance and instruction (Durkin 1966; Anbar 1986).

Considerable diversity in children's oral and written language experiences occurs in these years (Hart & Risley 1995). In home and child care situations, children encounter many different resources and types and degrees of support for early reading and writing (McGill-Franzen & Lanford 1994). Some children may have ready access to a range of writing and reading materials, while others may not; some children will observe their parents writing and reading frequently, others only occasionally; some children receive direct instruction, while others receive much more casual, informal assistance.

What this means is that no one teaching method or approach is likely to be the most effective for all children (Strickland 1994). Rather, good teachers bring into play a variety of teaching strategies that can encompass the great diversity of children in schools. Excellent instruction builds on what children already know, and can do, and provides knowledge, skills, and dispositions for lifelong learning. Children need to learn not only the technical skills of reading and writing but also how to use these tools to better their thinking and reasoning (Neuman 1998).

The single most important activity for building these understandings and skills essential for reading success appears to be **reading aloud to children** (Wells 1985; Bus, Van Ijzendoorn, & Pellegrini 1995). High-quality book reading occurs when children feel emotionally secure (Bus & Van Ijzendoorn 1995; Bus et al. 1997) and are active participants in reading (Whitehurst et al. 1994). Asking predictive and analytic questions in small-group settings appears to affect children's vocabulary and comprehension of stories (Karweit & Wasik 1996). Children may talk about the pictures, retell the story, discuss their favorite actions, and request multiple rereadings. It is the talk that surrounds the storybook reading that gives it power, helping children to bridge what is in the story and their own lives (Dickinson & Smith 1994; Snow et al. 1995). Snow (1991) has described these types of conversations as "decontextualized language" in which teachers may induce higher-level thinking by moving experiences in stories from what the children may see in front of them to what they can imagine.

A central goal during these preschool years is to enhance children's **exposure to and concepts about print** (Clay 1979, 1991; Holdaway 1979; Teale 1984; Stanovich & West 1989). Some teachers use Big Books to help children distinguish many print features, including the fact that print (rather than pictures) carries the meaning of the story, that the strings of letters between spaces are words and in print correspond to an oral version, and that reading progresses from left to right and top to bottom. In the course of reading stories, teachers may demonstrate these features by pointing to individual words, directing children's attention to where to begin reading, and helping children to recognize letter shapes and sounds. Some researchers (Adams 1990; Roberts 1998) have suggested that the key to these critical concepts, such as developing word awareness, may lie in these demonstrations of how print works.

Children also need opportunity to practice what they've learned about print with their peers and on their own. Studies suggest that the physical arrangement of the classroom can promote time with books (Morrow & Weinstein 1986; Neuman & Roskos 1997). A key area is the classroom library—a collection of attractive stories and informational books that provides children with immediate access to books. Regular visits to the school or public library and library card registration ensure that children's collections remain continually updated and may help children develop the habit of reading as lifelong learning. In comfortable library settings children often will pretend to read, using visual cues to remember the words of their favorite stories. Although studies have shown that these pretend readings are just that (Ehri & Sweet 1991), such visual readings may demonstrate substantial knowledge about the global features of reading and its purposes.

Storybooks are not the only means of providing children with exposure to written language. Children learn a lot about reading from the labels, signs, and other kinds of print they see around them (McGee, Lomax, & Head 1988; Neuman & Roskos 1993). Highly visible print labels on objects, signs, and bulletin boards in classrooms demonstrate the practical uses of written language. In environments rich with print, children incorporate literacy into their dramatic play (Morrow 1990; Vukelich 1994; Neuman & Roskos 1997), using these communication tools to enhance the drama and realism of the pretend situation. These everyday, playful experiences by themselves do not make most children readers. Rather they expose children to a variety of print experiences and the processes of reading for real purposes.

For children whose primary language is other than English, studies have shown that a strong basis in a first language promotes school achievement in a second language (Cummins 1979). Children who are **learning English as a second language** are more likely to become readers and writers of English when they are already familiar with the vocabulary and concepts in their primary language. In this respect, oral and written language experiences should be regarded as an additive process, ensuring that children are able to maintain their home language while also learning to speak and read English (Wong Fillmore, 1991). Including non-English materials and resources to the extent possible can help to support children's first language while children acquire oral proficiency in English.

A fundamental insight developed in children's early years through instruction is the **alphabetic principle**, the understanding that there is a systematic relationship between letters and sounds (Adams 1990). The research of Gibson and Levin (1975) indicates that the shapes of letters are learned by distinguishing one character from another by its type of spatial features. Teachers will often involve children in comparing letter shapes, helping them to differentiate a number of letters visually. Alphabet books and alphabet puzzles in which children can see and compare letters may be a key to efficient and easy learning.

At the same time children learn about the sounds of language through exposure to **linguistic awareness** games, nursery rhymes, and rhythmic activities. Some research suggests that the roots of phonemic awareness, a powerful predictor of later reading success, are found in traditional rhyming, skipping, and word games (Bryant et al. 1990). In one study, for example (Maclean, Bryant, & Bradley 1987), researchers found that three-year-old children's knowledge of nursery rhymes specifically related to their more abstract phonological knowledge later on. Engaging children in choral readings of rhymes and rhythms allows them to associate the symbols with the sounds they hear in these words.

Although children's facility in **phonemic awareness** has been shown to be strongly related to later reading achievement, the precise role it plays in these early years is not fully understood. Phonemic awareness refers to a child's understanding and conscious awareness that speech is composed of identifiable units, such as spoken words, syllables, and sounds. Training studies have demonstrated that phonemic awareness can be taught to children as young as age five (Bradley & Bryant 1983; Lundberg, Frost, & Petersen 1988; Cunningham 1990; Bryne & Fielding-Barnsley 1991). These studies used tiles (boxes) (Elkonin 1973) and linguistic games to engage children in explicitly manipulating speech segments at the phoneme level. Yet, whether such training is appropriate for younger-age children is highly suspect. Other scholars find that children benefit most from such training only after they have learned some letter names, shapes, and sounds and can apply what they learn to real reading in meaningful contexts (Cunningham 1990; Foorman et al. 1991). Even at this later age, however, many children acquire phonemic awareness skills without specific training but as a consequence of learning to read (Wagner & Torgesen 1987; Ehri 1994). In the preschool years sensitizing children to sound similarities does not seem to be strongly dependent on formal training but rather from listening to patterned, predictable texts while enjoying the feel of reading and language.

Children acquire a working knowledge of the alphabetic system not only through reading but also through writing. A classic study by Read (1971) found that even without formal spelling instruction, preschoolers use their tacit knowledge of phonological relations to spell words. **Invented spelling** (or phonic spelling) refers to beginners' use of the symbols they associate with the sounds they hear in the words they wish to write. For example, a child may initially write *b* or *bk* for the word *bike*, to be followed by more conventionalized forms later on.

Some educators may wonder whether invented spelling promotes poor spelling habits. To the contrary, studies suggest that *temporary* invented spelling may contribute to beginning reading (Chomsky 1979; Clarke 1988). One study, for example, found that children benefited from using invented spelling compared to having the teacher provide correct spellings in writing (Clarke 1988). Although children's invented spellings did not comply with correct spellings, the process encouraged them to think actively about letter-sound relations. As children engage in writing, they are learning to segment the words they wish to spell into constituent sounds.

Classrooms that provide children with regular opportunities to express themselves on paper, without feeling too constrained for correct spelling and proper handwriting, also help children understand that writing has real purpose (Graves 1983; Sulzby 1985; Dyson 1988). Teachers can organize situations that both demonstrate the writing process and get children actively involved in it. Some teachers serve as scribes and help children write down their ideas, keeping in mind the balance between children doing it themselves and asking for help. In the beginning these products likely emphasize pictures with few attempts at writing letters or words. With encouragement, children begin to label their pictures, tell stories, and attempt to write stories about the pictures they have drawn. Such novice writing activity sends the important message that writing is not just handwriting practice—children are using their own words to compose a message to communicate with others.

Thus the picture that emerges from research in these first years of children's reading and writing is one that emphasizes wide exposure to print and to developing concepts about it and its forms and functions. Classrooms filled with print, language and literacy play, storybook reading, and writing allow children to experience the joy and power associated with reading and writing while mastering basic concepts about print that research has shown are strong predictors of achievement.

In kindergarten

Knowledge of the forms and functions of print serves as a foundation from which children become increasingly sensitive to letter shapes, names, sounds, and words. However, not all children typically come to kindergarten with similar levels of knowledge about printed language. Estimating where each child is developmentally and building on that base, a key feature of all good teaching, is particularly important for the kindergarten teacher. Instruction will need to be adapted to account for children's differences. For those children with lots of print experiences, instruction will extend their knowledge as they learn more about the formal features of letters and their sound correspondences. For other children with fewer prior experiences, initiating them to the alphabetic principle, that a limited set of letters comprises the alphabet and that these letters stand for the sounds that make up spoken words, will require more focused and direct instruction. In all cases, however, children need to interact with a rich variety of print (Morrow, Strickland, & Woo 1998).

In this critical year kindergarten teachers need to capitalize on every opportunity for enhancing children's **vocabulary development.** One approach is through listening to stories (Feitelson, Kita, & Goldstein 1986; Elley 1989). Children need to be exposed to vocabulary from a wide variety of genres, including informational texts as well as narratives. The learning of vocabulary, however, is not necessarily simply a byproduct of reading stories (Leung & Pikulski 1990). Some explanation of vocabulary words prior to listening to a story is related significantly to children's learning of new words (Elley 1989). Dickinson and Smith (1994), for example, found that asking predictive and analytic questions before and after the readings produced positive effects on vocabulary and comprehension.

Repeated readings appear to further reinforce the language of the text as well as to familiarize children with the way different genres are structured (Eller, Pappas, & Brown 1988; Morrow 1988). Understanding the forms of informational and narrative texts seems to distinguish those children who have been well read to from those who have not (Pappas 1991). In one study, for example, Pappas found that with multiple exposures to a story (three readings), children's retelling became increasingly rich, integrating what they knew about the world, the language of the book, and the message of the author. Thus, considering the benefits for vocabulary development and compre-

hension, the case is strong for interactive storybook reading (Anderson 1995). Increasing the volume of children's playful, stimulating experiences with good books is associated with accelerated growth in reading competence.

Activities that help children clarify the **concept of word** are also worthy of time and attention in the kindergarten curriculum (Juel 1991). Language experience charts that let teachers demonstrate how talk can be written down provide a natural medium for children's developing word awareness in meaningful contexts. Transposing children's spoken words into written symbols through dictation provides a concrete demonstration that strings of letters between spaces are words and that not all words are the same length. Studies by Clay (1979) and Bissex (1980) confirm the value of what many teachers have known and done for years: Teacher dictations of children's stories help develop word awareness, spelling, and the conventions of written language.

Many children enter kindergarten with at least some perfunctory knowledge of the alphabet letters. An important goal for the kindergarten teacher is to reinforce this skill by ensuring that children can recognize and discriminate these letter shapes with increasing ease and fluency (Mason 1980; Snow, Burns, & Griffin 1998). Children's proficiency in **letter naming** is a well-established predictor of their end-of-year achievement (Bond & Dykstra 1967, Riley 1996), probably because it mediates the ability to remember sounds. Generally a good rule according to current learning theory (Adams 1990) is to start with the more easily visualized uppercase letters, to be followed by identifying lowercase letters. In each case, introducing just a few letters at a time, rather than many, enhances mastery.

At about the time children are readily able to identify letter names, they begin to connect the letters with the sounds they hear. A fundamental insight in this phase of learning is that a letter and letter sequences map onto phonological forms. Phonemic awareness, however, is not merely a solitary insight or an instant ability (Juel 1991). It takes time and practice.

Children who are phonemically aware can think about and manipulate sounds in words. They know when words rhyme or do not; they know when words begin or end with the same sound; and they know that a word like *bat* is composed of three sounds /b/ /a/ /t/ and that these sounds can be blended into a spoken word. Popular rhyming books, for example, may draw children's attention to rhyming patterns, serving as a basis for extending vocabulary (Ehri & Robbins 1992). Using initial letter cues, children can learn many new words through analogy, taking the familiar word *bake* as a strategy for figuring out a new word, *lake*.

Further, as teachers engage children in shared writing, they can pause before writing a word, say it slowly, and stretch out the sounds as they write it. Such activities in the context of real reading and writing help children attend to the features of print and the alphabetic nature of English.

There is accumulated evidence that instructing children in phonemic awareness activities in kindergarten (and first grade) enhances reading achievement (Stanovich 1986; Lundberg, Frost, & Petersen 1988; Bryne & Fielding-Barnsley 1991, 1993, 1995). Although a large number of children will acquire phonemic awareness skills as they learn to read, an estimated 20%

will not without additional training. A statement by the IRA (1998) indicates that "the likelihood of these students becoming successful as readers is slim to none.… This figure [20%], however, can be substantially reduced through more systematic attention to engagement with language early on in the child's home, preschool and kindergarten classes." A study by Hanson and Farrell (1995), for example, examined the long-term benefits of a carefully developed kindergarten curriculum that focused on word study and decoding skills, along with sets of stories so that children would be able to practice these skills in meaningful contexts. High school seniors who early on had received this type of instruction outperformed their counterparts on reading achievement, attitude toward schooling, grades, and attendance.

In kindergarten many children will begin to read some words through recognition or by processing letter-sound relations. Studies by Domico (1993) and Richgels (1995) suggest that children's ability to read words is tied to their ability to write words in a somewhat reciprocal relationship. The more opportunities children have to write, the greater the likelihood that they will reproduce spellings of words they have seen and heard. Though not conventional, these spellings likely show greater letter-sound correspondences and partial encoding of some parts of words, like *SWM* for *swim*, than do the inventions of preschoolers (Clay 1975).

To provide more intensive and extensive practice, some teachers try to integrate writing in other areas of the curriculum, like literacy-related play (Neuman & Roskos 1992), and other project activities (Katz & Chard 1989). These types of projects engage children in using reading and writing for multiple purposes while they are learning about topics meaningful to them.

Early literacy activities teach children a great deal about writing and reading but often in ways that do not look much like traditional elementary school instruction. Capitalizing on the active and social nature of children's learning, early instruction must provide rich demonstrations, interactions, and models of literacy in the course of activities that make sense to young children. Children must also learn about the relation between oral and written language and the relation between letters, sounds, and words. In classrooms built around a wide variety of print activities, then in talking, reading, writing, playing, and listening to one another, children will want to read and write and feel capable that they can do so.

The primary grades

Instruction takes on a more formal nature as children move into the elementary grades. Here it is virtually certain that children will receive at least some instruction from a commercially published product, like a basal or literature anthology series.

Although research has clearly established that no one method is superior for all children (Bond & Dykstra 1967; Snow, Burns, & Griffin 1998), approaches that favor some type of **systematic code instruction along with meaningful connected reading** report children's superior progress in reading. Instruction should aim to teach the important letter-sound relationships, which once learned are practiced through having many oppor-

tunities to read. Most likely these research findings are a positive result of the Matthew Effect, the rich-get-richer effects that are embedded in such instruction; that is, children who acquire alphabetic coding skills begin to recognize many words (Stanovich 1986). As word recognition processes become more automatic, children are likely to allocate more attention to higher-level processes of comprehension. Since these reading experiences tend to be rewarding for children, they may read more often; thus reading achievement may be a by-product of reading enjoyment.

One of the hallmarks of skilled reading is **fluent, accurate word identification** (Juel, Griffith, & Gough 1986). Yet instruction in simply word calling with flashcards is not reading. Real reading is comprehension. Children need to read a wide variety of interesting, comprehensible materials, which they can read orally with about 90 to 95% accuracy (Durrell & Catterson 1980). In the beginning children are likely to read slowly and deliberately as they focus on exactly what's on the page. In fact they may seem "glued to print" (Chall 1983), figuring out the fine points of form at the word level. However, children's reading expression, fluency, and comprehension generally improve when they read familiar texts. Some authorities have found the practice of repeated rereadings in which children reread short selections significantly enhances their confidence, fluency, and comprehension in reading (Samuels 1979; Moyer 1982).

Children not only use their increasing knowledge of letter-sound patterns to read unfamiliar texts. They also use a variety of strategies. Studies reveal that early readers are capable of being intentional in their use of **metacognitive strategies** (Brown, & DeLoache 1978; Rowe 1994) Even in these early grades, children make predictions about what they are to read, self-correct, reread, and question if necessary, giving evidence that they are able to adjust their reading when understanding breaks down. Teacher practices, such as the Directed Reading-Thinking Activity (DRTA), effectively model these strategies by helping children set purposes for reading, ask questions, and summarize ideas through the text (Stauffer 1970).

But children also need time for **independent practice**. These activities may take on numerous forms. Some research, for example, has demonstrated the powerful effects that children's reading to their caregivers has on promoting confidence as well as reading proficiency (Hannon 1995). Visiting the library and scheduling independent reading and writing periods in literacy-rich classrooms also provide children with opportunities to select books of their own choosing. They may engage in the social activities of reading with their peers, asking questions, and writing stories (Morrow & Weinstein 1986), all of which may nurture interest and appreciation for reading and writing.

Supportive relationships between these communication processes lead many teachers to **integrate reading and writing** in classroom instruction (Tierney & Shanahan 1991). After all, writing challenges children to actively think about print. As young authors struggle to express themselves, they come to grips with different written forms, syntactic patterns, and themes. They use writing for multiple purposes: to write descriptions, lists, and stories to communicate with others. It is important for teachers to expose children to a range of text forms, including stories, reports, and informational texts, and to help children select vocabulary and punctuate simple sentences that meet the demands of audience and purpose. Since handwriting instruction helps children communicate effectively, it should also be part of the writing process (McGee & Richgels 1996). Short lessons demonstrating certain letter formations tied to the publication of writing provide an ideal time for instruction. Reading and writing workshops, in which teachers provide small-group and individual instruction, may help children to develop the skills they need for communicating with others.

Although children's initial writing drafts will contain invented spellings, learning about spelling will take on increasing importance in these years (Henderson & Beers 1980; Richgels 1986). **Spelling instruction** should be an important component of the reading and writing program since it directly affects reading ability. Some teachers create their own spelling lists, focusing on words with common patterns, high-frequency words, as well as some personally meaningful words from the children's writing. Research indicates that seeing a word in print, imagining how it is spelled, and copying new words is an effective way of acquiring spellings (Barron 1980). Nevertheless, even though the teacher's goal is to foster more conventionalized forms, it is important to recognize that there is more to writing than just spelling and grammatically correct sentences. Rather, writing has been characterized by Applebee (1977) as "thinking with a pencil." It is true that children will need adult help to master the complexities of the writing process. But they also will need to learn that the power of writing is expressing one's own ideas in ways that can be understood by others.

As children's capabilities develop and become more fluent, instruction will turn from a central focus on helping children learn to read and write to helping them read and write to learn. Increasingly the emphasis for teachers will be on encouraging children to become **independent and productive readers**, helping them to extend their reasoning and comprehension abilities in learning about their world. Teachers will need to provide challenging materials that require children to analyze and think creatively and from different points of view. They also will need to ensure that children have practice in reading and writing (both in and out of school) and many opportunities to analyze topics, generate questions, and organize written responses for different purposes in meaningful activities.

Throughout these critical years **accurate assessment** of children's knowledge, skills, and dispositions in reading and writing will help teachers better match instruction with how and what children are learning. However, early reading and writing cannot simply be measured as a set of narrowly-defined skills on standardized tests. These measures often are not reliable or valid indicators of what children can do in typical practice, nor are they sensitive to language variation, culture, or the experiences of young children (Shepard & Smith 1988; Shepard 1994; Johnston 1997). Rather, a sound assessment should be anchored in real-life writing and reading tasks and continuously chronicle a wide range of children's literacy activities in different situations. Good assessment is essential to help teachers tailor appropriate instruction to young children and to know when and how much intensive instruction on any particular skill or strategy might be needed.

By the end of third grade, children will still have much to learn about literacy. Clearly some will be further along the path to independent reading and writing than others. Yet with high-quality instruction, the majority of children will be able to decode words with a fair degree of facility, use a variety of strategies to adapt to different types of text, and be able to communicate effectively for multiple purposes using conventionalized spelling and punctuation. Most of all they will have come to see themselves as capable readers and writers, having mastered the complex set of attitudes, expectations, behaviors, and skills related to written language.

Statement of position

IRA and NAEYC believe that achieving high standards of literacy for every child in the United States is a shared responsibility of schools, early childhood programs, families, and communities. But teachers of young children, whether employed in preschools, child care programs, or elementary schools, have a unique responsibility to promote children's literacy development, based on the most current professional knowledge and research.

A review of research along with the collective wisdom and experience of members has led IRA and NAEYC to conclude that learning to read and write is a complex, multifaceted process that requires a wide variety of instructional approaches, a conclusion similar to that reached by an esteemed panel of experts for the National Academy of Sciences (Snow, Burns, & Griffin 1998).

Similarly, this review of research leads to a theoretical model of literacy learning and development as an interactive process. Research supports the view of the child as an active constructor of his or her own learning, while at the same time studies emphasize the critical role of the supportive, interested, engaged adult (e.g., teacher, parent, or tutor) who provides scaffolding for the child's development of greater skill and understanding (Mason & Sinha 1993; Riley 1996). The principle of learning is that "children are active learners, drawing on direct social and physical experience as well as culturally transmitted knowledge to construct their own understandings of the world around them" (Bredekamp & Copple 1997, 13).

IRA and NAEYC believe that goals and expectations for young children's achievement in reading and writing should be developmentally appropriate, that is, *challenging but achievable*, with sufficient adult support. A continuum of reading and writing development is generally accepted and useful for teachers in understanding the goals of literacy instruction and in assessing children's progress toward those goals. (An abbreviated continuum of reading and writing development appears on pp. 14–15; for more detailed examples, see Chall 1983; Education Department of Western Australia 1994a–d; Whitmore & Goodman 1995; Snow, Burns, & Griffin 1998). Good teachers understand that children do not progress along this developmental continuum in rigid sequence. Rather, each child exhibits a unique pattern and timing in acquiring skills and understanding related to reading and writing.

Like other complex skills, reading and writing are outcomes that result from the continual interplay of development and learning, and therefore a range of individual variation is to be expected in the rate and pace at which children gain literacy skills. Given exposure to appropriate literacy experiences and good teaching during early childhood, most children learn to read at age six or seven, a few learn at four, some learn at five, and others need intensive individualized support to learn to read at eight or nine. Some children who do not explore books and other print during their early years are likely to need more focused support for literacy development when they enter an educational program, whether at preschool, kindergarten, or first grade (since preschool and even kindergarten attendance is not universal). Other children who enter school speaking little or no English are likely to need instructional strategies in their home language (Snow, Burns, & Griffin 1998).

Given the range within which children typically master reading, even with exposure to print-rich environments and good teaching, a developmentally appropriate expectation is for most children to achieve beginning conventional reading (also called early reading) by age seven. For children with disabilities or special learning needs, achievable but challenging goals for their individual reading and writing development in an inclusive environment are established by teachers, families, and specialists working in collaboration (DEC Task Force 1993; DEC/ CEC 1994).

IRA and NAEYC believe that early childhood teachers need to understand the developmental continuum of reading and writing and be skilled in a variety of strategies to assess and support individual children's development and learning across the continuum. At the same time teachers must set developmentally appropriate literacy goals for young children and then adapt instructional strategies for children whose learning and development are advanced or lag behind those goals. Good teachers make instructional decisions based on their knowledge of reading and writing, current research, appropriate expectations, and their knowledge of individual children's strengths and needs.

A continuum of reading and writing development is useful for identifying challenging but achievable goals or benchmarks for children's literacy learning, remembering that individual variation is to be expected and supported. Using a developmental continuum enables teachers to assess individual children's progress against realistic goals and then adapt instruction to ensure that children continue to progress. During the preschool years most children can be expected to function in phase 1 of the developmental continuum, Awareness and Exploration. In kindergarten an appropriate expectation is that most children will be at phase 2, Experimental Reading and Writing. By the end of first grade, most children will function in phase 3, Early Reading and Writing. An appropriate expectation for second grade is Transitional Reading and Writing (phase 4), while the goal for third grade is Independent and Productive Reading and Writing (phase 5). Advanced Reading is the goal for fourth grade and above.

As fundamental as the principle of individual variation is the principle that human development and learning occur in and are influenced by social and cultural contexts. Language, reading, and writing are strongly shaped by culture. Children enter early childhood programs or schools having learned to communicate and make sense of their experiences at home and in their communities. When the ways of making and communicating meaning are similar at home and in school, children's transitions are eased. However, when the language and culture of the home and school are not congruent, teachers and parents must work together to help children strengthen and preserve their home language and culture while acquiring skills needed to participate in the shared culture of the school (NAEYC 1996a).

Most important, teachers must understand how children learn a second language and how this process applies to young children's literacy development. Teachers need to respect the child's home language and culture and use it as a base on which to build and extend children's language and literacy experiences. Unfortunately teachers too often react negatively to children's linguistic and cultural diversity, equating difference with deficit. Such situations hurt children whose abilities within their own cultural context are not recognized because they do not match the cultural expectations of the school. Failing to recognize children's strengths or capabilities, teachers may underestimate their competence. Competence is not tied to any particular language, dialect, or culture. Teachers should never use a child's dialect, language, or culture as a basis for making judgments about the child's intellect or capability. Linguistically and culturally diverse children bring multiple perspectives and impressive skills, such as code-switching (the ability to go back and forth between two languages to deepen conceptual understanding), to the tasks of learning to speak, read, and write a second language. These self-motivated, self-initiating, constructive thinking processes should be celebrated and used as rich teaching and learning resources for all children.

Recommended teaching practices

During the infant and toddler years. Children need relationships with caring adults who engage in many one-on-one, face-to-face interactions with them to support their oral language development and lay the foundation for later literacy learning. Important experiences and teaching behaviors include but are not limited to

- talking to babies and toddlers with simple language, frequent eye contact, and responsiveness to children's cues and language attempts;
- frequently playing with, talking to, singing to, and doing fingerplays with very young children;
- sharing cardboard books with babies and frequently reading to toddlers on the adult's lap or together with one or two other children; and
- providing simple art materials such as crayons, markers, and large paper for toddlers to explore and manipulate.

During the preschool years. Young children need developmentally appropriate experiences and teaching to support literacy learning. These include but are not limited to

- positive, nurturing relationships with adults who engage in responsive conversations with individual children, model reading and writing behavior, and foster children's interest in and enjoyment of reading and writing;

- print-rich environments that provide opportunities and tools for children to see and use written language for a variety of purposes, with teachers drawing children's attention to specific letters and words;
- adults' daily reading of high-quality books to individual children or small groups, including books that positively reflect children's identity, home language, and culture;
- opportunities for children to talk about what is read and to focus on the sounds and parts of language as well as the meaning;
- teaching strategies and experiences that develop phonemic awareness, such as songs, fingerplays, games, poems, and stories in which phonemic patterns such as rhyme and alliteration are salient;
- opportunities to engage in play that incorporates literacy tools, such as writing grocery lists in dramatic play, making signs in block building, and using icons and words in exploring a computer game; and
- firsthand experiences that expand children's vocabulary, such as trips in the community and exposure to various tools, objects, and materials.

In kindergarten and primary grades. Teachers should continue many of these same good practices with the goal of continually advancing children's learning and development (see the continuum of reading and writing development for appropriate grade-level expectations). In addition every child is entitled to excellent instruction in reading and writing that includes but is not limited to

- daily experiences of being read to and independently reading meaningful and engaging stories and informational texts;
- a balanced instructional program that includes systematic code instruction along with meaningful reading and writing activities;
- daily opportunities and teacher support to write many kinds of texts for different purposes, including stories, lists, messages to others, poems, reports, and responses to literature;
- writing experiences that allow the flexibility to use nonconventional forms of writing at first (invented or phonic spelling) and over time move to conventional forms;
- opportunities to work in small groups for focused instruction and collaboration with other children;
- an intellectually engaging and challenging curriculum that expands knowledge of the world and vocabulary; and
- adaptation of instructional strategies or more individualized instruction if the child fails to make expected progress in reading or when literacy skills are advanced.

Although experiences during the earliest years of life can have powerful long-term consequences, human beings are amazingly resilient and incredibly capable of learning throughout life. We should strengthen our resolve to ensure that every child has the benefit of positive early childhood experiences that support literacy development. At the same time, regardless of children's prior learning, schools have the responsibility to educate every child and to never give up even if later interventions must be more intensive and costly.

Recommended policies essential for achieving developmentally appropriate literacy experiences

Early childhood programs and elementary schools in the United States operate in widely differing contexts with varying levels of funding and resources. Regardless of the resources available, professionals have an ethical responsibility to teach, to the best of their ability, according to the standards of the profession. Nevertheless, the kinds of practices advocated here are more likely to be implemented within an infrastructure of supportive policies and resources. IRA and NAEYC strongly recommend that the following policies be developed and adequately funded at the appropriate state or local levels:

1. *A comprehensive, consistent system of early childhood professional preparation and ongoing professional development* (see Darling-Hammond 1997; Kagan & Cohen 1997).

   Such a professional preparation system is badly needed in every state to ensure that staff in early childhood programs and teachers in primary schools obtain specialized, college-level education that informs them about developmental patterns in early literacy learning and about research-based ways of teaching reading and writing during the early childhood years. On-going professional development is essential for teachers to stay current in an ever-expanding research base and to continually improve their teaching skills and the learning outcomes for children.

2. *Sufficient resources to ensure adequate ratios of qualified teachers to children and small groups for individualizing instruction.*

   For four- and five-year-olds, adult-child ratios should be no more than 1 adult for 8 to 10 children, with a maximum group size of 20 (Howes, Phillips, & Whitebook 1992; Cost, Quality, and Child Outcomes Study Team 1995). Optimum class size in the early grades is 15 to 18 with one teacher (Nye et al. 1992; Nye, Boyd-Zaharias, & Fulton 1994). Young children benefit most from being taught in small groups or as individuals. There will always be a wide range of individual differences among children. Small class size increases the likelihood that teachers will be able to accommodate children's diverse abilities and interests, strengths and needs.

3. *Sufficient resources to ensure classrooms, schools, and public libraries that include a wide range of high-quality children's books, computer software, and multimedia resources at various levels of difficulty and reflecting various cultural and family backgrounds.*

   Studies have found that a minimum of five books per child is necessary to provide even the most basic print-rich environment (Morrow & Weinstein 1986; Neuman & Roskos 1997). Computers and developmentally appropriate software should also be available to provide alternative, engaging, enriching literacy experiences (NAEYC 1996b).

4. *Policies that promote children's continuous learning progress.*

   When individual children do not make expected progress in literacy development, resources should be available to provide more individualized instruction, focused time, tutoring by trained and qualified tutors, or other individualized intervention strategies. These instructional strategies are used to accelerate children's learning instead of either grade retention or social promotion, neither of which has been proven effective in improving children's achievement (Shepard & Smith 1988).

5. *Appropriate assessment strategies that promote children's learning and development.*

Teachers need to regularly and systematically use multiple indicators—observation of children's oral language, evaluation of children's work, and performance at authentic reading and writing tasks—to assess and monitor children's progress in reading and writing development, plan and adapt instruction, and communicate with parents (Shepard, Kagan, & Wurtz 1998). Group-administered, multiple-choice standardized achievement tests in reading and writing skills should not be used before third grade or preferably even before fourth grade. The younger the child, the more difficult it is to obtain valid and reliable indices of his or her development and learning using one-time test administrations. Standardized testing has a legitimate function, but on its own it tends to lead to standardized teaching—one approach fits all—the opposite of the kind of individualized diagnosis and teaching that is needed to help young children continue to progress in reading and writing.

6. *Access to regular, ongoing health care for every child.*

Every young child needs to have a regular health care provider as well as screening for early diagnosis and treatment of vision and hearing problems. Chronic untreated middle-ear infections in the earliest years of life may delay language development, which in turn may delay reading development (Vernon-Feagans, Emanuel, & Blood 1992). Similarly, vision problems should never be allowed to go uncorrected, causing a child difficulty with reading and writing.

7. *Increased public investment to ensure access to high-quality preschool and child care programs for all children who need them.*

The National Academy of Sciences (Snow, Burns, & Griffin 1998) and decades of longitudinal research (see, for example, Barnett 1995) demonstrate the benefits of preschool education for literacy learning. Unfortunately, there is no system to ensure accessible, affordable, high-quality early childhood education programs for all families who choose to use them (Kagan & Cohen 1997). As a result, preschool attendance varies considerably by family income; for example, 80% of four-year-olds whose families earn more than $50,000 per year attend preschool compared to approximately 50% of four-year-olds attending preschool from families earning less than $20,000 (NCES 1996). In addition, due primarily to inadequate funding, the quality of preschool and child care programs varies considerably, with studies finding that the majority of programs provide only mediocre quality and that only about 15% rate as good quality (Layzer, Goodson, & Moss 1993; Galinsky et al. 1994; Cost, Quality, & Child Outcomes Study Team 1995).

Conclusion

Collaboration between IRA and NAEYC is symbolic of the coming together of the two essential bodies of knowledge necessary to support literacy development of young children: knowledge about the processes of reading and writing and knowledge of child development and learning. Developmentally appropriate practices (Bredekamp & Copple 1997) in reading and writing are ways of teaching that consider

1. what is generally known about children's development and learning to set achievable but challenging goals for literacy learning and to plan learning experiences and teaching strategies that vary with the age and experience of the learners;

2. results of ongoing assessment of individual children's progress in reading and writing to plan next steps or to adapt instruction when children fail to make expected progress or are at advanced levels; and

3. social and cultural contexts in which children live so as to help them make sense of their learning experiences in relation to what they already know and are able to do.

To teach in developmentally appropriate ways, teachers must understand *both* the continuum of reading and writing development *and* children's individual and cultural variations. Teachers must recognize when variation is within the typical range and when intervention is necessary, because early intervention is more effective and less costly than later remediation.

Learning to read and write is one of the most important and powerful achievements in life. Its value is clearly seen in the faces of young children—the proud, confident smile of the capable reader contrasts sharply with the furrowed brow and sullen frown of the discouraged nonreader. Ensuring that all young children reach their potentials as readers and writers is the shared responsibility of teachers, administrators, families, and communities. Educators have a special responsibility to teach every child and not to blame children, families, or each other when the task is difficult. All responsible adults need to work together to help children become competent readers and writers.

References

Adams, M. 1990. *Beginning to read*. Cambridge, MA: MIT Press.

Anbar, A. 1986. Reading acquisition of preschool children without systematic instruction. *Early Childhood Research Quarterly* 1: 69–83.

Anderson, R.C. 1995. *Research foundations for wide reading*. Paper presented at invitational conference on "The Impact of Wide Reading" at Center for the Study of Reading, Urbana, IL.

Applebee, A.N. 1977. Writing and reading. *Language Arts* 20: 534–37.

Barnett, W.S. 1995. Long-term effects of early childhood programs on cognitive and school outcomes. *The Future of Children* 5: 25–50.

Barron, R.W. 1980. Visual and phonological strategies in reading and spelling. In *Cognitive processes in spelling*, ed. U. Frith, 339–53. New York: Academic.

Berk, L. 1996. *Infants and children: Prenatal through middle childhood*. 2d ed. Boston: Allyn & Bacon.

Bissex, G. 1980. *GYNS AT WRK: A child learns to write and read*. Cambridge, MA: Harvard University Press.

Bond, G., & R. Dykstra. 1967. The cooperative research program in first-grade reading instruction. *Reading Research Quarterly* 2: 5–142.

Bradley, L., & P.E. Bryant. 1983. Categorizing sounds and learning to read: A causal connection. *Nature* 301: 419–21.

Bredekamp, S., & C. Copple, eds. 1997. *Developmentally appropriate practice in early childhood programs*. Rev. ed. Washington, DC: NAEYC.

Brown, A.L., & J.S. DeLoache. 1978. Skills, plans and self-regulation. In *Children's thinking: What develops?* ed. R. Siegler, 336. Hillsdale, NJ: Erlbaum.

Bryant, P.E., M. MacLean, L. Bradley, & J. Crossland. 1990. Rhyme and alliteration, phoneme detection, and learning to read. *Developmental Psychology* 26: 429–38.

Bryne, B., & R. Fielding-Barnsley. 1991. Evaluation of a program to teach phonemic awareness to young children. *Journal of Educational Psychology* 83: 451–55.

Bryne, B., & R. Fielding-Barnsley. 1993. Evaluation of a program to teach phonemic awareness to young children: A 1-year follow-up. *Journal of Educational Psychology* 85: 104–11.

Bryne, B., & R. Fielding-Barnsley. 1995. Evaluation of a program to teach phonemic awareness to young children: A 2- and 3-year follow-up and a new preschool trial. *Journal of Educational Psychology* 87: 488–503.

Bus, A., J. Belsky, M.H. van IJzendoorn, & K. Crnic. 1997. Attachment and book-reading patterns: A study of mothers, fathers, and their toddlers. *Early Childhood Research Quarterly* 12: 81–98.

Bus, A., & M. Van IJzendoorn. 1995. Mothers reading to their 3-year-olds: The role of mother-child attachment security in becoming literate. *Reading Research Quarterly* 30: 998–1015.

Bus, A., M. Van IJzendoorn, & A. Pellegrini. 1995. Joint book reading makes for success in learning to read: A meta-analysis on intergenerational transmission of literacy. *Review of Educational Research* 65: 1–21.

Chomsky, C. 1979. Approaching reading through invented spelling. In *Theory and practice of early reading*, vol. 2, eds. L.B. Resnick & P.A. Weaver, 43–65. Hillsdale, NJ: Erlbaum.

Clarke, L. 1988. Invented versus traditional spelling in first graders' writings: Effects on learning to spell and read. *Research in the Teaching of English* 22: 281–309.

Clay, M. 1975. *What did I write?* Portsmouth, NH: Heinemann.

Clay, M. 1979. *The early detection of reading difficulties.* Portsmouth, NH: Heinemann.

Clay, M. 1991. *Becoming literate.* Portsmouth, NH: Heinemann.

Cost, Quality, and Child Outcomes Study Team. 1995. *Cost, quality, and child outcomes in child care centers, public report.* 2d ed. Denver: Economics Department, University of Colorado, Denver.

Cummins, J. 1979. Linguistic interdependence and the educational development of bilingual children. *Review of Educational Research* 49: 222–51.

Cunningham, A. 1990. Explicit versus implicit instruction in phonemic awareness. *Journal of Experimental Child Psychology* 50: 429–44.

Darling-Hammond, L. 1997. *Doing what matters most: Investing in quality teaching.* New York: National Commission on Teaching and America's Future.

DEC (Division for Early Childhood) Task Force on Recommended Practices. 1993. *DEC recommended practices: Indicators of quality in programs for infants and young children with special needs and their families.* Reston, VA: Council for Exceptional Children.

DEC/CEC (Division for Early Childhood of the Council for Exceptional Children). 1994. Position on inclusion. *Young Children* 49 (5): 78.

Dickinson, D., & M. Smith. 1994. Long-term effects of preschool teachers' book readings on low-income children's vocabulary and story comprehension. *Reading Research Quarterly* 29: 104–22.

Domico, M.A. 1993. Patterns of development in narrative stories of emergent writers. In *Examining central issues in literacy research, theory, and practice*, eds. C. Kinzer & D. Leu, 391–404. Chicago: National Reading Conference.

Durkin, D. 1966. *Children who read early.* New York: Teachers College Press.

Durrell, D.D., & J.H. Catterson. 1980. *Durrell analysis of reading difficulty.* Rev. ed. New York: Psychological Corp.

Dyson, A.H. 1988. Appreciate the drawing and dictating of young children. *Young Children* 43 (3): 25–32.

Education Department of Western Australia. 1994a. *First Steps reading developmental continuum.* Portsmouth, NH: Heinemann.

Education Department of Western Australia. 1994b. *First Steps writing developmental continuum.* Portsmouth, NH: Heinemann.

Education Department of Western Australia. 1994c. *First Steps spelling developmental continuum.* Portsmouth, NH: Heinemann.

Education Department of Western Australia. 1994d. *First Steps oral language developmental continuum.* Portsmouth, NH: Heinemann.

Ehri, L. 1994. Development of the ability to read words: Update. In *Theoretical models and processes of reading*, eds. R. Ruddell, M.R. Ruddell, & H. Singer, 323–58. Newark, DE: International Reading Association.

Ehri, L., & J. Sweet. 1991. Finger-point reading of memorized text: What enables beginners to process the print? *Reading Research Quarterly* 26: 442–61.

Ehri, L.C., & C. Robbins. 1992. Beginners need some decoding skill to read words by analogy. *Reading Research Quarterly* 27: 13–26.

Elkonin, D.B. 1973. USSR. In *Comparative Reading*, ed. J. Downing, 551–80. New York: Macmillian.

Eller, R., C. Pappas, & E. Brown. 1988. The lexical development of kindergartners: Learning from written context. *Journal of Reading Behavior* 20: 524.

Elley, W. 1989. Vocabulary acquisition from listening to stories. *Reading Research Quarterly* 24: 174–87.

Feitelson, D., B. Kita, & Z. Goldstein. 1986. Effects of listening to series stories on first graders' comprehension and use of language. *Research in the Teaching of English* 20: 339–55.

Foorman, B., D. Novy, D. Francis, & D. Liberman. 1991. How letter-sound instruction mediates progress in first-grade reading and spelling. *Journal of Educational Psychology* 83: 456–69.

Galinsky, E., C. Howes, S. Kontos., & M. Shinn. 1994. *The study of children in family child care and relative care: Highlights of findings.* New York: Families and Work Institute.

Gibson, E., & E. Levin. 1975. The psychology of reading. Cambridge, MA: MIT Press.

Graves, D. 1983. *Writing: Teachers and children at work.* Portsmouth, NH: Heinemann.

Hannon, P. 1995. *Literacy, home and school.* London: Falmer.

Hanson, R., & D. Farrell. 1995. The long-term effects on high school seniors of learning to read in kindergarten. *Reading Research Quarterly* 30: 908–33.

Hart, B., & T. Risley. 1995. *Meaningful differences.* Baltimore: Paul Brookes.

Henderson, E.H., & J.W. Beers. 1980. *Developmental and cognitive aspects of learning to spell.* Newark, DE: International Reading Association.

Holdaway, D. 1979. *The foundations of literacy.* Portsmouth, NH: Heinemann.

Howes, C., D.A. Phillips, & M. Whitebook. 1992. Thresholds of quality: Implications for the social development of children in center-based child care. *Child Development* 63: 449–60.

IRA (International Reading Association). 1998. *Phonics in the early reading program: A position statement.* Newark, DE: Author.

Johnston, P. 1997. *Knowing literacy: Constructive literacy assessment.* York, ME: Stenhouse.

Juel, C. 1991. Beginning reading. In *Handbook of reading research*, vol. 2, eds. R. Barr, M. Kamil, P. Mosenthal, & P.D. Pearson, 759–88. New York: Longman.

Juel, C., P.L. Griffith, & P. Gough. 1986. Acquisition of literacy: A longitudinal study of children in first and second grade. *Journal of Educational Psychology* 78: 243–55.

Kagan, S.L., & N. Cohen. 1997. *Not by chance: Creating an early care and education system for America's children.* New Haven, CT: Bush Center in Child Development and Social Policy, Yale University.

Karweit, N., & B. Wasik. 1996. The effects of story reading programs on literacy and language development of disadvantaged pre-schoolers. *Journal of Education for Students Placed At-Risk* 4: 319–48.

Katz, L., & C. Chard. 1989. *Engaging children's minds.* Norwood, NJ: Ablex.

Layzer, J., B. Goodson, & M. Moss. 1993. *Life in preschool: Volume one of an observational study of early childhood programs for disadvantaged four-year-olds.* Cambridge, MA: Abt Associates.

Leung, C.B., & J.J. Pikulski. 1990. Incidental learning of word meanings by kindergarten and first grade children thorough repeated read aloud events. In *Literacy theory and research: Analyses from multiple paradigms*, eds. J. Zutell & S. McCormick, 231–40. Chicago: National Reading Conference.

Lundberg, I., J. Frost, & O.P. Petersen. 1988. Effects of an extensive program for stimulating phonological awareness in preschool children. *Reading Research Quarterly* 23: 263–84.

Maclean, M., P. Bryant, & L. Bradley. 1987. Rhymes, nursery rhymes, and reading in early childhood. *Merrill-Palmer Quarterly* 33: 255–81.

Mason, J. 1980. When do children begin to read: An exploration of four-year-old children's word reading competencies. *Reading Research Quarterly* 15: 203–27.

Mason, J., & S. Sinha. 1993. Emerging literacy in the early childhood years: Applying a Vygotskian model of learning and development. In *Handbook of research on the education of young children*, ed. B. Spodek, 137–50. New York: Macmillian.

McGee, L., R. Lomax, & M. Head. 1988. Young children's written language knowledge: What environmental and functional print reading reveals. *Journal of Reading Behavior* 20: 99–118.

McGee, L., & D. Richgels. 1996. *Literacy's beginnings*. Boston: Allyn & Bacon.

McGill-Franzen, A., & C. Lanford. 1994. Exposing the edge of the preschool curriculum: Teachers' talk about text and children's literary understandings. *Language Arts* 71: 264–73.

Morrow, L.M. 1988. Young children's responses to one-to-one readings in school settings. *Reading Research Quarterly* 23: 89–107.

Morrow, L.M. 1990. Preparing the classroom environment to promote literacy during play. *Early Childhood Research Quarterly* 5: 537–54.

Morrow, L.M., D. Strickland, & D.G. Woo. 1998. *Literacy instruction in half- and whole-day kindergarten*. Newark, DE: International Reading Association.

Morrow, L.M., & C. Weinstein. 1986. Encouraging voluntary reading: The impact of a literature program on children's use of library centers. *Reading Research Quarterly* 21: 330–46.

Moyer, S.B. 1982. Repeated reading. *Journal of Learning Disabilities* 15: 619–23.

NAEYC. 1996a. NAEYC position statement: Responding to linguistic and cultural diversity—Recommendations for effective early childhood education. *Young Children* 51 (2): 412.

NAEYC. 1996b. NAEYC position statement: Technology and young children—Ages three through eight. *Young Children* 51 (6): 11–16.

NCES (National Center for Education Statistics). 1996. *The condition of education*. Washington, DC: U.S. Department of Education.

Neuman, S.B. 1997. Literary research that makes a difference: A study of access to literacy. *Reading Research Quarterly* 32 (April-June): 202–10.

Neuman, S.B. 1998. How can we enable all children to achieve? In *Children achieving: Best practices in early literacy*, eds. S.B. Neuman & K. Roskos. Newark, DE: International Reading Association.

Neuman, S.B., & K. Roskos. 1992. Literacy objects as cultural tools: Effects on children's literacy behaviors in play. *Reading Research Quarterly* 27: 202–25.

Neuman, S.B., & K. Roskos. 1993. Access to print for children of poverty: Differential effects of adult mediation and literacy-enriched play settings on environmental and functional print tasks. *American Educational Research Journal* 30: 95–122.

Neuman, S.B., & K. Roskos. 1997. Literacy knowledge in practice: Contexts of participation for young writers and readers. *Reading Research Quarterly* 32: 10–32.

Nye, B.A., J. Boyd-Zaharias, & B.D. Fulton. 1994. *The lasting benefits study: A continuing analysis of the effect of small class size in kindergarten through third grade on student achievement test scores in subsequent grade levels—seventh grade (1992–93), Technical report*. Nashville: Center of Excellence for Research in Basic Skills, Tennessee State University.

Nye, B.A., J. Boyd-Zaharias, B.D. Fulton, & M.P. Wallenhorst. 1992. Smaller classes really are better. *The American School Board Journal* 179 (5): 31–33.

Pappas, C. 1991. Young children's strategies in learning the "book language" of information books. *Discourse Processes* 14: 203–25.

Read, C. 1971. Pre-school children's knowledge of English phonology. *Harvard Educational Review* 41: 134.

Richgels, D.J. 1986. Beginning first graders' "invented spelling" ability and their performance in functional classroom writing activities. *Early Childhood Research Quarterly* 1: 85–97.

Richgels, D.J. 1995. Invented spelling ability and printed word learning in kindergarten. *Reading Research Quarterly* 30: 96–109.

Riley, J. 1996. *The teaching of reading*. London: Paul Chapman.

Roberts, B. 1998. "I No EverethENGe": What skills are essential in early literacy? In *Children achieving: Best practices in early literacy*, eds. S.B. Neuman & K. Roskos. Newark, DE: International Reading Association.

Rowe, D.W. 1994. *Preschoolers as authors*. Cresskill, NJ: Hampton.

Samuels, S.J. 1979. The method of repeated readings. *The Reading Teacher* 32: 403–08.

Shepard, L. 1994. The challenges of assessing young children appropriately. *Phi Delta Kappan* 76: 206–13.

Shepard, L., S.L. Kagan, & E. Wurtz, eds. 1998. *Principles and recommendations for early childhood assessments*. Washington, DC: National Education Goals Panel.

Shepard, L., & M.L. Smith. 1988. Escalating academic demand in kindergarten: Some nonsolutions. *Elementary School Journal* 89: 135–46.

Shepard, L., & M.L. Smith. 1989. *Flunking grades: Research and policies on Retention*. Bristol, PA: Taylor & Francis.

Snow, C. 1991. The theoretical basis for relationships between language and literacy in development. *Journal of Research in Childhood Education* 6: 510.

Snow, C., M.S. Burns, & P. Griffin. 1998. *Preventing reading difficulties in young children*. Washington, DC: National Academy Press.

Snow, C., P. Tabors, P. Nicholson, & B. Kurland. 1995. SHELL: Oral language and early literacy skills in kindergarten and first-grade children. *Journal of Research in Childhood Education* 10: 37–48.

Stanovich, K.E. 1986. Matthew Effects in reading: Some consequences of individual differences in the acquisition of literacy. *Reading Research Quarterly* 21: 360–406.

Stanovich, K.E., & R.F. West. 1989. Exposure to print and orthographic processing. *Reading Research Quarterly* 24: 402–33.

Stauffer, R. 1970. *The language experience approach to the teaching of reading*. New York: Harper & Row.

Strickland, D. 1994. Educating African American learners at risk: Finding a better way. *Language Arts* 71: 328–36.

Sulzby, E. 1985. Kindergartners as writers and readers. In *Advances in writing research*, ed. M.Farr, 127–99. Norwood, NJ: Ablex.

Teale, W. 1984. Reading to young children: Its significance for literacy development. In *Awakening to literacy*, eds. H. Goelman, A. Oberg, & F. Smith, 110–21. Portsmouth, NH: Heinemann.

Tierney, R., & T. Shanahan. 1991. Research on the reading-writing relationship: Interactions, transactions, and outcomes. In *Handbook on reading research*, vol. 2, eds. R. Barr, M. Kamil, P. Mosenthal, & P.D. Pearson, 246–80. New York: Longman.

Vernon-Feagans, L., D. Emanuel, & I. Blood. 1992. About middle ear problems: The effect of otitis media and quality of day care on children's language development. *Journal of Applied Developmental Psychology* 18: 395–409.

Vukelich, C. 1994. Effects of play interventions on young children's reading of environmental print. *Early Childhood Research Quarterly* 9: 153–70.

Wagner, R., & J. Torgesen. 1987. The nature of phonological processing and its causal role in the acquisition of reading skills. *Psychological Bulletin* 101: 192–212.

Wells, G. 1985. *The meaning makers*. Portsmouth, NH: Heinemann.

Whitehurst, G., D. Arnold, J. Epstein, A. Angell, M. Smith, & J. Fischel. 1994. A picture book reading intervention in day care and home for children from low-income families. *Developmental Psychology* 30: 679–89.

Whitmore, K., & Y. Goodman. 1995. Transforming curriculum in language and literacy. In *Reaching potentials: Transforming early childhood curriculum and assessment*, vol. 2, eds. S. Bredekamp & T. Rosegrant. Washington, DC: NAEYC.

Wong Fillmore, L. 1991. When learning a second language means losing the first. *Early Childhood Research Quarterly* 6: 323–46.

Continuum of Children's Development in Early Reading and Writing

Note: this list is intended to be illustrative, not exhaustive. Children at any grade level will function at a variety of phases along the reading/writing continuum.

Phase 1: Awareness and exploration (goals for preschool)

Children explore their environment and build the foundations for learning to read and write.

Children can

- enjoy listening to and discussing storybooks
- understand that print carries a message
- engage in reading and writing attempts
- identify labels and signs in their environment
- participate in rhyming games
- identify some letters and make some letter-sound matches
- use known letters or approximations of letters to represent written language (especially meaningful words like their name and phrases such as "I love you")

What teachers do

- share books with children, including Big Books, and model reading behaviors
- talk about letters by name and sounds
- establish a literacy-rich environment
- reread favorite stories
- engage children in language games
- promote literacy-related play activities
- encourage children to experiment with writing

What parents and family members can do

- talk with children, engage them in conversation, give names of things, show interest in what a child says
- read and reread stories with predictable text to children
- encourage children to recount experiences and describe ideas and events that are important to them
- visit the library regularly
- provide opportunities for children to draw and print, using markers, crayons, and pencils

Phase 2: Experimental reading and writing (goals for kindergarten)

Children develop basic concepts of print and begin to engage in and experiment with reading and writing.

Kindergartners can

- enjoy being read to and themselves retell simple narrative stories or informational texts
- use descriptive language to explain and explore
- recognize letters and letter-sound matches
- show familiarity with rhyming and beginning sounds
- understand left-to-right and top-to-bottom orientation and familiar concepts of print
- match spoken words with written ones
- begin to write letters of the alphabet and some high-frequency words

What teachers do

- encourage children to talk about reading and writing experiences
- provide many opportunities for children to explore and identify sound-symbol relationships in meaningful contexts
- help children to segment spoken words into individual sounds and blend the sounds into whole words (for example, by slowly writing a word and saying its sound)
- frequently read interesting and conceptually rich stories to children
- provide daily opportunities for children to write
- help children build a sight vocabulary
- create a literacy-rich environment for children to engage independently in reading and writing

What parents and family members can do

- daily read and reread narrative and informational stories to children
- encourage children's attempts at reading and writing
- allow children to participate in activities that involve writing and reading (for example, cooking, making grocery lists)
- play games that involve specific directions (such as "Simon Says")
- have conversations with children during mealtimes and throughout the day

Phase 3: Early reading and writing (goals for first grade)

Children begin to read simple stories and can write about a topic that is meaningful to them.

First-graders can

- read and retell familiar stories
- use strategies (rereading, predicting, questioning, contextualizing) when comprehension breaks down
- use reading and writing for various purposes on their own initiative
- orally read with reasonable fluency
- use letter-sound associations, word parts, and context to identify new words
- identify an increasing number of words by sight
- sound out and represent all substantial sounds in spelling a word
- write about topics that are personally meaningful
- attempt to use some punctuation and capitalization

What teachers do

- support the development of vocabulary by reading daily to the children, transcribing their language, and selecting materials that expand children's knowledge and language development
- model strategies and provide practice for identifying unknown words
- give children opportunities for independent reading and writing practice
- read, write, and discuss a range of different text types (poems, informational books)
- introduce new words and teach strategies for learning to spell new words
- demonstrate and model strategies to use when comprehension breaks down
- help children build lists of commonly used words from their writing and reading

What parents and family members can do

- talk about favorite storybooks
- read to children and encourage them to read to you
- suggest that children write to friends and relatives
- bring to a parent-teacher conference evidence of what your child can do in writing and reading
- encourage children to share what they have learned about their writing and reading

Phase 4: Transitional reading and writing (goals for second grade)

Children begin to read more fluently and write various text forms using simple and more complex sentences.

Second-graders can

- read with greater fluency
- use strategies more efficiently (rereading, questioning, and so on) when comprehension breaks down
- use word identification strategies with greater facility to unlock unknown words
- identify an increasing number of words by sight
- write about a range of topics to suit different audiences
- use common letter patterns and critical features to spell words
- punctuate simple sentences correctly and proofread their own work
- spend time reading daily and use reading to research topics

What teachers do

- create a climate that fosters analytic, evaluative, and reflective thinking
- teach children to write in multiple forms (stories, information, poems)
- ensure that children read a range of texts for a variety of purposes
- teach revising, editing, and proofreading skills
- teach strategies for spelling new and difficult words
- model enjoyment of reading

What parents and family members can do

- continue to read to children and encourage them to read to you
- engage children in activities that require reading and writing
- become involved in school activities
- show children your interest in their learning by displaying their written work
- visit the library regularly
- support your child's specific hobby or interest with reading materials and references

Phase 5: Independent and productive reading and writing (goals for third grade)

Children continue to extend and refine their reading and writing to suit varying purposes and audiences.

Third-graders can

- read fluently and enjoy reading
- use a range of strategies when drawing meaning from the text
- use word identification strategies appropriately and automatically when encountering unknown words
- recognize and discuss elements of different text structures
- make critical connections between texts
- write expressively in many different forms (stories, poems, reports)
- use a rich variety of vocabulary and sentences appropriate to text forms
- revise and edit their own writing during and after composing
- spell words correctly in final writing drafts

What teachers do

- provide opportunities daily for children to read, examine, and critically evaluate narrative and expository texts
- continue to create a climate that fosters critical reading and personal response
- teach children to examine ideas in texts
- encourage children to use writing as a tool for thinking and learning
- extend children's knowledge of the correct use of writing conventions
- emphasize the importance of correct spelling in finished written products
- create a climate that engages all children as a community of literacy learners

What parents and family members can do

- continue to support children's learning and interest by visiting the library and bookstores with them
- find ways to highlight children's progress in reading and writing
- stay in regular contact with your child's teachers about activities and progress in reading and writing
- encourage children to use and enjoy print for many purposes (such as recipes, directions, games, and sports)
- build a love of language in all its forms and engage children in conversation

From *Young Children*, July 1998, Vol. 53, No. 4, pp. 30-46. Copyright © 1998 by National Association for the Education of Young Children. Reprinted by permission.

Early literacy instruction in the climate of No Child Left Behind

Recent U.S. education reforms are having an impact on early literacy instruction.

Margaret Taylor Stewart

The No Child Left Behind Act (NCLB) of 2001 is changing the literacy climate of classrooms and schools in the United States. Regardless of whether individuals agree with its mandates, the impact of that law is being felt by districts and schools receiving Reading First funds, and often, in more indirect ways, by other U.S. educators. I wrote this article to assist teachers who are trying to adapt valued classroom techniques—some of which may be based on research into developmentally appropriate practices (e.g., Hart, Burts, & Charlesworth, 1997) or qualitative methodologies (e.g., case study, ethnography, teacher research)—to the new focus set forth by NCLB (i.e., that reading instruction must be derived from scientifically based reading research). Early childhood teachers in Reading First schools are expected to immediately implement mandated practices; often other teachers have to as well.

As they work with their classes, preservice and inservice teachers in my graduate literacy seminars search for ways to teach a wide range of learners. Even though my teaching has now shifted to the university setting, I continue to identify with classroom roles and responsibilities I had during my many years of teaching grades 1, 2, and 3. Because of that classroom background, I use the pronoun we to include myself as an insider in the discussion. This article grew out of conversations with teachers and administrators, studies of existing research, and more than 10 years of teacher research in classrooms of young learners. (All names used are pseudonyms.)

The No Child Left Behind Act focuses reading instruction on the following five components: phonemic awareness, phonics, vocabulary, fluency, and comprehension. It is essential to include, in addition to those five, emphasis on oral language and literacy experiences, as well as con- nections between reading and writing. Snow (2002), referencing a longitudinal empirical study of language and literacy development that showed the central place of oral language development in reading success (Snow, Dickinson, & Tabors, 2002), said, "If reading success is so dependent on oral language skills, should we not be placing more emphasis on vocabulary and rich language environments in preschool and the primary grades, rather than assuming that teaching word reading skills alone will suffice?" (slide 18). We must also continue to value the interrelatedness of reading and writing (e.g., Nelson & Calfee, 1998) and ways children go about reading and writing (e.g., Calkins, 1986, 2001; Clay, 1979, 1993a, 1998; Graves, 1983, 1994), among other important aspects of literacy.

Children deserve teachers who understand them, know the content of the subjects they teach, and are able to effectively engage students in learning that content; that is, as Imig (2002) phrased it, teachers who are learned professionals who also can address NCLB mandates. This article examines the law's requirements, discusses some ways to address those, and mentions several issues concerning the complexities of literacy classrooms.

What does the law require?

This section provides some key references and definitions that directly affect Reading First classrooms across the U.S. and indirectly affect classrooms not governed by Reading First legislation. Reading First is a grants program for schools that fail to meet standards. Over a three-year period, qualifying schools will receive federal money, routed through their states, to provide teacher education, programs, materials, remedial programs, and ongoing monitoring of student progress. All expenditures and activities must be aligned with findings of the National Reading Panel (NRP). Although most schools will not receive this money, it is important for all to understand the law because of its various effects (e.g., publishers create programs to match these requirements). In subsequent sections I interpret what quoted provisions mean for teachers.

Title I statement of purpose

The opening of section 1001 of NCLB states, "The purpose of this title is to ensure that all children have a fair, equal, and significant opportunity to obtain a high-quality education and reach, at a minimum, proficiency on challenging State academic achievement standards and state [sic] academic assessments" (Pub. L. 107-110, Title I, §1001, 115 Stat. 1439, 2002, ¶1). The law provides specific ways to do this.

Purposes of Part B—Student Reading Skills Improvement Grants, Subpart 1—Reading First:

(1) To provide assistance to State educational agencies and local educational agencies in establishing reading programs for students in kindergarten through grade 3 that are based on scientifically based reading research, to ensure that every student can read at grade level or above not later than the end of grade 3....

(4) To provide assistance to State educational agencies and local educational agencies in selecting or developing effective instructional materials (including classroom-based materials to assist teachers in implementing the essential components of reading instruction), programs, learning systems, and strategies to implement methods that have been proven to prevent or remediate reading failure within a State. (Pub. L. 107-110, §1201, 115 Stat. 1535, 2002)

Sample essential definitions from NCLB of 2001

(3) ESSENTIAL COMPONENTS OF READING INSTRUCTION.—The term "essential components of reading instruction" means explicit and systematic instruction in—(A) phonemic awareness; (B) phonics; (C) vocabulary development; (D) reading fluency, including oral reading skills; and (E) reading comprehension strategies....

(5) READING.—The term "reading" means a complex system of deriving meaning from print that requires all of the following: (A) The skills and knowledge to understand how phonemes, or speech sounds, are connected to print. (B) The ability to decode unfamiliar words. (C) The ability to read fluently. (D) Sufficient background information and vocabulary to foster reading comprehension. (E) The development of appro-

priate active strategies to construct meaning from print. (F) The development and maintenance of a motivation to read. (Pub. L. 107-110, §1208, 115 Stat. 1550-1551, 2002)

What do these requirements mean for classrooms?

I see no quick or simple way to implement requirements of the law in classrooms where teachers must consider multiple layers of complexity. Implementation requires extremely knowledgeable, thoughtful, well-prepared teachers who adjust instruction for learners' needs.

High-quality education for all children

As stated, the main purpose of NCLB is "to ensure that all children have a fair, equal, and significant opportunity to obtain a high-quality education" (Pub. L. 107-110, Title I, § 1001, 115 Stat. 1439, 2002, ¶1). This is a worthwhile goal indeed. Nonetheless, these complex issues cannot be fully resolved at the classroom level. Teachers in individual classrooms have little control over conditions of physical facilities in which they teach or programs mandated by administration. They have even less control over students placed in their classes, out-of-school conditions in those children's lives, caregivers with whom they live, peers with whom they interact outside of school, or number of days or months students remain in teachers' classrooms. Teachers *do*, however, have charge of students' education for whatever time period students are with them. In order to be used by Reading First schools, quantitative research must have proven the effectiveness of classroom procedures. Such research suggests ways effective teachers help students become engaged in learning through manageable challenges (e.g., Marzano, 2003). While not yet proven by quantitative research, descriptive research suggests ways effective teachers focus first on what students *can* do, building on that learning as a foundation (e.g., Clay, 1998; Stewart, 2003; Strickland, Ganske, & Monroe, 2002).

> Teachers who try to find out what children do not know (and much testing is directed to this) are looking for initial points of contact in the wrong places. What they need to do is find points of contact in children's prior learning, the things that children can do, and spend a little time helping children firm up their grasp of what they already know.... Learner-centered instruction is less about interest and motivation than it is about starting where the learner already is and helping that learner to move toward a new degree of control over novel tasks, teaching so that learners are successful and are able to say, "I am in control of this." From there they go on to extend their own learning. Even at a low level of simple perfor-

mance a sense of control and a sense of being effective will generate attention, interest, and motivation. (Clay, 1998, pp. 3–4)

Fostering engaged learning is not easy. But rigorous, research-based descriptive studies document teachers who have shaped their groups of disconnected individuals with personal agendas into bonded communities of learners (e.g., Dyson, 1989, 1993; Fraser & Skolnick, 1994; Stewart, 2002a). Such work shows learning communities in which students are challenged by depth of content and interested in working together to learn as much as they can. Research shows effective teachers are not all alike (e.g., Morrow, Tracey, Woo, & Pressley, 1999; Taylor, Pearson, Clark, & Walpole, 1999, 2000). These descriptive studies, while not generalizable to all teachers, show that teachers do have different teaching styles, personalities, beliefs, and values. One thing these teachers have in common is a belief that students are at the center of teaching. They treat their students as respected individuals worthy of attention and support (e.g., Ladson-Billings, 1994), recognize the learner in every individual, and work to "hook" that learner in multiple ways. These teachers look for ways to make learning personal—to fit curriculum to the needs of learners (e.g., Knapp et al., 1995). They recognize that "the quality of teacher-student interactions and collaborative talk, especially during scaffolded teacher assistance periods, can hasten students' development" (Block & Pressley, 2002, p. 3).

Effective teachers in these studies are dynamic—adjusting to the needs of their students (e.g., Block, Oakar, & Hurt, 2002). They make sure that entire blocks of learning time are fully used, establishing with their students thoughtful, appropriate routine procedures to deal with required, but tangential, tasks of running classrooms and schools. For example, McCollum (1995) discussed the impact of "orderly, enabling learning environments . . . [which were] highly productive learning environments, where students not only completed assigned tasks but also clearly enjoyed being and learning" (pp. 16–17). Teachers' attention to and care of each individual learner is the best assurance that every child receives a high-quality education fitted to her or his specific needs, regardless of whatever elements outside that classroom are less than fair, equal, or significant. Research shows that the teacher is key—the most important element in the effectiveness of classrooms (e.g., Berliner & Biddle, 1995; Bond & Dykstra, 1967/1997; Darling-Hammond, 1997; Haycock, 1998; Marzano, 2003; Wright, Horn, & Sanders, 1997).

Putting reading first

The law specifies that reading programs must be established in kindergarten through third grade in Reading First schools to "ensure that every student can read at grade level or above not later than the end of grade 3" (Pub. L. 107-110, §1201, 115 Stat. 1535, 2002). These pro-

grams must use scientifically based reading research as defined in the law.

The law does not mandate a published or scripted program for use with students. In fact, there is no exact definition of "reading programs" given. However, the U.S. Department of Education (USDOE) has been charged by Congress with interpreting the law and has put in place governing regulations to administer that law. These require schools receiving Reading First funds to use a portion of those funds to purchase a comprehensive reading program (a published program) that meets requirements as determined by the states. I have recently witnessed that approval process in my own state. I attended a session sponsored by the state Department of Education in which districts having eligible schools and interested in writing Reading First grant applications heard publishers of the seven state-approved programs explain them. It was encouraging to hear that all of the programs included strong emphasis on the five essential elements of reading as determined by the National Reading Panel (NRP) and included in NCLB. It was even more encouraging to hear that most of them also valued oral language, higher order thinking, writing, the reading-writing connection, and parental involvement, all of which I consider crucial to learners' literacy success. As teams from schools and districts write applications for Reading First funds, it is important that they look closely and carefully at the purchased programs they select. They must scrutinize the authors of those programs, as well as the programs themselves. They must be very sure that the programs have a strong base upon which knowledgeable teachers can build as they modify instruction to fit their particular students and settings—including the specifics of reading named in the law and discussed here, as well as broader aspects of literacy.

Knowledgeable teachers—armed with understandings gleaned from research that is scientifically based, rigorous, and pertinent (e.g., Adams, 1990; Beck, McKeown, & Kucan, 2002; Dickinson & Tabors, 2001; Snow, Burns, & Griffin, 1998)—can implement instruction tailored to their specific students in order to accomplish the NCLBA mandates. Let us briefly examine the five reading and literacy components promoted by the NCLBA: phonemic awareness and phonics (grouped here as word study), vocabulary, fluency, and comprehension. I include examples of ways teachers might choose to fit instruction to the needs of individual learners.

Word study. Word study integrates instruction in phonemic awareness, phonics, spelling, high-frequency word recognition, and vocabulary. The two sections of the law discussed in this subsection are phonemic awareness (PA) and phonics. PA is the "ability to focus on and manipulate phonemes in spoken words" (National Institute of Child Health and Human Development, 2000, p. 2-1). Phonemes are the smallest units of spoken language. "Systematic phonics instruction is a way of teaching reading that stresses the acquisition of letter-sound correspondences and their use to read and spell words" (p. 2-89), a definition taken from Harris and Hodges (1995). The National Reading Panel Reports of the Subgroups (NRPRS; National Institute of Child Health and Human Development, 2000) encouraged a planned, sequential set of phonics elements that are taught explicitly and systematically. These sections of the law are based on empirical research included in the Panel's meta-analysis and named in Parts I and II of Chapter 2 of the NRPRS (e.g., Ball & Blachman, 1991; Oakland, Black, Stanford, Nussbaum, & Balise, 1998). The NRP included in its meta-analysis only experimental studies "that included a PA treatment and a control group and that measured reading as an outcome of the treatment" (p. 2-1). Many studies measured reading through reading lists of isolated words.

The NRP recommended that PA instruction would be most effective when it was "focused on one or two types of phoneme manipulations rather than multiple types, and when students are taught in small groups" (p. 2-6). It notes that PA instruction is only one part of learning to read. Effective early childhood teachers have been fostering PA development for years by regularly using activities that "play" with language, such as playing rhyming games, singing, doing finger plays, clapping out syllables of names and words, and reading books by authors such as Dr. Seuss (e.g., Adams, Foorman, Lundberg, & Beeler, 1998; Neuman, Copple, & Bredekamp, 2000).

Word study is "an active decision-making process [that] uses comparing and contrasting; attends to sounds, spelling, and meaning; anchors letter-sound correspondence [in writing and meaning]; promotes fluency through automaticity; is aimed at the goal of comprehension; and systematically targets developmental needs" (Juel, 2002, slide 4). Researchers have described many ways to accomplish word study. For example, Gaskins, Ehri, Cress, O'Hara, and Donnelly (1997) discussed ways they taught children via explicit instruction to become "word detectives" (p. 319) to analytically study words. Invernizzi, Juel, and Rosemary (1996/1997) pace instruction in alphabet, phonics, word recognition, and spelling based on developmental word knowledge of each learner, as revealed through students' invented spellings. They use lessons that include "(a) rereading familiar story books, (b) word study, (c) writing, and (d) reading a new book" (p. 306).

Various researchers explain ways to carry out word study within classroom settings. For example, Cunningham and Cunningham's (1992) strategy for making words enhanced phonemic awareness, phonics, and spelling—children learned how the alphabetic system works as they explored letter-sound correspondences, spelling patterns, and word families. Cunningham and Hall (1994) explained that making words has three empirical supports. First is Treiman's (1985) experimental work that suggested children and adults find it easier to break words into their onsets (letters coming before the vowel) and times (the vowel

and letters following it). As an example, it is easier to break *Dan* into *D-an* than into *Da-n* or *D-a-n*. It is also easier to make *pan* or *fan* from *Dan* than it is to make *dab* or *dash*. A second empirical support is the work of Wylie and Durrell (1970), who identified 37 high-utility phonograms that can be found in almost 500 primary words. These are: "-ack, -ail, -ain, -ake, -ale, -ame, -an, -ank, -ap, -ask, -at, -ate, -aw, -ay, -eat, -ell, -est, -ice, -ick, -ide, -ight, -ill, -in, -ine, -ing, -ink, -ip, -it, -ock, -oke, -op, -ore, -ot, -uck, -ug, -ump, -unk" (pp. 787-788). A third source of empirical research supporting spelling patterns is the work of Goswami and Bryant (1990) that investigated spelling by analogy. This research taught us that once children can read and spell some words, they can use those words to help unlock unknown words (e.g., using the known words *bake* and *cake* to help unlock *snake*).

A child-friendly way to differentiate instruction in word study is by using Clay's (1993b) word boxes, which built on Elkonin's (1963) experimental research with sound boxes. Clay's technique helps children attend to sounds in spoken language and connect print and sounds as they identify and spell words. It also helps children hear the order of sounds and pay attention to orthographic features of words (visual patterns and letter sequences) as they write them (Joseph, 1998/1999). Walker (2003) cited use of Elkonin's sound boxes as helpful to struggling readers. Use of word or sound boxes scaffolds children's phonemic awareness, phonics, word identification, and spelling. It also acts as a window onto a child's understanding of phonics, builds on sounds and strategies she or he knows, pushes for greater conventionality in spelling, and roots letter sounds and word building in the very meaningful context of a child's own writing and reading.

Classroom teachers have many opportunities to plan differentiated instruction in word study (or other focus areas) as they observe and note the strengths of individual students during their ongoing daily instruction. Using techniques as simple and unobtrusive as preparing a clipboard sheet that holds a small sticky note for each student (with each child's name already on a separate note) allows busy teachers to quickly record and date what (and when) they notice a child doing well so that they can nudge students forward by offering assignment modifications that challenge each individual. For example, when I noticed second grader Jessica's ability to capture her ideas on paper, to use conventional punctuation and spelling (for most "second-grade" appropriate words), and to take risks in attempting difficult words in her writing, I noted, "Jessica, 8-18-97, + ideas, + conventions. Intro. circling" (Stewart, 1997). That was my shorthand annotation to myself that she was able to write strong content, had good punctuation and spelling, and could be introduced to a circling technique. For this technique, I encouraged students to pay attention first to *what* they were saying but, at the same time, to become aware of times they were not sure if the way they spelled a word was the way it would be spelled in a book. In order not to stop their flow of ideas, I asked them to think mainly about what they were writing and to simply circle words of which they were unsure so that later they could return to give those words more attention. Because some children were so unsure of many spellings that this would have been confusing to them, I introduced this technique individually as children demonstrated command of conventional spellings. (See Stewart, 2002b, pp. 181–183; 2002a, pp. 93, 137–138 for sequential examples of Jessica's writing growth using this technique.) At each day's end I placed completed sticky notes from the clipboard page onto the appropriate child's page in a binder. I put the sticky notes in date order so that I could see growth in a child's processing and strengths over time. This management tool helped guide my instruction in word study (and other focus areas) to fit individuals, and it documented growth to show students and parents in conferences.

Vocabulary. Vocabulary, as described in the law, is based on the work of the NRP. The NRP reviewed vocabulary as an aspect of comprehension and determined both vocabulary instruction and measurement to be important. The NRP found many studies that "describe aspects of vocabulary without specifically addressing questions of how vocabulary instruction is conducted" (p. 4-16). It recognized the importance of many studies but analyzed studies only if "they contained at least some experimental work on instructional methods" (p. 4-16). The NRP found that

> There are so many dimensions on which vocabulary instruction can be categorized that each implementation often appears to be unique…. A formal meta-analysis was not possible. Inspection of the research studies that were included in the database revealed a heterogeneous set of methodologies, implementations, and conceptions of vocabulary instruction. As noted, the Panel found no research on vocabulary measurement that met the NRP criteria; therefore, implicit evidence is presented … on the issue. (p. 4-17)

Although references (e.g., Beck, Perfetti, & McKeown, 1982; Durkin, 1993; McKeown, Beck, Omanson, & Pople, 1985) were listed for the vocabulary chapter of the NRPRS and vocabulary instruction methods were summarized in Appendix A (National Institute of Child Health and Human Development, 2000, pp. 4-33–4-35), no meta-analysis was done. As stated in the previous citation, this section of the law is based on implicit evidence.

Complex issues in vocabulary development require flexibility. Beck and McKeown (1991) said, "any question on vocabulary, be it how readily words are learned … or what kind of instruction works best, must be answered by 'it's conditional; it depends on the situation'" (p. 808). Wide reading builds vocabulary, language, and world knowledge. Beck and McKeown noted that strong, motivated readers gain more vocabulary from their reading than do less able readers. They endorse explicit instruction that teaches students to use context effectively and that builds rich vocabulary. They suggest focusing instruction on the most useful words (i.e., high-frequency words that occur in a mature vocabulary and that have broad utility across various domains of knowledge) and having students apply word knowledge in multiple contexts.

Beck and McKeown (2002) encouraged teachers to take advantage of students' "listening and speaking competencies [which are usually ahead of children's competence in reading and writing] to enhance their vocabulary development" (p. 48). They explained a comprehensive program of rich vocabulary instruction, encouraging teachers to provide students with friendly explanations, expand the context (because many times students cannot go beyond the context in which a word is used), and provide activities that encourage children to interact with words.

Expert teachers promote vocabulary growth and language development in meaningful ways, especially as they discuss books they read aloud to children (Dickinson & Smith, 1994). Consistent empirical findings reveal the importance of home support for literacy, rare word density, preschool exposure to rare words, and extended teacher discourse (Dickinson & Tabors, 2001).

Vocabulary development is an outgrowth of wide reading, especially nonfiction reading; observation and discussion; and explicit and thoughtful instruction. Students build an ever-expanding vocabulary through continual daily attention to—and talk about—words. In more than 10 years of teacher research I found that my young learners built vocabulary daily and in many ways. They learned vocabulary as we read together and discussed a variety of genres; as we discussed and wrote about discoveries from our daily "Elsewhere Expeditions," which were purposeful journeys outside our classroom to learn through close observation; as they shared family adventures through books they created during writing workshops; and as they deliberated in order to find strong words—just the right words—for their writing (see Stewart, 2002a, 2002b).

One way teachers may differentiate vocabulary instruction is by emphasizing words with groups and individuals in contexts that integrate oral language, reading, and writing. For example, to build on a whole-class read-aloud of *Awful Aardvark* (Mwalimu & Kennaway, 1989) in which I followed the reading with a discussion of the author's strong vocabulary choices, I assigned individuals a written retelling of the story for writing workshop. As I circulated throughout the class, I noticed one student, Adam, becoming frustrated as he struggled with his writing. Sensing a teachable moment, I modified his assignment so that I took a few minutes to act as his scribe as he orally retold the story to me. In the process of his retelling, he used strong vocabulary from the original story. My favorite example of his attention to vocabulary was when he said, "He said he was going to eat them." Then he said,

"No. Stop the tape. Do that over. He *threatened* to eat them" (Stewart, 2002a, p. 121). I became very excited and said, "Do you know what smart thing you just did?" He grinned and said, "Yes, I went back and used a better word—a word from the story!" Later, when I was sharing with the class his retelling that I had later typed, I pointed out to him (and to the class) what a "smart" thing Adam did in going back to use a strong word from the original story to improve his retelling. We had discussed many times that it is not a mistake to change a word—that often it strengthens the piece and shows the good thinking of the speaker or reader or writer. I never missed an opportunity to make a positive comment when I noticed a student editing or self-correcting in this way. My attention to strong vocabulary was reflected in students' attention to vocabulary in their speaking, writing, and reading.

Fluency. Fluency is another aspect of NCLB that is based on the work of the National Reading Panel. In the NRPRS (National Institute of Child Health and Human Development, 2000) report on fluency, the stated purpose was "to review the changing concepts of fluency as an essential aspect of reading and to consider the effectiveness of two major instructional approaches to fluency development and the readiness of these approaches for wide use by the schools" (p. 3-5). The NRP performed a meta-analysis only on the first approach, use of "procedures that emphasize repeated oral reading practice or guided oral reading practice" (p. 3-5). The second approach, "all formal efforts to increase the amounts of independent or recreational reading that children engage in, including sustained silent reading programs" (p. 3-5), was analyzed more informally due to the fact that there were too few experimental studies available. Five appendices at the end of the fluency chapter (pp. 3-35–3-43) list studies that were considered (e.g., Dowhower, 1987; Levy, Nicholls, & Kohen, 1993).

> Fluent readers can read text with speed, accuracy, and proper expression. Fluency depends upon well-developed word recognition skills, but such skills do not inevitably lead to fluency…. There is common agreement that fluency develops from reading practice. What researchers have not yet agreed upon is what form such practice should take to be most effective. (National Institute of Child Health and Human Development, 2000, p. 3-1)

Pressley (2002) described skilled reading as that which is fluent, with little effort being required for word-by-word reading—in other words, readers recognize most words without having to sound them out. He explained that this is important because "reading, both decoding and comprehension, takes place in and depends on short-term memory, and short-term capacity is very limited … word recognition skills matter in comprehension" (p. 292).

The process of reading is very different for beginning and fluent readers. Beginning readers must attend to so many tasks at the same time that many bog down in the decoding and then have to read a passage again in order to comprehend. Fluent readers are able to decode and comprehend simultaneously. Samuels (2002) explained that the differences between these two types of readers seem to be in the reading experience they have had and the way they process text. Novice readers attend to words letter-by-letter (or in a way that focuses on units greater than letter-by-letter but less than whole word), whereas fluent readers process words holistically. Fluent readers decode quickly and automatically, seemingly unaware of the process. Samuels said this ease of decoding stems from fluent readers' automatic recognition of the approximately 300 words that comprise about 85% of words encountered in everyday reading.

He reported a developmental sequence in the size of the visual unit used in recognizing words and that it depended upon how much reading a student has done rather than the reading method used by the teacher (p. 170).

Researchers have found that one of the best ways to develop automaticity and fluency in reading is to spend a lot of time doing it (e.g., Allington, 1977, 2001; Nagy & Anderson, 1984). Students who read more have more encounters with common words, and that seems to be the primary reason for increases in fluency (e.g., Jenkins, Stein, & Wysocki, 1984). Repeated reading is a technique for increasing fluency (e.g., Chomsky, 1978; Samuels, 1979). The NRP Report (National Institute of Child Health and Human Development, 2000) did not endorse or criticize this method, yet said that "repeated reading and other guided oral reading procedures … clearly … improve fluency and overall reading achievement" (p. 3-28). Samuels (2002) reported a consistent finding of more than 100 published studies in this area: "repeated reading practice produces statistically significant improvement in reading speed, word recognition, and oral reading expression on the practiced passages" (p. 179).

An example of a way I differentiated instruction and scaffolded my second graders' fluency was to turn stories we were reading into Readers Theatre productions. In the process of preparing their respective parts, students read and reread for the very real purpose of giving a good performance. I was able to group readers and assign parts in ways that allowed every individual to gain from the experience. In my classes I found it helpful to (a) select different pieces appropriate to the various readers' levels, (b) group students according to the number of parts in a selection geared to their reading level, sometimes with more than one group preparing the same Readers Theatre script, (c) have multiple Readers Theatre productions in process at once so that every child had an active and challenging part with sufficient practice time, and (d) send groups of students out to "perform" for other willing classes. There was enthusiasm in the rereading, as well as in the performing. In the process, the students gained fluency, expression, and self-motivation to read that carried over to other reading experiences. Martinez, Roser, and

Strecker (1999) discussed the important impact of Readers Theatre on fluency and meaning.

Comprehension. This section of the law also rests on the work of the NRP (National Institute of Child Health and Human Development, 2000), which decided to organize the overall comprehension report into three subareas, each with its own subreport: vocabulary instruction, text comprehension instruction, and teacher preparation and comprehension strategies instruction. Comprehension subgroup members divided the 203 studies that met NRP criteria into 16 categories, summarized in various ways in Appendix A and Appendix B (pp. 4-69–4-115). Once again, "a formal meta-analysis was not possible because even the studies identified in the same instructional category used widely varying sets of methodologies and implementations" (p. 4-42). While the NRP found few research studies that met all of its criteria, it did provide a list of references (pp. 4-55–4-68) upon which this section of the report is based (e.g., Palincsar & Brown, 1984; Pressley & Afflerbach, 1995).

It is generally agreed that comprehension, or understanding, is the goal of reading. In fact, the NRP terms comprehension the "essence of reading" (citing Durkin, 1993), "essential not only to academic learning but to lifelong learning as well" (p. 4-11). Duke and Pearson (2002) described much of what we know about how good readers read—that good readers (a) are active; (b) have clear reading goals in mind (which they evaluate as they read); (c) preview text (noting structure and sections that might be most helpful); (d) make predictions; (e) read selectively (based on their decisions about what to read carefully, quickly, or not at all); (f) *construct, revise,* and *question* the meanings they make as they read" (p. 205); (g) work to understand unfamiliar words or concepts and deal with gaps and inconsistencies; (h) "draw from, compare, and *integrate their prior knowledge* with material in the text" (p. 206); (i) think in depth about the authors of what they read; (j) *"monitor their understanding* of the text, making adjustments in their reading as necessary" (p. 206); and (k) evaluate and react to a text's value and quality (p. 206). Duke and Pearson reminded us that readers *"read different kinds of texts differently"* (p. 206). For example, they mentioned that good readers pay close attention to the characters and setting in narrative text and often create and revise summaries as they read expository text. They explained that good readers process texts even when they are not reading, so that they are thinking about the ideas as they take short breaks during and even after they have finished the formal process of reading. Other researchers have discussed effective comprehension instruction (e.g., Block & Pressley, 2002; Pearson, Roehler, Dole, & Duffy, 1992; Pressley & Afflerbach, 1995).

Duke and Pearson (2002) reminded readers of other important considerations for balanced comprehension instruction—meaning "comprehension instruction [that] includes both explicit instruction in specific comprehension strategies and a great deal of time and opportunity for actual reading, writing, and discussion of text" (p. 207). Their comprehension instruction model has teachers explicitly describe various comprehension strategies and teach students when and how to use each. It is important that teachers give explicit feedback that lets students know how and why their use of comprehension strategies is successful (Hattie, Biggs, & Purdie, 1996).

Duke (2002) denoted five components of effective comprehension instruction: "a clear vision of effective comprehension; appropriate attention to underlying skills and dispositions; many opportunities to read and be read to (and for compelling reasons); lots of talk, writing, and thinking about text; and explicit instruction in comprehension strategies" (slide 7).

Comprehension is critical for effective reading. As teachers work to provide good comprehension instruction, we must ground that instruction in relevant reading for real purposes (e.g., Searfoss, Readence, & Mallette, 2001) and remember to foster comprehension even when students are still learning the words (Ivey, 2002). We must engage students often in shared book experiences (Eldredge, Reutzel, & Hollingsworth, 1996) in order to enhance children's comprehension development, oral reading, fluency, and vocabulary development, as well as increase their desire to read for themselves. Our goal must be to have students grow into and remain self-motivated readers who choose to read (e.g., Gambrell, 1996; Guthrie & Anderson, 1999). Self-motivated readers continue to read long after they leave our classrooms and schools.

Teachers often differentiate instruction in comprehension by working with students in flexible groups. For example, by assessing comprehension on an ongoing basis, both informally and formally, I was able to group students so that they made steady progress toward increasingly higher levels of understanding. One of the most effective ways of differentiating comprehension instruction occurred informally as students demonstrated their comprehension through projects of various sorts. Using conversations and questioning, students built deeper understandings as they worked on individual and group projects. As they struggled with understanding concepts, explaining those concepts, and polishing their presentations (whether written or oral), students grew individually in comprehension and in demonstrations of that comprehension.

Considering complexities of literacy instruction in early childhood settings

From years of high-caliber descriptive, correlational, and experimental research, we know that classrooms and schools are complex places in which many aspects must be considered (e.g., Darling-Hammond, 1997; Marzano, 2003). In a paper commissioned by the National Reading Conference, Pressley (2001) called attention to a range of knowledge about effective literacy instruction. Skills are important, as documented in the NRPRS; yet teaching involves more than imparting skills (e.g., Pressley, 2001; Strickland & Morrow, 2000; Stronge, 2002).

Researchers are building consensus about areas to further examine regarding effective practice. For example, in discussing the effective first-grade classrooms that he and his colleagues studied (e.g., Pressley, Allington, Wharton-McDonald, Block, & Morrow, 2001; Pressley, Wharton-McDonald, et al., 2001), Pressley (2001) summarized their findings by describing the extremely complicated nature of instruction in first grade. Instruction in effective classrooms evidences excellent classroom management, and there is a generally cooperative atmosphere in which teachers often reinforce students. There is explicit instruction in many skills at the word level and in comprehension and writing. Classrooms are inundated with literature for the children to encounter, and excellent literature experiences take place. "Excellent classrooms are very busy academically, with the students doing a great deal of actual reading (i.e., in contrast to reading-related activities, such as completing worksheets) and writing" (p. 24). Tasks students do match their competency level, and demands on students increase as competencies improve. Teachers support student learning through scaffolding—carefully monitoring when students need assistance, then giving just enough help to get them started in the right direction rather than doing the task for them. "Effective teachers encourage students to self-regulate, to do academic tasks for themselves as much as possible" (p. 24). Reading and writing are an integral part of content area learning (pp. 24–25). The work of Pressley and his colleagues provides focus for further study of classroom practices used by effective teachers.

Whatever else is mandated, teachers must create time in classrooms to attend to the needs of individual learners. Knowledgeable, caring teachers are key to implementing NCLB in ways that help children experience learning success and become lifelong learners who choose to read and write in their daily lives. We must never forget that teaching reading—or teaching anything, for that matter—is more than science alone; it is also an art.

> The art of teaching is rooted in the experience, skill, judgment, and intuition of the teacher dedicated to the best interests of the students he or she serves, while the scientific knowledge revealed by effective, contextually relevant research forms the rational knowledge base for instructional decisions. (Farstrup, 2002, p. 1)

References

Adams, M.J. (1990). *Beginning to read: Thinking and learning about print.* Cambridge, MA: MIT Press.

Adams, M.J., Foorman, B.R., Lundberg, I., & Beeler, T. (1998). *Phonemic awareness in young children: A classroom curriculum.* Baltimore: Paul H. Brookes.

Allington, R. (1977). If they don't read much, how they ever gonna get good? *Journal of Reading, 21,* 57-61.

Allington, R.L. (2001). *What really matters for struggling readers: Designing research-based programs.* New York: Longman.

Ball, E., & Blachman, B. (1991). Does phoneme awareness training in kindergarten make a difference in early word recognition and developmental spelling? *Reading Research Quarterly, 26,* 49-66.

Beck, I., & McKeown, M. (1991). Conditions of vocabulary acquisition. In R. Barr, M. Kamil, P. Mosenthal, & P.D. Pearson (Eds.), *The handbook of reading research* (Vol. 2, pp. 789-814). New York: Longman.

Beck, I., McKeown, M.G., & Kucan, L. (2002). *Bringing words to life: Robust vocabulary development.* New York: Guilford.

Beck, I.L., Perfetti, C.A., & McKeown, M.G. (1982). Effects of long-term vocabulary instruction on lexical access and reading comprehension. *Journal of Educational Psychology, 74,* 506-521.

Berliner, D.C., & Biddle, B.J. (1995). *The manufactured crisis: Myth, fraud, and the attack on America's public schools.* Reading, MA: Addison-Wesley.

Block, C.C., Oakar, M., & Hurt, N. (2002). The expertise of literacy teachers: A continuum from preschool to grade 5. *Reading Research Quarterly, 37,* 178-206.

Block, C.C., & Pressley, M. (2002). *Comprehension instruction: Research-based best practices.* New York: Guilford.

Bond, G.L., & Dykstra, R. (1997). The cooperative research program in first-grade reading instruction. *Reading Research Quarterly, 32,* 348-427. (Original work published 1967)

Calkins, L.M. (1986). *The art of teaching writing.* Portsmouth, NH: Heinemann.

Calkins, L.M. (2001). *The art of teaching reading.* New York: Longman.

Chomsky, C. (1978). When you still can't read in third grade: After decoding, what? In S.J. Samuels (Ed.), *What research has to say about reading instruction* (pp. 13-30). Newark, DE: International Reading Association.

Clay, M.M. (1979). *The early detection of reading difficulties* (3rd ed.). Portsmouth, NH: Heinemann.

Clay, M.M. (1993a). *An observation survey of early literacy.* Portsmouth, NH: Heinemann.

Clay, M.M. (1993b). *Reading recovery: A guidebook for teachers in training.* Portsmouth, NH: Heinemann.

Clay, M.M. (1998). *By different paths to common outcomes.* York, ME: Stenhouse.

Cunningham, P.M., & Cunningham, J.W. (1992). Making words: Enhancing the invented spelling-decoding connection. *The Reading Teacher, 46,* 106-115.

Cunningham, P.M., & Hall, D.P. (1994). *Making words: Multilevel, hands-on, developmentally appropriate spelling and phonics activities.* Torrance, CA: Good Apple.

Darling-Hammond, L. (1997). *The right to learn: A blueprint for creating schools that work.* San Francisco: Jossey-Bass.

Dickinson, D., & Smith, M. (1994). Long-term effects of preschool teachers' book readings on low-income children's vocabulary and story comprehension. *Reading Research Quarterly, 29,* 104-122.

Dickinson, D.K., & Tabors, P.O. (Eds.). (2001). *Building literacy with language.* Baltimore: Brookes.

Dowhower, S.L. (1987). Effects of repeated reading on second-grade transitional readers' fluency and comprehension. *Reading Research Quarterly, 22,* 389-406.

Duke, N.K. (2002, August 19). *Comprehension.* PowerPoint session presentation, Institute for Statewide Literacy Initiatives. Cambridge, MA: Harvard Graduate School of Education. Retrieved November 8, 2003 from http://www.ppe.gse.harvard.edu/coursewebsites/literacy

Duke, N.K., & Pearson, P.D. (2002). Effective practices for developing reading comprehension. In A.E. Farstrup & S.J. Samuels (Eds.), *What research has to say about reading instruction*, (3rd ed., pp. 205-242). Newark, DE: International Reading Association.

Durkin, D. (1993). *Teaching them to read* (6th ed.). Boston: Allyn and Bacon.

Dyson, A.H. (1989). *Multiple worlds of child writers: Friends learning to write*. New York: Teachers College Press.

Dyson, A.H. (1993). *Social worlds of children learning to write in an urban primary school*. New York: Teachers College Press.

Eldredge, J.L., Reutzel, D.R., & Hollingsworth, P.M. (1996). Comparing the effectiveness of two oral reading practices: Round-robin reading and the shared book experience. *Journal of Literacy Research, 28* (2), 201-225.

Elkonin, D.B. (1963). The psychology of mastery elements of reading. In B. Simon & J. Simon (Eds.), *Educational psychology in the USSR* (pp. 165-179). London: Routledge & Kegan Paul.

Farstrup, A.E. (2002). There is more to effective reading instruction than research. In A.E. Farstrup & S.J. Samuels (Eds.), *What research has to say about reading instruction* (3rd ed., pp. 1-7). Newark, DE: International Reading Association.

Fraser, J., & Skolnick, D. (1994). *On their way: Celebrating second graders as they read and write*. Portsmouth, NH: Heinemann.

Gambrell, L. (1996). Creating classroom cultures that foster reading motivation. *The Reading Teacher, 50,* 14-25.

Gaskins, I.W., Ehri, L.C., Cress, C., O'Hara, C., & Donnelly, K. (1997). Procedures for word learning: Making discoveries about words. *The Reading Teacher, 50,* 312-327.

Goswami, U., & Bryant, P. (1990). *Phonological skills and learning to read*. Hove, UK: Psychology Press.

Graves, D.H. (1983). *Writing: Teachers & children at work*. Portsmouth, NH: Heinemann.

Graves, D.H. (1994). *A fresh look at writing*. Portsmouth, NH: Heinemann.

Guthrie, J.T., & Anderson, E. (1999). Engagement in reading: Processes of motivated, strategic, knowledgeable, social readers. In J.T. Guthrie & D.E. Alvermann (Eds.), *Engaged reading: Processes, practices, and policy implications* (pp. 17-45). New York: Teachers College.

Harris, T., & Hodges, R. (Eds.). (1995). *The literacy dictionary*. Newark, DE: International Reading Association.

Hart, C.H., Burts, D.C., & Charlesworth, R. (Eds.). (1997). *Integrated curriculum and developmentally appropriate practice: Birth to age eight*. Albany: State University of New York Press.

Hattie, J., Biggs, J., & Purdie, N. (1996). Effects of learning skills interventions on student learning: A meta-analysis. *Review of Educational Research, 66,* 99-136.

Haycock, K. (1998). Good teaching matters … a lot. *Thinking K-16, 3*(2), 1-14.

Imig, D.G. (2002, October 7). President's briefing: Preparing professionals who can address NCLB, too. *AACTE Briefs, 23*(11), 2. Retrieved October 29, 2002 from http://www.aacte.org/publications/brf100702.pdf

Invernizzi, M., Juel, C., & Rosemary, C. (1996/1997). A community volunteer tutorial that works. *The Reading Teacher, 50,* 304-311.

Ivey, G. (2002). Building comprehension when they're still learning to read the words. In C.C. Block & M. Pressley, (Eds.), *Comprehension instruction: Research-based best practices* (pp. 234-246). New York: Guilford.

Jenkins, J., Stein, M., & Wysocki, K. (1984). Learning vocabulary through reading. *American Educational Research Journal, 21,* 767-788.

Joseph, L.M. (1998/1999). Word boxes help children with learning disabilities identify and spell words. *The Reading Teacher, 52,* 348-356.

Juel, C. (2002, August 20). *What teachers need to know about word study*. PowerPoint session presentation, Institute for Statewide Literacy Initiatives. Cambridge, MA: Harvard Graduate School of Education. Retrieved November 8, 2003 from http://www.ppe.gse.harvard.edu/coursewebsites/literacy

Knapp, M.S., with Adelman, N.E., Marder, C., McCollum, H., Needels, M.C., Padilla, C., et al. (1995). *Teaching for meaning in high-poverty classrooms*. New York: Teachers College Press.

Ladson-Billings, G. (1994). *The dreamkeepers: Successful teachers of African American children*. San Francisco: Jossey-Bass.

Levy, B.A., Nicholls, A., & Kohen, D. (1993). Repeated readings: Process benefits for good and poor readers. *Journal of Experimental Child Psychology, 55,* 303-327.

Martinez, M., Roser, N.L., & Strecker, S. (1999). "I never thought I could be a star": A Readers Theatre ticket to fluency. *The Reading Teacher, 52,* 326-334.

Marzano, R.J. (2003). *What works in schools: Translating research into action*. Alexandria, VA: Association for Supervision and Curriculum Development.

McCollum, H. (1995). Managing academic learning environments. In M.S. Knapp, with N.E. Adelman, C. Marder, H. McCollum, M.C. Needels, C. Padilla, et al., *Teaching for meaning in high-poverty classrooms* (pp. 11-32). New York: Teachers College Press.

McKeown, M.G., Beck, I.L., Omanson, R.C., & Pople, M.T. (1985). Some effects of the nature and frequency of vocabulary instruction on the knowledge and use of words. *Reading Research Quarterly, 20,* 522-535.

Morrow, L.M., Tracey, D.H., Woo, D.G., & Pressley, M. (1999). Characteristics of exemplary first-grade literacy instruction. *The Reading Teacher, 52,* 462-476.

Mwalimu, & Kennaway, A. (1989). *Awful aardvark*. Boston: Little, Brown.

Nagy, W., & Anderson, R.C. (1984). How many words are there in printed school English? *Reading Research Quarterly, 19,* 304-330.

National Institute of Child Health and Human Development. (2000). *Report of the National Reading Panel: Teaching children to read: An evidence-based assessment of the scientific research literature on reading and its implications for reading instruction. Reports of the subgroups*. Washington, DC: U.S. Government Printing Office.

Nelson, N., & Calfee, R.C. (1998). *The reading-writing connection: 97th yearbook of the National Society for the Study of Education*. Chicago: University of Chicago Press for the National Society for the Study of Education.

Neuman, S.B., Copple, C., & Bredekamp, S. (2000). *Learning to read and write: Developmentally appropriate practices for young children*. Washington, DC: National Association for the Education of Young Children.

No Child Left Behind Act of 2001, Pub. L. No. 107-110, §1001, 115 Stat. 1439. (2002). Retrieved May 29, 2002 from http://edworkforce.house.gov/issues/107th/education/ nclb/nclb.htm

No Child Left Behind Act of 2001, Pub. L. No. 107-110, §1201, 115 Stat. 1535. (2002). Retrieved May 29, 2002 from http://edworkforce.house.gov/issues/107th/education/ nclb/nclb.htm

No Child Left Behind Act of 2001, Pub. L. No. 107-110, §1208, 115 Stat. 1550, 1551. (2002). Retrieved May 29, 2002 from http://edworkforce.house.gov/issues/107th/education/ nclb/nclb.htm

Oakland, T., Black, J., Stanford, G., Nussbaum, N., & Balise, R. (1998). An evaluation of the dyslexia training program: A multisensory method for promoting reading in students with reading disabilities. *Journal of Learning Disabilities, 31,* 140-147.

Palincsar, A.S., & Brown, A.L. (1984). Reciprocal teaching of comprehension fostering and comprehension-monitoring activities. *Cognition and Instruction, 2,* 117-175.

Pearson, P.D., Roehler, L., Dole, J., & Duffy, G. (1992). Developing expertise in reading comprehension. In S.J. Samuels & A.E. Farstrup (Eds.), *What research has to say about reading instruction* (2nd ed., pp. 145-199). Newark, DE: International Reading Association.

Pressley, M. (2001). *Effective beginning reading instruction: Executive summary and paper commissioned by the National Reading Conference.* Chicago: National Reading Conference. Retrieved February 4, 2003 from `http:// nrc.oakland.edu/documents/2001/ pressleywhite2.PDF`

Pressley, M. (2002). Metacognition and self-regulated comprehension. In A.E. Farstrup & S.J. Samuels (Eds.), *What research has to say about reading instruction* (3rd ed., pp. 291-309). Newark, DE: International Reading Association.

Pressley, M., & Afflerbach, P. (1995). *Verbal protocols of reading: The nature of constructively responsive reading.* Hillsdale, N J: Erlbaum.

Pressley, M., Allington, R., Wharton-McDonald, R., Block, C.C., & Morrow, L.M. (2001). *Learning to read: Lessons from exemplary first grades.* New York: Guilford.

Pressley, M., Wharton-McDonald, R., Allington, R., Block, C.C., Morrow, L., Trace, D., et al. (2001). A study of effective grade 1 literacy instruction. *Scientific Studies of Reading, 5,* 35-58.

Samuels, S.J. (1979). The method of repeated readings. *The Reading Teacher, 32,* 403-408.

Samuels, S.J. (2002). Reading fluency: Its development and assessment. In A.E. Farstrup & S.J. Samuels (Eds.), *What research has to say about reading instruction* (3rd ed., pp. 166-183). Newark, DE: International Reading Association.

Searfoss, L.W., Readence, J.E., & Mallette, M.H. (2001). *Helping children learn to read: Creating a classroom literacy environment* (4th ed.). Boston: Allyn and Bacon.

Snow, C.E. (2002, August 19). *The central place of oral language development.* PowerPoint session presentation, Institute for Statewide Literacy Initiatives. Cambridge, MA: Harvard Graduate School of Education. Retrieved November 8, 2003 from `http://www.ppe.gse.harvard.edu/ coursewebsites/literacy`

Snow, C.E., Burns, M.S., & Griffin, P. (Eds.). (1998). *Preventing reading difficulties in young children.* Washington, DC: National Academy Press.

Snow, C.E., Dickinson, D.K., & Tabors, P.O. (2002). *The home-school study of language and literacy development.* Retrieved January 26, 2003 from `http://www.gseharvard.edu/ ~pild/homeschoolstudy.htm`

Stewart, M.T. (1997). [Field notes from second-grade class]. Unpublished raw data.

Stewart, M.T. (2002a). *"Best Practice"? Insights on literacy instruction from an elementary classroom.* Newark, DE: International Reading Association & Chicago: National Reading Conference.

Stewart, M.T. (2002b). *WRITING: "It's in the bag." Ways to inspire your students to write.* Peterborough, NH: Crystal Springs Books.

Stewart, M.T. (2003). Building effective practice: Using small discoveries to enhance literacy learning. *The Reading Teacher, 55,* 540-547.

Strickland, D.S., Ganske, K., & Monroe, J.K. (2002). *Supporting struggling readers and writers: Strategies for classroom intervention 3-6.* Portland, ME: Stenhouse and Newark, DE: International Reading Association.

Strickland, D.S., & Morrow, L.M. (2000). *Beginning reading and writing.* New York: Teachers College Press and Newark, DE: International Reading Association.

Stronge, J.H. (2002). *Qualities of effective teachers.* Alexandria, VA: Association for Supervision and Curriculum Development.

Taylor, B.M., Pearson, P.D., Clark, K.F., & Walpole, S. (1999). Effective schools/accomplished teachers. *The Reading Teacher, 53,* 156-159.

Taylor, B.M., Pearson, P.D., Clark, K.F., & Walpole, S. (2000). Effective schools and accomplished teachers: Lessons about primary reading instruction in low-income schools. *Elementary School Journal, 101,* 121-166.

Treiman, R. (1985). Onsets and rimes as units of spoken syllables: Evidence from children. *Journal of Experimental Psychology, 39,* 161-181.

Walker, B.J. (2003). Instruction for struggling readers contains multiple features. *The Reading Teacher, 57,* 206-207.

Wright, S.P., Horn, S.P., & Sanders, W.L. (1997). Teacher and classroom context effects on student achievement: Implications for teacher evaluation. *Journal of Personnel Evaluation in Education, 11,* 57-67.

Wylie, R.E., & Durrell, D.D. (1970). Teaching vowels through phonograms. *Elementary English, 47,* 787-791.

Stewart teaches at Louisiana State University (College of Education, Department of Curriculum & Instruction, 223 Peabody Hall, Baton Rouge, LA 70803, USA). E-mail to mstewa6@lsu.edu.

Literacy, Learning and Libraries: Common Issues and Common Concerns

Ken Haycock

Librarians are highly effective in enabling customers and clients to make informed decisions based on the best evidence available. We seem less successful in applying those same standards and approaches to our own professional practice, particularly with regard to literacy and learning programs. The result is programs that do not have the effect for the dollar that would otherwise be possible.

Consider these recent examples reported in the professional and scholarly literature.

Role clarification

What is the role of libraries and librarians in literacy? We have never been very clear or consistent about this. Are we in the library business? The information business? Or the community development business? Are we advocates talking "library, library, library" or players at the table, talking "literacy, learning, student achievement"?

The teaching role of librarians is becoming more apparent and more sophisticated, whether we are working with students in classes and other groups or providing staff development and training programs for support staff. Teaching students and staff is a highly skilled occupation; indeed, graduate degrees are given in these areas. Can we really expect to master these skills and

strategies in one-day workshops? How can we ensure that our staff are well trained if we have only sporadic staff development programs that are not aligned to organizational goals and have a low priority in budget deliberations? Too often, recent graduates in librarianship are hired for their technological expertise rather than for their ability to fill the overall and long-term needs of the system, due to the absence of a well-coordinated and well-supported staff training program.

And what of the role of our staff?

If youth literacy is a priority, are we better served by children's librarians serving children directly or by reorienting their role to train others—daycare supervisors, community centre leaders, and preschool and primary school teachers—in selecting literature, telling stories and programming around quality books? The former leads to a quality library-based program, while the latter increases our influence and position in the community. Each has its points, but we can rarely afford both. We often leave these choices to individual preference rather than focusing on organizational priorities and community outcomes.

Partnerships

Many public libraries are developing highly focused and professional

family literacy programs in response to community needs. Many school districts are simultaneously doing the same thing. Rarely are the two agencies aware of the plans and programs of the other; rarely do the two agencies collaborate as equal partners (and with other community groups) to ensure that all the pieces of the puzzle fit together. How odd that our history leads us to think that "partnerships 'r' us," yet we seem unable to bridge the gap between these two education and learning institutions. Of course there are exceptions, but the exception merely spotlights the norm.

Homework centres are common public library services in the United Kingdom and United States, although not so common here, and they do make a difference to students. Rarely, however, is the school district involved in promoting the service, referring specific students or participating in studies of effect on attendance and performance. We even let the district off the hook for training tutors, their area of expertise. We are oriented to providing service, which is certainly laudable, but we are less oriented to assessing outcomes and impact beyond the anecdotal "I enjoyed myself and it made a difference."

Similarly, one might argue that the only difference between a high school senior and a university freshman is two months, and yet high school and academic librarians know little of each other's worlds, let alone the issues and priorities that preoccupy them.

... student achievement results more from collaboration with faculty.

Collaboration

More than 40 years' research in teacher-librarianship makes clear that student achievement is affected by teacher-librarians only when they collaborate with classroom teachers to integrate information skills and strategies. Recent research in academic librarianship is drawing the same conclusions. Nevertheless, we proceed with our own interests and at our own comfort levels. We offer more stand-alone classes and courses in information literacy (or bibliographic instruction or even library skills) rather than working to integrate our work with that of faculty, which would be more difficult but also more successful.

What are our measures of success? Librarians prefer stand-alone classes and seminars in the library and are generally happy with them. Although attendance at these sessions tends to be low, students seem pleased with the program. However, studies tell us that improved student achievement results more from collaboration with faculty. In fact, students do better when there is collaboration between two partners, librarian and instructor, for a more integrated instructional approach. Students also do better in critical thinking when the instruction is embedded in an articulated information process model.

The information process

Libraries are moving from providing "physical" access to information and ideas (the book in hand, the text or video on the screen) to "intellectual" access (the ability to assess the information, derive meaning from it and synthesize it to share with others). While these labels and figures of speech are useful, they need to be translated into practice.

If libraries and librarians are serious about information literacy, then the entire information cycle needs to be incorporated into our programs. Any good reference librarian knows this. What is the sense of searching for information if the task is not articulated and understood? What is the sense of evaluating information from several sources if the student is unable to synthesize and present the results? Research from the U.K. dating from the 1970s and from the U.S. more recently provides guidance on creating effective programs through analysis of students' feelings, abilities and needs from the initiation of the project to completion and evaluation. Ample opportunity is typically provided for students to locate and evaluate information. But there is often insufficient time to determine the parameters of the problem or task. And there is relatively little guidance or time to think—to analyse and synthesize and to assess one's own effectiveness in the process and the product.

A consistent model for developing the information process incorporated into faculty assignments would better support student learning. If our challenge is the assignment given by the faculty member, it makes intuitive sense to integrate information process instruction and the research bears this out.

Are any of these easy? Of course not. Do they make a difference? Yes they do. Libraries are effective in building community, and librarians are catalysts for adding value to services and programs. By using our own research and by making a commitment to evidence-based practice, we can not only be more effective in our practice, but we will also demonstrate clearly our alignment with the overall goals of the institution, whether school, university or government agency. We know children benefit from our literacy programs, but their effect would be enhanced through formal partnerships with other community players. We know students benefit from our information literacy programs, but their effect would be enhanced through formal partnerships with faculty. If we wish to add value, prove our worth and be rewarded for it in return, then we must embrace evidence-based practice and insist on evidence for decision making. These stances can only make us stronger and more effective as a profession.

Ken Haycock is a professor in the School of Library, Archival and Information Studies at the University of British Columbia.

Public Libraries and Early Literacy: Raising the Reader

ALA's Preschool Literacy Initiative educates librarians on how to play a role in teaching reading to children

By Renea Arnold

It's Saturday morning at Multnomah County Library's Belmont branch in Portland, Oregon, where a librarian leads a lively crowd of 30 babies and their parents through an interactive routine of stories and songs. A 7-month-old stares at the librarian's hands, entranced by her rhythmic and animated motions. A 1-year-old toddles around the circle, seemingly oblivious to the adults' enthusiastic singing.

At the same time, a group of day-care providers gathers at Phoenix (Ariz.) Public Library's Ocotillo branch to learn new research-based ways to work with their 4- and 5-year-olds. The caregivers laugh at the interactive games designed to sharpen preschoolers' phonological sensitivity and are intrigued with the six skills that researchers have identified as early-literacy building blocks.

Are public libraries helping to teach these new parents and caregivers how to get their children ready to read, or are these families just having a good time? Will research-based practices and library workshops really change the behaviors of overworked and underpaid daycare providers? Can libraries really become key players in the Bush administration's No Child Left Behind goals? How will public libraries document their impact and know whether they are successful players in preparing children to read?

In 2000, the National Institute of Child Health and Human Development (NICHD) and ALA's Public Library Association created the Preschool Literacy Initiative. The project is designed to link reading research to action; to get the word out to parents and caregivers that learning to read is not instinctual, but must be taught; and to assess the ability of libraries to effect the desired change. ALA's Association for Library Service to Children joined the effort in 2001, to create accompanying project materials and to form a joint division task force.

Since 2001, 20 demonstration public-library sites have used a variety of ways to encourage parents and caregivers to actively participate in their children's literacy development. Through subtle changes in regular library story hours and the addition of parent-education classes, the libraries have introduced adults to new concepts and strategies to help prepare children for reading. A sampling of participants has completed testing to determine the impact on caregivers' behavior.

Six essential skills

According to NICHD's National Reading Panel, children should enter kindergarten with six early-literacy skills that begin to develop at birth: vocabulary, print motivation, print awareness, narrative skills, letter knowledge, and phonological sensitivity (see Figure 1). The Preschool Literacy Initiative focuses attention on activities to foster these emergent-literacy skills and on the parents or adult caregivers—the essential participants in children's learning.

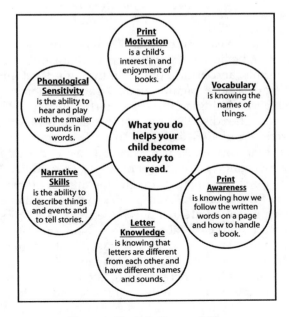

Figure 1. Six early literacy skills.

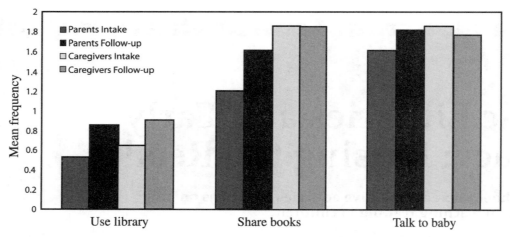

Figure 2. Early literacy behaviors of parents and caregivers of before and after program.

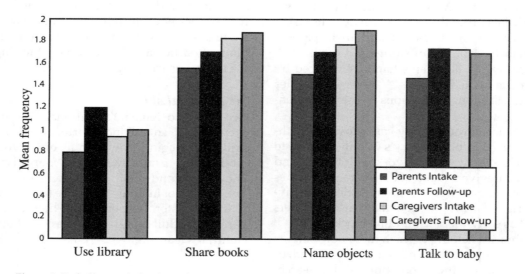

Figure 3. Early literacy behaviors of parents and caregivers of talkers (2-3years), intake and follow-up.

For many years, traditional library story hours have encouraged children's vocabulary, print awareness, narrative skills, and print motivation through developmentally appropriate picture books, songs, rhymes, and finger-plays. Using a Story-time Early Literacy Self-Observation Checklist, librarians at the demonstration sites utilized stimulation activities in each category or age group that answered such questions as: Did I … Sing rhyming chants and songs (phonological sensitivity)? Allow children to participate in retelling the story (narrative skills)? Encourage children to clap out the syllables of words (phonological sensitivity)? (See Figures 2, 3, and 4.)

Provo (Utah) City Library inserted emergent-literacy components in each of its age-specific storytimes for children. Children's Services Manager Carla Morris said, "Patrons have increased respect and confidence in the librarians and storytellers who use and understand correct emergent-literacy terms. They are pleased to take part in storytimes that 'have substance.' One child

told his mother that he likes to go to 'library school,' referring to storytimes."

To call adults' attention to the techniques that support early-literacy techniques used during storytime, librarians in Portland inserted taglines or comments for parents and caregivers such as "Children learn the most from books when they are actively involved, so be sure to ask them questions" or "Your child doesn't need worksheets or flashcards to learn to read; instead, make up silly words, rhyme words, and clap syllables in words."

Educating caregivers

Recognizing that parents and caregivers are children's primary teachers, the Preschool Literacy Initiative offers three age-specific classes for parents and caregivers of babies, toddlers, and preschoolers. Each class has the latest information on reading development in easy-to-understand terms and incorporates practical, hands-on activi-

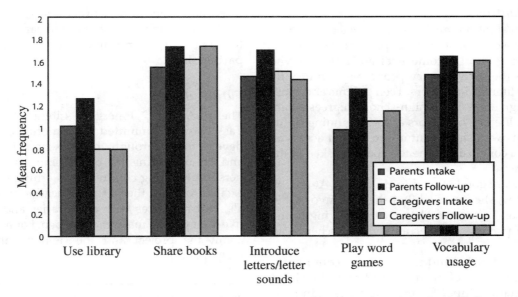

Figure 4 Early literacy behaviors of parents and caregivers of prereaders (4-5 years), intake and follow-up.

ties. Each participant was asked questions before and after class sessions to help assess whether libraries made a difference in parents' behavior.

The first class, Bonding with Baby, encourages the use of wordless books to talk about the pictures, and encourages singing songs and reciting rhymes such as "Eensy Weensy Spider." The Montgomery County (Md.) Public Libraries worked with the public school's English as a Second Language Department to adapt the workshops for families whose first language is Spanish. Following one of the workshops, the mother of an 8-month-old said she would start singing and talking more with her daughter. She wanted her daughter to learn English despite her own limited English-speaking skills that resulted in her hardly speaking at all to her baby. Following the workshop, she realized the importance of talking with and reading to her child.

A dialogic reading class at Multnomah County Library known as Hear and Say encourages interactive reading techniques with toddlers. Reading aloud has maximum learning potential when children are given opportunities to actively participate and respond. Asked why she came to the parent class, a 32-year-old Hispanic mother from Portland replied, "I came because I want to learn better ways of helping my daughter learn. I want her to be a good reader someday." Four weeks later, the mother was asked about how she had changed her interactions with her toddler after attending early-literacy classes. Her response: "I used to correct her pronunciation. Now, I ask her questions and she has more fun."

The Sound Awareness session for preschoolers teaches how to play language games to help children hear the different phonemes in words—phonological sensitivity. Sue Tracy, early childhood specialist at Hennepin County Library in Minnetonka, Minnesota, coached Head Start parents and caregivers as well as teen parents in high schools. After teaching a phonological awareness class she noted, "Many parents left excited and felt empowered to try new literacy interactions with their children."

Readying a reader

The most significant research to impact library programming is the clear evidence that phonological sensitivity and letter-knowledge skills are highly predictive of later reading success. Although children need direct instruction to gain these skills, the skills are not reached through drills, but by engaging them in fun, interactive, age-appropriate activities.

Literacy development can be greatly enhanced by simple interactions. Repeated reading of rhymes, poems, or stories with rhyming words help children notice sound patterns. Clapping out the syllables in their names or characters in a book helps children begin to separate sounds in words. Other fun games include searching for things on a page that begin with the "n" sound, or singing songs like "Willoughby, Wolloughby Woo" to heighten awareness of speech sounds.

The NICHD National Reading Panel reports that a minimal amount of phonemic instruction could have a positive effect on word-reading outcomes. It indicates that "the best effects of phonemic awareness instruction were found within programs that used between 5 and 18 hours total in the course of a school year." Libraries are well suited to provide this amount of instruction as part of existing programming.

In the past decade, library staff may have shied away from formally introducing the alphabet because it seemed too school-like. But now libraries are introducing letter-sound relationships by sharing appropriate children's books as well as encouraging play with felt or foam letters, or reading from alphabet books.

Positive evaluations

Second-year evaluation analysis, conducted by Sara Laughlin and Associates, shows that parents of every age, educational background, income level, and ethnicity who participated in the early-literacy programs significantly increased their literacy behaviors. Teen parents and those parents or caregivers without high-school degrees exhibited the fewest literacy behaviors at the beginning of the program, but showed significant improvement across all behaviors at the conclusion. One teen parent asked at the intake interview:

"What books are good to read to children?" At the follow-up interview, she reported that she was involved in such activities as "using the library card, singing to my daughter more, playing with her, and talking to her about her toys."

Participating libraries and their various community partners in the literacy effort described how they built on existing relationships. Several partners admitted that they were not aware of the library's knowledge of research-based literacy practices. They are now enthusiastic about the impact of the library's training and interested in continuing and expanding their partnerships.

Future plans

The PLA/ALSC Emergent Literacy/Early Childhood Task Force is committed to promoting children's literacy development through the Preschool Literacy Initiative and demonstrating that public libraries are valuable partners in preparing children for learning to read. They are excited to share the parent-education programs, materials, and resources with all libraries and have created a five-year plan to make that happen. For more information about the project and the demonstration sites, visit www.pla.org.

RENEA ARNOLD is program manager for Early Childhood Resources at the Multnomah County Library in Portland, Oregon.

"The best way is always through the children":
The impact of family reading

Low standards of adult literacy in an English borough prompted the local Library Service to initiate a nine-month family reading project.

By Sarah J. McNicol and Pete Dalton

Traditionally, the London Borough of Barking and Dagenham has been an area of low attainment; it is the 15th most deprived borough in England and has the highest proportion of adults without higher education qualifications. Supporting adult literacy is a priority because the borough was fourth from bottom in the U.K. Basic Skill Agency's 1998 index of adult literacy, and there are currently over 30,000 adults with very low levels of literacy (Barking & Dagenham Library Service, 2000). The borough has identified the improvement and support of adult literacy as a priority which it intends to implement through a range of services, including libraries.

The DCMS/Wolfson Public Libraries Challenge Fund is a partnership between the an Department for Culture, Media and Sport and The Wolfson Foundation to enhance the facilities and services provided by public libraries in England. The Reader Development Programme aimed to enhance public libraries' traditional strength in promoting reading as a skill and pleasure. Barking and Dagenham's bid for funding in 2000–2001 was based on a partnership between the Library Service, the Adult College, and the Education Service. The Library Service had recently merged with the Education Department, and this project was a practical way to help to strengthen connections and links and improve communication by working together.

The Partnership With Parents course run by Barking and Dagenham's Adult College is a taster course consisting of six two-hour sessions that aims to help the parents of 5- to 7-year-old children to support their children's literacy development by teaching them how children are taught to read, spell, and write at school and ways to help children at home. The course involves a high proportion of group work, and learners are encouraged to interact with a variety of fictional and factual texts, including reports, narratives, journalism, and poetry. The involvement of the Library Service was a novel feature of Barking and Dagenham's project.

Under the scheme, a family reading librarian took library materials for the whole family into the schools, led one session in the course, demonstrated the range of library services, and encouraged families to join and use the library. A taster collection of children's and adults' reading materials was left in each school for the course participants to borrow. Tutors allocated time for parents to exchange their books every week. Titles were initially selected by library staff, working on the advice of the Adult College tutors. However, as the project developed, the parents themselves frequently suggested additional resources. As a follow-up, further sessions in local libraries were planned and family reading groups set up. Provision was made for all library staff to be trained in family reading.

Evaluation formed an integral part of the project from the start. The activities undertaken by the Centre for Information Research (CIRT) at the University of Central England in Birmingham focused on (a) the impact of the family reading project on parents and library staff and (b) the partnerships it fostered between organisations involved in the initiative. This article is based on the evaluation team's findings.

Family literacy and family reading

Meek (1991) stated that "there is no single literacy, no definable set of common activities that produces the literateness of individuals. Instead there are series and sets of literate practices which individuals choose to engage in" (p. 232). However, as Brown (1998) pointed out, all literacies are not equally valued in society. Although it is just one of many literacy practices, family literacy is significant because it has the potential to engender lasting changes in some fundamental aspects of literacy education, particularly the role of local communities. As Behrman (2002) pointed out, "reading and writing are social as well as personal activities" and, as such, are affected by the community in which they take place. Family learning brings together the British tradition of nonformal adult literacy provision and conventional school provision, providing "the opportunity for a productive confrontation between distinct philosophies of education" (Barton & Hamilton, 1998, p. 206).

According to the U.K. National Literacy Trust, "family literacy" involves working "through parents to improve the reading and writing of their children, as well as the parents' literacy" (Bird, 2001, p. 2). However, other commentators (e.g., Morrow, 1995; Wolfendale & Topping, 1996) have adopted a wider definition of family literacy, using the term to include any approach that explicitly addresses the family dimension in literacy. With its emphasis on family use of libraries and parental involvement in schools, the Barking and Dagenham family reading project forms part of this wider concept of family literacy.

In the 1980s, there was a broad acceptance that parents had an important role to play in helping their children learn to read. However, it was not until the following decade that initiatives to support parents in relation to their own literacy development began to be introduced in the United Kingdom. Several projects attempted to improve parents' and children's literacy by providing parents with information about the English National Curriculum and education system and supporting them in developing their own strategies to help their children learn to read and write. An example is the British Government's Standards Fund Family Literacy Programme, developed by the Basic Skills Agency; this 12-week course targets parents with poor literacy skills and their children, providing a mixture of separate and joint activities for both.

While many family literacy programmes have been criticised because they are restrictive in terms of who can participate and how the programme is structured (e.g., Hannon, 2000), the Partnership With Parents course is intended to provide flexibility and engage a wider parental audience. Barking and Dagenham's family reading project aimed to encourage adults to read and use libraries for their own benefit and enjoyment, as well as to assist their children, while recognising that supporting their children's learning is a great motivator for parents who might not necessarily be interested in reading for their own development (Hammond & Gough, 2000).

Impact on parents

The family reading project aimed to have a significant impact on parents by assisting those who wished to become more actively involved in their children's education, breaking down barriers to library use, improving standards of adult literacy, encouraging parents to participate in adult learning, and widening reading choices. It recognised that literacy is not simply about the development of discrete skills, but has much wider benefits, such as helping people to voice ideas and to take independent action for the good of their families and communities (Stein, 1995).

Encouraging parental involvement

It was hoped that, by gaining an understanding of how children develop as readers, parents in Barking and Dagenham would be better placed to support them in choosing and enjoying books. It was also thought likely that families who attended the Partnership With Parents sessions would be more likely to contribute to the school in other ways and to encourage their children. A danger associated with family literacy is the potential to create a "deficit model" that blames families for children's lack of progress in school (Barton, 1996). The project partners were careful to avoid attaching blame, instead focusing on the positive outcomes of the courses.

Around one third of the headteachers involved were interviewed towards the end of the project. They confirmed that parents had, indeed, benefited from taking part in the courses by becoming more involved with the school and being better able to support their children. They claimed that the courses had raised parents' expectations and allowed them to gain an insight on what the schools are doing and what teachers are trying to achieve. As parents became more aware of what is being taught in schools, they began to feel more included and informed. Several parents said the family reading librarian's session had helped them to develop a greater understanding of their child's education.

Although the impact on children may only become evident over a longer period, several headteachers believed they had seen an improvement in the literacy skills of those children whose parents have been involved. Although this accounted for only a limited number of pupils, as one teacher said, "anything we can do to improve literacy is a help."

Family literacy activities provide schools with valuable opportunities to increase parental involvement. However, the true value of family literacy can be realised only if it provides "the possibility of new educational practices which need not be constrained by traditions of formal schooling" (Barton & Hamilton, 1998, p. 206). The involvement of other agencies, such as libraries, has a crucial role to play in this respect; these agencies can help to synthesise a range of literacies from the home and community to situate learners in both individual and community contexts.

Breaking down barriers to library use

Being community-based, libraries are "the key places for learning for most adults" (Barking and Dagenham Literacy and Cultural Services representative) who are not able to afford books and other items and who lack opportunities to learn and access information. The Partnership With Parents courses encourage adults to become involved in libraries through supporting their children. This project was a unique venture for Barking and Dagenham Library Service because it provided staff with an opportunity to give a clear explanation of what is on offer for families in local libraries, and parents had the chance to ask questions in a way that is not normally possible in a busy library. By taking the Library Service to schools and adopting an informal approach, librarians aimed to reach more adults, especially those who felt apprehensive or uncomfortable using libraries. The library staff felt that providing parents with an opportunity to find out more about libraries and simplifying joining procedures were two of the most successful aspects of the project.

Around one quarter of the 198 parents attending the 25 Partnership With Parents courses throughout the year were not current library members. By the end of their course, 83% had joined the library. However, out of the 65 adults and 113 children who joined the library as a direct result of attending a partnership course, just 26% of the adults and 21% of the children had actually made use of their library tickets by the end of the project. Library staff recognised that entering a library was a huge step for some parents and accepted that it would take longer than six weeks to progress from borrowing from the readily available taster collections to using the full library facilities. Nevertheless, it is an unquestionable achievement that, as a result of the family reading project, some parents have gained the confidence to use a library for the first time. When parents were asked about factors that discouraged them from making greater use of the library, the most common response was that loan periods are too short. The distance of the public library from their home and the general atmosphere in the library were also clearly important factors.

Some parents thought the family reading librarian's session had been worthwhile because they had been able to find out more about local libraries, in particular about new facilities such as videos and computing facilities. The most common response when parents were asked about the usefulness of the session was surprise at the range of books and library services available. One commented, "Although I already belong to the local library, this session made me realise just exactly how wide the library's range covers. It's useful to know the different

services the library offers." Both frequent library users and nonmembers said they had learned something new at the session. The few parents who did not find the session helpful were already aware of the services offered by the local library.

The evaluation team regularly reported its findings to the project steering group. This meant that the family reading librarian could constantly develop her session by responding to parents' comments. She was keen to use parents' current literacy practices and general interests as a starting point to involve them more fully in the session—for example, by including information about the computer facilities in the library, the local history collection, and ideas for new ways of choosing books. The contributions made by the parents were valued by the project partners, confirming the findings of Tett and St Clair (1997): "If parents are to be genuine partners in their children's education, then they must be able to share power, responsibility, and ownership in ways which show a high degree of mutuality" (p. 111).

The taster collections allowed parents who were not already library users to see the range of resources and services on offer and encouraged current users to try things they had not considered before, like nonbook materials. A few parents remarked that using the taster collection had prompted them to visit their local library. As one said, "It has actually given me a boost into taking my children into the local library and sitting and reading books . . . on a regular basis." Overall, just under one quarter of parents said they intended to use the library for a new purpose, such as borrowing videos or finding information, after attending the course. Around two thirds of these were infrequent users who had not used a library for at least three months.

In general, the family reading librarian's sessions and taster collections were very successful. However, enticing parents into libraries proved to be a more complex issue and still requires further work. The planned follow-up sessions were generally acknowledged as the least successful aspect of the project, and the number of parents attending family reading groups was very modest. A tutor reported that some parents' aversion to libraries was so strong that they simply had not turned up when they knew that a librarian would be speaking. This obviously limited the session's impact on those parents who might benefit the most.

Improving standards of adult literacy

Local schools and the Library Service both acknowledge the role they can play in improving adult literacy levels in the borough. Although many parents want to help their children, they expressed less concern about developing their own literacy and reading habits. This attitude led one headteacher to reflect, "the best way is always through the children" if parents are to be encouraged to improve their own literacy skills. Tellingly, several parents thought the section on adult reading in the family reading librarian's session was irrelevant and argued that there should be fewer adult titles in the taster collections. A number said that they were not interested in the adult collection because they did not read a great deal themselves. One said they could "see lots of good books, but I don't have time to read now." However, works on interior design and local history were mentioned by a number of parents as being enjoyable.

It was hoped that the partnership courses would encourage some parents to attend further Adult College courses. The positive attitude of the adult tutors was seen as key to the success of the courses. Headteachers felt that, even when parents described the course as "difficult" or "challenging," the tutors were very supportive and responded to parents "at their level"; the tutors were "key players" in making parents feel at ease.

As a college tutor commented, it has been "amazing" how much some of the parents taking part in the sessions have gained in terms of confidence, skills, and overall approach. However, despite the anecdotal evidence, measurable gains for parents in terms of their own learning are difficult to evaluate; this is a more long-term issue that cannot be adequately addressed through a single nine-month project.

Widening reading choices

The taster collections were a particularly successful aspect of the project, and one that the Library Service will continue beyond the official end date. The library staff were surprised by parents' responses to the taster collections; they "hadn't realised how special that would be." Much of this success is attributed to the fact that the collections were developed throughout the project from comments made by parents, with the Library Service responding to their needs.

In total, over a thousand items were loaned from taster collections during the course of the project. The vast majority of these, 88%, were children's titles. Each week 64% of parents borrowed books from the taster collection, and a further 14% did so every few weeks. Only one parent said the family had no intention of borrowing any books, adding that they had books of their own at home. Many parents praised the variety of material in the taster collection; one pointed out that there were "books that suit all family members—not just one age group."

The most common observation was surprise at the variety of material on offer. Materials available ranged from adult fiction and books about cookery, local history, and car maintenance to dual-language texts and titles suitable for children of all ages. From their comments, it appeared that some parents borrowed books for younger and older children and other adults in their household as well as for themselves and their 5- to 7-year-old children.

Several particularly commented on the inclusion of books for babies and preschool children. Almost half the parents remarked on the choice of books in the collection.

The wide range of material led to some problems, however; one parent found the selection a little confusing and would have liked more guidance on the type of books to choose for children of different ages. There is evidence that this problem was quickly addressed as, in later sessions, a number of parents said they appreciated the advice about which books were suitable for each age group.

Tutors also felt that parents had gained a lot from the taster collection. It allowed parents to experience books without the trouble of going to a library and may have helped some "get back on track" with their own reading. Of all the parents, 41% borrowed some adult material from the taster collection, with nonfiction material being more popular then fiction among adults. This compares with 73% who borrowed books for children. Seven out of 10 parents borrowed books from the taster collection, either to read with their children or by themselves. In a number of families, other adults and children also read books borrowed from the taster collection. An additional favourable feature of the taster collection was the newness of the books; parents and children appreciated having access to titles that were not yet available in the library.

Impact on public libraries

In addition to the benefits for parents involved, it was hoped that the family reading project would result in gains for the Library Service itself. Library staff felt the project had provided a good opportunity to promote the library in a more focussed and specific way; the Service has gained a higher profile through local publicity. Many parents became more aware of the facilities offered for both themselves and their children. In addition, the important role that libraries play in family learning and adult literacy was officially recognised, not just by librarians, teachers, and adult tutors, but more generally within the borough.

Staff training began towards the end of the project, and eventually this will provide all library staff with an opportunity to improve their customer care skills and gain a greater understanding of local families. It is hoped that long-lasting changes in the attitude and image of library staff may result. In addition, the project evaluation has provided an ideal opportunity for consultation with both users and nonusers. Perhaps most important, through the project, the librarians gained an opportunity to try out new ideas and a different style of service to see how various innovations can increase library use and membership.

Impact on schools

Teachers felt that involving the Library Service in schools would be beneficial to both organisations because it reinforces the message that family learning should not focus solely on the formal education system. Although the involvement of the Library Service did not figure in the decision to become involved in the family reading initiative at any of the schools that participated in the evaluation interviews, teachers did identify many benefits likely to result from the collaboration. These included

- more children taking books home from the school library,
- an increased interest in books,
- improved literacy levels among pupils,
- better liaison and "more of an open relationship" with parents, and
- fewer queries from parents as they gained a better understanding of the education system.

The interviewees all agreed that involvement in the Partnership With Parents courses had helped to address two fundamental concerns: raising standards and involving parents. Literacy had been identified as an area in need of improvement in the development plans of several schools; in some cases, involvement was related to the recommendations of recent Office for Standards in Education (OFSTED) inspections, which seek to improve standards of achievement and quality of education. Involving parents in their children's reading and encouraging children to visit the library are seen as vital parts of any strategy to improve standards in most schools. Most schools already operate informal schemes to promote greater parental involvement, such as requesting parents read with their children as well as running courses such as Partnership With Parents. However, even at the largest infants' school, it proved difficult to recruit parents, despite organising promotional activities such as coffee mornings and sending information home. We hope it will be possible to increase the number of parents participating in future courses at all schools by sharing information about successful approaches.

Remaining problems

Many of the parents who attended the Partnership With Parents courses already read and did activities with their children. However, there was a significant number of parents who did not respond or participate. Velazquez (1996) suggested that a large number of adults with low literacy levels do not participate because they equate literacy education with school. For some parents, a course lasting half a term or longer represented a serious commitment, one they were reluctant to make. As is the case with many family reading initiatives (e.g., Barton, 1996), few fathers took part in this project. Library staff

suggested that this may have been due to work commitments; the proportion of single-parent families in the borough; or the style and "hands-on" approach of the course, which appeals more to mothers. One school hoped to attract a slightly different group of parents by running the courses after school. Although this was very popular, some parents were still reluctant or unable to attend.

Although it is an inclusive model, the Partnership With Parents course was not suitable for all parents. Participants were not those individuals with the very lowest literacy levels; they needed to be in a position to develop their existing skills in English. Some parents dropped out part way through the course, and more still were not regular attendees for personal, as well as educational, reasons. However, in many schools, course members formed their own support groups. One parent commented that it was useful to hear "other parents' views and opinions; many were similar to my own." Several headteachers noted this and commented that the opportunity to meet other parents and share problems was one of the main benefits of the course for some participants.

Partnership course benefits

The Partnership With Parents course, and in particular the library session, can be seen as a useful way of alerting parents to the importance of books and reading. One headteacher expressed the hope that, through the project, homes as well as schools would become "book environments," as family reading became established in the borough. Although schools played a central role in the family reading project, the project partners acknowledged that the purpose, value, and role of literacy in the home differ from those in formal schooling. As Barton and Hamilton (1998) pointed out, "the home reveals a richer view of literacy than that which is often portrayed or assumed by schools" (p. 207). In narrow interpretations of family literacy, school literacy dominates and the result is simply school practices invading the home. This approach is inadequate because it fails to build on the strengths of the home and the family. The project attempted to connect elements of school and home or family literacies to centre learning on real life applications of literacy skills and draw on the experiences and strengths of families. Situating literacy within the family acknowledges its broad social and cultural nature.

Perhaps one of the most important benefits of the partnership courses was pleasure parents gained from attending. All the schools reported that parents seemed to enjoy the course and were enthusiastic about it. One headteacher described how, after they had gotten over their initial apprehension, many parents treated the classes as a social event. Many enjoyed the taster collections and used them to return to the habit of reading. Being able to choose from a more manageable selection also stimulated both parents and children to broaden their reading habits and try different kinds of books.

Throughout the project, the Library Service needed to be flexible and adapt its original proposal to ensure the family reading project was successful in practice. Many researchers have reported that involving learners is an important aspect of programme development (e.g., Fingeret, 1992; Velazquez, 1996). Using feedback from parents provided by the evaluation activities, the Library Service adapted and tried to meet parents' needs, thereby assisting them to become more actively involved in their child's education, breaking down barriers to library use, improving standards of adult literacy encouraging participation in adult learning, and widening reading choices.

The borough has been awarded a further year's funding to build on the success achieved and address many of the problems identified through the evaluation. For example, taster collections will be extended to more venues beyond the school environment, such as leisure centres, community centres, and workplaces to attract a wider range of participants, particularly fathers. CIRT will continue to evaluate the project as it develops and works with the other partners to extend beyond family literacy to encompass workplace and community literacy practices.

REFERENCES

Barking & Dagenham Library Service. (2000). *Annual library plan.* London: Author.

Barton, D. (1996). Family literacy programmes and home literacy practices. In D. Baker, J. Clay, & C. Fox (Eds.), *Challenging ways of knowing* (pp. 52-62). London: Falmer Press.

Barton, D., & Hamilton, M. (1998). *Local literacies: Reading and writing in one community.* London: Routledge.

Behrman, E.H. (2002). Community-based literacy learning. *Reading: Literacy and Language, 36*(1), 26-32.

Bird, V. (2001). *National developments in family literacy.* London: National Literacy Trust.

Brown, B.L. (1998). *Family literacy: Respecting family ways.* ERIC Digest No. 203. Columbus, OH: ERIC Clearinghouse on Adult Career and Vocational Education.

Fingeret, H.A. (1992). *Adult literacy education: Current and future directions, an update.* U.S. Department of Education, Information Series No. 355. Columbus, OH: National Center for Research in Vocational Education.

Hammond, C., & Gough, M. (2000). *A note on family learning.* London: Department for Education and Employment.

Hannon, P. (2000). Rhetoric and research in family literacy. *British Educational Research Journal, 25*(5), 121-138.

Meek, M. (1991). *On being literate.* London: Bodley Head.

Morrow, L.M. (Ed.). (1995). *Family literacy: Connections in schools and communities.* Newark, DE: International Reading Association.

Stein, S.G. (1995). *Equipped for the future: A customer-driven vision for adult literacy and lifelong learning.* Washington, DC: National Institute for Literacy.

Tett, L., & St Clair, R. (1997). Family literacy in the educational marketplace: A cultural perspective. *International Journal of Lifelong Education, 16*(2), 109-120.

Velazquez, L.C. (1996). Voices from the fields: Community-based migrant education. In P.A. Sissel (Ed.), *A community-based approach to literacy programs: Taking learners' lives into account. New directions for adult and continuing education* (No. 70, pp. 27-36). San Francisco: Jossey-Bass.

Wolfendale, S., & Topping, K. (Eds.). (1996). *Family involvement in literacy: Effective partnerships in education.* London: Cassell.

McNicol is research fellow and Dalton is research development manager at the Centre for Information Research, Faculty of Computing, Information, and English, at the University of Central England, Birmingham (Perry Barr, Birmingham, B42 2SU, U.K.). E-mail for McNicol is Sarah.McNicol@uce.ac.uk.

Enhancing Phonological Awareness, Print Awareness, and Oral Language Skills in Preschool Children

The preschool years are critical to the development of emergent literacy skills that will ensure a smooth transition into formal reading. Phonological awareness, print awareness, and oral language development are three areas associated with emergent literacy that play a crucial role in the acquisition of reading. This article presents an overview of these critical components of emergent literacy. The overview includes a brief review of recent research and provides strategies for developing phonological awareness, print awareness, and oral language in the preschool classroom.

PAIGE C. PULLEN AND LAURA M. JUSTICE

The literacy concepts, knowledge, and skills developed in early childhood are excellent predictors of children's future success in reading (Adams, 1990; Donaldson, 1978; Snow, Burns, & Griffin, 1998; Whitehurst & Lonigan, 1998). Children who grow up in rich literate environments enter school with an advanced understanding of the concepts underlying reading; some of these children may, in fact, already know how to read before entering school (Adams, 1990; Dickinson & Tabors, 2001). In contrast, recent research in the field of reading has provided compelling evidence that children who start off poorly in reading typically remain poor readers throughout their schooling and beyond (Adams, 1990; Francis, Shaywitz, Stuebing, Shaywitz, & Fletcher, 1996; Juel, 1988; Stanovich, 1986; Torgesen & Burgess, 1998). Stanovich described this phenomenon as the Matthew Effect—the rich get richer and the poor get poorer. If we are to make a difference in the lives of children, we must provide appropriate supports and experiences during the early childhood years to prevent the development of reading difficulties.

A growing body of research has indicated that three emergent literacy factors associated with later reading achievement are (a) phonological awareness, (b) print awareness, and (c) oral language (Whitehurst & Lonigan, 1998). In fact, these areas of emergent literacy represent a significant source of the individual differences in later reading achievement (e.g., Lonigan, Burgess, & Anthony, 2000; Stuart, 1995). This article provides an overview of the research on the relationship of these emergent literacy

skills to reading acquisition and describes strategies to enhance the development of each of these areas.

Precursors to Literacy: An Overview

Phonological Awareness

A powerful predictor of reading achievement that has garnered much attention over the last two decades is phonological awareness (e.g., Blachman, 1984, 2000; Bradley & Bryant, 1983; Byrne & Fielding-Barnsley, 1991; for review, see National Reading Panel [NRP], 2000). *Phonological awareness* refers to an individual's implicit and explicit sensitivity to the sublexical structure of oral language. Running speech comprises various phonological units ranging in size from large (words, syllables) to small (morphemes, phonemes). Children gradually become aware of the phonological composition of spoken language, with awareness moving from larger to smaller units; the most sophisticated level of phonological awareness represents the ability to analyze oral language at the level of the phoneme (Lane, Pullen, Eisele, & Jordan, 2002; Lonigan et al., 2000). A lack of this awareness may impede an individual's ability to acquire accurate and fluent word reading skills, and as such, is a primary source of difficulty for children with reading disabilities (Torgesen, Wagner, & Rashotte, 1997). Convergent evidence from both correlational and training studies has shown that phonological awareness is critical to the acquisition of early decoding skills (e.g., Ball & Blachman, 1991; Brady, Fowler, Stone, & Winbury, 1994; Byrne & Fielding-Barnsley, 1991; Rack, Snowling, & Olsen, 1992; Stanovich, 1992; Torgesen & Wagner, 1998).

Although phonological awareness is necessary to the development of skilled decoding, it is not sufficient for acquiring the ability to read words (NRP, 2000; Stanovich, 1992; Tunmer, Herriman, & Nesdale, 1988). In addition to phonological awareness, understanding of the alphabetic principle is necessary for developing word recognition and decoding skills (Chard, Simmons, & Kameenui, 1998); however, the *alphabetic principle* makes little sense to children with deficits in phonological awareness (Uhry & Shepherd, 1997). The alphabetic principle refers to the systematic relationship between letters and sounds; children must understand that the individual phonemes in words are represented by letters and that those sounds can be analyzed and synthesized in the decoding process (Nicholson, 1997). Children without this understanding are unable to develop adequate word recognition and decoding abilities.

The preschool period is an important source of development for phonological awareness (Ball & Blachman, 1991; Lonigan et al., 2000). In fact, very young preschool children's performance on phonological awareness tasks has been shown to be a robust predictor of early reading achievement (Blachman, 2000; Bryant, Bradley, Maclean, & Crossland, 1989; Lonigan et al., 2000; for review, see Scarborough, 1998). The development of phonological awareness occurs along a continuum reflecting a transition from shallow to deep levels. In other words, children gradually move from shallow to more heightened levels of awareness, with awareness of the phoneme representing the most sophisticated level of skill (Stanovich, 1992). Accordingly, preschool phonological awareness indicators examine children's performance on shallow tasks, that is, tasks examining sensitivity to large phonological features (e.g., words, syllables).

In the earliest stages of development, phonological awareness is best represented by children's abilities to produce and comprehend rhymes (Chaney, 1992; Goswami & East, 2000; Maclean, Bryant, & Bradley, 1987) and to sort words on the basis of beginning, middle, or ending sounds (Bradley & Bryant, 1983; Lonigan et al., 2000; Maclean et al., 1987). Additional indicators of the advent of phonological awareness include word awareness (understanding that sentences contain words) and syllable awareness (understanding that words comprise syllables). Promoting the development of these foundational aspects of phonological awareness in young children may help avoid "a causal chain of negative effects" initiated by the absence of phonological sensitivity (Stanovich, 1986, p. 364).

Print Awareness

In addition to phonological awareness, young children's knowledge of the forms and functions of written language influences their later reading attainment (Adams, 1990; Badian, 2001; Stuart, 1995; Weiss & Hagen, 1988). This knowledge is acquired by most children during the preschool years and sets the stage for eventual reading achievement. Three aspects of print awareness have received particular attention: print concepts, environmental print recognition, and alphabet knowledge.

According to numerous research studies, assessments measuring a child's understanding of print concepts have successfully predicted future reading success (e.g., Badian, 2001; Clay, 1993; Stuart, 1995; Tunmer et al., 1988; for review, see Adams, 1990, or Scarborough, 1998). Furthermore, awareness of print concepts has been related to other measures of reading readiness, such as phonological awareness. According to Adams (1990) and to Mason (1980), a child's awareness of the forms, functions, and uses of print provide the foundation upon which reading and writing abilities are built.

Children begin building concepts about print through literacy-based interactions with the adults in their lives at a very young age. Infants as young as 8 months of age begin handling books, turning pages, and actually babbling in a "reading-like" manner (see Snow et al., 1998). This foundation, however, is not built automatically. It requires active participation with adults in print-focused interactions that are age appropriate in a cognitive, emotional, social, and physical sense (Adams, 1990; Snow et al., 1998).

Indeed, it is during the preschool years that children come to know that print conveys meaning, and they acquire an increasingly sophisticated understanding of print forms (Justice & Ezell, 2001). Through experiences in being read to, children move beyond this understanding to a more comprehensive view of "book knowledge." Clay (1991) asserted that children who have heard many stories read to them develop awareness that book language, or literary forms of language, is different from spoken language. Clay's assertion was supported in a series of recent applied studies by Justice and Ezell (2000, 2002; Justice, Weber, Ezell, & Bakeman, 2002), which showed that adult–child shared storybook reading experiences that involve discussion about print increases children's knowledge of important print concepts.

A child with well-developed print concepts knows several essential points that are necessary to reading acquisition. For example, a child may know that

4. the print tells the story,
5. text on a page is read from left to right,
6. progression through text moves from the top of the page to the bottom of the page,
7. when one page of text is read, the story continues on the following page, and
8. the white spaces between groups of letters represent a break between spoken words or word boundaries (Clay, 1993; Justice & Ezell, 2001).

A student's knowledge about concepts of print has been found to support reading acquisition (Clay, 1993) and to moderately predict reading ability in the primary grades (for review, see Scarborough, 1998, or Snow et al., 1998).

In addition to knowledge about the concepts of print, children's interaction with environmental print is another key aspect of the attainment of print awareness. The knowledge that a symbol can stand for an actual object is a prerequisite to understanding the sound–symbol relationship of the alphabetic principle. For example, as described by Snow et al. (1998), very young children recognize the golden arches as a representation of McDonald's®. This is believed to be an important first step in understanding the concept of print-to-speech mapping, critical to attainment of the alphabetic principle. Not until children are able to move from understanding that print is like pictures and that written words comprise letters that map to speech sounds, will they be able to begin visual word recognition (Snow et al., 1998). Consequently, although environmental print is a necessary step in reading attainment, children must move beyond that understanding to an understanding of the alphabetic principle.

Another critical area of emergent literacy is letter knowledge, which is a reliable and particularly robust predictor of a child's later reading achievement (Adams, 1990; Catts, Fey, Zhang, & Tomblin, 1999; Scanlon & Vellutino, 1996; Whitehurst & Lonigan, 1998). In fact, knowledge of the alphabet has been described as the best predictor of future reading attainment. In a study of 1,000 kindergarten students, Scanlon and Vellutino (1996) found that 83% of the children would have been correctly identified as being successful or having difficulty with learning to read using a letter identification assessment. Although simple letter recognition can be as successful a predictor of future reading success compared to any other assessment, Adams (1990) posits that it is much more than simply naming the letters that supports reading acquisition—an overall familiarity with the letters and their sounds is necessary in the attainment of early reading skills.

Oral Language

Oral language proficiency has also long been associated with later reading achievement, particularly in the area of reading comprehension. Prediction studies have consistently shown that prekindergarten and kindergarten children's performance on vocabulary (semantic) and grammar (syntax) tasks accounts for a significant amount of variance in later elementary–grade reading ability (e.g., Catts et al., 1999, 2001; for review, see Scarborough, 1998). Likewise, investigations of poor readers' oral language abilities have shown semantic–syntactic language abilities to represent particular, albeit occasionally subtle, areas of weakness (e.g., Bishop & Adams, 1990; Catts et al., 2001; Scarborough, 1990).

In a particularly interesting and innovative study of oral language precursors to later reading achievement, Scarborough (1990) followed 52 children from approximately 2 years of age through second grade and conducted six evaluations of oral language skills (e.g., vocabulary knowledge, grammatical abilities) when children were between 2 and 5 years of age. Thirty-four children were at significant risk for developing reading problems due to familial incidence of reading disability. Of these children, 22 (65%) developed substantial reading problems by second grade. Detailed examination of these 22 children's oral language development over the preschool years showed a relatively greater number of grammatical errors at 2 years of age and poorer receptive and expressive vocabulary knowledge at 4 years, relative to those children who did not develop reading problems.

To this end, Scarborough (1990) has argued that preschool oral language difficulties represent an early manifestation, or symptom, of reading disability. This assertion, which has been supported by more recent studies (e.g., Lombardino, Riccio, Hynd, & Pinheiro, 1997), holds true even for children who are not at explicit risk for developing reading problems (see Snow et al., 1998). Generally speaking, children who show early difficulties with the development of vocabulary knowledge and grammatical skills are more likely to experience literacy problems, relative to children acquiring oral language, according to expected milestones. Taken together, such findings argue the need for promoting semantic–syntactic proficiency during the critical years of early childhood.

Strategies for Promoting Emergent Literacy

Phonological Awareness Activities

Support for phonological awareness should be integrated into the everyday activities of the preschool classroom. Indeed, phonological awareness for children at particular risk for early literacy achievement may best be encouraged through formalized lessons. That is, for young children with limited opportunities for language play at home, or who are at risk for developing a reading disability, explicit instruction in phonological awareness should be provided daily. *Explicit* does not refer to drill-like activities but rather the structuring of engaging, meaningful, and enjoyable activities that help children to actively attend to the phonological structure of oral language. Activities should focus on those skills acquired during the preschool years, which have been identified as predictive of later reading achievement. These include activities to promote rhyme and alliteration awareness, as well as those designed for promoting blending and segmenting skills. Blending and segmenting skills should begin at the word and syllable level and for older and more capable preschool children may include activities that help children begin developing skills at the onset–rime and phoneme levels.

Table 1. Activities to Promote Rhyming Abilities

Activity	Instruction
Read aloud rhyming	Rhyming activities can be effectively embedded in read aloud time. Select books with rhyme patterns. See appendix for suggested titles.
Explicit instruction in concept of rhyme	Often, children are told that words that rhyme sound the same at the end. This can be confusing, because *seen* and *sun* sound the same at the end. Words that rhyme sound the same in the middle and at the end. Help students isolate the rime of words to develop an understanding of rhyming. For example, say "*Fat* has *at*, does *bat* have *at*? Does *ban* have *at*?" (Lane & Pullen, 2004).
Sorting rhymes	Select a variety of objects (e.g., small plastic toys) to use for sorting rhymes and place them in a bag. Begin with three target rime patterns. Have the child pull a toy from the bag and sort based on the rhyme pattern.
Rhyme pockets	Create a picture card file by gluing pictures on the front of 3" x 5" index cards. Make a rhyming pockets game board using library pockets and poster board. Place a picture on the front of the library pocket (use Velcro to make board versatile). The child then takes a stack of picture cards and matches the rhymes by placing the picture card into the corresponding library pocket (Lane & Pullen, 2004).

For children in the emergent stages of literacy development, it is critical to realize that exposure long precedes mastery; increasing explicit engagement in and exposure to phonological awareness activities is more important than relentlessly pursuing mastery of such concepts. Likewise, it is also important to note that children's attainment of phonological awareness moves from shallow to increasingly deep levels of awareness; fostering attention to larger phonological units, such as words and syllables, precedes awareness of phonemes.

RHYMING AND ALLITERATION. Both rhyme and alliteration awareness reflect shallow levels of phonological awareness, based on the perspective that awareness ranges from shallow to deep levels. Preschool children acquire shallow sensitivity to phonological structure of language, which precedes and develops into eventual deep understanding. In this way, rhyme and alliteration awareness can be viewed as foundational to later attainment of deep levels of phonological awareness.

Both rhyme and alliteration reflect children's ability to focus sublexically on the phonological structure of spoken language, that is, to consider the sound structure of language as separate from meaning. *Rhyme* refers to two words' sharing of a rime structure (the part of a word following the onset, as in *at* in *cat*, *flat*, or *splat*), whereas *alliteration* refers to two words' sharing of a phoneme in the initial, medial, or final position (as with *s* in *sat* and *sun* or *m* in *plum* and *ram*).

Rhyme and alliteration can be difficult concepts for children to acquire, especially for young children with weak oral language skills (Boudreau & Hedberg, 1999) or limited oral language experiences. Explicit, repeated instruction may be necessary to promote the development of these skills. Rhyme instruction should begin with eas-

ier tasks such as rhyme recognition and move to more difficult tasks such as rhyme generation. The same holds true for alliteration awareness. Multiple exposures and opportunities should be provided. Table 1 provides specific examples of rhyming activities appropriate for young children, and Table 2 provides examples of alliteration activities.

BLENDING AND SEGMENTING ACTIVITIES. Although rhyming activities are important in the development of phonological awareness, alone these activities may not be adequate in preparing young children for the task of learning to read (Blachman, 2000). In numerous studies of nonreading children in kindergarten, blending and segmenting activities have been shown to improve the skills of children with low phonological awareness (Fox & Routh, 1984; O'Connor, Jenkins, & Slocum, 1995; Torgesen, Morgan, & Davis, 1992). For example, Torgesen and associates investigated the effects of blending and segmenting tasks for children in kindergarten with low levels of phonological awareness. Children were assigned to one of three intervention groups: (a) blending tasks, (b) blending and segmenting tasks, and (c) language experience (no phonological awareness). Children who received instruction in blending and segmenting performed better on phonological awareness tasks and on a reading analog task than either of the other two groups.

The success demonstrated by nonreaders who received blending and segmenting instruction on reading analog tasks may be because these phonological skills are most similar to reading and spelling. Children utilize blending skills as they learn to decode words and learn segmenting skills in spelling words (NRP, 2000). Instruction at the preschool level necessarily must begin with

Table 2. Activities to Promote Alliteration

Activity	Teacher's role
Alliterative sentences	Recite a sentence with alliteration (e.g., *Peter Piper picked a peck of pickled peppers*). Ask children to help identify the sound that is at the beginning of the words in that sentence.
Sound sleuth	Play word games to help children begin to recognize beginning sounds in words. Give children a target word, such as *boat*, then ask a child to identify the word that has the same beginning sound (e.g., *cap*, *bird*, or *song*).
Sound sorts	Provide children with a stack of picture cards or small plastic toys. Have each child sort the picture cards or toys based on the beginning sound.

Table 3. Activities to Promote Blending and Segmenting Abilities

Activity	Teacher's role
Sound tapping	Preschool children love to play with percussion instruments such as sand blocks, cymbals, and rhythm sticks. These instruments can be used to segment the units of sounds in sentences and words. As the teacher reads a short sentence aloud, the child can tap for each word in the sentence. Likewise, given a multisyllable word, the child can segment the word into syllables by tapping the percussion instruments (Lane & Pullen, 2004).
Bead counting	Bead counting can be used with individual children, small groups, or large groups. String six large wooden beads of a single color on thick cord (see Figure 1). Ask children to count the words in sentences or the syllables in words and to move a bead, one word or syllable at a time. After children complete the targeted segmenting task, ask them to hold up their bead strings. The teacher can quickly assess the childrens responses (Lane & Pullen, 2004; Sindelar, Lane, Pullen, & Hudson, 2002). This activity can be modified for the various levels of phonological awareness as children progress in phonological awareness.
Nursery rhyme sound blending	Recite a common nursery rhyme to your class. Segment some words into syllables or onset–rime units. Pause and ask children to blend the sounds together to make the whole word. For example, *"Jack be nimble, Jack be quick, Jack jump over the candle st-ick. What did Jack jump over?"* Children would blend the onset and rime together to form the word stick.

easier blending tasks, such as blending syllables or onsets and rimes into words. Segmenting tasks can therefore focus on tapping and counting syllables in words or words in sentences or segmenting words into onsets and rimes. Table 3 provides specific examples of activities to promote blending and segmenting skill.

Print Awareness Activities

Two powerful ways to support the development of print awareness in young children is through adult–child shared storybook reading and print-enriched play. Children benefit in many ways from daily doses of such opportunities (Justice & Ezell, 2002; Neuman & Roskos, 1990; Whitehurst et al., 1988); in addition, these interactions can be explicitly structured to accelerate children's print awareness.

ADULT–CHILD SHARED STORYBOOK READING. One strategy for encouraging the development of print concepts, environmental print awareness, and alphabet knowledge

Figure 1. Bead strings are useful for segmenting words into syllables or phonemes.

is by increasing children's participation in reading interactions that feature books with salient print. Salient print features include large narrative print, redundant text, and contextualized print embedded within the illustrations (Justice & Kaderavek, 2002). Children are more likely to visually attend to print when they are reading books in which print is a salient feature (Justice & Lankford, 2002). Reading of electronic storybooks, in which print is made particularly salient through graphic means (e.g., high-lighted links), appears to help children internalize knowledge of print concepts and features (de Jong & Bus, 2002). Additionally, when reading typical storybooks, adults can encourage children to attend to print features (including print embedded within illustrations) by asking questions, making comments about print, and tracking the print while reading.

Studies have shown that adult use of these print-referencing behaviors can be a powerful strategy for enhancing preschool children's print awareness. For instance, Justice and Ezell (2002) recently used these print-referencing strategies (i.e., talking about print, tracking the print) during an 8-week reading program for 3- to 5-year-old children in Head Start. Children made substantial gains on a variety of print awareness measures, including environmental print recognition (for words occurring in the storybooks), alphabet knowledge, and print concepts. Accelerated growth in print awareness has also been observed when parents use these print-referencing strategies during home-based reading interactions (Justice & Ezell, 2000). However, despite the benefits of doing so, adults are unlikely to reference print, verbally or nonverbally, when reading with children (Ezell & Justice, 2000); therefore, teachers and parents may need instruction in structuring book reading interactions to include an explicit focus on print.

PRINT-ENRICHED PLAY. Children in preschool classrooms frequently engage in play-based interactions, including dramatic play. A number of studies have shown that integrating literacy artifacts into children's play settings can encourage children's print awareness (e.g., Neuman & Roskos, 1990, 1992). Such artifacts may include functional signs, such as building labels (e.g., *grocery store, post office*), as well as literacy tools (e.g., paper, pens, books). Children will naturally integrate these artifacts into their play at increasing rates when made available.

An additional strategy for increasing children's print awareness through play is to use adult mediation. Applied studies have indicated that adults can play an important role in encouraging children to embed literacy artifacts into their play and that this can produce more powerful effects on print awareness relative to simply providing increased access to such artifacts (Christie & Enz, 1992; Neuman & Roskos, 1993). Adults can guide children in how to use artifacts during play (e.g., writing a shopping list prior to going to the grocery store); these mediated opportunities provide additional support for children's increased understanding of the forms and functions of written language. Table 4 provides examples of materials that can be added to classroom centers to increase literacy-related play.

Oral Language Activities

The intricate and robust association between oral language and other aspects of emergent literacy—namely, phonological awareness and print awareness—argues the importance of helping children to develop a strong oral language foundation. As previously described, critical oral language domains include semantics and syntax. The preschool years provide the developing child a brief and singularly critical window of opportunity to develop sophisticated oral language skills; at the end of the preschool years, children's rapid pace of oral language growth slows, as many adults who have attempted to acquire a foreign language know. Importantly, emergent and conventional literacy abilities are built upon this oral language foundation.

Two approaches identified in the language intervention literature that may be particularly useful for enhancing preschool children's oral language performance are focused stimulation and interactive storybook reading. These approaches are described in the following sections.

FOCUSED STIMULATION. Children acquire language proficiency through their interactions with others, such as parents, teachers, and peers. Indeed, despite their innate biological propensity for language acquisition, without environmental input children will not develop language to any substantial degree. The quality and quantity of input experienced by young children serve as important sources of variation in vocabulary and syntactic development (Baumwell, Tamis-LeMonda, & Bornstein, 1997; Bloom, 1993; Tamis-LeMonda, Bornstein, & Baumwell, 2001).

Adults interacting with young children can emphasize the use of various input strategies known to be particularly influential for oral language growth. These input strategies help children to map the associations between the environment and particular linguistic forms and functions; their use provides substantial opportunities for children to hear oral language models and to produce increasingly sophisticated productions of their own. The specific strategies discussed here can be integrated into myriad daily activities, including classroom routines (e.g., snack time) and dramatic play interactions (Fey, Cleave, Long, & Hughes, 1993; Girolametto, Pearce, & Weitzman, 1996):

1. *Self-talk* and *parallel talk* are two adult-input strategies that provide frequent models of key linguistic forms and labels; these models are incorporated into children's common daily routines. *Self-talk* refers to an adult's ongoing description of her own activities or thoughts (e.g., I am washing the baby); with parallel talk, the adult provides an ongoing description of the child's activities (e.g., You are putting on the diaper). Self-talk and parallel talk can be structured to provide increased exposure to specific language concepts, for instance, adjectival comparisons (e.g., big vs. little), syntactic devices (e.g., interrogatives, pronouns, auxiliary verbs, elaborated nouns), and discourse events (e.g., questions vs. comments vs. requests).

Table 4. Literacy-Enriched Play Materials for Centers

Center	Materials	Teacher's role
Block Center	Clipboards with paper and pencil Labels for block containers Building plans with diagrams (i.e., "blueprints") Books about construction	Children will learn important text structure features by following plans for buildings. Provide simple step-by-step directions for children to follow. Encourage children to write about the buildings they have created on the clipboards provided in the center.
Restaurant	Menus Pens Order notepads Nametags Cookbooks Coupons	A restaurant center provides opportunities for children to learn about print and engage in meaningful writing activities.
Post Office	Envelopes Pens Pencils Stationery Stickers Mail cubby for each child Mailbox	Create a class mail center and have "mail time" during morning circle. Encourage parents, older book buddies, and resource teachers to write to your students. Parent volunteers can guide students learning in the mail center during the school day and help them reply to their mail.
Housekeeping	Telephone book Message pads Pens and pencils Shopping list pads Cookbooks Magazines Recipe cards (with recipes) Blank recipe cards	The housekeeping center is common to preschool classrooms and can be enhanced by adding a few literacy-related materials.

2. *Repetitions*, in which children's utterances are followed by the adult's exact reproduction of what the child said (e.g., Child: Boy eating; Adult: Boy eating), also provide children with increased exposure to language use and help children recognize the associations between their own language use and their communicative environment. Repetitions can be coupled with praise and encouragement (e.g., You're right! Boy eating) to show children the importance and emerging accuracy of their communicative behaviors.

3. *Expansions* occur when children's utterances are followed by the adult's production of a slightly more sophisticated rendition (e.g., Child: Boy eating. Adult: The boy is eating). The adult's expansion provides one additional element of semantic or syntactic information beyond that which was provided in the child's utterance. By their very nature, expansions provide children a language model that is only slightly beyond their current level of linguistic independence; therefore, expansions serve as an excellent stimulation strategy. Expansions may be coupled with requests for elaboration to encourage the child's exposure to and use of more sophisti-

cated linguistic productions (e.g., Child: Walking. Adult requests elaboration: Who walking? Child: Boy walking. Adult expands: The boy is walking!).

Again, it is important to recognize that children acquire increasingly refined knowledge of oral language forms and labels through exposure. Exposure that is lacking in quality or quantity, as may occur when children are exposed to little language or to language of little variation, can have an inverse relationship with the rate of oral language acquisition. To this end, it is particularly relevant to point out that children do not need to produce language to acquire language; exposing children to linguistic models of high quality is effective on its own. What this means is that children do not need to imitate language models, nor is there any evidence showing the benefit of young children's participation in language drills. Indeed, these kinds of activities do little to promote oral language expertise.

INTERACTIVE READING. In addition to accelerating children's print awareness, as discussed previously in this article, storybook reading has been found to be a powerful enhancer of oral language proficiency, particularly in the area of vocabulary development (e.g., Bus, van Ijzendoorn, & Pellegrini, 1995; Ninio, 1983; Pellegrini, Galda, Jones, & Perlmutter, 1995; Scarborough & Dobrich, 1994; Teale, 1986). Adult–child storybook reading interactions have been used in a number of recent studies as a deliberate context for encouraging children's oral language proficiency, as seen in a research program conducted by Whitehurst and his colleagues (e.g., Crain-Thoreson & Dale, 1999; Whitehurst et al., 1988, 1994).

These studies, as well as several others, have unequivocally shown that adults' reading with young children can incorporate specific interactive strategies into book reading interactions to encourage oral language development. Although book reading by itself has been positively associated with oral language achievements (see Scarborough & Dobrich, 1994), the following strategies, when incorporated directly into reading interactions, appear to accelerate the pace of language growth. Such strategies are designed to

- provide children with quality inputs of oral language labels, forms, and functions;
- encourage children's active participation in shared reading events; and
- scaffold children's gradual use of more sophisticated productions.

The research program conducted by Whitehurst and colleagues (e.g., see Whitehurst et al., 1988, 1994) has shown adults' use of the following behaviors during storybook reading to be effective for advancing oral language skills in preschool children, including those who are at risk. Use of these strategies has been shown to influence vocabulary knowledge as well as mean length of utterance, a general index of syntactic development.

1. **Repetitions:** The adult repeats what the child says verbatim.
2. **Expansions:** The adult repeats what the child says but adds additional linguistic information.
3. **Open-Ended Questions:** The adult asks the child questions requiring more than a yes/no response, such as *who* and *what* questions.
4. **Praise:** The adult gives the child positive feedback regarding participation in the book reading activity.

Senechal and associates (e.g., Hargrave & Senechal, 2000; Senechal, 1997; Senechal & Cornell, 1993; Senechal, LeFevre, Thomas, & Daley, 1998; Senechal, Thomas, & Monker, 1995), as well as other researchers in child language acquisition (Robbins & Ehri, 1994; Wasik & Bond, 2001), have identified additional strategies that can be used to promote oral language achievement, particularly vocabulary, in young children within the storybook reading context. A summary of these techniques is provided below:

1. **Active Participation:** Active participation occurs when children are asked to name and point to items with novel names occurring in illustrations; this is more powerful to oral language growth than simply hearing new words spoken in the context of a story.
2. **Repeated Readings:** Ongoing exposure to new words through repeated storybook readings positively influences children's receptive vocabulary skills; children are more likely to acquire words that they have heard repeatedly.
3. **Story Props:** Providing children with opportunities to interact with props associated with particular stories (e.g., musical instruments for a story involving a musician) increases the likelihood that children will acquire new words associated with the stories.

Summary

The preschool years are critical to the development of emergent literacy skills that will help prevent later reading problems. Early literacy skills, such as phonological awareness and letter knowledge, represent the best predictors of later achievement in reading (see Adams, 1990; Snow et al., 1998), and oral language is highly correlated with emergent literacy knowledge. Parents and teachers of preschool children play an important role in helping to develop these skills, and fortunately, activities that promote phonological awareness, oral language development, and print awareness can be easily incorporated into preschool activities at home and at school.

Throughout the school day, teachers should look for opportunities to incorporate activities that promote emergent literacy skills. Circle time provides the opportunity to play group games that develop phonological awareness; share big books, focusing on print concepts; and engage children in meaningful conversation that develops oral language. Parent volunteers are an excellent resource for shared storybook reading; train volunteers to engage in storybook reading that promotes oral language development and print awareness. Centers throughout the preschool classroom can incorporate literacy-related props, and parents and teachers can guide children's play in meaningful ways. Incorporating activities that promote phonological awareness, print concepts, and oral language development can enhance the preschool experience for young children. The activities presented in this article provide opportunities for parents and teachers of young children to capitalize on this critical learning period and help ensure children a smooth transition into formal reading.

ABOUT THE AUTHORS

Paige C. Pullen, PhD, is an assistant professor in curriculum, instruction, and special education at The University of Virginia. Her current interests include early literacy development and learning disabilities. **Laura M. Justice**, PhD, is an assistant professor in curriculum, instruction, and special education at The University of Virginia. Her current interests include early literacy development and communication disorders. Address: Paige C. Pullen, University of Virginia, PO Box 400273, Charlottesville, VA 22904-4273.

Authors' Note

Several of the phonological awareness activities described in this manuscript are based on collaboration between the first author and Dr. Holly B. Lane at the University of Florida.

References

Adams, M. J. (1990). *Beginning to read: Thinking and learning about print*. Cambridge: MIT Press.

Badian, N. A. (2001). Phonological and orthographic processing: Their roles in reading prediction. *Annals of Dyslexia, 51,* 179–202.

Ball, E. W., & Blachman, B. A. (1991). Does phoneme awareness training in kindergarten make a difference in early word recognition and developmental spelling? *Reading Research Quarterly, 26,* 49–66.

Baumwell, L., Tamis-LeMonda, C. S., & Bornstein, M. H. (1997). Maternal verbal sensitivity and child language comprehension. *Infant Behavior and Development, 20,* 247–258.

Bishop, D. V. M., & Adams, C. (1990). A prospective study of the relationship between specific language impairment, phonological disorders, and reading impairment. *Journal of Speech and Hearing Research, 38,* 446–462.

Blachman, B. A. (1984). Relationship of rapid naming ability and language analysis skill to kindergarten and first grade reading achievement. *Journal of Educational Psychology, 76,* 610–622.

Blachman, B. A. (2000). Phonological awareness. In M. L. Kamil, P. B. Mosenthal, P. D. Pearson, & R. Barr (Eds.), *Handbook of reading research* (Vol. 3, pp. 483–502). Mahwah, NJ: Erlbaum.

Bloom, L. (1993). *The transition from infancy to language*. New York: Cambridge University Press.

Boudreau, D. M., & Hedberg, N. L. (1999). A comparison of early literacy skills in children with specific language impairment and their typically developing peers. *American Journal of Speech-Language Pathology, 8,* 249–260.

Bradley, L., & Bryant, P. E. (1983). Categorizing sounds and learning to read—A causal connection. *Nature, 301,* 419–421.

Brady, S., Fowler, A., Stone, B., & Winbury, N. (1994). Training phonological awareness: A study with inner-city kindergarten children. *Annals of Dyslexia, 44,* 26–59.

Bryant, P. E., Bradley, L., Maclean, M., & Corossland, J. (1989). Nursery rhymes, phonological skills and reading. *Journal of Child Language, 16,* 407–428.

Bus, A. G., van Ijzendoorn, M. H., & Pellegrini, A. D. (1995). Joint book reading makes for success in learning to read: A meta-analysis on intergenerational transmission of literacy. *Review of Educational Research, 65,* 1–21.

Byrne, B., & Fielding-Barnsley, R. (1991). Evaluation of a program to teach phonemic awareness to young children. *Journal of Educational Psychology, 83,* 451–455.

Catts, H. W., Fey, M. E., Zhang, X., & Tomblin, J. B. (1999). Language bases of reading and reading disabilities: Evidence from a longitudinal investigation. *Scientific Studies of Reading, 3,* 331–362.

Catts, H. W., Fey, M. E., Zhang, X., & Tomblin, J. B. (2001). Estimating the risk of future reading difficulties in kindergarten children: A research-based model and its clinical instrumentation. *Language, Speech, and Hearing Services in Schools, 32,* 38–50.

Chaney, C. (1992). Language development, metalinguistic skills, and print awareness in 3-year-old children. *Applied Psycholinguistics, 13,* 485–514.

Chard, D. J., Simmons, D. C., & Kaméenui, E. J. (1998). *Understanding the primary role of word recognition in the reading process: Synthesis of research on beginning reading*. Retrieved November 18, 2002, from http://darkwing.uoregon.edu/~ncite/reading/WordSyn.html

Christie, J. F., & Enz, B. (1992). The effects of literacy play interventions on preschoolers' play patterns and literacy development. *Early Education and Development, 3,* 205–220.

Clay, M. M. (1991). Introducing a new storybook to young readers. *The Reading Teacher, 45,* 264–273.

Clay, M. M. (1993). *Reading recovery: A guidebook for teachers in training*. Portsmouth, NH: Heineman.

Crain-Thoreson, C., & Dale, P. S. (1999). Enhancing linguistic performance: Parents and teachers as book reading partners for children with language delays. *Topics in Early Childhood Special Education, 19,* 28–39.

de Jong, M. T., & Bus, A. G. (2002). Quality of book reading matters for emergent readers: An experiment with the same book in a regular or electronic format. *Journal of Educational Psychology, 94,* 145–155.

Dickinson, D. K., & Tabors, P. O. (2001). *Beginning literacy with language*. Baltimore: Brookes.

Donaldson, M. (1978). *Children's minds*. New York: Norton.

Ezell, H. K., & Justice, L. M. (2000). Increasing the print focus of shared reading interactions through observational learning. *American Journal of Speech-Language Pathology, 9,* 36–47.

Fey, M. E., Cleave, P. L., Long, S. H., & Hughes, D. L. (1993). Two approaches to the facilitation of grammar in children with language impairment: An experimental evaluation. *Journal of Speech and Hearing Research, 36,* 141–157.

Fox, B., & Routh, D. (1984). Phonemic analysis and synthesis as word-attack skills: Revisited. *Journal of Educational Psychology, 76,* 1059–1064.

Francis, D., Shaywitz, S., Stuebing, K., Shaywitz, B., & Fletcher, J. (1996). Developmental lag versus deficit models of reading disability: A longitudinal, individual growth curves analysis. *Journal of Educational Psychology, 88*(1), 3–17.

Girolametto, L., Pearce, P. S., & Weitzman, E. (1996). Interactive focused stimulation for toddlers with expressive vocabulary delays. *Journal of Speech and Hearing Research, 39,* 1274–1283.

Goswami, U., & East, M. (2000). Rhyme and analogy in beginning reading: Conceptual and methodological issues. *Applied Psycholinguistics, 21,* 63–93.

Hargrave, A. C., & Senechal, M. (2000). A book reading intervention with preschool children who have limited vocabularies: The benefits of regular reading and dialogic reading. *Early Childhood Research Quarterly, 15,* 75–90.

Juel, C. (1988). Learning to read and write: A longitudinal study of 54 children from first through fourth grades. *Journal of Educational Psychology, 80,* 437–447.

Justice, L. M., & Ezell, H. K. (2000). Enhancing children's print and word awareness through home-based parent intervention. *American Journal of Speech-Language Pathology, 9,* 257–269.

Justice, L. M., & Ezell, H. K. (2001). Written language awareness in preschool children from low-income households: A descriptive analysis. *Communication Disorders Quarterly, 22,* 123–134.

Justice, L. M., & Ezell, H. K. (2002). Use of storybook reading to increase print awareness in at-risk children. *American Journal of Speech-Language Pathology, 11,* 17–29.

Justice, L. M., & Kaderavek, J. (2002). Using shared storybook reading to promote emergent literacy. *Teaching Exceptional Children, 34,* 8–13.

Justice, L. M., & Lankford, C. (2002). *Preschool children's visual attention to print during storybook reading.* Manuscript in review.

Justice, L. M., Weber, S., Ezell, H. K., & Bakeman, R. (2002). A sequential analysis of children's responsiveness to parental references to print during shared storybook reading. *American Journal of Speech-Language Pathology, 11*, 30–40.

Lane, H. B., & Pullen, P. C. (2004). Phonological awareness assessment and instruction: A sound beginning. Needham Heights, MA: Allyn & Bacon.

Lane, H. B., Pullen, P. C., Eisele, M. R., & Jordan, L. (2002). Preventing reading failure: Phonological awareness assessment and instruction. *Preventing School Failure, 46*, 11–15.

Lombardino, L. J., Riccio, C. A., Hynd, G. W., & Pinheiro, S. B. (1997). Linguistic deficits in children with reading disabilities. *American Journal of Speech-Language Pathology, 6*, 71–78.

Lonigan, C. J., Burgess, S. R., & Anthony, J. L. (2000). Development of emergent literacy and early reading skills: Evidence from a latent-variable longitudinal study. *Developmental Psychology, 36*, 596–613.

Maclean, M., Bryant, P., & Bradley, L. (1987). Rhymes, nursery rhymes, and reading in early childhood. *Merrill-Palmer Quarterly, 33*, 255–281.

Mason, J. M. (1980). When do children begin to read: An exploration of four year old children's letter and word reading competencies. *Reading Research Quarterly, 15*, 203–227.

National Reading Panel. (2000). *A report of the National Reading Panel: Teaching children to read.* Washington, DC: National Institute of Child Health and Human Development.

Neuman, S. B., & Roskos, K. (1990). Play, print, and purpose: Enriching play environments for literacy development. *The Reading Teacher, 44*, 214–221.

Neuman, S. B., & Roskos, K. (1992). Literacy objects as cultural tools: Effects on children's literacy behaviors in play. *Reading Research Quarterly, 27*, 202–225.

Neuman, S. B., & Roskos, K. (1993). Access to print for children of poverty: Differential effects of adult mediation and literacy-enriched play settings on environmental and functional print tasks. *American Educational Research Journal, 30*, 95–122.

Nicholson, T. (1997). Closing the gap on reading failure: Social background, phonemic awareness, and learning to read. In B. Blachman (Ed.), *Foundations of reading acquisition and dyslexia: Implications for early intervention* (pp. 381–408). Mahwah, NJ: Erlbaum.

Ninio, A. (1983). Joint book reading as a multiple vocabulary acquisition device. *Developmental Psychology, 19*, 445–451.

O'Connor, R., Jenkins, J., & Slocum, T. (1995). Transfer among phonological tasks in kindergarten: Essential instructional content. *Journal of Educational Psychology, 87*, 202–217.

Pellegrini, A. D., Galda, L., Jones, I., & Perlmutter, J. (1995). Joint reading between mothers and their Head Start children: Vocabulary development in two text formats. *Discourse Processes, 19*, 441–463.

Rack, J. P., Snowling, M. J., & Olsen, R. K. (1992). The nonword reading deficit in developmental dyslexia: A review. *Reading Research Quarterly, 27*(1), 29–53.

Robbins, C., & Ehri, L. C. (1994). Reading storybooks to kindergarteners helps them learn new vocabulary words. *Journal of Educational Psychology, 86*, 56–64.

Scanlon, D. M., & Vellutino, F. R. (1996). Prerequisite skills, early instruction, and success in first grade reading: Selected results from a longitudinal study. *Mental Retardation and Developmental Research, 2*, 54–63.

Scarborough, H. S. (1990). Very early language deficits in dyslexic children. *Child Development, 61*, 1728–1743.

Scarborough, H. S. (1998). Early identification of children at risk for reading difficulties: Phonological awareness and some other promising predictors. In B. K. Shapiro, P. J. Accardo,

& A. J. Capute (Eds.), *Specific reading disability: A view of the spectrum* (pp. 75–199). Timonium, MD: York Press.

Scarborough, H., & Dobrich, W. (1994). On the efficacy of reading to preschoolers. *Developmental Review, 14*, 245–302.

Senechal, M. (1997). The differential effect of storybook reading on preschoolers' acquisition of expressive and receptive vocabulary. *Journal of Child Language, 24*, 123–138.

Senechal, M., & Cornell, E. H. (1993). Vocabulary acquisition through shared reading experiences. *Reading Research Quarterly, 28*, 360–374.

Senechal, M., LeFevre, J., Thomas, E., & Daley, K. (1998). Differential effects of home literacy experiences on the development of oral and written language. *Reading Research Quarterly, 32*, 96–116.

Senechal, M., Thomas, E., & Monker, J. (1995). Individual differences in 4-year-old children's acquisition of vocabulary during storybook reading. *Journal of Educational Psychology, 87*, 218–229.

Sindelar, P. T., Lane, H. B., Pullen, P. C., & Hudson, R. F. (2002). Remedial interventions for students with reading decoding problems. In M. R. Shinn, H. M. Walker, & G. Stoner (Eds.), *Intervention for academic and behavior problems II: Preventive and remedial approaches* (pp. 703–729). Bethesda, MD: National Association of School Psychologists.

Snow, C. E., Burns, M. S., & Griffin, P. (Eds.). (1998). *Preventing reading difficulties in young children.* Washington, DC: National Academy Press.

Stanovich, K. E. (1986). Matthew effects in reading: Some consequences of individual differences in the acquisition of literacy. *Reading Research Quarterly, 21*, 360–406.

Stanovich, K. E. (1992). Speculations on the causes and consequences of individual differences in early reading acquisition. In P. B. Gough, L. C. Ehri, & R. Treiman (Eds.), *Reading acquisition* (pp. 307–342). Hillsdale, NJ: Erlbaum.

Stuart, M. (1995). Prediction and qualitative assessment of five- and six-year old children's reading: A longitudinal study. *British Journal of Educational Psychology, 65*, 287–296.

Tamis-LeMonda, C. S., Bornstein, M., & Baumwell, L. (2001). Maternal responsiveness and children's achievement of language milestones. *Child Development 72*, 748–767.

Teale, W. H. (1986). Home background and young children's literacy development. In W. H. Teale & E. Sulzby (Eds.), *Emergent literacy: Writing and reading.* Norwood, NJ: Ablex.

Torgesen, J. K., & Burgess, S. R. (1998). Consistency of reading-related phonological processes throughout early childhood: Evidence from longitudinal-correlational and instructional studies. In J. Metsala & L. Ehri (Eds.), *Word recognition in beginning reading.* Hillsdale, NJ: Erlbaum.

Torgesen, J. K., Morgan, S. T., & Davis, C. (1992). Effects of two types of phonological awareness training on word learning in kindergarten children. *Journal of Educational Psychology, 84*, 364–370.

Torgesen, J. K., & Wagner, R. K. (1998). Alternative diagnostic approaches for specific developmental reading disabilities. *Learning Disabilities Research and Practice, 13*, 220–232.

Torgesen, J. K., Wagner, R. K., & Rashotte, C. (1997). Approaches to the prevention and remediation of phonologically based reading disabilities. In B. Blachman (Ed.), *Foundations of reading acquisition and dyslexia* (pp. 287–304). Mahwah, NJ: Erlbaum.

Tunmer, W. E., Herriman, M. L., & Nesdale, A. R. (1988). Phonemic segmentation skill and beginning reading. *Journal of Educational Psychology, 77*, 417–427.

Uhry, J. K., & Shepherd, M. J. (1997). Teaching phonological recoding to young children with phonological processing deficits: The effect on sight-vocabulary acquisition. *Learning Disability Quarterly, 20*, 104–125.

Wasik, B. A., & Bond, M. A. (2001). Beyond the pages of a book: Interactive book reading and language development in preschool classrooms. *Journal of Educational Psychology, 93,* 243–250.

Weiss, J. J., & Hagan, R. (1988). A key to literacy: Kindergarteners' awareness of the functions of print. *The Reading Teacher, 41,* 574–579.

Whitehurst, G., Arnold, D., Epstein, J., Angell, A., Smith, M., & Fischel, J. (1994). A picture-book reading intervention in day care and home for children from low-income families. *Developmental Psychology, 30,* 679–689.

Whitehurst, G. J., Falco, F. L., Lonigan, C. J., Fischel, J. E., De-Baryshe, B. D., Valdez-Menchaca, M. C., et al. (1988). Accelerating language development through picture book reading. *Developmental Psychology, 24,* 552–559.

Whitehurst, G. J., & Lonigan, C. J. (1998). Child development and emergent literacy. *Child Development, 69,* 848–872.

Appendix A:

Children's Literature with Multiple Rhyme Patterns

Brown, M. W. (1989). *Goodnight moon.* New York: Scholastic.
Brown, M. W. (1999). *Another important book.* New York: HarperCollins.
Charlip, R. (1999). *Sleepytime rhyme.* New York: Greenwillow.
Degen, B. (1983). *Jamberry.* New York: Harper & Row.
Dodd, L. (1999). *Hairy Maclary and Zachary Quack.* Wellington, New Zealand: Mallinson Rendel.
DuQuette, K. (1999). *The house book.* New York: Putnam.
Ehlert, L. (2000). *Market day.* San Diego: Harcourt.
Fleming, D. (1991). *In the small, small pond.* New York: Holt, Rinehart & Winston.
Fleming, D. (1991). *In the tall, tall grass.* New York: Holt, Rinehart & Winston.
Fleming, D. (1994). *Barnyard banter.* New York: Holt, Rinehart & Winston.
Gleman, R. G. (1979). *Hello, cat, you need a hat.* New York: Scholastic.
Hoberman, M. A. (1996). *One of each.* Boston: Little, Brown.
Katz, M. J. (1990). *Ten potatoes in a pot.* New York: Harper & Row.
Langstaff, J. (1974). *Oh, a-hunting we will go.* New York: Atheneum.
Lowery, L. (1995). *Twist with a burger, jitter with a bug.* Boston: Houghton Mifflin.
Maccarone, G. (1992). *Itchy, itchy chicken pox.* New York: Scholastic.
McPhail, D. (1993). *Pigs aplenty, pigs galore!* New York: Dutton.
Reid, B. (1999). *The party.* New York: Scholastic.
Shaw, N. (1991). *Sheep in a shop.* Boston: Houghton Mifflin.
Shaw, N. (1992). *Sheep out to eat.* Boston: Houghton Mifflin.
Suen, A. (1998). *Window music.* New York: Viking.
Winthrop, E. (2001). *Dumpy La Rue.* New York: Holt, Rinehart & Winston.

CLASSIFIED

Doctoral Study in Behavior Disorders

Parent involvement in children's acquisition of reading

Sharon Darling, Laura Westberg

Parent involvement has a positive influence on student achievement (Epstein, Clark, Salinas, & Sanders, 1997; Jordan,. Snow, & Porche, 2000; Shaver & Walls, 1998; Westat & Policy Studies Associates, 2001). In addition, evidence demonstrates that parent involvement at home has a more significant impact on children than it does in school activities (Christenson & Sheridan, 2001; Hickman, Greenwood, & Miller, 1995; Izzo, Weissberg, Kasprow, & Fendrich, 1999; Trusty, 1999).

The National Reading Panel (National Institute of Child Health and Human Development, 2000) report provided educators with important scientific evidence about effective classroom practices for reading instruction in the United States. This report, however, did not address the impact parents have on their children's reading achievement or how educators might support parents in helping their children learn to read.

The lack of clear scientific evidence on the effectiveness of parent involvement in children's reading acquisition led the National Center for Family Literacy, with funding from the National Institute for Literacy, to conduct a meta-analysis of the research literature to determine the effect of parent involvement on the reading acquisition of children from kindergarten to grade 3 (Sénéchal, in press). The primary goal of this meta-analysis was to inform those working in family literacy and related fields so that they may better equip parents to support their children's literacy development. A second goal was to extend the scientific evidence provided by the National Reading Panel and supplement the current evidence on parent involvement in general. In this column, we describe the methodology of the meta-analysis, share the results, and outline some implications for practice.

Methodology

For the purposes of this meta-analysis, parent involvement in literacy acquisition was narrowly defined to include parent-child activities that focus on reading. Reading acquisition, as a general term, refers to the early literacy behaviors of children in kindergarten as well as the more advanced behaviors of children in grade 3. Thus, reading acquisition includes early literacy behaviors such as knowledge of letter names and letter sounds, phoneme awareness, and early decoding abilities, as well as word recognition and reading comprehension.

Three categories of questions were addressed. The first two were related to whether the characteristics of (a) the interventions and (b) the sample affected the impact of parent involvement. Interventions were defined for purposes of this study as intentional teacher-parent interactions intended to influence the way parents support their children's reading; these interventions may have included direct training, parent workshops, and materials sent home to parents. The third category concerned questions about the design of studies. This article focuses on the first two categories; those interested in the third category may contact the National Center for Family Literacy at www.famlit.org for the complete technical report.

A search of the research literature was conducted through electronic databases, review articles, and reference lists from the selected databases and review articles. For the electronic searches, three categories of search terms on parent involvement, literacy, and grade level were used. Articles selected for coding had to be studies that

a. were published in a peer-reviewed journal;
b. used an experimental or quasi-experimental design or a pretest-posttest design;
c. tested the hypothesis that parent involvement affects the acquisition of reading;
d. included at least five participants; and
e. reported statistics permitting the calculation or estimation of effect sizes, or reported effect sizes.

The coding instrument included three sections with studies coded on dimensions for intervention, participant, and study characteristics.

Results

A total of 20 interventions representing 1,583 families were meta-analyzed. Results clearly show that parent involvement has a positive effect on children's reading acquisition. The three types of parent involvement (see Figure) identified in this research differed in their effectiveness.

Training parents to teach their children reading with specific exercises produced greater results than having parents listen to their child read with or without training. In addition, training parents to listen to their child read was two times more effective than having parents listen to their child read without training.

Types of parent involvement

Type	Description
Listen to child read (3 studies)	In these studies, parents were encouraged to listen to their child read. Teachers provided specific suggestions to the parents. Suggestions included reading locations, talking about a story before reading it, encouraging children, avoiding criticism, and using good reading practices. In all of these studies, books were sent home from school.
Trained to listen (7 studies)	Techniques to train parents varied and included corrective feedback; the paired reading technique; using sentence context to determine the correct word; using initial phoneme sound to guide word choice; encouraging children to self-correct; praising children; using meaning, context, and phonic cues instead of direct word prompts; and delaying intervention when children struggled to read a word. In two of these studies, parents read books to their children. In all but one of the studies in this category books were sent home from school.
Trained to teach (10 studies)	Parents were trained to teach their children specific reading skills. Strategies included using flashcards with children learning to read new words, sentences with these new words, and letter names; selecting reading environments; correcting children's errors; teaching letter-sound correspondence and letter-sound blending; helping children learn to read one-syllable words; recognizing and saying beginning consonant and ending vowel-consonant sounds; and blending beginning and ending sounds to sound out new words. In four studies, parents were given a structured program that included exercises and texts with controlled difficulty levels. In some cases, the texts promoted specific letter-sound knowledge or reading specific words. In three studies parents were trained to use reading programs: Teach Your Child to Read in 100 Easy Lessons (Engelmann, Haddox, & Bruner, 1983), the Reading Recovery model, and the Reading Made Easy program (Harrison, 1981).

Due to considerable variability of the studies within the three intervention types, results must be interpreted with caution.

Interventions four months or shorter were more effective than interventions longer than five months. The amount of training and any supportive feedback the parents received had no impact on the effectiveness of the intervention.

Parent involvement had a positive effect on children from kindergarten to grade 3. In addition, the interventions were as effective for children at risk for or experiencing reading difficulties as they were for typically developing children. Socioeconomic status of the participating families did not affect the positive effect of the interventions.

Implications for practice

How should these findings influence the ways educators work with families? These findings support efforts by family literacy experts and other educators to emphasize literacy development through intentional activities and strategies that engage parents in their children's reading acquisition. On the basis of the results reported here, educators may want to assess their literacy program's strengths in implementing specific strategies for supporting parents in helping their children learn to read. Interventions that actively serve parents seeking to improve their own literacy skills as well as support their children's learning, such as family literacy programs, are ideal settings for developing systematic training for parents to teach their children to read. As parents learn about the essential skills for reading and practice those skills with their children, they can support their children's reading acquisition while improving their own. Parent involvement strategies that incorporate education and family literacy might produce greater results for children learning to read than strategies that do not address parents' knowledge of their children's literacy development. Training for parents can align with evidence-based reading instruction provided by children's classroom teachers.

The results of this research synthesis on parent involvement in children's acquisition of reading provide another layer of evidence for implementing effective reading instruction that increases children's reading achievement and builds stronger families of readers.

References

Christenson, S.L., & Sheridan, S.M. (2001). *Schools and families: Creating essential connections for learning.* New York: Guilford.

Engelmann, S., Haddox, P., & Bruner, E. (1983). *Teach your child to read in 100 easy lessons.* New York: Simon & Shuster.

Epstein, J.L., Clark, L., Salinas, K.C., & Sanders, M.G. (1997, March). *Scaring up school-family-community connections in Baltimore: Effects on student achievement and attendance.* Paper presented at the annual meeting of the American Educational Research Association, Chicago, IL.

Harrison, G.V. (1981). *Reading made easy: A handbook for parents.* Provo, UT: Metra.

Hickman, C.W., Greenwood, G., & Miller, M.D. (1995). High school parent involvement: Relationships with achievement, grade level, SES, and gender. *Journal of Research and Development in Education, 28* (3), 125-134.

Izzo, C.V., Weissberg, R.P., Kasprow, W.J., & Fendrich, M. (1999). A longitudinal assessment of teacher perceptions of parent involvement in children's education and school performance. *American Journal of Community Psychology, 27,* 817-839.

Jordan, G.E., Snow, C.E., & Porche, M.V. (2000). Project EASE: The effect of a family literacy project on kindergarten students' early literacy skills. *Reading Research Quarterly, 35,* 524-546.

National Institute of Child Health and Human Development. (2000). *Report of the National Reading Panel: Teaching children to read: An evidence-based assessment of the scientific research literature on reading and its implications for reading instruction. Reports of the subgroups.* Washington, DC: U.S. Government Printing Office.

Senechal, M. (in press). *The effect of parent involvement on their children's acquisition of reading from kindergarten to grade 3.* Louisville, KY: National Center for Family Literacy.

Shaver, A.V., & Walls, R.T. (1998). Effect of Title I parent involvement on student reading and mathematics achievement. *Journal of Research and Development in Education, 31* (2), 90-97.

Trusty, J. (1999). Effects of eighth-grade parental involvement on late adolescents' educational experiences. *Journal of Research and Development in Education, 32,* 224-233.

Westat, & Policy Studies Associates. (2001). *The longitudinal evaluation of school change and performance in Title I schools.* Washington, DC: U.S. Department of Education.

Darling is the president and founder of the National Center for Family Literacy (325 W. Main St., Suite 300, Louisville, KY 40202, USA). Westberg is a senior project manager for the National Center for Family Literacy.

Beyond Shared Book Reading: Dimensions of Home Literacy and Low-Income African American Preschoolers' Skills

Pia Rebello Britto, Jeanne Brooks-Gunn

The home environment is always cited as an influence on the development of young children's literacy and school achievement skills (Snow and others, 1991; Sugland and others, 1995). However, we do not know exactly *how* home environments foster this development. If, as has been stated, literacy begins in infancy for families where print is the mediator for life's activities (Purcell-Gates, 1996), then what aspects of family literacy environments promote children's emerging literacy? Is it parent and child shared book reading, following a recipe or directions to a destination, parents' instructing children in the alphabet or similar school readiness skills, or telling stories and singing songs, or some combination of these? Are there aspects of family literacy that we have not even tapped yet? If so, where might we start looking? And how do families emphasize different dimensions of family literacy?

According to Wasik (2001), there are at least three ways in which the term *family literacy* is currently being used: to describe the study of literacy in the family, to describe a set of interventions related to the literacy development of young children, and to refer to a set of programs designed to enhance the literacy skills of more than one family member. This study explores family literacy in the first sense—specifically, the dimensions of family literacy environments associated with children's literacy outcomes. Emergent literacy is the knowledge, attitudes, and skills that are developmental precursors to more established forms of literate behavior (Whitehurst and Lonigan, 1998). Thinking of the development of literacy in terms of emerging skills is a shift away from the traditional schools of thought that defined this stage in terms of reading readiness. According to emergent literacy theorists, children become readers through a series of experiences that encourage active engagement with meaningful forms of reading, writing, and spoken language and through supportive environments that foster learning, risk taking, and active experimentation with print (Crawford, 1995; Shapiro and Doiron, 1987; Sonnenschein, Brody, and Munsterman, 1996). In other words, there is a naturalness to emergent literacy that gives importance to out-of-school literacy experiences. Though much has been written about both family literacy and emergent literacy separately, few studies have connected them.

In this chapter we explore some of the possible dimensions of family literacy. Then we examine the relative and

differential importance of these dimensions for young children's emerging literacy skills. Finally, we discuss implications of the results for future research and practice in the area of child and family literacy.

Dimensions of Family Literacy Environments

Our work focuses on literacy in the family. In our review of the literature, we found that three dimensions of family literacy environments were identified: language and verbal interactions, the learning climate, and the social and emotional climate. Each of these three dimensions, and the facets embedded in them, is discussed in terms of definitions and constructs, measures of these constructs, and the links between these constructs and child outcomes (children's expressive and receptive vocabulary and school readiness).

Language and Verbal Interactions. Oral language, or talking, begins before literacy and then parallels it (Strickland and Morrow; 1990). Both of these skills are closely connected and similar in many ways. For instance, both learning to read and learning to talk are challenging tasks, maturation plays a role in the development of both sets of skills, and social interaction is central to the expansion of literacy and language (Snow; 1983).

An extensive longitudinal investigation by Hart and Risley (1995) demonstrated that a richer early exposure to language in the home is associated with better vocabulary skills in early and middle childhood. Topics of conversations and use of words during conversations have also been linked with children's emerging literacy skills. In the Home School Study of Language and Literacy Development, a longitudinal observation of language use in eighty-four low-income families with young children, use of rare or uncommon words was associated with child verbal ability scores (Snow, 1993). An analysis of standardized tests of verbal ability indicates that tests may stress rare words at the top end of the continuum; therefore it is unclear whether it is the oral or written language in the home that contributes to children's verbal ability (see Chapter One of this volume).

The current empirical and theoretical literature on emergent literacy emphasizes that experience with decontextualized language is a critical ingredient to school success (Dickinson and Snow, 1987; Dickinson and Tabors, 1991; Snow; 1993). For instance, decontextualized language use is noted most commonly in written language and to some extent in oral language, where the topic and situation dictate the degree of disembeddedness (see Chapter One of this volume). Decontextualized, or disembedded, language skills reflect an ability to talk about ideas and nonpresent objects or events—for example, referring to past and future events, requesting or sharing information, and expressing ideas and opinions unrelated to the immediate physical context (Olson, 1977; Snow, 1991). In the Home School Study of Language and Literacy Development, Snow and colleagues found a wide range in decontextualized language use across four activities: book reading, talking about a past event, mealtime conversation, and talking while playing with toys (Snow, 1991; Beals, De Temple, and Dickinson, 1994; De Temple and Beals, 1991). They also noted that decontextualized language use was associated with the literacy environment in the home. In homes where children had more literacy exposure, there was greater use of decontextualized language compared with homes where children had fewer literacy experiences.

Learning Climate. A "learning culture" may exist in families, which may or may not be academic in the conventional sense of the term. At least two aspects of the learning climate have been identified—structure and function. The structure of the learning environment, the more studied aspect of the two, consists of the presence and availability of, and the access to, printed matter in the home. Children's experience with printed matter through parental teaching and reading styles characterizes the functional aspect of the learning climate.

Children's exposure to printed material in the home appears to be facilitated through parents' teaching and reading styles. Parents use printed matter in one or more of a variety of ways while interacting with their children: as a source of entertainment, as a skill to be learned, and as an integral ingredient of daily life. Direct skill instruction has been compared with more informal ways of teaching to examine its effect on children's emerging literacy skills. For instance, children whose parents tend to view and use reading as a source of entertainment appear to have a more positive attitude toward reading and better reading skills compared with children of parents who tend to use more direct skill instruction while engaging their children with print (Baker, Scher, and Mackler, 1997; Baker, Serpell, and Sonnenschein, 1995; Sonnenschein, Brody, and Munsterman, 1996).

Strong links between maternal teaching and reading styles and children's emergent literacy skills (such as language usage, word recall, and story comprehension) have been demonstrated (Haden, Reese, and Fivush, 1996; Pellegrini, Galda, Jones, and Perlmutter, 1995; Senechal, 1997; Senechal, Thomas, and Monker, 1995).

Social and Emotional Climate. Supportive environments have been defined in terms of their responsiveness to the developing child's social and emotional needs. A positive link exists between children's well-being and the socioemotional support available to them in the home (Bradley and others, 1989; Gottfried, Gottfried, and Bathurst, 1995). However, in the realm of family literacy, such evidence is lacking (Baker, Afflerbach, and Reinking, 1996; Edwards and Pleasants, 1997). The social and emotional aspects of family literacy have yet to evolve. For instance, the affective and emotional interaction between an adult and child during shared book reading is understudied. We do not know how parent and child physical closeness, warmth, and positive interactions during storytelling or recounting events affect children's verbal abilities.

Social interactions between parents and children during activities like shared book reading may influence children's emerging literacy skills (Fitzgerald, Schuele, and Roberts, 1992), as do parent-child verbal interactions around everyday routines (Pellegrini, Galda, and Charak, 1997; Schaefer and Edgerton, 1985). In addition to opportunities to engage in discourse, the *number* of people with whom children converse may be important (Pellegrini, Galda, and Charak, 1997).

The emotional warmth and motivational support in the home during literacy activities may modulate children's experiences with literacy (Edwards and Pleasants, 1997; Leichter, 1984, 1997; Shapiro and Doiron, 1987). Parents' general supportive presence and warmth have been associated with children's language ability (Berlin, Brooks-Gunn, Spiker, and Zaslow, 1995; Foster, 1997).

In terms of parent-child attachment, Bus and van IJzendoorn (1995, 1997) have demonstrated that mothers in insecure relationships with their children (as measured by the strange-situation episode) engage in less shared book reading in the home and that when they do read, they tend to engage in more disciplining types of talk during the book reading. In addition, the children are less inclined to share books with their mothers. Bus and van IJzendoorn conclude that shared book reading is a social process and that learning to read is in part associated with the affective dimension of the mother-child relationship.

Conclusion. A comparison of the three broad dimensions of family literacy identified here indicates that the first dimension, language and verbal interactions, has received the most attention in the literature. The conclusion of three decades of research is that children who are exposed to a richer linguistic environment earlier in life demonstrate a richer vocabulary and early acquisition of literacy skills. The second dimension, learning climate, has also been investigated, although to a lesser extent. The social and emotional climate in the home has been the least studied dimension of family literacy. However, these three dimensions have not been examined under the rubric of a single study.

In our work we expect that these dimensions may play a role in children's emerging literacy. The relative contribution of each is explored, with the expectation that although the language and verbal interactions are believed to be predominant, the learning climate may be just as salient as any other dimension.

Despite the vast body of literature on family and child literacy, comparisons of methodology and measures across studies is very difficult (Scarborough and Dobrich, 1994). As a result, we do not know much about the relative and differential importance of the dimensions. Consequently, in this study we address not only the association between the three dimensions of family literacy environments but also their relative and differential importance via multiple measurement techniques of the dimensions and child outcomes.

Design. The sample in this study included participants from the Newark Young Family Study (NYFS), an observational study embedded in the Teenage Parent Demonstration Program (TPD). Begun in 1986, TPD was designed to test the feasibility and explore the implications of making welfare eligibility contingent on teenage mothers' participation in employment-directed activities, schooling, working, and job training. This program used an experimental design in which six thousand first-time, welfare-eligible adolescent mothers from three sites (Chicago, Illinois, and Camden and Newark, New Jersey) were enrolled and then assigned randomly to one of two groups—intervention or control. For the intervention, support from Aid to Families with Dependent Children (AFDC) was contingent on the mothers' participation in self-sufficiency activities. Mothers who did not participate in self-sufficiency activities had part of their AFDC stipend reduced. At the same time, the intervention mothers received special services, such as case management, job training, life skills workshops, assistance in making child-care arrangements, and financial subsidies for child care, to facilitate their compliance with program requirements. Control mothers received financial and other forms of assistance already provided under the regular AFDC program.

The evaluation of TPD was primarily collected through survey instruments—interviews and self-report questionnaires that could be implemented through large-scale data collection efforts (Maynard, 1993, 1995). The aim of the NYFS was to examine, in more detailed ways than is possible in survey studies, whether participation in self-sufficiency activities has any influence on interactions in families or on developmental processes (Aber, Brooks-Gunn, and Maynard, 1995). Families were seen in their homes approximately forty months after baseline.

Sample. Participants in the NYFS were a representative random subsample of 126 African American mothers from the Newark site whose children were seven months of age or younger at baseline (time 1). The sample was equally divided between intervention (48 percent) and control (52 percent) groups.

At entrance into the study (time 1), the participants, who were all teenage mothers, were between 14 and 20 years of age ($M = 17.47$, $SD = 1.13$). No mother had completed high school or received a GED certificate. As measured by the Test of Adult Basic Education, the average reading grade level was seventh grade. Although the mothers were of high school age, a majority of them (65 percent) were reading at a middle school level or below a seventh-grade level; 11 percent were reading at a seventh-grade level, and 24 percent were reading above a seventh-grade level. Only 16 percent of the mothers were reading at or above a tenth-grade level. Virtually all mothers reported that they had never been married (98 percent). The majority (65 percent) lived with one or both of their parents. The children ranged in age from two weeks old to 27 months old ($M = 7$ months, $SD = 7.16$ months), and 54 percent were girls.

At the follow-up (time 2—about two years after baseline), on average, the mothers were 20 years of age, and the children were 36 months old. Only 20 percent of the mothers had finished high school by this time. The average reading grade level had gone up by a grade; the mothers were now reading at an eighth-grade level. Almost half of the mothers (46 percent) were reading below a seventh-grade level, 17 percent at a seventh-grade level, 11 percent at an eighth- or ninth-grade level, and 26 percent at a tenth-grade level or higher. The vast majority of the mothers were still unmarried (93 percent), and over half lived with their parents. In addition, one-third of the mothers had borne a second child, and approximately 10 percent had borne three children.

The shared book-reading observation (time 3) occurred three years after baseline. The mothers' mean age was 21 years ($SD = 1.25$ years), and the children's mean age was 48 months ($SD = 7.36$ months). The mothers' average receptive language ability, as indexed by their Peabody Picture Vocabulary Test-Revised (PPVT-R) (Dunn and Dunn, 1981) standard score, was 74.63 ($SD = 16.21$). This receptive language score was more than a standard deviation below the normative mean for the test ($M = 100$, $SD = 15$ for the PPVT-R). Only 25 percent of the mothers had scores above the mean.

Procedure. The families in this study were seen three times: at baseline, or time 1 (interview and assessment of maternal reading ability); at a twenty-four-month follow-up, or time 2 (interview and assessment of maternal reading ability); and at a thirty-six-month follow-up, or time 3 (NYFS observation—observation of mother-child interactions and child assessment). Data collection at times 1 and 2, as part of the TPD project, primarily involved interview and survey measures (with the exception of the maternal reading test).

At time 3 data were collected during a three-and-one-half-hour home visit conducted by two intensively trained field staff workers. During the visit, the field staff administered an extensive series of demographic questions and a set of standard questionnaires to the mothers, evaluated several aspects of the children's development and the home environment, and coordinated several videotaped sessions, including shared book-reading and puzzle-solving sessions.

During the mother-child shared book reading, each mother was handed the book *Sounds I Hear* (Kriss, 1983) and asked to read the book to her child. (*Sounds I Hear* is a concept book that has fifteen pages of illustrations and text comprising forty-seven independent clauses. The purpose of the book was to enhance children's preschool readiness skills vis-à-vis recognition of sounds made by animals, objects, and vehicles found in both urban and rural settings.) The book-reading session lasted approximately seven minutes.

The mother and child were given two puzzles, one "easy" (chosen to be relatively simple for the child to complete) and one "hard" (chosen to be difficult for the children to complete without the help of their mothers). The mother was instructed to allow the child to try the puzzles alone and then to give "whatever help you think he/she needs to do it him/herself." The puzzle-solving task lasted approximately ten minutes.

Measures

The measures are described in terms of the three dimensions of family literacy environment—language and verbal interactions, the learning climate, and the social and emotional climate.

Language and Verbal Interactions. The language and verbal interactions dimension was assessed by coding maternal decontextualized and expressive language use from videotaped interactions of the book reading at time 3. Maternal verbal interactions were transcribed using the Codes for Human Analysis of Transcripts transcription system (MacWhinney, 1991). All transcripts underwent a two-step verification process to ensure 100 percent accuracy of the spoken word and transcribing conventions in the transcription.

Maternal Decontextualized Language. Individual mother utterances were coded from the verbal transcripts of the book-reading interaction using the Home-School Coding System (De Temple, 1993). An utterance is equivalent to a single unit of talk, such as a word, phrase, comment, or a single turn during a conversation. Maternal utterances were distinguished according to whether they were contextual (that is, using information that is readily available from the illustrations or the text) or decontextual (that is, going beyond the text or the illustrations to make predictions, draw inferences, analyze or make connections to the real world, and so on). Two independent coders evaluated all 126 transcripts. For the decontextualized and contextualized dimensions of talk, initial intercoder agreement was 80 percent. Then the coders compared each transcript and resolved all disagreements to achieve 100 percent agreement.

Maternal Expressive Language. Expressive language was measured by the total number of different words used during the shared book-reading interaction. This measure was estimated by running the FREQ analyses in the Computerized Language Analysis (CLAN) program

(MacWhinney, 1991). A composite variable was created by summing maternal decontextual and expressive language use ($M = 12.89$, $SD = 8.79$).

Learning Climate. The learning climate in the home was assessed at time 3 based on coding of Maternal Quality of Assistance from videotaped interactions of mother-child puzzle solving and based on Academic Stimulation in the home, rated by observers using the Home Observation for Measurement of the Environment (HOME) inventory (Bradley, 1994).

Maternal Quality of Assistance. Quality of assistance during problem solving was coded using a system adapted by Chase-Lansdale, Zamsky, and Brooks-Gunn (1989; see also Spiker, Ferguson, and Brooks-Gunn, 1993) from a system developed by Sroufe, Matas, and Rosenberg (1980). This scale measures the mother's overall skill in assisting the child in a manner that helps the child stay interested and motivated while allowing a maximum amount of exploration and learning. Mothers were coded on a 7-point scale ranging from no assistance to excellent assistance ($M = 3.75$, $SD = 1.49$, minimum = 1, maximum = 7). The intercoder reliability within 1 point was 100 percent.

Academic Stimulation. The standard fifty-five-item early childhood version of the HOME inventory was administered at time 3. The HOME inventory is the most widely used assessment of children's home environments in the field of developmental psychology. The HOME inventory is intended to measure the quality and quantity of stimulation and support available to a child in the home environment. The procedure for scoring the inventory involves a semistructured observation and an interview conducted to minimize obtrusiveness. The seven-item academic subscale of the HOME inventory assesses the degree to which the child is encouraged to learn skills related to school readiness ($M = 6.71$, $SD = 1.54$, minimum = 0, maximum = 7).

Social and Emotional Climate. The Warmth subscale of the early childhood HOME inventory was administered at time 3 to assess the encouragement and warmth in the home environment ($M = 5.65$, $SD = 1.50$, minimum = 1, maximum = 8).

Child Outcomes

Three measures of children's emerging literacy were assessed: receptive vocabulary, expressive language, and school readiness.

Receptive Vocabulary. Child receptive vocabulary was assessed using the PPVT-R (Dunn and Dunn, 1981) at time 3. The child is expected to identify correctly one of four pictures that match a stimulus word. This standardized test has a mean of 100 and a standard deviation of IS, with higher scores indicating a larger receptive vocabulary ($M = 82.69$, $SD = 12.85$, range = 56–121). These scores are low, more than one standard deviation below the standardized mean of the test. However, they are in accordance with other studies of low-income young children (Campbell and Ramey, 1994; Lee, Brooks-Gunn, Schnur, and Liaw, 1990; Pellegrini, Galda, Jones, and Perlmutter, 1995).

Expressive Language. The children's expressive language was assessed by the number of *different* words spoken by the child during the shared book-reading session at time 3. This measure is not to be confused with the total number of words spoken by the child. The expressive language score was obtained by running the FREQ analyses in CLAN ($M = 10$, $SD = 5.88$, range = 0–30).

School Readiness. Children's school readiness was assessed using the Caldwell Preschool Inventory, Revised Version (Cooperative Tests and Services, 1970). Forty-eight items were administered to the children at time 3. The items tap children's knowledge of colors, shapes, and general information. Higher scores are indicative of greater preparedness for school. The average score for the children was 28.49 ($SD = 8.72$, range = 10–46). In a parallel sample of low-income preschool-age children, similar scores on the Caldwell Preschool Inventory were noted ($M = 28.72$) (Schnur, Brooks-Gunn, and Shipman, 1992).

Results

Our research question—"What are the associations between dimensions of family literacy environments and young children's literacy skills?"—was explored via regression analyses. A taxonomy of regression models was built. Children's age, mothers' age at the birth of the target child, treatment status, and number of children were entered as control variables in all the models. For the language and verbal interactions model, the maternal decontextualized and expressive language use variable was entered as the predictor. For the learning climate model, two variables were entered-maternal quality of assistance and the academic stimulation in the home. The social and emotional climate model had one variable—warmth in the home. Separate direct effects models tested the association between each dimension of family literacy environment and children's receptive and expressive language and school readiness. In the final model, maternal educational characteristics of verbal ability and high school completion were entered.

As noted, three different child outcomes were examined: receptive vocabulary, expressive language, and school readiness. In terms of children's receptive language, children with a score lower than were omitted from the analyses, as this score is 3 standard deviations below the standardized mean of the test ($N = 11$ children omitted). For the Caldwell Preschool Inventory, children with outlier scores of more than 2.5 standard deviations above the mean were also omitted from the analyses ($N = 3$ omitted).

Language and Verbal Interactions Dimension. Children's expressive language was associated with the language and verbal interactions dimension ($F[5,l03] = 26.18$, $p < .0001$). This model explained nearly 56 percent of the variance in the children's expressive language. In particular,

children's expressive language appeared to be strongly associated with maternal decontextual and expressive language use during book reading ($\beta = 0.72$, $p < .0001$). Mother's age at birth of the child emerged as a significant correlate, with children of older mothers having a higher vocabulary. Even after maternal educational correlates were added, the association between maternal language and children's expressive language remained. In terms of control variables, a greater number of siblings appear to have a detrimental effect on children's expressive language ($\beta = -0.14$, $p < .05$). Surprisingly, mothers' high school completion was negatively associated with children's expressive language use during shared book reading ($\beta = -0.16$, $p < .05$).

The children's receptive language skills (PPVT-R) were not associated with maternal language and verbal interactions. Maternal high school completion was positively and significantly associated with higher child receptive vocabulary scores (PPVT-R, $\beta = 0.33$, $p < .01$). On average, children of mothers who had a high school diploma scored 10 points higher on the PPVT-R test compared with children whose mothers did not have a high school diploma, which indicates that maternal educational attainment is an important correlate of children's receptive vocabulary skills.

The model testing the association between children's school readiness and the language and verbal interactions dimension was significant ($F[7,76] = 7.23$, $p < .0001$). However, maternal decontextualized and expressive language use during book reading was not associated with school readiness. In particular, maternal high school completion was associated with this skill ($\beta = 0.24$, $p < .01$). The other significant factors that emerged were child age ($\beta = 0.44$, $p < .0001$) and number of siblings ($\beta = -0.17$, $p < .05$).

Learning Climate Dimension. Maternal quality of assistance during the puzzle task was positively and significantly associated with the children's expressive language ($\beta = 0.32$, $p < .0001$). No associations were seen between children's receptive vocabulary (PPVT-R) scores and the learning climate. Children's school readiness was associated with the learning climate in the home ($F[8,76] = 8.10$, $p < .0001$). This model explained 42 percent of the variance in children's school readiness skills.

Social and Emotional Climate Dimension. Children's receptive and expressive language skills were not associated with the social and emotional climate in the home. However, the social and emotional climate in the home appeared to be associated with children's school readiness skills ($F[7,77] = 7.97$, $p < .0001$). This model explained 35 percent of the variance in preschool children's school readiness skills.

Association Between Family Literacy Environments and Children's Skills. In order to test the *relative* contribution of each dimension of family literacy environment on preschool-age children's literacy skills, a regression model was built that included aspects from each of the three dimensions. The controls entered in the model were the same as for the individual-dimension models. This was followed by the three dimensions of the family literacy environment. Maternal high school completion and receptive vocabulary were added in the final model. Separate models were run for each of the three outcomes.

The overall model for children's expressive language was significant ($F[10,95] = 14.01$, $p < .0001$). Maternal decontextualized and expressive language use emerged as a significant predictor ($\beta = 0.72$, $p < .0001$), and maternal warmth approached significance ($\beta = 0.12$, $p < .1$). Thus even though the language and verbal interactions in the home might be relatively important for children's expressive language development, the warmth in the home also might contribute to the development of this ability.

The overall model for children's receptive vocabulary was not significant. However, maternal quality of assistance, characterizing the learning dimension, approached significance ($\beta = 0.22$, $p < .1$).

The overall model for children's preschool readiness was significant ($F[10,71] = 6.73$, $p < .0001$). In particular, maternal quality of assistance was significantly associated with children's school readiness ($\beta = 0.27$, $p < .01$). The other two family literacy measures were not. The results suggest that the learning climate might be relatively more important for children's school readiness skills compared with the language and verbal interaction or social and emotional climate dimensions.

Discussion

The purpose of this study was to look at family literacy environments from a dimensional rather than "the environment-in-its-entirety" perspective vis-à-vis associations with literacy skills of low-income African American young children.

In this sample, maternal decontextualized and expressive language use was associated with preschoolers' expressive language. The learning climate dimension was associated with school readiness skills and expressive language. As part of the learning climate, quality of assistance provided by the mothers, as opposed to the academic stimulation in the home, was most strongly associated with these early literacy skills. Finally, the social and emotional climate dimension, specifically the warmth in the home, was associated with the children's school readiness skills. These results suggest that the three dimensions of the family literacy environments in low-income homes differentially foster African American preschool-age children's emerging literacy. Their relative importance appears to vary by the skill being acquired.

Even though the language and verbal interactions dimension was significantly associated with children's expressive language, it was not associated with the children's receptive vocabulary. Several possibilities for these results exist.

First, use of extended language, such as decontextual talk, is associated with certain aspects of children's literacy development during the preschool years (Snow, 1991), and experiences at home relate differentially to children's contextualized language skills. Hence it is plausible that children's receptive vocabulary may not be closely linked to decontextual language exposure in the home, as it does not capture aspects of decontextualized language.

Second, it could be that higher levels of decontextual talk are needed to foster children's emergent literacy skills. In this study relatively low levels of such talk were noted. For instance, less than 5 percent of maternal utterances were coded as extending the conversation during the book reading to make predictions or inferences about the text or as relating the text to the child's real world.

Third, it is possible that the nature of the book (a concept book) limited the use of maternal decontextual language. A concept book typically does not have a story line or characters; hence it might limit the extent to which parents can use it to extend the children's conversation beyond the text. The low levels of decontextualized language seen in the current study may not be adequate to foster certain literacy skills.

Fourth, mothers may be using more decontextualized forms of language in interactions other than the book-reading interaction—a limitation of this study because those other interactions were not examined. Purcell-Gates (Chapter One of this volume) notes differences in decontextualized language use across reading of a wordless storybook and retelling of a significant event.

Fifth, related to the preceding point, other aspects of language interaction not tied to books could have been associated with children's receptive vocabulary.

The learning climate in the home was associated with preschoolers' school readiness and expressive language skills. The findings in this study suggest that the manner in which parents interact with their children is associated with children's literacy development. This finding is especially strong in that the learning climate was assessed during the puzzle-solving activity and the child expressive language skills during the shared book-reading activity. Other work has also noted an association between parental teaching and young children's literacy skills (see Chapter Three of this volume).

Of the two functional aspects investigated, academic stimulation in the home was not significantly associated with child literacy outcomes compared with maternal quality of assistance during problem solving. Perhaps no association was found for academic stimulation because very little variability was noted for this scale ($M = 6.7$ for a 7-point scale). Perhaps because of social desirability, most of the mothers reported that they encouraged these activities; however, the actual interactions around these activities are not assessed by the HOME inventory. In addition, the correlation between maternal quality of assistance and the academic stimulation in the home was not significant. It appears that informal teaching around a puzzle-solving activity was more strongly linked with children's school readiness and expressive language. Assisting the child in a manner that helps the child stay interested and motivated in the task while also allowing a maximum amount of exploration and learning may foster children's developing literacy skills.

The social and emotional climate in the home was significantly associated with preschoolers' school readiness skills and modestly associated with their expressive language. Based on the HOME inventory, it was the encouragement and warmth in the home (understood in terms of more "positive" interactions) that were associated with children's emerging literacy. The findings in this study advance our knowledge about the association between social and emotional interactions in the home and children's literacy skills.

Maternal education has been strongly associated with reading and literacy activities in the home (Bradley and others, 1989; Hart and Risley, 1995; Klebanov, Brooks-Gunn, and Duncan, 1994; Klebanov, Brooks-Gunn, McCarton, and McCormick, 1998; Snow, 1993). In addition, the links between children's IQ scores and quality of learning opportunities and emotional support in the home are stronger for children of more educated mothers than for children of mothers who have not completed high school (Brooks-Gunn, Klebanov, and Duncan, 1996). Mothers themselves state that education gives them a sense of empowerment and the ability to assist their children (Gadsden, 1995). Our results confirm those of other studies (even with the truncated range of education).

Besides the expected link between maternal education and child literacy outcomes, an interesting finding emerged. Children whose mothers did not graduate from high school demonstrated a greater expressive language compared with children whose mothers did graduate, even controlling for mothers' language use in the book reading. This was a counterintuitive and anomalous finding.

The associations between literacy environment and child outcomes remained significant despite the significance of maternal education. By controlling for maternal education and receptive vocabulary (PPVT-R), we held constant factors that have been held responsible for child literacy outcomes (Scarborough and Dobrich, 1994). In this and other studies (see Chapter Four of this volume), the unique influence of the family literacy environment has pervaded.

Conclusion

Literacy skills are akin to a complex tapestry, woven together by threads of different dimensions. The intricate patterns that emerge are a function of the interactions between the dimensions. In the current sample of low-income, low-education families, associations were seen between the three dimensions of family literacy environment and preschool-

ers' emergent literacy skills. The relative importance of each dimension varied based on the skill being acquired.

Given the complex nature of literacy acquisition, global processes may not be particularly useful in identifying more specific dimensions of literacy processes, and employing multidimensional models is warranted. For instance, in the current sample of African American teenage mothers and young children, all three family processes were implicated in at least one child outcome.

This study is based on a demonstration program and evaluation funded by the Administration for Children, Youth and Families and by the assistant secretary for planning and evaluation, U.S. Department of Health and Human Services. The primary evaluation was conducted by Mathematica Policy Research, Inc., under the direction of Rebecca Maynard. Supplementary data collection and analysis were funded by the Rockefeller Foundation, the Foundation for Child Development (conducted in collaboration with Lawrence Aber and Jeanne Brooks-Gunn at Columbia University and George Carcagno at Mathematica Policy Research, Inc.), and the Spencer Foundation (conducted by Jeanne Brooks-Gunn and Pia Rebello Britto). We would like to thank the National Institute for Child Health and Human Development Research Network on Child and Family Well-Being for its advice and assistance in connection with this study.

References

Aber, J. L., Brooks-Gunn, J., and Maynard, R. "The Effects of Welfare Reform on Teenage Parents and Their Children." *Future of Children*, 1995, 5, 53–71.
Baker, L., Afflerbach, P., and Reinking, D. (eds.). *Developing Engaged Readers in School and Home Communities*. Mahwah, N.J.: Erlbaum, 1996.
Baker, L., Scher, D., and Mackler, K. "Home and Family Influences on Motivations for Reading." *Educational Psychologist*, 1997, 32, 69–82.
Baker, L., Serpell, R, and Sonnenschein, S. "Opportunities for Literacy Learning in the Homes of Urban Preschoolers." In L. Morrow (ed.), *Family Literacy: Connections in Schools and Communities*. Newark, Del.: International Reading Association, 1995.
Beals, D. E., De Temple, J. M., and Dickinson, D. K. "Talking and Listening That Support Early Literacy Development of Children from Low-Income Families." In D. K Dickinson (ed.), *Bridges to Literacy: Children, Families, and Schools*. Cambridge, Mass.: Blackwell, 1994.
Berlin, L.J., Brooks-Gunn, J., Spiker, D., and Zaslow, M. J. "Examining Observational Measures of Emotional Support and Cognitive Stimulation in Black and White Mothers of Preschoolers." *Journal of Family Issues*, 1995, 16, 664–686.
Bradley, R H. "The HOME Inventory: Review and Reflections." In. H. W. Reese (ed.), *Advances in Child Development and Behavior*. Orlando, Fla.: Academic Press, 1994.
Bradley, R H., and others. "Home Environment and Cognitive Development in the First Three Years of Life: A Collaborative Study Involving Six Sites and Three Ethnic Groups in North America." *Developmental Psychology*, 1989, 25, 217–235.
Brooks-Gunn, J., Klebanov, P. K, and Duncan, G. "Ethnic Differences in Children's Intelligence Test Scores: Role of Economic Deprivation, Home Environment, and Maternal Characteristics." *Child Development*, 1996, 67, 396–408.
Bus, A. G., and van IJzendoorn, M. H. "Mothers Reading to Their Three-Year-Olds: The Role of Mother-Child Attachment Security in Becoming Literate." *Reading Research Quarterly*, 1995, 40, 998–1015.
Bus, A. G., and van IJzendoorn, M. H. "Affective Dimension of Mother-Infant Picturebook Reading." *Journal of School Psychology*, 1997, 35, 47–60.
Campbell, F. A., and Ramey, C. T. "Effects of Early Intervention on Intellectual and Academic Achievement: A Follow-Up Study of Children from Low-Income Families." *Child Development*, 1994, 65, 684–698.
Chase-Lansdale, P. L., Zamsky, E. S., and Brooks-Gunn, J. *Manual for Scoring the Puzzle Task for Adolescent Mothers*. New York: Center for

Young Children and Families, Teachers College, Columbia University, 1989.

Cooperative Tests and Services. *The Preschool Inventory Revised Edition—1970: Handbook.* Princeton, N.J.: Education Testing Service, 1970.

Crawford, P. A. "Early Literacy: Emerging Perspectives." *Journal of Research in Childhood Education,* 1995, 10, 71–86.

De Temple, J. M. *Coding System for Home Book Reading.* Unpublished manuscript, Harvard University, 1993.

De Temple, J. M., and Beals, D. E "Family Talk: Sources of Support for the Development of Decontextualized Language Skills." *Journal of Research in Childhood Education,* 1991, 6, 11–19.

Dickinson, D. K., and Snow, C. E. "Interrelationships Among Prereading and Oral Language Skills in Kindergartners from Two Social Classes." *Early Childhood Research Quarterly,* 1987, 2, 1–25.

Dickinson, D. K, and Tabors, P. O. "Early Literacy: Linkages Between Home, School, and Literacy Achievement at Age Five." *Journal of Research in Childhood Education,* 1991, 6, 30–46.

Dunn, L. M., and Dunn, L. M. *Peabody Picture Vocabulary Test-Revised.* Circle Pines, Minn.: American Guidance Service, 1981.

Edwards, P. A., and Pleasants, H. M. "Uncloseting Home Literacy Environment: Issues Raised Through Telling of Parent Stories." *Early Child Development and Care,* 1997, 127–128, 27–46.

Fitzgerald, J., Schuele, C. M., and Roberts, J. E. "Emergent Literacy: What Is It and What Does the Teacher of Children with Learning Disabilities Need to Know About It?" *Reading and Writing Quarterly,* 1992, 8, 71–85.

Foster, M. "Family Literacy: Questioning Conventional Wisdom." In D. Taylor (ed.), *Many Families, Many Literacies: An International Declaration of Principles.* Portsmouth, N.H.: Heinemann, 1997.

Gadsden, V. L. "Representations of Literacy: Parents' Images in Two Cultural Communities." In L. M. Morrow (ed.), *Family Literacy: Connections in Schools and Communities.* Newark, Del.: International Reading Association, 1995.

Gottfried, A. E, Gottfried, A. W., and Bathurst, K. "Maternal and Dual-Earner Employment Status and Parenting." In M. Bornstein (ed.), *Handbook of Parenting,* Vol. 2: *Biology and Ecology of Parenting.* Mahwah, N.J.: Erlbaum, 1995.

Haden, C. A., Reese, E., and Fivush, R. "Mothers' Extratextual Comments During Storybook Reading: Stylistic Differences over Time and Across Texts." *Discourse Processes,* 1996, 21, 135–169.

Hart, B., and Risley, T. R. *Meaningful Differences in the Everyday Experience of Young American Children.* Baltimore: Brookes, 1995.

Klebanov, P. K., Brooks-Gunn, J., and Duncan, G. J. "Does Neighborhood and Family Poverty Affect Mothers' Parenting, Mental Health, and Social Support?" *Journal of Marriage and the Family,* 1994, 56, 441–455.

Klebanov, P. K., Brooks-Gunn, J., McCarton, C., and McCormick, M. C. "The Contribution of Neighborhood and Family Income upon Developmental Test Scores over the First Three Years of Life." *Child Development,* 1998, 69, 1420–1436.

Kriss, D. *Sound I Hear* (O. Gelbart, trans.). Jerusalem: Home Institution Program for Preschool Youngsters, Hebrew University, 1983.

Lee, V., Brooks-Gunn, J., Schnur, E., and Liaw, T. "Are Head Start Effects Sustained? A Longitudinal Follow-Up Comparison of Disadvantaged Children Attending Head Start, No Preschool, and Other Preschool Programs." *Child Development,* 1990, 61, 495–507.

Leichter, H. J. "Families as Environments for Literacy." In H. Goelman, A. Oberg, and F. Smith (eds.), *Awakening to Literacy.* Portsmouth, N.H.: Heinemann, 1984.

Leichter, H. J. "Some Perspectives on the Family." In D. Taylor (ed.), *Many Families, Many Literacies: An International Declaration of Principles.* Portsmouth, N.H.: Heinemann, 1997.

MacWhinney, B. *The CHILDES Project: Tools for Analyzing Talk.* Mahwah, NJ: Erlbaum, 1991.

Maynard, R. *Building Self-Sufficiency Among Welfare-Dependent Teenage Parents: Lessons from the Teenage Parent Demonstration.* Princeton, N.J.: Mathematica Policy Research, 1993.

Maynard, R. "Teenage Childbearing and Welfare Reform: Lessons from a Decade of Demonstration and Evaluation Research." *Children and Youth Services Review,* 1995, 17, 309–332.

Olson, D. "From Utterance to Text." *Harvard Educational Review,* 1977, 47, 257–281.

Pellegrini, A. D., Galda, L., and Charak, D. "Bridges Between Home and School Literacy: Social Bases for Early School Literacy." *Early Child Development and Care,* 1997, 127–128, 99–109.

Pellegrini, A. D., Galda, L., Jones, I., and Perlmutter, J. "Joint Reading Between Mothers and Their Head-Start Children: Vocabulary Development in Two Text Formats." *Discourse Processes,* 1995, 19, 441–463.

Purcell-Gates, V. "Stories, Coupons, and the TV Guide: Relationships Between Home Literacy Experiences and Emergent Literacy Knowledge." *Reading Research Quarterly,* 1996, 31, 406–428.

Scarborough, H. S., and Dobrich, W. "On the Efficacy of Reading to Preschoolers." *Developmental Review,* 1994, 14, 245–302.

Schaefer, E., and Edgerton, M. "Parental and Child Correlates of Parental Modernity." In I. E. Siegel (ed.), *Parental Belief Systems: The Psychological Consequences for Children.* Mahwah, N.J.: Erlbaum, 1985.

Schnur, E. S., Brooks-Gunn, J., and Shipman, V. "Who Attends Programs Serving Poor Children? The Case of Head Start Attendees and Nonattendees." *Journal of Applied Developmental Psychology,* 1992, 13, 405–421.

Sénéchal, M. "The Differential Effect of Storybook Reading on Preschoolers' Acquisition of Expressive and Receptive Vocabulary." *Journal of Child Language,* 1997, 24, 123–138.

Sénéchal, M., Thomas, E., and Monker, J. "Individual Differences in 4-Year-Old Children's Acquisition of Vocabulary During Storybook Reading." *Journal of Educational Psychology,* 1995, 87, 218–229.

Shapiro, J., and Doiron, R. "Literacy Environments: Bridging the Gap Between Home and School." *Childhood Education,* 1987, 63, 262–269.

Snow, C. E. "Literacy and Language: Relationships During the Preschool Years." *Harvard Educational Review,* 1983, 53, 165–189.

Snow, C. E. "The Theoretical Basis for Relationships Between Language and Literacy in Development." *Journal of Research in Childhood Education,* 1991, 6, 5–10.

Snow, C. E. "Families as Social Contexts for Literacy Development." In C. Daiute (ed.), *The Development of Literacy Through Social Interaction.* New Directions for Child Development, no. 61. San Francisco: Jossey-Bass, 1993.

Snow, C. E., and others. *Unfulfilled Expectations: Home and School Influences on Literacy.* Cambridge, Mass.: Harvard University Press, 1991.

Sonnenschein, S., Brody, G., and Munsterman, K. "The Influences of Family Beliefs and Practices on Children's Early Reading Development." In L. Baker, P. Afflerbach, and D. Reinking (eds.), *Developing Engaged Readers in School and Home Communities.* Mahwah, N.J.: Erlbaum, 1996.

Spiker, D., Ferguson, J., and Brooks-Gunn, J. "Enhancing Maternal Interactive Behavior and Child Social Competence in Low Birth Weight, Premature Infants." *Child Development,* 1993, 64, 754–768.

Sroufe, L. A., Matas, L., and Rosenberg, D. M. *Manual for Scoring Mother Variables in Tool-Use Task Applicable for Two-Year-Old Children.* Minneapolis: Mother-Child Project, University of Minnesota, 1980.

Strickland, D. S., and Morrow, L. M. "Family Literacy: Sharing Good Books." *Reading Teacher,* 1990, 43, 518–519.

Sugland, B. W., and others. "The Early Childhood HOME Inventory and HOME-Short Form in Differing Racial/Ethnic Groups: Are There Differences in Underlying Structure, Internal Consistency of Subscales, and Patterns of Prediction?" *Journal of Family Issues,* 1995, 16, 632–663.

Wasik, B. H. "Overview of Family Literacy Programs." Unpublished manuscript, University of North Carolina, Chapel Hill, 2001.

Whitehurst, G. J., and Lonigan, C. J. "Child Development and Emergent Literacy." *Child Development,* 1998, 69, 848–872.

PIA REBELLO BRITTO is research scientist at the Center for Children and Families: Advancing Policy, Education and Development, at Teachers College, Columbia University.

JEANNE BROOKS-GUNN is Virginia and Leonard Marx Professor of Child Development and Education at Teachers College, Columbia University.

UNIT 2

Creating a Literacy Culture

Unit Selections

9. **Family Literacy: Perspective and Practices**, Lesley Mandel Morrow, Jeanne Paratore, Devron Gaber, Colin Harrison, and Diane Tracey
10. **The Role of Child Development and Social Interaction in the Selection of Children's Literature to Promote Literacy Acquisition**, C. Denise Johnson
11. **The Many Rewards of a Literacy-Rich Classroom**, David K. Dickinson and Lori Lyman DiGisi
12. **Building Walls of Words**, Edna Greene Brabham and Susan Kidd Villaume

Key Points to Consider

- What is the role of the family in initiating, developing, and supporting literacy?

- How can schools and families work together to promote literacy learning and development?

- How can schools implement developmentally appropriate practices and still be standards based?

- What effect does or should brain research have on teaching practices?

- How can meeting the needs of the whole child enhance literacy learning?

- How can schools meet the literacy needs of bilingual and limited English proficiency students?

 **Links: www.dushkin.com/online/**
These sites are annotated in the World Wide Web pages.

National Literacy Trust
http://www.literacytrust.org.uk/index.html

We teachers are naïve if we think we are the only ones who have the power or expertise to teach children. Unit 1 provided clear evidence of how children's pathway for becoming literate doesn't begin on their first day of school, but many years before they even set foot in a classroom. This Unit will expand on the ideas presented in the first unit by framing the discussion around a particular theoretical perspective for understanding social and cultural impacts on literacy development. Vygotsky's sociocultural theory will be used to explain these connections.

According to Vygotsky, children use language as a tool for developing higher-order mental functioning. In the words of Wink and Putney (2002), "we use language, in our action of speaking, as a tool for developing thought, and, at the same time, we develop language through thought." Since language is culturally bound, it is difficult to separate cognitive functioning from the cultural context in which it sprang. Thus, as educators, we cannot ignore the power that families have to influence a child's success in school. As children transition from home to school, we must join as partners to support and integrate each other's work so all children can succeed.

Researchers have found that the methods used to teach literacy in schools are different from the ways children learn in the home environment—an anomaly which often causes confusion in children and hesitancy in parents. The degree of dissimilarity between these two contexts will influence how much cognitive restructuring must occur before the child can learn concepts pre-

sented at school (Bodrova & Leong, 1996). How parents expose their children to and interact with them in the context of literacy varies according to their specific cultural backgrounds. Thus, this author describes how culture operates on at least two different levels: the culture of the greater society and the culture of each individual family. Educators must be sensitive to these variations while striving to understand all their students' familial nuances and how these may affect literacy learning, as future language and literacy development build on previous accomplishments (Bodrova & Leong, 1996).

Teachers, like parents, have a wide repertoire of strategies that they can employ to assist children with the construction of language and literacy knowledge. Careful consideration to the physical and social environments within the classroom assists children with constructing and reconstructing their understanding of literacy. Some of the most popular and well-known program models found in preschools, such as the Reggio Emilia and Montessori, were developed in response to the unique sociocultural needs of young children, stressing their role of being active authors of their own development and the value of partnering with parents. Johnson's article, "The Role of Child Development and Social Interaction in the Selection of Children's Literature to Promote Literacy Acquisition," implies that literature that most appeals to children will be connected to their stage of development. Making sense of their reading and writing will be most meaningful when shared with their peers and other significant adults.

Children's early literacy learning continues as they enter elementary schools with print-rich environments where developmentally appropriate practices and differentiation are common. While Johnson's article focuses mainly on the role of literature and a print-rich classroom and home environment, Dickinson and DiGisi, in "The Many Rewards of a Literacy-Rich Classroom," look at the benefits of a classroom where the joy of writing is also nurtured and valued. Their findings confirm that the amount and types of writing children do is related to their reading achievement. Children who wrote narrative and informational pieces in writing across the curriculum had higher reading scores.

Another strategy of particular use to teachers is scaffolding behaviors within the zone of proximal development. A primary tenant of best practices is creating challenging but achievable curriculum (NAEYC, 1997). In other words, teachers must recognize the tasks that children can accomplish independently and those that are just beyond their current capabilities. Teachers then create a context that bridges the gap, helping children accomplish tasks with assistance.

The ultimate goal of all teaching professionals is for their students to learn critical information to become successful and productive citizens in their adult years. With a culture steeped in literacy, there is no question that to be literate is one of the vital tools that provides the key for unlocking doors of opportunity in our society. As teachers we have a moral obligation to ensure that all students acquire the literacy skills that will put them on the road to a bright future.

Penny Sholl and Terri Jo Swim

References

Bodrova, E., & Leong, D.J. (1996). *Tools of the mind: The Vygotskian approach to early childhood education.* Columbus, OH: Merrill Prentice Hall.

National Association for the Education of Young Children (NAEYC, 1997). *Developmentally appropriate practice in early childhood programs* (Rev. ed.). Washington, DC: Author.

Wink, J., & Putney, L. (2002). *A vision of Vygotsky.* Boston: Allyn and Bacon.

Family Literacy: Perspective and Practices

Lesley Mandel Morrow
Jeanne Paratore
with Devron Gaber, Colin Harrison, and Diane Tracey

The authors define and provide a current perspective on the state of family literacy.

In 1991, the Board of Directors of the International Reading Association (IRA) formed the Commission on Family Literacy to study issues and initiatives in family literacy from a global perspective.

Earlier approaches to family literacy centered primarily on parents as partners in helping their children learn to read. That perspective is naturally important, but with vast changes in the demographics of schools and communities, family literacy needs to be approached in a much broader context.

Specifically, the commission will maintain the earlier perspective, but also focus on issues related to "environments which enable adult learners to enhance their own literacies, and at the same time provide environments which promote the literacies of their children" (Braun, 1991, p. 1).

A major goal of the Commission on Family Literacy is to disseminate information that defines family literacy, provides information about existing programs, and describes relevant work of agencies and professional associations. The scope of that dissemination will include both school and community programs ranging in levels of interest and activity from infancy through adult life. It is hoped that such dissemination will increase general recognition of the significance of the family's crucial role in the development of literacy.

It is clear that if we do not attend to the home when we discuss literacy development, whatever strategies we carry out in school will never be completely successful. It is time for issues in family literacy to get front-page treatment. They should be viewed by schools and other community agencies as the most important element in literacy development. They need focus equal in importance to that given such other issues as whole language, assessment, and connections between reading and writing. Within appropriate attention to family literacy, implementing strategies such as holistic instruction seems relatively unimportant. Schools need to view family literacy as part of the curriculum.

Family literacy: A broad perspective

As early as 1908 in the U.S., Huey suggested that children's learning in school begins with parents reading to them at home. Research now supports a strong link between home environment and children's acquisition of school-based literacy. Such practices in the home as shared reading, reading aloud, making a variety of print materials available, and promoting positive attitudes toward literacy have been found to have a significant impact on children's literacy learning (Clark, 1984; Cochran-Smith, 1986; Morrow, 1993; Teale, 1984).

But research also points out that the types and forms of literacy practiced in some homes are largely incongruent with those that children will encounter in school (Auerbach, 1989; Heath, 1983; Taylor & Dorsey-Gains, 1988). Despite the fact that literacy activity is present in some form or another in most home settings, the particular kinds of events that some parents share with their children may have little influence on their children's school success. Conversely, the kinds of literacy practiced in classrooms may have little meaning for those children outside school walls.

The nature of such conflicts can make it difficult for some parents to integrate school-based literacy events into their children's lives. There seems to be a strong correlation, for instance, between poverty and illiteracy. However, it is important to review the evidence thoroughly. It is also essential to follow Auerbach's (1989) lead in critically examining the assumptions which underpin evidence that supports such apparent correlation and to review the growing body of evidence that many low-income, minority, and immigrant families cultivate rich (though perhaps not school-like) contexts for literacy development and that they, indeed, support family literacy with exceptional effort and imagination.

Given all the evidence, it is essential to adopt an eclectic approach in surveying family literacy and to accept from the outset that what is to be learned will come from parents and children as well as from scholarly publications, agencies, and professionals. Family literacy must be studied from the widest possible perspective by respecting cultures, for instance, in which no books exist but in which storytelling is a common practice, as well as by reporting on cultures within which print is a dominant medium.

Defining family literacy

It is notoriously difficult to agree on definitions in the field of literacy; indeed, no definition is more resistant to consensus than the term literacy itself. Yet, the importance of literacy is universally accepted. Beliefs about literacy inevitably carry with them various assumptions and implications for subsequent action, any of which might conflict with those that undergird other beliefs and definitions.

Family literacy must be studied from the widest possible perspective. . . .

Those who work in family literacy or comment on it vary greatly in the theoretical stances they hold. From political and economic perspectives, for instance, the focus of discussions and programs in family literacy is often shaped by a desire to promote educational and, ultimately, economic advancement, both personally and nationally. Some people in the field believe that while it is important to support programs aimed at arresting what is perceived as a cycle of illiteracy, that focus may represent a deficit view because it does not take into account certain literacy events that occur within families. This perspective acknowledges the complexities of literacy activities and environments within families where literacy events may not be school like and, consequently, may go unnoticed by those outside the family or culture.

Proponents of this latter view suggest that literacy is not an all-or-nothing state but rather a function of individual interactions with print within a multidimensional range of literacy and personal experiences (Auerbach, 1989; Taylor & Dorsey-Gaines, 1988; Weinstein-Shr, 1991). Such accounts go well beyond school-based definitions of literacy. In their broader view, they support literacy as part of the fabric of everyday life. This viewpoint suggests that rather than accomplishing academically defined skills and activities, literacy occurs as family members go about their daily lives.

Current family literacy initiatives

The wide range of perspectives on family literacy is evident in the types of initiatives that have been labeled or described in the professional literature as "family literacy." Such initiatives might be spearheaded by schools, adult literacy programs, community groups, colleges, government agencies, researchers, or any combination thereof. A re-

view suggests that family literacy initiatives seem to fall within one or another of at least three distinct categories: (1) home-school partnership programs, (2) intergenerational literacy programs, and (3) research that explores uses of literacy within families. Initiatives sampled below are generally well known. Outlining them here does not necessarily represent an endorsement by the IRA Family Literacy Commission; rather, it simply provides a source for describing representative efforts within each of the three categories the commission has identified to date.

Home-school partnerships include programs designed to involve parents in literacy activities and events that support school-based goals. Such efforts focus on parents as agents or intervenors in support of the child's literacy learning in school. They are often designed to reflect the emphasis a particular school places on strategies for literacy development. As programs, they change as the school changes its ideas about how literacy develops. Through home-school partnerships parents are informed about the goals, objectives, and strategies used in literacy programs in school and are included as active participants.

First implemented by the Solano Beach School District in California, USA, a program called Books and Beyond, for example, is designed to increase students' recreational reading at home, decrease their indiscriminate television viewing, and consequently improve reading ability. Children, parents, and administrators are asked to participate in a Read-A-Thon which involves keeping track of the number of books children read, the amount of time they spend reading, and the amount of time they spend watching television. The project aims to develop recreational readers who treat reading as an ongoing habit.

Bookmates: Family Literacy Projects in Winnipeg, Manitoba, Canada, also focuses on extending the literacy development of children through the help of their parents. It provides instruction for parents of innercity preschoolers on why, what, and how to read to their children, with special emphasis on the use of children's literature and environmental print.

Talking to Literacy Learners: A Parent Education Project in Western Sydney, Australia, provides 18 months of comprehensive training for parents to improve parent-child interactions during reading and writing.

Intergenerational literacy programs are designed explicitly to improve the literacy development of both adults and children. Because parents and children are viewed as colearners, such efforts are generally characterized by planned and systematic instructional events for parents and children working either collaboratively or in parallel settings. Intergenerational programs offer basic literacy skill development for parents in need, teach parents how to help their children with literacy skills, and give parents the opportunity to practice these skills in school settings. In addition, support groups are organized for parents, where discussions about parenting, life coping skills, and educational goals are emphasized.

The Kenan Family Literacy Model Program, for example, administered by the National Center for Family Literacy in Louisville, Kentucky, USA, brings parents and children together 3 days each week in an elementary school. In neighboring classrooms, the children participate in a comprehensive preschool program while the adults study a variety of academic subjects. The parents also learn how to participate directly in their children's preschool classrooms and how to apply the classroom strategies at home.

Other similar intergenerational family literacy programs are described by Auerbach (1989), Nuckolls (1991), Paratore (1992), Parker (1989), and Quintero and Velarde (1990), some in school contexts, others in homes.

Research that explores uses of literacy within families involves the observation and description of literacy events that occur in the routine of daily lives. This research often does not have deliberate or explicit connections to the school curriculum or the school-based goals. Rather, it focuses on how families use literacy to mediate their social and community lives. In contrast to the first two categories, which describe programs where the focus is on helping parents and children learn from and about schooling, efforts that fall into this third category tend to focus on what educators can learn from and about families.

Taylor and Dorsey-Gaines (1988), for example, provide detailed descriptions of how literacy events were woven into the daily lives of the families they studied. Madigan (1992) describes how adults use reading and writing as a means of understanding themselves and their relationship to the worlds in which they live. Chapman (1991) describes the writing and oral communication in three African-American families. Such investigations draw attention to the mismatch that often exists between school and home literacies.

Each study cited here explores the responsibility of schools and community agencies in better understanding the children and parents with whom they work. Then they can build on the literacies that exist in both mainstream and nonmainstream homes, drawing on experiences from these homes to enhance literacy instruction in the school and community.

The range of initiatives described within these three categories demonstrates the diversity of perspectives on family literacy and the importance of defining the field broadly. Unfortunately, review of existing ideas and programs also suggests that families are too often viewed in their deficits and dilemmas rather than in the richness of their heritages and experiences. A full review of the literature leaves one with the impression that schools strongly emphasize how parents can learn from schools but give little attention to how schools might learn from parents. Families can, of course, learn a great deal about literacy development from the school, but it is also true that teachers need to learn more about how parents and children share literacy on a daily basis and to explore how such events can serve school learning.

Future directions

Educators have become increasingly convinced of the promise of family literacy programs in promoting successful learning experiences for children and their parents. Policymakers at all levels and from a wide range of agencies have been called upon to join in the effort to create and support effective family literacy programs. The emphasis placed on collaboration and partnerships in support of family literacy is evident in the number and diversity of agencies involved in implementing or investigating programs. They include adolescent, adult education, and alternative education centers; churches and clergy; corporations and industries; day care centers; elementary and secondary schools, both public and private; federal, state/provincial, and local governments; Head Start programs for preschool underprivileged children in the U.S.; hospitals and health care centers; human resource agencies; immigrant and refugee agencies; libraries; migrant education programs; professional associations (e.g., International Reading Association and the National Association for the Education of Young Children); preschools, both public and private; prisons; private foundations; universities and colleges; and welfare agencies.

A full review of the literature leaves one with the impression that schools strongly emphasize how parents can learn from schools, but give little attention to how schools might learn from parents.

The existence of such a variety of organizations and their potential for collaboration represent an invaluable strength in the continued study of family literacy. Only by hearing from a broad range of viewpoints in a field so complex will we come to understand it fully.

Program planning and initiatives

In a clear example of how collaborative family literacy programs can take shape, the Canadian federal and Alberta provincial governments in partnership support several different projects. They include a Spanish/English program for mothers and children operated through the Catholic School Board in Calgary and a Homespun Literacy Project in which mothers with beginning literacy abilities are taught how to read children's books and share them with their children. Other programs represent partnerships among local governments and public and private agencies. The Edmonton School Board, for instance, leads a program that provides literacy instruction to adults and their preschool children. A hospital in the province of Saskatchewan provides new mothers with an information kit intended to raise their awareness of the need for reading and writing with their children.

Similar collaborative efforts are evident in the United States. At the federal level, the largest family literacy initiative to date is the Even Start Program, which funds local agencies to implement direct services related to family literacy. More than 150 family literacy programs have been initiated since September 1989. Each program shares three major goals: to help parents become full partners in the education of their children, to assist children in reaching their full potential as learners, and to provide literacy instruction for parents.

In the United States at the state level, family literacy programs are increasing in priority. Alaska's Department of Education, for example, has targeted funding for literacy programs for teenage parents and their children. Kansas has a statewide plan to implement family literacy programs on community college campuses and military bases. In South Carolina, Head Start, adult education, and social service agencies are collaborating in a statewide family literacy campaign. The Massachusetts Bureau of Adult Education gives priority to funding proposals which include a family literacy component, thus giving such programs an edge in the competitive funding process.

Research, development, and evaluation

The majority of initiatives are presently aimed at direct service programs; more emphasis needs to be placed on the evaluation of such initiatives. Some funding supports the study of the effectiveness of specific programs and practices; for example, the U.S. Department of Education's FIRST Program and the Barbara Bush Foundation for Family Literacy support studies that evaluate family literacy efforts. The National Center for Family Literacy recently reported the results of studies of parents and children who participated in the Kenan Trust Model for Family Literacy. The U.S. Department of Education has engaged ABT Associates to conduct a national evaluation of programs supported by Even Start. Data from these and other investigations will be critical in determining the kinds of practices most beneficial in promoting family literacy.

Dissemination

Dissemination activities have to date been supported by professional associations largely through special interest groups, conferences and seminars, special task forces and committees, and publications and monographs. As noted earlier, the International Reading Association recently established the Commission on Family Literacy to examine and report the status of existing family literacy programs. Similar efforts have been undertaken at state and provincial levels by boards of education and other groups. The Ontario Ministry of Education has sponsored a series of meet-

ings throughout the province on children's literacy, with particular emphasis on the importance of family literacy. The Manitoba Reading Association, an affiliate of the International Reading Association, has developed a pamphlet for parents on how and why to read to their children.

In the United States, the National Center for Family Literacy supports expansion of family literacy programs through its Affiliate Program, which prepares participants to conduct training and technical assistance in the Kenan Family Literacy Model (Darling & Hayes, 1988-89). The center also routinely hosts conferences and training seminars throughout the United States to introduce educators to the Kenan Model. A partnership between the National Center for Family Literacy and the community affairs department of Apple computer corporation enables teachers to share activities, strategies, and problems through AppleLink, Apple's telecommunications systems.

Over the last few years, several major research organizations, including the National Research Conference, the American Educational Research Association, and the International Reading Association, have supported dissemination of information by selecting papers on family literacy to be presented at their annual meetings. Over the next few years, the IRA Commission on Family Literacy expects to offer sessions at IRA conferences; produce a themed issue of *The Reading Teacher*; publish a pamphlet that includes a set of succinct issues, suggestions, and plans for action; and prepare an annotated bibliography of programs, associations, and research relevant to home activities and programs in family literacy. We are also in the process of preparing an edited book on family literacy and establishing liaisons and partnerships with other organizations that deal with the issue.

Summary

The purpose of this article is to heighten awareness about the importance of family literacy and its many complex perspectives. There is widespread agreement about the importance of family literacy, but substantially less agreement on the goals of family literacy programs and how families and schools can collaborate to learn from each other. Although we agree that they are important, family literacy programs are not yet a priority in schools. Schools need to incorporate the concept of family literacy into their curriculum just as they incorporate holistic strategies for literacy instruction. Before such programs are implemented or designed, the following questions should be addressed:

- How can we make family literacy a priority in our schools?
- What are the components of quality home-school partnership programs?
- What are the components of quality intergenerational programs?

- How can educators be confident that they are providing families with beneficial, rather than intrusive, experiences?
- How can schools provide programs that take into account the needs of families from diverse cultural backgrounds, who possess different literacies from the schoollike activities we are familiar with?
- How can program effectiveness best be assessed, documented, collected, and shared?
- What kinds of outcomes should we expect as a result of family literacy programs?

In *The Reading Teacher* articles we expect solutions, strategies, and suggestions, rather than questions. With family literacy, we are still at the stage of posing questions. Obviously, the Commission on Family Literacy is faced with a delicate task. It is widely held within the political community that poverty and lack of educational resources are major causes of low literacy among adults and children. Furthermore, it is often because those factors are generally accepted as causal that family literacy projects are funded at all. At the same time, commission members hope to avoid supporting a view that family literacy flourishes only under conditions of economic strength or when externally imposed programs are introduced.

In our deliberations thus far, we have found such tensions to be productive and stimulating, rather than divisive, and it is our hope that as we continue our explorations, we shall be able to produce reports that recognize and respect the importance of both political perspectives and family-focused perspectives.

Editors' note: This article was based on a document compiled by members of the IRA Family Literacy Commission. The Commission was formed by IRA in 1991 to disseminate information about the many perspectives that exist concerning family literacy and to make it a priority issue within the organization.

References

Auerbach, E.R. (1989). Toward a Socio-contextual approach to family literacy. *Harvard Educational Review, 59,* 165–181.

Braun, C. (1991). *Commission on Family literacy. Proposal to International Reading Association Board of Directors.* Newark, DE: International Reading Association.

Chapman, C. (1991, March). *Lessons from the workplace: Writing and oral communication in three African American families.* Paper presented at the Conference on College Composition and Communication, Boston, MA.

Clark, M. (1984). Literacy at home and at school: Insights from a study of young fluent readers. In H. Goelman, A. Oberg, & F. Smith (Eds.), *Awakening to literacy* (pp. 122–130). Portsmouth, NH: Heinemann.

Cochran-Smith, M. (1986). Reading to children: A model for understanding texts. In B.B. Schieffelin & P. Gilmore (Eds.). *The acquisition of literacy: Ethnographic perspectives* (pp. 35–54). Norwood, NJ: Ablex.

Darling, S., & Hayes, A.E. (1988–89). *Breaking the cycle of illiteracy: The Kenan family literacy model program.* Louisville, KY: The National Center for Family Literacy.

Heath, S.B. (1983). *Ways with words.* Cambridge, England: Cambridge University Press.

Huey, E. (1908). *The psychology and pedagogy of reading.* New York: Macmillan.

Madigan, D. (1992). Family uses of literacy: A critical voice. In C. Kinzer & D.J. Leu (Eds.). *Literacy research, theory and practices: Views from many perspectives* (pp. 87–100). Chicago, IL: National Reading Conference.

Morrow, L.M. (1993). *Literacy development in the early years: Helping children read and write.* Boston: Allyn & Bacon.

Nuckolls, M. (1991). Expanding students' potential through family literacy. *Educational Leadership, 49,* 45–46.

Paratore, J.R. (1992, December). *A three-year study of an intergenerational approach to literacy on the reading/writing practices of adults and their children.* Paper presented at the National Reading Conference, San Antonio, TX.

Parker, J.M. (1989). Building bridges in midtown Manhattan: An intergenerational literacy program. *Urban Education, 24,* 109–115.

Quintero, E., & Velarde, M.C. (1990). Intergenerational literacy: A developmental, bilingual approach. *Young Children, 45*(4), 10–15.

Taylor, D., & Dorsey-Gaines, C. (1988). *Growing up literate.* Portsmouth, NH: Heinemann.

Teale, W.H. (1984). Reading to young children: Its significance for literacy development. In H. Goelman, A. Oberg, & F. Smith (Eds.), *Awakening to literacy* (pp. 110–121). Portsmouth, NH: Heinemann.

Weinstein-Shr, G. (1990). *Family and intergenerational literacy in multilingual families.* Washington, DC: Office of Educational Research and Improvement.

Morrow chairs the IRA Family Literacy Commission and teaches at Rutgers University. Paratore, also a member of the commission, teaches at Boston University, Devron Gaber, Colin Harrison, and Diane Trace are also members of the Family Literacy Commission. Morrow can be contacted at Rutgers University, Graduate School of Education, 10 Seminary Place, New Brunswick, NJ 08903, USA.

The Role of Child Development and Social Interaction in the Selection of Children's Literature to Promote Literacy Acquisition

C. Denise Johnson
The College of William and Mary

Introduction

She laughed and she cried as she read, and she exclaimed aloud in the high and echoing room: "Wow!" (Spinelli, 1997, p. 74)

A book can serve as a kind of magic ticket to far away or even imaginary places. In the book *The Library Card*, author Jerry Spinelli tells the story of how a magic library card turns out to be the ticket to finding what each young character needs most at the time. This fantastic story certainly illustrates the point that good books can have an important influence on the mind of the reader. Indeed, most of us still remember a favorite book as a child that left a lasting impression. As a toddler, many remember the silly antics and language of a Dr. Seuss book such as *Green Eggs and Ham* or perhaps the comfort and security of Margaret Wise Brown's *Goodnight Moon* or the rhyme and rhythm of the *Mother Goose Tales*. Upon entering the elementary grades, many remember the beautiful friendship between Wilbur and Charlotte in E. B. White's *Charlotte's Web*, the mystery and intrigue in Frances Hodgson Burnett's *The Secret Garden*, or the fanciful imaginary world of Lewis Carroll's *Alice's Adventures in Wonderland*. These books continue to bring joy to our lives today and will live on forever as adults help children experience this joy.

The Importance of Child Development to Teaching, Learning, and Literature

Our images of children-as-learners are reflected, inevitably, in our definition of what it means to teach (Wood, 1988, p. 1).

The "magic" of literature for children is necessarily bound with the nature of their development. Research in past decades reflects our changing view of how children develop and learn. Children have their own unique needs, interests, and capabilities. We are born with the ability to organize, classify, and impose order on our environment, re-sulting in the construction of our own unique theory of the world (O'Donnell & Wood, 1999; Wood, 1988). Very little of the content and order of our theory is the result of direct instruction; rather, it is the interaction of biological, cultural, and life experiences that greatly affects the substance of our theory and the way we organize our experiences. As children encounter new experiences, existing memory structures in the brain or schema are reshaped, impacting the linguistic, cognitive, social, and emotional development of children over time. Therefore, "knowledge cannot be *given* directly from the teacher to the learner, but must be *constructed by the learner and reconstructed* as new information becomes available" (Ryan & Cooper, 2000, p. 346). From this point of view, learning is not the result of development; rather, learning *is* development.

"From this perspective, which places instruction at the heart of development, a child's *potential* for learning is revealed and indeed is often *realized* in interactions with more knowledgeable others" (Wood, 1988, p. 24). For example, not too long ago, I visited my friend Diane who has a 4-year-old daughter. We were sitting in her living room talking when her little girl, Rachel, came running into the room with her favorite book *Brown Bear, Brown Bear, What Do You See?* by Bill Martin, Jr., and illustrated by Eric Carle. On each page of the book, a different tissue-paper collage animal is introduced who urges the reader onward to discover which creature will show up next, with a repeated, rhyming, patterned text. She proceeded to crawl into Diane's lap, open the book, and start reciting the text, pointing and commenting on the various illustrations. Anyone looking at this scene would know that Rachel has been read to many, many times and finds great joy in the experience. A closer look might provide insight into how this experience will assist in Rachel's development:

- Positive emotions are created from the established lap reading routine that generates an intimate closeness and feeling of security.
- Interactive social dialogues between Rachel and her mother build on prior knowledge and provide immediate feedback as they discuss each animal as the story progresses.

- The language they use to label, compare, explain, and classify creates a supportive context for structuring the processes of thinking and concept formation.

Each of the domains of development—linguistic, cognitive, social, and emotional—is affected during Rachel's experience, and all play an important role in her development. Although each domain constitutes an entire theoretical approach to child development, no single theory can explain the rich complexity of development (Santrock, 1999).

Supporting Children's Experiences with Literature

Linguistic, social, emotional, and cognitive development are complementary processes that ultimately work together to shape a child's literacy growth (Vygotsky, 1978). Vygotsky, a 20th-century Russian psychologist, theorized that social interaction is the primary means by which children arrive at new understanding. Rachel, for example, has acquired quite a bit of knowledge about the act of reading when she demonstrates how to hold a book, which end of the book goes up, and which side is the front; when she takes care to turn the pages, always looks to the right page before moving on to the left page, and starts at the top of the page and moves down; when she reads with tone, inflection, enthusiasm, and expresses excitement and joy; when she points to pictures and words as she reads and pauses to discuss what she is thinking; and when she responds appropriately to Rachel's comments or questions. Rachel is also learning about storybook language, which is different from oral language, and the structure of stories. Vocabulary and concept development are also affected as Diane and Rachel work together to construct a meaningful experience around a common literacy event. From the first time Diane read *Brown Bear, Brown Bear, What Do You See?* aloud to Rachel, she has scaffolded, or made adjustments, in her support based on constant feedback received from Rachel. As Rachel began to internalize the actions and language of her mother, she began to use these tools to guide and monitor her own processing behavior until she is now able to take over much of the responsibility for reading the book (Dorn, French, & Jones, 1998).

Barbara Rogoff (1990) considers children to be apprentices as they acquire a diverse repertoire of skills and knowledge under the guidance and support of more knowledgeable persons. "In an apprenticeship setting, adults model the significance of written language as an important tool for documenting and communicating information. As adults and children engage in interactive oral discussions about written language, children acquire important tools of the mind for literacy acquisition" (Bodrova & Leong, 1996, as cited in Dorn, French, & Jones, 1998, p. 3).

Selecting "Just Right" Literature

The selection of literature is key to providing an experience that results in promoting literacy development in that if the literature is not developmentally appropriate then what the child takes from the book and how he responds to the book will be limited or nonexistent. The book *Brown Bear, Brown Bear, What Do You See?* is perfect for Rachel because of its layout; repeated, rhyming, patterned text format; and simple concepts that promote cognitive development. On the other hand, a preservice teacher once told me that she read the very humorous *Piggie Pie* by Margie Palatini aloud to a group of preschoolers; but to her dismay, the preschoolers did not find the book nearly as funny as she did. In the story, a witch, hungry for piggie pie, visits a farm in order to get the main ingredient—pigs. The clever pigs disguise themselves as other farm animals and successfully fool the witch into thinking that the farm has no pigs. She is consoled in the end by a wolf that has also had difficulty finding pigs, and they go off together to "have lunch."

It is not uncommon for there to be differences between what children and adults find to be funny. The reason for this difference is the vast developmental gap between children and adults. "Often when humorous books fail to amuse children, it is indicative of a poor match between children's cognitive-developmental level and the reading material" (Jalongo, 1985, p. 109). Jalongo's research identifies characteristics of children's humor such as "cognitive challenge," or the intellectual ability required to understand a particular joke, and "novelty," or surprise, which is really the cornerstone of humor. If a child doesn't have the correct set of expectations, the unexpected is not surprising. Throughout the story, *Piggy Pie* draws much of its humor from references to other stories and songs such as *The Wizard of Oz, The Three Little Pigs, Old MacDonald Had a Farm, To Grandmother's House We Go*, and an advertising campaign for the *Yellow Pages*, "let your fingers do the walking." The majority of preschoolers, not being familiar with these references, did not find *Piggie Pie* to be very funny.

The preschoolers did find parts of the story to be funny, especially when the pigs dress up like other farm animals. Jalongo (1985) points out, "Because young children are learning to distinguish between fantasy and reality, events that are incongruous with their expectations are considered to be funny" (p. 110). But the level of scaffolding that the teacher would have had to provide to assist the children in meeting the cognitive challenge to understand the expectations on which much of the humor in the book depended would have been considerable. As a result, this literature experience was not as beneficial for the majority of these preschoolers as perhaps another book selection might have been.

Although books at a variety of levels can and should be read to, with, or by children for a variety of reasons, books that are within a child's zone of proximal development are more likely to be intellectually stimulating. According to Vygotsky (1978), the zone of proximal development is "the distance between the actual developmental level as determined through problem-solving under adult guidance or in collaboration with more capable peers" (p. 86). The book *Brown Bear, Brown Bear, What Do You See?* is within Rachel's zone of proximal development, and she derives great joy from it, while many of the textual references from which *Piggie Pie* draws its humor were outside the preschool children's zone of proximal development. A child who is not developmentally ready for a particular book will derive less joy and meaning from it and will respond differently to it. Teachers need to know each child as an individual—his or her level of development, rate of development, and varying interests—in order for the child to receive maximum benefit from his or her experiences with literature.

A Framework for Integrating Child Development, Social Interaction, and Literature Selection

A framework for understanding the interrelated nature of the cognitive, social, emotional, linguistic, and literacy development of children; social interaction; and literature selection in grades K-4 is provided in the appendix. The purpose of the framework is to provide a general guide for teachers, parents, and other caregivers in the appropriate selection of books that takes into consideration the importance of child development. In the far left-hand column of the framework, an overview of the general developmental characteristics of children in the areas of cognitive, language, social, emotional, and literacy development is provided. The middle column gives examples of important experiences that adults can provide when interacting with children and books based on the implications from the developmental characteristics for each grade level. The column at the far right is a list of suggested books appropriate for each stage of development. The books were selected based on recommendations from teachers, children, parents, and professional literature resources such as children's literature journals and books.

This framework is only approximate and should be informed by ongoing observational information acquired about individual children. With this in mind, the framework will assist in planning appropriate literature experiences and in understanding children's responses to books and book preferences at different levels of development.

Conclusion

Wood (1988) states, "Our ideas about the nature of infancy and childhood dictate the ways in which we think about teaching and education" (p. 1). As teachers, if we believe that child development, teaching, and learning share a reciprocal relationship, then a clear understanding of the general characteristics of child development and our role through social interaction can assist us in selecting books that reflect a child's current developmental needs while promoting progress toward literacy development and the "magic" of reading.

References

Bodrova, Elena, & Leong, Deborah J. (1996). *Tools of the mind: The Vygotskian approach to early childhood education*. Englewood Cliffs, NJ: Merrill.

Dorn, Linda J.; French, Cathy; & Jones, Tammy. (1998). *Apprenticeship in literacy*. York, ME: Stenhouse.

Fountas, Irene C., & Pinnell, Gay Su. (2001). *Guiding readers and writers, grades 3–6: Teaching comprehension, genre, and content literacy*. Portsmouth, NH: Heinemann. ED 451 503.

Jalongo, Mary Renck. (1985). Children's literature: There's some sense to its humor. *Childhood Education, 62*(2), 109–114. EJ 328 574.

O'Donnell, Michael P., & Wood, Margo. (1999). *Becoming a reader: A developmental approach to reading instruction* (2nd ed.). Boston: Allyn & Bacon. ED 428 322.

Rogoff, Barbara. (1990). *Apprenticeship in thinking: Cognitive development in social context*. New York: Oxford University Press.

Ryan, Kevin, & Cooper, James M. (2000). *Those who can, teach* (9th ed.). Boston: Houghton Mifflin.

Santrock, John W. (1999). *Life-span development* (7th ed.). Boston: McGraw-Hill.

Snow, Catherine E.; Burns, M. Susan; & Griffin, Peg (Eds.). (1998). *Preventing reading difficulties in young children*. Washington, DC: National Academy Press. ED 416 465.

Vygotsky, L. S. (1978). *Mind in society: The development of higher psychological processes* (Michael Cole, Vera John-Steiner, Sylvia Scribner, & Ellen Souberman, Eds. & Trans.). Cambridge, MA: Harvard University Press.

Wood, David. (1988). *How Children think and learn*. Cambridge, MA: Blackwell.

Children's Literature Cited

Martin, Jr., Bill. (1992). *Brown Bear, Brown Bear, What do you see?* (Eric Carle, Illus.). New York: Henry Holt.

Palatini, Margie. (1997). *Piggie pie!* (Howard Fine, Illus.). New York: Houghton Mifflin.

Spinelli, Jerry. (1997). *The library card.* New York: Scholastic.

Author Information

Denise Johnson is an assistant professor of reading education at the College of William and Mary, Williamsburg, Virginia. She received her Ed.D. in reading from the University of Memphis, Tennessee. She has worked as an elementary classroom teacher, a middle school reading specialist, and a Reading Recovery teacher. She now teaches graduate and undergraduate courses in literacy education and conducts research on the integration of technology into preservice and inservice education courses and within elementary classrooms. Her articles on literacy and technology have been published in a variety of journals, and she is active in several professional organizations. She enjoys traveling with her family and reading to her son, Derek.

Denise Johnson, Ed.D.
Assistant Professor of Reading Education
The College of William and Mary
313 Jones Hall, School of Education
Williamsburg, VA 23187
Telephone: 757-221-1528
Fax: 757-221-2988
Email: cdjohn@wm.edu
http://faculty.wm.edu/cdjohn/

Appendix
A Framework for Integrating Child Development, Social Interaction, and Literature Selection

Preschool—Kindergarten

Readers seek out and enjoy experiences with books and print; become familiar with the language of literature and the patterns of stories; understand and follow the sequence of stories read to them; begin to acquire specific understandings about the nature, purpose, and function of print; experiment with reading and writing independently, through approximation; and see themselves as developing readers and writers.*

General Characteristics of Children	Implications for Adults for Social Interaction	Literature Selection
Cognitive Development • Begins to understand spatial, perceptual, and attributional relationship • Can retell a short story; has a vague concept of time; can count to 10 and knows primary colors Language Development • Experiences rapid vocabulary growth and speech development; uses correct verb and pronoun tense; uses language to explore the environment; enjoys playing with sound and rhythm in language • Enjoys dramatic/role/creative play • Understands that there is a connection between language and print Social and Emotional Development • Begins to develop relationships with other children and enjoys participating in group activities and games that use imagination • Understands that others have feelings, too; expresses feelings through facial expressions • Wants to help around the house and with younger siblings; takes pride in accomplishments; exhibits anxiety or fears (e.g., of the dark); likes to go to new places; likes to play with favorite toys	• Importance of reading aloud simple picture books with easily identifiable characters and happy endings and poetry several times a day at school and at home • Importance of actively involving children in shared reading in which they can participate in the reading process • Importance of selecting literature about everyday experiences that also expands language and concept development, encourages curiosity about the world, and engages the imagination • Importance of providing opportunities to respond to literature with peers and the teacher and also through writing/drawing • Importance of providing, with guidance, opportunities for students to self-select fiction and nonfiction books, including alphabet, number, and concept books and books that include environmental print	• *Today I feel Silly* (Jamie Lee Curtis) • *Look! Look! Look!* Tana Hoban) • Mother Goose rhymes • *Ten, Nine, Eight* (Molly Bang) • *ABC I Like Me!* (Nancy L. Carlson) • *No, David!* (David Shannon) • *A Color of His Own* (Leo Lionni) • *Red Light, Green Light* (Margaret Wise Brown) • *A House Is a House for Me* (Mary Ann Hoberman) • *Peter's Chair* (Ezra Jack Keats) • *Mouse Paint* (Ellen Stoll Walsh) • *Noisy Nora* (Rosemary Wells) • *Five Little Monkeys* (Eileen Christelow) • *Bashi, Baby Elephant* (Theresa Radcliffe) • *Color Zoo* (Lois Ehlert) • *Brown Bear, Brown Bear, What Do You See?* (Bill Martin, Jr.) • *From Head to Toe* (Eric Carle) • *Chicka Chicka Boom Boom* (Bill Martin, Jr.) • *The Three Little Pigs* (James Marshall) • *Hop on Pop* (Dr. Suess) • *Harold and the Purple Crayon* (Crockett Johnson) • *The Tale of Peter Rabbit* (Beatrix Potter) • *Millions of Cats* (Wanda Gag) • *Tell Me A Story, Mama* (Angela Johnson) • *Feast for 10* (Cathryn Falwell) • *The Bus for Us* (Suzanne Bloom) • *Dear Zoo* (Rod Campbell) • *Trucks, Trucks, Trucks* (Peter Sis)

Literacy Development**

• Enjoys listening and talking about stories and understands that print carries a message
• Identifies letters and letter-sound relationships and writes letters or approximations of letters and high frequency words
• Demonstrates logographic knowledge by identifying labels, signs, and cereal boxes, and other types of environmental print
• Begins to pretend-read and engage in paper-and-pencil activities that include various forms of scribbling and written expression
• Understands basic concepts of print, such as left-to-right, top-to-bottom orientation
• Enjoys being read to and begins to engage in sustained reading and writing activities
• Becomes familiar with rhyming
• Develops a sense of story/story grammar/storybook reading behavior through interaction with storybooks

First and Second Grades

Readers understand that reading is a meaning-making process; acquire sight vocabulary; make balanced use of the cueing systems in written language (syntax, semantics, and graphophonemics) to identify words not known at sight; and see themselves as readers and writers. *

General Characteristics of Children	Implications for Adults for Social Interaction	Literature Selection
Cognitive Development • Enjoys listening to stories read aloud and can listen to longer stories due to an increased attention span; still needs concrete experiences to learn • Understands relationships among categories • Has a vague understanding of time • Is beginning to understand the difference between fantasy and reality Language Development • Continues to add words to the his or her vocabulary and uses increasingly complex sentences Social and Emotional Development • Begins to develop a sense of humor • Has definite, inflexible ideas of right and wrong • Occasionally challenges parents and argues with siblings but continues to need security of family relationships • Continues to take pride in accomplishments, sometimes showing assertiveness and initiative • Seeks teachers' praise • Is curious about gender differences	• Continued importance of reading aloud picture books and poetry several times a day at school and at home • Importance of reading aloud short chapter books in which each chapter contains independent episodes • Continued importance of small group and whole group opportunities to respond to literature with peers and the teacher and through writing/drawing—becoming more sustained overtime • Continued importance of actively involving children in shared reading in which they observe the teacher demonstrate concepts about print and model using appropriate reading strategies with both fiction and nonfiction texts and involving student participation • Importance of initial reading experiences being enjoyable using books with familiar concepts and experiences with predictable, repeated patterned text and then moving into longer texts with more complex structure • Importance of giving children, with guidance, ample opportunities to select both fiction and nonfiction books on their own from a wide variety of topics and to recommend books through book talks to other children • Importance of providing children with opportunities for storytelling and dramatization of stories	• *Where the Wild Things Are* (Maurice Sendak) • *Ramona* books (Beverly Cleary) • *Junie B. Jones* books (Arnold Lobel) • *Frog and Toad* books (Arnold Lobel) • *A Chair for My Mother* (Vera B. Williams) • *When Sophie Gets Angry—Really, Really Angry* (Molly Garrett Bang) • *Pete's Pizza* (William Steig) • *Crow Boy* (Taro Yashima) • *Julius* (Angela Johnson) • *Tops and Bottoms* (Janet Stevens) • *Ira Sleeps Over* (Bernard Waber) • *The Terrible, Horrible, No Good Very Bad Day* (Judith Viorst) • *Toasting Marshmallows: Camping Poems* (Kristine O'Connell George) • *Too Many Tamales* (Gary Soto) • *Make Way for Ducklings* (Robert McCloskey) • *Henry and Mudge* books (Cynthia Rylant) • *The Relatives Came* (Cynthia Rylant) • *My Little Sister Ate One Hare* (Bill Grossman) • *The Talking Eggs: A Folktale from the American South* (Robert D. San Souci) • *Sam, Bangs, and Moonshine* (Evaline Ness) • *Lilly's Purple Plastic Purse* (Kevin Henkes) • *How Babies Are Made* (Andrew C. Andry and Steven Schepp) • *Grandfather's Journey* (Allen Say) • *A Light in the Attic* (Shel Silverstein) • *The Bee Tree* (Patricia Polacco) • *10 Minutes till Bedtime* (Peggy Rathmann)

Literacy Development**

• Begins to read, write, and retell simple stories transitioning to longer stories with an increase in fluency and use of cognitive and metacognitive strategies more efficiently when comprehending and composing

• Develops greater word identification strategies, sight word recognition, conventional spelling, and sustained silent reading

• Reads orally initially and begins to read silently

• Uses letter-sound information along with meaning and language to solve words

Third and Fourth Grades

Readers increase fluency in reading and writing, increase motivation to read and write, and focus on meaning in reading and writing. *

General Characteristics of Children	Implications for Adults for Social Interaction	Literature Selection
Cognitive Development • Begins to exhibit independence in reading, but a wide range of reading abilities and interests prevail • Continues to develop concept of time and space • Exhibits improved memory with increased attention span • Begins to connect ideas and concepts as thoughts become flexible and reversible, increasing capacity for problem solving, categorizing, and classifying **Language Development** • Exhibits increasing vocabulary • Increases use of connectors such as *meanwhile, unless,* and *although* **Social and Emotional Development** • Begins to be influenced by social situation and peers • Exhibits more interest in sports and hobbies • Searches for values and is influenced by models other then the family—TV, movies, music, sports, books • Begins to develop empathy for others as concepts of right and wrong become more flexible	• Continued importance of reading aloud more sophisticated picture books and poetry every day • Importance of reading aloud longer chapter books with more variety, perspectives, and issues to promote interest and appreciation for a variety of genre • Continued importance of sustained small group and whole group opportunities to respond to literature with peers and the teacher and through writing • Continued importance of actively involving children in small group and whole group shared reading in which the teacher engages students in discussion/modeling/demonstrations of more complex reading strategies that promote understanding of literary devices, vocabulary development, connections to text, and graphic aids in fiction and nonfiction texts • Importance of providing, with guidance, opportunities for students to self-select fiction and nonfiction books, including series books, biographies, how-to-books, riddles, comics, and magazines • Continued importance of providing children with opportunities for storytelling and dramatization of stories, reader's theatre, and choral reading	• *Mufaro's Beautiful Daughters: An African Tale* (John Steptoe) • *The Boy Who Drew Cats: A Japanese Folktale* (Arthur A. Levine) • *Tales of a Fourth Grade Nothing* (Judy Blume) • *Little House* books (Laura Ingalls Wilder) • *Attaboy, Sam!* (Lois Lowry) • *The Girl Who Loved Wild Horses* (Paul Goble) • *Martin's Big Words* (Doreen Rappaport) • *Just A Dream* (Chris Van Allsburg) • *More Rootabagas* (Carl Sandburg) • *Joey Pigza Loses Control* (Jack Gantos) • *The Lion, the Witch, and the Wardrobe* (C. S. Lewis) • *A Bear for Miguel* (Elaine Marie Alphin) • *Magic Schoolbus* Books (Joanna Cole) • *Finding Out about Whales* (Elin Kelsey) • *Harry Potter and the Sorcerer's Stone* (J. K. Rowling) • *Time Warp Trio* Books (Jon Scieszka) • *Can Jensen* books (David Adler) • *When Marian Sang* (Pam Munoz Ryan) • *George Washington's Breakfast* (Jean Fritz) • *The American Girl* books (Connie Rose Porter et al.) • *Nate the Great* books (Marjorie Weinman Sharmat) • *Joyful Noise: Poems for Two Voices* (Paul Fleischman) • *Because of Winn-Dixie* (Kate DeCamillo) • *Encounter* (Jane Yolen) • *Earth Lines: Poems for the Green Age* (Pat Moon) • *Stone Fox* (John Reynolds Gardner) • *Wilma Unlimited: How Wilma Rudolph Became the World's Fastest Woman* (Kathleen Krull)

Literacy Development**

• Reads silently most of the time and reads fluently when reading aloud
• Has a large core of known words that are recognized automatically
• Is moving toward sustained reading of texts with many pages that require reading over several days or weeks
• Knows how to read differently in different genres
• Connects texts with previously read texts
• Begins to identify with characters in books and to see himself or herself in the events of the stories
• Becomes absorbed in books
• Is in a continuous process of building background knowledge and realizes that he or she needs to bring his or her knowledge to reading
• Has systems for learning more about the reading process as he or she reads so that he or she builds skills simply by encountering many different kinds of texts with a variety of new words
• Interprets and uses information from a wide variety of visual aids in expository texts Analyzes words in flexible ways and makes excellent attempts at new, multisyllable words

*Adapted from *Becoming a Reader: A Developmental Approach to Reading Instruction* (O'Donnell & Wood, 1999).

**Adapted from *Preventing Reading Difficulties in Young Children* (Snow, Burns, & Griffin, 1998) and *Guiding Readers and Writers, Grades 3–6: Teaching Comprehension, Genre, and Content Literacy* (Fountas & Pinnell, 2001).

The Many Rewards of a Literacy-Rich Classroom

The Center for Children and Families is discovering the kinds of teaching practices that stimulate language and literacy development.

David K. Dickinson and Lori Lyman DiGisi

In the primary grades, reading and writing instruction have traditionally been two of the three basics that all children must master. Traditional wisdom is bolstered by research that has tracked children's reading success from kindergarten and 1st grade into later elementary and high school years. These longitudinal studies confirm that the process of becoming literate begins early in life and that children's early experiences affect school readiness and later school success (Hart and Risley 1995, Juel 1988, Snow et al. 1991).

To better understand the factors that influence literacy, the Center for Children and Families at the Education Development Center, Inc., is working with Harvard University on the Home-School Study. By following more than 60 children over a period of 10 years, we are learning about the types of environments and teaching practices that stimulate language and literacy development

Two Classrooms

As part of the study, researchers visited 69 1st grade classrooms in 11 school systems. During these visits, we observed the classrooms, instructional materials, and samples of children's work, and interviewed the teachers. In addition to identifying factors that support literacy, we discovered enormous variability in how educators conceptualize and foster literacy. Two vignettes illustrate the variations.

William's classroom has centers for math, science, language, writing, and art. The classroom library area, appealingly decorated with a rug and a blanket, has more than 40 books. Children's stories about beavers and their poems about spiders and ants line the science center walls. Elsewhere their stories about their vaca-

tions, a hungry tomato, and what happened one dark night fill the walls alongside colorful posters displaying letters, numbers, and nursery rhymes. As William joins the reading group, his teacher, Ms. Kerlan, is discussing current events with the children, using a map to show them where events occurred. Later she will meet with them individually to assign tasks such as alphabetizing words, reading silently, and writing synopses of stories they have read.

Christine's classroom has no centers, library area, or evidence of written work in social studies or science. In reading group, her teacher, Ms. Green, asks the children to make umbrellas to put on the windows. "It is April," Ms. Green says. "What happens in April?" When there is no response, she replies, "It rains a lot. If it rains a lot we need an umbrella." The children cut out umbrellas and write *umbrella* on their cut-outs. Christine is the first one done. Ms. Green sees that the *b* is written as a *d* and offers to change it for her. She then writes the word *umbrella* on the board and asks the children to write their names on their umbrellas.

These vignettes illustrate two ends of the spectrum in literacy instruction. In William's classroom, children are surrounded by print and books, and they undertake a wide range of writing tasks. They write about personal experiences, integrating reading and writing as they create new endings for stories. Writing is part of their science and social studies work. Although Ms. Kerlan occasionally focuses instruction on isolated letters, her primary goal is to encourage reading and writing for many purposes.

In contrast, Christine's classroom provides comparatively few opportunities to read books, and Ms. Green limits writing to exercises that build skills (for example, copying words, practicing handwriting) and that reinforce basic knowledge of sound-symbol correspondence. Her concern that children arrive at correct answers makes it hard for her to allow them to write for self-expression or to explore what they are learning in science and social studies through reading and writing tasks. On the other hand, the daily activities help Christine to focus on individual letters and sound-symbol relationships, a vital skill for many children (Foorman et al. 1997).

The Reading-Writing Link

How do such diverse classroom environments and learning experiences affect young children's ability to learn the basics of reading and writing? To identify the correlations between instructional practices and literacy learning, we tested children, beginning in kindergarten, using a battery of language and literacy assessments. In 1st grade, we gave them individualized reading tests (oral reading, comprehension, decoding) and a spelling test. To examine the effects of 1st grade programs on reading growth, we statistically controlled for students' vocabulary at the end of kindergarten and for whether they were identified as needing remedial help in reading. We then examined the impact of 1st grade classroom experiences on children's reading at the end of 1st grade.

We found that the amount of writing children did in class was correlated with 1st grade reading achievement ($r = .32$, $p < .01$). Students with higher reading achievement scores were in classrooms where teachers asked students to engage in narrative and informational writing. Both narrative writing and writing related to content studies were positively associated with reading, but content-related writing was an especially important predictor of reading level. Consistent with these overall findings, William was one of the highest-scoring children in 1st grade, while Christine was among the lower-scoring children.

These findings illustrate the value of integrating writing activities into reading and content area studies in the primary grades. When children have many opportunities to write and when reading and writing are integrated into content area studies, children become better readers and writers. This conclusion is consistent with research showing that reading and writing are closely linked processes and that participation in strong writing programs benefits children's reading and writing development (Shanahan and Lomax 1988, Tierney and Shanahan 1991).

Frequent writing helps beginning writers in multiple ways. As they produce invented spelling, children may become intensely engaged in figuring out how to spell words they want to write to communicate. Such attention to the individual sounds of words and the pairing of sounds to symbols enhances children's spelling and

decoding, with low achievers benefiting most (Clarke 1988). As they listen and respond to each other's work, they develop skill in identifying sources of confusion as well as effective compositional techniques (Hansen 1983, Hindley 1996, Zaragoza and Vaughn 1995). Such composition skills may benefit children's reading comprehension as well, because reading can be thought of as a process of composing meaning (Langer 1986).

Integrating writing and reading into content area projects appears to have special benefits. Such linkages encourage children to extend their thinking, to be more critical, and to adopt multiple perspectives (Many et al. 1996, Tierney et al. 1989). Further, linking content area instruction and literacy also can help to enhance children's literacy growth while deepening content learning (Guthrie et al. 1996, Morrow et al. 1997).

Links with National Standards

Too frequently, education research stands apart from the real world of schools. However, current standards-based reforms indicate an increasing convergence between research and broad-based policy movements. The approach to writing that we found most likely to support literacy growth is consistent with practices described in the Standards for the English Language Arts developed by the International Reading Association and the National Council of Teachers of English. These standards state that children should write for different purposes, including research. In an example of the standards in practice (Crafton 1996), 2nd graders studying the Iditarod dog race read *Stone Fox*, a book about the race. The class brainstormed questions together and listed people who might ask such questions. Individual children then assumed a particular perspective (veterinarian, historian, reporter) and generated additional questions. Finally, small groups conducted research (using a toll-free phone number to call Alaska; watching the dog race; reading) that culminated in projects.

By following more than 60 children over a period of 10 years, we are learning about the kinds of teaching practices that stimulate language and literacy development.

Another standards-based reform effort that is encouraging the integration of writing and reading into content areas comes from the National Board for Professional Teaching Standards, a voluntary national teacher certification movement. The board has developed and adopted standards in several certification areas. One of these, the Early Childhood/Generalist certificate, is for teachers of children from ages 3 to 8 years (National Board 1995). The standards value integration of subjects and varied uses of writing. Teachers create portfolios that display how they integrate subject areas, using reading and writing in varied ways. Their work is scored by other practicing teachers, who are trained by seeing examples of highly accomplished teaching. Thus, the standards are being translated into classroom practices for both those teachers completing the assessments and those scoring them.[2]

Where Literacy Is Basic

Early literacy instruction is indisputably basic. Discussions about its key ingredients typically have focused on the importance of phonics. While children undoubtedly must learn how to connect sounds to symbols and that phonics helps some children make this vital connection (Adams 1990), children also must have reasons to use print.

At a time of hope for educational reform, it is reassuring to see research and reform efforts come together. As awareness and acceptance of standards-based reforms grow, we can expect to see school systems supporting teachers as they engage young children in different content areas through reading and writing experiences.[3]

: *Current standards-based reforms indicate*
: *an increasing convergence between research*
: *and broad-based policy movements.*

Our own hope is that, in the coming years, we will hear fewer debates about what constitutes effective reading instruction and see more primary classrooms like William's—classrooms where literacy is basic to all learning.

Notes

6. The names of the teachers and students have been changed,

7. The Early Childhood/Generalist assessment and scoring system were developed by researchers in the Center for Children and Families researchers at the Educational Development Center, Inc.

8. Such a teacher development effort is currently underway. Project AS-SIST (funded by the U.S. Office of Special Education Programs) is collaborating with elementary school teachers to deepen students understanding of science, using reading, writing, and technology in addition to inquiry projects.

Authors' note: The work reported here has been supported by grants from the Spencer Foundation and the U.S. Department of Health and Human Services Administration on Children and Families, Grant. Colleagues on the Home-School Study—Patton Tabors, Catherine Snow, Kevin Rourke, and Brenda Kurland—contributed to this report. Sharon Grollman reviewed earlier drafts of our manuscript.

References

Adams, M.J. (1990). *Beginning to Read: Thinking and Learning About Print.* Cambridge, Mass.: MIT Press.

Clarke, L.K. (1988). "Invented Versus Traditional Spelling in First Graders' Writings: Effects on Learning to Spell and Read." *Research in the Teaching of English* 22, 3: 281–309.

Crafton, L.K. (1996). *Standards in Practice Grades K–2.* Urbana, Ill.: National Council of Teachers of English.

Foorman, B.R., D.J. Francis, T. Beeler, D. Winikates, and J.M. Fletcher. (1997). "Early Interventions for Children with Reading Problems: Study Designs and Preliminary Findings." *Learning Disabilities: A Multi-Disciplinary Journal* 8, 1: 63–71.

Guthrie, J.T., P. Van Meter, A.D. McCann, A. Wigfield, L. Bennett, C.C. Poundstone, M.E. Rice, F.M. Faibish, B. Hunt, and A.M. Mitchell. (1996). "Growth of Literacy Engagement: Changes in Motivations and Strategies During Concept-oriented Reading Instruction." *Reading Research Quarterly* 31, 3: 306–332.

Hansen, J. (1983). "Authors Respond to Authors." *Language Arts* 60, 8: 970–976.

Hart, B., and T.R. Risley. (1995). *Meaningful Differences in the Everyday Experience of Young American Children.* Baltimore: Paul H. Brookes.

Hindley, J. (1996). *In the Company of Children.* York, Maine: Stenhouse.

Juel, C. (1988). "Learning to Read and Write: A Longitudinal Study of Fifty-four Children from First Through Fourth Grades." *Journal of Educational Psychology* 80, 4: 437–447.

Langer, J.A. (1986). *Children Reading and Writing: Structures and Strategies.* Norwood, N.J.: Ablex.

Many, J.E., R. Fyfe, G. Lewis, and E. Mitchell. (1996). "Traversing the Topical Landscape: Exploring Students' Self-Directed Reading-Writing-Research Processes." *Reading Research Quarterly* 31, 1: 12–35.

Morrow, L.M., M. Pressley, J.K. Smith, and M. Smith. (1997). "The Effect of a Literature-based Program Integrated into Literacy and Science Instruction with Children from Diverse Backgrounds." *Reading Research Quarterly* 32, 1: 54–76.

National Board for Professional Teaching Standards. (1995). *Early Childhood/Generalist: Standards for National Board Certification.* Detroit, Mich.: Author.

Shanahan, T., and R.G. Lomax. (1988). "A Developmental Comparison of Three Theoretical Models of the Reading-Writing Relationship." *Research in the Teaching of English* 22, 2: 196–212.

Snow, C.E., W.S. Barnes, J. Chandler, I.F. Goodman, and L. Hemphill. (1991). *Unfulfilled Expectations: Home and School Influences on Literacy.* Cambridge, Mass.: Harvard University Press.

Tierney, R.J., and T. Shanahan. (1991). "Research on the Reading-Writing Relationship: Interactions, Transactions, and Outcomes." In *Handbook of Reading Research 2,* edited by R. Bart, M.L. Kamil, P. Mosenthal, and P.D. Pearson. White Plains, N.Y.: Longman.

Tierney, R.J., A. Soter, J.F. O'Flahavan, and W. McGinley. (1989). "The Effects of Reading and Writing upon Thinking Critically." *Reading Research Quarterly* 24, 2: 134–173.

Zaragoza, N., and S. Vaughn. (1995). "Children Teach Us to Teach Writing." *The Reading Teacher* 49, 1: 42–47.

David K. Dickinson is Senior Research Scientist at the Center for Children and Families. **Lori Lyman DiGisi** is Senior Research Associate at the Center for Family, School, and Community. Both centers are parts of the Education Development Center, Inc., 55 Chapel St., Newton, MA 02158 (e-mail: DDickins@EDC.org and LDigisi@EDC.org).

Building walls of words

Edna Green Brabham, Susan Kidd Villaume

Words here, words there, walls of words everywhere! We invite readers to join us in an exploration of word walls and how they are transforming not only walls but also conversations in U.S. classrooms. In the November 2000 and February 2001 columns, we responded to questions and answers about literature discussions and the role of peer talk in writing classes that we encountered on the RTEACHER list-serv and in personal interactions with teachers. We reflected on ways that Literature Circles and Authors Circles provide conversational scaffolds that help shift the control and domination of talk about reading and writing from teacher to students. In this column, we will explore how word walls and the activities related to them function as conversational and, in addition, as visual scaffolds that help students take control of literacy skills and strategies.

Word walls are more apparent every day in our own and other teachers' classrooms, but there is more to a word wall than meets the eye. Word walls have great potential for transferring responsibility and control for reading and writing from teacher to students, but their novelty makes many teachers unsure of their purpose and effectiveness. Like other innovative practices, word walls will be effective only if we are willing to ask questions about their use. And questions about word walls abound! In discussions on the RTEACHER listserv with teachers and reading specialists and in classes with pre-service teachers, we have encountered and asked many questions about word walls and how to "do" them. In the sections that follow, we share our questions and answers that are evolving about what word walls are, the purposes they serve, and how they can meet readers' needs at different points in literacy development.

What are word walls?

Although teachers make different decisions about how to display, arrange, and use word walls in their classrooms, most word walls share common characteristics.

- All are collections of words that are developmentally appropriate for study by students in the classroom.
- Words are selected for specific instructional purposes.
- Collections are cumulative; as new words are introduced, familiar words remain for further study.
- Activities and talk about word walls provide conversational scaffolds that structure the ways that students study, think about, and use words.
- Words on walls serve as visual scaffolds that temporarily assist students in independent reading and writing.

What purposes do word walls serve?

Purposes for word walls vary. Some teachers use them to facilitate word analysis; other teachers use them to provide models of commonly misspelled words; still others use them to build vocabulary from units of study. In some classrooms, teachers create separate word walls for these three purposes. In others, teachers use a single word wall to serve several purposes. All word walls, however, provide references that enable students to become more independent and strategic problem solvers as they read and write.

Word walls not only empower students, they also empower teachers. As students work with them, words on the wall become anchored in long-term memory in ways that allow quick and easy access, promote detection of patterns, and encourage connections between words. The words themselves become the materials of instruction as students use them to construct knowledge in minds-on conversations and hands-on activities. Word walls make the students' reading and writing the hub of the literacy curriculum and can provide an alternative to commercially produced programs and worksheets.

At the same time, word walls display a visible record of skills taught and content studied. Word walls let teachers and students see and monitor what has been taught and learned, and they serve as guides for determining what needs to be added to make word study systematic and to avoid gaps in the curriculum. Used effectively, word walls can be the core of a systematic phonics and spelling program and document what has been the focus of study in both planned instruction and in moments that teachers seize as unplanned instructional opportunities.

How do you use word walls with beginning readers and writers?

Students at different points in literacy development benefit from different kinds of word walls and different kinds of word-wall activities. Many kindergarten and first-grade teachers begin with an ABC word wall of student names (Cunningham, 2000). Each day a name is added, and the teacher engages children in counting letters, clapping syllables, comparing word lengths, chanting letters, and matching beginning sounds in their names.

These activities promote phonemic awareness, letter-name knowledge, and letter sound relationships. After all students' names are on the wall, many teachers add high-frequency words, making sure that all 26 letters have example words. Many of the high-frequency words contain common endings or rimes such as -ay that can be used to read and spell hundreds of other words.

Some teachers whom we have read about and observed introduce other kinds of word walls by the end of kindergarten or in first grade. Word walls with theme words, which build and change as units of study are conducted and completed, are now common in primary classrooms. Wagstaff (1998, 1999) suggested a modified ABC word wall featuring words that are examples of the many different sounds that each letter can represent. She also recommended a words-we-know wall with high-frequency words such as because, they, and other words that lack predictable spelling patterns. Finally, Wagstaff invited teachers to make a chunking wall that organizes common spelling patterns by vowels.

No matter what kind of word wall we create, the mileage that children will get from the words seems to be an important consideration when deciding what words go on the wall. Our own experiences have led us to parsimony in selecting words for walls. We now avoid adding words that offer no new spelling patterns. For example, if say is already on the wall, we will not add play. Although play is a word that frequently occurs in children's books, we want students to find and use the word say to help them read and write play. Similarly, if eat is on the wall, it is not necessary to add the word each because students can use the vowel combination in eat to read and spell each. As we continue to work with word walls, we learn more about conserving space and selecting key anchor words that will help beginning readers and writers maximize what they know to figure out how to read and write the words they do not know.

In our professional readings and classroom observations, we have found that many primary teachers support word recognition by posting words on pictures, different colors of paper, and cards that outline the shapes of words to emphasize positions of tall and short letters. Observations of children using word walls, however, have caused us to be cautious about recommending these practices. We have found that these well-intentioned prompts distract some beginning readers and writers and keep them from paying full attention to the letters.

Cunningham (2000) reminded us that having a word wall is unproductive unless we are also doing the word wall. Similarly, Pinnell and Fountas (1998) emphasized the importance of interactive word walls. For word walls to be effective with beginning readers and writers, teachers must plan activities that invite students to develop deeper understandings of the relationships between letters and sounds and that explicitly show them how to use word parts as springboards for reading and spelling other words. To energize word study and maximize attention, teachers may ask students to clap between words; alternate sitting and standing; and write the words in the air, with letter tiles or shaving cream, or on dry erase boards. Word searches, I Spy, and flash card games promote word identification and connections among words on walls. Classroom centers may be equipped with materials for sorting words or building new words using the word wall. Some teachers use word walls for spelling tests, calling out words in full view to see if students can locate them; however, they also call out words that are not on the wall but that can be spelled using clues in anchor words on the wall. For example, a first-grade teacher might ask the class to spell clam using Sam's name.

Powerful instruction using word walls also occurs during conversations about word-solving problems that come up as students read and write. For example, when a child asks how to spell feet, we point out the word need on the wall and ask how it can help. When a child stumbles on the word right as she reads, we ask her to find the word night on the wall to help solve the problem. These conversations are scaffolds that support the development of chunking and decoding-by-analogy strategies used by skillful readers. When we see students glance at the word wall during independent reading and writing and smile triumphantly as they solve a new word, we know that we are doing the word wall instead of just having one in the room.

How do you use word walls with developing readers and writers?

Developing readers and writers are ready to construct more refined understandings of spelling patterns and to analyze the structural components of words in more sophis-

ticated ways. We have read about and observed teachers in the upper elementary grades and in middle schools who are exploring differentiated uses of word walls. Many have posted a word wall of commonly misspelled words that includes confusing homophones and contractions and serves as an easily accessible reference. Some teachers of developing readers and writers also use word walls to explore different spellings of vowel phonemes. For example, a word wall organized by long vowels might include anchor words such as boat, though, rope, and beau. As students come across other spelling patterns for /O/ in their reading, they add words to the wall. The talk and excitement generated when students discover a new spelling pattern assures us that this type of word wall is a powerful instructional tool. Similarly, when we hear one student prompt another to spell soap like boat, we know that the word walls we have created are succeeding as visual and conversational scaffolds.

Cunningham and Hall (1998) suggested that teachers make a nifty-thrifty-fifty word wall that highlights common prefixes and suffixes and spelling patterns associated with these (e.g., doubling the consonant before adding the suffix). Words such as unfriendly and irresponsible support work with other words containing those morphemes. The authors described a brandname-phonics wall that reminds students of common spelling patterns and uses trade names like Sprite, Coke, and Snack Pack as scaffolds for reading and spelling the words ignite, provoke, and attacked. Teachers of developing readers and writers also construct word walls that display content vocabulary and theme words and use these words in multiple ways. For example, they may ask students to do word sorts, features analysis charts, or maps to find common spelling patterns, similarities in meaning, and conceptual relationships (Bear, Invernizzi, Templeton, & Johnston, 2000).

How do you use word walls with struggling readers and writers?

Struggling readers often benefit from revisiting previous instruction in systematic, explicit, and personalized ways. Word walls promote these activities, but those constructed for general classroom use may not serve the needs of struggling readers. As a solution, Cunningham (2000) suggested portable word walls that can be transported easily and that evolve as teachers work with struggling readers in one-on-one conferences or small groups. We find that these portable word walls hold much promise because they provide teachers with activities, materials, and records that promote systematic instruction guided by the needs of the learners. As our second-grade students struggle with /ou/ words, for example, we record an anchor word such as *out* on the wall and revisit it often as students practice reading and spelling words using *out* as an anchor. Recently, one of these readers noticed that adding *s* to *say* produced *says* and a new spelling pattern to put in our word wall column for short-*e* words. When struggling readers become that sensitive to the ways that words work, we know that we are on the right track!

The ongoing challenge

As we keep working with word walls, we ask ourselves how we can make them continue to serve as scaffolds for thoughtful, probing word analysis and internalization of word-solving strategies instead of becoming static, external devices that promote copying and memorization. We are learning that the ongoing challenge is finding ways to use word walls so that they create independence rather than reliance. How do we change and when do we discard words to ensure that word walls really function as visual and conversational scaffolds rather than as crutches? Exploring the use of word walls with readers and writers at different points in their development is an invigorating endeavor. We hope that you, too, will be challenged to put word walls to work as scaffolds for literacy development, and we look forward to seeing your results as this conversation about word walls continues in our schools and on the RTEACHER listserv.

References

Bear, D., Invernizzi, M., Templeton, S., & Johnston, F. (2000). *Words their way: Word study for phonics, vocabulary, and spelling instruction.* Upper Saddle River, NJ: Merrill.

Cunningham, P. (2000). *Phonics they use: Words for reading and writing* (3rd ed.). New York: Longman/Addison Wesley.

Cunningham, P., & Hall, D.P. (1998). *Month-by-month phonics.* Greensboro, NC: Carmen-Dellosa.

Pinnell, G.S., & Fountas, I. (1998). *Word matters: Teaching phonics and spelling in the reading/writing classroom.* Portsmouth, NH: Heinemann.

Wagstaff, J.M. (1998). Building practical knowledge of letter-sound correspondences: A beginner's word wall and beyond. *The Reading Teacher, 51,* 298-304.

Wagstaff, J.M. (1999). *Teaching reading and writing with word walls: Easy lessons and fresh ideas for creating interactive word walls that build literacy skills.* New York: Scholastic.

The editors welcome reader comments on this department. E-mail: brabhed@auburn.edu. Mail: Edna Greene Brabham and Susan Kidd Villaume, Department of Curriculum and Teaching, Auburn University, 5040 Haley Center, Auburn, AL 36849-5212, USA.

UNIT 3

Current Theory Guiding Best Practices

Unit Selections

Key Points to Consider

- What role should phonemic awareness play in early literacy instruction?

- Has the 2000 National Reading Panel's questionable interpretation of research led to the nation's current administration's emphasis on skill based instruction?

- Given all the different components of a balanced literacy program and budget concerns, how can teachers select books for guided reading, shared reading, independent reading, and read alouds?

- How can teachers evaluate their reading and writing programs and make the changes necessary to meet the needs of their students?

- Will technology change the skills students need for reading and writing in the future?

 **Links: www.dushkin.com/online/**
These sites are annotated in the World Wide Web pages.

Center for Academic and Reading Skills
http://cars.uth.tmc.edu/debate/understand.shtml

Over the past half century, the pendulum has swung wildly over the debate between whole language and phonics-based instruction. As a result, many educators struggle to maintain their classroom's literacy curriculum, repeatedly restructuring to match their school district's adopted language program and current best practices. Our current administration's No Child Left Behind legislation has proponents of both sides, once again, in heated debate.

With little effort, one can easily identify former teachers or colleagues as skill-based or holistic teachers. How did they form their beliefs? What experiences led them to develop their literacy curriculum? One colleague shared that when she entered first grade, already knowing how to read, her teacher placed her in a corner with a book. She had no idea if her teacher taught her classmates with a phonics approach. Twenty years later, as a college student, her language arts professor advocated whole language, giving only one lecture on phonics instruction. She was hired as a teacher because she agreed to use "real literature" and not use the district's basal series. Imagine her distress seven years later, when a new principal wanted her to teach phonics.

This story typifies the experiences many teachers have on either side of the skill-based or holistic approach debate. When the pendulum swings or administrations change, teachers often find themselves throwing out their literacy programs to try something new. In time, many teachers come to realize that each new program has its weaknesses and begin to create literacy programs that include components of both skill-based instruction and whole language. On their own, they identify what their students need and create a combined approach using skill-based instruction and good literature.

The articles in this unit examine current theories guiding best practices in literacy instruction today. They reflect the wide range of opinions and options teachers must weigh as they make informed decisions on how to develop their literacy curriculums. As many educators have discovered, prepackaged curriculum rarely meet the needs of diverse student populations or match individual state standards. As local, state, and national policies change and as budgets are tightened, teachers must make sound decisions on curriculum adoption committees and budget expenditures. Only close examination of identified effective approaches, tested best practices, and interactive classroom environments that foster collaborative learning will prepare our students for the future.

The article "Phonemic Awareness: A Crucial Bridge to Reading," supports the necessity of phonemic awareness skills for emergent readers. The authors conclude that phonological sensitivity to sound is a key indicator to identifying children at risk for reading development and believe teachers can use it for early identification and intervention.

In "False Claims About Literacy Development," author Stephen Krashen, disputes the 2000 National Reading Panel's conclusions about literacy development. In his rebuttal to key statements in the report, he questions their claim that skill-based approaches are superior to whole language approaches and offers research to support the effectiveness of whole language. He further challenges educators to inquire if the National Reading Panel's report has led state and local reading policies to misdirect federal funding.

The question remains: how can current and future teachers learn to find that balance? In "Matching Texts and Readers: Leveling Early Reading Materials for Assessment and Instruction," Canadian teachers discuss how their school district worked together to create a leveling system to support emergent literacy and identify strategies students must develop for each reading level. In "Guided Reading: Who is in the Driver's Seat?" the authors question how teachers can help students become independent, strategic readers if their guided lessons are structured to teach specific skills and strategies. By closely examining guided reading procedures, these teachers found ways to step back and give themselves the freedom to take ownership of their instructional practices, reflecting the needs of their students within the context of a balanced literacy curriculum.

Mem Fox (2001), popular author and college professor warns teachers about the dangers of throwing away one orthodoxy after another as something new comes along.[1] Teachers no longer need to "re-invent the wheel," but must continue to grow as they develop their own knowledge base of effective approaches and classroom practices. Using a balanced literacy approach can empower teachers to become instructional specialists capable of making choices to best meet their students' needs and prepare them for the future. Educators must offer their voices on major policy issues and learn from one another as they create interactive learning environments which foster collaborative learning between educators.

Denise Jean Cross

Reference
1.) Have We Lost Our Way? Mem Fox, Language Arts, November 2001

Phonemic Awareness: A Crucial Bridge to Reading

Before man's arrival on earth [language] did not exist. And what is it? barely a breath! A few noises strung together. … It's a mystery impossible to fathom.

—Montessori (1967a, pp. 108-110)

By Carol S. Woods

These few noises that are strung together so mysteriously are receiving much focus as educators examine the all-too-frequent failure of our children to read at the appropriate grade level. Increasingly, research is focusing on language experiences in early childhood, the years prior to formal schooling. The findings support Maria Montessori's emphasis on the value of early language experiences: the foundation for reading and writing is laid during the sensitive period for language. Muchcan be done to prepare children for literacy during these early years.

Language is multifaceted with elements that are interrelated and interdependent: it includes listening, speaking, writing, and reading. It provides the means for interpersonal relationships and logical thought. A weakness in any one area can have a negative impact on other areas (Grimes, 2001).

The earliest language experiences are oral in nature, including listening and vocalizing. Infants' behavior indicates the brain's propensity for language: they watch our mouths as we talk, and they begin to imitate the sounds of our speech pattern very early in life. Their joy in language is apparent from their happy wriggling as they absorb the speech sounds and vocalize their own sounds. These oral language skills develop and refine at an astounding rate through the early years.

Researchers have identified a relationship between strong oral language skills and later success with written language (Grimes, 2001; Birsh, 1999). Increasingly, they are studying a specific area of oral language, phonological awareness, as they seek ways to improve the literacy rate. Phonological awareness is a general ability relating to awareness of the "sound structure of oral language" (Birsh, 1999, p. 63). This type of awareness highlights the sounds rather than the meaning of language (National Research Council [NRC], 1998). For example, the words *plant* and *can't* may be paired because they contain similar sounds (i.e., they rhyme), but they are unrelated in semantics and syntax.

Phonemic awareness is a part of phonological awareness: it is the understanding that words consist of individual, discrete sounds in particular sequences (Blevins, 2000). Phonemic awareness is crucial for learning the relationship between speech and the written word, and it is one part of the foundation for success with the written form of the language (NRC, 1998).

Typically developing children begin to understand the phonological basis of speech during the preschool years (NRC, 1998). A language-rich environment, with many individual and group opportunities for conversing, singing, exploring books, and writing, helps prepare children for literacy. The language materials in the early childhood Montessori environment offer much support for developing and refining the child's phonemic awareness. However, other kinds of activities address the specific skills related to phonological and phonemic awareness and offer preliminary and supplemental support. Stimulation includes both group activities and individual work choices found in the environment.

Activities to Develop Phonological and Phonemic Awareness

Songs

Any songs that include word play, such as *Willowby Wallaby* or *Banana Fan*a, are helpful. Children quickly master the words and sound substitutions and enjoy the silly, nonsense words that result from these types of songs.

The Alphabet

Montessori noted that "an analysis of the sounds of speech is intimately connected with the learning of the alphabet" (1967b, p. 148). Each letter has four qualities: its name, sound, shape, and feel. The only quality that is stable is the name; the sound, shape, and feel all can change. The names of the letters provide children with one unchanging element, a constant, for each symbol (Birsh, 1999).

Frequent singing of the *Alphabet Song* (so that each letter name is clearly articulated) helps children learn the names and sequence of the letters. Including exercises for matching and sequencing the letters provides practice in associating the auditory learning from the song to the visual images of the specific symbols. Some studies suggest that capital letters are easier than lower-case letters for children to master (Birsh, 1999). Including activities with them is beneficial, since so much environmental print is in the upper case.

Rhyming Activities

Marilyn Adams (1990) noted that children's rhyming abilities are strong indicators of reading readiness. Research suggests that rhyming skills develop during the preschool years, so any activities that support the emergence of this ability will help prepare children for literacy (NRC, 1998). For a list of suggested exercises, see "The Role of Rhyme" (Woods, 1998).

The National Research Council publication *Preventing Reading Difficulties in Young Children* noted that phonemic awareness starts with recognizing when two words begin with the same sound, such as *tooth* and *turtle*.

I Spy provides a vehicle for stimulating this early level of phonemic awareness. The first experience is with one object, isolated to assure success. With repeated practice, the child will select correctly one object with a particular beginning sound from among many and eventually discriminate ending and medial sounds.

Word Games

Word games provide multiple levels of manipulating words and sounds. The young child may begin with compound words: the adult says a compound word; the child repeats the word; then the adult asks the child to say the word again without a part of the original word. For example, "Say *raincoat*…now say it without *coat*." With practice, the first part of the word may be dropped instead of the second part (Grimes, 2001).

As the child experiences the movable alphabet, the above exercise is repeated with single words, deleting one sound: "Say *bag*…now say it without /g/." Later,

the beginning sound may be dropped: "Say *fin*…now say it without /f/."

Children who are proficient with the movable alphabet may be asked to substitute one sound for another: "Say *hat*…now change the /a/ to /i/."

According to Grimes (2001), children should be able to participate in all the above levels successfully by age 6. In a language-rich Montessori environment, 5-year-old children can perform most of the levels successfully (possible exception: sound substitution).

Word Segmentation

Research indicates that the child's understanding of language shifts during the preschool years from a focus on whole words to a perception of the sounds in words (NRC, 1998). Word segmentation supports this emerging awareness: the child says a familiar word, then says each sound individually, sequentially breaking the word into its individual sounds.

Assigning one sound to each finger provides kinesthetic reinforcement: the child taps each finger in turn while vocalizing each sound. For example, the child is asked to say a word such as *cap*, then say each sound in order: /c/, /a/, /p/. As each sound is vocalized, a finger taps the table or floor. The focus is on sounds, not on spelling. Thus, *ship* is segmented into three sounds as /sh/, /i/, /p/; *tape* is segmented as /t/, /a/, /p/, with the /a/ sounded as a long vowel sound. Consonant blends are segmented into their sounds: *blast* is segmented as /b/, /l/, /a/, /s/, /t/.

The *Yopp-Singer Test of Phoneme Segmentation* (Yopp, 1995) is a simple tool for assessing children's skills in this area. It is designed to provide teachers with the ability to identify children who might benefit from additional stimulation (Gillingham & Stillman, 1997).

A Case Study

The activities described above can support children in developing phonemic awareness, as demonstrated by Edward, who attended our school for 3 years. He was a highly verbal child and enjoyed conversing about the events in his daily life. His long stories included interesting and varied vocabulary that sometimes seemed beyond his age.

Early in his second school year, Edward began to play *I Spy* successfully, so he started work on the sandpaper letters. He progressed steadily with the sound/symbol

relationships, and after learning five sounds, he began to compose words with the movable alphabet. Since his expressive language was strong, the teaching staff anticipated that this work would be pleasurable for him. However, the movable alphabet proved challenging, and his struggles with composing only a few words at a time puzzled the staff. Adding to the mystery was the fact that he continued to learn sound/symbol relationships easily.

Early in Edward's third year with us, I attended a workshop presented by Dr. Sally Grimes (2001). Dr. Grimes discussed phonological awareness and talked about the expected phonological skills of a child entering first grade. She listed rhyme, word segmentation, and word play that includes sound omissions and substitutions as being among the important abilities that support reading development.

Eagerly I took the skills I'd learned back to the classroom and began experimenting with several exercises. I quickly discovered that although Edward could rhyme and segment words into their individual sounds, he could not engage in word play.

Orally, Edward could not omit a sound from a word or substitute one sound for another within a word. For example, when asked to say a word such as *tag* and then say it again without either the first or last sound ("say it again without /t/" or "say it again without /g/"), he would say an unrelated word. He also was unable to change one sound to another; when asked to say a word such as *fun*, then change the /u/ to /a/, he could not respond. Despite his high level of expressive language, he did not understand how to manipulate sounds orally. His ability level contrasted with that of the other kindergarten-age children; all of them were able at least to omit sounds correctly.

Even though Edward's expressive language seemed well developed, his articulation often made his speech difficult to understand for anyone not acclimated to his speech pattern. After we discovered that he could not manipulate sounds in the word play games, we referred him to a speech and language pathologist, who concluded that his articulation errors were age appropriate. She declined both to test his phonological abilities and to refer him for any intervention, suggesting another evaluation in a year.

The teaching staff began at once to engage Edward in word games. Furthermore, we explained the games to his parents, who early agreed to play them at home. Since he had not developed the skill through auditory experiences, we sought ways to make use of other senses to support his learning. Thus we used the movable alphabet to provide visual clues in support of the auditory input. A teacher would dictate a three-letter word, such as *wag*. After Edward composed the requested word with the movable alphabet, he would be asked to change a sound, such as "change the /w/ to /s/." Next he might be asked to change the /g/ to /t/, etc. With each request, he replaced one letter with another.

Within 3 months, the results were remarkable. He developed the ability to omit sounds, as requested, and his facility with the movable alphabet improved. His early efforts at reading had been painfully slow, as he sounded out every letter and struggled to blend. Gradually, he began to blend sounds into words with increased ease, and his reading progressed accordingly. By the end of his third school year, he was reading short-vowel books fluently.

As an Orton-Gillingham tutor, I work with children ranging in age from early elementary grades to junior high school. All are struggling with the printed word in both reading and writing, and many are dyslexic. The majority of these students experience auditory processing difficulties of some sort, as did Edward. Often as I work with these students, I wonder what might have changed in their lives if at least some of their problems had been identified in the preschool/kindergarten years.

I believe that early detection and intervention can help many children. Teachers in early childhood environments can serve children well by looking closely at language problems, seeking outside intervention as needed, and offering extra stimulation to support appropriate devel-

opment. I do not know if Edward will experience additional problems, but I am certain that the teaching staff at his school helped him to move into early literacy.

Conclusion

Some researchers believe that phonemic awareness is a stronger predictor of reading achievement than vocabulary, intelligence, and reading readiness. However, recent studies have indicated that phonemic awareness does not just predict success; it is a necessary skill for learning to read (Gillingham, 1997). The exciting part is that extra practice may provide the needed support for some children who are deficient in this area.

Montessori identified the preschool years as the sensitive period for language, the period of the "keenest interest" (1967a, p. 133). Recent research has upheld her view: young children delight in all aspects of language.

During preschool years, phonological awareness gradually emerges, often beginning with word games such as "butterfly...flutterby" (NRC, 1998). Capitalizing on this innate sensitivity supports children in understanding that this mysterious thing called language consists of noises or sounds strung together sequentially. Such understanding prepares them for learning the alphabetic nature of our language, a necessary understanding for reading success (NRC, 1998). An environment that is rich in language experiences includes activities that emphasize the phonemic nature of language, and the Montessori early childhood environment offers an ideal setting. Furthermore, the child's keen interest

in language makes these exercises fun for everyone!

References

Adams, M. J. (1990). *Beginning to read.* Cambridge, MA: MIT Press.

Birsh, J. R. (Ed.). (1999). *Multisensory teaching of basic language skills.* Baltimore: Brookes.

Blevins, W. (2000). Playing with sounds. *Instructor, 109*(6), pp. 16-17.

Gillingham, A., & Stillman, B.W. (1997). *The Gillingham manual.* Cambridge, MA: Educators Publishing Service.

Grimes, S. C. (2001, November 3). Teaching reading in the 21st century. International Dyslexia Association Fall Conference, Ohio Valley Branch.

Montessori, M. (1967a). *The absorbent mind* (C. Claremont, Trans.). New York: Dell. (Original work published 1949)

Montessori, M. (1967b). *The discovery of the child* (M. J. Costelloe, Trans.). Notre Dame, IN: Fides. (Original work published 1948)

National Research Council (NRC). (1998). *Preventing reading difficulties in young children.* Washington, DC: National Academy Press.

Woods, C. S. (1998). The role of rhyme. *Montessori Life, 10*(4), pp. 34-36, 48.

Yopp, H. K. (1995 September). A test for assessing phonemic awareness in young children. *Reading Teacher, 49*(1), pp. 20-29.

CAROL S. WOODS is teaching coordinator at Montessori Center Room, Cincinatti, OH, and a member of the Academy of Orton-Gillingham Practitioners.

False Claims About Literacy Development

Despite what many people believe, the National Reading Panel's conclusions about literacy development are not proven facts.

By Stephen Krashen

The 2000 National Reading Panel report makes various claims about reading and reading instruction, including the following:

- Phonemic awareness training significantly improves children's reading ability.
- Systematic phonics instruction is more effective than less systematic phonics instruction.
- Skills-based approaches are superior to whole language approaches.
- There is no clear evidence that encouraging students to read more in school improves reading achievement.

In fact, sufficient evidence exists to challenge all four claims.

Rebutting the Evidence

False Claim #1:Phonemic awareness training significantly improves children's reading ability.

Phonemic awareness is the ability to divide a word into its component sounds. Looking at a number of studies involving students who received direct teaching or "training" in phonemic awareness, some individuals have claimed that such training is "clearly effective," helps students "learn to read and spell," and improves reading comprehension and word reading (National Reading Panel, 2000, p. 40).

In my review of the research on phonemic awareness (Krashen, 2001a), I sought studies that looked at pure phonemic awareness—not phonemic awareness combined with phonics—and that tested students on reading comprehension, not just on phonemic awareness or reading isolated words. I found only six published studies, covering a total of 11 comparisons of phonemic awareness-trained students and students untrained in phonemic awareness. Only three of the six studies dealt with English-speaking students; the others dealt with students who spoke Spanish, Hebrew, or Norwegian.

The overall results were unimpressive. The average effect size for the 11 comparisons was +.35 in favor of phonemic awareness training. (Effect size is a measure of the impact of a treatment in an experiment.) An effect size of +.35 falls between a small effect (+.2) and a medium effect (+.5) (Wolf, 1986). Moreover, the findings of a number of individual studies raise doubt about the value of phonemic awareness training:

- In one study (Weiner, 1994), the effect size was positive for one of two comparisons (+.40) but negative for the other (–.41).
- In three comparisons (two from Defior & Tudela, 1994; one from Hatcher, Helm, & Ellis, 1994), effect sizes were low: +.13 or less.
- In four studies (six comparisons), the number of students who underwent phonemic awareness training was small: Bradley & Bryant, 1983, 13 students; Defior & Tudela, 1994, 9 students; Kozminsky & Kozminsky, 1995, 15 students; Weiner, 1994, 5 students.
- Only one study reported substantial effect sizes as well as statistically significant results in favor of phonemic awareness training: a study

conducted in Israel with Hebrew-speaking students, involving only 15 students who underwent phonemic awareness training (Kozminsky & Kozminsky, 1995).

No reasonable person would conclude on the basis of this evidence that phonemic awareness training is essential, or even particularly important. Evidence supporting the phonemic awareness claims that appear to have gripped the schools in a kind of hysteria should be made of much sterner stuff.

The National Reading Panel's comments on my conclusions expressed no real disagreement (Ehri, Shanahan, & Nunes, 2002), noting that when we consider only studies dealing with English speakers, the average effect size is +.28, which, they point out, falls short of statistical significance. Ehri and colleagues conclude that this "supports Krashen's claim," but they add that "more comparisons would yield a firmer conclusion" (p. 129). Of course, I agree. But most important, they do not contest the claim that few studies have been conducted to test the impact of phonemic awareness training on reading comprehension.

There are other reasons to suspect that phonemic awareness is not a crucial element in learning to read. For example, children without phonemic awareness or with very low phonemic awareness often learn to read quite well (Bradley & Bryant, 1985; Stuart-Hamilton, 1986), and some adults who are excellent readers do poorly on tests of phonemic awareness (Campbell & Butterworth, 1985).

False Claim #2: Systematic phonics instruction is more effective than less systematic phonics instruction.

The National Reading Panel claimed to find

> solid support for the conclusion that systematic phonics instruction makes a bigger contribution to children's growth in reading than alternative programs providing unsystematic or no phonics instruction. (2000, p. 92)

A close look, however, reveals that the National Reading Panel's analysis actually showed that intensive, systematic phonics instruction has a limited impact. The Panel reported an overall effect size of +.46 favoring systematic, intensive phonics programs over programs providing less or no phonics instruction. The effect, however, depended on the kind of measure used, with systematic phonics showing a greater effect (+.67) on reading single, regularly spelled words aloud, and a smaller effect (+.27) on tests involving reading texts (for details, see Garan, 2001, 2002).

The +.27 effect size for reading comprehension deserves more comment. The Panel found a small, nonsignificant relationship between systematic phonics training and performance on tests of reading comprehension for older students (grades 2–6; +.12). Garan (2001, 2002) argues that the relationship between intensive phonics instruction and reading comprehension is stronger for younger students because reading comprehension tests for young students contain short passages with many phonetically regular words. The relationship diminishes when passages become more complex and include more words with irregular sound-spelling correspondences, as is the case with reading comprehension measurements used with older students.

Children without phonemic awareness or with very low phonemic awareness often learn to read quite well.

Camilli, Vargas, and Yurecko (2003) have come to similar conclusions. They examined the same studies that the National Reading Panel reviewed and used a more sophisticated statistical model, one that takes into account more than one fac-

tor at a time. These researchers concluded that the effect of systematic phonics instruction was considerably less than that reported by the National Reading Panel and that other factors—individual tutoring and "language activities" (defined as whole word or whole language activities)—had a significant effect as well.

False Claim #3: Skills-based approaches are superior to whole language approaches.

The National Reading Panel concluded that systematic phonics approaches were superior to whole language approaches, claiming that the average effect size in favor of phonics was +.32 (based on 12 comparisons). They did not, however, analyze effect sizes separately for each kind of measurement used. Some measurements involved reading single, isolated words; some involved real texts. Also, the issue should not center on whether a treatment is labeled "whole language" or "skills-based," but rather on how much reading the students actually do. In Evans and Carr (1985), for example, the skills-based, "traditional" group did significantly more silent reading than the "whole language" group did.

I reanalyzed these studies considering only tests of reading comprehension (Krashen, 2002). I also considered not whether a treatment was labeled "whole language" or "phonics" but whether the students in one treatment did more real reading than the students in the other treatment did. In addition, I included some studies that the National Reading Panel had missed. In the end, I found a small advantage favoring whole language on tests of reading comprehension (+.17).

False Claim #4: There is no clear evidence that encouraging children to read more in school improves reading achievement.

The National Reading Panel reached this startling conclusion on the basis of only 10 studies of sustained silent reading with control groups. In sustained silent reading, some class time is set aside for free voluntary reading with little or no "accountability." The 10 studies contained 14 separate comparisons. Of the 14 comparisons, 4 had positive results (students who engaged in free voluntary reading outperformed control groups in traditional language arts classes), and 10 showed no difference between the two groups. In no case did students in sustained silent reading do worse.

The Panel considered this result to be unimpressive.

The Panel report left out many studies. A look at additional studies of sustained silent reading and similar in-school recreational reading programs showed that sustained silent reading students did as well as or better than students in traditional language arts classes in 50 out of 53 comparisons (Krashen, 2001b). In long-term studies (those longer than one year), sustained silent reading students performed better in 8 out of 10 studies, and the remaining 2 studies showed no difference. The Panel did not include any studies lasting longer than one year.

In addition, the Panel misinterpreted some of the studies that it did include and included some that it should have omitted. In one study (Carver & Liebert, 1995), students in the reading group were limited to only 135 titles; "the regular library stacks were off limits during the study" (p. 33). Students in this study were provided with incentives, had to take tests on what they read, and had to read in two-hour blocks. Successful sustained silent reading programs do not use extrinsic motivators, do not test students on what they read, provide a wide variety of books, and typically meet for a short time each day over a long period.

Axioms or Hypotheses?

The National Reading Panel's conclusions have become "the law of the land," reflected in reading plans developed by state and local agencies across the United States. Federal funding requires adherence to these conclusions. They have, in fact, become axioms, considered by some to be proven facts rather than hypotheses. Obviously, if the National Reading Panel's claims are false, the implications are staggering. At a minimum, educators and policymakers should demote the status of the Panel's conclusions from axioms back to hypotheses.

References

Bradley, L., & Bryant, P. (1983). Categorizing sounds and learning to read—a causal connection. *Nature, 301,* 419-421.

Bradley, L., & Bryant, P. (1985). *Rhyme and reason in reading and spelling.* Ann Arbor, MI: University of Michigan Press.

Camilli, G., Vargas, S., & Yurecko, M. (2003). Teaching children to read: The fragile link between science and federal policy. *Education Policy Archives,*

11(15). Available: http://epaa.asu.edu/epaa/v11n15

Campbell, R., & Butterworth, B. (1985). Phonological dyslexia and dysgraphia in a highly literate subject: A developmental case with associated deficits of phonemic processing and awareness. *Quarterly Journal of Experimental Psychology, 37A,* 435-475.

Carver, R., & Liebert, R. (1995). The effect of reading library books at different levels of difficulty upon gains in reading. *Reading Research Quarterly, 30,* 26-48.

Defior, S., & Tudela, P. (1994). Effect of phonological training on reading and writing acquisition. *Reading and Writing, 6,* 299-320.

Ehri, L., Shanahan, T., & Nunes, S. (2002). Response to Krashen. *Reading Research Quarterly, 37*(2), 128-129.

Evans, M., & Carr, T. (1985). Cognitive abilities, conditions of learning, and the early development of reading skill. *Reading Research Quarterly, 20*(3), 327-350.

Garan, E. (2001). Beyond the smoke and mirrors: A critique of the National Reading Panel report on phonics. *Phi Delta Kappan, 82*(7), 500-506.

Garan, E. (2002). *Resisting reading mandates.* Portsmouth, NH: Heinemann.

Hatcher, P., Helm, C., & Ellis, A. (1994). Ameliorating early reading failure by integrating the teaching of reading and phonological skills: The phonological linkage hypothesis. *Child Development, 65,* 41-57.

Kozminsky, L., & Kozminsky, E. (1995). The effects of early phonological awareness training on reading success. *Learning and Instruction, 5,* 187-201.

Krashen, S. (200la). Does "pure" phonemic awareness training affect reading comprehension? *Perceptual and Motor Skills, 93,* 356-358.

Krashen, S. (200lb). More smoke and mirrors: A critique of the National Reading Panel report on fluency. *Phi Delta Kappan, 83,* 119-123.

Krashen, S. (2002). The NRP comparison of whole language and phonics: Ignoring the crucial variable in reading. *Talking Points, 13*(3), 22-28.

National Reading Panel. (2000). *Teaching children to read: An evidence-based assessment of the scientific research literature on reading and its implications for reading instruction.* Washington, DC: National Institute of Child Health and Human Development.

Stuart-Hamilton, I. (1986). The role of phonemic awareness in the reading style of beginning readers. *British Journal of Educational Psychology, 56,* 271-285.

Weiner, S. (1994). Effects of phonemic awareness training on low- and middle-achieving first graders' phonemic awareness and reading ability. *Journal of Reading Behavior, 26*(3), 277-300.

Wolf, F. (1986). *Meta-analysis.* Thousand Oaks, CA: Sage.

Stephen Krashen is Professor Emeritus of Education at the University of Southern California; krashen@usc.edu

From *Educational Leadership,* Vol. 60, No. 6, March 2004, pp. 18-21. Reprinted by permission of the Association for Supervision and Curriculum Development. Copyright © 2004 by ASCD. All rights reserved. The Association for Supervision and Curriculum Development is a worldwide community of educators advocating sound policies and sharing best practices to achieve the success of each learner. To learn more, visit ASCD at www.ascd.org

Matching Texts and Readers: Leveling Early Reading Materials for Assessment and Instruction

The authors describe a book leveling system developed to support emergent literacy in one Canadian school district.

Lori Jamison Rog and Wilfred Burton

For too long, we have tried to teach children to read using materials that may not be at an appropriate level of difficulty for them. If students are to learn and apply reading strategies, they need texts that provide a balance between support and challenge. That is, story text should be easy enough to develop students' confidence and facilitate comprehension, but difficult enough to provide a challenge and require the reader to do some "reading work" (Clay, 1991a).

Simple grade-level approximations provided by readability formulas are not accurate at the early primary level because they fail to take into account the many additional kinds of information provided by illustrations. Nor are the gradients fine enough to deal with the substantial difference in reading ability between a child entering Grade 1 and the same child at the end of the year.

A number of researchers (Clay, 1991a; Fountas & Pinnell, 1999; Hiebert, 1999b; Peterson, 1991) and publishers (Scholastic, Wright Group, Pearson Education) have developed means of leveling text for reading instruction. We have analyzed these systems and synthesized them into a process that helps teachers in our district to identify the most appropriate texts for their students at varying developmental levels. In this article, we will discuss the kinds of texts that are appropriate for students at various stages of their reading development and share our criteria for determining the difficulty levels of early reading materials.

What is a "just-right" text?

We know that a "just-right" text for instructional purposes is one in where the reader can read about 9 out of 10 words and comprehend the meaning of the passage with little difficulty (Clay,

1991a). A text in which a child can read 90–95% of the words easily is considered to be at that child's instructional reading level—where instruction will be most effective. Text that is easier is considered to be at the student's independent reading level. More difficult text is considered to be at the child's frustration level, and is not appropriate for reading instruction.

All students should receive reading instruction using texts at their instructional reading levels (Fountas & Pinnell, 1996). A procedure for leveling reading materials according to difficulty provides teachers with guidelines to quickly and easily select appropriate reading materials for each student.

Leveling reading materials is a complex task. Although traditional readability formulas rely on numerical calculations of sentences, words, and syllables, we know that there are many more factors that influence the degree of difficulty of a text for a particular reader. Some of these factors include the following (Fountas & Pinnell, 1996; Hiebert, 1999b; Weaver, 2000):

- the length of the book,
- the appearance and placement of print on the page,
- the degree of support offered by the illustrations,
- the complexity of concepts and familiarity of subject matter,
- the degree of predictability of the text, and
- the proportion of unique or repeated words to familiar words.

The concept of leveled reading materials is not new. It is an integral aspect of most models of literacy intervention, such as Reading Recovery (Clay, 1991a). Various attempts have been made to provide "appropriate" texts for young readers (Hiebert, 19998). Basal programs contained strictly controlled vocabulary that was introduced in a prescribed sequence, often teaching children only a core of sight words rather than working on decoding strategies. Decodable texts also used controlled vocabulary with regular letter-sound correspondences. Sometimes, however, meaning was sacrificed in the interest of repeating a particular pattern. The children's literature or whole language movement provided a rich literary experience for children, but often contained concepts and vocabulary beyond the reading ability of many students. We concur with Clay (1991a) and Hiebert (1999a) that appropriate reading materials for emergent readers contain meaningful and natural language patterns and many high-frequency words. These texts should be interesting and engaging for children, contain high-quality illustrations, and have literary merit.

Developing our leveling system

An abundance of early reading materials published during the last decade support early readers through natural language, meaningful concepts, and appealing format. When we first started examining these materials in the mid-1990s, we found that many publishers were creating texts at increasing gradients of difficulty, sorted by numbers, letters, or icons. Unfortunately, each publisher used its own leveling system. Therefore, the readability of a Level 3 book from one program might not compare to that of a Level 3 book from another program. Furthermore, none of the publishers explicitly defined the criteria by which their materials were leveled. Nor did they describe the characteristics of the texts at each level. At that time, the only explicitly described leveling system was Clay's (1991a) Reading Recovery program, which we felt was an excellent model but one not designed for general classroom use.

Faced with this dilemma, teachers in our school district examined hundreds of trade books and early literacy materials and sorted them into a 10-step leveling system for beginning reading instruction, using the following five considerations: vocabulary, size and layout of print, predictability, illustration support, and complexity of concepts. See Figure for criteria.

Vocabulary. The number of words on a page is an important consideration for level of difficulty (Fountas & Pinnell, 1996). Hiebert (1999a) added that the number of high-frequency ("sight") words and decodable (phonetically regular) words affects the difficulty of the text. For example, beginning texts will have only one or two words on a page, including such high-frequency words as *a* or *the*. Key vocabulary is often repeated several times throughout the text. At higher levels, more complex, multisyllable words are evident. Furthermore, early texts use oral language structures, such as sentence fragments and repetitive phrasing, that may sound choppy. At higher levels, literary vocabulary and flowing phrases are used.

Size and layout of print. The appearance of the print and the amount of text have an impact on a book's readability (Fountas & Pinnell, 1996). At the earliest levels, the print is in a large, clear font and consistently placed on every page. One-word or two-word labeling of pictures evolves into phrases, sentences, and ultimately paragraphs of a story as levels increase.

There is a further graduation when line breaks for sentences are considered. At the lowest level, each line contains a sentence. Later, line breaks are found at the end of key phrases to

help a child retain meaning. It is not until the highest levels that line breaks are made when there is no more space at the end of the line.

Predictability. All literary patterns, including rhyme, rhythm, and repetition as well as cumulative or chronological text structures, help to make text predictable (Clay, 1991a). Beginning levels should contain consistent patterns of a few words or a sentence that may be repeated on each page, with only one or two words changed each time. At mid-range levels, patterns are longer with more word changes. At the highest levels there is unlikely to be any pattern at all; occasionally, single words or key phrases may be repeated, but this is for literary effect rather than predictability.

Illustration support. At the earliest levels, pictures are simple, clear, and directly support the text; in fact, the text is generally little more than a labeling of the pictures. Two factors influence the amount of contextual support that illustrations provide: the extent to which the vocabulary can be associated with clear and concrete images, and the reader's familiarity with the vocabulary (Clay, 1991a). A very clear and explicit illustration of a totem pole, for example, will not offer much support to a child who is unfamiliar with the concept or the word. At higher levels, the illustrations become more complex and ultimately serve to enhance and extend the story line without offering much support for decoding.

Complexity of concepts. Most beginning texts simply label illustrations that are familiar to the reader. Low-level story lines are based on events and experiences common to most young readers, such as visiting Grandma or having a birthday party. These stories become less predictable as more characters are involved in the story and the reader is expected to make inferences. Stories at higher levels tend to be unique and more engaging, with a strong plot, individualized characters, descriptive language, and literary text structures. Although there is little information in the research about concept complexity, it is our experience that this is a significant factor in the difficulty of text for students.

What do books look like at each level?

Guided by these five general considerations, teachers in our district began sorting texts used for beginning reading instruction. When we started, there were a variety of different systems for leveling books in use in the district, ranging from publishers' lists to Clay's (1991a) Reading Recovery levels. Using Clay's system as a foundation, we developed a framework that teachers could use for strategy instruction with students at all levels. Our goal was to extend the system for general classroom use. With this goal in mind, we developed a 10-level rubric. The intent of this process was not to create an infallible leveling system. We realize there are many exceptions to the criteria provided, and the background experiences of the students will play a role in determining what kinds of texts are most appropriate for them. Our leveling system provides teachers with a pedagogical and professional development tool to support them in making informed choices about reading materials. Our provincial curriculum advocates a resource-based approach to instruction,

Criteria for leveling books

Level	Vocabulary	Print	Predictability	Illustrations	Content and concepts	Anchor book
1	• 0–2 words per page • Sight words: *a, the, an, my* • Title may be more difficult	• Large print found in the same place on every page • Short book (probably eight pages)	• No rhyme or pattern	• Simple, clear, no clutter • Provide strong, direct support for text	• No story line • Labeling of pictures of familiar objects and actions	*The Big Chase* by Karen Anderson and Lyn Kriegler
2	• Simple, familiar language • Some sight words repeated in the text pattern • Usually a repeated phrase or short sentence	• Consistent placement of print • Short length	• Usually a consistent pattern that may change slightly at the beginning or end of the book	• Text is usually labeling of pictures • Very strong picture support for text	• Familiar objects or actions • No evident story line	*A Garden* by Jill Mitchell and Marjory Gardner
3	• Usually complete sentences • May see verb changes in the pattern, such as singular to plural, or addition of /ing/ or /s/ • More sight words	• May have one or two sentences per page • May include questions • Consistent placement of print on the page	• Usually a pattern with one or two words changing on each page	• Direct support for text	• Familiar objects and actions • No evident story line	*In the Park* by Nicola Barrie and Marjorie Scott
4	• Simple, familiar language • Increased sight words • May include prepositional phrases	• Consistent placement of print • Longer sentences	• Strong pattern which may have two or more word changes on each page	• Illustrations with familiar objects or actions provide strong support	• Usually about common experiences of young children	*Animals* by Paul Reeder and Graham Meadows
5	• Increased number of sight words • Mostly decodable words	• 1–3 sentences per page, require reader to make a return sweep • More punctuation	• Similar to Level 4 at first, but ending may be completely different pattern • May have 2–3 pattern changes	• Still high support for text • Familiar objects and actions	• Starting of simple story line • May have more than one character talking	*The Busy Mosquito* by Helen Depree and Helen Casey
6	• Mostly decodable text and sight words • Some two-syllable words	• 2–3 sentences per page • Short, choppy sentences • Conventional punctuation • Print is large and usually consistently placed on the page	• Repetitive patterns may occur • Some cumulative or chronological patterns (e.g., days of the week)	• Continue to provide high support for text	• Many familiar objects and actions • Simple sequence of events • Predictable • Simple story line • More conversation	*Our Cat* by Helen Depree and Veronica Alkema
7	• More new words introduced in each sentence	• Longer, more detailed sentences	• Sometimes rhythmic • May have 2–3 different sentence	• Picture cues provide moderate to high support	• More detail in story line	*Where is the Milk?* by Sandra Iverson and Julie McCormack

(continued)

Criteria for leveling books (continued)

Level	Vocabulary	Print	Predictability	Illustrations	Content and concepts	Anchor book
8	• More unique words introduced per page, but still dominated by high-frequency words • New vocabulary repeated often in text • Stilted language	• Longer stories, more words per page	• Sentence pattern still apparent, but doesn't dominate text • Lots of repeated text • Highly predictable	• More detailed, less supportive of text	• Book language begins • More sophisticated sequence of events • Single event continues over several pages with a variation in sentence patterns	*The New Nest* by Sandra Iversen and Peter Paul Bajer
9	• Beginning of "literary language;" blend of oral and written language structures • More print on the page, mostly high-frequency • More new vocabulary, less likely to be repeated	• Longer sentences, compound and simple • Increased length of books	• Few patterns	• Picture cues less supportive of text	• Predictable story line with increasing sophistication; "twist" at the end • Conversations among several characters	*Dad's New Path* by Darrel and Sally Odgers and Grant Lodge
10	• Increasingly difficult vocabulary • More unfamiliar words per page, less likely to be repeated • May contain "book language"	• Longer sentences, little pattern • Increasing amounts of print • Longer stories, longer sentences • Line breaks at phrases • Up to a full page of text • Still likely to be enlarged font	• Patterns of phrases may be variable or no pattern at all • Predictability through rhyme, cumulative structure	• Pictures provide less direct support to text	• Conversations among many characters • More connected story line • May have "twist" at the end • Figurative or poetic language may appear • Single event continues over several pages	*Nobody Knew My Name* by Jan McPherson and Lyn Kriegler

Note. Anchor books have been selected from the Foundations series, distributed by the Wright Group.

empowering teachers to make choices about the materials that best suit the needs of their students. This leveling system continues to be a work in progress as teachers collaborate to identify ways to match texts to an increasingly diverse population of readers.

The leveling system we created involves explicit descriptions of what texts look like at each level of development.

Level 1 books have one or two words on each page to label illustrations of familiar concepts, such as *a ball* or *the moon*. The print is in a large, clear font and located in the same place on every page. This text should be accessible to any child who knows enough about English print to read from left to right and front to back, and who has the vocabulary base to identify the illustrations.

Level 2 books still tend to describe illustrations of familiar objects or actions, although they usually contain repeated phrases or simple sentences. Usually there is a pattern repeated throughout the book, with one word changed on each page, such as, *Here is a horse. Here is a dog. Here is a cow.* This sentence pattern may be slightly altered on the first or last page, such as *Here are the animals.*

Level 3 books contain a few more words per page, usually in complete sentences. Sometimes there are two sentences on a page. Two pattern changes (such as the verb and the noun) are not uncommon, such as, *At my party I ate some cake. At my party I played some games. At my party I opened some presents.* These books are still highly predictable, with clear, uncluttered pictures that directly support the text.

Level 4 books maintain a strong language pattern, often with two word changes in the pattern, or a changing prepositional phrase, such as, *The dog jumped over the fence. The fish swam in the lake. The birds flew in the sky.* The text essentially describes the illustrations; there is usually not a story line at this point. There is more text on each page than in previous levels, but the language continues to be simple and familiar, with many high-frequency words and concept words matching the illustrations. Sentences are longer, but the line breaks are usually at the ends of phrases. There is often a distinct space between lines.

By *Level 5*, the "reading work" has begun. Students must rely on more strategies than just looking at pictures or reciting patterns. They must have a repertoire of high-frequency words and some decoding skills. Rather than simply labeling pictures, there is usually a predictable story line, which requires the reader to attend more to meaning. The increasing length of sentences requires an understanding of syntax to support comprehension and decoding. There is more text on the page, and there may be dialogue among characters. Although the text structure may follow a pattern, it generally changes distinctly on the last page.

Level 6 texts move away from reliance on repetition on every page, but some repeated language patterns may appear throughout the text. A simple, predictable story line is evident, with strong direct support from illustrations. Sentences tend to be short and choppy, but there is more print on each page than in previous levels. Print continues to be large and placed consistently on each page. High-frequency and decodable words predominate.

By *Level 7*, some literary language and structure begin to emerge. There may be more than one event in the story and more detail in the story line. Sentences are still simple and, in general, the language still tends to be stilted and choppy. If sentence patterns are used, there may be two or three different ones throughout the story. The text is still dominated by high-frequency and decodable words. When new vocabulary is introduced, it is repeated several times throughout the book. Illustrations may represent ideas rather than specific words.

Level 8 books are longer with noticeably more text on each page, though the text is usually enlarged. There are more new words, often repeated throughout the text. Most vocabulary is high frequency, phonetically regular, or accessible from context. Students will need a range of cueing strategies to read at this level. There is a more sophisticated story line, with multiple events or a single event continuing over several pages. There may be a variety of forms of punctuation, including dialogue among characters. Illustrations are more detailed and support the concept of the story. Repetitive language patterns may be used, but do not continue throughout the book.

In *Level 9*, the books begin to take on the characteristics of a "real story," with occasional use of literary language. The story line continues to be predictable, but begins to demonstrate more sophistication, such as a surprise twist at the end. The books are longer. There are many compound sentences, such as, *Billy jumped on his skateboard and sped down the street.* Several characters may take part in the dialogue. There may be four or five lines of text on each page, consisting of predominantly high-frequency words. More new vocabulary is also introduced at this level.

Level 10 contain more unfamiliar words. There may be full pages of text, but it is still likely to be enlarged print. There are more compound sentences. The concepts continue to be familiar to most children, such as going to school or playing with friends. Shorter books with poetic language, expository text, or sophisticated concepts may be found at Level 10. The illustrations are more subtle and detailed, enhancing the story line rather than providing cues to the text.

Reading strategies

An additional support for teachers in our district is a description of the strategies needed by the reader to access text at each of the levels. This information lets teachers focus on the specific reading strategies needed by students to move to the next level.

Level 1
- Uses concepts about print (Clay, 1991b), such as directionality
- Understands the difference between picture and text
- Begins to match voice to print (number of words spoken equal to number of words in print)
- Reads pictures

Level 2
- Uses language patterns to predict
- Relies heavily on pictures to access text
- Relies on own speaking vocabulary and oral language structures

Level 3
- Predicts using text patterns
- Can return sweep to read two lines of text
- Begins to notice initial consonants
- "Gets mouth ready" to say the words
- Uses illustrations to check and confirm

Level 4
- Can return sweep with eyes to read one sentence spaced over two lines
- Uses language structures of prepositional phrases
- Notices punctuation
- Remembers repeated words
- Uses a core of high-frequency words
- Uses initial consonant to predict words

Level 5
- Uses patterns that consist of several words or an entire sentence
- Uses sentence syntax to predict text
- Notices differences and similarities in sentence patterns
- Begins to monitor comprehension (may pause before an uncertain word or after a miscue has been made)
- May self-correct miscues
- May reread a line for clarification
- Is building a small repertoire of sight words

Level 6

- Notices similarities and differences in parts of words
- Can skip a difficult word and read on for context
- Uses graphophonic cues beyond initial consonant: ending sounds, medial vowels, little words in big words, or onset-rimes
- Begins to rely on comprehension strategies such as self-monitoring
- Can retell key elements of the story

Level 7

- Begins to use structural cues such as root words and endings to decode
- Self-monitors reading for comprehension by pausing if a word doesn't make sense or going back and rereading
- Self-corrects when word doesn't make sense
- Uses story sense to predict story line

Level 8

- Begins to integrate visual, contextual, and syntactic cues for decoding
- Reads with more fluency and speed; uses punctuation and phrasing
- Can follow a single sentence or event over several pages
- Relies less on picture cues and more on large chunks of text for comprehension
- Has a large repertoire of sight words
- Sustains interest and motivation with longer text

Level 9

- Accesses more than one reading strategy; will try another if one doesn't work
- Can retell the story, recalling important details and omitting irrelevant points
- Notices conversations among characters and reflects differences in oral reading
- Notices and uses punctuation cues
- Begins to make inferences about stories

Level 10

- Reads with increased fluency and phrasing
- Continues to experiment with a variety of reading strategies
- Demonstrates willingness to take risks
- Notices and appreciates "book language" or new forms of text
- Can retell figurative language in own words
- Uses rhyme as a prediction strategy
- Has mastery of basic sight words

How does this system compare with other leveling systems?

Our leveling system is based on the work of such researchers as Clay (1991a), Fountas & Pinnell (1996), Hiebert (1999a, 1999b), and Peterson (1991). Clay's (1991a) Reading Recovery Levels were designed for intensive early intervention with children at risk for reading difficulties. It was Clay who impressed upon us the importance of teaching students to read using texts at their instructional levels, and laid the foundation for applying the "best practices" of Reading Recovery to all students. However, in view of the unique purpose for which Reading Recovery was designed, we felt that the gradients were too fine for general classroom use.

Fountas and Pinnell contributed much to extending leveled reading to classroom use, stressing the importance of "good first teaching for *all* children" (Fountas & Pinnell, 1996). Their leveling system uses similar criteria to Reading Recovery, such as amount and format of text, degree of predictability, and decodability and familiarity of vocabulary. We found their work to be a valuable resource. We agree that the process of analyzing, sorting, and categorizing text was an important step in teachers' professional understanding of reading instruction. We found that we were able to define our criteria more explicitly to meet the needs of our teachers and our own resource collections.

Many published collections, such as Foundations (Wright Group Canada), Little Celebrations (Pearson Education Canada), Shoebox Libraries (Scholastic Canada), PM Storybooks (Nelson Thompson Canada), and various others, are marketed as "leveled" collections. However, each uses its own system that may not be consistent with any others and is usually not clearly defined. This inconsistency makes it very difficult for teachers to integrate a variety of resources into their programs and emphasizes the need for a clearly defined process that teachers can use to incorporate new materials into their leveled reading collections. This was the impetus behind developing our own leveling system.

How to use leveled reading materials

As student populations become increasingly diverse, the need for ways to accommodate diversity has become ever more critical. We recognize that there is no single text that is appropriate for all students, just as there is no single method of teaching reading that works for all students. Leveled reading materials help teachers select texts at the instructional levels of their students. "Instructional level" implies that the teacher will prepare the students for potentially unfamiliar vocabulary and concepts using a picture walk or other prereading strategies. Our rule of thumb is that materials should be at least two levels below a student's instructional level for independent reading practice.

Leveled books are only one type of reading resource available to students. If we restrict all of the students' independent reading choices to our collections of leveled books, we jeopardize the motivation that comes from self-selection of reading materials. Interest and background knowledge will have a significant impact on the readability of a text for a particular student. Therefore, it is important for all students to learn to self-select reading materials that will be interesting and accessible to them.

Matching books to readers cannot be reduced to a formula. It requires a great deal of professional judgment on the part of the teacher. In order to make decisions about appropriate books for students, the teacher must know the students, the books, and the reading process. Texts within the same level have different degrees of appropriateness for different students, depending on their background knowledge and personal interests. For example, some urban children may be unfamiliar with farm animals, and prairie-born children may struggle with the easiest text on ocean life. It is important to remember that emergent readers usually cannot decode words that are not in their speaking vocabularies.

Many teachers worry that matching students to leveled reading materials represents a return to the stigmatized "reading groups" of the past. There are, however, three key differences:

- Using leveled reading materials for strategic reading instruction is only one component of a balanced literacy program, along with shared reading, independent reading, reading aloud, writing, and other activities.
- Groupings are flexible. As students progress in their ability to decode and comprehend increasingly difficult text, the groups are adjusted. Students do not remain in the same group all year.
- The teacher continually assesses the students' progress from one level to the next, so the students move to increasingly difficult texts at a pace that is appropriate for them.

Reading benchmarks

Part of our district's early literacy initiative has been to provide all teachers with a set of benchmark books representative of each of the levels from 1–10 and with inservice support in taking Running Records, analyzing miscues, and assessing comprehension. We do not use standardized tests for early reading assessment, but collect data on the instructional reading levels of our first- and second-grade students at two points in the year.

Collecting district data on first- and second-grade students' reading levels helps teachers know where their students fit in relation to others in the district. The data gives the administration information to share with the elected board and the public about what our students can do and where the needs for early intervention are greatest. We take a proactive approach to large-scale assessment by using authentic classroom assessment tools to gather data about reading achievement in our school district.

Ongoing professional development and continuing resource development help teachers refine their use of Running Records and benchmark books for classroom instruction. Teachers are brought together regularly to level new materials using our existing criteria and benchmark books. This information is added to a database. Teachers do not always agree on the level of a particular book, but it is the professional dialogue around coming to consensus that is the truly valuable process and that enhances our understanding of children, books, and reading. Our goal is not to achieve 100% consistency in leveling books; it is to help teachers understand the reading process and how best to teach it.

We continue to refine our leveling process as we extend our understanding of what matters in text selection for beginning readers. The process will be constantly modified and adapted as teachers apply it to classroom use and develop it into a structure that honors both the diversity of students and the professionalism of teachers.

References

Clay, M. (1991a). *Becoming literate: the construction of inner control.* Auckland, New Zealand: Heinemann.

Clay, M. (1991b). *The early detection of reading difficulties* (3rd ed.) Auckland, New Zealand: Heinemann.

Fountas, I., & Pinnell, G. (1996). *Guided reading: Good first teaching for all children.* Portsmouth, NH: Heinemann.

Fountas, I., & Pinnell, G. (1999). *Matching books to readers: A leveled book list for guided reading, K–3.* Portsmouth, NH: Heinemann.

Hiebert, E. (1999a). *Text matters in learning to read* (CIERA Report #1-001). Ann Arbor, MI: Center for the Improvement of Early Reading Achievement, University of Michigan School of Education. Available online: http://www.ciera.org

Peterson, B. (1991). Selecting books for beginning readers. In D. Deford, C. Lyons, & G. Pinnell (Eds.), *Bridges to literacy: Learning from reading recovery* (pp. 119–147). Portsmouth, NH: Heinemann.

Weaver, B. (2000). *Leveling books K–6: Matching readers to texts.* Newark, DE: International Reading Association.

Rog is a language arts consultant for Regina Public Schools (1600 4th Avenue, Regina SK S4R 8C8, Canada). She may be reached by e-mail at lrog@rbe.sk.ca. Burton is an instructor at the Gabriel Dumont Institute of the University of Regina.

From *The Reading Teacher*, Vol. 55, No. 4, December 2001/January 2002, pp. 348-356. Copyright © 2002 by International Reading Association. Reprinted by permission.

Guided Reading: Who is in the Driver's Seat?

By Susan Kidd Villaume and Edna Greene Brabham

Many of our discussions with teachers at different grade levels are marked by numerous questions about guided reading: Should basals, children's literature, or decodable texts be used? Should grouping be homogeneous or heterogeneous? Should instruction be systematic or responsive? Should students read orally or silently? These questions and others recur and bring guided reading into focus frequently on the RTEACHER listserv, in talks with teachers, at inservice sessions, in university courses, and during professional conferences. Our stance on all these questions is that the answer is "Yes!" Even though each question includes the word *or* and suggests choices, we feel that we risk losing sight of purposes for guided reading by privileging or dismissing any options. If we hang our hats on one correct answer, we limit opportunities to meet the individual and diverse needs of students. By extending our understandings of guided reading in action and in reading the professional literature (see Sidebar), we became convinced that effective guided reading instruction depends less on doing it the "right" way and more on reflecting on its purposes. We believe that a willingness to assume personal ownership for the concept of guided reading is at the core of effective implementation. This column is devoted to examples that show why and how

we and other teachers are probing purposes and taking ownership for guided reading instruction.

As we recalled the ways we once planned and implemented reading instruction, we were reminded of the U.S. Greyhound bus slogan "Leave the driving to us." Too often, we took the wheel and led students through predetermined lessons. In contrast, the concept of guided reading challenged us to think deeply about how to help students become independent, strategic, and self-extending readers. Focusing on these purposes for guided reading, the question "Who is in the driver's seat?" came to the forefront of our instructional decisions, and it provides the framework for this column. First, we tackle what it means to let the students do the driving during guided reading lessons. Next, we probe specific questions about how to maximize student time behind the wheel during different parts of these lessons. Finally, we offer our insights as to what challenges we face as we continue to explore effective guided reading instruction.

What does it mean to put students in the driver's seat?

Our early explorations of guided reading reflected our initial understandings of what it means to put

students in the driver's seat. As we met with students in small groups, we explicitly taught word-analysis skills and word-solving strategies. We selected texts based on assessments of students' needs. We became more sensitive to the frustration and shutdown that occurred when we asked students to read texts that were too difficult, and we developed an understanding of what is meant by instructional-level text. We watched with pride as students sat in the driver's seat and dealt strategically with unfamiliar words they encountered while reading. However, becoming independent and self-extending readers involves much more than developing expertise at the word level. Skillful readers build meaning in thoughtful and self-regulating ways as they activate and integrate numerous word-analysis and comprehension strategies; they also deftly and expertly maneuver their ways through many different types of texts and genres.

These realizations made us ask "Who is in the driver's seat?" as we scrutinized other aspects of guided reading lessons. Knowing that all teachers—ourselves included—must take the wheel and provide explicit instruction at times, we wrestled with this question, especially as we began to wonder if we were still spending too much time in the driver's seat. We also began to wonder if we were giving students sufficient opportunity to become competent behind the wheel as they read and studied informational texts. As a result of these reflections, we began to uncover previously untapped opportunities for putting students in the driver's seat by integrating expository materials and guided reading lessons. To illustrate these changes in our understandings, we use examples from a guided reading lesson with second graders who read and responded to an informational article about dinosaurs.

Who is in the driver's seat when text-related knowledge is activated?

Acknowledging that skillful readers link what they are reading to what they already know in thoughtful ways, we often positioned ourselves in the driver's seat to jumpstart the process. Sometimes we announced text-related topics and asked students to share what they knew about them. Often we recorded their responses using a K-W-L chart (What I Know-What I Want to Know-What I Learned; see Donna Ogle, *The Reading Teacher, 39,* 1986, pp. 564–570), or we created webs of information that they shared. At other times, we prepared anticipation guides and asked the students to respond to text-related statements. Although we successfully prompted students to probe their knowledge and beliefs about topics in texts, we realized that we were asking the students to leave most of the driving to us. We began to contemplate ways to allow students to take more responsibility for this aspect of guided reading.

We recalled that picture walks invite young readers to talk about what they see in the illustrations before they begin tackling the print. In this activity, students sit in the driver's seat as they identify topics and engage in spontaneous discussions of knowledge related to the text. We tried a similar strategy with older readers. We invited them to preview texts and to discuss what they noticed. We discovered that students could use clues from titles, illustrations, chapter headings, and bold print to identify text-related topics and activate prior knowledge. We also realized that encouraging students to do the driving during this aspect of a guided reading lesson provided them with opportunities to practice careful observations and to build on one another's knowledge by sharing their thoughts.

In our example of the second-grade guided reading lesson, the teacher began by prompting the students to look at the pictures and describe what they thought the article would be about. The children carefully examined the pictures and began talking excitedly about the two kinds of dinosaur depicted on the first page. They accurately noted that the illustration included a meat-eating and a plant-eating dinosaur. Encouraging students to dig deeper, the teacher pulled a Venn diagram from a file of graphic organizers. Using this familiar scaffold, she prompted the students to think about what was the same and different about these two types of dinosaur. From their positions in the driver's seat, the students launched into an animated and lively discussion in which they identified differences in teeth, neck lengths, overall size, and front legs. To remind students that they also needed to think about similarities, the teacher simply pointed to the overlapping portion of the Venn diagram. The students paused to think. Then one student blurted out that both types of dinosaur have been extinct for a long time.

From observations like this, we learned that graphic organizers are powerful conversational scaffolds even when we do not write on them. We discovered that just pointing (often silently) to different parts of familiar graphic organizers such as Venn diagrams, K-W-L charts, and word maps provides subtle but sufficient prompts to keep students in the driver's seat as they probe what they know about text-related topics. Some of our colleagues reminded us that written records of students' thinking are important, but we found that writing interferes with the pace of conversations. Many discussions that began as lively and dynamic conversations disintegrated into turn-taking rounds when we started transcribing student responses. Interestingly, we also realized that selectively pulling graphic organizers to fit topics at hand encourages students to think about logical structures for organizing and discussing information. This insight became apparent when a fourth grader paused during a conversation on cloning and remarked, "I think this calls for an agree/disagree chart."

Who is in the driver's seat when word problems are addressed?

Like many other teachers, we became aware that teaching words prior to reading denies students important opportunities to sit in the driver's seat and to acquire the problem-solving expertise demonstrated by skillful readers. We began to see that introducing vocabulary positions us in the driver's seat but found that a few minutes behind the wheel, when used wisely, allow us to contribute significantly to the development of independent, strategic, and self-extending readers. Consequently, we began to make more deliberate and thoughtful decisions about which potential problems, what skills, and how many words we introduce prior to reading.

In our second-grade example, the teacher predicted that several words in the article, including the dinosaurs' names, would provide challenges for students. Anticipating that the sheer length of these terms would be overwhelming, she decided to use a few minutes behind the wheel to review how to chunk long words and to practice with two of the dinosaurs' names. After this brief word-analysis lesson, she moved out of the driver's seat and let the students take the wheel to face

Further reading

Allen, J. (2000). *Yellow brick roads: Shared and guided paths to independent reading 4–12*. Portland, ME: Stenhouse.

Baumann, J.F., Hooten, H., & White, P. (1999). Teaching comprehension through literature: A teacher-research project to develop fifth graders' reading strategies and motivation. *The Reading Teacher, 53*, 38–51.

Brown, K.J. (1999/2000). What kind of text—for whom and when? Textual scaffolding for beginning readers. *The Reading Teacher, 53*, 292–307.

Clay, M. (1991). *Becoming literate: The construction of inner control*. Portsmouth, NH: Heinemann.

Cunningham, P., & Hall, D. (2001, May 9). Guided reading, self-selected reading, working with words, writing: The four blocks in classrooms that work. [Online]. Available: `http://www.wfu.edu/~cunningh/fourblocks`

Cunningham, P., Hall, D., & Defee, M. (1998). Nonability-grouped, multilevel instruction: Eight years later. *The Reading Teacher, 51*, 652–664.

Dowhower, S.L. (1999). Supporting a strategic stance in the classroom: A comprehension framework for helping teacher help students to be strategic. *The Reading Teacher, 52*, 672–688.

Fawson, P.C., & Reutzel, D.R. (2000). But I only have a basal: Implementing guided reading in the early grades. *The Reading Teacher, 54*, 84–89.

Fountas, I.C., & Pinnell, G.S. (1996). *Guided reading: Good first teaching for all children*. Portsmouth, NH: Heinemann.

Fountas, I.C., & Pinnell, G.S. (2001). *Guiding readers and writers grades 3–6: Teaching comprehension, genre, and content literacy*. Portsmouth, NH: Heinemann.

Headley, K.N., & Dunston, P. (2000). Teachers' Choices books and comprehension strategies as transaction tools. *The Reading Teacher, 54*, 260–268.

Hicks, C.P., & Villaume, S.K. (2000/2001). Finding our own way: Critical reflections on the literacy development of two Reading Recovery children. *The Reading Teacher, 54*, 398–412.

Mesmer, H.A.E. (1999). Scaffolding a crucial transition using text with some decodability. *The Reading Teacher, 53*, 130–142.

Opitz, M.F., & Ford, M.P. (in press). *Take five: Innovative and flexible strategies for guided reading*. Portsmouth, NH: Heinemann.

Routman, R. (2000). *Conversations: Strategies for teaching, learning, and evaluating*. Portsmouth, NH: Heinemann.

Short, R.A., Kane, M., & Peeling, T. (2000). Retooling the reading lesson: Matching the right tools to the job. *The Reading Teacher, 54*, 284–295.

the remaining word challenges as they encountered them in the text. When reading "This giant plant-eating dinosaur was discovered in 1987 in Argentina," one student stumbled on the word *discovered*. The teacher listened patiently as the student carefully chunked the word: "dis-coh-ver-ed." Noting the student's puzzled look, the teacher whispered, "That got you close. Don't forget to think what makes sense." The student, situated squarely in the driver's seat, smiled. She then backed up and reread the entire sentence correctly.

Our understandings of how to support students as they sit in the driver's seat and deal with word problems continue to evolve. We are becoming increasingly aware of the many different kinds of word problems that emerge. Sometimes the problem is similar to the one the student faced with the word *discovered*—students are familiar with a word's oral form but do not immediately recognize its written form. At other times, students pronounce a word accurately but find the meaning troublesome. For example, the teacher asked the second graders to pause while reading the dinosaur article and share any problems they had experienced. One student announced that he was confused about what the word *cast* meant in the sentence "He led the team that made the cast, or model skeleton, for the museum."

Providing assistance without grabbing the wheel, the teacher invited students to think about different meanings for this word by pulling a word map from the file of graphic organizers. She pointed to the part of the word map labeled "What are some examples?" One student recalled the cast he had when he broke his arm. Another described the casts of hands that he and his classmates made for their mothers when they were in kindergarten. A third student shared that her sister had a cast of her teeth made when she went to the orthodontist for braces. The teacher tapped the part of the word map that read "What is it?" Students concluded that "dinosaur casts" must be kind of like "teeth casts" and made out of that "plaster junk." The word map provided the support that the students needed to expand understandings of the word and, at the same time, to remain in the driver's seat.

Who is in the driver's seat during discussions of text?

In discussions intended to help students comprehend text, we often found ourselves sitting squarely in the driver's seat again. Time after time, we realized that we were retaking the wheel to ask our questions as we attempted to monitor and direct the ways that students constructed meaning. Reminding ourselves that the purpose of guided reading is to help students develop as independent, strategic, and self-extending readers, we began using our time behind the wheel more productively.

We taught specific comprehension strategies such as asking questions, making connections, and visualizing. When we paused for discussion during and after reading, we prompted students to stay in the driver's seat and to reflect on what had happened in their heads during their reading. Another look at the second-grade reading lesson provides an example.

After students finished reading the article, the teacher asked "What questions popped into your head when you were reading?" This simple prompt sparked a volley of inquiries: "What happens to the real dinosaur bones after they make the cast of them?" "How do they hook the cast bones together?" "Why are plant-eating dinosaurs so much bigger than meat-eating dinosaurs?" These questions, along with the discussion stemming from them, provided evidence that the students were situated in the driver's seat and actively building meaning in thoughtful and probing ways.

The ongoing challenge

For us, guided reading is a dynamic concept. It continues to evolve as we become increasingly aware of the complexity of the reading process and more adept at keeping students behind the wheel during their reading endeavors. We also remain convinced that our answer to each of the questions posed in the first paragraph of the column is a firm and resounding "Yes!" We believe that options presented in each question must be evaluated in light of whether they enable students to develop as independent, strategic, and self-extending readers. Because of students' different instructional needs and the complexity of the reading process, we find ourselves exploring the value of all options for guided reading. Sometimes we use basals, sometimes children's literature, sometimes decodable texts, and sometimes informational articles or content area textbooks. Sometimes we create groups of students who are reading on similar instructional levels; sometimes we form groups of students who will benefit from a particular strategy focus; and sometimes we group students heterogeneously to provide extended opportunities for sharing similar interests, collaborating, and peer modeling. Sometimes we provide systematic word analysis and comprehension instruction, and sometimes we teach in more spontaneous and responsive ways. Sometimes we ask students to take turns reading orally, sometimes we listen as they whisper read, and sometimes we have them read silently. Our in-structional decisions are grounded in ongoing assessments of students and their needs; they are not governed by "right" answers. We resist adopting a set of correct procedures that limits our expanding understandings and the potentials of guided reading.

As we think about the challenges involved in keeping students in the driver's seat during guided reading lessons, we are struck by the accompanying and parallel challenge to maintain our place behind the wheel in ongoing explorations of this topic. We cannot allow others to do the driving for us. Although professional literature and conversations continue to contribute significantly to our growth, we are committed to steering our own course as we probe purposes and take ownership of concepts behind guided reading. The books and articles in the Sidebar are important travel guides for ongoing explorations. We invite you to buckle up in your own driver's seat and journey along with us as you ask your own questions and create your own responses for guiding reading.

UNIT 4

Implementing Best Practices in the Field

Unit Selections

Key Points to Consider

- How can teachers incorporate the components of a balanced literacy program without giving up anything they are already doing?

- How much of what teachers are currently doing can be adequately justified in the climate of NCLB?

- How will teacher's attitudes help or hinder the balanced literacy process?

 **Links: www.dushkin.com/online/**
These sites are annotated in the World Wide Web pages.

Teaching Strategies
http://www.teachingstrategies.com

"**B**ut this is the way we've always done it," or "This, too, shall pass," are words we've often heard spilling from the lips of teachers. Perhaps we've even said them ourselves when asked to perform new methodologies which seem to conflict with the old. With the findings of the National Reading Panel and the establishment of No Child Left Behind, we are indeed expected to change *something*. However, we are left confused after teaching for years and seeing language arts programs and methods come and go. Change can not only be very painful, but frustrating, especially if it does not fit into our scheme of the way the world works, and no one is there to clear it up for us. So we rightfully resist in varying degrees. We hope the days of change for change's sake are gone. We are making a transition in the twenty-first century from various techniques which had validity, but were not effective in *isolation,* to using a variety of specific techniques *in the context* of reading, writing, and phonological awareness.

During the last thirty-plus years, educators have provided us with an abundance of data on literacy acquisition. Coupled with fresh action research, we are able to identify strategies that provide for appropriate, effective literacy learning in our classrooms. The key is to take a child from what is known to what is unknown no matter where the known begins. In some cases the known is lower than grade level, and in others it is above grade level (see Units 3 and 6).

It is often difficult to make sense of the overwhelming amount of research-based methods, but this unit offers educators a palette of best practices for literacy instruction. For successful implementation in the classroom, it is extremely important to have a keen awareness of the students' abilities, together with a positive attitude and high expectations for all.

The articles in this unit address and go beyond, the five key areas (phonemic awareness, phonics, fluency, vocabulary, and text comprehension) put forth by the National Reading Panel for K-3 reading instruction. Unit 3 established that effective literacy curriculum is balanced in its approach and applies to elementary, (4-6 grades) as well. Although there are some differing interpretations regarding the National Reading Panel's findings, the components promulgated therein are echoed in the position statements of the IRA & NAEYC.

Many teachers are already engaged in best practices; however, they can feel alienated and resistant when approached with new methods, before having their current practices validated. As suggested in Unit 2, teachers' professional development must be built upon like a scaffold just as they build upon children's learning. We can effect change with our students if we are constantly thinking about what is best for them. We must also bear in mind that there is not one magical teaching approach that works for every child, rather good teachers employ a variety of strategies to reach all children.

When I was thrust into a first grade classroom, I was consumed with fear. I did not know how I was to start the reading process with these children. I assumed that if I placed books in front of them, they would read. I pushed them into books that were too difficult and I drilled them on the textbook's opinion of what should be new vocabulary. I gave them spelling tests on words that they would rarely use in their writing, especially in first grade. I simply did not know what was appropriate. I improved as time went on, but the pivotal point in my career came when I began teaching Reading Recovery. The Reading Recovery learning was concurrent with my teaching. I saw immediately that what I lacked was not enthusiasm, but a global understanding of how "for-granted" we take children's learning to read. Until

I thought about my own literacy learning, I was unable to understand what tools a child needed to not only decode, but also make sense of what they read.

Once I became more introspective, I was able to synthesize my new learning into my classroom. When I started to see recognizable change that was directly linked to the new approaches I was implementing, I began to really believe that I could make a difference. As with anything, there is still some trial and error. As long as I stayed balanced in my attention to reading, writing, and phonological awareness, my students reached my high expectations. When I got out of balance, from time to time, my students' performance indicated that an adjustment was necessary.

Once I recognized that my Reading Recovery training had given me a gift that I needed to continue sharing, I sought out any teacher who was willing to be part of what I had learned. I encountered several, but one stands out in my memory.

Sara was a teacher that I observed wanting to continue in her own way. When asked to describe her way, she provided a litany of wonderful literacy activities including Teacher Read-Aloud, Shared Reading, and Shared Writing. It was easy to see the value in what she was already doing. Once she was validated, she was more willing to accept steps toward an even more effective approach. First, she added metacognition to her reading and writing lessons; then, she added phonological awareness to assist her student's reading and writing abilities. She began making connections herself. She had never stopped to realize that the things she, as a good reader and writer took for granted, were things that her students were unfamiliar with. After she modeled these behaviors for her students, they began to verbalize what had been modeled. She saw how a small shift in her practice could impact the students in such a positive way. Sara also began to use her students' strengths and weaknesses to drive her teaching. She took baby steps, and over time became an instrument of change. She became a model for colleagues, while simultaneously helping her students achieve new academic heights. Sara's class added one new learner—herself.

As you read the articles in this unit you will identify with them on a variety of planes. It is my sincere hope that you will validate yourself for the strong literacy work that you already have in place, and replace any less effective strategies with more powerful ones.

For a taste of what a balanced literacy program looks like, read "The Essentials of Early Literacy Instruction" and "Just Think of the Possibilities: Formats for Reading Instruction in the Elementary Classrooms." To delve in a little deeper, "Using Centers to Engage Children During Guided Reading Time: Intensifying Learning Experiences Away From the Teacher" provides a variety of strong literacy learning that needn't be teacher-directed once they are introduced.

In "Digging Up the Past, Building the Future: Using Book Authoring to Discover and Showcase a Community's History," there are embedded gems of literacy learning that students will participate in, unknowingly. It is an authentic vehicle for learning with a balanced approach as its backdrop.

Since comprehension is critical to reading, articles in this unit are devoted to it. "Our Students are Ready For This: Comprehension Instruction in the Elementary School," "A Comprehension Checklist: What if it Doesn't Make Sense," and "How Do You Know? A Strategy to Help *Emergent* Readers Make Inferences," all deal with comprehension as an integral part of the classroom. Special attention can be paid to "Our Students . . ." because it provides an extensive look at comprehension strategies with actual field examples. This benefits new and experienced teachers alike.

We are a nation in need of a literate work force. That strong work force starts in our classrooms. We have the ability to prepare our students for the challenges they will face. It is up to you to decide how to thoughtfully proceed from here.

Ingrid Laidroo

THE ESSENTIALS OF EARLY LITERACY INSTRUCTION

Kathleen A. Roskos, James F. Christie, and Donald J. Richgels

The cumulative and growing research on literacy development in young children is rapidly becoming a body of knowledge that can serve as the basis for the everyday practice of early literacy education (IRA & NAEYC 1998; National Research Council 1998; Yaden, Rowe, & MacGillivary 2000; Neuman & Dickinson 2001; NAEYC & NAECS/SDE 2002). Although preliminary, the knowledge base outlines children's developmental patterns in critical areas, such as phonological and print awareness. It serves as a resource for designing early literacy programs and specific instructional practices. In addition, it offers reliable and valid observational data for grounding approaches to early reading assessment.

That we know more about literacy development and acquisition, however, does not let us escape a central issue of all early education: What *should* young children be learning and doing before they go to kindergarten? What early literacy instruction should children receive? What should it emphasize—head (cognition) or heart (motivation) or both?

Real-life answers to these questions rarely point directly to this or that, but rather they are somewhere in the middle, including both empirical evidence and professional wisdom. While we will continue to wrestle with these complicated questions, we must take practical action so that our growing understanding in early literacy supports the young child as a wholesome, developing person.

What then are the essentials of early literacy instruction? What content should be included, and how should it be taught in early education settings? Our first response to these complex questions is described below in a skeletal framework for action. We briefly define early literacy, so as to identify what young children need to know and be able to do if they are to enjoy the fruits of literacy, including valuable dispositions that strengthen their literacy interactions. Then we describe two examples of instruction that support children's reading and writing learning before they enter the primary grades.

With the imagery of Pip's remark from *Great Expectations* in mind, we hope to show that well-considered early literacy instruction is certainly not a bramble-bush for our very young children, but rather a welcoming environment in which to learn to read and write.

THE LEARNING DOMAIN

Today a variety of terms are used to refer to the preschool phase of literacy development—emerging literacy, emergent reading, emergent writing, early reading, symbolic tools, and so on. We have adopted the term *early literacy* as the most comprehensive yet concise description of the knowledge, skills, and dispositions that precede learning to read and write in the primary grades (K–3). We chose this term because, in the earliest phases of literacy development, forming reading and writing concepts and skills is a dynamic process (National Research Council 1998, 2000).

Young children's grasp of print as a tool for making meaning and as a way to communicate combines both oral and written language. Children draw and scribble and "read" their marks by attributing meaning to them through their talk and action. They listen to stories read aloud and learn how to orient their bodies and minds to the technicalities of books and print.

When adults say, "Here, help me hold the book and turn the pages," they teach children basic conventions of book handling and the left-to-right, top-to-bottom orientation of English. When they guide children's small hands and eyes to printed words on the page, they show them that this is the source of the reading and that the marks have meaning. When they explain, "This says 'goldfish'. Do you remember our goldfish? We named it Baby Flipper. We put its name on the fishbowl," they help children understand the connection between printed words, speech, and real experience.

Children's early reading and writing learning, in other words, is embedded in a larger developing system of oral communication. Early literacy is an emerging set of relationships between reading and writing. These relationships are situated in a broader communication network of speaking and listening, whose components work together to help the learner negotiate the world and make sense of experience (Thelen & Smith 1995; Lewis 2000; Siegler 2000). Young children need

Essential Early Literacy Teaching Strategies

Effective early literacy instruction provides preschool children with developmentally appropriate settings, materials, experiences, and social support that encourage early forms of reading and writing to flourish and develop into conventional literacy. These basics can be broken down into eight specific strategies with strong research links to early literacy skills and, in some cases, with later elementary-grade reading achievement. Note that play has a prominent role in strategies 5, 6, and 8. Linking literacy and play is one of the most effective ways to make literacy activities meaningful and enjoyable for children.

1. Rich teacher talk

Engage children in rich conversations in large group, small group, and one-to-one settings. When talking with children,

- use rare words—words that children are unlikely to encounter in everyday conversations;
- extend children's comments into more descriptive, grammatically mature statements;
- discuss cognitively challenging content—topics that are not immediately present, that involve knowledge about the world, or that encourage children to reflect on language as an object;
- listen and respond to what children have to say.

2. Storybook reading

Read aloud to your class once or twice a day, exposing children to numerous enjoyable stories, poems, and information books. Provide supportive conversations and activities before, during, and after reading. Repeated reading of favorite books builds familiarity, increasing the likelihood that children will attempt to read those books on their own.

3. Phonological awareness activities

Provide activities that increase children's awareness of the sounds of language. These activities include playing games and listening to stories, poems, and songs that involve
rhyme—identifying words that end with the same sound (e.g., Jack and Jill went up the hill);
alliteration—recognizing when several words begin with the same sound (e.g., Peter Piper picked a peck of pickled peppers);
sound matching—deciding which of several words begins with a specific sound (e.g., show a child pictures of a bird, a dog, and a cat and ask which one starts with the /d/ sound).
Try to make these activities fun and enjoyable.

4. Alphabet activities

Engage children with materials that promote identification of the letters of the alphabet, including

- ABC books
- magnetic letters
- alphabet blocks and puzzles
- alphabet charts

Use direct instruction to teach letter names that have personal meaning to children ("Look, Jennifer's and Joey's names both start with the same letter. What is the letter's name? That's right, they both start with j").

5. Support for emergent reading

Encourage children to attempt to read books and other types of print by providing

- a well-designed library center, stocked with lots of good books;
- repeated readings of favorite books (to familiarize children with books and encourage independent reading);
- functional print linked to class activities (e.g., daily schedules, helper charts, toy shelf labels);
- play-related print (e.g., signs, menus, employee name tags in a restaurant play center).

6. Support for emergent writing

Encourage children to use emergent forms of writing, such as scribble writing, random letter strings, and invented spelling, by providing

- a writing center stocked with pens, pencils, markers, paper, and book-making materials;
- shared writing demonstrations in which the teacher writes down text dictated by children;
- functional writing opportunities that are connected to class activities (e.g., sign-up sheets for popular centers, library book check-out slips, Do not touch! signs);
- play-related writing materials (e.g., pencils and notepads for taking orders in a restaurant play center).

7. Shared book experience

Read Big Books and other enlarged texts to children, and point to the print as it is read. While introducing and reading the text, draw children's attention to basic concepts of print such as

- the distinction between pictures and print;
- left-to-right, top-to-bottom sequence;
- book concepts (cover, title, page).

Read favorite stories repeatedly, and encourage children to read along on the parts of the story they remember.

8. Integrated, content-focused activities

Provide opportunities for children to investigate topics that are of interest to them. The objective is for children to use oral language, reading, and writing to learn about the world. Once a topic has been identified, children can

- listen to the teacher read topic-related information books and look at the books on their own;
- gather data using observation, experiments, interviews, and such;
- use emergent writing to record observations and information; and
- engage in dramatic play to consolidate and express what they have learned.

As a result of such projects, children's language and literacy skills are advanced, and they gain valuable background knowledge.

writing to help them learn about reading, they need reading to help them learn about writing; and they need oral language to help them learn about both.

What early literacy instruction should children receive? What should it emphasize—head (cognition) or heart (motivation) or both?

Young children need writing to help them learn about reading, they need reading to help them learn about writing; and they need oral language to help them learn about both.

NECESSARY CONTENT AND DISPOSITIONS IN EARLY LITERACY

Early literacy holds much that young children might learn. Yet we cannot teach everything and must make choices about what content to teach and which dispositions to encourage. High-quality research provides our best evidence for setting priorities for what to address and how.

Recent reviews of research indicate at least three critical content categories in early literacy: oral language comprehension, phonological awareness, and print knowledge. They also identify at least one important disposition, print motivation—the frequency of requests for shared reading and engagement in print-related activities, such as pretend writing (Senechal et al. 2001; Layzer 2002; Neuman 2002; Lonigan & Whitehurst in press).

Children need to learn mainstay concepts and skills of written language from which more complex and elaborated understandings and motivations arise, such as grasp of the alphabetic principle, recognition of basic text structures, sense of genre, and a strong desire to know. They need to learn phonological awareness, alphabet letter knowledge, the functions of written language, a sense of meaning making from texts, vocabulary, rudimentary print knowledge (e.g., developmental spelling), and the sheer persistence to investigate print as a meaning-making tool.

Content of Early Literacy Instruction

Teaching preschool children
- what reading and writing can do
- to name and write alphabet letters
- to hear rhymes and sounds in words
- to spell simple words
- to recognize and write their own names
- new words from stories, work, and play
- to listen to stories for meaning

Valuable Dispositions of Early Literacy Instruction

Cultivating preschool children's
- willingness to listen to stories
- desire to be read to
- curiosity about words and letters
- exploration of print forms
- playfulness with words
- enjoyment of songs, poems, rhymes, jingles, books, and dramatic play

WRITTEN LANGUAGE IS HARDER TO LEARN THAN ORAL

Learning an alphabetic writing system requires extra work. Both spoken and written language are symbol systems for representing and retrieving meanings. In spoken language, meaning making depends on phonemes or sounds. As children gain experience with the language of their community, they learn which words (or sequences of phonemes) stand for which concepts in that language. For example, children learn that the spoken word *table* in English or *mesa* in Spanish names a four-legged, flat-topped piece of furniture.

Writing and reading with an alphabetic system involve an extra layer of symbols, where the phonemes are represented by letters. This means that beginners must both learn the extra symbols—the letters of the alphabet—and raise their consciousness of the phonemes (because, while speaking and understanding speech, we unconsciously sequence and contrast phonemes).

Speakers, for example, understand the two very different concepts named by the words *nail* and *lane* without consciously noticing that those words are constructed from the same three phonemes (/n/, /A/, and /l/), but in different sequences. When children learn to read, however, they must pay attention to those three phonemes, how they are sequenced, and what letters represent them.

Invented spelling is a phonemic awareness activity that has the added advantage of being meaningful and functional (Richgels 2001). Children nonconventionally but systematically match sounds in words that they want to write with letters that they know. For example, they may use letter names and sounds in letter names (/ch/ in H, /A/ as the name of the letter A, and /r/ in R) when spelling *chair* as HAR. Invented spelling begins before children's phonemic awareness is completely developed and before they know all the names of the letters of the alphabet. With encouragement from adults, it develops through stages that culminate in conventional spelling.

The meanings of both spoken and written language serve real purposes in our daily lives (Halliday

1975). We usually do not speak without wanting to accomplish something useful. For example, we might want to influence others' behavior ("Would you turn that down, please?"), express our feelings ("I hate loud music"), or convey information ("Habitual listening to loud music is a danger to one's hearing"). Similarly, with written messages we can influence behavior (NO SMOKING), express feelings (I ❤ NY), and inform (Boston 24 mi) while serving such added purposes as communicating across distances or preserving a message as a record or a reminder.

These added purposes require that written messages be able to stand on their own (Olson 1977). Written language is decontextualized; that is, the sender and receiver of a written communication usually do not share the same time and space. The writer is not present to clarify and extend his or her message for the reader. This means that young readers' and writers' extra work includes, in addition to dealing with phonemes and letters, dealing with decontextualization.

WHY DO THE EXTRA WORK?

Historically, societies have found the extra work of writing and reading to be worthwhile. The extra functions of written language, especially preserving messages and communicating across distances, have enabled a tremendous growth of knowledge. Individual children can experience similar benefits if teachers help them to acquire the knowledge and skill involved in the extra work of reading and writing while always making real to them the extra purposes that written language serves. We must cultivate their dispositions (curiosity, desire, play) to actively seek, explore, and use books and print. As they learn what letters look like and how they match up with phonemes, which strings of letters represent which words, and how to represent their meanings in print and retrieve others' meanings from print, they

must see also how the fruits of those labors empower them by multiplying the functionality of language.

With speech, children can influence the behavior of others, express their feelings, and convey information. A big part of motivating them to take on the extra work of reading and writing must be letting them see how the permanence and portability of writing can widen the scope of that influencing, expressing, and informing. Young children who can say "No! Don't!" experience the power of spoken words to influence what others do or don't do—but only when the speakers are present. Being able to write *No* extends the exercise of that power to situations in which they are not present, as morning kindergartners Eric, Jeff, Zack, and Ben realized when they wrote *NOStPN* (No stepping) to keep afternoon kindergartners from disturbing a large dinosaur puzzle they had assembled on the classroom floor (McGee & Richgels 2000, 233–34).

W ritten language is decontextualized; that is, the sender and receiver of a written communication usually do not share the same time and space.

THE PRACTICE OF EARLY LITERACY INSTRUCTION: TWO EXAMPLES

Unlike the very real and immediate sounds and meanings of talk, print is silent; it is obscure; it is not of the here and now. Consequently, early literacy instruction must often be explicit and direct, which is not to say that it must be scriptlike, prescriptive, and rigid (Schickedanz 2003). Rather it should be embedded in the basic activities of early learning long embraced by early education practice and research. These include reading aloud, circle time, small

group activities, adult-child conversations, and play.

Teachers can embed reading and writing instruction in familiar activities, to help children learn both the conventions of print and how print supports their immediate goals and needs. The two examples below show how what's new about early literacy instruction fits within tried-and-true early education practice.

INTERACTIVE STORYBOOK READING

Reading aloud has maximum learning potential when children have opportunities to actively participate and respond (Morrow & Gambrell 2001). This requires teachers to use three types of scaffolding or support: (a) before-reading activities that arouse children's interest and curiosity in the book about to be read; (b) during-reading prompts and questions that keep children actively engaged with the text being read; and (c) after-reading questions and activities that give children an opportunity to discuss and respond to the books that have been read.

Instruction can be easily integrated into any of these three phases of story reading. This highly contextualized instruction should be guided by children's literacy learning needs and by the nature of the book being read:

- information books, such as Byron Barton's *Airport*, can teach children new vocabulary and concepts;
- books, songs, and poems with strong rhymes, such as Raffi's *Down by the Bay*, promote phonological awareness; and
- stories with strong narrative plots, such as *There's an Alligator under My Bed*, by Mercer Mayer, are ideal for generating predictions and acquainting children with narrative structure, both of which lay a foundation for reading comprehension.

In addition, most books can be used to teach print recognition, book

Shared Reading to Learn about Story Plot

Here is how one teacher reads *There's an Alligator under My Bed*, by Mercer Mayer, to a group of four-year-olds.

Before reading. The teacher begins by saying, "Let's look at the picture on the cover of the book. [Shows a boy in bed with an alligator sticking out from beneath] The boy in this story has a *big* problem. Can anyone guess what that problem is?"

After the children make their guesses, the teacher points to the title and says, "The title of this book is *There's an Alligator under My Bed.* So Suzy and Joey were correct in guessing what the boy's problem is. How do you think the boy will get rid of the alligator?"

After several children share their predictions, the teacher begins reading the book aloud.

During reading. After reading the first section of the book, which introduces the boy's problem, the teacher pauses and asks, "Do you have any other ideas about how the boy might get rid of the alligator?"

The teacher reads the next two pages, which detail the boy's plan to leave a trail of bait to the garage, and then pauses to ask the children what the word bait means.

After reading the next section, in which the boy lays out a trail of food, the teacher asks, "What do you think the alligator is going to do?"

Finally, after reading the rest of the story, in which the alligator gets trapped in the garage, the teacher points to the note the boy left on the door to the garage and asks, "What do you think the boy wrote in his note?"

After reading. The teacher sparks a discussion of the book by asking several open-ended questions, such as "What did you like best about the story?" and "How would *you* have gotten rid of that alligator?"

Later, the teacher does a follow-up small group activity—to reinforce a sense of story plot, she helps children sequence a few pictures of the main story events.

---

concepts (e.g., cover, page), and concepts of print (e.g., print vs. pictures). Of course, instruction should be limited to several brief teaching points per reading so children can enjoy the read-aloud experience. Enjoyment and building positive dispositions should always be given high priority when reading aloud. For an example of how a teacher might do an interactive story reading session with *There's an Alligator under My Bed*, see "Shared Reading to Learn about Story Plot."

LITERACY IN PLAY

The general benefits of play for children's literacy development are well documented, showing that a literacy-enriched play environment exposes children to valuable print experiences and lets them practice narrative skills (Christie & Roskos 2003). In the following example, two preschoolers are playing in a restaurant activity center equipped with wall signs (Springville Restaurant), menus, pencils, and a notepad:

Food server: Can I take your order?

Customer: [Looks over the menu] Let's see, I'd like some cereal. And how about some orange juice. And how about the coffee with that too.

Food server: We don't have coffee. We're all runned out.

Customer: Okay, well . . . I'll just take orange juice.

Food server: [Writes down order, using scribble writing] Okay. I'll be right back with your order. (Roskos et al. 1995)

Here, the customer is using the literacy routine of looking at a menu and then placing an order. If the menu is familiar and contains picture cues, some emergent reading might also be taking place. The food server is using another routine—writing down customer orders—and is practicing emergent writing. In addition, the children have constructed a simple narrative story, complete with a problem (an item is not available) and a resolution (drop that item from the order).

A Vygotskian approach to developing mature dramatic play also illustrates the value of tangible play plans for helping children to self-regulate their behaviors, to remember on purpose, and to deliberately focus their attention on play activity—foundational cognitive skills of reading and writing (Bodrova & Leong 1998). We have found that preschoolers often spend more time preparing for their dramatizations than they spend acting out the stories. For example, one group of four-

year-olds spent more than 30 minutes preparing for a pizza parlor story (organizing felt pizza ingredients, arranging furniture for the pizza kitchen, making play money, and deciding on roles) and less than 10 minutes acting out the cooking, serving, and eating of the pizza meal. One would be hard pressed to find another type of activity that can keep young children focused and "on task" for this length of time.

Specific to early literacy, descriptive research shows that a literacy-in-play strategy is effective in increasing the range and amount of literacy behaviors during play, thus allowing children to practice their emerging skills and show what they have learned (Neuman & Roskos 1992). Evidence is also accumulating that this strategy helps children learn important literacy concepts and skills, such as knowledge about the functions of writing (Vukelich 1993), the ability to recognize play-related print (Neuman & Roskos 1993), and comprehension strategies such as self-checking and self-correction (Neuman & Roskos 1997). Like storybook reading, the literacy learning potential of play can be increased when it includes before-, during-, and after types of scaffolding as illustrated in "Guided Play to Explore New Words and Their Sounds."

Guided Play to Explore New Words and Their Sounds

With the teacher's help, the children are creating a gas station/garage play center as part of an ongoing unit on transportation.

Before play. The teacher provides background knowledge by reading *Sylvia's Garage*, by Debra Lee, an information book about a woman mechanic. She discusses new words, such as *mechanic, engine, dipstick, oil*.

Next, the teacher helps the children plan the play center. She asks children about the roles they can play (e.g., gas station attendant, mechanic, customer) and records their ideas on a piece of chart paper. She then asks the children to brainstorm some props that they could use in their center (e.g., signs, cardboard gas pump, oil can, tire pressure gauge) and jots these down on another piece of chart paper. The children then decide which props they will make in class and which will be brought from home, and the teacher or a child places an *m* after each make-in-class item and an *h* after each from home item.

During the next several days, the teacher helps the children construct some of the make-in-class props, such as a sign for the gas station ("Let's see...*gas* starts with a *g*. Gary, your name also starts with a *g*. Can you show us how to write a *g*?").

The list of props from home is included in the classroom newsletter and sent to families.

During play. The teacher first observes the children at play to learn about their current play interests and activities. Then she provides scaffolding that extends and enriches children's play and at the same time teaches important literacy skills. She notices, for example, that the mechanics are not writing out service orders or bills for the customers, so she takes on a role as an assistant mechanic and models how to write out a bill for fixing a customer's car. She monitors her involvement to ensure close alignment with children's ongoing activity.

After play. During small group activity time, the teacher helps children with a picture-sort that includes pictures of people and objects from their garage play. They sort the pictures into labeled columns according to beginning sounds—/m/ *(mechanic, man, map, motor)*; /t/ *(tire, tank, top, taillight)*; and /g/ *(gas, gallon, garden, goat)*. They explore the different feel of these sounds in the different parts of their mouths. They think of other words they know that feel the same way.

After modeling, the teacher gives the children a small deck of picture cards to sort, providing direct supervision and feedback.

CLOSING

We are gaining empirical ground in understanding early literacy learning well enough to identify essential content that belongs in an early childhood curriculum. Increasingly, the field can articulate key concepts and skills that are significant and foundational, necessary for literacy development and growth, research-based, and motivational to arouse and engage children's minds. The need to broadly distribute this knowledge is great—but the need to act on it consistently and carefully in instructional practice is even greater, especially if we are to steer children clear of the bramble-bushes and on to be successful readers and writers.

REFERENCES

Bodrova, E., & D. Leong. 1998. Development of dramatic play in young children and its effects on self-regulation: The Vygotskian approach. *Journal of Early Childhood Teacher Education* 19 (2): 115–24.

Christie, J., & K. Roskos. 2003. Literacy in play. In *Literacy in America: An encyclopedia of history, theory and practice*, ed. B. Guzzetti, 318–23. Denver, CO: ABC-CLIO.

Halliday, M.A.K. 1975. *Learning how to mean*. New York: Elsevier.

IRA & NAEYC. 1998. Joint Position Statement. Learning to read and write: Developmentally appropriate practices for young children. *Young Children* 53 (4): 30–46. Online (overview): www.naeyc.org/resources/position_statements/psread0.htm

Layzer, C. 2002. Adding ABCs to apple juice, blocks and circle time. Paper presented at the conference, Assessing Instructional Practices in Early Literacy and Numeracy, September, in Cambridge, Massachusetts.

Lewis, M. 2000. The promise of dynamic systems approaches for an integrated account of human development. *Child Development* 71: 36–43.

Lonigan, C., & G. Whitehurst. In press. Getting ready to read: Emergent literacy and family literacy. In "Family literacy programs: Current status and future directions," ed. B. Wasik. New York: Guilford.

McGee, L.M., & D.J. Richgels. 2000. *Literacy's beginnings: Supporting young readers and writers*. 3d ed. Needham, MA: Allyn & Bacon.

Morrow, L., & L. Gambrell. 2001. Literature-based instruction in the early years. In *Handbook of early literacy research*, eds. S. Neuman & D. Dickinson, 348–60. New York: Guilford.

NAEYC & NAECS/SDE (National Association of Early Childhood Specialists in State Departments of Education). 2002. Joint Position Statement. Early learning standards: Creating the conditions for success. Online: naeyc.org/resources/position_statements/earlylearn.pdf

National Research Council. 1998. *Preventing reading difficulties in young children*. Washington, DC: National Academy Press.

National Research Council. 2000. *From neurons to neighborhoods: The science of early childhood development*. Washington, DC: National Academy Press.

Neuman, S.B. 2002. What research reveals: Foundations for reading instruction in preschool and primary education. Handout of the U.S. Department of Education's Early Educator Academy, 14–15 November, in Los Angleles.

Neuman, S.B., & D. Dickinson, eds. 2001. *The handbook of early literacy research*. New York: Guilford.

Neuman, S.B., & K. Roskos. 1992. Literacy objects as cultural tools: Effects on children's literacy behaviors in play. *Reading Research Quarterly* 27 (3): 202–35.

Neuman, S.B., & K. Roskos. 1993. Access to print for children of poverty: Differential effects of adult mediation and literacy-enriched play settings on environmental and functional print tasks, *American Educational Research Journal* 30 (91): 95–122.

Neuman, S.B., & K. Roskos. 1997. Literacy knowledge in practice: Contexts of participation for young writers and readers. *Reading Research Quarterly* 32 (1): 10–33.

Olson, D.R. 1977. From utterance to text: The bias of language in speech and writing. *Harvard Educational Review* (47): 257–81.

Richgels, D.J. 2001. Invented spelling, phonemic awareness, and reading and writing instruction. In *Handbook of early literacy research*, eds. S.B. Neuman & D. Dickinson, 142–55. New York: Guilford.

Roskos, K., C. Vukelich, J. Christie, B. Enz, & S. Neuman. 1995. Linking literacy and play. Videotape (12 min.) and facilitator's guide. International Reading Association.

Schickedanz. J. 2003. Engaging preschoolers in code learning. *In Literacy and young children*, eds. D. Barone & L. Morrow, 121–39. Newark, DE: International Reading Association.

Senechal. M., J. LeFevre, K.V. Colton, & B.L. Smith. 2000. On refining theoretical models of emergent literacy. *Journal of School Psychology* 39 (5): 439–60.

Siegler, R. 2000. The rebirth of children's learning. *Child Development* 71 (1): 26–35.

Thelen, E., & L.B. Smith. 1995. *A dynamic systems approach to the development of cognition and action.* Cambridge, MA: The MIT Press.

Vukelich, C. 1993. Play: A context for exploring the functions, features, and meaning of writing with peers. *Language Arts* 70: 386–92.

Yaden, D., D. Rowe, & L. MacGillivary. 2000. Emergent literacy: A matter (polophony) of perspectives. In *The handbook of reading research*, vol. 3, eds. M. Kamil, P.B. Mosenthal, P.D. Pearson, & R. Barr, 425–54. Mahwah, NJ: Erlbaum.

Kathleen A. Roskos, Ph.D., is the director of the Ohio Literacy Initiative at the Ohio Department of Education and is a professor at John Carroll University in Cleveland. She coordinated Bridges and Links, one of the first public preschools in Ohio, and is instrumental in the development of content guidelines in early literacy. Kathleen studies early literacy development, teacher cognition, and the design of professional education for teachers.

James F. Christie, Ph.D., is a professor of curriculum and instruction at Arizona State University in Tempe, where he teaches courses in language, literacy, and early childhood education. His research interests include children's play and early literacy development. James is the president of the Association for the Study of Play.

Donald J. Richgels, Ph.D., is a professor in the literacy education department at Northern Illinois University in DeKalb, where he teaches graduate and undergraduate courses in language development, reading, and language arts.

Beyond the Journal. This article also appears on NAEYC's Website: www.naeyc.org.

Illustrations © Diane Greenseid.

Just Think of the Possibilities: Formats for Reading Instruction in the Elementary Classroom

The purpose of this article is to describe six basic formats that can be used to teach reading in the elementary classroom: shared reading, read-aloud, guided reading, Readers Theatre, sustained silent reading, and literature circles. Each format is discussed by describing the focus of instruction, suggestions for implementation strategies, and examples of materials that could be utilized. For each approach, a description of the focus of instruction is offered, along with suggestions for implementation, examples of instructional materials, and a list of print resources.

Kimberly Kimbell-Lopez

In the elementary classroom, a variety of approaches or formats are used to instruct children in how to read. Merriam-Webster Online defines format as "the general plan of organization, arrangement, or choice of material." In terms of reading instruction, the term "format" correlates well with the many different options that can be used to most effectively meet the literacy needs of our students. The formats that will be discussed in this article are shared reading, read-aloud, guided reading, Readers Theatre, sustained silent reading, and literature circles.

Each of these formats differs in terms of the number of students involved, the amount and type of materials used, the structural elements included in the lesson, and the specific focus or content emphasized. Some of the options for decision making that must be addressed once the reading format is selected are identified below:

How are the students grouped?
- heterogeneous versus homogeneous (visit Education World for a discussion)
- whole group, small group, or one-on-one (Education Place features an article)

What type of reading materials will be used?
- big book or text written on chart paper or overhead (see the Patchogue-Medford Literacy Initiative for more information)
- guided reading sets (visit Suite 101.com for a discussion)

- novel sets by theme (the SESD Teacher Resource page features a list of themes)
- picture books (go to the New York Public Library site for suggestions)

What is the focus of the lesson?
- modeling of concepts about print (North Central Regional Educational Library provides a definition)
- reading for enjoyment (visit Saskatchewan Learning for some guidelines)
- monitoring student use of reading strategies (go to the NCTE site to access an article)
- modeling how to use a particular strategy using think aloud (Suite 101.com features a discussion)

Using a combination of these six reading formats, it is possible for students to have multiple interactions with a text and thereby to practice and apply word recognition, fluency, and reading comprehension strategies. Morrow, Strickland, and Woo (1998, p. 82) have stated that grouping children in a variety of arrangements eliminates the stigmas attached to a single grouping system and allows children to interact with all others in the class. The amount of teacher or peer modeling of strategy use will vary depending on the particular format that is selected. Strickland (2002, online document) and Opitz (2000, online document) both expand on the concept of flexible grouping to facilitate the teaching of reading.

It is also important to consider which of the formats would be most developmentally appropriate based on the needs of individual children in the classroom. The International Reading Association (IRA) has produced a joint position statement with the National Association for the Education of Young Children (NAEYC) that includes a continuum of children's development in early reading and writing (IRA/NAEYC, 1998, online document).

Varying Instruction Using These Formats

The students in our classrooms today vary greatly in their needs and ability levels. As a result, it is necessary to provide multiple opportunities for students to read so that they can develop their ability to read and comprehend text. Teacher or peer modeling of different reading formats can help to ensure that students see effective application of strategies, and that they have the opportunity to practice and apply these strategies within the context of real reading. The Center for the Improvement of Early Reading Achievement (CIERA) identifies 10 research-based principles for improving reading achievement. Addressed within these principles is the need for primary-level instructional activities to promote growth in word recognition through instructional activities that include repeated reading of text, guided reading and writing, strategy lessons, reading aloud with feedback, and conversations about texts children have read. CIERA (1998) also states that proficient reading in third grade and above is sustained and enhanced by programs that adhere to four fundamental features:

1. Deep and wide opportunities to read
2. The acquisition of new knowledge and vocabulary, partially through wide reading but also through explicit attention to acquiring networks of new concepts through instruction
3. An emphasis on the influence that the kinds of text (e.g., stories versus essays) and the ways writers organize particular texts has on understanding
4. Explicit attention to assisting students in reasoning about text

Duffy-Hester (1999, p. 489) states that through reading aloud, students hear quality literature read to them; through guided reading, they read materials written on their instructional level with teacher guidance and minimal support; through shared reading, they read materials that may be too difficult for them to read independently with the support of other students and the teacher; and through independent reading, they read easy materials. One other format, literature circles, makes it possible to transform power relationships in the classroom, to make students both more responsible for and more in control of their own education, to develop lifelong readers, and to nurture a critical, personal stance toward ideas (Daniels, 1994, p. 31). In addition, the use of Readers Theatre provides an opportunity to enhance comprehension of text (Burns, Roe, & Ross, 1999, p. 204) as well as to create interest in and enthusiasm for learning (Ruddell, 1999, p. 236).

How Much Time Is Enough?

An issue raised by many educators is the amount of time that should be spent reading. In describing observations of more ef-
fective versus less effective teachers, Allington (2001) states that the more effective teachers had students reading for longer periods of time than the less effective teachers. Typically, the more effective teachers engaged their students in reading for 40 to 45 minutes per every hour allocated to reading instruction. In contrast, the less effective teachers had their students reading approximately 25 minutes of this one-hour block. The less effective teachers spent more time doing follow-up such as response activities, workbook exercises, story review, and vocabulary checks. Allington observed similar disparities in social studies and science classrooms where the more effective teachers had students reading two to three times as much material in these content areas as did the less effective teachers.

Allington (2001) discusses the fact that there is no exact time identified by research as being ideal for readers to develop proficiency in reading. He further states:

> Time spent reading, my preferred measure of volume, is important. The research does not provide clear evidence on whether one type of reading is better than another. In other words, increasing the volume of oral or silent or choral or paired reading or almost any combination of these has been shown to enhance achievement. It does seem reasonable that older and more experienced readers might read more often silently and beginning readers might more often read aloud. But as long as children and adolescents are reading, the type of reading seems less critical. (p. 35)

When considering the possibilities for reading instruction, remember the needs of the students in your classroom. What works best for one student might not necessarily work for another. When the possible formats for reading are varied, there is an increased probability that the student will receive an appropriate amount of skill and strategy instruction as well as the time and opportunity to practice reading in authentic contexts. In addition, the probability of pressing the "magic button" that turns a child on to reading is much greater.

Shared Reading

> Shared reading is a time when the entire class gathers together to share a variety of literacy experiences by reading and discussing a variety of texts (Fisher & Medvic, 2000, p. 3).

What Is Shared Reading?

Shared book experience is a reading format that is useful for developing a sense of story and narrative. It involves a daily time set aside for reading and rereading favorite rhymes, songs, poems, chants, and stories to and with children in order to demonstrate that reading is a pleasurable and meaningful experience (Butler & Turbill, 1987, p. 61). In shared reading, children participate in reading, learn critical concepts of how print works, and get the feel of learning (Fountas & Pinnell, 1996, p. 1). This format is a great way to share and demonstrate the pleasure of reading a good book with young children.

The Montgomery County Public School Department of Academic Programs provides an early literacy guide at their website that addresses basic elements of the shared reading activity. It features information focusing on conducting the shared reading session, procedures to follow, learning that can be observed, and ideas for after the shared reading activity. LingualLinks provides further information about using shared reading through a summary and guidelines for implementation. A third resource on shared reading is provided by the University of West Florida through its discussion Shared Reading: A Strategy That Leads Towards Better Readers. Specific topics that are addressed pertain to maintaining student interest in shared reading, selecting a lesson focus, choosing resources and materials, and creating your own shared reading lesson.

Cathy Corrado (May/June, 1999) discusses Shared Reading and Writing: Directing the Tour Through Text from *Perspectives in Education and Deafness: Practical Ideas for the Classroom and Community*. Corrado discusses how she uses the shared reading experience when working with deaf and hard-of-hearing second through fifth graders. As she reads a story, students are invited to read along silently or to sign along with her. She and her students look for main ideas and predict what will happen in the storyline as she teaches reading strategies and the basic concepts needed to decode print. She makes note of how repeated readings of a text can help all students develop confidence in their ability to read.

Familiarity With the Text

Students can join in shared reading as they become more familiar with the text, or in some cases listen as the rest of the class reads the story. Fisher and Medvic (2000, p. 29) state that familiarity supports learning to read, independence in reading, fluency, comprehension, vocabulary development, and love of learning. Eventually, most children join in with the shared reading once they have become familiar with the text. As the teacher reads aloud from the big book, the students are able to follow along or read along with her. The teacher models concepts about print through the left to right movement of text on the page, and the return sweep as the reader moves from top to bottom in the text. Students experience the inflections and rhythm of the teacher's voice when she foreshadows events in the text by lowering or raising her voice or by the pace in which she reads the story. Through subsequent readings, an understanding of capitalization and punctuation increases as the students begin to read along with the teacher. The shared reading introduces students to colorful language and presents new vocabulary and concepts in a safe and supportive atmosphere. Best of all, it scaffolds the student's learning experience so that eventually, each can go and read the book independently based on the shared-book experience.

Types of Books

McCracken and McCracken (1995) suggest that some of the books we read to children should be those that are easily memorized. Use of these types of books helps children to learn about how print works, about story structures, word recognition, and the fact that books can be a source of enjoyment as well as information. McCracken and McCracken (1995) suggest six types of books that provide these learning opportunities (pp. 41-64):

Rhythmic books. The rhythm of the text enables children to anticipate some of the words. An example would include Leland B. Jacobs book, *Good Night, Mr. Beetle* where each line follows the format, "Good night, _____," with a culminating line for "The moon's in the sky."

Repetitive books. Many books contain repetitive text by which children can easily learn and join in during that part of the reading. The classic story of the *Three Little Pigs* provides an example of repetition:

I'll huff and I'll puff, and I'll blow your house in.

Cumulative books. This type of text continually builds each page by repeating text from previous pages and adding a new line of text with each new page. For example, in the *House that Jack Built*:

This is the house that Jack built.

This is the malt that lay in the house that Jack built.

This is the rat, that ate the malt, that lay in the house that Jack built.

Basic sentence pattern books. In this type of book, a basic sentence pattern is used to provide support for the reader. For example, the basic pattern could be represented by, "This is my _____," which is repeated on every page with variations in the last blank of the sentence (i.e., dog, cat, etc.). Dick Bruna's *My Shirt Is White* and Lois Lenski's *Mr. Small* books provide examples of this type of book.

Two-part books. Brown, Brown Bear, What do You See? by Bill Martin Jr, is a good example of a two-part book. This type of text reads like a conversation in which a question is asked by one animal over two lines in the book, and a response from another animal is given with a subsequent two lines.

Information books. These books do not follow a storyline, but are instead full of information about content-related topics. Use of information books is a good way to support students as they learn vocabulary, facts, and concepts. Examples include *Antarctica* by Helen Cowcher, *Sharks* by Russel Freedman, and *Pumpkin, Pumpkin* by Jeanne Titherington.

Using information books as part of the shared reading activity also provides an opportunity to teach about tables of contents, reading tables, charts and diagrams, and the index and glossary. The use of these books also provides a support structure where children can easily practice and rehearse what they are learning about books, stories, story structures, language patterns, and language structures. For additional resources, the Montgomery County Public Library's website provides a listing organized by type that includes cumulative, repetitive, rhyme, and pattern books.

Connections and Extensions

- Write the story, or a portion of the story on sentence strips so that students can retell or build the story in a pocket chart (McCracken & McCracken, 1995).
- Cover up key portions of the text to focus on vocabulary or graphophonic elements of particular words.
- Assign children roles by giving them index cards labeled with each character's name. The students then wear the role tag and act out the story as a creative drama activity (Fisher & Medvic, 2000).
- Have children write a big book that extends from the storyline by predicting what would happen next if the story were to continue.
- Use puppets for role-playing so that students can dramatize and become the character (Fisher & Medvic, 2000).

Read-Aloud

Three keys to the success of read-aloud is that it is fun, it is simple, and it is cheap (Trelease, 1989b).

A read-aloud session is a method framework often used by teachers to develop independent readers (Leu & Kinzer, 1999). Jim Trelease's *The New Read-Aloud Handbook* is a wonderful resource for teachers and parents. It provides information on getting started with read-alouds, along with a collection of recommended books. The read-aloud event involves social relationships among people—teachers and students, parents and children, and authors and readers (Morrow and O'Connor, 1995, p. 102). By participating in the read-aloud experience, children are able to see that print differs from speech and that it carries a message.

As part of the read-aloud, the teacher models good oral reading—expression and intonation—and introduces children to a variety of language patterns as well as new vocabulary and concepts. The enjoyment children receive from read-alouds sparks their desire to read for themselves in a way that worksheets can not (Campbell, 2001, p. 91). Reading aloud can easily be used as a way to model thinking aloud about what is being read and to highlight strategies that good readers use. This type of format is appropriate across all grade levels from kindergarten up to college.

For more information on how to do a read-aloud, the Montgomery County Public Schools' website addresses the rationale for using read-aloud, the most effective way to read aloud, procedures for implementation, and criteria for selection. Another resource, which features activities written by Teresa Matthews and used with fifth graders is provided by the Yale-New Haven Teachers Institute: Beyond R. L. Stine: Read-Aloud Books and Group Activities for Fifth Graders.

Guidelines

The National Education Association's website includes tips for reading aloud from the Public Broadcast System's *Between the Lions*. The Bank Street College of Education also provides helpful hints for reading tutors to follow when conducting read-aloud sessions.

Trelease (1989a), author of *The New Read-Aloud Handbook*, also offers some general guidelines to follow when reading aloud to your class:

1. Start with picture books and build to storybooks and novels. A sampling of recommended books can be found at a website hosted by Jim Trelease and Reading Tree Productions. The full *Treasury of Read-Alouds* can be found in the print version of *The New Read-Aloud Handbook.*
2. Practice the story ahead of time to get a feel for voice inflection and expression.
3. Adjust your voice tone and pace for exciting and suspenseful parts of the book.

In addition to a list of what should be done, Trelease also provides a list of what should not be done so that students are not turned off to the read-aloud experience:

1. Do not read books that you do not enjoy yourself.
2. Choose another book if the one selected turns out not to be a good choice.
3. If your students have seen the book as a movie or on television, then select another book. It is likely their interest will be diminished if they know the plot and outcome ahead of time.

In addition, when choosing books for read-aloud, try not to be influenced by the awards a book may have won. Awards such as the Caldecott and Newbery are given for the quality of the writing, and how well a book might read aloud to an audience is not necessarily considered. Instead, select books that are recommended by children, such as those identified by the International Reading Association's Children's Choices book awards cosponsored with the Children's Book Council. For a list of other favorites, try out *Education World Online*, which features a list of book titles recommended by school principals to be used when reading aloud to children.

Don't Forget Informational Books

Remember to include information books when selecting the book for your read-aloud session. Moss (1995, pp. 122-123) identifies five reasons why it is important to read nonfiction books aloud.

1. It expands children's knowledge, thereby contributing to schema development, a critical factor in comprehension.
2. It sensitizes children to the patterns of exposition.
3. It provides excellent tie-ins to various curricular areas.
4. It promotes personal growth and moves children to social response.
5. It whets children's appetite for information, thus leading to silent, independent reading of this genre.

Through selection of information books that cover such topics as the rainforest, dinosaurs, World War II, and the Civil War, children are provided opportunities to explore the world around them. CreativeClassroomOnline hosts a page about non-fiction features, which discusses organizational features, language features, and the ways that reading nonfiction differs from reading other types of texts.

Interactive Read-Aloud

A variation of the read-aloud is the interactive read-aloud, which encourage verbal interaction with the text, peers, and teacher (Barrentine, 1996a; Campbell, 2001). The interactive read-aloud is an instructional practice that uses dialogue to assist and enable novices in the meaning-making process (Barrentine, 1996b). In addition to assisting meaning construction and developing shared meanings, interactive read-alouds can promote intimate familiarity with a story, enhance enjoyment of stories, allow for positive social interaction, and provide rehearsal of comprehension strategies (Barrentine, 1996b, p. 53). Interactive Read-aloud with First Grade ELLs discusses how one teacher used the read-aloud in her dual language classroom of language-minority students whose home language is Spanish.

Connections and Extensions

- Take the time to discuss the book before reading each day, but also leave time at the end of the read-aloud session to do so as well. Go back and reread special sections of the book and talk about your students' different interpretations of the particular event. Invite them to talk about why a character reacted in a certain way.

- Provide opportunities for students to share their thoughts through journals writing. Encourage them to write about what was read, evaluate the material, ask questions about what is happening in the book, and make connections to self and connections to movies or other books.

- Have students reenact the story as a creative drama activity. For books that are longer, students can work in groups to select key events from the story to reenact.

- Listen to music that reflects the content or time period of the story.

- Embark on an Internet information search about the author or illustrator to learn more about each one. Many authors now have webpages that highlight their lives and books. The Children's Book Council features a webpage that provides links to a variety of authors and illustrators. Some authors have e-mail addresses listed at their websites for those who are interested to correspond them. For example, when visiting the website for Jane Yolen, there is an e-mail link that can be selected to send her a message.

The Development and Dissemination Schools Initiative, a five-year project of the New York City Board of Education's Office of English Language Learners and the Education Alliance at Brown University, features information on its website on how to adapt the interactive read-aloud in dual-language classrooms. This resource, Adapting the Interactive Read-Aloud, addresses the use of read-aloud with second-language learners and provides a description of the strategies that were used as part of the project during the 1999-2000 school year.

Guided Reading

It is through Guided Reading that teachers can show children how to read and can support children as they read (Fountas & Pinnell, 1996, p. 1).

In IRA's summary of the National Reading Panel Report, guided oral reading with feedback was found to positively impact word recognition, reading fluency, and comprehension. The use of this format across grade levels was found to help children recognize new words, read with more accuracy, read with more ease, and understand what they were reading.

The teacher's goal during guided reading is to interest the children in the story, relate it to their experience, and provide a frame of meaning that will support problem solving (Fountas & Pinnell, 1996, p. 8). During the guided reading session, the teacher works with a small group of children who use similar reading processes and are able to read similar levels of text with support. The teacher introduces the book and ties it in to their prior knowledge. She then walks the students through the text, highlighting vocabulary and concepts they may come across when they read the book independently. As the students read the book softly to themselves, the teacher monitors individuals for evidence of reading strategies that are being applied, or in some cases, not applied.

During the session, one to two teaching points may be addressed (i.e., calling attention to a word in context; locating and noticing specific features such as beginning or ending). The ultimate goal of the guided reading is for students to be able to read text independently and silently. A discussion of guided reading at the Montgomery County Public School's website provides additional information about the benefits, principles, materials, and evaluation procedures.

Patricia Cunningham's website details how guided reading is an integral part of her Four Blocks approach. In contrast to Fountas and Pinnell, Cunningham advocates the use of heterogeneous groups versus homogeneous groups when working with the guided reading groups. Cunningham uses a variety of partner, small group, and whole group formats in order to make the guided reading session as multilevel as possible. The students who meet in these groups change regularly and better readers are included who serve as models for the struggling readers.

Selecting the Text

A general rule of thumb when selecting texts for guided reading is that the children should be able to read the text with 90% or higher accuracy. A text that is within this range enables children to draw on their knowledge of visual as well as meaning and structure cues. When the student is reduced to simple word calling because the text is too difficult, then he or she becomes unable to construct meaning or to cross-check and self-monitor. Staying within the 90% range allows "children to sustain attention while problem solving an extended piece of text and, in doing so, build a system of strategies that they can use for reading other texts" (Fountas & Pinnell, 1996, p. 9).

One key to the success of guided reading is the selection of books that are on the level of readers in the group. One website about leveled books allows the user to search for books according to the reading recovery level or by title of book, author, imprint, or publisher. Other resources that allows readers to search an interactive database for leveled books include the Beaverton School District and Portland Public Schools websites. Selecting from a range of materials that includes fiction and nonfiction guarantees that children are also exposed to different types of text features.

The text selection should also be based on the focus of instruction for the lesson, which will be dependent on the interventions that are needed by each child. In other words, students will be placed in groups based on strategic behaviors that they may already have or may be missing or need additional work. This placement should then build on previous strengths to help improve weaknesses that have been noted during instructional activities. Carolyn Schmidt's website includes a discussion on strategies, minilessons, and assessment.

The Dynamic Aspect of Grouping

Another important aspect of guided reading is that the groups are dynamic (Fountas & Pinnell, 1996), and constantly changing, based on the teacher's ongoing observation and assessment of each child. The teacher's use of running records for each child enables her to effectively monitor the student's use of reading strategies. The teacher keeps careful records of guided reading, including books read, running records, and any notes on specific reading behaviors.

What About the Rest of the Class?

The most common concern among teachers wishing to implement this format relates to what the rest of the class is doing when the teacher is working with the guided reading group. The answer is the use of literacy centers, which are ideal for classrooms at all levels of learning—not just primary but also intermediate levels. It is important to introduce the centers slowly so that learning routines and procedures can become established.

Kathy Shrock's Guide for Educators offers a listing of links for more information on possible literacy centers that can be used in the classroom. In addition, Fountas and Pinnell (1996) recommend a variety of centers that can be managed using a workboard. The purpose of the workboard is to diagram the names of children in groups, along with names and pictures of routine tasks in the classroom, thereby providing a flexible way of rotating students through the centers. Fountas and Pinnell describe the use of an ABC center involving letter or word activities using magnetic letters, a listening center with a variety of stories on tape, a writing center where children's journals and other writing resources are stored, a drama center with puppets or other props to role play or act out the story, a poetry center with a box of poems the children have heard the teacher read or children have learned to read during shared reading, and a computer center where children can learn to write their own stories

using publishing software or play games that extend and enrich language and literacy.

Connections and Extensions

- Build on the grammar of the story and write a class big book using the format.
- Retell the story by acting out using puppets or other props.
- Draw a picture and write about your favorite part of the story.
- Make a list of interesting words (i.e., describing/adjective, action/verb, naming/noun, etc.) or high-frequency words that were found in the story. To reference lists of high-frequency words, the Dolch list can be found at The School Bell website.
- Look back through the book and write targeted words on chart paper (i.e., words ending in -ed, -s, -es, -ing; words beginning with certain sounds—sh, th, wh; different ways to say "said"—shouted, whispered).

Readers Theatre

The Reader's Theater format offers a way for readers to participate in repeated readings in a meaningful and purposeful context (Martinez, Roser, & Strecker, 1998/1999).

Readers Theatre is another way to enhance comprehension of text (Burns, Roe, & Ross, 1999, p. 204) as well as to create interest in and enthusiasm for learning (Ruddell, 1999, p. 236). Readers Theatre is unlike a traditional play where students have costumes, sets, and have memorized lines. Instead, students read aloud from a script using their voices and facial expressions to share the story. This format provides an opportunity for students to develop fluency in reading through the multiple readings of the text, using expressiveness, intonation, and inflection when rehearsing the text. The Readers Theatre format offers a way for readers to participate in repeated readings in a meaningful and purposeful context (Martinez, Roser, and Strecker, 1998/1999). Carrick (2001, online document) provides a description of Readers Theatre along with sources for scripts and for information on implementation, additional classroom applications, and assessment.

Types of Scripts

In this format, readers can develop a script after reading a literature selection, which helps to draw their attention to story elements, thus developing an understanding of characters, setting, problem, key events, and solution. Another option is for students to use a script such as those found in websites hosted by Aaron Shepard and Rick Swallow. FictionTeachers.com also provides links to scripts and lesson plans that can be used for Readers Theatre.

Guidelines for writing scripts and other tips can be also found at Aaron Shepard's website. Here, he addresses script roles, cuts and changes, narration, script format, and team scripting. The Internet School Library Media Center and LiteracyConnections.com also provide lists of Web resources related to Readers Theatre.

The use of Readers Theatre can offer a different context in which children are exposed to texts focusing on poetry, science, social studies, or other content related topics. Educational consultant Lisa Blau offers biographical scripts that focus on the lives of Helen Keller and Eleanor Roosevelt, as well as informational scripts such as "Stupendous Snakes" and "Japan—The Land of the Rising Sun."

Connections and Extensions

- Analyze personality traits of major characters in the story. Cite examples from the script that support each personality trait identified for the character.
- Develop a story map that details character, setting, problem, events, and solution.
- Identify examples in the script of colorful and vivid language that are used to create images in the script.
- Use the scripts for Readers Theatre to illustrate how to use dialogue to show spoken language by a character.
- Follow the lesson plan written by Jean Rusting to conduct a Readers Theatre for the English folktale *Cap o' Rushes* (a variant on Cinderella).

Sustained Silent Reading

Only by providing quality SSR programs can we truly attain the goal of creating readers who both *can* and *do* read (Pilgreen, 2000, p. 70).

Sustained Silent Reading (SSR) is a time when everyone, including the teacher, reads silently for a given period of time (Butler & Turbill, 1987, p. 49). Uninterrupted Sustained Silent Reading (USSR), Drop Everything And Read (DEAR), and Sustained QUIet Reading Time (SQUIRT) are other names for this concept. In their survey of seventh-grade teachers, Nagy, Campenni, and Shaw (2000, online document) found that the practice of setting aside time during the school day for silent reading is alive and well. The teachers surveyed expressed satisfaction with the use of SSR, in part because it helped them to achieve curricular goals, helped students develop positive attitudes toward reading, and fostered students' habit of reading for information and enjoyment (Nagy et al., 2000). Noted educators John Pikulski and J. David Cooper state that independent reading in school should be increased and cite relevant research that supports this argument.

In *Becoming a Nation of Readers*, Anderson, Hiebert, Scott, and Wilkinson (1985) report that independent reading is associated with gains in reading achievement in school or out of school; therefore, children should spend more time in independent reading. By the time students are in third or fourth grade, they should be reading a minimum of two hours a week (Anderson et. al, 1985). Allington (2001) looks at the volume of reading in his book *What Really Matters for Struggling Readers*. He examines research studies and states that what these studies have consistently shown is "that there exists a potent relationship between volume of reading and reading achievement" (Allington, 2001, p. 33).

Stephen Krashen, a major proponent of sustained silent reading, offers a critique of the National Reading Panel Report and the review of studies that were completed regarding SSR. In comments at a National Reading Panel Forum, he states that "despite their repeated claims of rigor and completeness, the section on free reading/sustained silent reading is very sloppy." His main argument pertains to the fact that the report restricted the review of studies conducted since 1984. By doing so, 41 studies were left out of the panel's review, of which 38 of these studies showed that readers in silent sustained reading programs did as well or better on tests of reading than children who spent an equivalent amount of time in traditional instruction. Krashen (Pilgreen, 2000) has stated that when studies are allowed to run for a sufficient length of time, then those who do SSR do better.

In his foreword in Pilgreen's (2000) text on sustained silent reading, Krashen discusses specific studies that support the use of SSR as part of classroom literacy activities. One teacher, William Marson, corroborates Krashen's claims about the success of free voluntary reading. At Education World's website, Marson discusses his success in motivating sixth graders in his article Free Voluntary Reading (FVR) Pays Big Dividends!

Guidelines

The most critical elements to sustained silent reading are that students must have the time and opportunity to read. A major benefit of SSR is that during this time students develop proficiency in reading independently for an extended period of time. Students may only read three to five minutes at the beginning of the school year. The goal is to gradually increase the amount of time children spend reading so that they are reading for longer, sustained periods of time. Through involvement with SSR, students develop an appreciation and enjoyment of literature while they are reinforcing those skills and strategies in which they are proficient. This reading format gives students time to practice emerging reading skills and strategies.

In a chapter excerpt from *The Read-Aloud Handbook*, Jim Trelease addresses the issue of sustained silent reading. He includes a structure for SSR recommended by Robert and Marlene McCracken, discusses Stephen Krashen's research on SSR, which he calls Free Voluntary Reading (FVR), and describes the benefits of using this reading format. Trelease also considers the pros and cons of using computerized "reading incentive" programs such as Advantage Learning System's *Accelerated Reader* and Scholastic's *Reading Counts*.

Factors for Success

In *The SSR Handbook: How To Organize and Manage a Sustained Silent Reading Program*, Pilgreen (2000) identifies eight factors for SSR success: 1) access, 2) appeal, 2) conducive environment, 4) encouragement, 5) staff training, 6) non-accountability, 7) follow-up activities, and 8) distributed time to read.

Access and appeal. The children need to be able to select from a variety of interesting reading materials during the SSR time (Pilgreen, 2000). In addition to picture books and novels, also include nonfiction texts, newspapers, magazines, comic books, books created in class with students, and any other free and appropriate reading materials that can be accessed. It is also important to determine what type of materials appeal to students by administering interest surveys or conducting informal class discussions about what students would like to have available for reading materials. Using this information, the next step is to include materials that range from easy to more difficult so that a variety of reading levels are available from which to choose.

Conducive environment and encouragement. The classroom using sustained silent reading should provide an environment that is conducive to free reading (Pilgreen, 2000). Some basic characteristics of the reading environment should include comfortable surroundings, a consistent structure in terms of procedures, a low-risk atmosphere (i.e., quiet music or book covers to maintain privacy of reading selections), and acknowledgement of the sacred time through insistence on no interruptions. Teacher modeling is also a critical component, since the students are more likely to value reading when the teacher values it as well.

Staff training. Pilgreen (2000) emphasizes the necessity "for the entire staff to believe in the benefits of SSR and wholeheartedly support its implementation" (p. 522). When all involved understand the philosophy underlying SSR, then the level of commitment they bring to its implementation will be stronger.

Non-accountability and follow-up activities. The non-accountability component means that after the free reading period, the students are not required to complete a record or report (Pilgreen, 2000). Freedom from this aspect enables children to make mistakes without feeling embarrassed for failing to demonstrate competence. It also means children are able to experience the joy of reading and develop confidence in the selection of more difficult reading material.

When discussing SSR, Pilgreen (2000) is careful to distinguish between accountability measures versus follow-up activities. Interactive or sharing activities can provide positive contributions to the SSR program. These interactive activities can also involve collaborative opportunities for the student to work together on a joint project. Most important to this component is the need for students to self-select the activity. Pilgreen (2000) points out that "the more freedom the students have to develop their own ideas, the greater the degree of ownership and engagement they will have in the activities" (p. 67).

Time to read. When starting SSR, USSR, or DEAR time, it is best to set a time goal that will be easily attainable for the students. The students must be able to sustain the reading time which may only be three or four minutes in the beginning. Older students can begin with 10 minutes (Pilgreen, 2000, p. 68). Gradually, the time can be extended until students are reading 20 to 30 minutes or longer (Butler & Turbill, 1987).

Connections and Extensions

- Volunteers give 60-second reviews of in-progress highlights about their book; the class develops student-produced newspapers with "book recommendation" sections; or have a book and author luncheon (Pilgreen, 2000, p. 65-66).
- Students read aloud or share thoughts about their book while sitting in the Author's Chair (Harste, Short, & Burke, 1988).
- Teacher holds monthly "book sales" where students who have finished a book and want to sell it explain the main points of the book, tell about the authors, characters, or setting, or give their personal reactions to the book (Revel-Wood, 1988).

Literature Circles

When teachers value their students' responses, literature discussion groups provide a safe place for children to use language to explore important ideas and issues (Wells, 1995, p. 132).

A major purpose of the literature discussion groups is to change the way children talk about the texts they read. Key features include: a) children choosing their own reading materials; b) formation of small temporary groups; c) group readings of different books; d) groups meeting periodically to discuss what has been read since the last meeting; e) the teacher acting as facilitator; and f) evaluation consisting of teacher observation, group evaluation, and self-evaluation (Daniels, 1994; Gambrell & Almasi, 1996; Roser & Martinez, 1995).

A useful resource for learning more about literature circles is LiteratureCircles.com, which features discussions about this format, book recommendations, research on effectiveness, ideas for classroom management, links to related sites and organizations, and news of relevant publications and events. This site also includes a featured article of the month as well as a section called In the Classroom that discusses management, logistics, troubleshooting, and problem solving for literature circles in the classroom. Other resources include Laura Candler's Literary Lessons and *Education World's* Literature Circles Build Excitement for Books! by Mary Daniels Brown, which offers advice about how to begin using literature circles.

Guidelines

Harvey Daniels and the team of teachers he has worked with identifies literature circles by using the following definition:

Literature circles are small, peer-led discussion groups whose members have chosen to read the same story, poem, article, or book. While reading each group-assigned portion of the text (either in or outside of class), members make notes to help them contribute to the upcoming discussion, and everyone comes to the group with ideas to share. Each group follows a reading and meeting schedule, holding periodic discussions on the way through the book. When they finish a book, the circle members may share highlights of their reading with wider community; then they trade members with other finishing groups, select more reading, and move into a new cycle (Daniels, 2002, p. 2).

Daniels (2002), in his book *Literature Circles: Voice and Choice in Book Clubs and Reading Groups* (2nd ed.), expands on the concept of role sheets in the chapter on books and materials. He explains the concept of role sheets as a type of support structure that may actually be beneficial to more experienced book clubs as opposed to those students first beginning literature circles. He describes the role sheets as temporary devices to help students internalize and practice making multiple cognitive perspectives on texts. He cautions against the overuse of the role sheets because it can cause children's conversations to become stilted and mechanical. In the second edition of his book on literature circles, Daniels advises that the role sheets should be used for only about three to four weeks at which point they can be replaced with a reading log (Daniels, 2002). The reading logs become a place where students can write down connections they make, questions they might have for the author, any criticisms or opinions they want to share, or drawings of pictures or ideas that were triggered by the story.

Daniels (2002) emphasizes that literature circles are not to be used only with fiction books. Texts for nonfiction can be pulled from whole books about animals, people, and places. There are also books about notable historical figures, sports, entertainment, adventure tales, and science series like Eyewitness books. Shorter pieces can be taken from magazines, newspapers, or even historical documents related to a unit of study. Daniels (2002) states that readers will require the same discussion skills whether they are reading fiction or nonfiction texts. "Kids need to know how to keep a response log, mark important sections of a text, participate effectively in a group, reflect on and improve discussions, and so forth" (Daniels, 2002, p. 202).

Adapting Literature Circles for Different Grade Levels

Literature circles are more often used with children in third or fourth grades and up, but can also be an appropriate format for younger children. In order for them to be most successful, it is helpful for the students to have developed some independence in reading. At Multiage-Education.Com, Linda Geist writes about how literature circles can be adapted for young children. She discusses the group size that she recommends as well as the roles the students used as part of the literature circles in her first- and second-grade classroom.

Seattle University's School of Education hosts the Literature Circles Resource Center, which features information on topics such as structure for literature circles in the primary grades and structure for literature circles in middle school. Each of these topics links to a webpage focused on a specific teacher's classroom and gives an overview of its process by the day, by the week, and by the year. This site also has a section of general

guidelines that provides useful information on planning, choosing books, reading the books, and extension projects.

Another Web resource that focuses on using literature circles with fifth grade was developed by Marjorie Duby at Joseph Lee School. This website, hosted by *Inquiry Unlimited* includes links to pages that discuss the roles these fifth graders used, delineate how evidence of participation would be determined, and address how the students rotated through the various roles during the literature circles.

An example of a literature study unit using *The Cay* and *Timothy of the Cay* has been developed by Sara Bork, Carrie Kriescher, Candice Murphy, and Melissa Randall as part of the St. Norbert College Ocean Voyagers Program. These teachers identify how to implement a unit involving these two books. Their 10-day unit breaks down how the book is introduced, how roles are rotated so that each student is responsible for each role at least once, and how assessment of the literature circles is determined.

Role of the Teacher

The role of the teacher during this process is usually identified as that of a facilitator. However, when first introducing the concept of literature circles to children, the teacher might need to take a more active role by modeling discussion tactics and written responses. The Literature Circles Resource Center's Making Discussions Work, adapted from *Getting Started with Literature Circles* by Katherine L. Schlick Noe and Nancy L. Johnson (1999), addresses selecting a discussion format, teaching students how to discuss, helping students prepare for discussion, and debriefing after the discussion to cover skills. Another useful resource at this site, Sample Forms for Discussion, provides examples of templates for the discussion log, comment cards, self-evaluation, and focus questions.

Connections and Extensions

- The *Literature Circles Resource Center* discuss a variety of extension projects that can last anywhere from a day to a week to complete. The projects discussed range from beginning projects such as character bookmarks and accordion books to more complex projects that include the collection of artifacts for a jackdaw or creation of a story quilt.

- Samples of sharing devices are addressed in Harvey Daniels's book *Literature Circles*. The chapter on forming, scheduling, and managing groups includes a listing of projects such as posters advertising the book, videotaped dramatizations, a timeline of the story, and collages representing the different characters.

Addressing Skills and Strategies

Minilessons highlighting particular skills are easily incorporated into the classroom using the literature circles as a format for reading instruction. For example, *Amelia Bedelia* by Peggy Parish could be used to teach figurative language, *The Little House in the Big Woods* by Laura Ingalls Wilder could be used to look at description, and *Hatchet* by Gary Paulsen could be used to examine character development. Carol Hurst's Children's Literature Site models how to use good literature to model comprehension strategies. She includes minilessons that address reading for detail along with inferencing using *Shiloh* by Phyllis Reynolds Naylor, making inferences with *Holes* by Louis Sachar, visualizing using Lois Lowry's *Autumn Street*, and making predictions using *Crabbe* by William Bell.

Frameworks for Organizing Instruction

Reading Workshop

The formats that have been discussed can be used as part of the reading workshop framework that is most commonly associated with Nancie Atwell's book, *In the Middle* (1998). Major components of this framework include a short minilesson, time for independent reading, responding, conferencing, and sharing. The time that is set aside for the independent reading, responding, and conferencing is the largest chunk of time that could be anywhere from 30 minutes to 1 hour of the instructional block. The teacher may opt to start off the workshop with a shared reading or read aloud session. During the independent time, students can participate in guided reading groups, literature circles, or Readers Theatre. The sustained silent reading portion of reading workshop is when students have the opportunity to read the literature club selection, reread a previous text, or self-select other material that is of interest.

For more information on how to organize instruction for reading workshop, visit the Reading Language Arts webpage. Other useful resources include the article Making the Difference with Reading Instruction: Reader's Workshop, by Richard Wulf-McGrath, which offers further insight into reading workshop; tips on management and grouping posted on Scholastic's Teacher Resource website by Laura Robb, author of *Teaching Reading in Middle School*; and Reading Workshop Assessments and Mini Lessons by Sarah Crocker.

Book Club

Another framework is that of Book Club, which was begun in 1989-1990 by Susan McMahon and Taffy Raphael. These researchers developed a framework for this program that includes four contexts for instruction and participation in language and literacy: (a) community share, (b) reading, (c) writing, and (d) student-led book clubs. A primary goal of the Book Club program was to create a context within which students could engage in meaningful conversations, on their own, about the texts they read (McMahon & Raphael, 1997, p. 4).

Considering the Options

These formats for reading instruction can be considered as a reminder of the many different options that are available to us throughout the day. The options that are best for each teacher would be dependent on the needs of the students in his or her class. For example, a first grade or second grade class might

start the morning with a shared reading activity followed by the teacher working with a guided reading group while other students are working at literacy centers. Later in the morning, the class could gather around for a read-aloud by the teacher. A third grade, fourth grade, or fifth grade class might start their day with sustained silent reading, followed by sessions where students work on a Reader's Theater story or meet together to discuss a book they have been reading as part of a literature discussion group. This does not mean that the first grade class will not at some point during the day also participate in Sustained Silent Reading. It means that the choices that a teacher makes about which formats to use during a particular day or week will be based on the literacy needs of the students in the classroom.

It is also important to provide numerous opportunities for children to participate in meaningful writing experiences. Used in conjunction with the formats that have been discussed, it becomes simple to provide such opportunities. Children can write stories modeled on favorite books read or listened to during read-aloud, shared reading, sustained silent reading, or guided reading. Another option is to write personal reflections in a journal or literature log after participating in literature circles. Budding screenwriters have the chance to adapt an existing script or write an original script about a book as part of activities associated with Readers' Theater. The bottom line is authentic writing experiences that enable children to connect to what has been read is one other way to enrich their literacy growth.

One last note—the formats discussed in this article are by no means the only formats for teaching reading in the elementary school. However, each can easily be used to address skill areas that children need to learn while modeling these skills within the context of real books. We must remember that in order for our children to read, they also need the time and opportunity to practice what they are being taught. Again, the use of these formats can accomplish that task. In combination, these formats for reading instruction provide a much needed balance between independence and instruction that will support our students as they learn to read.

References

Allington, R.L. (2001). *What really matters for struggling readers: Designing research-based reading programs.* New York: Longman.

Anderson, R.C., Hiebert, E.H., Scott, J.A., & Wilkinson, I.A.G. (1984). *Becoming a nation of readers: The report of the Commission on Reading.* Washington, DC: National Institute of Education.

Barrentine, S.J. (1996a). Engaging with reading through interactive read-alouds. *The Reading Teacher, 50,* 36-43.

Barrentine, S.J. (1996b). Storytime plus dialogue equals interactive read-aloud. In L.B. Gambrell & J.F. Almasi (Eds.), *Lively discussions: Fostering engaged reading* (pp. 52-62). Newark, DE: International Reading Association.

Burns, P.C., Roe, B.D., & Ross, E.P. (1999). *Teaching reading in today's elementary school* (7th ed.). Boston: Houghton Mifflin.

Butler, A., & Turbill, J. (1987). *Towards a reading-writing classroom.* Portsmouth, NH: Heinemann.

Campbell, R. (2001). *Read-alouds with young children.* Newark, DE: International Reading Association.

Carrick, L. (2001, July/August). Internet resources for conducting Readers Theatre. *Reading Online, 5*(1). Available: `http://`

www.readingonline.org/electronic/elec_index.asp?HREF=carrick/index.html

CIERA (1998, Summer). Improving the reading achievement of America's children: 10 research-based principles. Available (retrieved July 5, 2002): http://www.ciera.org/library/instresrc/principles/index.html

Daniels, H. (1994). *Literature circles: Voice and choice in the student-centered classroom.* York, ME: Stenhouse.

Duffy-Hester, A.M. (1999). Teaching struggling readers in elementary school classrooms: A review of classroom reading programs and principles of instruction. *The Reading Teacher, 52,* pp. 480-495.

Fisher, B., & Medvic, E.F. (2000). *Perspectives on shared reading: Planning and practice.* Portsmouth, NH: Heinemann.

Fountas, I.C., & Pinnell, G.S. (1996). *Guided reading: Good first teaching for all children.* Portsmouth, NH: Heinemann.

Gambrell, L.B., & Almasi, J.F. (1996). *Lively discussions: Fostering engaged reading.* Newark, DE: International Reading Association.

Harste, J.C., Short, K.G., & Burke, C. (1988). *Creating classrooms for authors: The reading-writing connection.* Portsmouth, NH: Heinemann.

IRA/NAEYC (May,1998). Learning to Read and Write: Developmentally Appropriate Practices for Young Children, part 4: Continuum of Children's Development in Early Reading and Writing. Available: http://www.naeyc.org/resources/positionstatements/psread4.htm

Leu, D.J., & Kinzer, C.K. (1999). *Effective literacy instruction* (4th ed.). UpperSaddle River, NJ: Merrill.

McCracken, M.J., & McCracken, R.A. (1995). *Reading, writing, and language* (2nd ed.). Winnipeg Manitoba Canada: Peguis.

McMahon, S.I., & Raphael, T.E. (1997). *The book club connection: Literacy and learning and classroom talk.* Newark, DE: International Reading Association and Teachers College Press.

Martinez, Roser, & Strecker (1998/1999). "I never thought I could be a star": A reader's theater ticket to fluency. *The Reading Teacher, 52,* 326-334.

Morrow, L.M., & O'Connor, E.M. (1995). Literacy partnerships for change with "at-risk" kindergartners. In R.L. Allington & S.A. Walmsley (Eds.), *No quick fix* (pp. 97-115). Newark, DE: International Reading Association.

Morrow, L.M., Strickland, D.S., & Woo, D.G. (1998). *Literacy instruction in half- and whole-day kindergarten.* Newark, DE: International Reading Association.

Moss, B. (1995). Using children's nonfiction tradebooks as read-aloud. *Language Arts, 72,* pp. 122-126.

Nagy, N.M., Campenni, C.E., & Shaw, J.N. (2000). A survey of sustained silent reading practices in seventh-grade classrooms. *Reading Online, 4*(5). Available: http://www.readingonline.org/articles/art_index.asp?HREF=/articles/nagy/

Opitz, M. (2000). Meeting special needs: Empowering the reader in every child. *Instructor.* Available (retrieved July 5, 2002): http://www.scholastic.ca/education/professional articles/langarts/opitz.html

Pilgreen, J. (2000). *The SSR handbook: How to organize and manage a sustained silent reading program.* Portsmouth, NH: Heinemann.

Revel-Wood, M. (1988). Invitations to read, to write, to learn. In J.C. Harste, K.G. Short, & C. Burke (Eds.), *Creating classrooms for authors: The reading-writing connection.* Portsmouth, NH: Heinemann.

Roser, N.L., & Martinez, M.G. (1995). *Book talk and beyond: Children and teachers respond to literature.* Newark, DE: International Reading Association.

Ruddell, R.B. (1999). *Teaching children to read and write: Becoming an influential teacher* (2nd ed.). Needham Heights, MA: Allyn and Bacon.

Schlick Noe, K.L., & Johnson, N.J. (1999). *Getting started with literature circles.* Norwood, MA: Christopher Gordon.

Strickland, D. (2000). Balanced literacy: Teaching the skills and thrills of reading. *Instructor.* Available (retrieved July 5, 2002): http://www.scholastic.ca/education/professional articles/langarts/balancedlit.html

Trelease, J. (1989a). *The new read-aloud handbook* (4th ed.). New York: Penguin Books.

Trelease, J. (1989b). Jim Trelease speaks on reading aloud to children. *The Reading Teacher, 49,* 200-206.

Wells, D. (1995). Leading Grand Conversations. In N.L. Roser & M.G. Martinez (Eds.), *Book talk and beyond: Children and teachers respond to literature* (pp. 132-139). Newark, DE: International Reading Association.

Kimberly Kimbell-Lopez is an assistant professor at Louisiana Tech University. She teaches undergraduate and graduate courses in literacy and technology. She may be contacted by e-mail (kklopez@latech.edu) or via mail (P.O. Box 3161, Ruston, LA 71272).

Our students *are* ready for this: Comprehension instruction in the elementary school

This article offers instructional methods to help young readers deepen their understanding of the comprehension process and demonstrates how elementary students respond to this approach.

James Barton; Donna M. Sawyer

There is general, sustained agreement that comprehension instruction is a central component in the language arts curriculum (Duffy, Roehler, & Mason, 1984; Durkin, 1993; Graves, Juel, & Graves, 2001; Pressley, 1998; Roehler & Duffy, 1991). However, as Pressley (2000) noted in a recent review of comprehension instruction, there is room for improvement in the ways that elementary students are taught to comprehend. Given the great diversity of written materials available to readers, the act of comprehension is by nature so sophisticated that no single instructional method can be sufficient for all readers with all texts in all learning situations (Snow, Burns, & Griffin, 1998). Given this lack of consensus, how can we help young readers learn bow to comprehend? This is the question we tried to answer with our research in Donna's (second author's) third-grade classroom.

Donna teaches at an elementary school in Pawtucket, Rhode Island, USA. Her 25 vivacious students represent an urban mix of cultural and socioeconomic backgrounds. Eight students speak both Spanish and English, and several of them moved to the United States recently. At the time of this writing, 9 students read at or above grade level while 4 of the remaining 16 are beginning readers. Donna uses the writing process to integrate her curriculum, and, on average, her students spend between four and five hours each school day engaged in literacy-related activities. These activities are interactive, as Donna emphasizes sharing and community building to help her students take responsibility for their own scholarship. Together, Donna's third graders gradually become "reasoners" about text, consciously learning how to comprehend and reevaluate their incipient interpretations from new perspectives.

Jim (first author) teaches courses in literacy education at Rhode Island College, located about six miles from Donna's classroom in Pawtucket. We collaborated to plan and implement our vision of comprehension instruction in the elementary grades. Our approach owes its origins to the related fields of cognitive psychology and reader-response theory, which, to our thinking, are connected by their common emphasis on the reader's construction of meaning. Cognitivists believe readers shape meaning by connecting new information in texts with existing background knowledge (Graves et al., 2001; Rumelhart, 1980). Advocates of reader-response theory believe sophisticated transactions take place between reader and text, resulting in the development of personalized interpretations (Rosenblatt, 1983; Spiegel, 1998). For our instructional purposes, we approached Donna's third graders as thoughtful meaning makers and anticipated they would generate a rich variety of compelling interpretations in response to the materials we read together.

In this article, we share our mutual learning experiences in hopes of assisting other elementary teachers in their efforts to deepen young students' understanding about the comprehension process. We begin with an overview of the key components of our comprehension instruction, followed by a lesson Donna conducted using these components with her students. Next, we share additional examples to help other teachers think creatively about their own instructional options. We conclude the article with some thoughts about the challenges and benefits of using this comprehension approach with our students.

Understanding comprehension

Comprehension instruction has many facets (Pressley, 2000), each with its own set of creative possibilities and chal-

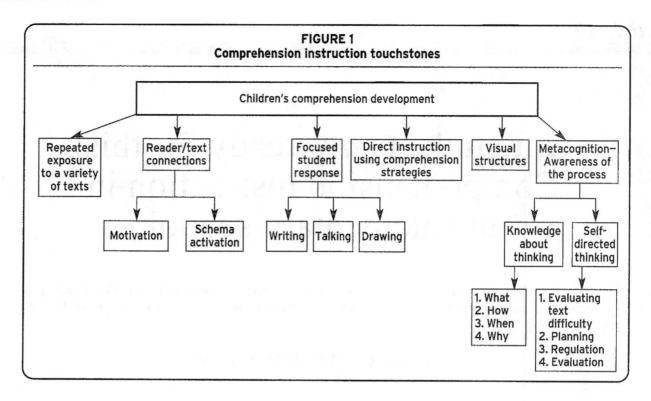

FIGURE 1
Comprehension instruction touchstones

lenges for teachers and students. In Donna's classroom, we focused on six instructional touchstones (see Figure 1).

Repeated exposure to different kinds of writing

Introducing young readers to a variety of texts prepares them to deal with more complex texts (and complex issues) in the future (Fisher, Flood, & Lapp, 1999; Snow et al., 1998). In Donna's classroom, this exposure included different genres of narrative, expository, and poetic and dramatic writing, with particular emphasis on texts that support more than one interpretation. She introduced her young readers to the rich variety of illustrations that accompany and embellish the ideas in texts. She acquainted her students with a diversity of cultural voices that communicate unique perspectives and shared experiences. She also helped them see how different authors use stylistic devices (such as authentic voice and dramatic build) to convey meaning to the reader.

Reader/text connections

Students who find themselves in the texts they read become more sensitive to poetic imagery, authors' styles, and text structure (Marshall, 2000; Rosenblatt, 1983). The act of making personal connections also aids comprehension through schema activation—connecting what the reader already knows about a given topic with the new information offered in the text (Anderson & Pearson, 1984; Bransford, Brown, & Cocking, 1999; Hudson & Slackman, 1990). Many young readers (and some older ones) have little experience at making these kinds of productive connections (Williams, 1993). Donna encouraged this important process through frequent, explicit modeling of relevant

CHILDREN'S BOOKS CITED

Anzaldua, G. (1993). *Friends from the other side*. San Francisco: Children's Book Press.

Brown, M. (1998). *Locked in the library*. Boston: Little, Brown.

Bunting, E. (1999). *I have an olive tree*. New York: HarperCollins.

Collins, P. (1992). *I am an artist*. Brookfield, CT: Millbrook.

Conrad, P. (1989). *The tub people*. New York: HarperCollins.

Couric, K. (2000). *The brand new kid*. New York: Doubleday.

Fitzpatrick, M.L. (1998). *The long march*. Hillsboro. OR: Beyond Words.

Granowsky, A. (1996). *The little red hen*. Austin, TX: Steck-Vaughn.

Guthrie, W. (1998). *This land is your land*. Boston: Little, Brown.

Hoose, P., & Hoose, H. (1998). *Hey, little ant*. New York: Scholastic.

Knight, M. (1992). *Talking walls*. Gardiner, ME: Tilbury House.

Mitchell, M. (1993). *Uncle Jed's barbershop*. New York: Simon & Schuster.

Shannon, D. (1998). *A bad case of stripes*. New York: Scholastic.

Yashima, T. (1955). *Crow Boy*. New York: Puffin.

associations between her students' lives and the characters, situations, settings, emotions, and ideas in the texts they read.

Focused student response

Talking, writing, and drawing help readers reflect about what they've read and share their insights with others. These kinds of responses can take many forms, but, without response, comprehension of a text is rarely deepened (Beach, 1993; Guthrie &

Anderson, 1999). Donna helped develop her third graders' response repertoires by encouraging them to ask questions about the texts they read. Her students' comprehension was further enhanced by Donna's use of a variety of questions and writing prompts to stimulate different kinds of responses. For example, she included affective ("How would it feel?") and imaginative ("What would happen if …?") questions and prompts as well as analytic ones ("What happened next?"). Donna's students also learned to reflect on and extend their initial interpretations of a text through her practice of consistent emphasis on the importance of careful listening and thoughtful reaction to classmates' responses.

Direct instruction in using comprehension strategies

Thinking strategies interact with readers' prior knowledge to develop complex understandings of the ideas in a text (Pressley, 2000: Pressley & Afflerbach, 1995). The ability to employ appropriate reasoning strategies, such as making predictions or drawing conclusions, is the essence of the comprehension process. To become fluent comprehenders, readers must determine which strategies to use depending on the content and difficulty of the text (Alexander & Jetton, 2000; Bransford et al., 1999: Paris & Jacobs, 1984). Due to the sophisticated nature of this process, Donna's students needed a great deal of explicit direction and guided practice to become adept strategic readers. Her experiences reinforced Paris, Wasik, and Turner's (1991) finding that direct instruction in strategies is a necessary prerequisite for awareness of the comprehension process. We also found, as we illustrate in our demonstration lesson, that whole-group direct instruction was most effective when coupled with guided practice in small groups.

Strategy knowledge plays an important role in strengthening elementary readers' comprehension abilities (Pressley et al.,

1998). However, many different comprehension strategies of varying importance exist (Tierney & Readence, 2000), making it difficult to design a coherent comprehension curriculum. In her classroom, Donna focused instruction on a limited set of the most essential strategies. To be considered essential, a strategy had to meet the following criteria:

- The strategy must be powerful (i.e., very effective in promoting understanding).
- The strategy must be relatively ubiquitous (i.e., applicable to a wide array of texts, including difficult ones).

The 10 comprehension strategies shown in Figure 2 met these two criteria. The strategies and their definitions are as follows:

Locating details—finding specific information in a text.

Sequencing—arranging specific events into an accurate chronological order.

Comparing and contrasting—explaining how two or more things, people, places, or ideas are alike or different from one another.

Summarizing—distinguishing important dramatic events from relatively trivial details.

Envisioning character change—pinpointing how characters change and grow.

Drawing conclusions—going beyond literal information to make supportable guesses about ideas that are not completely spelled out.

Determining cause and effect—understanding how one thing leads to another.

Making predictions—using available clues to make supportable guesses about what might happen next.

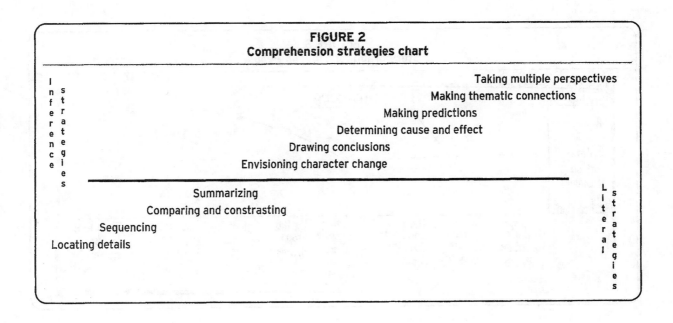

FIGURE 2
Comprehension strategies chart

Inference strategies

Taking multiple perspectives
Making thematic connections
Making predictions
Determining cause and effect
Drawing conclusions
Envisioning character change

Summarizing
Comparing and constrasting
Sequencing
Locating details

Literal strategies

Making thematic connections—connecting a text's message to the reader's own life.

Taking multiple perspectives—considering two or more points of view.

Literal strategies (such as locating details and sequencing) appear at the bottom of the chart and gradually lead up to more abstract inference strategies (such as making predictions and taking multiple perspectives). This arrangement is not meant to suggest, however, that these essential strategies should be taught in any particular order. Donna's decisions about which strategies to emphasize at a given point were based on the texts her students were reading at the time and her perceptions about students' particular instructional needs (Barton, 2001). Donna found there was no such thing as the "right" text for a particular strategy. Her text choices were versatile enough to support many strategy options.

Visual structures to support comprehension

Visual structures are powerful tools for comprehension instruction because they offer concrete, memorable representations of abstract thinking processes (Alvermann & Boothby, 1986; Calfee & Patrick, 1995; Norton, 1992). Donna employed visual structures to help her students to organize large amounts of textual information, to establish strong reader/text connections, and to introduce and reinforce essential comprehension strategies. In the course of our explorations, we discovered that certain visual representations worked better than others for modeling particular comprehension strategies. For example, see the story graph Donna and her students created to summarize the key plot events in *The Tub People* (Conrad, 1989), a narrative picture book about the adventures of a family of toys that lives together on the edge of a bathtub (Figure 3). This visual structure helped students distinguish important dramatic events from relatively trivial details in the story. First, Donna assisted her students in listing each story event along the horizontal axis, and then they determined which of these events carried the greatest degree of dramatic impact along the vertical axis. The dramatic events that appear above the dotted line became the students' summary of *The Tub People*.

Donna found it was necessary to model and practice these visuals with a variety of texts to support her students' attempts to learn new ways of reasoning. She also used these visual structures to help her students identify specific links between different texts. Her young readers were quick to assimilate the visuals she introduced, moving rapidly from initial confusion to manipulating the visuals with ease. This scaffolding process (Brandt, 1998; Bruner, 1985; Roehler & Cantlon, 1997) was most effective when the students constructed their own visual representation (with Donna's guidance) during the course of a whole-class discussion about a particular text and followed this activity with additional practice in small groups. In fact, this visual approach achieved its purpose and gradually became unnecessary; over the course of the school year, many of the third graders internalized particular ways of thinking and no longer needed visual support to employ appropriate comprehension strategies.

Awareness of the comprehension process

Paris, Cross, and Lipson (1984) referred to this awareness as metacognition and defined it as knowledge about thinking and self-directed thinking. Knowledge about thinking includes declarative knowledge (knowing which comprehension strategy to use in a given situation), procedural knowledge (knowing how to successfully employ a strategy), and conditional knowledge (knowing the purpose of a strategy and when to employ it). Self-directed thinking includes evaluating the difficulty of a text, planning (allocating appropriate time and effort), regulating (staying focused on a plan), and evaluating (monitoring a

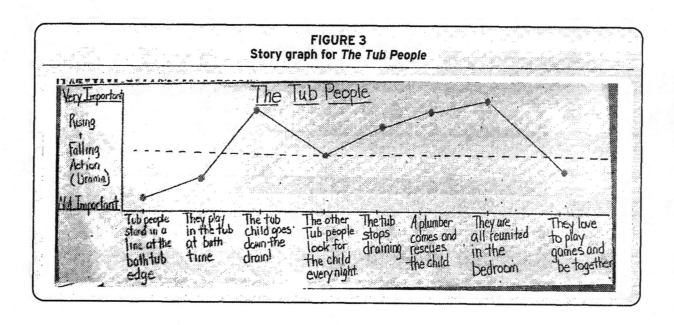

FIGURE 3
Story graph for *The Tub People*

124

plan's effectiveness and modifying it as needed). Metacognitive practices help readers set comprehension goals for themselves and control the processes for reaching these goals (Schunk & Zimmerman, 1998).

Donna helped her students become metacognitive thinkers by explicitly modeling and discussing the components of comprehension with them on a routine basis. Her lessons invariably concluded with an interactive discussion about the particular strategies they had been practicing. Specifically, the class members regularly reviewed the name of each strategy they had just employed, discussed how to go about using it with flexibility, speculated about when it could be useful to a reader, and determined why it was an effective comprehension tool. Donna also encouraged her third graders to comment on the relative difficulty of each text they read and consider how different strategies might be applied to new texts they would read in the future. These "metadiscussions" helped make the comprehension process more understandable and purposeful for her students.

Putting it all together

Donna's comprehension instruction took many forms as she blended her key components (e.g., diverse text exposure, reader/text connections, student response, direct strategy instruction, visual support, metacognitive awareness) in different combinations throughout the school year.

Making predictions

The following lesson is based on *A Bad Case of Stripes* (1998), a narrative picture book by David Shannon. This lesson took place early in the year and illustrates how Donna employed whole-group and small-group instruction to encourage her students' active participation in this learning process. *A Bad Case of Stripes* relates the trials of a young girl named Camilla who is so eager to impress others that she ignores her own feelings, especially her desire for lima beans. Camilla comes down with a disease that morphs her appearance into whatever anyone else wishes her to become, be it covered in purple polka dots or a giant fungus. She comes to realize that the price of trying to fit in isn't worth the cost to her own peace of mind. The "miracle cure" for her disease turns out to be ... lima beans!

Donna's comprehension lesson with this text took place over several class sessions. She gave each student a copy of the book and set the stage for reading by encouraging an initial reader/text connection and involving her third graders in speculating about the contents of the book.

Before we read this new story, *A Bad Case of Stripes*, I have a question for each one of you. What do you think is the very yuckiest food? In other words, if someone said, "We're having *this* for dinner," you would say, "YUCK!" (Student responses included broccoli, peas, Brussels sprouts, spinach, squash, turkey, lima beans, and pork.) You know what I don't like? I think cottage cheese and liver are yucky. Do any of you like any of the foods your classmates say are yucky? Would you eat them anyway? (Several stu-

dents indicated they would still like broccoli and turkey no matter what their classmates say.)

Now, let's look at the cover of the book. What do you suppose my questions and your answers have to do with this story? Can anyone predict the connection? (The students speculated about the connection. One student guessed that the girl on the cover doesn't like some kinds of foods, but she has to eat them anyway, "Like when you eat chicken soup to get better when you have a fever." Another student surmised, "Maybe she is gonna get sick from eating some yucky food.")

Let's read the book to see if your predictions come true. Please pay close attention to our main character, Camilla. Her story begins on the first day of school, and her experiences at school may remind you of some other books we have read together.

As the class read *A Bad Case of Stripes* together, Donna paused at appropriate spots to reinforce connections between the students and Camilla. At the end of the story, she solicited the students' reactions and helped them forge a personal connection with Camilla.

Any reactions now that we've finished this story? (Representative comments included "It was really, really funny when she turned into a pill"; "She looked like an alien when she turned into a plant"; "It wasn't nice for the other kids to make fun of her"; and "I liked it when the little old lady came and helped her.") Some of your predictions came true, didn't they? Have you ever stopped yourself from doing something you really wanted to do because you were afraid of what other people might think? (A general discussion ensued. Three students offered the following life experiences: "I like black-eyed peas. But I don't eat them because my friend doesn't like them." "One time I was planning my birthday party. I wanted to have a skating party. My friends argued with me to do it their way and have a swimming party instead. We ended up doing it their way on my birthday." "When I go to my friend's house we have to play her games. One time when I chose my game she sent me home.")

Sequencing

To explore the strategy of sequencing with her class, Donna prepared her students to select specific details from the text and work together in small groups to organize their choices into a story circle visual structure.

What were some of the different things Camilla turned into in the story? (A flag, a checkerboard, a pill, a fungus, her room, herself.) Let's take a closer look. Everyone, please take out a sheet of paper. Here are some colored pencils. I'd like you to each draw your favorite Camilla. You can draw her any way you imagine her. You can look back through the book, but your pictures don't have to look exactly like the illustrations. (Donna gave her class ample time to draw.) Now, in groups of five, please share your pictures to see who drew

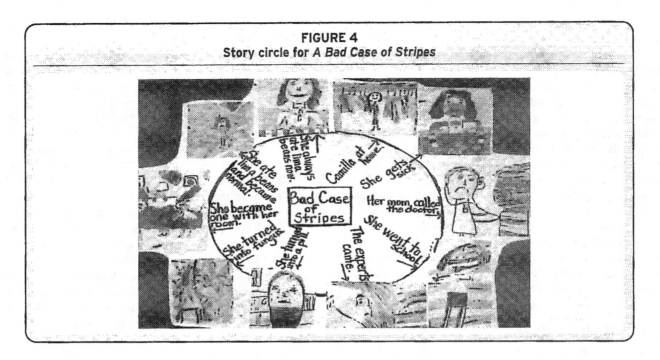

FIGURE 4
Story circle for *A Bad Case of Stripes*

which Camilla. Then, put your pictures in the order that each one happened to Camilla in the story. (Each small group was given sufficient time to complete this task.)

To share your work, I'd like each group to complete a story circle using the events in your illustrations. Be sure to fill in the story circle completely by including any story events that may be missing from your group's pictures.

Donna handed out copies of the story circle chart and monitored each group's progress. One group's completed visual is shown in Figure 4.

At this juncture, Donna reinforced the students' comprehension efforts by explicitly reviewing the strategy and its payoffs.

What comprehension strategy are we practicing here? ("Sequencing.") How do you sequence a story? ("You put the events in order.") When does the sequencing strategy help you as a reader? ("When a story has a lot of events.") Why is sequencing a useful strategy? ("It helps me remember more about a story after I'm done reading it.")

One things leads to another

Donna's lesson could have ended at this point. Instead, because her students' interest showed no sign of flagging, she chose another strategy to practice with them.

Nice work, class. Let's practice another way of thinking about *A Bad Case of Stripes*. We're going to discuss how one thing leads to another in this story. Does anyone know the name for this comprehension strategy? ("Cause and effect.") Cause and effect means that

one thing happens and this, in turn, makes something else happen. We'll use an episode analysis chart to determine the cause and effect relationships. I'll use your responses to create this chart on the board. Let's start with a literal question. Do you remember what the word *literal* means? ("It means you can find the answer right in the story.") Okay, here's the question: What is Camilla's problem in this story? ("She turns into stuff.") What is her response to this problem? How does the problem make her feel? ("Weird, scared, embarrassed, shocked.") What actions does she take to try to solve her problem? ("She tries lots of different cures from different doctors. Then she decides to eat lima beans.") What outcome does this action lead to? ("She turns back into herself.")

Next, Donna challenged her young thinkers by adding a layer of sophistication to her strategic instruction.

Well done, class. Let's review the cause-and-effect relationships in the story. (The students read through the four-part chart.) Let's try a more difficult version of episode analysis by asking inference questions about this story. Do you remember what the word *inference* means? ("To make a guess about something that isn't spelled out in the story by using evidence from the book and our lives.") Right, we think about what's in the text, what's in our heads, and what's in our hearts. Let me start this episode analysis chart with a problem taken directly from the first page of the book: Camilla wants to fit in. What is her response to this problem? ("She ignores her real feelings.") What actions does this response lead to? ("She keeps changing into things. Camilla can't get comfortable until she pays at-

FIGURE 5
Episode analysis chart

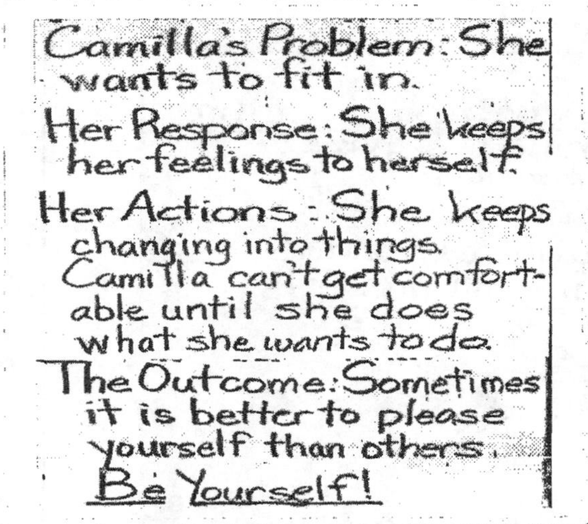

Camilla's Problem: She wants to fit in.

Her Response: She keeps her feelings to herself.

Her Actions: She keeps changing into things. Camilla can't get comfortable until she does what she wants to do.

The Outcome: Sometimes it is better to please yourself than others. Be Yourself!

tention to her feelings and does what she wants to do.") Given this problem, response, and action, what inferences can you make about the outcome of this story? What point is the author trying to make? Think for a minute about the story and your own life, and then come up with a theme, or lesson about life, that you find in *A Bad Case of Stripes*. Remember, a story can have more than one theme. Write your personal theme statement next to the outcome space in the episode analysis chart.

Donna gave individual students the support they needed to complete this task. One third grader's completed episode analysis chart can be seen in Figure 5.

To complete this comprehension lesson, Donna summarized and reinforced her students' accomplishments with the complementary strategies of cause and effect and making thematic connections.

We'll share some of your theme statements in just a moment. But first, what comprehension strategy have we been using our episode analysis charts to practice? ("Cause and effect.") How do you use cause and effect? ("You decide how a character's problem makes him or her feel, and then you figure out how he or she acts and why.") When does cause and effect help you as a reader? ("When it is not clear why certain events are happening and you need to make inferences about a book.") Why is cause and effect a useful comprehension strategy? ("It helps you to understand the point of the story.")

OK, now let's share some of your theme statements. Does everybody remember what the word *theme* means? ("A lesson about life.") Any volunteers? (The students generated four themes: "You need to listen to your feelings." "Don't lie to your friends, or they

won't trust you." "People who are mean to you aren't your friends. You don't need to please them to be happy." "Do what you want to do.") Donna wrote these theme statements on the board and asked, "Can you think of other stories that could fit these themes?" (The students offered the following text connections: *The Little Red Hen* (Granowsky, 1996)—she did what the other animals said to do, but by the time she made the bread she didn't want to share with them anymore." "*Locked in the Library* (Brown, 1998)—Arthur is busy doing his homework, but his friend wants him to play a game. They start to get into a fight, but then they work it out so he plays with his friend as soon as his homework is finished." "*Friends From the Other Side* (Anzaldua, 1993)—Prietita stood up for the new kid even though her friends wanted her to be mean to him, just like what happened in *The Brand New Kid* (Couric, 2000)." "*Crow Boy* (Yashima, 1955)—the other kids made fun of Crow Boy because he was different, but it turned out he could do some cool things that they couldn't do.")

Instructional options

Donna created visual structures with her third graders for each of the seven additional comprehension strategies we have identified in this article. Each visual, accompanied by a brief strategy explanation, is applied to a trade book Donna read and discussed with her students. In keeping with our desire to offer students experiences with a variety of genres, three of these trade books are fiction, two are nonfiction, one is a poem, and one is in play form.

Locating details

Finding specific information in a text can be introduced with the aid of a semantic web to map the connections among important details. The example in Figure 6 features the poetic picture book *This Land Is Your Land* (1998), based on Woody Guthrie's famous protest song about life in the United States during the Great Depression.

Comparing and contrasting

Explaining how two or more things, people, places, or ideas are alike or different from one another can be introduced with the aid of a weave chart to highlight similarities and differences. A chart created for *Talking Walls* (1992), an expository picture book by Margy Knight about the different kinds of walls people have built around the world throughout recorded history, appears in Figure 7.

Envisioning character change

Pinpointing how characters change and grow can be introduced with the aid of a character continuum to track character development throughout the course of a story. The continuum in Figure 8 features *The Long March* (1998), a narrative picture book by Marie-Louise Fitzpatrick about the compassionate re-

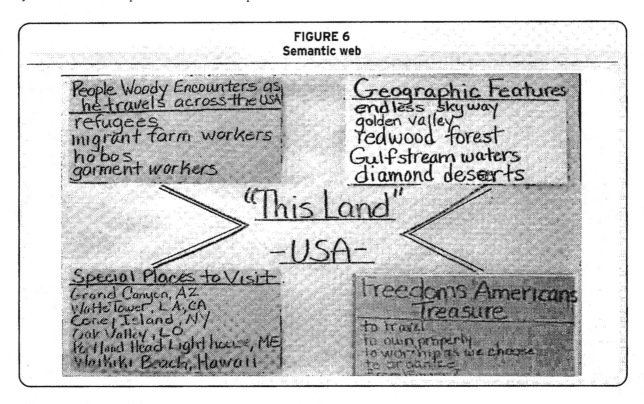

FIGURE 6
Semantic web

People Woody Encounters as he travels across the USA
refugees
migrant farm workers
hobos
garment workers

Geographic Features
endless sky way
golden valley
redwood forest
Gulfstream waters
diamond deserts

"This Land"
-USA-

Special Places to Visit
Grand Canyon, AZ
Watte Tower, LA, CA
Coney Island, NY
Oak Valley, LO
Portland Head Lighthouse, ME
Waikiki Beach, Hawaii

Freedoms Americans Treasure
to travel
to own property
to worship as we choose
to organize

sponse of the Choctaw people to the Irish Potato Famine in the mid-1800s.

FIGURE 7
Weave chart

Wall	Location	Construction	Purpose
Great Wall of China	across China	large stones and granite boulders	to keep out invaders
Berlin Wall	Berlin, Germany	built as an Iron Curtain to separate Eastern and Western Europe	to divide and control
Mahabalipuram's Well	Bay of Bengal, India	carved figures into the cliffs with chisels & hammers	a place to worship and pray.
City of the Sun	Cuzco Peru (in the Andes Mountains)	enormous stones.. moved by levers and ?	to celebrate with song and dance
Vietnam Veterans Wall	Washington, DC (USA)	black granite- chiseled with names designed by Maya lin	to remember a war and loved ones who died in it.

Drawing conclusions

Going beyond literal information to make supportable guesses about ideas that are not completely spelled out can be introduced with the aid of a conclusion hierarchy chart to focus readers on subtle foreshadowing clues in a text.

The hierarchy in Figure 9 features *I Have an Olive Tree* (1999), a narrative picture book by Eve Bunting about a young Greek American girl's awakening to her cultural heritage.

Making predictions

Using available clues to make supportable guesses about what might happen next can be introduced with the aid of a modified story graph to trace the pattern of a character's behavior and unfolding plot events. The example (see Figure 10) features *Hey, Little Ant* (1998), a dramatic encounter between a skeptical young boy and a quick-thinking ant by Phillip and Hannah Hoose. Readers take on, in turn, the roles of both participants as they debate the ant's continued existence.

FIGURE 8
Character continuum

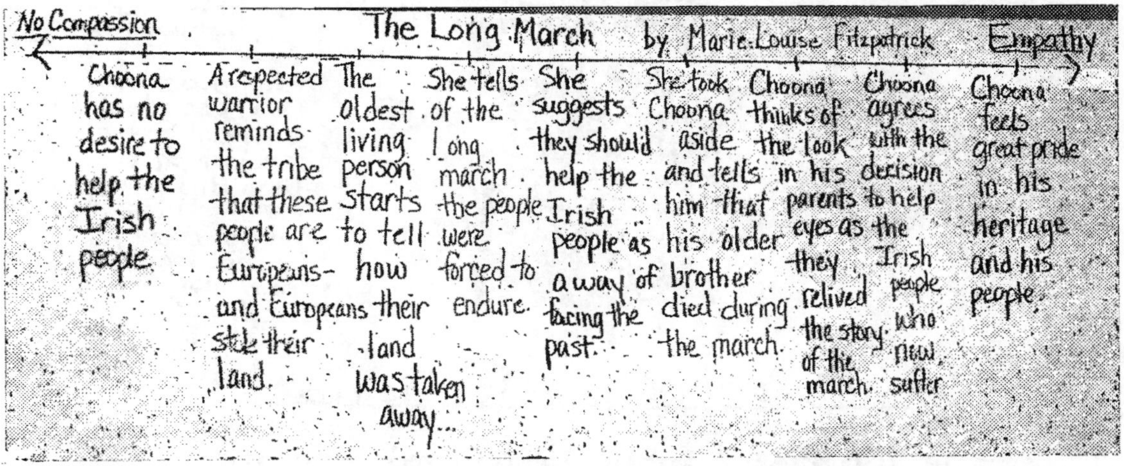

Making thematic connections

Connecting a text's message to the reader's own life can be introduced with a life lesson chart to accentuate the power of thematic lessons in young readers' lives. The chart in Figure 11 features *Uncle Jed's Barbershop* (1993), a narrative picture book by Margaree Mitchell about a man who balances his own dreams with the needs of his community.

Taking multiple perspectives

Considering two or more points of view can be introduced with the aid of a perspective lens to illustrate how perception is shaped by the ways we choose to look at the world. The example in Figure 12 features *I Am an Artist* (1992), an expository picture book by Pat Collins that encourages the creative impulse in all readers.

What difference does it make?

Donna began her comprehension exploration with clear goals in mind for her budding readers. Initially, she wanted them to learn appropriate words (e.g., *literal, inference, strategies, visual structures*) to talk about the comprehension process and become aware of how it works. We knew she had approached this goal when her students started to use this language among themselves. For example, we might overhear them saying, "Why don't you do a weave chart to compare and contrast these two settings?" The approach was difficult for some of Donna's third graders. In the beginning, some children struggled as they tried to learn the strategies and understand their purposes. Helping Donna's students become purposeful in

their strategy use was a yearlong effort. As they became more aware of the process, the children developed deeper personal connections with the texts they read and employed comprehension strategies with greater regularity. As the year progressed, our gauge for student growth became their ability to think flexibly. They began to use different strategies independently with different texts and make increasingly sophisticated connections between texts.

However, not all students progressed at the same rate. The children who actively participated in these lessons became more adept at using the strategies. Donna worked to keep them all involved by focusing on their thoughts and ideas. The students who talked more began to understand the strategies by using them. For these young readers, the payoffs were clear. This approach to comprehension instruction helped them become better thinkers. Now, they comprehend new texts and life situations with more ease. This outcome made us realize that adults use these same strategies in daily life.

From our perspective, some students' comprehension difficulties could be alleviated if more elementary teachers made comprehension instruction a central part of their literacy curriculum. We can only speculate beyond Donna's classroom about the kinds of support needed to help other teachers feature comprehension instruction, but our experiences suggest the following areas for future research:

- How much knowledge do elementary teachers and students already possess about specific comprehension strategies?

- Under what conditions do teachers become metacognitively aware of strategy use in their own classroom practice?

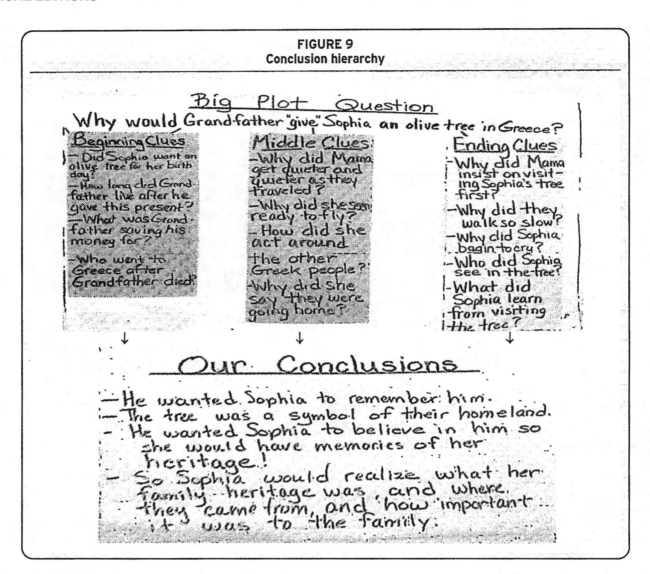

FIGURE 9
Conclusion hierarchy

Big Plot Question
Why would Grandfather "give" Sophia an olive tree in Greece?

Beginning Clues
- Did Sophia want an olive tree for her birthday?
- How long did Grandfather live after he gave this present?
- What was Grandfather saving his money for?
- Who went to Greece after Grandfather died?

Middle Clues
- Why did Mama get quieter and quieter as they traveled?
- Why did she seem ready to fly?
- How did she act around the other Greek people?
- Why did she say they were going home?

Ending Clues
- Why did Mama insist on visiting Sophia's tree first?
- Why did they walk so slow?
- Why did Sophia begin to cry?
- Who did Sophia see in the tree?
- What did Sophia learn from visiting the tree?

Our Conclusions
- He wanted Sophia to remember him.
- The tree was a symbol of their homeland.
- He wanted Sophia to believe in him so she would have memories of her heritage!
- So Sophia would realize what her family heritage was, and where they came from, and how important it was to the family.

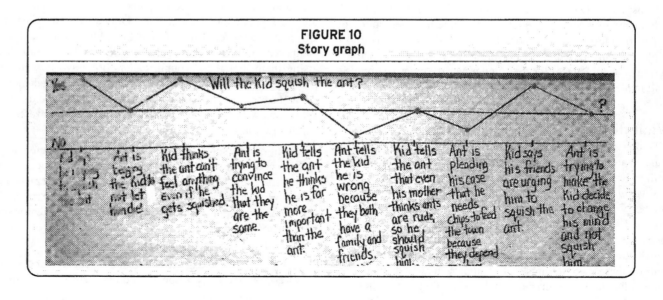

FIGURE 10
Story graph

Will the Kid squish the ant?

| Ant is begging the kid to not let him die | Kid thinks the ant can't feel anything even if he gets squished. | Ant is trying to convince the kid that they are the same. | Kid tells the ant he thinks he is far more important than the ant. | Ant tells the kid he is wrong because they both have a family and friends. | Kid tells the ant that even his mother thinks ants are rude, so he should squish him. | Ant is pleading his case that he needs chips to feed the town because they depend | Kid says his friends are urging him to squish the ant. | Ant is trying to make the kid decide to change his mind and not squish him. |

FIGURE 11
Life lesson chart

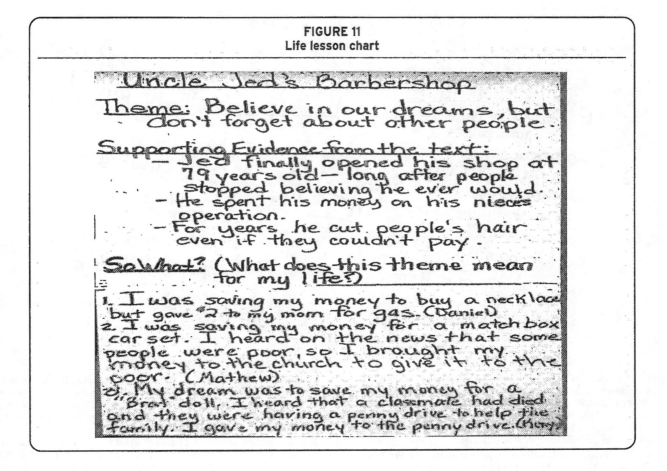

- What kinds of texts support (and hinder) teachers in their efforts to model specific comprehension strategies and articulate their purposes?
- How can other teachers build on the knowledge Donna's students now possess about the comprehension process as they make their way into the upper grades?

No prescription for comprehension

The instructional ideas in this article are adaptable to a wide variety of texts and student needs. However, comprehension instruction is a creative process, and no two teachers will approach it exactly the same way. Therefore, we encourage other elementary teachers to modify these methods to complement their individual teaching styles. For example, visual structures are most effective when used judiciously. Too much structure can constrain understanding and limit a reader's engagement with a text. On the other hand, young readers can never be given too much support and encouragement in their efforts to become more sophisticated thinkers. The creative instruction students receive in learning how to comprehend during elementary school will accrue over time in heightened reasoning abilities as they make their way through the grades to high school and beyond.

References

Alexander, P., & Jetton, T. (2000). Learning from text: A multidimensional and developmental perspective. In M.L. Kamil, P.B. Mosenthal, P.D. Pearson, & R. Barr (Eds.), *Handbook of reading research* (Vol. 3, pp. 545-561). Mahwah, NJ: Erlbaum.

Alvermann, D., & Boothby, P. (1986). Children's transfer of graphic organizer instruction. *Reading Psychology, 7*(2), 87-100.

Anderson, R., & Pearson, D. (1984). A schema-theoretic view of basic processes in reading. In P.D. Pearson, R. Barr, M.L. Kamil, & P. Mosenthal (Eds.), *Handbook of reading research* (Vol. 1, pp. 255-291). New York: Longman.

Barton, J. (2001). *Teaching with children's literature.* Norwood, MA: Christopher-Gordon.

Beach, R. (1993). *A teacher's introduction to reader-response theories.* Urbana, IL: National Council of Teachers of English.

Brandt, R. (1998). *Powerful learning.* Washington, DC: Association for Supervision and Curriculum Development.

Bransford, J., Brown, A., & Cocking, R. (Eds.). (1999). *How people learn: Brain, mind, experience, and school.* Washington, DC: National Academy Press.

Bruner, J. (1985). On teaching and thinking: An afterthought. In S. Chipman, J. Segal, & R. Glaser (Eds.), *Thinking and learning skills, Vol. 2: Research and open questions* (pp. 597-607). Hillsdale, NJ: Erlbaum.

Calfee, R., & Patrick, C. (1995). *Teach our children well: Bringing K-12 education into the 21st century.* Stanford, CA: Stanford Alumni Association.

Duffy, G., Roehler, L., & Mason, J. (Eds.). (1984). *Comprehension instruction: Perspectives and suggestions.* New York: Longman.

Durkin, D. (1993). *Teaching them to read* (6th ed.). Boston: Allyn & Bacon.

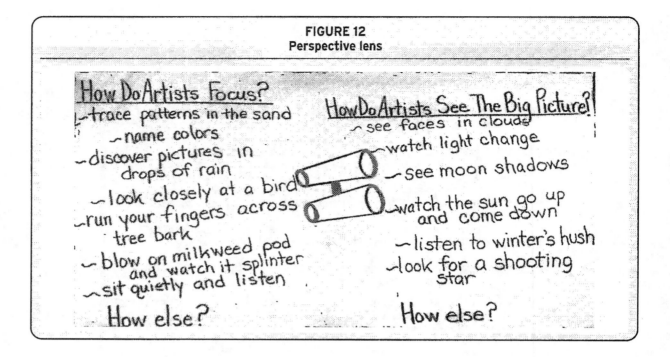

FIGURE 12
Perspective lens

How Do Artists Focus?
- trace patterns in the sand
- name colors
- discover pictures in drops of rain
- look closely at a bird
- run your fingers across tree bark
- blow on milkweed pod and watch it splinter
- sit quietly and listen

How else?

How Do Artists See The Big Picture?
- see faces in clouds
- watch light change
- see moon shadows
- watch the sun go up and come down
- listen to winter's hush
- look for a shooting star

How else?

Fisher, D., Flood, J., & Lapp, D. (1999). The role of literature in literacy development. In L. Gambrell, L. Morrow, S. Neumann, & M. Pressley (Eds.), *Best practices in literacy instruction* (pp. 119-135). New York: Guilford.

Graves, M., Juel, C., & Graves, B. (2001). *Teaching reading in the 21st century* (2nd ed.). Boston: Allyn & Bacon.

Guthrie, J., & Anderson, E. (1999). Engagement in reading: Processes of motivated, strategic, knowledgeable, social readers. In J. Guthrie & D. Alvermann (Eds.), *Engaged reading: Processes, practices, and policy implications* (pp. 17-46). New York: Teachers College Press.

Hudson, J., & Slackman, E. (1990). Children's use of scripts in inferential text processing. *Discourse Processing, 13,* 375-385.

Marshall, J. (2000). Response to literature. In M.L. Kamil, P.B. Mosenthal, P.D. Pearson, & R. Barr (Eds.), *Handbook of reading research* (Vol. 3, pp. 545-561). Mahwah, NJ: Erlbaum.

Norton, D. (1992). *The impact of literature-based reading.* New York: Merrill.

Paris, S., Cross, D., & Lipson, M. (1984). Informed strategies for learning: A program to improve children's reading awareness and comprehension. *Journal of Educational Psychology, 76,* 1239-1252.

Paris, S., & Jacobs, J. (1984). The benefits of informed instruction for children's reading awareness and comprehension skills. *Child Development, 55,* 2083-2093.

Paris, S., Wasik, B., & Turner, J. (1991). The development of strategic readers. In R. Barr, M.L. Kamil, P.B. Mosenthal, & P.D. Pearson (Eds.), *Handbook of reading research* (Vol. 2, pp. 186-212). White Plains, NY: Longman.

Pressley, M. (1998). *Reading instruction that works: The case for balanced teaching.* New York: Guilford.

Pressley, M. (2000). What should comprehension instruction be the instruction of? In M.L. Kamil, P.B. Mosenthal, P.D. Pearson, & R. Barr (Eds.), *Handbook of reading research* (Vol. 3, pp. 545-561). Mahwah, NJ: Erlbaum.

Pressley, M., & Afflerbach, P. (1995). *Verbal protocols of reading: The nature of constructively responsive reading.* Mahwah, NJ: Erlbaum.

Pressley, M., El-Dinary, P., Wharton-McDonald, R., & Brown, R. (1998). Transactional instruction of comprehension strategies in the elementary grades. In D. Schunk & B. Zimmerman (Eds.), *Self-regulated learning: From teaching to self-reflective practice* (pp. 54-76). New York: Guilford.

Roehler, L., & Cantlon, D. (1997). Scaffolding: A powerful toot in social constructivist classrooms. In K. Hogan & M. Pressley (Eds.), *Scaffolding student learning: Instructional approaches and issues* (pp. 6-42). Cambridge, MA: Brookline.

Roehler, L., & Duffy, G. (1991). Teachers' instructional actions. In R. Barr, M.L. Kamil, P.B. Mosenthal, & P.D. Pearson (Eds.), *Handbook of reading research* (Vol. 2, pp. 861-883). White Plains, NY: Longman.

Rosenblatt, L. (1983). *Literature as exploration* (4th ed.). New York: Modern Language Association.

Rumelhart, D. (1980). Schemata: The building blocks of cognition. In R. Spiro, B. Bruce, & W. Brewer (Eds.), *Theoretical issues in reading comprehension* (pp. 33-58). Hillsdale, NJ: Erlbaum.

Schunk, D., & Zimmerman, B. (Eds.). (1998). *Self-regulated learning: From teaching to self-reflective practice.* New York: Guilford.

Snow, C., Burns, M., & Griffin, P. (1998). *Preventing reading difficulties in young children.* Washington, DC: National Academy Press.

Spiegel, D. (1998). Reader response approaches and the growth of readers. *Language Arts, 76,* 41-56.

Tierney, R., & Readence, J. (2000). *Reading strategies: A compendium* (5th ed.). Boston: Allyn & Bacon.

Williams, J. (1993). Comprehension of students with and without learning disabilities: Identification of narrative themes and idiosyncratic text representations. *Journal of Educational Psychology, 85,* 631-641.

Barton teaches at Rhode Island College (Department of Elementary Education, 210 Horace Mann, Rhode Island College, Providence, RI 02908, USA). E-mail jbarton@ric.edu. Sawyer is a third-grade teacher at Henry J. Winters Elementary School in Pawtucket, Rhode Island.

From *Reading Teacher,* Vol. 57, No. 4, January 2003, pp. 334-347. Copyright © 2003 by International Reading Association. Reprinted by permission.

A comprehension checklist: What if it doesn't make sense?

Dixie D. Massey

"What can you do if what you're reading doesn't make sense?" I asked a girl I'll call Hunter. "I don't know," was her reply. I have found that Hunter's reply is typical for struggling and nonstruggling readers, but *typical* makes it no less frustrating. There are plenty of suggestions for students who are trying to decode an unknown word (e.g., looking for familiar chunks, looking at the picture). Strategies that students can use when their comprehension breaks down are much harder to find. Texts and journals give multiple suggestions for teaching comprehension, such as K-W-L (What I know, What I want to know, What I have learned) charts and DR-TAs (Directed Reading-Thinking Activities), but these suggestions are hard for individual students to apply when they are trying to understand a text.

We know that good readers employ fix-up strategies (Pressley, 2002) and that poor readers lack the knowledge necessary to correct their comprehension breakdowns. Even the tutoring manuals and texts on reading difficulties seem to lack definite suggestions for dealing with comprehension breakdowns for transitional and older elementary readers, yet comprehension is the point of difficulty for most elementary and middle school readers (Gunning, 2002; Morris, 1999).

Comprehension checklist

This article was born of the present dilemma. I provide here one method for dealing with students' comprehension breakdowns by proposing a comprehension checklist. This checklist is designed to give struggling readers a starting point for fixing their own comprehension breakdowns by suggesting strategies and helping them self-regulate their learning, as recommended by researchers (Buettner, 2002; Pressley, 2000). On the basis of my experience as an elementary teacher, a university educator, and a tutor of struggling readers, I began forming the checklist shown in Figure 1. It lists multiple student-di-

rected strategies and serves as an idea list for teachers to pull from—although there are other strategies that could be included, such as graphic organizers, questioning strategies, and additional self-monitoring strategies (Baker, 2002; Dowhower, 1999).

The checklist is divided into prereading comprehension strategies, during-reading comprehension strategies, and postreading comprehension strategies. The strategies included on the checklist are student directed and, after appropriate modeling, do not need to be teacher led. The steps in using the checklist are listed in the Sidebar. To ensure appropriate instruction, the checklist should be individualized around students' strengths and needs, as described in the following two examples.

Individualized comprehension checklist

I worked with Bradley (pseudonym) when he was in the second and third grades. His decoding ability was limited; his ability to comprehend was almost nonexistent. He did not want to think about what was going on or what was going to happen. When asked what he thought would happen, he invariably answered "I don't know." What Bradley did well was look at the pictures before he started to read. While he had been taught to look at the pictures, Bradley didn't know what he was looking for when he previewed the pictures. Thus, asking him to look at the pictures (using what he already knew) and predict what the story was going to be about (new strategy) provided the first step in my instruction. I also added an after-reading strategy, checking predictions, and created an individualized comprehension checklist for Bradley on a laminated bookmark-sized copy of the comprehension checklist. I asked him to check off the strategies he used. Because we practiced these strategies, I did not use picture cues; however, picture cues may be necessary for some students.

FIGURE 1
A comprehension checklist

When you read, ask yourself: Does it make sense? If it doesn't make sense, place a check beside which of the following comprehension strategies you used.

Prereading: Before you started reading, did you
- Set a purpose for reading—what do you need to find or figure out?
- Think about what you already know about the topic—a lot or a little?
- Look at the pictures and predict what the story is going to be about?
- Read the captions?
- Read the bold words?
- Read the table of contents?
- Read any summaries?
- Read the questions at the end of the chapter?

During reading: While you were reading, did you
- Skip the word—is it one word that doesn't make sense? Did you try skipping that word and reading to the end of the sentence or paragraph? Did you go back to see if you knew what the word was or if you knew what it meant?
- Reread the paragraph and look for new information?
- Keep a mental picture of what's happening in your head?
- Summarize—stop every page or two pages and summarize the main points?
- Find that you could go on, or do you need more information from another student or teacher?

After reading: After you finished reading, did you
- Do a text check—was this text too hard, too easy, or just right?
- Reread the section, looking for new details?
- Develop questions—what might the teacher ask? What might be on a test?
- Check your predictions—were you right? If you weren't, did you decide why?

FIGURE 2
Bradley's individualized comprehension checklist

When you read, ask yourself: Does it make sense? If it doesn't make sense, place a check beside which of the following comprehension strategies you used.

Prereading: Before you started reading, did you
- Look at the pictures?

After reading: After you read, did you
- Check your predictions to see if you were right?
- Go back and reread if your predictions were wrong?

As I modeled these new strategies, Bradley began making and checking his predictions. Sometimes, he made an incorrect prediction. We talked about what it meant if he made the wrong prediction. Sometimes there was an incomplete or tricky picture. Through think-alouds, I began to build on our strategy list, this time adding rereading. If our prediction wasn't right and we were still confused, rereading the page of text might help us find where and why we went wrong. Because we were still dealing with short texts, I added this to the after-reading section of Bradley's checklist. His individualized checklist at this point in the tutoring is as shown in Figure 2.

In this manner, we gradually built the checklist to include numerous strategies, all of which were modeled and scaffolded until Bradley could use them independently. As Bradley was introduced to more and more genres and texts, the number of comprehension strategies grew. In the process, he was able to suggest new strategies of his own, becoming more metacognitively aware of his own reading processes. When I started working with Bradley at the end of his second-grade year, his comprehension was at a late primer level. At the end of his third-grade year, he was able to read and comprehend at a late second level.

Ongoing comprehension checklist

Kendra (pseudonym) was a rising ninth grader who came to me for tutoring over a summer. Our first tutoring session was abysmal. She was sullen, barely raising her eyes to acknowledge me or answer a question. What I was able to assess showed me that she was able to comprehend complex plots from narrative texts, particularly sci-

FIGURE 3
Kendra's ongoing comprehension checklist

When you read, ask yourself: Does it make sense? If it doesn't make sense, check which of the following comprehension strategies you used.

During reading: Before you started reading, did you
Keep a mental picture in your mind or on paper?
Summarize—stop every page or two pages and summarize the main points?

After reading: After you read, did you
Reread and add at least two details to your picture or mental image?
Ask yourself questions—what questions might the teacher ask or might there be on a test?

ence fiction. However, her ability to comprehend other text structures was minimal. She was quite clear about not wanting to be tutored. I found out that what she did like was art. Her notebook was full of drawings.

With this very limited information, I decided to list making mental pictures of the text as a strategy during reading. I also included a postreading strategy—rereading and adding at least two details to her physical or mental image. This strategy extended what she already knew and liked to do. We began with the Harry Potter text she was reading (Rowling, 1999). I asked her to read two pages draw the pictures she saw in her mind. After glancing up to let me know she was surprised that I would ask her that in a reading session, she went to work—if not happily, at least willingly. When she finished her picture, I asked her to tell me about what she selected. We verified certain details in the text. Next, I asked her to reread, looking for two more details she could add to her picture.

From this initial list of strategies, I gradually modeled (using Kendra's physical pictures to summarize the selection and to write questions pertaining to the information) strategies validated as effective in improving comprehension for older students (Pressley, 2002). Kendra's checklist began to expand.

As our tutoring proceeded, I bargained with Kendra, She could bring in a text of her choosing for us to read and practice with, then I would bring in a text that I liked. I always chose a content area text—usually social studies, because it was a problem area for Kendra. Up until this point, there were no prereading strategies on Kendra's checklist (see Figure 3). I modeled setting the purpose and previewing (particularly the pictures) as prereading strategies and added these to her list. Kendra's checklist was in no way complete when she finished her summer with me, but she did leave with more strategies than when she came.

A COMPREHENSION CHECKLIST: STEP BY STEP

1. Assess the students' strengths and weaknesses through informal reading inventories and interest surveys. (I used the Qualitative Reading Inventory—3, 2001.)
2. Begin a personalized checklist, listing the strengths of the students first.
3. Identify one to two new comprehension strategies from Figure 1 that are within the students' reading abilities and needs.
4. Model the new strategy several times, then allow the students to participate in the strategy use with you.
5. Allow the students to read a passage independently. Students then check off the strategies that they used from their new checklist. This passage should be one that is at an instructional level for the students and will allow them to use the old and new strategies.
6. Discuss using the checklist as a guide. Allow students to think about other strategies they used to understand the passage and might wish to add to their checklist.

Meeting individual needs

The comprehension checklist offers teachers and tutors a concrete way to help students become aware of comprehension strategies and monitor their own progress, and it includes strategies that are different from those used by a teacher to guide understanding of complex stories. The checklist may be used with individual students or in small groups. The key to its effective use is individualizing the checklist around the students' strengths and adding pre-, during-, and postreading strategies through modeling and ample practice with a variety of texts.

When using the comprehension checklist with culturally or linguistically diverse students, the teacher will want to spend extra time building background knowledge of reading strategies and text content through thinkalouds and hands-on experiences before introducing the comprehension strategies included on the list. For all children, the strategies added must be ones that the students can use independently, without teacher direction (see also Baker, 2002; Dowhower, 1999, for further self-monitoring strategies). Through the checklist, we begin to address the need for helping students monitor their own comprehension (Pressley, 2002).

References

Baker, L. (2002). Metacognition in comprehension instruction. In C.C. Block & M. Pressley (Eds.), *Comprehension instruction: Research-based best practices* (pp. 77-95). New York: Guilford.

Buettner, E.G. (2002). Sentence by sentence self-monitoring. *The Reading Teacher, 56*, 34-44.

Dowhower, S. (1999). Supporting a strategic stance in the classroom: A comprehension framework for helping teachers help students to be strategic. *The Reading Teacher, 52,* 672-688.

Gunning, T.G. (2002). *Assessing and correcting reading and writing difficulties* (2nd ed.). Boston: Allyn & Bacon.

Morris, D. (1999). *The Howard Street training manual. Teaching at-risk readers in the primary grades.* New York: Guilford.

Pressley, M. (2000). What should comprehension instruction be the instruction of? In M.L. Kamil, P.B., Mosenthal, P.D. Pearson, & R. Barr (Eds.), *Handbook of reading research* (Vol III, pp. 545-562). Mahwah, NJ: Erlbaum.

Pressley, M. (2002). Comprehension strategies instruction: A turn-of-the-century status report. In C.C. Block & M. Pressley (Eds.), *Comprehension instruction: Research-based best practices* (pp. 11-27). New York: Guilford.

Rowling, J.K. (1999). *Harry Potter and the prisoner of Azkaban.* New York: Scholastic.

Massey teaches at North Carolina A&T University in Greensboro, USA. She may be contacted at ddmassey@ncat.edu.

How do you know?
A strategy to help emergent readers make inferences.

Janet C. Richards; Nancy A. Anderson

Inferencing has been described as central "to the overall process of comprehension"—(Anderson & Pearson, 1984, p. 269) and as the glue that cements the construction of meaning (see Suh & Trabasso, 1993). It is the strategic process of generating assumptions, making predictions, and coming to conclusions based upon given information in text and in illustrations. Theories that attempt to explain inference generation conclude that inferring requires readers to spontaneously engage in complex thinking as they encode and process text information (Long, Seely, Oppy, & Golding, 1996).

Causal and relational inferences

Distinctions can be made between two main types of inferences. Causal inferences in part require readers to infer the antecedent or consequences of an action. Here is an example: "David did not feel well. He had eaten five hamburgers, 11 cookies, and three ice cream cones at the school fair." Readers must conclude that David felt ill because he ate a large amount of food. Relational inferences require readers to integrate information across sentences, as in this example: "Morgan sat at the kitchen table doing addition problems. She could hear the TV. It was her favorite show. Morgan sighed and got to work." Readers must deduce here that Morgan was doing her homework, the TV was not in the kitchen, and Morgan wanted to watch her favorite TV program.

In nearly every quality children's picture book, emergent readers must infer information from text *and* illustrations to fully comprehend and enjoy the story. For example, in *Gregory Cool* (Binch, 1994), Gregory flies to a tropical island where his grandmother meets him at the airport. With a broad smile, she says, "My, my, Gregory, you just like your photos…. It's your granny got to kiss you at last." It is vital that young students infer from

Granny's greeting that Gregory had never visited his grandmother because this piece of information explains his reluctant attitude and indecisive behavior throughout much of the story.

Readers have to make another important inference in the Creole folk tale *The Talking Eggs* (San Souci, 1989) when the author explains that Blanche had to iron the clothes each morning using an old iron filled with hot coals. Unless young readers conclude that Blanche's farmhouse had no electricity, they gloss over two important pieces of information—the setting (i.e., in the past) and the family's poverty, which is the reason Blanche's mother hungered for riches.

In the Latino story *Too Many Tamales* (Soto, 1993), emergent readers must generate inferences from the text and the illustrations to build a complete understanding of Maria's multifaceted personality and her goals and actions. Early in the story, Maria and her mother happily make tamales. Maria's mother leaves the kitchen, and an illustration shows Maria wiping her hands on her apron with a sly yet triumphant smile on her face as she looks at her mother's diamond ring on the kitchen counter. When she glances furtively at the doorway, readers must deduce that Maria knows she is about to do something wrong and wants to be sure her mother won't return while she puts on the ring, "just for a minute." A later illustration shows Maria with her cousins—she looks down at her hand and screams, "The ring!" Emergent readers must infer that Maria has panicked because the ring is missing from her finger.

Helping emergent readers

In our work with young students, we often note that they do not generate inferences naturally and spontaneously. They can usually deduce information from one segment of the text, but they fail to integrate it with implied information in other parts of the story or in storybook illustrations. Often, emergent readers experience problems because of text constraints, such as syntactic or vocabulary difficulty (Dewitz & Dewitz, 2003). Their underdeveloped reasoning abilities, lack of prior knowledge for story content, or overdependence on prior knowledge that causes them to invent plausible but inaccurate answers also may create barriers to comprehension (Anderson & Pearson, 1984; Dewitz & Dewitz, 2003; Neuman, 1990; Trabasso & Suh, 1993).

Readers can improve their abilities to infer information when teachers model how to reason, make assumptions, and come to conclusions (Hansen, 1981; Hansen & Pearson, 1983; Mantione & Smead, 2003; Raphael & Wonnacott, 1985). Therefore, we have developed a think-aloud questioning strategy to develop emergent readers' abilities to make causal and relational inferences. We call it How Do You Know? The strategy helps emergent readers focus their attention on important information that is explicitly stated in storybooks and depicted in their illustrations. It also helps emergent readers to (a) make connections between given and implied information and (b) examine their thinking and reasoning so that they can verbalize how they arrived at their assumptions and conclusions.

Preparing for How Do You Know?

Before introducing this questioning strategy, teachers should carefully preview quality children's literature to identify what types of inferential connections can and should be made. For example, in *Doctor De Soto* (Steig, 1982), a mouse, who is a dentist, reluctantly accepts a sly, hungry fox as a patient. Near the midpoint of the story, the mouse gives the fox anesthesia so he can extract an infected tooth. The fox starts dreaming and mumbles, "M-m-m, yummy…. How I love them raw … with just a pinch of salt." The mouse and his spouse make their own clever inference and immediately put a long pole in the fox's mouth to keep it open.

STEPS IN HOW DO YOU KNOW?

- Read a picture book aloud and stop where students should make an inference.
- Ask a question that prompts students to infer important information (e.g., "Do you think Gregory got to see his grandmother often?").
- When students respond, confirm their answer and ask, "Does the author say that?"
- When students reply, "No," ask them, "Then how do you know?"
- When students are familiar with the strategy, ask them, "Are there any inferences you can make in this paragraph? Explain how you figured out the connections."

Presenting How Do You Know?

To introduce this questioning strategy, tell your students they are going to learn a new way to understand stories by making inferences. Explain that inferences are two or more connections that readers make as they read and listen to stories and view their illustrations. Next, model the strategy by reading a picture book aloud, stopping at a place in the story where an inference can and should be made. For example, in presenting the scene in *Gregory Cool* (Binch, 1994) where Granny greets Gregory, we stopped and asked, "Do you think Gregory got to see his grandmother often?" The students replied, "No," and we confirmed, "Good thinking. Does the story say Gregory did not get to see his grandmother often?" When the students said, "No," we asked them, "Then, *how do you know*?" With some probing, they explained their reasoning. One boy answered, "The part when Granny said 'got to kiss you at last' and 'You just like your photos' gave me clues."

We followed the same questioning procedure with *The Talking Eggs* (San Souci, 1989). When we read the part where the author explained that Blanche had to iron the clothes each morning using an old iron filled with hot coals, we stopped and asked, "Do you think the family had electricity?" When the students said, "No," we responded, "Good thinking?' Then, we asked, "Does the author say that the family didn't have electricity? When the students replied, "No," we probed, "Then, *how do you know*?" One student explained, "Because if the family had electricity, Blanche could plug the iron in an electric socket, and she wouldn't need to use hot coals."

Expanding How Do You Know?

When emergent readers are familiar with the think-aloud questioning strategy, teachers can gradually shift responsibility for identifying inferential connections to them. For example, the teacher can identify relevant paragraphs in stories and ask students, "Can you think of any inferences you might make in this paragraph? Explain your thinking. How did you figure out the connections?" These types of questions provide opportunities for emergent readers to communicate their developing understanding of inferences and to interact with peers as they share the processes they used to construct meaning from text (Kucan & Beck, 1997).

As students become more proficient in recognizing inferential linkages in picture books, teachers can encourage them to engage in a reading and writing connection and to work with a partner, filling in charts (see Sample Chart). In addition, teachers can provide opportunities for students to participate in multiple literacy experiences by portraying inferential connections through informal dramatic enactments, such as Readers Theatre, puppet shows, and role-play (Paris & Upton, 1976; Richards & McKenna, 2003). Students also can engage in multiple literacy activities by creating illustrations that depict causal and relational inferences they discover in stories (see Sa-

<table>
<tbody>
<tr><td colspan="2" style="text-align:center">**SAMPLE CHART**
How DO YOU Know?</td></tr>
<tr><td>Book title:</td><td>*The Talking Eggs* *</td></tr>
<tr><td>Page and paragraph number:</td><td>page 2, paragraph 3</td></tr>
<tr><td>My inference:</td><td>Blanche's family had no electricity.</td></tr>
<tr><td>How Do I Know?</td><td>Blanche had to fill the iron with hot coals so she could iron the clothes.</td></tr>
</tbody>
</table>

* (San Souci, 1989)

doski & Paivio, 2001, for an explanation of the connection between imagery and mental models of inferences).

Benefits and assessments

The ability to make inferences is vital to emergent readers' effective comprehension of picture books. Our think-aloud questioning strategy helps these readers learn how to make connections between given and implied information. It also helps them examine their thinking and reasoning so they can verbalize how they arrived at their assumptions and conclusions. Keeping a record of student responses to the think-aloud questions provides an alternative way to document growth in students' abilities to make inferential connections in picture books, frame relevant questions independently, engage in more complex reasoning, and share their thinking with peers.

Our strategy can be used with individual students and with small or large groups of readers. We have found that it promotes student interactions and discussions that help narrow the cultural and linguistic distance between the backgrounds of ethnically diverse students and the vocabulary and concepts presented in stories (Barnitz, 2002). Student discussions about their inferences provide opportunities for second-language learners to hear peers' language and consider peers' disparate views and thinking (Mora & Grisham, 2001). Struggling readers and older readers of content material can also benefit from How Do You Know?

References

Anderson, R., & Pearson, P.O. (1984). A schema-theoretic view of basic processes in reading comprehension. In P.D. Pearson (Ed.), *Handbook of reading research* (pp. 255-291). New York: Longman.

Barnitz, J. (2002). Language diversity foundations for literacy instruction. In J. Gipe (Ed.), *Multiple paths to literacy: Classroom techniques for struggling readers* (5th ed., pp. 50-64). Upper Saddle River, NJ: Merrill/Prentice Hall.

Dewitz, P., & Dewitz, P. (2003). They can read the words, but they can't understand: Refining comprehension assessment. *The Reading Teacher, 56,* 422-435.

Hansen, J. (1981). Inferential comprehension strategy for use with primary grade children. *The Reading Teacher, 34,* 665-669.

Hansen, J., & Pearson, P.D. (1983). An instructional study: Improving the inferential comprehension of fourth grade good and poor readers. *Journal of Educational Psychology, 75,* 821-829.

Kucan, L., & Beck, I. (1997). Thinking aloud and reading comprehension research: Inquiry, instruction, and social interaction. *Review of Educational Research, 67,* 271-299.

Long, D., Seely, R., Oppy, B., & Golding, J. (1996). The role of inferential processing in reading ability. In B. Britton & A. Graesser (Eds.), *Models of understanding text* (pp. 189-214). Mahwah, NJ: Erlbaum.

Mantione, R., & Smead, S. (2003). *Weaving through words: Using the arts to teach reading comprehension strategies.* Newark, DE: International Reading Association.

Mora, J., & Grisham, D. (2001). ¡What deliches tortillas! Preparing teachers for literacy instruction in linguistically diverse classrooms. *Teacher Education Quarterly, 28*(4), 51-70.

Neuman, S. (1990). Assessing children's inferencing strategies. In J. Zutell & S. McCormick (Eds.), *Literacy theory and research: Analysis from multiple paradigms* (pp. 267-274). Chicago: National Reading Conference.

Paris, S., & Upton, L. (1976). Children's memory for inferential relationships in prose. *Child Development, 47,* 660-668.

Raphael, T., & Wonnacott, C. (1985). Heightening fourth-grade students' sensitivity to sources of information for answering survey questions. *Reading Research Quarterly, 20,* 282-296.

Richards, J., & McKenna, M. (2003). *Integrating multiple literacies in K-8 classrooms: Cases, commentaries, and practical applications.* Mahwah, NJ: Erlbaum.

Sadoski, M., & Paivio, A. (2001). *Imagery and text: A dual coding theory of reading and writing.* Mahwah, NJ: Erlbaum.

Sub, S., & Trabasso, T. (1993). Inferences during reading: Converging evidence from discourse analysis, talk-aloud protocols and recognition priming. *Journal of Memory and Language, 32,* 270-301.

Trabasso, T., & Suh, S. (1993). Understanding text: Achieving explanatory coherence through on-line inferences and mental operations in working memory. *Discourse Processes, 16,* 3-34.

Children's books cited

Binch, C. (1994). *Gregory Cool.* New York: Dial.
San Souci, R. (1989). *The talking eggs.* New York: Dial.
Soto, G. (1993). *Too many tamales.* New York: G.P. Putnam's Sons.
Steig, W. (1982). *Doctor De Soto.* New York: Farrar, Straus & Giroux.

Richards teaches in the Childhood Education Department at the University of South Florida (College of Education, 4202 East Fowler Avenue-EDU 62, Tampa, FL 33620, USA). Anderson teaches at the same university. †

Using centers to engage children during guided reading time:

Intensifying learning experiences away from the teacher

When a teacher works with a small group, other students need independent activities that help them learn and practice reading and writing.

Michael P. Ford and Michael F. Opitz

While . . . small-group work is at the heart of guided reading, it must not be seen as an end in itself.... Small-group guided reading, as powerful as it is, must be understood as but one part of a comprehensive literacy program. (Routman, 2000, p. 140)

There is no question that the practice of meeting with readers in small groups to provide guided reading instruction is perceived as a critical part of literacy programs designed to create independent, lifelong readers (Cunningham, Hall, & Cunningham, 2000; Fountas & Pinnell, 1996; Mooney, 1990). The smaller groups provide a greater opportunity for teachers to use instruction that scaffolds the learning and engages the learner—two key characteristics of exemplary teachers in high-achieving primary classrooms (Pressley, 1998). These small groups allow for a more effective type of strategic coaching to take place, and strategic coaching appears to be one of the key elements that distinguish high-achieving classrooms from those with moderate or low performances (Taylor, Pearson, Clark, & Walpole, 1999). Seeing guided reading promoted and implemented by countless teachers is no surprise. Hearing questions emerge as teachers give their best efforts to implement guided reading is also no surprise. Regardless of the teaching strategy, our own teaching experiences have helped us to see that translating theory into practice takes time and effort. Why should guided reading be any different?

In our interactions with primary teachers working to effectively implement guided reading practices, many of the questions we receive relate to the issues Routman raised in the comments that introduce this article (Opitz & Ford, 2001). More specifically, questions relate to classroom organization and management. A review of articles and books focused on guided reading helps to explain why this is so (Cunningham,

Hall, & Cunningham, 2000; Mooney, 1995). Much of the attention in these publications focuses on the quality of instruction that occurs with the teacher during guided reading, leaving questions unanswered about what the other children should be doing and the quality of their instruction when they are away from the teacher. However, because students spend a significant amount of time away from the teacher during guided reading, the time question is critical. Clearly, the power of the instruction that takes place away from the teacher must rival the power of the instruction that takes place with the teacher.

This article offers some suggestions that can be used to maximize the literacy learning that can and needs to occur during this independent learning time. After presenting three possible classroom organizational structures, we elaborate on the one that many teachers are (re)discovering: learning centers.

Instruction away from the teacher: Three organizational structures

In traditional classroom organizational patterns, approximately two thirds of a student's time during the designated reading block would be spent away from the teacher (Baumann, Hoffman, Duffy-Hester, & Ro, 2000). For the teacher to focus on the small group at hand, the remaining students had to be engaged in an independent activity. That activity was often defined by workbooks and worksheets (Durkin, 1978–1979; Ford, 1991). In a more contemporary version of that pattern, small groups of children met to talk with their teacher about their books while others were independently engaged in a menu of cut, color, and paste response projects. Neither scenario seemed to provide a level of instruction away from the teacher that was as powerful as the instruction with the teacher.

While we believe strongly in small groups for instruction as one critical element in a balanced reading program, we offer a caution that the concerns of the past do not surface again with the increasing use of guided reading. In some diverse classrooms where guided reading groups are formed primarily with children who are reading texts at the same level, the classroom teacher may be juggling even more small groups than in the past. From what we have observed in some classrooms that are implementing guided reading, a student's time with the teacher is even less frequent than in the traditional models. So the question of just how we make that time away from the teacher as powerful as the time spent with the teacher becomes even more critical.

The success of guided reading as an instructional practice certainly depends on the implementation of a classroom structure that provides teachers with opportunities to effectively work with small groups of readers while keeping other readers independently engaged in meaningful literacy learning activities (Kane, 1995). Collaborating with others is one organizational structure that is sometimes used to make this happen. Some classroom teachers are fortunate enough to work in schools designed to encourage collaboration with other professionals such as reading specialists and special educators. The type of collaboration differs among schools and teachers. Sometimes specialists plan and team teach with teachers within the regular classroom setting. In this model there are two professionals in the room during the guided reading time, and each works with different guided reading groups. This makes work with several groups more likely and more manageable. Other times, specialists and teachers plan together for given groups of students, and some students leave the room to work with a specialist (Tilton, 1996).

Another classroom structure combines the use of an established program like writers' workshop with guided reading. If students are well versed and rehearsed in a more independent classroom routine like writers' workshop, then individual writing, revising, and editing times; peer conferences; and sharing times provide natural ways for students to stay engaged in powerful literacy activities away from the teacher. Teachers may have less need to develop an additional infrastructure for student engagement in order to secure time to work with small guided reading groups.

A third classroom structure involves using learning centers, small areas within the classroom where students work alone or together to explore literacy activities independently while the teacher provides small-group guided reading instruction.

There are many ways to implement centers (Morrow, 1997; Opitz, 1994). Sometimes one center is called "guided reading," and this is where the teacher is stationed. Children rotate through the centers according to a specified time schedule, thereby ensuring that every child does guided reading during the course of the day. Other times, children are grouped and then choose their own centers. The teacher then selects one or two children from the various groups to meet for guided reading instruction. Instead of a set rotation, students stay at the center until the task is completed and then move to other centers until center time is finished (Fountas & Pinnell, 1996). Regardless of

Figure 1
Word identification skills and strategies

Meaning cues
Using pictures
Using background knowledge
Using information in the selection
Visual memory cues
Letter-sound cues
Spelling patterns
Language structure cues
Comparing an unknown word to known words
Reading on
Rereading
Self-monitoring
Self-corrections

the way that one chooses to use learning centers, there are several considerations that ensure success for students and teacher alike.

Considerations for successful learning centers

1. As with any good teaching, decisions about learning centers need to be grounded in the teacher's knowledge about the children as readers, writers, and learners. In considering the learners, one often overlooked question for the teacher to answer has to do with independence. Just how well can the children function independently? What do they need to learn to function better as independent learners? Most often, children need to be taught how to be independent. Taking time to teach them how to be independent learners is well worth the effort. Opitz (1994) offered a framework for how to do just that. He emphasized that the teacher must watch children to see what needs to be taught. For example, children may need to learn how to work with others in a group, use a tape recorder, care for materials, and locate help. After identifying these needs, Opitz suggested planning a four-part minilesson focused on each need:

- A focus (purpose for the lesson);

- An explanation, in which children are provided with the information related to the stated purpose;

- Role playing, which gives students opportunities for guided practice; and

- Direct application, which provides children with time to use the information as they complete their center activities for the day.

2. Consider the types of activities in which children will be independently engaged. Children need activities that will advance their knowledge about literacy. Looking at what children are able to do on their own and how they perform on assessments and during guided reading can provide a wealth of information. Do students need repeated practice with a given story? Do they need to read with a partner to better understand a story?

Do they need to write a response to something they have read? Do students need to listen to a given story on tape to better understand how to read with fluency? Answers to questions such as these lead to specific learning center activities designed to address them.

It is important to distinguish between independent activities that create excitement about reading and writing and those that actually require students to interact with print while reading and writing. While any number of cut, color, and paste activities done in response to or in support of reading and writing experiences can help to create some excitement about reading and writing instruction, these activities do little to require students to actually interact with print. This interaction is essential for learning about print and intensifies the power of center-based instruction.

3. Consider state or district curricular expectations. Now more than ever, it seems, teachers are expected to follow curriculum guides and provide evidence that students have been exposed to (if not mastered) the curriculum. Designing centers with the literacy curriculum in mind is an excellent way to ensure that children are exposed to it. Of course, to make some of these documents user friendly, teachers may want to transform them into manageable lists for easy reference. These lists might be housed in a lesson plan book or affixed to a file folder. (See Figure 1.) In some cases, activities can be coded to these lists (Opitz, 1994.)

4. Consider what is known about engagement in instructional settings. According to Brophy (1987), there are two keys that motivate learning: perception of the possibility of success and perception that the outcome will be valued. The instructional activity must be within reach of the learner. In other words, the learner needs to be able to perceive the possibility of success. Most of us withdraw quickly from any activity when we perceive that success is not possible (especially when that perception is based on the real experience of repeated failure). And so it is with children. We need to set them up for success, and one way to do this is to provide appropriate activities. Another way is to make sure that the children fully understand the activity as the result of discussing, modeling, and practicing it in large- and small-group instructional settings guided by the teacher. By the time the activity is placed in a center for independent use, students can't help but be successful.

Students need to perceive not only that "I can do this!" but also that the outcome will be valued. Perhaps the best way to accomplish this is to offer purposeful and meaningful literacy activities. The challenge for teachers is knowing that students within one class vary quite significantly in their abilities to perceive success and in what outcomes they will value. Giving students a variety of activities is essential when one considers the diversity that exists within any one classroom. All students deserve to be successful, and some will need more support than others. Planning centers that operate with instructional density around multiple goals and outcomes is one way to guarantee this success. Opitz (1994) provided concrete suggestions for accomplishing this.

One example is to design an independent word-family activity. Teachers can identify an anchor word like *bug* but differentiate expectations for different groups moving through that center. Some groups might work with *bug* and create a word family based on the phonogram -*ug* with initial consonant substitutions (e.g., *rug, mug, tug, hug*). Other groups might start with bug as a root word and create a word family that is more structurally based by adding endings to the root word (e.g., *bugs, bugged, bugging, buggy*). Another group might start with bug at the center of a semantic map and map out meaning-based connections to the word (e.g., *bother, spy, insect*). The instruction at the center thus can address multiple goals and produce different outcomes.

5. Finally, consider the following guidelines for establishing an infrastructure of instruction away from the teacher. This infrastructure needs to do the following:

- Facilitate independent use by students. Any activity that has the potential to interrupt small-group instruction because of the complexity of sustaining its operation may be more of a deterrent than a learning tool.

- Operate with minimal transition time and management concerns. If implementing centers consumes more time, energy, and effort than the instruction and activities that take place at the centers, using them needs to be rethought.

- Encourage equitable use of activities among learners. If all center-based activities have value, it stands to reason that they would be important for all students. While some students may like some activities more than others, they need to be encouraged to participate in all activities. If the organization precludes some students from having access to the same centers as other students, arrangements need to be made to equalize access.

- Include a simple built-in accountability system. Engagement in the center-based activities is critical if students are going to learn what we would like them to learn as a result of completing them. True, we can be comfortable knowing that some students will stay productively engaged in the learning activities in the teacher's absence. At other times, we may well wonder whether all students were productively engaged. Simple accountability measures will motivate some students to stay productively engaged while serving as a window on the level of engagement for each student. One example is a center card issued to each student (see Figure 2). On it, a teacher can identify the independent activity options for students, and students can color in or mark off activities completed during independent time.

- Allow for efficient use of teacher preparation time. Elaborate centers that consume large amounts of teachers' limited preparation time without similar payoffs in duration of student engagement will lead to a quick abandonment of centers. Busy teachers need activities that can be easily changed or altered once established as part of center-based instruction.

- Build around class routines. Routines provide a predictable way for children to engage in learning. Routines also provide a predictable way for teachers to plan instruction that minimizes concerns, confusion, and chaos along the way. After they have been established and practiced with teacher guidance, routines can be performed without teacher guidance. The gradual release of responsibility (Pearson & Gallagher,

Figure 2
A student's center card

1983) gives the teacher greater assurance that the activities students are expected to complete independently are within their reach.

Centers that meet established criteria

The following section describes nine centers that meet the criteria we have discussed. They each build on classroom routines to encourage independent use by students and efficient use of teacher preparation time. While the structure of the center can stay the same, the activities within them can change with relative ease. Each center is designed to be accessible for all students and provide for individual differences because of the level of sophistication each learner brings to the task. Each can be linked to what the teacher knows about students as readers, writers, and learners as well as to standards, curricula, and assessments. With simple structures, transition time can be kept to a minimum, equitable use can be encouraged, and accountability can be ensured.

Listening post: The listening post provides learners with additional practice with print. By placing a story on tape and multiple copies of the text at the center, the teacher can easily create a changeable center that gives learners an opportunity to warm up before, review after, or extend beyond a guided reading session. One teacher we observed intensifies the practice at the listening post for a longer period of time by encouraging students

Figure 3
Listening post routine

1. Listen to the story on tape and follow along.
2. Listen to the story on tape and read along.
3. Turn off the tape and read together.
4. Turn off the tape and read with a partner.
5. Turn off the tape and read on your own.
6. Listen to the story on tape and read along again.
7. Talk about your improvement.
8. Be ready to share the story with the class.

to work through an identified routine that involved repeated practice of the text in a variety of ways (see Figure 3). Accountability can be built in by inviting students to orally perform a selection practiced at the listening post at the end of the language arts block.

Readers Theatre: Like the listening post, a Readers Theatre center can be easily created by a classroom teacher by designating a practice space, providing multiple texts, and identifying guidelines for practicing. Like with the listening post, it can be used as a warm-up, review, or extension from the guided reading instruction. It can also allow more heterogeneously grouped students to work together because appropriate parts can be assigned to students of differing abilities. A sequenced routine (see Figure 4) can engage students for longer periods of

Figure 4
Readers Theatre routine

1. Leader reads the story aloud.
2. Everyone reads the story together.
3. Partners read the story together.
4. Everyone is assigned a part.
5. Students practice their parts on their own.
6. Students practice their parts together.
7. Students share the story with the class.

Figure 5
Scavenger hunt routine

Find three words in our room that . . .

1. Have more than six letters.
2. End in -*ing* where the final letter was doubled.
3. Mean the same as *said*.
4. Have the same sound pattern as *boat*.
5. Are words from math.
6. Start with *sh*.
7. Have the same spelling pattern as *nice*.
8. Are contractions.
9. Rhyme with *she*.

time as they practice for a performance, which can serve as an accountability check. This type of practice provides a purposeful opportunity for building fluency, oral performance skills, and confidence. The addition of simple props, masks, or puppets can make the production of plays from practiced texts another way to engage students.

Reading/writing the room: This is often a popular way to become familiar with a print-rich classroom environment. Students can be encouraged to choose partners and use special pointers and glasses to "read the room"—one student points to words in the environment as the partner reads them. Clipboards and scrap paper might be available for students to use in "writing the room"—copying words from the environment. To engage students in a more challenging activity, teachers can easily create a scavenger hunt (see Figure 5) that invites students to look for specific examples to explore concepts of print, letter names, word identification, and vocabulary elements more closely grounded in curricular needs. These can be easily changed and designed in varying degrees of difficulty for diverse learners. It leaves a "paper trail" from the students' efforts that can be collected and quickly reviewed by the teacher.

Pocket chart: Any instructional tool and space used in large-group instruction can easily become a center for more independent activity during guided reading instruction. In one classroom the pocket chart was used to introduce common core poems used at the line, phrase, word, and word-part levels (Ford, 1996). When a poem was initially introduced on the pocket chart, the teacher used sentence strips to go through the verse line by line. Children were invited to point to different lines and read the words on the sentence strip for that line. The teacher would also say a line, and children would have to come up and point to it. The teacher would hand out copies of the sentence strips, and children would match them to the lines on the pocket chart or put the poem back together in order. As children showed mastery of the poem at the line level, the teacher would cut up the sentence strips into smaller chunks—phrases—and guide students through similar activities, requiring greater attention to print details and finer visual discrimination skills. As children showed mastery of the poem at the phrase level, the teacher would cut up the phrase strips into individual words.

Using the pocket chart as an independent center, students can conduct activities modeled by the teacher in large-group settings. One regular activity that can be linked to pocket charts that contain poems is providing students with blank paper grids and inviting them to copy each word from the poem in a box on

the grid. Students can cut the words apart and create a set of word cards that can be used to independently reconstruct the poem or to create innovations by changing the words around. Working with partners, students can play common word card games, which provide opportunities for independent skill practice. Activities chosen by students can vary in difficulty according to their needs. The introduction of a new poem provides new material and another opportunity to repeat the activity.

Poems/story packs: In another classroom, when the teacher retires a poem or story from large-group practice situations she places the words, phrases, or sentences created for word study in a large see-through envelope. These packs of story and poem parts are placed in a basket and made available to students during center time. Because they represent materials created from texts of varying difficulties, students can select packs appropriate for their level. Students find a quiet place to shake out the parts and engage in a variety of activities including reconstructing or innovating on the language of the familiar text. Working with partners or independently, they can engage in a variety of classifying and sorting activities that call attention to words and their features. Color-coding the parts for each text makes it easy to get the right parts back into the right pack.

Big Books: Again, teachers have discovered the importance of letting students independently explore materials previously introduced in large- and small-group settings. For example, revisiting Big Books used in shared reading experiences provides a natural opportunity for students to explore print more independently. Big Books placed in an easily accessible center can be made more inviting by giving students access to teaching tools like pointers, word frames, adhesive notes, and correcting tape so they can conduct activities modeled by the teacher in the large-group setting. As anyone who has worked with young children knows, children thoroughly enjoy taking on the role of teacher.

Responding through art: We have already noted concern about the difference between activities that generate excitement and those that actually engage students in reading and writing. Response activities placed in centers for students to work on independently may be a better use of limited class time than having students do activities as a whole group. We would argue, however, that response activities need to be designed in a way that minimizes teacher's preparation time. Planned, precut, prepared art projects may not be necessary for response. In one classroom, Shel Silverstein's (1974) poem "Spaghetti" was featured. The response center contained a variety of bags of pasta and large sheets of colored construction paper. Students designed projects as creative as any teacher-prepared art project might have been. By labeling pictures, adding talking bubbles, or writing descriptive sentences, the teacher could use these student responses to create a print-rich bulletin board, and later bind them into a book for the class reading center.

Writing: There is no question that one of the best ways to engage children with text is to have them generate their own. Writing demands much critical thinking in that the writer must organize ideas and use specific words to express thoughts to create text that is meaningful to self and others. Other times, writing is a form of response that enables the writer to show what was of personal value in the text or what was remembered. It is also a way for the writer to apply all known print conventions. The centers can be easily created by supplying students with access to a variety of writing tools, formats, and resources. Students can engage in writing activities that differ in their demands. The writing projects can be shared publicly and reviewed privately to hold students accountable.

Reading: We cannot emphasize enough that the best activity for students to become involved in away from the teacher is reading. Students should always be encouraged to read when they are waiting for instruction with the teacher. This can be done individually, with a classmate, or with a more competent coach. Teachers can easily create inviting reading centers that provide easy access and inviting opportunities to independently explore texts (Morrow, 1997). This exploration can be one additional way to warm up, review, or extend texts from guided reading instruction. In one classroom, students are encouraged to grab a text, a buddy, and a carpet square; find a quiet corner; and read to each other. Some teachers have developed structures to maximize the value of buddy reading (Samway, Whang, & Pippitt, 1995). Finally, additional people in the classroom may provide the students with the possibility of additional contact with a competent reader (an older student or adult classroom volunteer). These individuals may not be capable of conducting a separate guided reading group, but can certainly listen to individuals read texts. Like writing, practiced reading can be shared publicly or recorded in simple logging formats.

Instruction away from the teacher needs to be as powerful as instruction with the teacher. Like instruction with the teacher, it needs to be grounded in knowledge of the children—their reading and writing abilities and their degree of independence. It needs to be sensitive to the external demands of standards, curricula, and assessments. It should involve children in an unceasing cycle of self-improvement by continued engagement with print-rich activities. Children and adults must see learning

experiences away from the teacher as accessible and purposeful. Such activities must set up children for success so that they see themselves as independent readers—the ultimate goal of guided reading.

References

Baumann, J., Hoffman, J., Duffy-Hester, A., & Ro, J. (2000). The first R yesterday and today: U.S. elementary reading instruction practices reported by teachers and administrators. *Reading Research Quarterly, 35,* 338–377.

Brophy, J. (1987). Synthesis of research on strategies for motivating students to learn. *Educational Leadership, 54,* 40–45.

Cunningham, P., Hall, D., & Cunningham, J. (2000). *Guided reading the four-blocks way.* Greensboro, NC: Carson-Dellosa.

Durkin, D. (1978–1979). What classroom observations reveal about comprehension instruction. *Reading Research Quarterly, 10,* 481–533.

Ford, M.P. (1991). Worksheets anonymous: On the road to recovery. *Language Arts, 6,* 553–559.

Ford, M.P. (1996). Tightening up: Working toward balanced literacy. *The Whole Idea, 7,* 1, 12–15.

Fountas, I., & Pinnell, G. (1996). *Guided reading: Good first teaching for all children.* Portsmouth, NH: Heinemann.

Kane, K. (1995). *Keeping your balance: Teacher's guide for guided reading in the early grades.* Danbury, CT: Grolier.

Mooney, M. (1990). *Reading to, with, and by children.* Katonah, NY: Richard C. Owen.

Mooney, M. (1995). Guided reading: The reader in control. *Teaching K–8, 25,* 57–58.

Morrow, L. (1997). *The literacy center: Contexts for reading and writing.* York, ME: Stenhouse.

Opitz, M.F. (1994). *Learning centers: Getting them started, keeping them going.* New York: Scholastic.

Opitz, M.F., & Ford, M. (2001). *Reaching readers: Innovative and flexible strategies for guided reading.* Portsmouth, NH: Heinemann.

Pearson, P.D., & Gallagher, M.C. (1983). *The new instruction of reading comprehension* (Tech. Rep. No. 297). Urbana, IL: University of Illinois, Center for the Study of Reading.

Pressley, M. (1998). *Reading instruction that works: The case for balanced teaching.* New York: Guilford.

Routman, R. (2000). *Conversations: Strategies for teaching, learning and evaluating.* Portsmouth, NH: Heinemann.

Samway, K., Whang, G., & Pippitt, M. (1995). *Buddy reading: Cross-age tutoring in a multicultural school.* Portsmouth, NH: Heinemann.

Silverstein, S. (1974). *Where the sidewalk ends: The poems and drawings of Shel Silverstein.* New York: HarperCollins.

Taylor, B., Pearson, P.D., Clark, K.F., & Walpole, S. (1999). Effective schools/Accomplished teachers. *The Reading Teacher, 53,* 156–158.

Tilton, L. (1996). *Inclusion: A fresh look.* Shorewood, MN: Covington Cove.

Ford is Associate Dean at the University of Wisconsin Oshkosh (NE 113, College of Education and Human Services, Oshkosh, WI 54901, USA). Opitz teaches at the University of Northern Colorado, Greeley, Colorado, USA.

Digging up the past, building the future: using book authoring to discover and showcase a community's history

A classroom oral history project bolsters literacy skills
for these second graders and their families.

Dorothy J. Leal

"Good news! Today your child is bringing home a copy of the amazing book our class wrote about Coaltown [pseudonym]." So begins the letter sent home to families, accompanied by individual copies of *The Story of Coaltown*. The 20-page spiral-bound book was the culmination of a two-month project integrating literacy skills with learning about Coaltown's history. It began with the desire of two educators to help second-grade children expand their knowledge of their community and deepen their understanding of the reading and writing process.

Writing narrative stories about students' own lives has been shown to help children develop personal, social, and cultural connections (Allen et al., 2002). In addition, exploring life stories can provide a sense of direction and purpose for students (Muley-Meissner, 2002). Because we recognized the importance of student writing, the idea grew to help these second-grade students broaden their connections to the history of their community and provide them an increased sense of direction and purpose in their learning environment.

These second-grade students had the same literacy needs as all students: immersion in quality literature and a print-rich environment, many opportunities to read and write authentic material, individual assessment and intervention, instructional materials at appropriate levels, highly qualified teachers and tutors, and strong family support (Allington, 2000; Pressley, 1998). The challenge was how to address these needs in the limited amount of time teachers have today. I joined forces with a second-grade teacher to see what could be done. Because we believed that writing goes hand in hand with reading and that writing always includes some reading during production, a plan to write the history of the community began to take shape. It was hoped that if students and families "owned" the topic, they would be more ready to learn about and engage with good literacy practices. The following description documents the procedures and expected outcomes for carrying out such a project in the classroom.

Ready, set, write: A two-part writing experience

To guide students in the writing process, the project had two components. First the whole class would work on an illustrated book, to learn the writing process and see the published outcome. Following this step, each child would delve further into history and author the biography of a close relative. Because most of the students were born in the community, this project would become an extension for learning more about the history of Coaltown, a small town in rural Appalachia. The Coaltown area has a long salt- and coal-mining history.

Many of the students were not aware of the important place Coaltown has in the history of the state. The closing of the mines and the consolidation of the schools in the area have resulted in students' lack of understanding about the important place their communities play in history and in their own lives. Much of the local history, family stories, and understanding of the unique characteristics of Appalachia are also being lost due to the high rate of family illiteracy. Many of the children come from single-parent families where academic support is minimal. In addition, one out of four students at the school has special educational needs, and an additional one out of three students is designated as at risk for lack of school success. Eighty-six percent of the students qualify for free or reduced-cost lunch. This project sought to bring the students and their families together to research and write about the history of Coaltown in an effort to build community identity and foster connections to their rich heritage through increased literacy.

Class-authored book

The first project, the class-authored book, was an adventure for all. The process was defined and refined as we went. Two guest speakers who grew up in Coaltown came in to answer questions and talk to the children about what the town was like when they were young. Both speakers had rich memories of Coaltown many years ago. In addition, we obtained a film taken of the community back in the 1930s when Coaltown was thriving. The speakers, the film, and archived newspaper records served as the primary sources for our investigation. The steps followed for the two months of the project are shared here so that you may try similar projects in your own classrooms.

1. We planted a seed of excitement by doing a K-W-L exercise (Ogle, 1989). We wanted to find out what students already knew about Coaltown's history as well as what they wanted to know. Students generated questions to ask the "experts" on Coaltown's history such as the following: What did you eat? What did you do for fun? What was school like? What kind of clothes did you wear? What kind of jobs did your parents have?

2. We watched the film and invited the students to discuss what they saw and to share additional ideas and questions.

3. We did some prewriting activities, including a semantic web of the most interesting things they learned about Coaltown's history. We also did a "describing" activity to guide the children to "show" and not just "tell" with their writing.

4. We invited our first guest expert to answer questions about life and growing up in Coaltown. Students wrote down the answers the history experts gave to their questions. We audiotaped the oral history interview and listened to it again afterward. We also started an A to Z list of what they were learning about Coaltown.

5. Following the first guest's visit, the teacher elicited from the students a topic for the book's first chapter. The students were fascinated by the coal mines, so the title became "The History of the Coaltown Coal Mines." The children dictated sentences to the teacher, and she wrote their words on the chalkboard. She used this time to guide the students in editing their work, helping them add descriptive words as well as asking probing questions to help them expand on their ideas. The first paragraph of the book is one of my favorites: "When Coaltown became a village in 1834 the people worked in salt mines. After they were done salt mining they came up with coal mining. The mines were owned by the New York Coal Company."

6. The edited first chapter was entered into one of the class computers. Students each drew a picture of what they thought best illustrated this chapter.

7. We looked at the semantic web and decided on five other chapter topics we wanted in the book. We divided the children into five groups so that each group would be responsible for one chapter. Each group selected a topic and wrote a chapter for the book. Groups created the title and illustrations for their own chapters. The next five chapters are entitled Fun Things They Used to Do in Coaltown, Families and Homes in Coaltown During the Coal Mine Times, What the Schools Were Like, Jobs and Money Are Good, and The History of the Town of Coaltown.

8. During the writing process, more questions emerged. Each group developed a set of questions about its chapter topic to ask our next invited guest.

9. Our second guest expert came and answered these new questions as well as previous ones that needed more explanation.

10. Students worked two mornings a week for an hour for several weeks. When they finished authoring their chapters, they worked to edit their writing. A party was held to celebrate the editing process. Students ate popcorn while they edited. They also created illustrations for their chapters.

11. Students who were able to use the keyboard entered the text into the computer. Older students came in and helped students who were not comfortable with entering text on the class computers.

12. Near the end of the process, students discussed several titles for the book and decided on *The Story of Coaltown.* All the students drew illustrations for the cover and then discussed which one to use.

13. The class discussed how to evaluate the success of the project. The teacher guided and suggested categories while the students generated questions that would help them do the evaluation. Figure 1 depicts the evaluation form used. Together they answered the questions and decided the book was a great success.

14. When all the chapters were entered and illustrations completed, the books were copied and spiral bound. Each child received his or her own copy to take home with a letter to the parents inviting them to the Authors' Party.

15. We celebrated the learning with an Authors' Party. We invited our history experts to come and share the celebration and food. The children read their chapters aloud and showed the pictures. Copies of this first book were also presented to community friends as well as to each teacher and worker in the school.

Individually authored books

Family literacy and enhancing language and literacy development are important topics in today's schools (Kidd & Casey, 2001). Good teachers explore successful ways to engage their students and families in literacy learning. When students and families own the topic, they are more ready to learn and engage in literacy activities.

"What is next?" asked the letter sent home to parents by the teacher. "This spring your child will be writing and publishing his or her very own book! The children will be writing a book about someone in their family, possibly YOU! They will be interviewing the person and taking pictures and then using this information to

FIGURE 1
Second-grade writing evaluation form

	Yes	Some	No
I. Content			
Is the main idea clear?			
Is there a lot of good information?			
Does it describe the details in an interesting way?			
Is it well organized?			
Do the pictures help explain the information?			
II. Mechanics			
Are the sentences complete?			
Is the spelling correct?			
Do all the sentences have correct punctuation?			
Are all the right words capitalized?			
III. Response			
Is it easy to understand?			
Is it very interesting?			
Is it fun to read?			
What do you like most about this book?			
What can the author do to make it even better?			

write biographies." So began the next phase of the project, which covered another two months. Again we worked for one hour on Tuesday and Thursday mornings. The process followed these steps:

1. Agreement forms for the biography subjects were sent home. Children brought back signed forms from family members who agreed to be the focus for the book.

2. Picture book biographies and photobiographies were read aloud to the children and discussed. Sample titles included *All the Places to Love* (MacLachlan, 1994), *This Quiet Lady* (Zolotow, 1992), *Not So Very Long Ago: Life in a Small Country Village* (Fix, 1987), *Eleanor* (Cooney, 1996), *Lincoln: A Photobiography* (Freedman, 1987), and *Immigrant Kids* (Freedman, 1980) Formats and layouts were also examined and discussed.

3. Through a grant from the local College of Education, students were provided with disposable cameras to document what their biography subjects told them. We suggested that both the child and the biography subject take pictures. Before the cameras went home we had a lesson on the essentials of photography, demonstrating the procedures of winding, aiming, and shooting. Then each child took a photograph of someone else in the class. These were developed, and we discussed what made a good picture and what made a bad picture for a book.

4. Topics for the books were discussed, and the students selected four: The Early Years; The School Years; Family and Friends; and Jobs, Money, and Having Fun.

5. The cameras were sent home with a list of "cool ideas for photographs" as shown in Figure 2, as well as an invitation to family members to send in old photographs that could be scanned and used in the books. The following week the children returned the cameras so the film could be developed and the pictures integrated with the writing.

6. Each week the students authored and illustrated a different chapter, following the same process each time. First the class generated questions on each topic. Some sample questions they decided on for chapter 1 (The Early Years) included the following: Where were you born? What was your favorite food? What kind of pets did you have? One young writer's dad grew up in Syria, and for pets he had a cat and a camel. For chapter 2 on school days, questions included these: What was your school like? What was your favorite subject? What games did you play? Did you ever get in trouble? We had some really interesting and entertaining responses to that question. For chapter 3 on family and friends, sample questions included the following: Did you have sisters and brothers and aunts and uncles? What did you do together? What TV shows did you watch? Sample questions for chapter 4 included these: What kinds of jobs did you have? How much money did you get? Did you get vacations? Did you have favorite songs, movies, games, and sports? Responses often revealed strong family ties. One second-grade boy wrote in this chapter that "The most important thing my dad has done in his life is to be a loving father to his three children."

7. Every week students took copies of the questions home and asked their biography subjects to answer the questions that were most interesting to them. Students also worked on illustrations for each chapter; the product was often a combination of photographs and illustrations.

FIGURE 2
Cool Ideas for photos

You can use photos you already have or make new ones with your camera.

Take a picture of the person by himself or herself.
Take a picture of the person with different family members.
Take a picture of the person where he or she lives.
Take a picture of the person with his or her best friend(s).
Take a picture of the person with things that are important, such as trophies, musical instruments, pets, sports items, or souvenirs from trips.
Take a picture of the person where he or she works or a picture of something he or she does or makes on the job.
Take a picture of the person's special or favorite places.
Take a picture of things the person does for fun or vacations.
Take a picture of what kinds of transportation the person uses, such as cars, buses, or motorcycles.

8. As each chapter was written and edited, students entered their work on the computers. Older students came in and helped the young students type their stories.

9. Toward the end of the process the children created titles and cover pictures for their books.

10. When all written work was completed and all photographs selected and scanned, the books were printed out and spiral bound.

11. The students used the previously developed, class-designed evaluation form to evaluate their own books. Again, the books were a huge success.

12. A second Authors' Party was planned, and students wrote invitations to their families. The turnout was tremendous, with two to three family members per child coming to the event. Each biography subject was introduced and presented with his or her own copy of the book. Each child received a framed award certificate recognizing the work he or she had completed.

Digging up the past to build a future

When all the books were completed it was hard to tell who was prouder, the students or the subjects of the biographies. Clearly the project was a huge success for all. Even though some of the parents were not readers themselves, they were proud that their children had written a book especially about their family and their community. The experts interviewed for the first book were also invited to this celebration. After the celebration, one of the experts wrote,

I enjoyed my visit and feeling the atmosphere of the classroom and the enthusiasm shown by the kids. It did my heart good to see and hear the interaction they seemed to enjoy in doing this project. It undoubtedly began with their very capable teacher … It also made me feel a sense of pride reminiscing my childhood days in Coaltown—a wonderful place for a kid to be raised.

Having seen the products and enthusiasm coming from the second grade, this year the teachers at all grade levels are doing this in their classrooms as an all-school project. As copies of *The Story of Coaltown* circulated, many more stories and unwritten histories surfaced among teachers, school workers, and community members. There's a mine to be tapped and a wealth of community jewels to be polished. While digging up the past, we discovered that building the future has only just begun.

References

Allen, J., Fabregas, V., Hankins, K.H., Hull, G., Labbo, L., Lawson, H.S., et al. (2002). PhOLKS lore: Learning from photographs, families, and children. *Language Arts, 79,* 312–322.

Allington, R.L. (2000). *What really matters for struggling readers: Designing research-based programs.* New York: Addison-Wesley.

Cooney, B. (1996). *Eleanor.* New York: Viking.

Fix, P. (1987). *Not so very long ago: Life in a small country village.* New York: Dutton.

Freedman, R. (1980). *Immigrant kids.* New York: Dutton.

Freedman, R. (1987). *Lincoln: A photobiography.* New York: Clarion.

Kidd, J.K., & Casey, E. (2001). *Developing literacy through family stones and photos: A family literacy project.* Paper presented at the annual meeting of the National Council of Teachers of English, Baltimore, MD.

MacLachlan, P. (1994). *All the places to love.* New York: HarperCollins.

Muley-Meissner, M.L. (2002). The spirit of a people: Hmong American life stories. *Language Arts, 79,* 323–331.

Ogle, D.M. (1989). The know, want to know, learn strategy. In K.D. Muth (Ed.), *Children's comprehension of text: Research into practice* (pp. 205–223). Newark, DE: International Reading Association.

Pressley, M. (1998). *Reading instruction that works: The case for balanced teaching.* New York: Guilford.

Zolotow, C. (1992). *This quiet lady.* New York: Greenwillow.

Leal teaches at Ohio University (207 McCracken Hall, Athens, OH 45701, USA). E-mail leal@ohio.edu.

UNIT 5
Integrated Curriculum

Unit Selections

Key Points to Consider

• What role do trade books play in accessing textbook content?

• Does motivation theory have a role in content area literacy?

• What is the place of writing in learning?

• Do the arts have a place in content area literacy?

 **Links: www.dushkin.com/online/**
These sites are annotated in the World Wide Web pages.

California Reading Initiative
http://www.sdcoe.k12.ca.us/score/promising/prreading/prreadin.html

Early Childhood Education Online
http://www.umaine.edu/eceol/

International Reading Association
http://www.reading.org

Reggio Emilia
http://www.ericdigests.org/2001-3/reggio.htm

of accountability testing in most states that has resulted in literacy taking a central place.

I remember the transition during the eighties, when testing students' math skills became more a matter of testing students' ability to read and comprehend word problems than their ability to compute numbers. While accountability testing was limited to math, reading, and language arts during the last three decades of the twentieth century, the new century was ushered in with an expansion of testing to social studies and science in secondary grades. Some states are piloting social studies and science testing as early as fourth grade. Basic to this testing is students' ability to read and comprehend in all content areas.

There are no easy answers for addressing the complexities of teaching students to read to learn. Overall students dislike low-challenging tasks that require minimal thinking, and little risk-taking; yet, textbook writers continue, in many cases, to streamline texts to present only basic, isolated facts rather than to integrate texts with a narrative style. It is no wonder to educators why many students seem to have difficulty when it comes to reading textbooks—motivation and interest are not likely to be found in relationship to sterile texts. This is unlike the social studies texts that I read in the 1960s. At the same time, the more enjoyable to read narrative style texts of my youth presented another problem—a monocultural view of society with established social classes and gender roles.

In "Teaching Expository Text Structures Through Information Trade Book Retellings," Barbara Moss informs educators on how to use trade book retellings to define expository text structures. Teachers are encouraged to model retellings after introducing a particular text structure. This will then allow for participation as the teacher scaffolds students toward textbook comprehension.

Supplementing texts with trade books and projects across the curriculum have become well-accepted strategies for developing content area literacy. In "Mathematics Trade Books: Establishing Their Value and Assessing Their Quality," Patricia D. Hunsader affirms the value of supplemental literature to enhance instruction in mathematics, but she warns that not all publishers use quality as a gauge in recommending mathematical literature books. Hunsader challenges teachers to use an assessment scale in determining the value of these books.

Projects make it possible for students to connect the arts and literacy development. In "It's As Easy As A-B-C and Do-Re-Mi: Music, Rhythm, and Rhyme Enhance Children's Literacy Skills," Kantaylieniere Y. Hill-Clarke and Nicole R. Robinson highlight the interrelationship between music, language, and reading. They offer a brief discussion on Gardner's eight intelligences as a backdrop for all later learning, as music is the earliest developing intelligence. The article is teeming with specifics to integrate music into early childhood and elementary classrooms.

Reading in the content area, reading and writing across the curriculum, and reading to learn are all phrases frequently heard by in-service and pre-service teachers. All teachers must become reading and writing teachers no matter what subject they teach. Students must read and write to learn in all content areas.

I remember discovering in ninth grade that history and science textbooks had some of the same information. It was the first time I experienced integration of the various subjects I was studying. I noticed that the study of history sometimes relied on the sciences, especially anthropology, archeology, and geology. Before my discovery, textbooks were something I only used for defining terms and answering section questions for a grade. The weeks and months of school had a rhythm to them—define terms, answer section questions, take notes, and take a test. It was only when the teachers assigned projects that I read to find information. That reading was in the library and not in my textbooks.

While reading in the content area has become associated with a focus on secondary teachers becoming reading teachers within their content areas, elementary teachers have a long history of distinguishing expository text reading to learn science, math, and social studies, from narrative reading used for literacy development in the primary grades. A stronger emphasis has been placed on expository texts because

Finally, Rebecca New explores the Reggio Emilia approach to emergent literacy development. In "Reggio Emilia: New Ways to Think About Schooling," New suggests that not only is this "working-together" approach appealing to parents and students, but to educators across the country as well. In "Promoting Creativity for Life Using Open-Ended Materials," Walter F. Drew and Baji Rankin encourage teachers to take an active role in providing opportunities for exploring, manipulating, and creating with open-ended materials to promote growth of language skills. Corinna S. Bisgaier, Triada Samaras, and Michele J. Russo describe how "Young Children Try, Try Again: Using Wood, Glue, and Words to Enhance Learning." They explain how a wood project promoted language development, including building vocabulary for talking about the art-making process and answering open-ended questions. When coupled with paper and writing utensils, these dynamic strategies foster emergent literacy skills.

Unit 1 referred to the long and bumpy road of literacy development. It is only when all teachers on all levels and in all content areas consider themselves to be reading teachers, playing a role in each child's literacy development that NO child will be left behind!

Glenda Moss

Teaching expository text structures through information trade book retellings

Teachers can help students understand common expository text structures
by having them retell information trade books.

Barbara Moss

During the past few years, teachers at all grade levels have become increasingly interested in developing student understanding of expository text. At least two factors have helped to drive this interest. First, teachers are well aware of the demands of living in an era when information is increasing at an alarming rate. They recognize that if today's students are to survive in the Information Age, they must develop greater familiarity with and understanding of expository text.

Second, mounting pressures for improved student standardized test performance have resulted in increased attention to exposition. Because 70–80% of standardized reading test content is expository (Daniels, 2002), it is essential to provide students with the tools necessary to develop understanding of this type of text.

Teachers, too, are discovering that the proliferation of excellent children's informational literature available today can provide a vehicle for teaching children about exposition. The authors of these books are experienced in making the most complex concepts comprehensible, and children have the opportunity to explore the real world through texts that are inviting, accurate, and accessible. Today's information books contain wonderful examples of well-written exposition and are ideal for exposing even the youngest children to common expository text structures such as description, sequence, comparison and contrast, cause and effect, and problem and solution.

While most teachers are very familiar with the power of narrative retellings to improve student comprehension, they are less experienced with expository retellings. Involving students in retelling information trade books represents a promising means not only for engaging students with outstanding literature but also for improving their understanding of expository text. This article describes how teachers can use information trade book retellings to improve student comprehension of expository

text structures. First, I provide background information about retellings, expository text structure and teaching these text patterns through information trade books. In the second part of the article, I describe instructional strategies and procedures for teaching the various text structures through large-group, small-group, and paired retellings. In the final section of the article, I describe how teachers can assess individual student retellings.

Why teach about expository text?

Educators today are reexamining questions of what it means to be literate in the Information Age. Few would argue against the fact that technology is dramatically changing the way we live, and that the Internet, websites, e-mail, discussion boards, chat rooms, and other forms of communication have changed our views about what it means to be literate (Reinking, 1998). It is clear that the literacy demands of today's technological society require that students be able to read and write not only in the print world but also in the digital world (Schmar-Dobler, 2003).

The Internet arguably represents one of the most demanding forms of technology in terms of its literacy requirements. The ability to use the Internet to access information quickly, sift through volumes of text, evaluate content, and synthesize information from a variety of sources is central to success at school and in the workplace (Schmar-Dobler, 2003). All of these skills, however, require that students capably read the text found on Internet websites, most of which is expository (Kamil & Lane, 1997). For this reason, it is imperative that even young children begin to develop understanding of this text type.

For many years, experts assumed that children's ability to understand narrative text preceded the ability to comprehend exposition. Pappas's (1991) seminal study comparing 20 kindergartners' ability to retell information trade books with a fictional one called that assumption into question. She found that the children she studied were just as capable of retelling informational text as narrative. Even so, children have far less familiarity with expository texts and their underlying structures (Chambliss, 1995; Goldman, 1997) than with narrative. Knowledge of the structure of different text genres develops over time for children; older children have greater understanding of different text types than younger children (Goldman & Rakestraw, 2000). Despite this fact, students of all ages generally find reading expository text more difficult than reading narrative text (Langer, 1985).

There are at least two possible reasons for students' difficulty with this type of text. First, young children lack early exposure to exposition. Story continues to be the predominant genre in early elementary classrooms. Duke (2000), for example, found that very little informational text was available in the first-grade classrooms she studied, whether displayed on walls or in classroom libraries. Most important was that she found that students in these classrooms spent on average only 3.6 minutes with informational text per day.

The second possible reason is that in many cases students have not been taught how to read expository text. Children need more than exposure to informational texts; they need instruction that familiarizes them with its organization and structure. In a study involving more than 100 hours of observations in primary literacy classrooms, Fisher and Hiebert (1990) found there was not a single instance of teachers modeling strategies for reading expository text. Teaching common expository text structures such as description, sequence, comparison and contrast, cause and effect, and problem and solution facilitates reading and writing of exposition (Block, 1993; Goldman & Rakestraw, 2000; McGee & Richgels, 1985; Raphael, Kirschner, & Englert, 1988). Students who learn to use the organization and structure of informational texts are better able to comprehend and retain the information found in them (Goldman & Rakestraw, 2000; Pearson & Duke, 2002).

If today's students are to meet the literacy demands of the future, they need to engage in authentic literacy tasks with expository texts. Information trade book retellings can provide students rich opportunities for not only gaining exposure to expository text but also gaining expertise in understanding this text type.

What are retellings?

Teachers and students often confuse retellings with summaries. Retellings are oral or written postreading recalls during which children relate what they remember from reading or listening to a particular text. Conversely, a summary represents a short, to-the-point distillation of the main ideas in the text. Retellings provide a holistic representation of student understanding rather than the fragmented information provided by answering comprehension questions (Bromley, 1998). When students retell,

they attempt to recall as much of the information in the text as possible, not just the main points. Retellings are an important precursor to helping students develop summarization skills, both oral and written. Students who are unable to retell will find it difficult, if not impossible, to summarize effectively. As students gain facility in retelling in the early grades, their recounts of expository texts will become increasingly sophisticated. Through these experiences they will be well prepared to develop skills in summarizing as they move beyond the primary grades.

Research (Gambrell, Koskinen, & Kapinus, 1991; Gambrell, Pfeiffer, & Wilson, 1985; Morrow, 1986) clearly supports the usefulness of retellings in improving student understanding of story. Reconstructing texts through retellings helps children develop reading flexibility as well as knowledge of text forms, text conventions, and the processes involved in text construction. Retellings provide insights about children's ways of constructing meaning from texts and their ability to organize information. When students share retellings, they "read, reread and reread again" and engage with text much more intensely than at other times (Brown & Cambourne, 1990, p. 11). In addition, retellings let teachers see *how* as well as *how much* information children retain after reading or listening to a text (Irwin & Mitchell, 1983).

By retelling the expository text in information trade books, students can sense text organization and identify relationships among pieces of information and develop their oral language abilities. English-language learners may particularly benefit from this strategy, because the concrete nature of informational text can help them build bridges between their first and second languages. Through oral retellings of information trade books, children can develop deeper understanding of the forms and functions of exposition—a critical component to comprehending nonnarrative material.

Understanding expository text structures

Authors use different "tools" as they construct stories and information texts. Most of the time, stories are written in a narrative form, while information books are written in an expository one. Narrative and expository texts have different purposes. The main purpose of narrative texts is to tell a story, while expository text is intended to inform, describe, or report. Authors who create people and events from their imaginations use narrative structures to create stories. When authors write information books, they conduct research to gain information on the topic at hand. They organize the information as logically and interestingly as they can using various expository text structures.

Narrative texts have a specific, predictable structure that readers encounter over and over again. This structure, or story grammar, includes characters; a setting; a problem (or conflict); a climax, or high point to the action; and a resolution. Expository texts, like narrative ones,

---

FIGURE 1
Common expository text structures

- *Description* presents a topic and provides details that help readers understand characteristics of a person, place, thing, topic, or idea. No specific signal words are typically associated with description. When authors delineate a topic they use description. Semantic maps (a graphic organizer that resembles a spider web and groups information by categories) provide a visual representation for this structure.

Trade book examples: *Bats* by Gail Gibbons, *Amazing Snakes* by Richard Parsons, and *Ant Cities* by Arthur Dorros

- The *sequence* structure involves putting facts, events, or concepts in their order of occurrence. Signal words like *first, second, third, then, next, last, before, after,* and *finally* indicate order of events. Authors use sequence when giving directions for an experiment or explaining the stages in an animal's life cycle. Series of events chains are visual organizers that use boxes and arrows to illustrate a sequence of events and the steps in that sequence.

Trade book examples: *My Puppy Is Born* by Joanna Cole, *How Kittens Grow* by Millicent Selsam, and *The Buck Stops Here* by Alice Provensen

- The *comparison and contrast* structure involves identification of similarities and differences between facts, concepts, people, and so forth. Signal words include same as, *alike, similar to, resembles, compared to, different from, unlike, but,* and *yet.* Authors use this structure to compare and contrast crocodiles and alligators or life in ancient times with life today. Venn diagrams use interlocking circles to illustrate similarities and differences between two things. Individual characteristics appear in the left and right sections, while common characteristics appear in the overlapping sections.

Trade book examples: *Fire, Fire* by Gail Gibbons, *Gator or Croc* by Allan Fowler, and *Outside and Inside You* by Sandra Markle

- The *cause and effect* structure includes a description of causes and the resulting effects. Cause and effect is often signaled by *if, so, so that, because of, as a result of, since, in order to,* and the words *cause* and *effect.* When authors explain the effects of an oil spill or the reasons for animal extinction they use this structure. *Cause* and *effect* maps use circles or squares with connecting arrows to illustrate relationships between causes and their resulting effects.

Trade book examples: *What Makes Day and Night?* by Franklyn Bramley, *What Happens to a Hamburger?* by Paul Showers, *How Do Apples Grow?* by Guilio Maestro

- The *problem and solution* structure shows the development of a problem and its solution. Signal words include *problem, solution, because, cause, since, as a result,* and *so that.* Authors use this structure to explain why inventions are created, why money was invented, or why you should buy a particular product. Problem and solution outlines visually illustrate the problem-solving process by defining components of a problem and possible solutions.

Trade book examples: *A River Ran Wild: An Environmental History* by Lynn Cherry, *Cars and How They Go* by Joanna Cole, and *If You Traveled on the Underground Railroad* by Ellen Levine

---

have their own structures. These structures provide students with a map that guides them through a text. The greater children's awareness of expository text structures and organizational patterns, the better they can follow the author's message.

The five most common expository text structures include description, sequence, comparison and contrast, cause and effect, and problem and solution (Meyer, 1985). Signal words (or cue words) alert readers to the presence of these patterns. Often, however, signal words are implied rather than stated. Figure 1 describes each of these text structures and their characteristics.

Information trade books that reflect expository text patterns

Today's information trade books are ideally suited for teaching expository text structures because, unlike textbooks, they contain well-organized and clearly written texts. Books used for this purpose should, however, be selected with care. First and foremost, texts should be selected on the basis of literary quality. Information books should be well written, accurate in terms of content and

illustration, and appropriate to the age level of the child. They should not simply be "baskets of facts" but should be written in an engaging and appealing way. Second, teachers must choose books that don't overwhelm children with difficult technical vocabulary and numerous complex concepts. The best informational books make even the most difficult terms and concepts comprehensible to children. Finally, teachers need to select books that clearly illustrate the text structure being taught. In many information trade books signal words are implied rather than explicitly stated. If this is the case, teachers should choose books with page layouts, headings, and tables of contents that provide students with important clues about the pattern used.

Expository text structures work on two different levels. In books for younger children, these text patterns may provide the macrostructure, or overall structure for a particular book. Titles like *Amazing Snakes* (Parsons, 1990), for example, use a descriptive structure to teach children about different types of snakes.

At the microstructure, or paragraph level, however, authors may use many, or even all, of these structures within a given book or chapter, or even on a single page.

FIGURE 2
Sequence for teaching expository text structures

13. Introduce the organizational pattern.
14. Explain the pattern and when writers use it. Point out the signal words associated with the structure and share an example.
15. Model ways students can determine text structures when signal words are not used. The table of contents and headings can help in this area.
16. Introduce a graphic organizer for the pattern.
17. Read aloud a trade book or a section of a book illustrating the appropriate text structure. Ask students to listen for signal words that can help them identify the structure.
18. Using the overhead projector, involve the group in completing a graphic organizer illustrating the text type.
19. Ask students to work in pairs to locate examples of the structure in information trade books. They can search for examples of the signal words, as well as use headings and other text features to guide their search.
20. Have students diagram these structures using a graphic organizer.

Note. Adapted from Tompkins (2002).

FIGURE 3
Problem and solution outline for *Ospreys* (Patent, 1993)

Problem
Who has the problem? The osprey.
What was the problem? They nest on power poles.
Why was it a problem? Their nests can damage the wires. Sometimes the birds touch their wings to the wires and kill themselves and short out the power.

Solution
Some companies put up spiked poles where birds can't nest.

Teachers might, then, select portions of text from such titles to illustrate particular text structures. Not every expository text uses these structures; some combine structures or incorporate features of narrative as well as exposition. As students increase their understanding, they can begin to identify texts illustrating a variety of structures, such as their textbooks. Figure 1 provides examples of high-quality information trade books illustrative of each type of text structure at the macrolevel.

Introducing text structures through trade books

The teaching of expository text structures can begin as early as kindergarten and become increasingly sophisticated as students move through the grades. Each text structure should be taught individually; students need time to master one structure before learning another. Structures like sequence and comparison and contrast tend to be easier for students to grasp, while description, cause and effect, and problem and solution are more challenging. Figure 2 offers a clear sequence for teaching expository text structures through minilessons.

Teacher Alan Page wanted to teach his sixth graders the problem and solution text structure. His students were studying endangered animals. He introduced them to the problem and solution structure by asking, "What can we do to prevent endangered animals from disap-

pearing from the planet?" Students then brainstormed solutions to the problem. After that, Alan explained that authors may use the problem and solution pattern when discussing world problems, scientific inventions, and so on. He pointed out the signal words often used with this pattern. At this point, he presented the following paragraph from *Ospreys* (Patent, 1993) on the overhead projector. He read the paragraph aloud and asked students to note signal words that could indicate this pattern. He then underlined the words "solve this problem" to emphasize their usefulness in identifying the pattern.

> In some areas ospreys have become pests by nesting on power poles. Their large nests can damage the wires. Or even worse, the birds can touch their wings to two wires at once, killing themselves and shorting out the power. Some companies solve this problem by putting up spiked poles where the birds can't nest. (p. 53)

He then distributed copies of the problem and solution outline. Students worked together to complete the outline (see Figure 3). Students later searched for examples of this pattern on selected pages of their science text.

Teaching the retelling process

After students understand a particular text structure, experience retelling texts that illustrate that structure can provide understanding of how these texts are constructed. A two-phase sequence can facilitate student development of expository retelling skills. During Phase 1, teachers need to model the retelling process. During Phase 2, students need opportunities to practice retellings, in small groups or pairs.

Phase 1: Teacher modeling of retellings

Because expository text may he unfamiliar to students, teacher modeling is a critical first step in involving students in expository retellings. Teachers need to provide extensive scaffolding for students as they develop understanding of the process. Teachers should model retelling books with structures like sequence or comparison and contrast first and then gradually move to more complex structures such as cause and effect. With younger children it is best to model the retelling process using a read-aloud; older students may read the text silently.

Step 1: Before reading a text, develop links between children's experiences and the text itself. Use prereading activities designed to activate prior knowledge and stimulate thinking about the content of the book, such as KWL (what I *know,* what I *want* to know, what I *learned*), brainstorming, or problem solving. Make book concepts more concrete by using props, pictures, or actual examples of things mentioned in the story.

Step 2: During reading of the text, point out specific text features that facilitate retelling, such as signal words, the table of contents, headings, bolded words, maps, charts, or diagrams. Instruct students to read or listen carefully to remember as much about the text as they can.

Step 3: After reading, retell the text as completely as possible. Ask students to add any missing information, and model "look backs" by rereading or directing students to reread particular sections of the text that might have been missed during the retelling.

Step 4: Model more "embellished" retellings by including analogies, personal anecdotes, and imagery (Wood & Jones, 1998). This demonstrates to students that making the text their own is not only acceptable but desirable.

Phase 2: Students practice retelling

After students understand the concept of retelling, they need opportunities to practice. Involvement in large-group retellings allows students to experience the process again with peer support. Once students are comfortable with large-group retellings, they can begin to retell in pairs or small groups. To begin using large-group retellings, the following sequence may be useful:

Step 1: Involve students in before reading activities (see Step 1 of Phase 1) and then read the text aloud or ask students to read it. Encourage students to predict what the text might be about and to think about what the organization pattern of the text might be by previewing the text or the table of contents.

Step 2: Ask students what they can remember about the text. Record their responses on the whiteboard. Provide scaffolds and prompts that aid student recall, such as pictures from the text or questions such as the following: What did you find out first? What did you find out next? What did you learn after that?

Step 3: Reread the text or ask students to reread the text and encourage them to identify information missed during the first retelling. Add this information to what has already been recorded on the whiteboard.

Step 4: Encourage students to make personal connections between their lives and the text. Record these on the whiteboard as appropriate.

After reading *How Kittens Grow* (Selsam & Bubley, 1973), a sequential text, aloud to her first graders, teacher Andrea Craig engaged her class in a large-group retelling. To prompt students as they retold for the first time, she mounted key photographs from the text onto the whiteboard. She also prompted the students by asking questions like "What did we find out first about kittens? What did we find out after that?" and so on, modeling important signal words associated with a sequential structure. After students retold, Andrea reread the text, and the students filled the gaps in their retelling by noting details they neglected the first time.

Once students have experience with large-group retellings, they can move to small-group or paired retelling. These smaller groups can provide students with more independent retelling experiences but still give them some degree of peer support. Cumulative retellings (Hoyt, 1999) are ideal for small-group retelling practice. After reading a text, the first student in the group retells the first events from the story. The second student retells the next series of events but repeats the earlier events. The third student relates the events provided by the first two and then adds the next set of events. The process continues until the entire text has been retold.

After practice with group retellings, students can retell in pairs. Here are steps to follow for paired retellings:

Step 1: Ask students to select a trade book to read on their own silently or through paired reading. Remind them that they will want to remember the big ideas from the text as well as the details.

Step 2: Have students work in pairs to reconstruct the text. Each child in the pair can retell half of the text. One child can be identified as the reteller and one as the listener. They can then switch roles.

Step 3: Instruct students to listen carefully to one another as they retell. With older children, the listener can record the ideas recounted by the reteller.

Step 4: After each pair of students has retold, they can look back at the text and compare it with the ideas that have been recorded to identify information missed during their retelling.

To teach her students about the sequential text structure, fifth-grade teacher Maria Gomez involved her students in paired retellings of a section of *Mummies, Tombs, and Treasures* (Perl, 1987), dealing with the sequence of events in an ancient Egyptian funeral procession. Maria began the lesson by reviewing sequential text signal words. She then asked her students to read the text silently. Following this, students completed a series of events chains in pairs (see Figure 4). After that, students retold the information from the text in pairs, relying on their series of events chains as needed.

Individual retellings and assessment

While the focus of this article has been on using retellings as an instructional strategy, individual retellings represent a powerful means of assessment. Rubrics like the one adapted from Irwin and Mitchell (1983) provide a framework for teacher evaluation of student retellings

---

FIGURE 4
Series of events chain for *Mummies, Tombs, and Treasures* (Perl, 1987)

Event 1
The dead person was sent to be mummified.

Event 2
On the day of burial, a procession was formed starting at the house of the dead person. A new coffin was pulled on a wooden sled.

Event 3
Mourners and servants followed the coffin.

Event 4
The mummy was laid in its coffin.

Event 5
The procession continued into the foothills.

Event 6
At the tomb site, the mourners ate a funerary banquet.

Event 7
After the banquet, the mummy was sealed into its tomb.

(see Figure 5). This scale provides for holistic evaluation of retellings not unlike that used for evaluating writing samples. The scoring method acknowledges the child's response as a whole, with all its individual, unique features and richness. Moreover, it assesses a student's ability to identify main ideas, relevant details, and overall text structure, along with the ability to infer beyond the text, summarize, and relate text information to his or her own life.

The following steps can guide teachers as they use individual retellings for assessment:

Step 1: Before beginning the retelling assessment, ask the student to predict what a book might be about based upon the title. Ask the child to read the book or read it to that child. Instruct the student to remember everything he or she has heard or read.

Step 2: Ask the child to tell you everything he or she can about what has been read. Use prompts such as "Can you tell me more about that?" or "What else do you remember?" to ensure that the student shares as much information as he or she can about the text without looking back at the book.

Step 3: At the end of the retelling, use follow-up questions to elicit additional information about the student's understanding. For example, assess ability to summarize by asking, "If you were going to tell a friend what this book was about in just a few words, what would you say?" To learn about personal responses to the book, ask, "What was the most important thing you learned from this book? How did you

feel about this book? Why did you like or dislike it? Would you tell a friend to read it, and why or why not?"

Step 4: Encourage students to relate these texts to their own lives and schema.

Students must draw connections between their own lives and the text in order to obtain higher scores on the rubric (see Figure 5). Students need to "personalize" their retellings by demonstrating their own interest in and questions about the text rather than by providing dry recitations of the facts. The following is an example of a fourth grader's retelling of an excerpt from *Storms* (Simon, 1992) relating to hailstorms and downdrafts. The student obviously felt comfortable embellishing her retelling in ways that made it personal for her. This retelling clearly indicates that the student is connecting the text to her own life and experiences:

> It talked about hailstones and how they can harm you and other animals. I think that's pretty interesting, because they can kill chickens and rabbits and squirrels and I never knew that it could actually kill little animals. But if it hits you in the right way, it could kill you too. The hailstones are pretty interesting looking. They look like an onion. It's shaped like an onion.... It also talks about downdrafts and how they could hurt people in airplanes and how airplanes could crash in seconds because the downdrafts are so heavy. So if you ever go on an airplane and know that there are downdrafts—don't.

As this example indicates, it is possible for students to draw connections between expository text information and their own lives in many of the same ways they connect narrative text to their own experiences. As their comfort level with exposition increases, students will find it easier to move beyond the recitation of facts to more meaningful retellings.

Capitalize on enthusiasm

Information trade book retellings can acquaint students with the expository text patterns most commonly found in their reading. By engaging students in retelling information trade books, teachers can capitalize on students' enthusiasm for nonfiction literature while providing rich experiences for engagement with nonnarrative texts. Through carefully sequenced instruction involving introduction of each text pattern; teacher modeling; and the use of large-group, small-group, and paired retellings, teachers can ensure that students increase their familiarity with and understanding of expository text. In addition, careful assessment of information trade book retellings can provide teachers with valuable information about each student's emerging abilities in comprehending nonnarrative text—an essential literacy skill for success in our technological world.

FIGURE 5
Richness of retelling scale

Level	Criteria for establishing level
5	*Very cohesive and complete retelling.* Student includes all main ideas and supporting details, sequences material properly, infers beyond the text, relates text to own life, understands text organization, summarizes, gives opinion of text and justifies it, and may ask additional questions.
4	*Cohesive and complete retelling.* Student includes most main ideas and supporting details, sequences material properly, relates text to own life, understands text organization, summarizes, and gives opinion of text and justifies it.
3	*Fairly complete retelling.* Student includes some main ideas and details, correctly sequences most material, understands text organization, and gives opinion of text.
2	*Incomplete retelling.* Student includes a few main ideas and details, has some difficulty putting material in sequence, may give irrelevant information, and gives opinion of text.
1	*Very incomplete retelling.* Student gives details only, sequences material poorly, and gives irrelevant information.

Note. Adapted from Irwin & Mitchell (1983).

References

Block, C.C. (1993). Strategy instruction in a student-centered classroom. *Elementary School Journal, 94,* 137-153.

Bromley, K. (1998). *Language arts* (3rd ed.). Needham Heights, MA: Allyn & Bacon.

Brown, H., & Cambourne, B. (1990). *Read and retell: A strategy for the whole-language/natural learning classroom.* Portsmouth, NH: Heinemann.

Chambliss, M. (1995). Text cues and strategies successful readers use to construct the gist of lengthy written arguments. *Reading Research Quarterly, 30,* 778-807.

Daniels, H. (2002). Expository text in literature circles. *Voices From the Middle, 9,* 7-14.

Duke, N.K. (2000). 3.6 minutes per day: The scarcity of informational texts in first grade. *Reading Research Quarterly, 35,* 202-224.

Fisher, C.W., & Hiebert, E.H. (1990, April). *Shifts in reading and writing tasks: Do they extend to social studies, science, and mathematics?* Paper presented at the annual meeting of the American Educational Research Association, Boston, MA.

Gambrell, L.B., Koskinen, P.S., & Kapinus, B.A. (1991). Retelling and the reading comprehension of proficient and less-proficient readers. *Journal of Educational Research, 84,* 356-363.

Gambrell, L.B., Pfeiffer, W., & Wilson, R. (1985). The effects of retelling upon reading comprehension and recall of text information. *Journal of Educational Research, 78,* 216-220.

Goldman, S.R. (1997). Learning from text: Reflections on the past and suggestions for the future. *Discourse Processes, 23,* 357-398.

Goldman, S.R., & Rakestraw, J.A. (2000). Structural aspects of constructing meaning from text. In M. Kamil, P.B. Mosenthal, P.D. Pearson, & R. Barr (Eds.), *Handbook of reading research* (Vol. 3, pp. 311-336). Mahwah, NJ: Erlbaum.

Hoyt, L. (1999). *Revisit, reflect, retell.* Portsmouth, NH: Heinemann.

Irwin, P.A., & Mitchell, J.N. (1983). A procedure for assessing the richness of retellings. *Journal of Reading, 26,* 391-396.

Kamil, M., & Lane, D. (1997, May). *Using information text for first grade reading instruction: Theory and practice.* Paper presented at the National Reading Conference, Scottsdale, AZ.

Langer, J.A. (1985). Children's sense of genre: A study of performance on parallel reading and writing tasks. *Written Communication, 2,* 157-187.

McGee, L., & Richgels, D. (1985). Teaching expository text structure to elementary students. *The Reading Teacher, 38,* 739-748.

Meyer, B.J.F. (1985). Prose analysis: Purposes, procedures, and problems. In B.K. Britton & J.B. Black (Eds.), *Understanding expository text* (pp. 11-64). Hillsdale, NJ: Erlbaum.

Morrow, L.M. (1986). Effects of structural guidance in story retelling on children's dictation of original stories. *Journal of Reading Behavior, 28,* 135-152.

Moss, B. (2003). *Exploring the literature of fact: Children's nonfiction trade books in the elementary classroom.* New York: Guilford.

Pappas, C.C. (1991). Fostering full access to literacy by including information books. *Language Arts, 68,* 449-462.

Parsons, A. (1990). *Amazing snakes.* New York: Knopf.

Patent, D.H. (1993). *Ospreys.* New York: Clarion.

Pearson, P.D., & Duke, N.K. (2002). Comprehension instruction in the primary grades. In C.C. Block & M. Pressley (Eds.), *Comprehension instruction: Research-based best practice* (pp. 247-258). New York: Guilford.

Perl, L. (1987). *Mummies, tombs, and treasures: Secrets of ancient Egypt.* New York: Clarion.

Raphael, T.E., Kirschner, B.W., & Englert, C.S. (1988). Expository writing programs: Making connections between reading and writing. *The Reading Teacher, 41,* 790-795.

Reinking, D. (1998). Introduction: Synthesizing technological transformations of literacy in a post-typographic world. In D. Reinking, M.C. McKenna, L.D. Labbo, & R.D. Kieffer (Eds.), *Handbook of literacy and technology: Transformation in a post-typographic world* (pp. xi-xxx). Mahwah, NJ: Erlbaum.

Schmar-Dobler, E. (2003). Reading on the Internet: The link between literacy and technology. *Journal of Adolescent & Adult Literacy, 47,* 80-85.

Selsam, M.E., & Bubley, E. (1973). *How kittens grow.* New York: Scholastic.

Simon, S. (1992). *Storms.* New York: Mulberry.

Tompkins, G. (2002). *Language arts: Content and teaching strategies.* Saddle River, NJ: Merrill Prentice Hall.

Wood, K.D., & Jones, J. (1998). Flexible grouping and group retellings include struggling learners in classroom communities. *Preventing School Failure, 43,* 37-38.

Moss teaches at San Diego State University (Education 127, 5500 Campanile Drive, San Diego, CA 92182, USA). E-mail bmoss@mail.sdsu.edu.

From *Reading Teacher,* Vol. 57, No. 8, 2004, pp. 710-718. Copyright © 2004 by International Reading Association. Reprinted by permission.

Mathematics trade books: Establishing their value and assessing their quality

Patricia D. Hunsader

A rubric practical for teacher use in evaluating mathematics texts found that less than half of the texts received a high enough score for both literary and mathematical quality to be recommended.

Students are often intimidated by mathematics with its myriad rules and historical emphasis on speed, memory, and accuracy (Guiett, 1999). Although the recent shift away from isolated skills and algorithms toward an emphasis on problem solving and the development of conceptual understanding may relieve some students' anxiety, there are still too many children who lack confidence in dealing with mathematics (Hellwig, Monroe, & Jacobs, 2000).

The first section of this article provides justification and support, as well as methods and ideas, for using literature in the elementary mathematics classroom as a means of reaching all students, especially those for whom success in mathematics has seemed out of reach. The second section addresses the current lack of systematic assessment of mathematics literature and the potential and pitfalls of existing evaluation tools. The final section presents a time-efficient rubric to evaluate mathematics literature along with results of research on the quality of the mathematics literature recommended for use in third grade by two nationally known mathematics curriculum publishers.

The benefits of using literature in mathematics instruction

One of the keys to success in mathematics is being able to communicate mathematically (Schiro, 1997). The National Council of Teachers of Mathematics (NCTM) emphasizes the important role of communication in helping children construct understandings of mathematical concepts and develop connections between their informal knowledge and the abstract symbolism of mathematical concepts. "Many children's books present interesting problems and illustrate how other children solve them. Through these books students see mathematics in a different context while they use reading as a form of communication" (National Council of Teachers of Mathematics, 1989, p. 27). Literature can be used to engage learners in meaningful

conversations and investigations in mathematics. This engagement with literature provides a natural way for students to connect the abstract language of mathematics to their personal world (Whitin & Whitin, 1996), helping them overcome the common difficulty of communicating mathematically (Moyer, 2000). Literature provides a means for mathematics and language skills to develop simultaneously as children listen, read, write, and talk about mathematics (Hellwig et al., 2000).

The content of both English and mathematics requires development of many of the same skills: pattern recognition, classifying, examining relationships, organizing thoughts, and solving problems. By selecting quality children's literature and using it to find natural mathematical connections, teachers can create an environment for learning that is supported by both the National Council of Teachers of English (NCTE) and the NCTM (Moyer, 2000; Taylor, 1999). This integration benefits students by allowing them to develop their language and mathematical skills simultaneously (Hellwig et al., 2000).

Another important benefit of integrating literature with mathematics is that it provides a natural setting for observing mathematics in the real world, allowing it to convey real meaning to students, and making it come alive (Hellwig et al., 2000; Leitze, 1997). When numbers and their operations are embedded in meaningful real-world contexts, children are able to make sense of the mathematics, gain mathematical power (NCTM, 2000), and develop a wider view of the place of mathematics in their world (Schiro, 1997). Cognitive psychology and schema theory also support the use of real-world contexts, because information that fits into a student's existing schema is more easily understood, learned, and retained than information that does not fit into an existing schema (Slavin, 1991).

Children's literature has a unique advantage for visual learners over most other forms of mathematical representation because ideas are presented in a nonthreatening pictorial format (Guiett, 1999). Literature can help students bridge the gap between concrete representations and abstract concepts and can improve student attitude and motivation. While it is next to impossible for students to learn that which they feel incapable of learning, it is possible for teachers to present the "unlearnable" in such an engaging format that students' attitudes do not obstruct their learning. Literature seems to provide a way around the barriers to understanding and engagement that are erected by children who suffer from mathematics anxiety.

Using mathematics literature in the Classroom

In general, when a teacher uses a piece of children's literature to explore a mathematics concept, the concept should be reviewed before reading the book (Whitin & Whitin, 2001). Children should be given the opportunity through classroom discussion to activate their own prior knowledge about the mathematics content and the subject of the story. After discussion, the story should be read aloud in its entirety, pausing only to allow students to predict upcoming events. The act of predicting allows students to focus attention on reasoning, patterns, and problem solving while adjusting their personal schemata to fit the story (Ducolon, 2000). To take full advantage of literature's motivating influence on students, it is important for the first read of the story to focus on enjoyment and not on mathematical content (Narode, 1996).

When planning lessons for integrating literature and mathematics, teachers need to provide opportunities for children to actively engage in practicing their problem-solving skills (National Council of Teachers of Mathematics, 1989). Writing activities that are open-ended in nature not only give students of all abilities an opportunity to show what they know and understand (Dyer & Moynihan, 2000) but also provide the teacher with a window on students' thinking. For example, students can write about a specific math concept presented in a book for the purpose of explaining it to a younger child or an absent classmate. When exploring a book involving a mathematical pattern, students can independently or collaboratively create their own patterned stories. Because the very nature of mathematics allows for an infinite number of ways to visually represent a mathematical idea, students should also be encouraged to draw on their own personal backgrounds to illustrate math concepts that are explored in literature (Whitin & Whitin, 1996).

Although there is an abundance of mathematics situated in quality literature, it is largely ignored because it is often not explicitly communicated in traditional mathematical representations such as diagrams, number sentences, graphs, or algorithms. Teachers can model through a think-aloud session the process of focusing on the mathematics that is embedded in the text. Whole-class or small-group book discussions can assist students in making sense of difficult mathematical text and in ferreting out the mathematics that may not be overtly presented. Graphic organizers are also a beneficial tool for making connections between narrative text and mathematical problems. To enhance mathematics literature, teachers should not be afraid to add mathematical annotations and vocabulary. As a word of

caution, because one of the greatest benefits of using literature to teach mathematics concepts is the motivating influence of literature on students, care should be taken to ensure that alterations or annotations do not detract from children's enjoyment of the story (Halpern, 1996). Additional lesson ideas are available in Bresser (1995), Burns (1992), and Whitin and Wilde (1992).

Current lack of systematic assessment

Publishers have responded to the NCTM's endorsement of integrating literature and mathematics, and the subsequent increased demand for such literature, by filling the library shelves with books for that purpose. Unfortunately, mixed in with the books that provide meaningful and thought-provoking experiences with mathematics are many that have little value (Hellwig et al., 2000). Given the time constraints that govern teachers' instructional decisions, it is inefficient to use a math trade book for instruction that is not of high mathematical and literary quality. If teachers make repeated use of mathematics trade books that fail to enhance both mathematics and literacy instruction, not only will students fail to benefit from what could and should be a valuable learning experience but also teachers may fail to see this integration as worthwhile and abandon its practice.

There exists a wide range of research-supported writing on the benefits of using literature to improve comprehension of mathematics concepts in the classroom (Griffiths & Clyne, 1991; Kolakowski, 1992; National Council of Teachers of Mathematics, 1989; Welchman-Tischler, 1992). There have been numerous books written and tools developed for the purpose of simplifying classroom teachers' implementation of this integration. Many publishers of elementary mathematics curriculum now include a list of recommended literature, some sorted by content area, in their teacher materials. Although these lists appear to speed the teacher's selection of content-appropriate mathematics trade books for use in instruction, few teachers have questioned whether publishers have assessed the mathematics or literary quality of the books they recommend.

Teachers might also make use of annotated bibliographies of mathematics trade books; however, some of these bibliographies provide no stated measure of quality. The most sophisticated evaluation system being used in a published bibliography is a three-star rating of each book's mathematics content that fails to provide the rationale or criteria used to determine the rating (Roberts, 1990; Thiessen & Matthias, 1992). A book with a high rating may be little more than a glorified textbook that might be useful in an independent learning center, but has no place in the instructional day. None of the bibliographies provide any rating of the texts' literary quality. Although content specific activity books (Braddon, Hall, & Taylor, 1993; Evans, Leija, & Falkner, 2001) reduce the burden on the classroom teacher for designing lesson activities, there is insufficient attention paid in these books to the quality of the trade books around which activities are designed.

Existing tools for the evaluation of quality

If the integration of mathematics literature with mathematics instruction is as powerful a tool as research suggests, where is the outcry from practitioners over the lack of systematic assessment of the quality of the ever-increasing wealth of these books on the library shelf? Schiro (1997) stands as one of the few who have raised this issue. In *Integrating Children's Literature and Mathematics in the Classroom* he details the development of a comprehensive tool for assessing mathematics trade books individually against mathematical and literary standards of quality. While his 22-item rubric, including 11 mathematics criteria and 11 literary criteria, allows for a detailed evaluation, it is too time-intensive for classroom teacher use.

Hellwig et al. (2000) developed a simpler instrument using accuracy, visual and verbal appeal, connections, audience, and the "wow" factor as criteria. While their rubric is time-efficient, it lacks two key components of the Schiro (1997) instrument. First, a book's mathematical and literary quality are not rated independently. A text that scores very high in mathematics but is of poor literary quality would still be recommended for instructional use. Second, the Hellwig et al. rubric does not allow the evaluator to target a grade level. Schiro's criteria allow the classroom teacher to evaluate the developmental appropriateness of both the mathematics and language of the text.

The benefits of the use of mathematics literature in the classroom, coupled with the existing lack of systematic assessment of these texts, led me to conduct research into the development and application of a functional assessment tool for mathematics literature.

Getting familiar with Schiro's rubric

I conducted a pilot study using Schiro's (1997) original instrument to become familiar with its criteria and informally assess its strengths and weaknesses. In choosing the most appropriate grade level to study, my two major considerations were the extent of the mathematics content likely to be included in the texts and the percentage of recommended texts that were likely to be in the picture book format for which Schiro's rubric was designed. The third grade was chosen as the level most likely to provide an acceptable balance between these two criteria. Nine books were selected from nine different content strands and were evaluated using Schiro's instrument in its original form.

Adapting the instrument

My experience using Schiro's (1997) original instrument in the pilot study led me to adapt it. The adapted instrument serves to reduce the number of criteria for speed in assessment and eliminate or reduce the relative weight of nondiscriminating or trivial criteria. Some of Schiro's mathematics criteria that seemed to ask the same question were combined, while others that did not significantly contribute to the evaluation were eliminated. In the process, the original list of 11 mathematics criteria was narrowed to 6, and all criteria were scored on a 5-point

scale with 5 representing the best score. The mathematics standards for the adapted instrument are as follows. Specific examples are included where appropriate.

1. Is the book's mathematics content (text, computation, scale, vocabulary, and graphics) correct and accurate? This is determined through a careful review of both the text and the pictures and graphics. The most common problem area for this criterion is the artwork, as is evident in *The Doorbell Rang* (Hutchins, 1989). The number of cookies pictured on one page is not the same as on the next page, even though no cookies have been added to or taken from the tray in the story.

2. Is the book's mathematics content visible and effectively presented? For this criterion, look for the extent to which the author and illustrator showcase the mathematics in the story text and illustrations. For example, *Summer Wheels* (Bunting, 1992) is recommended for addition of whole numbers but contains no discernible mathematics except for one reference to time and a mention of the number of bicycles in the shed. While it is a beautiful story, only a very creative teacher could successfully integrate it with mathematics instruction.

3. Is the book's mathematics content intellectually and developmentally appropriate for its audience? If the book is to be used for third grade, the mathematics content should be within one grade level of third-grade curricular guidelines. *Cookie's Week* (Ward, 1997) walks the reader through a week of a cat's life. While days-of-the-week is an important concept for the primary grades, it does not merit mathematics classroom time in third grade.

4. Does the book facilitate the reader's involvement in, and use and transfer of, its mathematics? This criterion evaluates the extent to which the reader feels compelled to "do" the math that is embedded in the text, as well as the likelihood that the book will enable and encourage the reader's transference of the mathematics to other situations. *Math Curse* (Scieszka, 1995) is a prime example of a book that compels readers to become involved in mathematical problem solving.

5. Do the book's mathematics and story complement each other? The mathematics should enhance what is already a good story, and the story should be even better for the inclusion of the mathematics. A book that reads more like a mathematics lesson set to the tune of a story should not score well on this criterion.

6. How great are the resources needed to help readers benefit from the book's mathematics? This criterion guards teachers against books that require an extraordinary amount of time or money in the preparation of materials to enact an effective lesson. Readily available classroom supplies should be all that is required for students to benefit from a text's mathematics.

In the same manner as the mathematics criteria, some of Schiro's (1997) literary items were combined, while others were eliminated. All criteria are assessed using a 5-point scale, with 5 representing the highest possible score. The resulting six literary standards for the adapted instrument are as follows:

1. Does the plot exhibit good development, imagination, and continuity? Are the characters (if any) well developed? As with any good story, a strong plot and engaging characters are essential for a quality mathematics trade book.

2. Does the book contain a vivid and interesting writing style that actively involves the child? Some mathematics trade books suffer from either overly repetitive or terse text. Conveying quality mathematics should not detract from the inherent interest of the writing style or the extent to which the reader is drawn into the story. *Capacity: Math Counts* (Pluckrose, 1995) presents sound mathematics and good graphics, but the text is dull and does not invite engagement.

3. Are the book's illustrations and graphics text-relevant, appealing, and representative of a child's perspective? This item evaluates the age-appropriateness and appeal and effectiveness of the visual elements of the book.

4. Are the book's readability and interest level developmentally appropriate for the intended audience? The most common problem is text that is written at a much different level than the audience for which the book is recommended. In this study it was more common for the recommended books to be below rather than above the targeted interest level, as was the case with *You'll Soon Grow Into Them, Titch* (Hutchins, 1992) and *Zoo* (Gibbons, 1991).

5. Do the book's plot, style, and graphics/ illustrations complement one another? This criterion measures synergy. How well do all of the textual and visual elements of the book work together to create a product that children will enjoy?

6. Does the book respect the reader by presenting positive ethical and cultural values? Look for books that present positive models of men and women in both community and parental roles, highlight the value of diversity, and present morals and ethics appropriate for children. To accurately score this criterion, the evaluator must delve below the surface of the text to critically examine the messages and possible stereotypes embodied in the story. *Gator Pie* (Matthews, 1995) is one of the best books I have seen for the presentation of fractions, but the implied moral of the story is that whoever can incite others to fight will ultimately get the prize.

How good are the books recommended by publishers?

The value of integrating literature with the mathematics curriculum has been established, and a practical tool for assessing the quality of mathematics literature has been developed. The adapted instrument is presented in the Figure. The question remains as to the level of quality of the mathematics literature that is being recommended by publishers of mathematics curricula. To what extent are the recommended texts of high mathematics and literary quality, at the appropriate reading level, and well matched to the specified content?

Selection of texts for the full study

I chose two mathematics curricula, McGraw-Hill's *Mathematics* (2000) and Harcourt Brace's *Math Advantage* (1998), with which to conduct the study. Both publishers are well known throughout the United States, and both include a grade-specific list of recommended mathematics literature to be used in conjunction with their curricula. McGraw-Hill's bibliography is listed according to mathematics content and lends itself to additional scrutiny as to how well the content of the texts match the content for which they are recommended (content match). Because the original Schiro (1997) instrument and my adaptation were designed to evaluate texts written in a picture book or storybook format, texts on the publisher's lists not fitting that format were not included in the study. In addition, 6 texts on McGraw-Hill's list and 13 on Harcourt Brace's list, a significant 13% of all recommended texts, could not be found in any public county or university library in the state of Florida and were also eliminated from the study. After these eliminations, a total of 75 texts remained to be evaluated, only 2 of which appeared on both publishers' lists.

Assessing the texts and interpreting the scores

For the study, each book was read through once for enjoyment and coherence, then the text and graphics on each page were carefully perused during the scoring process. The scores were averaged to arrive at a single whole number rating between 1 and 5 for both mathematics and literary quality. Only those texts that received a 4 or 5 average rating for both mathematical and literary quality were deemed to be valuable for use in mathematics instruction. The issue of rounding became critical with books whose average of mathematics or literary scores was a 3.5. A careful review of the individual criteria led to the decision to round down. For many of the criteria, a score of 3 represents a neutral rating. Therefore, an average score of 3.5 represents a text that is barely above neutral and could not be recommended without some equivocation. *Cookie's Week* (Ward, 1997) is an example of a text with a 3.5 average for mathematics. The book received a high score for mathematical accuracy (sequencing of the days of the week), low for developmental appropriateness, and midrange for the remaining criteria. As a whole, this book would not contribute enough to student learning to justify a recommendation.

The mathematics and literary quality of a text should be assessed separately because a book that fails to be recommended for both may still have a place in the classroom. Books that are recommended for mathematics but not literary quality can be used in independent learning centers as tools for students' self-teaching but should not play a role in whole-class instruction. Books that receive a recommend vote for literary quality but not mathematics were likely never intended for use in mathematics

Mathematics trade book evaluation form by Patricia D. Hunsader *

Reviewer: _____ Date: _____

Book name:	Author:
Publisher and date:	
Mathematics content of book:	Target audience (circle all appropriate): preschool K 1 2 3 4 5 6 7 8 9

Answer the following based on an average of scores from the subsequent pages of this instrument

How good is the book from a mathematical perspective?	5 superb	4 recommended	3 acceptable	2 marginal	1 unacceptable
How good is the book from a literary perspective?	5 superb	4 recommended	3 acceptable	2 marginal	1 unacceptable

General comments:

Mathematical standards

Is the book's mathematics content (text, computation, scale, vocabulary, and graphics) correct and accurate?	5 correct	4	3 partially	2	1 incorrect	NA
Comments:						

Is the book's mathematics content visible and effectively presented?	5 optimally	4	3 partially	2	1 poorly
Comments:					

Is the book's mathematics content intellectually and developmentally appropriate for its audience?	5 optimally	4	3 partially	2	1 unsuited
Comments:					

Does the book facilitate the reader's involvement in, and use and transfer of, its mathematics?	5 optimally	4	3 no effect	2	1 inhibit
Comments:					

Do the book's mathematics and story complement each other?	5 optimally	4	3 no effect	2	1 detract
Comments:					

How great are the resources needed to help readers benefit from the book's mathematics?	5 optimally	4	3 average	2	1 excessive
Comments:					

Literary standards

Does the plot exhibit good development, imagination, and continuity? Are the characters (if any) well developed?	5 excellent	4	3	2	1 poor
Comments:					

(continued)

Mathematics trade book evaluation form (continued)					
Does the book contain a vivid and interesting writing style that actively involves the child?	5 excellent	4	3	2	1 poor
Comments:					
Are the book's illustrations and graphics text-relevant, appealing, and representative of a child's perspective?	5 excellent	4	3	2	1 poor
Comments:					
Are the book's readability and interest level developmentally appropriate for the intended audience?	5 excellent	4	3	2	1 poor
Comments:					
Do the book's plot, style, and graphics/illustrations complement one another?	5 excellent	4	3	2	1 poor
Comments:					
Does the book respect the reader by presenting positive ethical and cultural values?	5 excellent	4	3	2	1 poor
Comments:					

* Adapted with permission from Schiro, M. (1997). *Integrating children's literature and mathematics in the classroom: Children as meaning makers, problem solvers, and literary critics.* New York: Teachers College Press.

instruction. They may have value for use in another content area, and in the hands of a very creative and resourceful mathematics teacher may still be used in mathematics instruction. However, in and of themselves, they do not present enough valuable mathematics to be recommended for inclusion in mathematics instruction.

Disappointing findings

One would hope that mathematics curriculum publishers would recommend only texts that are high-quality literature, include high-quality mathematics, are appropriate for the audience, and contain real-world mathematical contexts for the content areas they are recommended. Unfortunately, that is not always the case. Of the 29 texts from McGraw-Hill's bibliography that were included in the study, 15 (52%) received high enough mathematical and literary scores to be recommended as mathematics literature. Five additional texts (17%) received a recommend rating for mathematics only, and 5 (17%) were recommended strictly as quality literature. The mean mathematics score for all texts was 3.6, and the mean literary score was 3.9. The average score for content match was less than 3 out of a possible 5, indicating that the texts contained content aligned to the content for which they were recommended slightly more than half of the time.

Of the 48 texts from Harcourt Brace's bibliography that were included in the study, 19 (40%) scored high enough in both categories to be recommended for use as mathematics literature. An additional 4 texts (8%) received a recommendation for mathematics only, and a significant 14 texts (29%) were recommended strictly as quality literature. The mean mathematics score for all texts on the list was 3.5 and the mean literary score was 3.9. It is interesting that only two texts appeared on both publishers' lists, both of which scored high for mathematics and literary standards. A combined total of 75 individual texts were reviewed, and 32 of those texts scored high enough on both sets of standards to be recommended for inclusion in the mathematics curriculum.

Tables 1 and 2 show the math and literary average scores, content match score (for the McGraw-Hill list only), and author recommendations for all texts on both publishers' lists. A bibliography (see Sidebar) is included for all texts that earned recommendations for both mathematical and literary quality, and the mathematics content addressed by each book is listed.

Implications

When quality mathematics literature is successfully integrated with mathematics instruction, children benefit by improving their mathematical communication, becoming actively and being motivated to challenge themselves. The

TABLE 1

Rating with adapted Schiro instrument—McGraw-Hill's *Mathematics*

Book title	Math average	Literary average	Content match	Recommendations
17 Kings and 42 Elephants	1	3	1	Neither
Alexander, Who Used to Be Rich Last Sunday	4	4	3	Math & Literary
Amanda Bean's Amazing Dream	5	5	5	Math & Literary
Anno's Magic Seeds	5	4	4	Math & Literary
Anno's Mysterious Multiplying Jar	4	4	4	Math & Literary
Big Numbers	4	3	5	Math only
Biggest House in the World, The	2	4	2	Literary only
Biggest Nose, The	3	4	3	Literary only
Biggest, Strongest, Fastest	5	4	5	Math & Literary
Cache of Jewels, A	2	3	1	Neither
Cloak for the Dreamer, A	5	5	5	Math & Literary
Deep Down Underground	4	4	1	Math & Literary
Gator Pie	4	3	4	Math only
Giant Jam Sandwich, The	1	4	1	Literary only
Greatest Guessing Game, The	4	4	5	Math & Literary
Greedy Triangle, The	5	5	5	Math & Literary
How Did Numbers Begin?	4	3	1	Math only
Marge's Diner	2	4	1	Literary only
Measuring Penny	5	5	5	Math & Literary
More M&Ms Brand Chocolate Candies Math	4	4	4	Math & Literary
Numbers	4	4	1	Math & Literary
One Grain of Rice	5	5	4	Math & Literary
Purse, The	4	4	1	Math & Literary
Sea Sums	3	3	2	Neither
Socrates and the Three Little Pigs	4	3	3	Math only
Spaghetti and Meatballs for All	4	5	4	Math & Literary
Summer Wheels	1	5	1	Literary only
You'll Soon Grow Into Them, Titch	1	3	1	Neither
Zero Is Nothing	4	2	1	Math only

operative word here is *quality*. If publishers of mathematics curricula seek to encourage and support this integration, they must also take measures to ensure that the literature they recommend is of high enough quality to be beneficial. It is not a question of whether high-quality mathematics literature exists, it is more a question of whether publishers are using due diligence in selecting and recommending that literature. More effort needs to be made by these publishers to verify the quality of texts before placing them on a list for classroom teacher use. In addition, publishers should assess the availability of a text before placing it on their list. Publishers have a duty to ensure that their recommendations are well thought out and thoroughly justified. Teachers have a right to expect that publishers will uphold this responsibility.

This research reveals that these two publishers have not upheld their responsibility, and, more often than not, teachers will be disappointed. It is unfortunate that this failure on the part of the publishers places increased burden on classroom teachers to do their own evaluation and selection of quality mathematics literature. The adaptation of Schiro's (1997) rubric provides a valid and time-efficient means of conducting the evaluations to aid in making selections. While there is some element of sub-

jectivity in using any holistic rating scale, this tool provides a more systematic approach than unguided judgment. Given the myriad benefits to students of including literature in the mathematics curriculum, the extra effort on the part of the teacher is warranted.

BIBLIOGRAPHY OF RECOMMENDED MATH LITERATURE BOOKS FROM MCGRAW-HILL'S *MATHEMATICS* GRADE 3

Anno, M. (1983). *Anno's mysterious multiplying jar.* New York: Philomel. Multiplication, factorial numbers.
Anno, M. (1995). *Anno's magic seeds.* New York: Philomel, Problem solving, multiplication.
Burns, M. (1994). *The greedy triangle.* New York: Scholastic. Properties of geometric shapes.
Burns, M. (1997). *Spaghetti and meatballs for all.* New York: Scholastic. Area and perimeter.
Caple, K. (1986). *The purse.* Boston: Houghton Mifflin. Operations with decimals.
Demi. (1997). *One grain of rice.* New York: Scholastic. Multiplication, the power of doubling.
Dunrea, O. (1989). *Deep down underground.* New York: Macmillan. Counting, addition.
Freidman. A. (1994). *A cloak for the dreamer.* New York: Scholastic. Tessellations.

	TABLE 2		
	Rating with adapted Schiro instrument-Harcourt Brace's Math Advantage		
Book title	**Math average**	**Literary average**	**Recommendations**
Alexander, Who Used to Be Rich Last Sunday	4	4	Math & Literary
Anno's Counting House	3	3	Neither
Anno's Mysterious Multiplying Jar	4	4	Math & Literary
Bag Full of Pups, A	3	3	Neither
Beach Feet	3	3	Neither
Bicycle Race	2	2	Neither
Brooklyn Bridge: A Wonders of the World Book, The	4	5	Math & Literary
Capacity: Math Counts	4	3	Math only
Chair for My Mother, A	3	5	Literary only
Cookie's Week	3	3	Neither
Counting on Frank	4	4	Math & Literary
Doorbell Rang, The	4	4	Math & Literary
Each Orange Had Eight Slices	4	3	Math only
Earthquakes	3	3	Neither
Echoes for the Eye: Poems to Celebrate Patterns	5	5	Math & Literary
Eight Hands Round	4	4	Math & Literary
Ellis Island: New Hope in a New Land	3	5	Literary only
Fraction Action	5	5	Math & Literary
Goat in the Rug, The	3	3	Neither
Grandfather Tang's Story	5	5	Math & Literary
Half-Birthday Party, The	3	4	Literary only
Harry's Birthday	2	3	Neither
How Big Is a Foot?	5	4	Math & Literary
How Big Were the Dinosaurs?	4	4	Math & Literary
How Many Days to America?	2	4	Literary only
How Much Is a Million?	5	4	Math & Literary
How Pizza Came to Queens	1	4	Literary only
If You Made a Million	5	4	Math & Literary
Jigsaw Jackson	2	5	Literary only
Librarian Who Measured the Earth, The	4	4	Math & Literary
Locks, Crocs, and Skeeters: The Story of the Panama Canal	3	2	Neither
Math Curse	5	5	Math & Literary
Millions of Cats	3	4	Literary only
Mountains	3	4	Literary only
My Place in Space	4	4	Math & Literary
Nine for California	2	5	Literary only
Old Home Day	3	4	Literary only
Paperboy	3	5	Literary only
Picture Book of Jesse Owens, A	2	4	Literary only
Pigs Will Be Pigs	5	4	Math & Literary
Ready, Set, Hop!	4	3	Math only
Remainder of One, A	4	4	Math & Literary
Round Trip	4	5	Math & Literary
Sam Johnson and the Blue Ribbon Quilt	2	4	Literary only
Seven Chinese Brothers, The	3	4	Literary only
Shopping Basket, The	3	3	Neither
Wildlife 1-2-3: A Nature Counting Book	4	3	Math only
Zoo	1	2	Neither

Froman, R. (1978). *The greatest guessing game.* New York: Thomas Y. Crowell, Probability and odds.

Jenkins, S. (1995). *Biggest, strongest, fastest.* New York: Houghton Mifflin. Scale, measurement.

Leedy, L. (1997). *Measuring penny.* New York: Henry Holt. Measurement.

McGrath, B.B. (1998) *More M&M's brand chocolate candies math.* Watertown, MA: Charlesbridge. Graphing, addition, subtraction, multiplication, ordinal numbers.

Neuschwander, C, (1998). *Amanda Bean's amazing dream.* New York: Scholastic. Multiplication basic facts.

Pluckrose, H. (1995). *Numbers.* Chicago: Children's Press. Uses of numbers.

Viorst, J. (1978). *Alexander, who used to be rich last Sunday.* New York: Macmillan. Decimals, subtraction.

BIBLIOGRAPHY OF RECOMMENDED MATH LITERATURE BOOKS FROM HARCOURT BRACE'S *MATH ADVANTAGE* GRADE 3

Anno, M; (1983). *Anno's mysterious multiplying jar.* New York: Philomel. Multiplication, factorial numbers.

Axelrod, A, (1994). *Pigs will be pigs.* New York: Simon & Schuster. Operations with decimals.

Clement, R. (1991). *Counting on Frank.* Milwaukee, WI: Gareth Stevens. Problem solving.

Esbensen, B.J. (1996). *Echoes for the eye: Poems to celebrate patterns in nature.* New York: HarperCollins. Patterns.

Hirst, R., & Hirst, S. (1988). *My place in space.* New York: Orchard. Measurement related to the solar system.

Hutchins, P. (1986), *The doorbell rang.* New York: Mulberry. Division.

Jonas, A. (1983). *Round tri*p. New York: Greenwillow. Geometry, perspective.

Lasky, K. (1994). *The librarian who measured the earth.* Boston: Little, Brown. Measurement, geometry.

Leedy, L. (1994). *Fraction action.* New York: Holiday House. Fractional parts.

Mann, E. (1996), *The Brooklyn bridge: A wonders of the world book.* New York: Mikaya Press. Measurement. geometry.

Most, B. (1994). *How big were the dinosaurs?* New York: Harcourt Brace. Measurement, proportional reasoning, estimation.

Myller, R. (1974). *How big is a foot?* New York: Atheneum. Measurement.

Paul, A.W. (1991); *Eight hands round.* New York: Houghton Mifflin. Division.

Schwartz, D.M. (1985). *How much is a million?* New York: Lothrop, Lee & Shepard, Large numbers, place value, proportional reasoning.

Schwartz, D. M. (1989). *If you made a million.* New York: Lothrop, Lee & Shepard, Large numbers, place value, proportional reasoning.

Scieszka, J. (1995). *Math curse.* New York: Penguin. Algebraic thinking, whole number operations, problem solving.

Tompert, A. (1990). *Grandfather Tang's Story.* New York: Crown. Spatial relations, geometry.

Viorst, J. (1978). *Alexander who used to be rich last Sunday.* New York: Macmillan. Decimals, subtraction.

References

Braddon, K., Hall, N., & Taylor, D. (1993). *Math through children's literature: Making the NCTM standards come alive.* Englewood, CO: Teacher Ideas Press.

Bresser, R. (1995). *Math and literature (4-6).* Sausalito, CA: Math Solutions.

Bunting, E. (1992). *Summer wheels.* New York: Harcourt Brace Jovanovich.

Burns, M. (1992). *Math and literature (K-3).* Sausalito, CA: Math Solutions.

Ducolon, C.K. (2000). Quality literature as a springboard to problem solving. *Teaching Children Mathematics, 6,* 442-446.

Dyer, M.K., & Moynihan, C. (2000). *Open-ended questions in elementary mathematics: Instruction and assessment.* Larchmont, NY: Eye on Education.

Evans, C.W., Leija, A.J., & Falkner, T.R. (2001). *Math links: Teaching the NCTM standards through children's literature.* Englewood, CO: Teacher Ideas Press.

Gibbons, G. (1991). *Zoo.* New York: Thomas Y. Crowell.

Griffiths, R., & Clyne, M. (1991). *Books you can count on: Linking mathematics and literature.* Portsmouth, NH: Heinemann.

Guiett, D. (1999). From alphabet to zebras: Using children's literature in the mathematics classroom. *Ohio Media Spectrum, 51,* 32-36.

Halpern, P.A. (1996). Communicating the mathematics in children's trade books using mathematical annotations. In P.C. Elliott (Ed.), *Communication in mathematics: K-12 and beyond, 1996 yearbook of the National Council of Teachers of Mathematics* (pp. 54-59). Reston, VA: National Council of Teachers of Mathematics.

Harcourt Brace. (1998). *Math advantage.* Orlando, FL: Author.

Hellwig, S., Monroe, E.E., & Jacobs, J.S. (2000). Making informed choices: Selecting children's trade books for mathematics instruction. *Teaching Children Mathematics, 7,* 138-143.

Hutchins, P. (1989). *The doorbell rang.* New York: Mulberry. Hutchins, P. (1992). *You'll soon grow into them, Titch.* New York: Greenwillow.

Kolakowski, J.S. (1992). *Linking math with literature.* Greensboro, NC: Carson-Dellosa.

Leitze, A.R. (1997). Connecting process problem solving to children's literature. *Teaching Children Mathematics, 3,* 398-405.

Matthews, L. (1995). *Gator pie.* New York: Dodd, Mead.

McGraw-Hill. (2000). *Mathematics.* Columbus, OH: Author.

Moyer, P.S. (2000). Communicating mathematically: Children's literature as a natural connection. *The Reading Teacher, 54,* 246-255.

Narode, R. (1996). Communicating mathematics through literature. In P.C. Elliott (Ed.), *Communication in mathematics K-12 and beyond, 1996 yearbook of the National Council of Teachers of Mathematics* (pp. 76-80). Reston, VA: National Council of Teachers of Mathematics.

National Council of Teachers of Mathematics. (1989). *Curriculum and evaluation standards for school mathematics.* Reston, VA: Author.

National Council of Teachers of Mathematics. (2000). *Principles and standards for school mathematics.* Reston, VA: Author.

Pluckrose, H.A. (1995). *Capacity: Math counts.* New York: Children's Press.

Roberts, P.L. (1990). *Counting books are more than numbers: An annotated action bibliography.* Hamden, CT: Library Professional Publications.

Schiro, M. (1997). *Integrating children's literature and mathematics in the classroom: Children as meaning makers, problem solvers, and literary critics.* New York: Teachers College Press.

Scieszka, J. (1995). *Math curse.* New York: Penguin.

Slavin, R.E. (1991). *Educational psychology* (3rd ed.). Needham Heights, MA: Allyn & Bacon.

Taylor, G.M. (1999). Reading, writing, arithmetic—Making connections. *Teaching Children Mathematics, 6,* 190-197.

Thiessen, D., & Matthias, M. (1992). *The wonderful world of mathematics.* Reston, VA: National Council of Teachers of Mathematics.

Ward, C. (1997). *Cookie's week.* New York: G.P. Putnam's Sons.

Welchman-Tischler, R. (1992). *How to use children's literature to teach mathematics.* Reston, VA: National Council of Teachers of Mathematics.

Whitin, D.J., & Whitin, P.E. (1996). Fostering metaphorical thinking through children's literature. In P.C. Elliott (Ed.), *Communication in mathematics: K-12 and beyond, 1996 yearbook of the National Council of Teachers of Mathematics* (pp. 60-65). Reston, VA: National Council of Teachers of Mathematics.

Whitin, P.E., & Whitin, D.J. (2001). Using literature to invite mathematical representations. In A.A. Cuoco (Ed.), *The roles of representation in school mathematics, 2001 yearbook of the National Council of Teachers of Mathematics* (pp. 228-237). Reston, VA: National Council of Teachers of Mathematics.

Whitin, D.J., & Wilde, S. (1992). *Read any good math lately: Children's books for mathematical learning.* Portsmouth, NH: Heinemann.

Hunsader is an advanced graduate teaching assistant in the Childhood Education Department at the University of South Florida, Tampa. She may be contacted at 6320 205th St. E, Bradenton, FL 34211, USA. E-mail hunsader@tempest.coedu.usf.edu.

Article 26

It's as Easy as A-B-C and Do-Re-Mi

Music, Rhythm, and Rhyme Enhance Children's Literacy Skills

Kantaylieniere Y. Hill-Clarke and Nicole R. Robinson

In recent years, the need to develop new, effective teaching strategies to further children's literacy learning increased with urgency. National organizations, as well as state policy makers, have developed reading standards and initiatives to address young children's literacy needs (Christie 2001). For example, the Reading First initiative encourages individual states to seek grants for creating programs that improve the literacy skills of children in prekindergarten through grade 3 (Reading First 2002). The purpose of these programs is to assist educators, as well as families, in meeting the diverse literacy needs of children.

The range of children's reading styles is extensive and thus requires a variety of teaching strategies and techniques. Teachers are encouraged to implement new strategies to increase literacy learning opportunities for all students (Ebeling 2001). Use of music is one effective vehicle for enhancing literacy instruction for young children (Jalongo & Ribblet 1997; Cornett 2003). This article suggests musical activities that support early literacy development.

Arts-based learning

"Strong support for arts-based learning comes from the work of researcher Howard Gardner" (Cornett 2003, 16). According to Gardner (1993), children use different forms of intelligences to make sense of the world around them. Gardner identifies eight intelligences that children use to approach various learning tasks and to problem solve.

linguistic—effective use of language to express thoughts, ideas and feelings
logical/mathematical—effective use of reasoning and inductive thinking skills
spatial—the ability to organize and visualize things in spatial terms
naturalist—awareness of and sensitivity toward living things and the natural world
interpersonal—the ability to understand and relate well with others
intrapersonal—the ability to understand and relate with oneself as an individual
bodily/kinesthetic—the ability to use the body to solve problems
musical—the ability to hear, recognize, and remember patterns

Music's important place

According to Gardner the earliest intelligence to emerge is musical (1993). A child's first exposure to music is in the womb, hearing the repeated rhythm of the mother's heartbeat. For this reason, children, including infants, are naturally guided through their inner kinesthetic sense to move to basic beats and rhythms, and as they grow older this natural desire increases (Bayless & Ramsey 1991).

Music is an important part of our lives and an intrinsic part of children's play (Cornett 2003). As children grow and develop, their musical involvement widens through opportunities for moving, listening, creating, and singing. "When we help children tap into their musical intelligence, we liberate them to make music and add beauty to their personal and shared worlds" (Cornett 2002, 340).

Singing and listening to nursery songs, folk songs, and jingles can extend and develop vocabulary and comprehension skills. Learning through music can build listening skills, enhance abstract thinking, improve memory, and encourage the use of compound words, rhymes, and images.

Because music is naturally woven into a child's day, learning through music can be inseparable from learning in other areas (Bayless & Ramsey 1991; Brown & Brown 1997). For example, singing and listening to nursery songs, folk songs, and jingles can extend and develop vocabulary and comprehension skills. Additionally, learning through music can build listening skills, enhance abstract thinking, improve memory, and encourage the use of compound words, rhymes, and images (Bayless & Ramsey 1991; Chandler 1999; Morrow 2001).

The interrelationship between music, language, and reading is extremely important; each subject requires similar skills mastery—concentration, memory, and understanding of abstract concepts (Bayless & Ramsey 1991). Rarely will one find a child who can

Early Literacy Activities

Interactive storytelling (for pre-K through grade 3) fosters creative expression, reinforces listening and word recognition skills, and encourages interactions with written text.

1. **Select a book** with various characters and a sequence of events (e.g., *The Stinky Cheese Man and Other Fairly Stupid Tales,* by Jon Scieszka; *The Grouchy Ladybug,* by Eric Carle; *Little Red Riding Hood,* by Grimm brothers).

2. **Ask the children to predict** what the story is about before beginning to read. Encourage them to make predictions based on the title and pictures in the story. Such an introduction gives children a purpose, and enticement, for reaching and listening.

3. **List the story's main characters** on the board or chart paper. Assign a no-pitch percussion instrument to represent each character (e.g., a rattle for the old woman, a ratchet for the old man). If instruments are not available, use household utensils, such as spoons and pots, or have children make instruments using various materials. As each character is introduced, play the corresponding instrument to introduce the sound and character association.

4. **Involve the children** in creating a simple song or melody to accompany the main character(s) of the book. For example,

> Grouchy, grouch lady bug,
> Grouchy as can be.
> When you look—you will see
> She's grouchy as can be!

5. **Invite children to represent each character.** Give the volunteers the instruments that represent their characters. Ask the children volunteering to listen carefully. When an assigned character speaks, the child should play his or her instrument. Have all children sing the song or melody the group created every time the story's main character is mentioned. Read the story aloud with enthusiasm and inflection, emphasizing all the characters' names. Cue the children when it's time to sing and play instruments.

6. **Lead a discussion** about the story (the characters, setting, plot and outcome). Ask the children why they think certain instruments were chosen to represent specific characters. Brainstorm together to find other instruments or classroom and household items whose sounds could represent the characters.

Nursery rhyme charades (for children kindergarten through grade 3) foster creative expression, develop literacy skills, and enhance physical movement.

1. **Display the words to a variety** of well-known nursery rhymes (e.g., "Hickory Dickory Dock," "Hey Diddle Diddle").

2. **Select and enthusiastically read** one of the rhymes to the class.

3. **Lead a discussion** about the events in the rhyme, focusing on sequential order and rhyming words. For example, discuss the events that occur at the beginning, middle, and end of the rhyme.

4. **Explain how to share** stories and nursery rhymes through movement. Demonstrate by retelling the rhyme using only movement. Use a different movement to represent each key word.

An extended activity is appropriate for older children, grades 2 and 3. Divide the class into small groups of three or four children and assign each group a nursery rhyme. One group of children can retell the rhyme through movement while other groups try to guess which rhyme is being presented.

Tuning in to rhyme (Appropriate for kindergartners through grade 3) reinforces children's rhyming skills and incorporates singing and movement.

1. **Review the concept** of rhyme. Ask children to share examples.

2. **Teach the children to sing** the following song [to the tune of "Mary Had a Little Lamb"]:

> Which of these are rhyming words,
> Rhyming words, rhyming words?
> Which of these are rhyming words,
> _____, _____ and _____?
> (*ring*) (*race*) (*sing*)

3. **Substitute words,** including two words that rhyme and one that does not. Ask the children to identify rhyming or not rhyming words.

4. **Repeat the song** and encourage children to insert their own rhyming words.

This tune makes me feel . . . (for children in kindergarten through grade 3) fosters creative expression, an appreciation for music, and writing skills.

1. **Prerecord examples** of various music genres (e.g., country, rhythm and blues, classical).

2. **Provide a journal sheet** with the title of each song and the following sentence starter, "This tune makes me feel …" Leave space for an illustration.

3. **Play an excerpt of music.** Tell the children to write about or draw an illustration of how this tune makes them feel.

4. **Continue this process** until all musical excerpts have been played.

5. **Collect the journal sheets** and create a class book titled "These Tunes Make Us Feel…." Read the book to the class and share the drawings.

6. **Discuss children's feelings** and how listening to the same song can evoke different feelings for each listener.

If I were a … integrates creative thinking and writing.

1. **Display a selection of instruments** (e.g., drum, piano, flute, tuba). If actual instruments and someone to play them are not available, use pictures and recordings or videotapes. Lead a discussion about each instrument's size, color, and sound. Ask how these instruments are alike and different. Record children's responses on a chart.

2. **Focus on one instrument** (e.g., drum) and have the children describe it. For example, they might say the drum is "big, loud, and heavy." Ask, What do you think it would be like to be a drum? How would you feel? What would your day be like? Provide examples and think aloud to model the activity. Record children's responses on a chart.

3. **Have the children complete a sentence starter** "If I were a _____." Next they can draw an illustration of the instrument, working alone, with a partner, or in small groups. Ask the children to share their responses with the class. Collect the journal sheets and create a class book.

---

read music but cannot read text. The coding systems for reading and music differ; however, the thinking process for deciphering each coding system is similar (Bayless & Ramsey 1991). Just as a child must have an awareness of music notation, symbol recognition, and sound relationships to interpret musical scores, so also must the child attend to basic letter recognition and sound relationships to interpret written text (Bayless & Ramsey 1991). When children engage in musical activities such as moving, singing, snapping, and clap-

ping, they strengthen listening, thinking, and word recognition skills (Collett 1992). Activities such as dramatic play, songwriting, and field trips to concerts can enhance literacy instruction as well as motivate learners.

Integrated classroom activities

Music in the classroom has three basic functions—primary, secondary, and music simply for music's sake. Primary functions consist of using music

to teach specific academic skills (e.g., word recognition, phonemic awareness, sentence structure, and context clues). Music serves too as a supplemental/secondary source (e.g., listening to background music during reading and writing activities, playing music during classroom transitions).

Activities such as dramatic play, songwriting, and field trips to concerts can enhance literacy instruction as well as motivate learners.

Music for the sake of music is learning the specifics of this discipline—notes, rhythms, tone, music production, and composers. When structured properly, each function provides meaningful learning experiences that can enhance young children's literacy learning.

Integrating music into daily activities allows teachers to meet the needs of students reading at varied levels. Effective integration of music and literacy creates an environment in which children can enjoy gaining specific academic skills (Wolverton 1990). Cornett recommends integrating music into the curriculum because music

- is a learning vehicle;
- unites affective, cognitive, and psychomotor domains;
- solves problems;
- bonds people;
- increases creativity, sensitivity, and self-discipline; and
- gives aesthetic enjoyment. (2003, 337–40)

Learning through music enhances literacy skills of creative expression, phonemic awareness, and creative writing. creative musical expression inspires personal responses from young readers and connects readers and the printed material (Pike, Compain, & Mumper 1997). Because reading is an active process that includes the reader, the text, and the situation, creative expression activities enhance comprehension and vocabulary skills (Carbo 1996; Pike, Compain, & Mumper 1997).

Phonemic awareness is noticing that speech is built from sounds (Yopp & Yopp 2000). To develop an awareness of speech sounds, children need opportunities to identify beginning and ending sounds, substitute one sound for another, and manipulate sounds (Reutzel & Cooter 1999; Morrow 2001). Phonemic awareness activities involving music should be interactive, stimulating, and developmentally appropriate.

Like reading, creative writing is "multidimensional and involves complex transactions between readers and writers" (Tompkins 2003, 324). Writing or drawing their ideas on pa-per helps children develop fluency, critical thinking, creative expression, and the ability to reflect (Morrow 2001). Young children need to be engaged in a variety of writing activities, supplemented by music, which let them explore and experiment with print (Pike, Compain, & Mumper 1997). Teachers should provide meaningful, purposeful writing experiences that are enjoyable and nurture personal response.

Conclusion

It is often suggested that educators go back to the basics of teaching. Bayless and Ramsey state that "we are turning 'back to the basics' without realizing and acknowledging that music is a true basic, essential to the development of the human personality" (1991, 104). Words are important in teaching children to read. Bayless and Ramsey add, "Words are meanings; words open doors; words have power; words are personal; words are humorous; words tell us what we are. Words are ribbons of the future, and words set to music lead us there" (1991, 104).

Each time children learn a chant or nursery rhyme, their reading skills grow. Each time children learn a rhythmic pattern, they strengthen their accenting and syllabication skills. Each time children learn a new song, their memorization and comprehension skills are enhanced (Bayless & Ramsey 1991).

References

Bayless, K.M., & M.E. Ramsey, 1991. *Music: A way of life for the young child*. 4th ed. New York: Merrill.
Brown, R., & N. Brown. 1997. Use songs to teach. *Reading and Writing Quarterly* 13: 349–54.
Carbo, M. 1996. Active learning promotes reading skills. *Education Digest* 62: 64–67.
Chandler, K. 1999. Home literacy activities and signs of children's emerging literacy, 1993 and 1999. Report #200026. Online: www.nces.ed.gov.
Christie, K. 2001. Lagging literacy. *Phi Delta Kappan* 82: 729–31.
Collett, M.J. 1992. Music as the basis for learning. *Education Digest* 57: 61–64.
Cornett, C.E. 2001. *Creating meaning through literature and the arts*. Upper Saddle River, NJ: Merrill-Prentice Hall.
Ebeling, D.G. 2001. Teaching to all learning styles. *Education Digest* 66: 41–45.
Gardner, H. 1993. *Frames of mind: The theory of multiple intelligences*. 2nd ed. New York: Basic.
Jalongo, M.R., & D.M. Ribblett. 1997. Using song picture books to support emergent literacy. *Childhood Education* 74: 15–22.
Morrow, L.M. 2001. *Literacy development in the early years: Helping children read and write*. 4th ed. Boston: Allyn & Bacon.
Pike, K., R. Compain, & J. Mumper. 1997. *New connections: An integrated approach to literacy*. New York: Longman.
Reading First. 2002. Online: www.ed.gov/programs/reading-first/index.html.
Reutzel, D.R., & R.B. Cooter. 1999. *Balanced reading strategies and practices: Assessing and assisting readers with special needs*. Upper Saddle River, NJ: Prentice Hall.
Tompkins, G.E. 2003. *Literacy for the 21st century: Teaching reading and writing in prekindergarten through grade 4*. Upper Saddle River, NJ: Pearson Education.
Wolverton, V.D. 1990. Facilitating language acquisition through music. *Update* 9: 24–30.
Yopp, H.K., & R.H. Yopp. 2000. Supporting phonemic awareness development in the classroom. *The Reading Teacher* 51: 130–33.

Kantaylieniere Y. Hill-Clarke, EdD, is an assistant professor of elementary education at the University of Memphis. Her research interests include best practices in literacy instruction for young children, family involvement, and effective teacher preparation.

Nicole R. Robinson, PhD, is an assistant professor of music education at the University of Memphis. Her research focus includes effective teacher preparation, community music education programs, and using music to reach and educate students who are at risk.

Reggio Emilia:
New Ways to Think About Schooling

The Reggio Emilia approach offers educators a catalyst for change and for developing new kinds of collaboration in teaching and learning.

Rebecca S. New

How can parents ensure that young children are ready for school? How should teachers prepare for the children who arrive? Which assessment strategies can enhance students' learning, inform teacher practice, and engage parents in their children's education experiences?

These questions continue to plague educators despite dramatic new insights into children's early brain development and vastly improved theoretical understandings of how children learn (Bransford, Brown, & Cocking, 2000). Faced with expanding curriculum mandates amid draconian budget cuts, U.S. public schools have become the target of political rhetoric and tough-love reform initiatives. Opinion surveys convey little improvement in public satisfaction with U.S. schools; worse still, students often describe school as "boring, irrelevant, and mindless" (Carpenter, 2000, pp. 383-384). What's a teacher to do?

Go to Italy! Over the past decade, a small but growing number of elementary educators across the United States have joined their early childhood colleagues in finding new ideas and inspiration from the early care and education pro-

gram of the city of Reggio Emilia in northern Italy. Reggio Emilia is also increasingly a source of new ideas for educators in more than 40 countries, from Brazil to Tanzania to the Philippines.

How Did It Begin?

The town of Reggio Emilia lies in a prosperous area of northern Italy known for its civic engagement. Following World War II, a small group of parents began Reggio Emilia's municipal early childhood program, which thrived under the leadership of early childhood educator Loris Malaguzzi and the hard work of hundreds of parents and teachers. After decades of innovation and experimentation, city leaders sent traveling exhibitions throughout Europe and to the United States to share the Reggio Emilia approach. As news of Reggio Emilia spread, educators, parents, and policymakers began to take note.

What Is the Reggio Emilia Approach?

Embedded in the Reggio Emilia approach to education is an image of children, families, and teachers working together to make schools dynamic and democratic learning environments. Reggio Emilia has attracted educators interested in

- The role of the classroom environment in children's learning;
- Long-term curriculum projects that promote inquiry among teachers and children;
- Partnerships with parents that include collaboration in the learning process;
- Documentation for observation, research, and assessment; and
- "The hundred languages of children"—children's multiple means of expression and understanding (Edwards, Gandini, & Forman, 1993, 1998).

A visitor to a Reggio Emilia classroom finds an inviting environment, with adult- and child-sized furnishings, plants and natural light, large panels documenting the children's ideas, and very few commercially produced materials. The children are deeply immersed in their own dramatic or constructive play, or perhaps they are in small groups with a teacher, exploring how best to design the highways around a block city, construct a functioning water fountain for the birds, or draw a life-size dinosaur to scale. Later on, the teachers, armed with tape recorders and their own drawings, discuss the children's ideas as they plan for the next day.

A return visit in the evening might find groups of parents poring over the teachers' photos and notes and discussing how best to help their children express their mathematical ideas about distance and speed, or their quandaries about the meanings of love, or their fears of the dark, or, more recently, of pending war. On another evening, parents work in the kitchen with the cook, sharing recipes and making friends as they debate current events. Imbued in these activities are a deep respect for children's intelligence and a commitment to adult engagement.

Reggio Emilia's education philosophy resonates with key ideas in contemporary education, including Howard Gardner's theory of multiple intelligences, Lev Vygotsky's notions of the role of symbolic languages in cognition, James Comer's ideas about parental involvement, and Nel Nodding's challenge to create caring schools. Many educators note Reggio Emilia's similarities to John Dewey's education philosophy and to the play-based learning of British Infant Schools in the early 1970s. These key ideas run counter to a subject-centered, outcomes-based view of education and have challenged educators to rethink the purpose and scope of what they do.

Reggio Emilia and Early Childhood Educators

Historically, such challenges to the utilitarian approach to education have been more popular among early childhood educators than among elementary school educators. Partly because of the relatively autonomous status of early education outside mainstream public education in the United States, its educators have often felt freer to consider alternative approaches to learning (New, 2002). Nearly a century ago, the ideas of Germany's Friedrich Froebel influenced the establishment of the U.S. kindergarten as a place for children to learn in a nurturing and carefully planned environment. Italy's Maria Montessori furthered the development of environments and materials designed specifically for young children. British Infant Schools and the project approach are more recent international influences on early childhood education.

Reggio Emilia's ideas did not, however, always resonate with early childhood educators. When the approach first came to the attention of U.S. educators in the 1980s, early childhood educators had translated Piaget's interpretations of children's cognitive development into an emphasis on individual children learning in isolation from classmates. They viewed play as central to children's learning and teacher-directed activity as unnecessary or even counterproductive. Reggio Emilia served as a powerful catalyst in reexamining these beliefs and their associated theories (New, 1997) and revealed some of the biases embedded within the field's traditional views (Bredekamp, 2002). The guidelines for developmentally appropriate practice developed in 1987 by the National Association for the Education of Young Children (Bredekamp, 1987) had paid scant attention to these ideas, but the 1997 guidelines frequently cite examples from Reggio Emilia to illustrate principles of social cognition, scaffolding, and the role of symbolic languages in knowledge construction (Bredekamp & Copple, 1997).

Reggio Emilia's Appeal for Elementary Educators

The academic goals of elementary education have often been at odds with the developmental approach of early childhood education. Many parents and teachers continue to raise concerns about children arriving in structured and academically focused elementary classrooms for which their previous child-centered classrooms have failed to prepare them.

Elementary educators find that Reggio Emilia offers new perspectives on many current issues, including notions of readiness and transitions from home to school, ways of promoting family engagement in children's learning, the benefits of looping and multi-age grouping for using children's relationships to promote academic achievement, and the importance of staffing practices, such as teams of teachers, to promote professional development. The greatest attraction, however, is the way in which Reggio Emilia stimulates a rethinking of what schools do.

Embedded in the Reggio Emilia approach to education is an image of children, families, and teachers working together to make schools dynamic and democratic learning environments.

Reggio Emilia has helped bridge the divide between early and elementary educators in three ways: by revealing new ways for promoting children's academic learning in the realm of big ideas; by offering documentation as a tool for studying, sharing, and planning children's education experiences; and by provoking a new way to think about the role of the teacher.

New Possibilities for Children's Learning

Reggio Emilia's optimistic and respectful image of the child has influenced educators' views of what and how children learn. Conflicts between academic goals and child-initiated activities have lost their punch as teachers have experienced the benefits of hypothesis-generating projects rich and varied enough to provide authentic learning experiences for both adults and children. As children work together—for example, to create the rules for an athletic event—teachers notice how far they stretch their mathematical skills of measurement, estimation, and computation. Signs and invitations for such events serve as forms of authentic assessment when they reveal emerging skills and future learning goals. As teachers provide materials and purposeful questioning, they relish the ease with which children become deeply engaged in their projects.

Many of the values and practices associated with Reggio Emilia's interpretation of curriculum appeal to U.S. educators who have tired of standardized interpretations of effective teaching and children's learning. Thus, an elementary special education teacher in New Hampshire was inspired by Reggio Emilia to use collaborative projects to address individual education plan goals, taking her students with special needs into the community to explore their curiosities about plumbing and public transportation. An intern in a 1st grade class in a small Massachusetts fishing town drew on state-mandated curriculum goals while responding to children's anxieties about the impact of changing fishing regulations on their families' lives. The resulting community-based project included interviews with parents, tours of fishing plants, and the creation of a board game based on new federal regulations.

Documentation for Discussion and Discovery

When U.S. educators first began to adopt the Reggio Emilia approach, they often confused Reggio Emilia's concepts of documentation with traditional child-centered observations. As teachers began to share and discuss the meanings of their photos, tape recordings, and samples of children's work with other colleagues and children's families, however, they learned how to "make learning visible"—their own and that of the children they teach. Project Zero's uses of documentation strategies to capture children's individual learning within the context of group experiences has also helped U.S. educators to see the value of the pedagogical strategy of long-term projects (Project Zero & Reggio Children, 2001). In groups and as individuals, U.S. teachers are now sharing their ideas, experiences, frustrations, and inspirations through national and statewide conferences, an e-mail forum, and a Reggio Emilia Web site (http://ericeece.org/reggio.html).

The Role of the Teacher

What attracts educators most to Reggio Emilia's approach is how it changes their understandings of themselves—as teachers, as citizens, and as learners. U.S. teachers have reached the limits of their tolerance for the go-it-alone approach to teaching. More than half of the teachers responding to a 1990 Carnegie Foundation survey noted the limited time for meeting with colleagues, and less than 10 percent were satisfied with the opportunities available for them to establish collegial relationships (Darling-Hammond & Sclan, 1996).

The role of the teacher inherent in Reggio Emilia's approach offers new hope for lonely educators and corresponds with recent research on teacher collaboration (Cochran-Smith & Lytle, 1993; Fu, Stremmel, & Hill, 2002). Teams of teachers, such as those at the Crow Island School in Winnetka, Illinois, now travel together to workshops and conferences, bringing back new ideas to discuss with the whole faculty. School-based groups in Ohio participate in monthly statewide Reggio study groups. Massachusetts teachers meet regularly to share their documentation of children's learning in gatherings sponsored by Project Zero at Harvard University. Collaboration also involves parents: Two teachers in Ohio, frustrated by the problem of birthday parties in an economically and religiously diverse classroom, turned the issue over to the parents, setting the stage for more active partnerships with children's families throughout the year. All of these experiences have transformed the teacher's role from single expert to collaborative participant in an adult learning community (New, 2000).

Challenges and Possibilities

The reasons for Reggio Emilia *not* having much impact on U.S. elementary education are numerous. International education research has a poor track record for influencing changes in U.S. education practice in grades 1-12. Skeptics of Reggio Emilia's relevance to U.S. classrooms cite cultural challenges associated with Italy's philosophical roots, including the cultural support for close relationships between teachers and parents. Reggio Emilia's goals also stand in sharp contrast to a growing emphasis in the United States on high-stakes testing, a view of teachers as tools rather than decision makers, and a focus on individual learning in a competitive environment.

Others point to the practical challenges of building sustained relationships in an increasingly fragmented and hurried society; of planning curriculum that will be responsive to the diverse needs of children and families; and of finding the time, resources, and support necessary for what is surely more rewarding work—but also more work. Still others join me in cautioning against the idea that any one city, program, or set of guidelines can adequately determine what and how children are educated.

And yet there are many reasons to be optimistic about Reggio Emilia's usefulness in helping U.S. educators rethink their approach to public education. Of all of its features, Reggio Emilia's reconceptualization of the working environment of teachers may have the most to offer. The respect for children and parents is central, but the international success of Reggio Emilia's example is surely due to the respect given to teachers—as capable of asking good questions, willing to debate with one another, and committed to consultation with children's families. Even middle school teachers are beginning to think about how to adapt the Reggio Emilia approach to their instruction (Hill, 2002).

> *Of all its features, Reggio Emilia's reconceptualization of the working environment of teachers may have the most to offer U.S. educators.*

Anderson (2000) notes that new ideas in education often weave in and out of public awareness for years, waiting for the right time and place for implementation. He argues that new common ground serves as a foundation for current reform initiatives, including the convergence of a shared understanding that

the rigid graded structure of schools must be overhauled; self-containment in any professional role is less than desirable.... classrooms must become busy, active, even noisy ... curriculum shouldn't be strictly compartmental-

ized; high expectations are good; participation of all players is essential and workable. (p. 403)

Reggio Emilia has much to contribute to helping to make these changes more desirable and, therefore, more likely. Such changes would go a long way toward contributing to a more dynamic culture of education as envisioned by Bruner (1996) and living up to John Dewey's faith in schools as catalysts for societal change. There has never been a better time to give it a try.

References

Anderson, R. H. (2000). Rediscovering lost chords. *Phi Delta Kappan, 81*(5), 402-404.

Bransford, J., Brown, A., & Cocking, R. R. (Eds.) & Committee on Developments in the Science of Learning, National Research Council. (2000). *How people learn: Brain, mind, experience, and school* (Expanded ed.). Washington, DC: National Academies Press.

Bredekamp, S. (1987). *Developmentally appropriate practice in early childhood programs serving children from birth through age 8.* Washington, DC: National Association for the Education of Young Children.

Bredekamp, S. (2002). Developmentally appropriate practice meets Reggio Emilia: A story of collaboration in all its meanings. *Innovations, 9*(1), 11-15.

Bredekamp, S., & Copple, C. (Eds.). (1997). *Developmentally appropriate practice in early childhood programs* (Rev. ed.). Washington, DC: National Association for the Education of Young Children.

Bruner, J. (1996). *The culture of education.* Cambridge, MA: Harvard University Press.

Carpenter, W. A. (2000). Ten years of silver bullets: Dissenting thoughts on education reform. *Phi Delta Kappan, 81*(5), 383-389.

Cochran-Smith, M., & Lytle, S. L. (Eds.). (1993). *Inside/outside: Teacher research and knowledge.* New York: Teachers College Press.

Darling-Hammond, L., & Sclan, E. M. (1996). Who teaches and why. In J. Sikula (Ed.), *Handbook of research on teacher education* (2nd. ed., pp. 67-101). New York: Macmillan Library Reference.

Edwards, C. P., Gandini, L., & Forman, G. (1993). *The hundred languages of children: The Reggio Emilia approach to early childhood education.* Norwood, NJ: Ablex.

Edwards, C. P., Gandini, L., & Forman, G. (1998). *The hundred languages of children: The Reggio Emilia approach—advanced reflections* (2nd ed.). Greenwich, CT: Ablex.

Fu, V. R., Stremmel, A. J., & Hill, L. T. (Eds.). (2002). *Teaching and learning: Collaborative exploration of the Reggio Emilia approach.* Upper Saddle River, NJ: Merrill/Prentice-Hall.

Hill, L. T. (2002). A journey to recast the Reggio Emilia approach for a middle-school. In V. Fu, A. Stremmel, & L. Hill (Eds.), *Teaching and learning: A collaborative exploration of the Reggio Emilia approach* (pp. 83-108). Upper Saddle, NJ: Merrill/Prentice-Hall.

New, R. (1997). Reggio Emilia: An approach or an attitude? In J. Roopnarine & J. Johnson (Eds.), *Approaches to early childhood education* (Rev. 3rd ed.). Columbus, OH: Merrill.

New, R. (2000). *Reggio Emilia: Catalyst for change and conversation.* (EDO-PS-00-15). Champaign, IL: ERIC/EECE Clearinghouse on Elementary and Early Childhood Education.

New, R. (2002). Culture, child development, and early childhood education:Rethinking the Relationship. In R. Lerner, F. Jacobs, & D. Wertleib (Eds.), *Promoting positive child, adolescent, and family development.* Thousand Oaks, CA: Sage.

Project Zero & Reggio Children. (2001). *Making learning visible: Children as individual and group learners.* Reggio Emilia, Italy: Reggio Children.

Rebecca S. New is an associate professor in the Eliot-Pearson Department of Child Development, Tufts University, 105 College Ave., Medford, MA 02155, becky.new@tufts.edu.

Promoting Creativity for Life Using
Open-Ended Materials

Walter F. Drew and Baji Rankin

Creative art is so many things! It is flower drawings and wire flower sculptures in clay pots created by kindergartners after visiting a flower show. It is a spontaneous leap for joy that shows up in a series of tempera paintings, pencil drawings of tadpoles turning into frogs, 3-D skyscrapers built from cardboard boxes or wooden blocks. It can be the movement and dance our bodies portray, the rhythmic sound of pie-pan cymbals and paper towel tube trumpets played by four-year-olds in their marching parade, the construction of spaceships and birthday cakes.

What is most important in the creative arts is that teachers, families, and children draw upon their inner resources, making possible direct and clear expression. The goal of engaging in the creative arts is to communicate, think, and feel. The goal is to express thought and feeling through movement, and to express visual perception and representation through the process of play and creative art making. These forms of creative expression are important ways that children and adults express themselves, learn, and grow (Vygotsky [1930–35] 1978a, 1978b; Klugman & Smilansky 1990; Jones & Reynolds 1992; Reynolds & Jones 1997; McNiff 1998; Chalufour, Drew, & Waite-Stupiansky 2004; Zigler, Singer, & Bishop-Josef 2004).

This article is based on field research, observations, and interviews about the use of creative, open-ended materials in early childhood classrooms and how their use affects the teaching/learning process. We identify seven key principles for using open-ended materials in early childhood classrooms, and we wrap educators' stories, experiences, and ideas around these principles. Included are specific suggestions for practice.

PRINCIPLE 1
Children's spontaneous, creative self-expression increases their sense of competence and well-being now and into adulthood.

At the heart of creative art making is a playful attitude, a willingness to suspend everyday rules of cause and effect. Play is a state of mind that brings into being unexpected, unlearned forms freely expressed, generating associations, representing a unique sense of order and harmony, and producing a sense of well-being.

Play and art making engender an act of courage equivalent in some ways to an act of faith, a belief in possibilities. Such an act requires and builds resilience, immediacy, presence, and the ability to focus and act with intention even while the outcome may remain unknown. Acting in the face of uncertainty and ambiguity is possible because pursuing the goal is worthwhile. These actions produce a greater sense of competence in children, who then grow up to be more capable adults (Klugman & Smilansky 1990; Reynolds & Jones 1997; McNiff 1998; Zigler, Singer, & Bishop-Josef 2004).

Children and adults who are skilled at play and art making have more "power, influence, and capacity to create meaningful lives for themselves" (Jones 1999). Those skilled at play have more ability to realize alternative possibilities and assign meaning to experiences; those less skilled in finding order when faced with ambiguity get stuck in defending things the way they are (Jones 1999).

In Reggio Emilia, Italy, the municipal schools for young children emphasize accepting uncertainty as a regular part of education and creativity. Loris Malaguzzi, founder of the Reggio schools, points out that creativity

> Seems to emerge from multiple experiences, coupled with a well-supported development of personal resources, including a sense of freedom to venture beyond the known. (1998, 68)

Many children become adults who feel inept, untalented, frustrated, and in other ways unsuited to making art and expressing themselves with the full power of their innate creative potential. This is unfortunate when we know that high-quality early childhood experiences can promote children's development and learning (Schweinhart, Barnes, & Weikart 1993).

The Association for Childhood Education International (ACEI) has enriched and expanded the definition of creativity. Its 2003 position statement on creative thought clarifies that "we need to do more than prepare children to become cogs in the machinery of commerce":

> The international community needs resourceful, imaginative, inventive, and ethical problem solvers who will make a significant contribution, not only to the Information Age in which we currently live, but beyond to ages that we can barely envision. (Jalongo 2003, 218)

Eleanor Duckworth, author of *The Having of Wonderful Ideas* (1996), questions what kinds of people we as a society want to have growing up around us. She examines the connection between what happens to children when they are young and the adults they become. While some may want people who do not ask questions but rather follow commands without thinking, Duckworth emphasizes that many others want people who are confident in what they do, who do not just follow what they are told, who see potential and possibility, and who view things from different perspectives. The way to have adults who think and act on their own is to provide them with opportunities to act in these ways when they are young. Given situations with interesting activities and materials, children will come up with their own ideas. The more they grow, the more ideas they'll come up with, and the more sense they'll have of their own way of doing things (E. Duckworth, pers. comm.).

PRINCIPLE 2
Children extend and deepen their understandings through multiple, hands-on experiences with diverse materials.

This principle, familiar to many early childhood educators, is confirmed and supported by brain research that documents the importance of the early years, when the brain is rapidly developing (Jensen 1998; Eliot 2000). Rich, stimulating experiences provided in a safe, responsive environment create the best conditions for optimal brain development. the years from birth to five present us with a window of opportunity to help children develop the complex wiring of the brain. After that time, a pruning process begins, leaving the child with a brain foundation that is uniquely his or hers for life. The key to intelligence is the recognition and creation of patterns and relationships in the early years (Gardner 1983; Jensen 2000; Shonkoff & Phillips 2000; Zigler, Singer, & Bishop-Josef 2004).

Rich, stimulating experiences provided in a safe, responsive environment create the best conditions for optimal brain development.

The importance of active, hands-on experiences comes through in the stories that follow, related by several early childhood educators.

At the Wolfson Campus Child Development Center in Miami, program director Patricia Clark DeLaRosa describes how four-year-old preschool children develop some early understandings of biology and nature watching tadpoles turn into frogs. The fact that this change happens right before their eyes is key to their learning. The children make simple pencil drawings of the characteristics and changes they observe.

One day during outdoor play, the teachers in another class see that children are picking flowers from the shaded area and burying them. This leads to a discussion with the children about how to prepare a garden in which to grow flowers and vegetables. Children and teachers work together to clear weeds and plant seeds. They care for the garden and watch for signs of growth. Over time they observe the plants sprouting, leaves opening, and colorful flowers blooming. The direct, hands-on experience inspires the children to look carefully and to draw and paint what they see.

Another group of children in the same class takes walks around downtown Miami. The children then talk about what they saw, build models, look at books, and explore their new understandings in the block play area.

DeLaRosa describes a classroom that includes a number of children who display challenging behaviors. Some of the architectural drawings the children produce during a project on architecture amaze her. They demonstrate that with a concrete project in which children are deeply interested, and with teachers who guide them and prompt them with stimulating materials and related books, children's accomplishments can far exceed expectations. Because the children have direct and compelling experiences and multiple ways to express their thoughts, curiosity, and questions, the teachers are able to help them focus and produce, expressing their thoughts and feelings in a positive way.

When an architect supplies actual building plans of a house, the children become even more active. They make room drawings and maps of the house, all the while conversing and building vocabulary. They roll up the plans in paper tubes and carry them around like architects. Because the children are deeply involved in the project, DeLaRosa reports, they experience significant growth in critical thinking and creative problem solving. With questions like "How can we build it so it stands up?" and "Where's the foundation?" they show a growing understanding of the structure of buildings and a deep engagement in the learning process.

Claire Gonzales, a teacher of four- and five-year-olds in Albuquerque, points out how open-ended materials allow children choices and independence, both crucial in stimulating genuine creativity. Children make things without preconceived ideas. When teachers support authentic expression, there is no one right or wrong way—there is space to create.

Gonzales describes a child who is fascinated by a stingray he sees on a visit to an aquarium. He is inspired to make a detailed, representational drawing of the stingray that goes beyond anything he has done before. Gonzales relates how he was able to use his memory and cognition to revisit the aquarium because the stingray made such a deep impression on him. The child recalled the connection he made with the stingray and represented the creature's details—the eyes, the stinger, the gills.

Key to this kind of work by children is the teacher's respect for both the child and the materials and the availability of open-ended materials like clay, paint, and tools for drawing and writing. materials can be reusable resources—quality, unwanted, manufacturing business by-products, otherwise destined for the landfill, which can serve as much-needed, open-ended resources: cloth remnants, foam, wire, leather, rubber and wood (See "A Word about Reusable Resources.") Open-ended materials are particularly effective because they have no predetermined use (Drew, Ohlsen, & Pichierri 2000)

Margie Cooper, in Atlanta, Georgia, works with Project Infinity, a group of educators inspired by the schools of Reggio Emilia. She speaks of the values of seeing art making not as a separate area of the curriculum but rather as an extension of thinking and communication. Art making can be especially valuable for young children whose verbal skills are not well developed because the diverse materials offer a variety of ways to communicate. We can learn a lot from children who show a natural affinity for materials, gravitating to them without fear or intimidation. Cooper notes that adults often approach materials, familiar or unfamiliar, with apprehension. Learning from children's openness to materials is important so as not to teach children the fears or discomforts we as adults may have.

PRINCIPLE 3
Children's play with peers supports learning and a growing sense of competence.

Duckworth underscores the importance of this principle, emphasizing that by working and playing together in groups, children learn to appreciate not only their own ideas and ways of ding things, but also each other's. a child can learn that others have interesting methods and ideas that are worth paying attention to and that can contribute to his or her interests as well.

In a kindergarten classroom in Worcester, Massachusetts, five- and six-year-old children study flowers together before a visit to a flower show. The children see and discuss with each other pictures of flowers painted by Vincent Van Gogh, Claude Monet, and Georgia O'Keeffe. They use some of these pictures as inspiration for their own sketches and paintings. They explore flowers with different colors, paints, paper, brushes, and print making.

To give the field trip a focus, the teacher, Sue Zack, organizes a scavenger hunt. At the flower show, the children work in small groups, searching for wolves,

> **B**y working and playing together in groups, children learn to appreciate not only their own ideas and ways of doing things, but also each other's.

sunflowers, tulips, a large fountain, waterfalls, goats, a yellow arrangement of flowers, and a Monet painting.

At school the children make flower creations using recycled materials. At first, they have difficulty making their top-heavy flowers stand up. Then one child discovers that he can use the recycled wire available on the table to hold the flower upright. Others encountering the problem use their classmate's solution.

When children discover how difficult it is to make flowers from clay, one child suggests, "We can use the clay to make a vase and put flowers in it instead." So the project turns into making clay pots. Zack describes the children as being so involved that they seem unaware of her presence nearby. They are engrossed in their flower pots, expressing their thoughts to each other while working and using adjectives such as *smooth, bigger, huge, longer, taller, bumpy, dusty, sticky,* and *cold.* All the children are proud of their work, eager to show and share with one another. "Did you make yours yet?" "Where did you put yours?" "What flowers do you have on yours?" "I have a dandelion and tulips." "My flowers go right from a side to the bottom."

Here are children excited to be working in small groups and deeply connected to a sense of themselves. They do not look for external motivation or recognition. Rather, they express something direct and clear from within themselves as individuals. This is a wonderful example of endogenous expression, where children draw on their inner resources and express themselves from within.

Learning in a social setting is extended when children use diverse materials and symbol systems such as drawing, building, talking, making, or writing. the interaction among these various symbol systems—that is, different languages children use to express themselves—promotes and extends thinking in individuals and within the group.

Promoting interaction among these expressive languages fosters children's development and learning. And the languages encompass a variety of subjects, which leads to the next principle.

PRINCIPLE 4
Children can learn literacy, science, and mathematics joyfully through active play with diverse, open-ended materials.

When children play with open-ended materials, Duckworth says, they explore the look and feel of the materials. They develop a sense of aesthetics by investigating what is beautiful and pleasing about the material. The wide variety of forms of different kinds of materials, along with suggestions of things to do and to look at, flows over into artistic and scientific creation. These experiences naturally lead to conversations among children that they can write or draw about or make into books or other literacy or science experiences. Play helps children develop a meaningful understanding of subject matter (Kamii 1982; Christie 1991; Stupiansky 1992; Althouse 1994; Owocki 1999; Jensen 2001; VanHoorn et al. 2002).

The more children use open-ended materials, the more they make them aesthetically pleasing by fiddling, sorting, and ordering, and the more they see the potential in the materials and in themselves. "Knowing your materials is the absolute basis for both science and art. You have to use your hands and your eyes and your whole body to make judgments and see potential," states Duckworth.

Cathy Weisman Topal, coauthor with Lella Gandini of *Beautiful Stuff* (1999), points out that children develop power when they build individual relationships with materials. When children have the chance to notice, collect, and sort materials, and when teachers respond to their ideas, the children become artists, designers, and engineers. When children are simply given materials to use without the chance to explore and understand them, the materials do not become part of their world. Weisman Topal relates,

> When a child says, "Oh, I need some of that red netting from onions," he demonstrates that he has experience, knowledge, and a relationship with the material, a connection. It is not somebody else's discovery; it is the child's. Whenever a child makes the discovery, it's exciting, it's fun. The child is the researcher and the inventor; this builds confidence. (Weisman Topal, pers. comm.)

Children's explorations come with stories. Histories, associations, and questions. From the questions come the next activities, investigations, and discoveries. A natural consequence is descriptive language; children naturally want to talk about—and maybe draw about—their discoveries. "Not many things can top an exciting discovery!" says Weisman Topal. Organizing and dealing with materials is a whole-learning adventure. Working in these modes, the child produces and learns mathematical patterns and rhythms, building and combining shapes and creating new forms.

When children have the chance to notice, collect, and sort materials, and when teachers respond to their ideas, the children become artists, designers, and engineers.

Teachers can promote language, literature, mathematics, and science through creative exploration. Margie Cooper points out that skill-based learning and standardized testing by themselves do not measure three qualities highly valued in our society—courage, tenacity, and a strong will. Yet these three characteristics may have more to do with success in life than the number of skills a person may have mastered.

PRINCIPLE 5
Children learn best in open-ended explorations when teachers help them make connections.

Working to strengthen a child's mind and neural network and helping the child develop an awareness of patterns and relationships are the teacher's job. Constructive, self-active, sensory play and art making help both children and adults make connections between the patterns and relationships they create and previous knowledge and experience. The brain, a pattern-seeking tool, constructs, organizes, and synthesizes new knowledge.

Teachers integrate playful, creative art making with more formal learning opportunities such as discussion, reading, writing, and storytelling. They ask questions and listen to the children so that the more formal learning activities are connected closely to the children's ideas and thinking. Teachers provide concrete experiences first: investigating, manipulating, constructing and reconstructing, painting, movement, and the drama of self-activity. Then the reflection and extension involving literacy, science, and mathematics that follow are meaningful. Zack in Massachusetts gives us a good example of this when she organizes a scavenger hunt at the flower show, encouraging children to make connections between their interests and activities at the show.

PRINCIPLE 6
Teachers are nourished by observing children's joy and learning.

A central tenet in the schools of Reggio Emilia is the idea that teachers are nourished by children's joy and intelligence. DeLaRosa clearly demonstrates this tenet as she describes teachers working with children on the architectural plans:

> Watching the teachers guide, interact, and work with the children makes me feel extremely excited—joyful just to see the gleam in their eyes. You know the children are thinking, you see them creating and producing and playing with purpose. I am proud to see teachers taking learning to higher levels, not sitting back festering about this problem or that. They could hang on to the fact that they have a hard time with some of the children … but they don't. They look at the positive and move on. (Pers. comm.)

Teachers and children learn together in a reciprocal process. The exciting work of the children inspires the teachers to go forward. Children are looking for more, and the teachers think, "What else can I do to bring learning to the next level?" "How can we entice them to go further?" "What new materials can I introduce?" and "I can see how to do this!" At times the teachers set up and move ahead of the children, and at times the children move ahead of the teachers. When teachers see what children can accomplish, they gain a greater appreciation for them and for the creative arts and materials.

In addition, the work that children do, while inspired by experiences teachers and parents provide, is at the same time an inspiration to all adults who notice. Sue Zack notes,

> The flower unit forced me to make the time to listen, reflect, and write down observations of the children. It felt good! It is what I need and what the class needs in order to be a group that communicates, experiences life, creates, learns, and cares about each other. (Pers. comm.)

PRINCIPLE 7
Ongoing self-reflection among teachers in community is needed to support these practices.

It is vital for teachers to work and plan together to promote children's creativity and thinking. By meeting together regularly over a few years, teachers connected with Project Infinity in Atlanta have developed the trust to have honest conversations with each other regarding observations of children and classroom experience—not an easy task. They are doing research and constructing knowledge together about how children build relationships (M. Cooper, pers. comm.). Just as children learn and grow in community, so do their teachers (Fosnot 1989).

Conclusion

Play and the creative arts in early childhood programs are essential ways children communicate, think, feel, and express themselves. Art making, fiddling around with bits of wood and fabric or pieces of plastic and leather, reveals the gentle spirit creating simple forms and arrangements, touching the hands, hearts, and minds of young children—and adults.

Children will succeed when they have access to a wide variety of art-making materials such as reusable resources, and when they are surrounded by adults who see and believe in the creative competence of all children and are committed to their success in expressing themselves. As we trust the process, as we encourage and observe the emerging self-initiative and choice making of the children, we come to more fully understand the intimate connection between the spirit of play and the art-making process.

Word about Reusable Resources

Many of the materials used in art-making and play experiences can be discards donated by local businesses. Fabric, yarn, foam, plastic moldings, gold and silver Mylar, paper products, wood, wire, and a world of other reusable materials provides early childhood teachers and families with hands-on resources for creative learning.

Most businesses generate an abundance of unwanted by-products, overruns, rejects, obsolete parts, and discontinued items and pay costly fees to dispose of them. Throughout the nation, manufacturers dispose of their discarded materials in landfills and incinerators.

Through the establishment of a local Reusable Resource Center, high-quality, unwanted materials serve much-needed resources for creative play, the arts, mathematics, science, and other creative problem-solving activities for early childhood education.

In this way businesses become a powerful force to improve early childhood education while reducing disposal costs, improving their bottom line, helping their community, and communicating a strong message that they are in business not just to make a profit but also to make a difference.

(For information on Reusable Resource Centers near you or for training and technical assistance in developing a reuse program in your community contact Reusable Resource Association, P.O. Box 511001, Melbourne Beach, FL 32951, or visit **www.reusableresources.org**.)

Given these optimum circumstances, children surprise and delight us—they create structures and thoughts no one has seen or heard before. We adults develop a greater appreciation for the children and for the power of creative art making and materials, thus providing a strong motivation for adults to continue teaching and children to continue learning in this way.

In this era of performance standards and skill-based/outcome-based education, it is more important than ever for educators and families to articulate the values and support the creativity of play and exploration as ways to meet the standards—and to go beyond them.

References

Althouse, R. 1994. *Investigating mathematics with young children*. New York: Teachers College Press.

Chalufour, I., W. Drew, & S. Waite-Stupiansky, 2004. Learning to play again. In *Spotlight on young children and play*, ed. D. Koralek, 50–58. Washington, DC: NAEYC.

Christie, J.F., ed. 1991. *Play and early literacy development*. Albany: State University of New York Press.

Drew, K., M. Ohlsen, & M. Pichierri. 2000. *How to create a reusable resource center: A guidebook for champions*. Melbourne, FL: Institute for Self Active Education.

Duckworth, E. 1996. *The having of wonderful ideas and other essays on teaching and learning*. 2nd ed. New York: Teachers College Press.

Eliot, L. 2000. *What's going on in there? How the brain and mind develop in the first five years of life*. New York: Bantam.

Fosnot, C.T. 1989. *Enquiring teachers, enquiring learners: A constructivist approach for teaching*. New York: Teachers College Press.

Gardner, H. 1983. *Frames of mind: The theory of multiple intelligences*. New York: Basic Books.

Jalongo, M.J. 2003. The child's right to creative thought and expression. *Childhood Education* 79: 218–28.

Jensen, E. 1998. *Teaching with the brain in mind*. Alexandria, VA: Association for Supervision and Curriculum Development.

Jensen, E. 2000. *Brain-based learning*. San Diego, CA: Brain Store.

Jensen, E. 2001. *Arts with the brain in mind*. Alexandria, VA: Association for Supervision and Curriculum Development.

Jones, E. 1999. The importance of play. Presentation for "The Play Experience: Constructing Knowledge and a Community of Commitment," symposium at the NAEYC Annual Conference, New Orleans.

Jones, E., & G. Reynolds. 1992. *The play's the thing: Teachers' roles in children's play*. New York: Teachers College Press.

Kamii, C. 1982. *Number in preschool and kindergarten: Educational implications of Piaget's theory*. Washington, DC: NAEYC.

Klugman, E., & S. Smilansky, eds. 1990. *Children's play and learning: Perspectives and policy implications*. New York: Teachers College Press.

Malaguzzi, L. 1998. History, ideas, and basic philosophy: Interview with Lella Gandini. In *The hundred languages of children: The Reggio Emilia approach—Advanced reflections*, 2nd ed., eds. C. Edwards, L. Gandini, & G. Forman, 49–97. Greenwich, CT: Ablex.

McNiff, S. 1998. *Trust the process: An artist's guide to letting go*. Boston, MA: Shambhala.

Owocki, G. 1999. *Literacy through play*. Portsmouth, NH: Heinemann. Available from NAEYC.

Reynolds, G., & E. Jones. 1997. Master players: Learning from children at play. New York: Teachers College Press.

Schweinhart, L.J., H.V. Barnes, & D.P. Weikart. 1993. *Significant benefits: The High/Scope Perry Preschool Study through age 27*. Monographs of the High/Scope Educational Research Foundation, no. 10. Ypsilanti, MI: High/Scope Press.

Shonkoff, J.P., & D.A. Phillips, eds. 2000. *From neurons to neighborhoods: The Science of early childhood development*. Report of the National Research Council, Washington, DC: National Academies Press.

Stupiansky, S.W. 1992. *Math: Learning through play*. New York: Scholastic.

VanHoorn, J., P. Nourot, B. Scales, & K. Alward. 2002. *Play at the center of the curriculum*. 3rd ed. Upper Saddle River, NJ: Merrill/Prentice Hall.

Vygotsky, L. [1930–35] 1978a. The role of play in development. in *Mind in society: The development of higher psychological processes*, eds. M. Cole, V. John-Steiner, S. Scribner, & E. Souberman, 92–104. Cambridge, MA: Harvard University Press.

Vygotsky, L. [1930–35] 1978b. The prehistory of written language. In *Mind in society: The development of higher psychological processes*, eds. M. Cole, V. John-Steiner, S. Scribner, & E. Souberman, 105–20. Cambridge, MA: Harvard University Press.

Weisman Topal, C., & L. Gandini. 1999. *Beautiful stuff: Learning with found materials*. New York: Sterling.

Zigler, E., D.G. Singer, & S.J. Bishop-Josef, eds. 2004. *Children's play: The roots of reading*. Washington, DC: Zero to Three Press.

Walter F. Drew, EdD, is a nationally known early childhood consultant whose inspiring workshops feature hands-on creative play with open-ended reusable resources. As founder of the Reusable Resource Association and the Institute for Self Active Education, he has pioneered the development of Reusable Resource Centers as community-building initiatives to provide creative materials for early childhood programs. He is an early childhood adjunct faculty member at Brevard Community College in Melbourne, Florida, and creator of Dr. Drew's Discovery Blocks.

Baji Rankin, EdD, is executive director of NMAEYC, lead agency for T.E.A.C.H. Early Childhood New Mexico. Baji studies the Reggio Emilia approach and is committed to building early childhood programs with well-educated and -compensated teachers who find renewal through promoting children's creativity.

From *Young Children*, July 2004, pp. 38-45. Copyright © 2004 by National Association for the Education of Young Children. Reprinted by permission.

Young Children Try, Try Again

Using *Wood, Glue,* and *Words* to Enhance Learning

During a wood sculpture residency, Ms. Soto, the teaching artist in a preschool classroom, has a profound experience with a child prone to aggressive behavior. Spending time with Phillip as he builds his sculpture, Ms. Soto sees the child's tender and sensitive side. Phillip makes a sculpture of himself sitting on his roof watching the sun go down. He creates a chair out of cardboard and makes a sculpture of a person seated in it. With a delicate wash of watercolor painted over the whole sculpture, he represents the reflection of the sunset on his apartment building, which he calls "the sun all around."

Corinna S. Bisgaier and Triada Samaras, with Michele J. Russo

*B*uilding sculptures from wood blocks, shapes, knobs, and scraps is a process that is easily explored in the classroom, rich with learning opportunities, and highly engaging for children. It allows children to learn new skills and the dispositions needed to create a work of art. Through a wood sculpture unit, children may learn the names of local trees; the different leaves, acorns, pinecones, and seeds that each tree produces; the types and colors of wood; the softness or hardness of wood from various trees; the customary uses of wood in our culture; a wood's suitability for sculpture or wood carving; the names of artists who use wood in their artwork. Opportunities abound for the teacher to help children make connections between their artwork and the world around them, relating the project to key curriculum areas such as science, math, and literacy while children develop as creative artists.

Artists in early childhood classrooms

To help early childhood teachers integrate the arts in their classrooms, Young Audiences of New Jersey implemented the Creative Beginnings program in 1997 in the traditionally underserved cities of Newark and Trenton, New Jersey. The program grew from an awareness that young children learn through play and that many early childhood teachers are no longer trained in the arts. Because of this gap between the teachers and the learners, Young Audiences of New Jersey

saw an opportunity to forge partnerships between early childhood education centers and professional artists with backgrounds in early learning. These ongoing partnerships have demonstrated the power of the arts to make a difference in children's lives.

In the Creative Beginnings program, artists work with preschool children and provide teachers with tools to bring the arts into their classrooms. One artist, coauthor Triada Samaras, who trained at Studio in a School in New York City and at Teachers College, Columbia University, focuses on helping teachers lead the children through a unit on building wood block sculptures. Artists model teaching methods, strategies, and language for teachers. Many of the skills teachers learn can be adapted to uses besides art projects.

Teachers may incorporate a wood block sculpture project for a week or several months, depending on their comfort with the process. Children enjoy the project no matter how much time is given to it because, as Loris Malaguzzi writes in *The Hundred Languages of Children*, children have "surprising and extraordinary strengths and capabilities linked with an inexhaustible need for expression and realization" (Edwards, Gandini, & Forman 1998, 72).

To facilitate a wood block sculpture unit in the classroom, there are two areas to focus on: organizing the process and using language appropriately. Both areas are integral to maximizing children's learning.

Organizing the process

In planning a wood block sculpture project, consider ways to tie the unit to other learning taking place in the class. Begin with the simplest, most obvious connections. For example, how do the shapes of the wood pieces reinforce the math curriculum? Can the children find circles, squares, ovals, rectangles, hexagons, and other polygons in the wood scrap bin? What shapes result when two or more blocks are combined? Connect the shape search to the larger environment outside the school. Does a nearby building have interesting configurations of shapes? Does its architecture use wood in an interesting way? The sculpture project provides an opportunity for children to explore resources in the community, such as nearby parks, churches, or buildings with interesting architecture.

Adjacent to Bethany Academy in Newark, for example, an unusual wood structure modeled after an African hut adorns the roof of a church. It was both a visual and cultural point of departure for children. The hut sparked children's interest in African art. Viewing a small collection of African sculptures, the children were fascinated by the fertility figures. They discussed the sculptures and learned about their meaning, then drew their own figures. This classroom connection to learning—not only about simple math concepts through a wood sculpture unit but also about neighborhood architecture, trees, wood, and art—makes the wood unit come alive in a unique way in each classroom.

Explore resources in the community, such as nearby parks, churches, or buildings with interesting architecture.

Connections to learning areas such as science and mathematics, physical development, social-emotional development, art, language arts, and social studies can be found in *The Block Book* (Hirsch 1996). The book provides concrete ways of using blocks in the classroom for exploration and learning. "The pleasure of blocks stems primarily from the aesthetic experience," states Hirsch. "It involves the whole person—muscles and senses, intellect and emotion, individual growth and social interaction. Learning results from the imaginative activity, from the need to pose and solve problems" (Hirsch 1996, vii). At Sarah Ward Preschool in Newark, a young child began building a cathedral during free block play. This led to much classroom discussion about a cathedral near the school and its striking appearance (especially at night). It resulted in a school trip to the cathedral.

Through extended discussions and natural curriculum links like these, wood block creations gain complexity in design and richness in meaning.

Suppliers

Nasco—www.enasco.com or 800-558-9595. Suggested items: Wood Whacking Sack (wood scraps)

Vanguard Crafts—www.vanguardcrafts.com or 800-662-7238. Suggested items: bag-o-wood (wood scraps/rounds); sack-o-scrap (wood scraps/flats); Craft Sticks; Elmer's Carpenter Wood Glue; Luan Plywood Plaques (for bases); Coated Cards (for bases)

S&S Worldwide—www.ssww.com or 800-243-9232. Suggested items: 10-pound carton of wood scraps

Note: Try martial arts competitions or ask local builders or instrument makers for scrap wood.

Steps of the process

The steps that follow guide teachers through the wood sculpture process. They are designed for use over several days or weeks (Samaras & Freer 2003).

1. Order wood scraps (see "Suppliers") or ask local lumberyards or home building stores for scraps. The children can collect twigs, small branches, nuts, acorns, leaves, and other natural resources. Bases for the sculptures can be purchased or made from cut-up corrugated cardboard boxes or larger scraps of wood. They need to be strong enough to hold a heavy block structure. A good size for a base is about 12 inches by 12 inches.

2. Identify books about building, sculpture, architecture, or wood to encourage discussion, vocabulary building, and exploration. Books for adults with pictures of interesting buildings or sculptures help children focus on specific elements of design. Introduce the books to the class and then make them available in the wood center (see #3) for children to look at. Read aloud children's books that address construction, change, or creativity (see "Children's Books Related to Wood Sculpture"). Discuss them with small groups of children to help them make sense of what they have seen and read. If they ask questions you cannot answer, work with them to find the answers, showing them that you are a learner as well.

3. Create a wood center. Leave the wood for sculptures loose in a bin for children to explore. Play and discovery are critical in yielding imaginative results later. During their wood explorations, children will use the ideas they have gotten from the books. Allow several days or weeks for this stage.

4. Put the sculpture bases in the wood center and suggest that children play with the loose wood pieces on a base. Join the children in the center. Talk about arranging the wood in various configurations and then making changes. Talk about balance, shapes, sizes, and textures of the wood pieces. Include new vocabulary in your discussions.

5. Introduce wood glue, distributed in deli containers and applied with Popsicle sticks or tongue depressors. Show the whole class how to use the glue. (Do not show the children how to build sculptures, since this may limit their creativity.) Explain how glue is used to attach wood pieces permanently to each other and to the base. Emphasize the importance of experimenting to see where a piece of wood best fits before gluing it.

Make a few mistakes when you demonstrate techniques: glue large pieces with too little glue and note that the piece will not stick. Glue small pieces with huge amounts of glue and note that the glue and the wood pieces slide or that the wood scrap drowns in the glue. Ask the children if you're doing things correctly and how you might do them better. Children love to help out on this. They learn to experiment if something doesn't work the first time. Talk to children about how difficult you find gluing, so they know that it's normal to get a bit frustrated, and so they will feel competent when they are able to do it themselves.

Now the children are ready to make their sculptures.

6. Have children glue larger wood pieces to the base first. Work with small groups in the wood center so you can provide help when children need it. Ask children questions about their work:

- How will adding this piece change the sculpture?
- When you look at your sculpture, what do you see?
- Is this sculpture made mostly of flat pieces or round pieces?

7. Continue the project for days or even weeks so children can add pieces to their sculptures. Encourage them to use a variety of shapes, sizes, and colors. Be sure children turn their bases around to look at their sculpture from different vantage points. This may give them new ideas about where to add pieces of wood and new perspectives on their work. Consider having the children paint and add collage items (fabric, paper, ribbon, string, pom-poms, feathers, beads) to their sculptures.

Continue discussing children's work with them. Introduce the concept *three-dimensional* in a discussion, explaining that sculpture is a three-dimensional art form. Introduce older children to the concept of positive and negative space. A teacher might explain that positive space is the wood and negative space is the air around the wood.

Just Enough Glue

Triada uses a rhyme to help children learn how to get just enough glue on a Popsicle stick, and then onto their wood pieces: "Tap, tap, tap, / Wipe, wipe, wipe, / Spread, spread, spread / Like jelly on the bread."

"Tap, tap, tap" is for tapping the Popsicle stick on the side of the container to get rid of some excess glue; "Wipe, wipe wipe" reminds children to wipe the Popsicle stick on the side of the container to get rid of more excess; and "Spread, spread, spread" tells children to spread the glue onto the wood piece to be attached.

Art Evolves

As children add pieces of wood to their sculptures, they may come up with new ideas, especially after some time has passed. A child's sculpture may start out as a vehicle that later changes to a creature and ends up a robot. Talk about making changes to what has already been done. Welcome such changes as evidence of the creative process. Talk to the children about what it means to be "finished" when they tell you they are done.

Change during the art-making process is similar to the revision/editing phase of the writing process. If the children have experienced the writing process, you can stress this link.

---

8. Hold a group discussion about the finished sculptures, encouraging individual children to share their work with their classmates. Ask children about the process of creating the sculpture as well as the finished product. Discuss with families how to talk to their children about art (more on this below). Explain the benefits children gain from participating in the project.

Have the children host a sculpture exhibition in their classroom. This makes a wonderful forum for family-school activity. Children can act as museum tour guides for the visitors—and for children from other classes.

Using language appropriately

Working with Triada, teachers in the Creative Beginnings program learn how to talk to children about the art-making process to maximize learning and the development of higher-order thinking skills such as analysis, synthesis, and evaluation (Bloom 1956).

Teaching through dialogue is not a laissez-faire pedagogical practice, nor a free-for-all conversation. For dialogue to promote learning, it needs to be thoughtfully structured around a sequence of questions that invite reflection. Sometimes a dialogue may be structured with specific learning in mind and at other times leading toward exploration and discovery. However, it always presupposes that the teacher knows enough about children's perceptions to pace the interchange to their needs, capacities, interests, and levels of understanding. (2000, 330)

In professional development sessions with teachers, Triada emphasizes the power of language used in all phases of the art-making process, from introduction of materials through closure of the activity: "The words used by the teachers can hamper or enhance the success of the visual art process, as words have the tremendous power to awaken the child to imagination, observation, investigation, exploration, planning, utilization, contemplation, and reflection with the art materials." The language used in this process falls into three categories: questions, vocabulary, and concepts.

Questions

Triada asks open-ended questions that require children to think about their creations and why they made particular choices. Here are some introductory questions to use early in the project, when children are first exploring wood pieces in the block center:

- Where did that block come from?
- How many ways can you place the block so that it will stand up?
- How can you make it higher in space?

These questions require children to analyze, synthesize, and evaluate.

Teachers' questions can lead to rich and thoughtful discussions that enhance children's thinking and promote learning.

It is important to avoid questions that do not facilitate the art-making process. Never begin with a "naming" question, such as "What is it?" or even worse, "Is that a car?" Questions like these limit the child's range of answers and may interrupt the art-making process because the child feels pressured to come up with a single word to describe a complex creation. Especially avoid declarative statements like "It's a bird!" because the sculpture may have noting to do with the child's concept of "bird."

The question "What is it?" can intimidate a child who has just built a block creation. It may elicit one-word answers—"A boat" or "A car" or "I don't know"—if any. Furthermore, merely naming an object requires less reflection than explaining how or why it was created. A good question is, "Can you tell me about how you made this?" or "What were you thinking about as you worked today?"

For example, a small group of four- and five-year-olds at Bethany Academy worked together in the wood center using the largest, sturdiest blocks to create a wood sculpture of the White House. When Triada asked them to talk about their work, they explained that they used strong blocks because "the White House can't move a muscle. When you shake the table, it won't move or fall. When you blow it, it can't fall."

"Tell Me about This"

Begin a dialogue with a child by urging gently, "Tell me about this." Take dictation from younger children. Write their explanations about their sculptures on sticky notes and attach them to the sculptures. (Some children will be able to write these notes themselves.) When a child sees that the teacher has documented the discussion on a sticky note, he or she is affirmed as an artist and a communicator.

The children continued, "The president lives there, George Bush. A lot of dollars live there too, maybe $120. It has a beach. George Bush makes copies of dollars with a machine in the White House. The White House also has a drum. George Bush plays the drum with his children."

Teachers' questions can lead to rich and thoughtful discussions that enhance children's thinking and promote learning. While children are creating their sculptures, teachers can help them consider their wood choices when they ask,

- Tell me about what you are doing.
- What made you think of using wood that way?
- Did you see anyone else at your table using wood the same way?
- Would you explain to your neighbor how you built that?

Triada emphasizes that teachers' asking children about their sculptures guides children in their dialogues with each other about their artwork. She often uses circle time to engage in this kind of communication. When a child shows his or her sculpture at circle time, Triada asks the child to tell the class about the piece. She then encourages other children to ask questions about it. for instance, Triada may begin by saying, "I notice that you used a lot of round pieces." She then asks other children to share what they notice about the sculpture.

Triada walks around the room and encourages children to talk to each other when they are working. She asks them to tell their neighbor about what they are doing or to notice what their neighbor is doing. Children soon catch on to how to talk to each other about their work. Verbalizing their ideas and explaining how they accomplished specific tasks substantially enriches the learning process for children.

Burton writes that "the virtues of teaching through dialogue in the arts are many … [I]t inhibits the kind of uniformity of outcome in making and appraising that is the consequence of 'telling and demonstration'" (2000, 330).

Vocabulary

Vocabulary building is woven into the art-making and questioning processes. Teachers can ask questions that build vocabulary, such as,

- Are the edges of this piece *smooth or rough*?
- Did you use more pieces with *straight* edges or with *round* edges?
- What shape is this piece that you put *beside/behind/ under/on top of/next to/near* the *rectangle*?

Introducing vocabulary words while giving instructions and reinforcing them while asking questions helps children learn new words in a meaningful context. It is a good way for children to learn about shapes because they can handle and examine a shape while learning its name. Introduce words like *rough, smooth, curved, straight, round, flat, edge, line, behind, beside, above, below, under, over, near*.

Teachers can use words posted on a wall in the classroom in dialogues with children during sculpture time or in contexts other than art making. Look for new words in children's books related to the sculpture unit (see

Wood Word Wall

Here are the contents of a word wall (see Houle & Krogness 2001) compiled by the children:

wood, branch, limb, tree, pine, maple, oak, birch, sawdust, driftwood, knot, plank, rectangle, square, circle, tall, small, short, fat, thin, narrow, wide, artist, sculptor, carpenter, architect, termite, ant, leaf, bud, root, light, dark, saw, hammer, nail, glue, wood glue, dowel, furniture, sculpture, paper, seasons of the tree (spring/summer/fall/winter), berry, change, sandpaper, shellac, wood scrap, base, attach, connect, fix, build, construct, sculpt, deciduous, evergreen, lumber, chain saw, log cabin.

"Children's Books Related to Wood Sculpture"). Words from the wall can be sent home for parents to use with their children and suggested for using during writing time both at home and in class.

Concepts

Teachers have a great deal of influence over children's developing creativity and the dynamic in the classroom. This influence is evident in an examination of the concepts or "slogans" Triada uses with young children.

When introducing the wood blocks, shapes, and pieces to the children, Triada takes time to experiment in front of the whole class, and she talks to them about her "failures." She stacks different shapes from the wood bin and says, "Now, what will happen if … I pile them up like this … and … Yikes! They all fell down!" Children seem to especially love this demonstration. They watch intently, seeing that it is okay for a teacher to "mess up." Triada says to the children, "Do I cry? No! I try, try, try again!" It is vital for children to understand that in making art, there are no mistakes.

Often, what seem like failures when making art can lead to new and better creative solutions and even more learning opportunities for the children. Triada asks, "Can we think of another way to make this work?" She explains that this is the way artists create—with a lot of imagination, patience, and hard work. Teachers can help children apply this concept to other areas of the classroom and to the larger world.

Conclusion

Burton states,

A good dialogue will allow an interweaving of personal sensory, affective, and cognitive responses as youngsters reflect on their experiences and,

through imaginative reconstruction, give them voice in and through visual materials. It will promote self-reflection, recognition, and tolerance for diversity, and an ability to listen to and learn from the thoughts of others. In addition, a thoughtful dialogue will offer youngsters insights into how ideas are constructed, relate to each other in sequence, and build in complexity to larger ideas. It gives meaning to an individual's personal development by opening them to the powers of scrutiny, investigation, inquiry, and questioning by others. (2000, 330)

At Sarah Ward Preschool, a young artist explained to Triada, "Last week, I made this sculpture and I only used a few blocks. That's because I was only still little then. Now I am big, and I am using many more blocks, and I can double stack them to build a very tall tower. Look! I don't cry! I try, try, try again!"

References

Bloom, B.S. 1956. *Taxonomy of educational objectives: The classification of educational goals: Handbook 1, cognitive domain.* Available online: **http://faculty.washington.edu/krumme/guides/bloom.html**.

Burton, J. 2000. The configuration of meaning: Learner-centered art education revisited. *Studies in Art Education* 41 (4): 330–42.

Edwards, C., L. Gandini, & G. Forman. 1998. *The hundred languages of children: The Reggio Emilia approach, advanced reflections.* Rev. ed. Greenwich, CT: Ablex.

Hirsch, E.S., ed. 1996. *The block book.* 3rd ed. Washington, DC: NAEYC.

Houle, A., & A. Krogness. 2001. The wonders of word walls. *Young Children* 56 (5): 92–93.

Samaras, T., & P.K. Freer. 2003. Sculpture and words: Constructing understanding. Presentation at the National Art Education Association Conference, April, in Minneapolis.

For more information about the Creative Beginnings program, contact Corinna Bisgaier at cbisgaier@yanj.org or visit the Young Audiences of New Jersey Web site at www.yanj.org.

Corinna S. Bisgaier, MA, is the education director at Young Audiences of New Jersey in Princeton. She is a former English teacher who believes in the power of the arts to transform the learning environment. Corinna works to bring artists into partnerships with schools across New Jersey.

Triada Samaras, BA, is a teaching artist and member for Young audiences of New Jersey, Studio in a School, and the Center for Arts Education. She holds a diploma and fifth year certificate from the School of the Museum of Fine Arts in Boston and is an MA candidate in art and art education at Teachers College, Columbia University, in New York.

Michele J. Russo, BA, is the early childhood project coordinator for Young Audiences of New Jersey. Michele is a former Montessori school teacher assistant; she now coordinates and facilitates all early learning residences in the Creative Beginnings program.

UNIT 6
Critical Teacher Leadership in Literacy Development

Unit Selections

Key Points to Consider

- What role does culture play in literacy development?

- Who is advantaged and who is disadvantaged by literacy practices under NCLB?

- How are you evaluating and utilizing multicultural literature in your classroom?

 **Links: www.dushkin.com/online/**
These sites are annotated in the World Wide Web pages.

Teacher Quick Source
http://www.teacherquicksource.com

Teachers Helping Teachers
http://www.pacificnet.net/~mandel/

Awesome Library for Teachers
http://www.neat-schoolhouse.org/teacher.html

Prospects: The Congressionally Mandated Study of Educational Growth and Opportunity
http://www.ed.gov/pubs/Prospects/index.html

Melting Pot or Salad Bowl? Conformity or Diversity? Monocultural Education or Multicultural Education? Assimilation or Pluralism? Monolingualism or Multilingualism? One Mode of Delivery or Multiple Styles of Learning? No Labeling or Labeling by Regular Education, Special Education, and Gifted and Talented? No Rights or Special Rights? Status Quo or Affirmative Action? Remediation or Acceleration? Autocracy or Democracy? While the title, *Annual Editions: Early Childhood and Elementary Literacy*, categorizes the contents within a certain age or grade range, educational level, or range of development, questions about ability grouping and labeling, philosophies of teaching and learning, and social and political issues that permeate educational policies and practices transcend all levels of education.

While my classroom teaching experiences were primarily in middle school, grades 6–8, and while I now prepare secondary classroom teachers, my research interest in education for social justice through democracy crosses all levels and aspects of education. I began page one of my dissertation work, conducted in 2001, by citing the position statement of the National Association for the Education of Young Children [NAEYC] (1996) as a standard against which to evaluate bilingual education program effectiveness.

For the optimal development and learning of all children, educators must accept the legitimacy of children's home language, respect (hold in high regard) and value (esteem, appreciate) the home culture, and promote and encourage the active involvement and support of all families, including extended and nontraditional family units.

This position implicates bilingual education in multiculturalism, in multiple language considerations, and in broader-based participation—three critical issues central to decades of educational reform initiatives across the United States. At the heart of these issues is literacy development for all children.

Literacy development issues are not limited to the United States, as a joint position statement of the International Reading Association (IRA) and the NAEYC (1998), which appears as the first article of unit one in this annual edition, indicates. The NAEYC (1998) stated:

Although reading and writing abilities continue to develop throughout the life span, the early childhood years—from birth through age eight—are the most important period for literacy development.

IRA and NAEYC are committed not only to helping young children learn to read and write but also to fostering and sustaining their interest and disposition to read and write for their own enjoyment, information, and communication.

The joint position statement of the IRA and NAEYC preceded the No Child Left Behind Act (NCLB) by several years. It includes all children, not only English-speaking children.

Educators would like to believe that the spirit of the federal act is aligned with the IRA/NAEYC's joint position statement—commitment to helping all children learn to read and write on levels that will allow them to fully participate in and contribute to making democracy a reality in the United States and world. Thus, the spirit of this joint position statement and the NCLB Act charges parents and classroom teachers to consider issues of diversity—cultural, social, physical, emotional, and psychological—that influence literacy development. Educators must examine the NCLB Act to determine what it means in practice for children. It must be evaluated by the educational standards set by the IRA and NAEYC, two organizations that continue to provide critical educational leadership by seeking to understand the complex needs of children in a multicultural society and determine most appropriate practices for literacy development.

Although children in any grade may function at a variety of levels, the IRA and NAEYC have provided a "continuum of children's development in early reading and writing."

Phase 1: Awareness and exploration (goals for preschool)

Phase 2: Experimental reading and writing (goals for kindergarten)

Phase 3: Early reading and writing (goals for first grade)

Phase 4: Transitional reading and writing (goals for second grade)

Phase 5: Independent and productive reading and writing (goals for third grade)

The full position statement, with review of literature to support recommendations, includes suggestions for what children can do, what teachers can do, and what parents and family members can do for children at each level.

The editors of this annual edition are committed to supporting the position statement of the IRA and NAEYC. As such, Unit 6 is intended to also be a position statement in practice. We believe that literacy educators (parents, teachers, administrators, policy makers) must provide critical leadership for literacy development. It has been suggested that legislators felt that a "NO" vote to NCLB would be misconstrued as wanting to leave children behind. It is the educators, not legislators, now faced with the complexity of implementing the letter of the law in the light of the position statement.

Thus, this unit builds on several articles presented in other units to give a focused view on research that addresses the complex issues of meeting the needs of special rights students, bilingual students, bicultural students, and socially disadvantaged students. We believe that educators must ground their practice in sound literacy theory and emerge as leaders in a complex learning environment held accountable by standardized testing. Educators must not lose sight of the standards set by the IRA and the NAEYC.

As readers engage articles in Unit 6, they may find it useful to reconnect with articles in Units 1-5. The second article of Unit 1 examines the requirements of NCLB, considers how educators can address the requirements, and frames the complexity of literacy development under the restrictions created by federally approved reading programs. In Unit 3, Stephen Krashen disputes the National Reading Panel's report that privileged phonics over whole language instruction. He further challenges educators to inquire if the National Reading Panel's report has led state and local reading policies to misdirect federal funding. Unit 4 is rich with sound practices that support the standards set by the IRA and NAEYC, and Unit 5 provides research on integrating literacy instruction in the content areas as students enter elementary grades. Unit six challenges educators to implement appropriate literacy instruction on ALL levels and for ALL children so that ALL children will have the privilege of education and social advancement in a country dedicated to democracy.

We are not asking teachers to choose between the joint position statement of the IRA and NAEYC, and the position of the NCLB Act. Rather, we are asking educators to use the literature to think about the complexity of literacy development in our diverse society. In other words, it is the work and moral responsibility of professional educators to assess the individual strengths and needs—cultural, family, and academic—of each learner, and match instructional strategies for successful achievement. This is reflective practice—best practices in action. That is the goal of this *Annual Edition.*

Glenda Moss

Article 30

Responding to Linguistic and Cultural Diversity Recommendations for Effective Early Childhood Education

---

A position statement of the
National Association for the Education of Young Children

Linguistically and culturally diverse is an educational term used by the U.S. Department of Education to define children enrolled in educational programs who are either non-English-proficient (NEP) or limited-English-proficient (LEP). Educators use this phrase, linguistically and culturally diverse, to identify children from homes and communities where English is not the primary language of communication (Garciá 1991). For the purposes of this statement, the phrase will be used in a similar manner.

This document primarily describes linguistically and culturally diverse children who speak languages other than English. However, the recommendations of this position statement can also apply to children who, although they speak only English, are also linguistically and culturally diverse.

Introduction

The children and families served in early childhood programs reflect the ethnic, cultural, and linguistic diversity of the nation. The nation's children all deserve an early childhood education that is responsive to their families, communities, and racial, ethnic, and cultural backgrounds. For young children to develop and learn optimally, the early childhood professional must be prepared to meet their diverse developmental, cultural, linguistic, and educational needs. Early childhood educators face the challenge of how best to respond to these needs.

The acquisition of language is essential to children's cognitive and social development. Regardless of what language children speak, they still develop and learn. Educators recognize that linguistically and culturally diverse children come to early childhood programs with previously acquired knowledge and learning based upon the language used in their home. For young children, the language of the home is the language they have used since birth, the language they use to make and establish meaningful communicative relationships, and the language they use to begin to construct their knowledge and test their learning. The home language is tied to children's culture and culture and language communicate traditions, values, and attitudes (Chang 1993). Parents should be encouraged to use and develop children's home language; early childhood educators should respect children's linguistic and cultural backgrounds and their diverse learning styles. In so doing, adults will enhance children's learning and development.

Just as children learn and develop at different rates, individual differences exist in how children whose home language is not English acquire English. For example, some children may experience a silent period (of six or more months) while they acquire English; other children may practice their knowledge by mixing or combining languages (for example, "Mi mamá me put on mi coat"); still other children may seem to have acquired English-language skills (appropriate accent, use of vernacular, vocabulary, and grammatical rules) but are not truly proficient; yet some children will quickly acquire English-language proficiency. Each child's way of learning a new language should be viewed as acceptable, logical, and part of the ongoing development and learning of any new language.

Defining the problem

At younger and younger ages, children are negotiating difficult transitions between their home and educational settings, requiring an adaptation to two or more diverse sets of rules, values, expectations, and behaviors. Educational programs and families must *respect* and *reinforce* each other as they work together to achieve the greatest benefit for all children. For some young children, entering any new environment—including early childhood programs—can be intimidating. The lives of many young children today are further complicated by having to communicate and learn in a language that may be unfamiliar. In the past, children entering U.S. schools from families whose home language is not English were expected to immerse themselves in the mainstream of schools, primarily through the use of English (Soto 1991; Wong Fillmore 1991). Sometimes the negative attitudes conveyed or expressed toward certain languages lead children to "give up" their home language. Early childhood professionals must recognize the feeling of loneliness, far, and abandonment children may feel when they are thrust into settings that isolate them from their home community and language. The loss of children's home language may result **in the disruption of family communication patterns, which may lead to the loss of intergenerational wisdom; damage to individual and community esteem; and children's potential nonmastery of their home language or English.**

NAEYC's position

NAEYC'S goal is to built support for equal access to high-quality educational programs that recognize and promote all aspects of children's development and learning, enabling all children to become competent, successful, and socially responsible adults. Children's educational experiences should afford them the opportunity to learn and to become effective, functioning members of society. Language development is essential for learning, and the development of children's home language does not interfere with their ability to learn English. Because knowing more than one language is a cognitive asset (Hakuta & García 1989), early education programs should encourage the development of children's home language while fostering the acquisition of English.

For the optimal development and learning of all children, educators must **accept** the legitimacy of children's home language, **respect** (hold in high regard) and **value** (esteem appreciate) the home culture, and promote and encourage the active involvement and support of all families, including extended and nontraditional family units.

When early childhood educators acknowledge and respect children's home language and culture, ties between the family and programs are strengthened. This atmosphere provides increased opportunity for learning because young children feel supported, nurtured, and connected not only to their home communities and families but also to teachers and the educational setting.

The challenges

The United States is a nation of great cultural diversity, and our diversity creates opportunities to learn and share both similar and different experiences. There are opportunities to learn about people from different backgrounds; the opportunity to foster a bilingual citizenry with skills necessary to succeed in a global economy; and opportunities to share one's own cherished heritage and traditions with others.

Historically, our nation has tended to regard differences, especially language differences, as cultural handicaps rather than cultural resources (Meier & Cazden 1982). "Although most Americans are reluctant to say it publicly, many are anxious about the changing racial and ethnic composition of the country" (Sharry 1994). As the early childhood profession transforms its thinking,

The challenge for early childhood educators is to become more knowledgeable about how to relate to children and families whose linguistic or cultural background is different from their own.

Between 1979 and 1989 the number of children in the United States from culturally and linguistically diverse backgrounds increased considerably (NCES 1993), and according to a report released by the Center for the Study of Social Policy (1992), that diversity is even more pronounced among children younger than age 6. Contrary to popular belief, many of these children are neither foreign born nor immigrants but were born in the United States (Waggoner 1993). Approximately 9.9 million of

the estimated 45 million school-age children, more than one in five, live in households in which languages other than English are spoken (Waggoner 1994). In some communities, however, the number of children living in a family in which a language other than English is spoken is likely to be much larger. Head Start reports that the largest number of linguistically and culturally diverse children served through Head Start are Spanish speakers, with other language groups representing smaller but growing percentages (Head Start Bureau 1995).

The challenge for teachers is to provide high-quality care and education for the increasing number of children who are likely to be linguistically and culturally diverse.

Families and communities are faced with increasingly complex responsibilities. Children used to be cared for by parents and family members who typically spoke the home language of their family, be it English or another language. With the increasing need of family members to work, even while children are very young, more and more children are placed in care and educational settings with adults who may not speak the child's home language or share their cultural background. Even so, children will spend an ever-increasing amount of their waking lives with these teachers. What happens in care will have a tremendous impact on the child's social, emotional, and cognitive development. These interactions will influence the child's values, view of the world, perspectives on family, and connections to community. This places a tremendous responsibility in the hands of the early childhood community.

Responding to linguistic and cultural diversity can be challenging. At times the challenges can be complicated further by the specific needs or issues of the child, the family, or the educational program. Solutions may not be evident. Individual circumstances can affect each situation differently. There are no easy answers, and often myths and misinformation may flourish. The challenges may even seem to be too numerous for any one teacher or provider to manage. Nonetheless, despite the complexity, it is the responsibility of all educators to assume the tasks and meet the challenges. Once a situation occurs, the early childhood educator should enter into a dialogue with colleagues, parents, and others in an effort to arrive at a negotiated agreement that will meet the best interest of the child. For example,

- A mother, father, and primary caregiver each have different cultural and linguistic backgrounds and do not speak English. Should the language of one of these persons be affirmed or respected above the others? How can the teacher affirm and respect the backgrounds of each of these individuals?
- The principal is concerned that all children learn English and, therefore, does not want any language other than English spoken in the early childhood setting. In the interest of the child, how should the educator respond?
- An educator questions whether a child will ever learn English if the home language is used as the primary language in the early childhood setting. How is this concern best addressed?

Solutions exist for each of these linguistic and cultural challenges, just as they do for the many other issues that early childhood educators confront within the early childhood setting. These challenges must be viewed as opportunities for the early childhood educator to reflect, question, and effectively respond to the needs of linguistically and culturally diverse children. Although appropriate responses to every linguistically and culturally diverse situation cannot be addressed through this document, early childhood educators should consider the following recommendations.

Recommendations for a responsive learning environment

Early childhood educators should stop and reflect on the best ways to ensure appropriate educational and developmental experiences for all young children. The unique qualities and characteristics of each individual child must be acknowledged. Just as each child is different, methods and strategies to work with young children must vary.

The issue of home language and its importance to young children is also relevant for children who speak English but come from different cultural backgrounds, for example, speakers of English who have dialects, such as people from Appalachia or other regions having distinct patterns of speech, speakers of Black English, or second- and third-generation speakers of English who maintain the dominant accent of their heritage language. While this position statement basically responds to children who are from homes in which English is not the dominant language, the recommendations provided may be helpful when working with children who come from diverse cultural backgrounds, even when they only speak English. The overall goal for early childhood professionals, however, is to provide every child, including children who are linguistically and culturally diverse, with a responsive learning environment. The following recommendations help achieve this goal.

A. Recommendations for working with children

Recognize that all children are cognitively, linguistically, and emotionally connected to the language and culture of their home.

When program settings acknowledge and support children's home language and culture, ties between the family and school are strengthened. In a supportive atmosphere young children's home language is less likely to atrophy (Chang 1993), a situation that could threaten the children's important ties to family and community.

Acknowledge that children can demonstrate their knowledge and capabilities in many ways.

In response to linguistic and cultural diversity, the goal for early childhood educators should be to make the most of children's potential, strengthening and building upon the skills they bring when they enter programs. Education, as Cummins states, implies "drawing out children's potential and making them more than they were" (1989, vii). Educational programs and practices must recognize the strengths that children possess.

Whatever language children speak, they should be able to demonstrate their capabilities and also feel the success of being appreciated and valued. Teachers must build upon children's diversity of gifts and skills and provide young children opportunities to exhibit these skills in early childhood programs.

The learning environment must focus on the learner and allow opportunities for children to express themselves across the curriculum, including art, music, dramatization, and even block building. By using a nondeficit approach (tapping and recognizing children's strengths rather than focusing the child's home environment on skills yet unlearned) in their teaching, teachers should take the time to observe and engage children in a variety of learning activities. Children's strengths should be celebrated, and they should be given numerous ways to express their interests and talents. In doing this, teachers will provide children an opportunity to display their intellect and knowledge that may far exceed the boundaries of language.

Understand that without comprehensible input, second-language learning can be difficult.

It takes time to become linguistically proficient and competent in any language. Linguistically and culturally diverse children may be able to master basic communication skills; however, mastery of the more cognitively complex language skills needed for academic learning (Cummins 1989) is more dependent on the learning environment. Academic learning relies on significant amounts of information presented in decontextualized learning situations. Success in school becomes more and more difficult as children are required to learn, to be tested and evaluated based on ever-increasing amounts of information, consistently presented in a decontextualized manner. Children learn best when they are given a context in which to learn, and the knowledge that children acquire in "their first language can make second-language input much more comprehensible" (Krashen 1992, 37). Young children can gain knowledge more easily when they obtain quality instruction through their first language. Children can acquire the necessary language and cognitive skills required to succeed in school when given an appropriate learning environment, one that is tailored to meet their needs (NAEYC & NAECS/SDE 1991; Bredekamp & Rosegrant 1992).

Although verbal proficiency in a second language can be accomplished within two to three years, the skills necessary to achieve the higher level educational skills of understanding academic content through reading and writing may require four or more years (Cummins 1981; Collier 1989). Young children may seem to be fluent and at ease with English but may not be capable of understanding or expressing themselves as competently as their English-speaking peers. Although children seem to be speaking a second language with ease, *speaking* a language does not equate to being *proficient* in that language. Full proficiency in the first language, including complex uses of the language, contributes to the development of the second language. Children who do not become proficient in their second language after two or three years of regular use probably are not proficient in their first language either.

Young children may seem to be fluent and at ease speaking a second language, but they may not be fully capable of understanding or expressing themselves in the more complex aspects of language and may demonstrate weaknesses in language-learning skills, including vocabulary skills, auditory memory and discrimination skill, simple problem-solving tasks, and the ability to follow sequenced directions. Language difficulties such as these often can result in the linguistically and culturally diverse child being over referred to special education, classified as learning disabled, or perceived as developmentally delayed.

B. Recommendations for working with families

Actively involve parents and families in the early learning program and setting.

Parents and families should be actively involved in the learning and development of their children. Teachers should actively seek parental involvement and pursue establishing a partnership with children's families. When possible, teachers should visit the child's community (for example, shops, churches, and playgrounds); read and learn about the community through the use of books, pictures, observations, and conversations with community members; and visit the home and meet with other family members.

Parents and families should be invited to share, participate, and engage in activities with their children. Parent involvement can be accomplished in a number of ways, including asking parents to share stories, songs, drawings, and experiences of their linguistic and cultural background and asking parents to serve as monitors or field trip organizers. Families and parents should be invited to share activities that are developmentally appropriate and meaningful within their culture. These opportunities demonstrate to the parent what their child is learning; increase the knowledge, information, and understanding of all children regarding people of different cultures and linguistic backgrounds; and establish a meaningful relationship with the parent. The early childhood educator should ensure that parents are informed and engaged with their child in meaningful activities that promote linkages between the home and the early care setting.

Encourage and assist all parents in becoming knowledgeable about the cognitive value for children of knowing more than one language, and provide them with strategies to support, maintain, and preserve home-language learning.

In an early childhood setting and atmosphere in which home language is preserved, acknowledged, and respected, all parents can learn the value of home-language development and the strength it provides children as they add to their existing knowledge and understanding. Parents and teachers can learn how to become advocates regarding the long-term benefits that result from bilingualism.

Parents and teachers recognize the acquisition of English as an intellectual accomplishment, an opportunity for economic growth and development, and a means for achieving academic success. There are even times when parents may wish for the ability, or have been mistakenly encouraged, to speak to their children only in English, a language of which the parents themselves may not have command. The educator should understand the effects that speaking only in English can have upon the child, the family, and the child's learning. The teacher must be able to explain that speaking to the child only in English can often result in communications being significantly hindered and verbal interactions being limited and unnatural between the parent and the child. In using limited English, parents may communicate to children using simple phrases and commands (for example, "Sit down" or "Stop"); modeling grammatically incorrect phrases (for example, "We no go store"); or demonstrating other incorrect usages of language that are common when persons acquire a second language. From these limited and incorrect verbal interactions, the amount of language the child is hearing is reduced, and the child's vocabulary growth is restricted, contributing to an overall decrease in verbal expression. When parents do not master the second language yet use the second language to communicate with their child, there is an increased likelihood that the child will not hear complex ideas or abstract thoughts—important skills needed for cognitive and language development. The teacher must explain that language is developed through natural language interactions. These natural interactions occur within the day-to-day setting, through radio and television, when using public transportation, and in play with children whose dominant language is English. The parent and the teacher must work collaboratively to achieve the goal of children's learning English.

Through the home language and culture, families transmit to their children a sense of identity, an understanding of how to relate to other people, and a sense of belonging. When parents and children cannot communicate with one another, family and community destabilization can occur. Children who are proficient in their home language are able to maintain a connectedness to their histories, their stories, and the day-to-day events shared by parents, grandparents, and other family members who may speak only the home language. Without the ability to communicate, parents are not able to socialize their children, share beliefs and value systems, and directly influence, coach, and model with their children.

Recognize that parents and families must rely on caregivers and educators to honor and support their children in the cultural values and norms of the home.

Parents depend on high-quality early childhood programs to assist them with their children's development and learning. Early childhood programs should make provisions to communicate with families in their home language and to provide parent-teacher encounters that both welcome and accommodate families. Partnerships between the home and the early childhood setting must be developed to ensure that practices of the home and expectations of the program are complementary. Linguistic and cultural continuity between the home and the early childhood program supports children's social and emotional development.

By working together, parents and teachers have the opportunity to influence the understanding of language and culture and to encourage multicultural learning and acceptance in a positive way.

C. Recommendations for professional preparation

Provide early childhood educators with professional preparation and development in the areas of culture, language, and diversity.

Efforts to understand the languages and cultural backgrounds of young children are essential in helping children to learn. Uncertainty can exist when educators are unsure of how to relate to children and families of linguistic and cultural backgrounds different from their own. Early childhood educators need to understand and appreciate their own cultural and linguistic backgrounds. Adults' cultural background affects how they interact with and/or teach young children. The educator's background influences how children are taught, reinforced, and disciplined. The child's background influences how the child constructs knowledge, responds to discipline and praise, and interacts in the early childhood setting.

Preservice and inservice training opportunities in early childhood education programs assist educators in overcoming some of the linguistic and cultural challenges they may face in working with young children. Training institutions and programs can consider providing specific courses in the following topic areas or include these issues in current courses: language acquisition; second-language learning; use of translators; working with diverse families; sociolinguistics; cross-cultural communication; issues pertaining to the politics of race, language, and culture; and community involvement.

Recruit and support early childhood educators who are trained in languages other than English.

Within the field of early childhood education, there is a need for knowledgeable, trained, competent, and sensitive multilingual/multicultural early childhood educators. Early childhood educators who speak more than one language and are culturally knowledgeable are an invaluable resource in the early childhood setting. In some instances the educator may speak multiple languages or may be able to communicate using various linguistic regionalisms or dialects spoken by the child or the family. The educator may have an understanding of sociocultural and economic issues relevant within the local linguistically and culturally diverse community and can help support language and in the acquisition of English. The early childhood teacher who is trained in linguistic and cultural diversity can be a much-needed resource for information about the community and can assist in the inservice cultural orientation and awareness training for the early childhood program. The bilingual educator also can be a strong advocate for family and community members.

Too often, however, bilingual early childhood professionals are called upon to provide numerous other services, some of which they may not be equipped to provide. For example, the bilingual professional, although a fluent speaker, may not have the vocabulary needed to effectively communicate with other adults or, in some instances, may be able to read and write only in English, not in the second language. In addition, bilingual teachers should not be expected to meet the needs of *all* linguistically and culturally diverse children and families in the program, especially those whose language they do not speak. Bilingual providers should not be asked to translate forms, particularly at a moment's notice, nor should they be required to stop their work in order to serve as interpreters. Bilingual teachers should not serve in roles, such as advising or counseling, in which they may lack professional training. These assignments may seem simple but often can be burdensome and must be viewed as added duties placed upon the bilingual teacher.

Preservice and inservice training programs are needed to support bilingual early childhood educators in furthering educators' knowledge and mastery of the language(s) other than English that they speak, and training should also credit content-based courses offered in languages other than English. Professional preparation instructors must urge all teachers to support multilingual/multicultural professionals in their role as advocates for linguistically and culturally diverse children. Early childhood professionals should be trained to work collaboratively with the bilingual early childhood teacher and should be informed of the vital role of the bilingual educator. Additionally, there is a need for continued research in the area of linguistic and cultural diversity of young children.

D. Recommendations for programs and practice

Recognize that children can and will acquire the use of English even when their home language is used and respected.

Children should build upon their current skills as they acquire new skills. While children maintain and build upon their home language skills and culture, children can organize and develop proficiency and knowledge in English. Bilingualism has been associated with higher levels of cognitive attainment (Hakuta & García 1989) and does not interfere with either language proficiency or cognitive development. Consistent learning opportunities to read, be read to, and see print messages should be given to linguistically and culturally diverse children. Literacy developed in the home language will transfer to the second language (Krashen 1992). Bilingualism should be viewed as an asset and an educational achievement.

Support and preserve home language usage.

If the early childhood teacher *speaks* the child's home language, then the teacher can comfortably use this language around the child, thereby providing the child with opportunities to hear and use the home language within the early childhood setting. Use of the language should be clearly evident throughout the learning environment (e.g., in meeting charts, tape recordings, the library corner). Educators should develop a parent information board, using a language and reading level appropriate for the parents. Teachers should involve parents and community members in the early childhood program. Parents and community members can assist children in hearing the home language from many different adults, in addition to the teacher who speaks the home language. Parents and community members can assist other parents who may be unable to read, or they can assist the teacher in communicating with families whose home language may not have a written form.

If the early childhood educator *does not speak* the language, he or she should make efforts to provide visible signs of the home language throughout the learning environment through books and other relevant reading material in the child's language and with a parent bulletin board (get a bilingual colleague to help review for accuracy of written messages). The teacher can learn a few selected words in the child's language, thus demonstrating a willingness to take risks similar to the risks asked of children as they learn a second language. This effort by the teacher also helps to validate and affirm the child's language and culture, further demonstrating the teacher's esteem and respect for the child's linguistic and cultural background. The teacher should model appropriate use of English and provide the child with opportunities to use newly acquired vocabulary and language. The teacher also must actively involve the parent and the community in the program.

If the teacher is *faced with many different languages* in the program or classroom, the suggestions listed above are still relevant. Often teachers feel overwhelmed if more than one language is spoken in the program; however, they should remember that the goal is for children to learn, and that learning is made easier when children can build on knowledge in their home language. The teacher should consider grouping together at specific times during the day children who speak the same or similar languages so that the children can construct knowledge with others who speak their home language. The early childhood educator should ensure that these children do not become socially isolated as efforts are made to optimize their learning. Care should be taken to continually create an environment that provides for high learning expectations.

Develop and provide alternative and creative strategies for young children's learning.

Early childhood educators are encouraged to rely on their creative skills in working with children to infuse cultural and linguistic diversity in their programs. They should provide children with multiple opportunities to learn and ways for them to demonstrate their learning, participate in program activities, and work interactively with other children.

To learn more about working with linguistically and culturally diverse children, early childhood educators should collaborate with each other and with colleagues from other professions. To guide the implementation of a developmentally, linguistically, and culturally appropriate program, collaborative parent and teacher workgroups should be developed. These committees should discuss activities and strategies that would be effective for use with linguistically and culturally diverse children.

Such committees promote good practices for children and shared learning between teachers and parents.

Summary

Early childhood educators can best help linguistic and culturally diverse children and their families by acknowledging and responding to the importance of the child's home language and culture. Administrative support for bilingualism as a goal is necessary within the educational setting. Educational practices should focus on educating children toward the "school culture" while preserving and respecting the diversity of the home language and culture that each child brings to the early learning setting. Early childhood professionals and families must work together to achieve high-quality care and education for all children.

References

Bredekamp, S., & T. Rosegrant, eds. 1992. *Reaching potentials: Appropriate curriculum and assessment for young children.* Vol 1. Washington, DC: NAEYC.

Center for the Study of Social Policy. 1992. *The challenge of change: What the 1990 census tells us about children.* Washington, DC: Author.

Chang, H.N.-L. 1993. *Affirming children's roots: Cultural and linguistic diversity in early care and education.* San Francisco: California Tomorrow.

Collier, V. 1989. How long: A synthesis of research on academic achievement in second language. *TESOL Quarterly* 23: 509-31.

Cummins, J. 1981. The role of primary language development in promoting educational success for language minority students. In *Schooling and language minority students: A theoretical framework,* eds. M. Ortiz, D. Parker, & F. Tempes. Office of Bilingual Bicultural Education, California State Department of Education. Los Angeles: Evaluation, Dissemination, and Assessment Center, California State University.

Cummins, J. 1989. *Empowering minority students.* Sacramento: California Association for Bilingual Education.

Garciá, E. 1991. *The education of linguistically and culturally diverse students: Effective instructional practices.* Santa Cruz: National Center for Research on Cultural Diversity and Second Language Learning, University of California.

Hakuta, K., & E. Garciá. 1989. Bilingualism and education. *American Psychologist* 44 (2): 374–79.

Head Start Bureau, Administration on Children, Youth, and Families, Department of Health and Human Services. 1995. *Program information report.* Washington, DC: Author.

Krashen, S. 1992. *Fundamentals of language education.* Torrance, CA: Laredo Publishing.

Meier, T.R., & C.B. Cazden. 1982. A focus on oral language and writing from a multicultural perspective. *Language Arts* 59: 504–12.

National Association for the Education of Young Children (NAEYC) and National Association of Early Childhood Specialists in State Departments of Education (NAECS/SDE). 1991. Guidelines for appropriate curriculum content and assessment in programs serving children ages 3 through 8. *Young Children* 46 (3): 21–38.

National Center for Education Statistics (NCES). 1993. *Language characteristics and schooling in the United States, a changing picture: 1979 and 1989.* NCES 93-699. Washington, DC: U.S. Department of Education, Office of Educational Research and Improvement.

Sharry, F. 1994. *The rise of nativism in the United States and how to respond to it.* Washington, DC: National Education Forum.

Soto, L.D. 1991. Understanding bilingual/bicultural children. *Young Children* 46 (2): 30–36.

Waggoner, D., ed. 1993. *Numbers and needs: Ethnic and linguistic minorities in the United States* 3 (6).

Waggoner, D. 1994. Language minority school age population now totals 9.9 million. *NABE News* 18 (1): 1, 24–26.

Wong Fillmore, L. 1991. When learning second language means losing the first. *Early Childhood Research Quarterly* 6: 323–46.

Resources

Banks, J. 1993. Multicultural education for young children: racial and ethnic attitudes and their modification. In *Handbook of research on the education of young children*, ed. B. Spodek, 236–51. New York: Macmillan.

Collier, V. 1989. How long: A synthesis of research on academic achievement in second language. *TESOL Quarterly* 23: 509–31.

Collier, V., & C. Twyford. 1988. The effect of age on acquisition of a second language for school. *National Clearinghouse for Bilingual Education* 2 (Winter): 1–12.

Derman-Sparks, L., & the A.B.C. Task Force. 1989. *Anti-bias curriculum: Tools for empowering young children.* Washington, DC: NAEYC.

McLaughlin, B. 1992. *Myths and misconceptions about second language learning: What every teacher needs to unlearn.* Santa Cruz: National Center for Research on Cultural Diversity and Second Language Learning, University of California.

Neugebauer, B., ed. 1992. *Alike and different: Exploring our humanity with young children.* Redmond, WA: Exchange Press, 1987. Reprint, Washington, DC: NAEYC.

Ogbu, J.U. 1978. *Minority education and caste: The American system in cross cultural perspective.* New York: Academic.

Phillips, C.B. 1988. Nurturing diversity for today's children and tomorrow's leaders. *Young Children* 43 (2): 42–47.

Tharp, R.G. 1989. Psychocultural variables and constants: Effects on teaching and learning in schools. *American Psychologist* 44: 349–59.

Not Made for Defeat

"Children come first." This core value sustained a
school's policy of inclusion and diversity in the face of
state-mandated standards and assessments.

Judy W. Kugelmass

I'll call it the Betsy Miller School.
Its 400 kindergarten through 5th
grade students are an ethnically and
linguistically diverse mix of white,
African American, Asian American,
and non-U.S.–born children. Its
teachers consistently articulate a
commitment to progressive reform,
diversity, and inclusion. Instructional practices and administrative
structures at the school support the
belief that "diversity is enriching; inclusion is central."

Although federal and state regulations continue to support these
commitments, the practices that are
central to the school's inclusive culture
are threatened by new "reforms": state
standards and high-stakes standardized testing.

Using a pseudonym reflects the
vulnerability that teachers at Betsy
Miller feel in the face of these new requirements. Their request for ano-
nymity is not a paranoid response,
but rather a carefully considered decision based on recent events in their
community. Recounting their responses to these events illustrates
how skilled collaboration has enabled
them to sustain and improve reforms
that began at their school in 1983.

I first learned about the Betsy
Miller School in 1993, when five of its

teachers participated in a graduate
course I offered. The journal of one
teacher, Karen, revealed a passionate
and insightful struggle to empower
children. When she invited me to
visit her 2nd grade class, I jumped at
the opportunity.

The visits began in fall 1994 and
continued for four years. In the dual
roles of researcher and supervisor of
student teachers, I visited other
classrooms and talked with teachers,
administrators, parents, and children. I discovered that Karen's classroom resembled other classrooms at
the school in significant ways. Every
teacher used constructivist practices
and shared a progressive approach
to instruction. Ethnic, racial, linguistic, and social diversity typified every classroom. Students classified as
eligible for special education were
also included in every class, and every room had more than one teacher.

The Evolution of
a Bias-Free Zone

The coteaching arrangements and instructional practices had evolved in response to events that began 10 years
earlier when a districtwide consolidation plan closed three elementary
schools. One hundred African American children from a low-income and

working-class neighborhood were
then bused to Betsy Miller. An additional 100 children of international
graduate students at the nearby university were also transferred there.
Many of these children did not speak
English. These 200 students merged
with 200 white students from the middle-class, professional community
who were already attending the
school. Although the school district's
expressed intent was to promote equity, the immediate impact on all the
children was devastating. Everyone I
spoke with who had been at the school
from 1983 to 1987 described those
years as chaotic.

Many of the students bused to
Betsy Miller in 1983 were eligible to
receive instruction in English as a
second language (ESL) or remedial
help for reading or mathematics or
were classified for special education.
Students identified as having significant management needs were placed
in self-contained special education
classrooms. Others were placed in
general education classrooms, but
were pulled out to receive a variety
of support services. As they passed
through the halls, some of these students disrupted classrooms by playing loudly or fighting. Others never
arrived at their destination. The ma-

jority of these students and those placed in special education classes were African American.

> # The staff and parents made a commitment to assure every child that the school was a bias-free zone.

The fifth principal in six years arrived in 1987. In the following year, he eliminated pullout services and separate special education and ESL classrooms. He believed that these practices reinforced racist stereotypes among children, teachers, and families and interfered with the development of supportive classroom communities. This decision was the needed catalyst for change.

The principal was not, however, solely responsible for the school's evolution. Rather, he recruited new teachers and supported those already at the school who shared his beliefs. They would shape the school. His openness to debate and his support for their assertiveness and instructional initiatives helped develop a shared commitment. By supporting teachers and providing staff development opportunities to empower teachers, the principal helped create new organizational structures and encouraged collaboration and instructional innovation.

In 1992, the school's staff and parents made a commitment to assure every child that Betsy Miller was a bias-free zone. This declaration was directed specifically at improving the educational performance of African American children. The staff agreed that the high dropout rate of these children reflected racism in the city's public schools.

Teachers at Betsy Miller participated in race relations workshops designed to help them examine their own racism. They also began investigating how cultural biases were embedded in instructional and assessment practices. They set out to

counteract racism by implementing instructional methods that strengthened the identity, pride, and performance of African American children. The teachers' discussions led to an understanding of how standardized assessments provided limited opportunities for children to demonstrate their strengths, interests, and talents.

The Narrative Reporting System

As teachers developed holistic approaches to literacy development, they incorporated anecdotal and running records into the assessment of children's work. They used mathematics assessments that determined the level of students' conceptual knowledge and competency. Teachers held conferences with students and introduced mathematics journals, self-assessments, and peer evaluations. These approaches came together when the school initiated a pilot project on assessment that teachers designed to develop a bias-free zone. Teachers built the schoolwide project on their reconceptualization of teaching and learning.

The project began with several days of intensive staff development, facilitated by consultants from the Prospect Center in Bennington, Vermont, and built on the work of Pat Carini (1986). After these workshops, teachers recorded their observations of children's work and behavior, focusing on children's strengths and potential. Teachers then met in small study groups to present their observations, using the descriptive review process developed by Carini (1982). This process helped teachers examine how their own values and assumptions shaped their understanding of children.

The pilot project eventually led to a narrative assessment process for monitoring the progress of every child. The compatibility of this system with the Individual Education Plans (IEPs) for children classified for special education supported the

inclusion of these children in general education classrooms.

Each child's unique development became the standard for establishing individual educational goals. At a face-to-face goal-setting meeting at the beginning of each year, teachers met with every child and his or her parent or caregiver. They collaboratively decided on goals by aligning the child's strengths, interests, and experiences with parental concerns and curricular objectives. The teacher then wrote a narrative summary that documented the agreed-on goals. Parents, teachers, and children met again at midyear to evaluate progress and, sometimes, to establish new goals. Another written report documenting each child's progress followed an end-of-year assessment conference. Classroom instruction was closely linked to this process.

Collaboration and Compromise

In 1996, a new district superintendent challenged the narrative assessment process. She directed every elementary school to use a uniform, skills-based, developmental checklist as the report card for all 1st and 2nd graders. The requirement reflected the shift of state and national educational reforms away from ensuring equity and toward measuring student performance. The superintendent believed that requiring students to demonstrate their progress toward a uniform set of external standards would improve academic achievement.

In 1996, composite scores on statewide standardized reading tests had placed Betsy Miller's students below expected levels on several subtests. In interpreting these results, the superintendent did not consider the disproportionate numbers of children from non-English-speaking and low-income families at the school and the smaller percentage of children classified for special education than at other elementary schools. Teachers at Betsy Miller rarely referred children for special education because their coteaching arrangements and individualized, learner-centered instructional practices supported student diversity within their classrooms. They were also sensitive to the overrepresentation of African American boys among special education students in this school district.

> The principal's openness to debate and support for teachers' assertiveness and instructional initiatives helped develop a shared commitment.

The relationship between scores on state tests and the number of students classified for special education was significant because the test scores of those special education children were not used to calculate a school's composite scores. By excluding the scores of special education students, a school could raise its composite score. Because Betsy Miller's philosophy of inclusion led to few students being officially classified as special education students, the scores of some children that another school might have excluded were averaged into Betsy Miller's composite score.

The superintendent saw the students' relatively poor performance on parts of the state tests as evidence that the narrative assessment process was inadequate. Using individual children's abilities as a reference point for establishing goals and determining progress might be appropriate for children classified for special education. However, she did not believe that this kind of individualized assessment was appropriate for typical children.

The dramatic response of Betsy Miller's staff and families was not surprising. Because the district re-port card was not directed at reporting children's strengths, interests, and goals and compared children in ways that ultimately identified some children as failing, the majority of teachers at Betsy Miller perceived its imposition, and the standardized approach to assessment that it represented, as a "violation of our culture." The initial response of some teachers was open resistance to, and defiance of, the superintendent's directive to use the report card for all 1st and 2nd grade students. A small group of parents, some of whom taught at the school, held public demonstrations and a sit-in at the district office. Although they appreciated parental support, other teachers realized that the superintendent could define direct opposition to her directive as an act of insubordination that might lead to dismissal or reassignment.

Teachers debated among themselves and with others to develop strategies and to critique the narrative reporting system at weekly staff meetings, the site-based decision-making council, and two town meetings open to the entire community. Their primary concern was maintaining the narrative assessment process and other practices that supported their belief in the value of inclusion and diversity. In spite of this commitment, they realized that the school's relative powerlessness within a bureaucratic system required strategically developed compromises that would accommodate the superintendent's demands.

By calling on the collaborative processes developed during their participation in the school's evolution, teachers were able to sustain practices that were central to supporting student diversity. Their shared commitment to combat racism and to serve all children in general education classrooms also supported their resolve to work with the school district to sustain the narrative assessment process.

Although some teachers and parents believed that imposing external performance standards was incon-sistent with the school's values, others did not see this practice as a contradiction of basic beliefs, but rather as an improvement. These parents and teachers focused on the political and social realities facing the school and its children. Not acknowledging statewide standards could jeopardize the school and fail to prepare students to meet the expectations of the document culture (Delpit, 1986). That, they argued, would violate the core value of the school: Children come first.

Sustaining Fundamental Values

By using their knowledge of the sociopolitical nature of schooling and their skills at collaboration, staff members secured a three-year waiver from the superintendent—if they would modify the narrative assessment system. The superintendent required the parents, teachers, and administrators to work together to develop performance standards consistent with both state standards and the school's constructivist curriculum. Goal-setting meetings could continue, but teachers would have to align parent and student goals with these standards. To meet this requirement, the teachers had to compromise their belief that children's interests, parental concerns, and their own assessment of children's abilities, talents, and development should be the only criteria for assessing student performance, while sustaining a practice that supported their fundamental beliefs.

> By calling on the collaborative processes developed during the school's evolution, teachers were able to sustain practices that were central to supporting student diversity.

By 1998, composite scores on statewide reading tests placed students at Betsy Miller within the average range expected by the state. It is impossible to determine whether the improvement on test scores reflected adaptations made by teachers in response to pressure from the school district, instructional changes that were already evolving within the school, or major revisions in the tests themselves. For example, that year, the process and content of new state tests reflected the whole-language and writing-process approaches used at Betsy Miller.

Regardless of which combination of factors might account for student performance, the external validation provided by these statewide assessments supported the school's efforts to sustain the narrative reporting system and other practices central to its culture.

Sustaining Change

During the revision process, teachers examined their instructional methods. They agreed to take a more eclectic approach to literacy instruction and to integrate direct instruction in phonemic awareness and guided reading into their reading programs. They investigated how well the revised narrative assessment process reported student progress in a way useful to teachers and parents. When the three-year waiver ended in 1999, two technical aspects of the narrative assessment process had changed:

- The goals established at the goal-setting conference became tied to state standards.
- Teachers refined the written narrative reports sent to parents during the year

These alterations had minimal impact on curriculum or instruction.

Currently, surveys are asking parents about their satisfaction with the process and asking teachers to examine its manageability and to suggest additional revisions. Teachers are developing a method for ensuring that the assessment process has a reliable continuum as children move from the developmental approach of the primary grades to the more academic focus of an intermediate curriculum.

Researchers have linked the failure to sustain progressive school reforms to the absence of a historical perspective among U.S. educators (Tyack & Cuban, 1995). Perhaps teachers at Betsy Miller were able to keep the narrative assessment process, a practice central to their school's culture, because they were aware of their own history.

The Chaos at Betsy Miller in the 1980s reflected the struggle to change a school culture to support and celebrate student diversity. Norms and traditions evolved over 10 years to support that new culture. They have, however, been difficult to sustain during the current historical period, when the focus of school reform has shifted from social justice to accountability.

Sustaining practices that keep children at the center of educational decisions will require teachers to develop an understanding of the political nature of school reform, the skills of effective negotiations, and the habit of critical reflection

References

Carini, P. F. (1982). *The school lives of seven children.* Grand Forks, ND: North Dakota Study Group on Evaluation.

Carini, P. F. (1986). *The Prospect Center documentary process: In progress.* North Bennington, VT: Prospect Archive and Center for Educational Research.

Delpit, L. D. (1986). Skills and other dilemmas of a progressive black educator. *Harvard Educational Review, 56*(4), 379–385.

Tyack, D., & Cuban, L. (1995). *Tinkering toward utopia: A century of public school reform.* Cambridge, MA: Harvard University Press.

Judy W. Kugelmass is Assistant Professor of Elementary and Special Education at the School of Education and Human Development, State University of New York at Binghamton. She may be reached at 3233 County Rd. 143, Interlaken, NY 14847 (e-mail: Jkugelmass@aol.com).

Vygotsky and the Blues: Re-Reading Cultural Connections and Conceptual Development

By Shuaib J. Meacham

THROUGHOUT THE HISTORY OF EDUCATIONAL research, the factor of cultural diversity has been traditionally associated with various forms of achievement deficit and academic failure. In particular, research on African American, Latino, and Native American students tends to focus on dropouts, literacy gaps, and educational delinquency (Garcia, 1994; Lee & Slaughter-Defoe, 1994; Lomawaima, 1994). The focus on reading education in our national discourse is accompanied by substantial attention on achievement gaps between Blacks and Whites (Schrag, 2000) and efforts to eliminate bilingual education (Porter, 1998). This history and the present discourse maintain a tradition where diversity, while increasingly celebrated, remains synonymous with deficit (Wilson, 1999).

A consistent characteristic of the discourse is the juxtaposition of the literacy competencies of children of color to a mainstream norm. This language has the conceptual effect of perpetually casting children of color in a "white shadow," where they are perpetually deficit. Educators are frequently unable to see the considerable cognitive competencies these children possess. As discussed in more detail below, students of color, particularly when they represent different cultures, are seldom represented in relationship to each other. We also rarely encounter students of color when the focus of the research examines learning strengths.

This article attempts to take up the work of sociocultural theorists who have provided the conceptual language and empirical evidence to conceive of and utilize cultural diversity as an educational and literacy learning resource. A theoretical foundation underlying much of the sociocultural literacy research is the work of Vygotsky, a seminal figure in cultural difference research (Moll & Greenburg, 1990; Tharp & Gallimore, 1990). The main argument of this article is that the implications of Vygotsky's writings support the idea that a culturally diverse learning environment, in contrast to the tradition of

deficit, may embody important advantages in higher-order conceptual development. By drawing connections between conceptual processes associated with jazz improvisation and Vygotsky's "generalization" (1986, p. 210), this article attempts to demonstrate that cultural connections, particularly within the context of reading comprehension, require cognitive processes nearly identical to those Vygotsky associates with higher-order conceptual development.

The argument is developed in three parts. First, I examine the discourse of cultural deficit, its historical patterns, and the manner in which sociocultural research has countered those patterns. Next, I compare Vygotsky's generalization to those of Murray's (1996) "blues idiom" to suggest the presence of an affinity between the culturally connective processes found in jazz improvisation and higher-order conceptual thinking. Finally, I provide examples from a culturally diverse classroom to illustrate how cultural connections, identified during text discussions, replicate higher-order conceptual processes reflective of Vygotsky's generalization.

Deficit Discourse and the Sociocultural Counter

The factor of cultural diversity has traditionally assumed a subordinate status within discussions of teaching and learning in general, and literacy learning in particular (Willis & Harris, 2000). This subordination is readily evident in the recent discussions of reading education that have occupied our national discourse. The current national emphasis on reading education has been defined exclusively in terms of the decoding of text (Allington & Woodside-Jiron, 2000; Gee, 1999) without any acknowledgment of the implications of cultural diversity for student learning.

Underlying this exclusion of culture from conceptions of reading is the longstanding conservative tendency in both literacy and literary studies to construct culture, linguistic, and class diversity as a kind of social and cognitive crisis (Gates, 1985; Shannon, 1989; West, 1993; Willinsky, 1990). Scholars of both literature and reading have feared that the influences of diverse and (assumed to be) inferior culture, language, and class traditions would precipitate a decline in literacy acquisition, literary study, and the social order. Subsequently, much of the educational research acknowledging cultural diversity has, until recently, emphasized the low achievement of students from non-mainstream cultural backgrounds, leaving a legacy of deficit (Garcia, 1994; Lee & Slaughter-Defoe, 1994; Lomawaima, 1994).

Sociocultural approaches to learning, by contrast, have attempted to integrate factors related to cultural diversity into the center of our understanding of literacy learning. According to Au (1995), these studies fall into the category of "cultural difference analyses" of literacy. The idea of cultural difference, whether intended or not, implicitly counters claims of cognitive and cultural deficit. Cultural difference research demonstrates that differences, not deficits, are largely responsible for achievement discrepancies between White middle-class students and students of color.

Specifically, cultural difference research shows "mismatches" (Au, 1995) between literacy assumptions of non-mainstream cultural students and those assumptions undergirding school-based literacy instruction. When educators make changes that create cultural matches between the assumptions of non-mainstream students and those of the school, significant improvements in literacy achievement can be attained (Au, 1980; Heath, 1983; Lee, 1995; Moll & Greenberg, 1990).

Cultural difference studies of literacy have effected undeniable advancement in scholarly understanding regarding the central role of culture in literacy learning and the validity of non-mainstream ways of knowing. However, most studies have examined cultural difference through a conceptual structure that continues to subordinate the factor of cultural diversity, albeit implicitly. In almost every study of cultural difference, the literacy assumptions and dispositions of a single non-mainstream population are juxtaposed to those of the mainstream, embodied by the school.

Thus, in a manner similar to the deficit discourse, the non-mainstream population is perceived only in relationship to a mainstream norm. That conception of norm stands implicitly superior as it is almost never questioned or critiqued, except for its limited openness to cultural diversity. The basic content of its literacy assumptions is never called into question, not only with respect to the non-mainstream population, but for all students. Consequently, cultural matching assumes a primarily adaptive posture with respect to the mainstream.

Vygotsky and cultural matching

Vygotsky's theories are important for cultural difference research in that they validate several assumptions

critical to the cultural matching scenario. First, Vygotsky (1986) affirms that learning does not take place in cognitive isolation, but within the context of activities and social interaction likely informed by the day-to-day contingencies of culture.

Second, Vygotsky suggests school learning is largely informed by the interaction between the conceptual domains of the home and the school, where children receive their primary conceptual and learning orientations. Finally, he asserts that regardless of cultural background, the most effective school learning occurs when learning assumptions in the home, or "spontaneous" conceptual domain, are meaningfully connected to the assumptions encountered in the school, the "schooled" conceptual domain.[1]

With respect to this last assumption, Vygotsky (1986) uses the analogy of a second language learner to describe the quality of conceptual learning that takes place at school. As in the learning of a second language, the learner does not grasp schooled concepts directly but indirectly through the more familiar conceptual frameworks taught in the home. Without meaningful connections to the spontaneous conceptual domain of the home, a mismatch exists and schooled learning becomes more difficult. Scholars have extended this principle to the area of reading comprehension by suggesting teachers employ reading texts that contain culturally familiar information, thereby facilitating the comprehension of texts for non-mainstream children (Au, 1980; Lee, 1995).

Vygotsky and "generalization"

Based on the affinity between cultural difference studies and the theories of Vygotsky, one might assume that he would advocate an adaptive ethos between home and school. However, a closer examination of his learning principles reveals a different scenario, the goal of conceptual learning is to reach a stage of "generalization" (Vygotsky, 1986, p. 218). Generalization occurs when a spontaneous conceptual understanding is dislodged from its exclusive identification with a specific local context and connected to a more general category of like concepts that integrate multiple contextual domains. Vygotsky describes this process of conceptual disruption and subsequent connection as a "new level of consciousness" (p. 203).

Students reach this consciousness when they begin to see their once exclusively home-based concept as merely "one language among many" (Vygotsky, 1986, p. 203). Therefore, according to Vygotsky, higher-order conceptual development is literally a multilingual phenomenon. This phenomenon is maximally realized when students break from limited applications of concepts and make connections among multiple conceptual languages. Thus, the schooled concept is not necessarily the endpoint of a conceptual application but how students connect to multiple contexts.

Lee (1995) suggests a similarly connective process takes place in the comprehension and analysis of literary texts, as students draw from a "nexus of schemata" (p. 619) to create conceptual understanding. As cultural difference research has demonstrated, that nexus includes a variety of cultural experiences. Comprehending text, therefore, requires cultural connections between the context of the book and the context of the reader. By extension within multiple diverse classrooms, reading comprehension necessarily becomes a process of intercultural connections, where connections are made across multiple cultural contexts. As the cultural composition of the multiple diverse classroom is too broad for one-to-one cultural matches between text and reader, readers have to identify the culturally familiar within the culturally different as they make the effort to comprehend.

While connective processes comprise a basic practice of reading comprehension in culturally diverse classrooms, the idea of intercultural connection is quite foreign to our sociological imaginations. Our cultural conceptions are delineated primarily in terms of borders or boundaries (Marable, 1995). Even multicultural education, the primary advocate for the importance of cultural understanding in schooling, is laid out according to "distinct" cultural traditions (Grant, 1994, p. 7). Thus, the prevailing qualities of thought and social consciousness in the society preclude the formation of intercultural connections that are conducive to higher order conceptual development.

The implications of this linkage between higher order conceptual development, reading comprehension, and culturally diverse connections is of considerable importance. They take us beyond casting the strengths of students of color only in relation to a dominant mainstream. This linkage suggests that cultural connections are beneficial to the conceptual development of all children and the mainstream perspective, by structurally discouraging such connections, may be a deficit conceptual construct. In other words, by consistently reinscribing boundaries with respect to the relationships and identities of cultural groups, the mainstream precludes the kinds of rich intercultural connections that are conducive to higher order conceptual development. By the same token, culturally diverse contexts, particularly those where connections between cultures are emphasized, may provide cognitive advantages in the development of higher order thought processes.

Given the prominence of boundaries within mainstream conceptions of cultural identity and social interaction, there are few areas in society where the act of intercultural connection is an acknowledged and historically valued practice. A prominent site of such intercultural connection, however, is that of jazz improvisation. The following section provides a brief account of processes traditionally associated with jazz improvisation, specifically the process of the "crossroads" (Thompson, 1984) and the "Blues Idiom" (Murray, 1996). In describing these processes, I make connections between jazz improvisation and Vygotsky's generalization. This enables us to identify similarities between cultural connections and processes associated with higher-order conceptual development.

Vygotsky at the Crossroads

Music in general, and jazz improvisation in particular, represents one of the few domains where one is rewarded for going outside of local tradition and integrating "foreign" sounds and ideas while maintaining the integrity of those ideas.[2] Intercultural connection has been a staple of jazz since its inception, particularly evident in its New Orleans origins. Many of the jazz world's most legendary figures have achieved their status precisely because of their powerful integration of jazz with other musical traditions.

The crossroads and jazz improvisation

A basic cultural concept underlying all jazz improvisation is that of the crossroads. Described as a definitive moment of challenge or crisis, a crossroad is reached when one is forced by circumstance to move beyond the familiar range of understanding and integrate new domains of information.

Specific to the contingencies posed by cultural diversity, the crossroads is also described as "a symbol of passage and communication between worlds . . . the point of intersection" (Thompson, 1984, p. 100). Often it is that meeting of different worlds, that intersection, which precipitates the crises that force movement beyond the familiar.

Vygotsky and the blues

Albert Murray (1996), perhaps the foremost theorist of jazz, came up with what he called "the blues idiom" to describe the basic aesthetic processes that inform jazz improvisation. The blues idiom may be perceived as an African American idiomatic expression of the universal experience of the crossroads. Murray describes it in terms of three interconnected phases: the break, improvisation, and affirmation. Each of these phases contains strong similarities to Vygotsky's higher order processes of generalization.

The break is that initial moment of a crossroads crisis when one's singular conceptual foundation has been disrupted. Musically, the break is that moment when supportive accompaniment and the map of written melody is removed, confronting the musician with a comparatively empty sonic landscape. Vygotsky also perceived development in terms of a crossroads crisis, going so far as to suggest that "crisis should be reconsidered as a positive, rather than as a negative (developmental) phenomenon" (Kozulin, 1986). Similar to the musical break, higher order conceptual thinking begins with instructional "interference," disrupting learners' singular conceptual identification with local contextual domains. Like the musician with an empty sonic landscape, the learner faces conceptual uncertainty, leading to the next phase of the process, improvisation.

Improvisation, I must emphasize, should not be confused with an anything goes or "winging-it" mentality. In many ways it is the opposite. The musician must fill the break with novel, on-the-spot applications of previously known repertoire, necessarily revised and altered in the middle of a performance. Appropriately, Murray (1996) refers to improvisation as that "moment of truth" (p. 95). Among the disruptions and upheavals of school-based conceptual development, Vygotsky also perceived learning as an improvisational, non-deterministic phenomenon. He described concept formation as a "creative, not a mechanical passive process" (Vygotsky, 1986, p. 99).

The final phase of the blues idiom is affirmation. Affirmation, however, is not a point of closure, as crossroads breaks and the need to improvise comprise inescapable elements of life. Affirmation is, in fact, a broadened and more flexible sense of relationships from which future crossroads will be encountered and acts of improvisation will be engaged. Affirmation represents the new awareness of musical relationships and possibilities that follow an improvisational performance.

In concept development, affirmation is analogous to the previously mentioned "new level of consciousness" (Vygotsky, 1986, p. 203). The new level of consciousness speaks to a sense of interconnected systems of relationships, consisting of elements once thought to be unrelated. Just as an expert musician moves between musical traditions to create unique improvisational expressions, higher order thinking enables students to "shift at will from one (conceptual) system to another" (p. 203). Tharp and Gallimore (1990) describe this new level of consciousness in terms of "a weave" (p. 110), specifically a basic pattern on which multiple connections are added.

As suggested above, our conceptual language with respect to reading achievement has historically regarded non-mainstream factors of cultural diversity in terms of deficit. This practice has been so pervasive that it becomes difficult to imagine cultural diversity in terms of cognitive equality, let alone cognitive and conceptual advantage. However, the processes involved in both jazz improvisation and Vygotsky's generalization suggest that the diversity of connections across contexts enhances conceptual development. While the above discussion implies this possibility conceptually, the final section of this article will provide a classroom-based example of how the processes of improvisation and generalization work in literacy instruction.

The blues in reading instruction

The following discussion is taken from a year-long study of a combined second and third grade classroom of 28 students with 11 different cultures and languages represented (Tharp & Gallimore, 1988). Gloria, the classroom teacher, had over 25 years of teaching experience. The

school was known throughout the district for its considerable cultural, language, and class diversity. Over the course of her career, Gloria had developed a metaphor that integrated her beliefs about literacy instruction and cultural diversity, which she refers to as "weaving." Weaving not only embodies Gloria's instructional ethos, but also constitutes an extension of her personal artistic pursuits, as she had spent several years as a weaver's apprentice. This integrative quality of the weave metaphor, connecting the personal, cultural, and educational, reflects Gloria's entire classroom ethos, especially her literacy instruction.

The weaving ethos and instruction

Gloria places a premium on using student cultural experiences and prior knowledge as a means of comprehending the thematic issues in the text. Prior knowledge, an important concept within schema theory toward the enhancement of reading comprehension, has profound implications for the quantity of cultural information in the classroom. In a classroom as diverse as Gloria's, prior cultural knowledge multiplies the quantity of culturally related concepts that are likely to emerge in classroom literacy instruction.

Regardless of the instructional context, questioning is the primary instructional vehicle Gloria uses to initiate processes of generalization. Especially when cultural themes and issues are prominent, Gloria regularly asked questions to assist thinking and stimulate creations by the student (Tharp & Gallimore, 1990). She asks questions that provoke students to weave their own connections between the themes discussed and their own prior cultural knowledge. In effect, Gloria supports students' connective processes until they are able to form such connections on their own. Through such questions, students move beyond their own, and society's, conceptual parameters to form connections across cultural domains.

In the following example, recorded during African American History Month, Gloria used questioning to provoke students to make generalizations between Native American culture and African American history:

Gloria: If you have a bear clan symbol, what does it mean? Greg, would you read it for us please?

Greg: "Gentleness and strength. It takes more strength not to raise your hand to strike someone than it does to strike them." I don't get that.

Gloria: You don't get that. What do you think that means?

Daniel: It takes more strength to stop yourself from hitting somebody else.

Gloria: We're talking about that inner strength right? Is there anybody who has said the same thing? (pause as no response) Think about who we've been honoring.

Gina: Martin Luther King.

Gloria: He said that, didn't he? (Dissertation Data, 1996)

Frequently in cultural diversity research and practice, cultural figures, events, and traditions are confined to an isolated and exclusive domain. In Vygotskian terms, this means cultural information is learned by children in isolated concepts. Gloria, through questioning, deploys her connective weaving consciousness as a means of helping students form connections beyond social norms.

Connections

The following example of connections between comprehension, culture, and higher order conceptual development took place in a discussion of Speare's (1983) *Sign of the Beaver*. The use of this text, both in the classroom and in research promoting culturally diverse pedagogy, is questionable in light of heavy criticisms levied against it (Slapin & Seale, 1992). It fails to name and accurately represent authentic Indian practices. Additionally, the text distorts Indian speech and represents problematic power relations between the White boy and the Indian. However, the story does disrupt dominant narratives involving categorical separations between mainstream and Indian worldviews and beliefs. Thus, the pedagogy of discursive disruption, not the book, is promoted.

An important aspect of the plot involves the grandfather of Attean, the Indian boy, requesting that Matt, the White boy, teach Attean to read. During these reading lessons, which include the *Bible* and *Robinson Crusoe*, the boys begin to identify cultural connections they share, as well as incompatible cultural assumptions. Thus, the plot mirrors practices that are a regular part of the literacy instruction in the classroom. Gloria used this mirroring quality between story and classroom to enhance the cultural connections identified by her students.

A key point in the story finds Attean having to leave Matt to carry out a rite of passage ceremony, called the Manitou. This ritual involves elements of fasting, purification, and prayer. Two students from different cultures, Ravi, a Nepalese Hindu, and Hugo, a Venezuelan Catholic, improvise conceptual connections between their own cultural traditions and those described in the text:

Gloria (reading from p. 108 of the text): He would stay there alone for many days. He would not eat anything at all. Even berries. After sundown he would drink a little water from a brook. He would sing the songs that his grandfather had taught him, and repeat the ancient prayers of his people so that his heart would be worthy. "... He would be a man, and a hunter. He would no longer be a ..." (upward inflection)

Many of the children: boy.

Gloria: (Nods at Ravi who has had his hand raised)

Ravi: In our country if we pray for our like this and we close our eyes or we're just standing up without eating or drinking anything while drinking water, just a drop (He stands up and makes a meditation sign with his hand, tilting his head in a Hindu meditative posture) we believe that the God will come for a long time.

Gloria: This sounds similar doesn't it?

Ravi: God comes and you turn back to yourself.

Gloria: Oh how interesting. Hugo.

Hugo: Before you can take your first Holy Communion. If you're Catholic, you have to go and say the bad things you remember about doing in life and then the priest gives you something to do and you have to do it, and the next day before you take your Holy Communion, you can't eat for one whole hour. Nothing to eat, just water.

The task of comprehending the Indian rite of Manitou represents a point of crossroads break and a Vygotskian (1986) point of "interference" with respect to the spontaneous conceptual understanding for both Ravi and Hugo. The Manitou fails to match either of their local cultural traditions. However, in their effort to understand the concept, they are able to abstract the elements of fasting, purification, prayer, and passage from out of their familiar conceptual domains into a broader, more generalized category.

Through this process, both Ravi and Hugo improvisationally weave intercultural conceptual connections and textual comprehension between their local cultural knowledge and the culturally different knowledge of the text. Consequently, for all of the students within Gloria's literacy ethos of conceptual weaving, Hindu, Catholic, and Indian spiritual categorical differences are modified by the higher order conceptual connections improvised in the classroom by Ravi and Hugo.

A second example of this process occurred when Gloria performed an account of the Iroquois "False Face Society." The False Face Society is a healing lodge with rites of rhythmic chanting, application of medicinal herbs, and dance. In the following passage, Gloria performs the account of the False Face ritual, during which Jason, an African American student, participates:

Gloria: Let me tell you a little bit about the Indian belief on health. The Indians knew a lot about plants and they knew which roots could cure which diseases. But sometimes, guess what happened. (dramatic pause) People would not get ...

Jason: *Well*.

Gloria: People would not get *well*. That's right. People continued to be very very sick, and they might have very bad dreams, while they were having this fever ...

Jason: Like a bad spirit.

Gloria: Now could you imagine what it would be like to be lying on your bed in the longhouse very very sick and all of a sudden these rattles would come in (Jason begins shaking an imaginary rattle) and these chants would be coming out of the longhouse (rhythmic cadence building, Maria gasps and raises her hand). Now what would your mind be saying if you really *believed* that the False Face society had power? What would your mind say? Jason?

Jason: I want to be *saved*.

Gloria's oral performance describing a spiritual practice in a rhythmical fashion where there is a leader and overtones of healing evoke practices associated with the African American church. In a sophisticated, yet tacit manner, Jason read cultural connections between his own cultural experience in the church, breaking the singularity of his own spiritual associations, engaging in spontaneous "call and response-like" participation. In the process, he improvised cultural connections between two socially and culturally separate domains.

Conclusion

This article began by discussing the idea of the consistent association between cultural diversity and deficit, which dominates our present literacy discourse. These associations have always relied heavily on test score results, which emphasize basic decoding and other linear cognitive tasks (Willis & Harris, 2000). However, as Au and Raphael (2000) point out, literacy assessments have rarely evaluated the kind of higher-order conceptual and sociocognitive thinking discussed here. Deficit conceptions rely on the constant juxtaposition of people of color to a mainstream norm. In representing students of color in relation to one another, sophisticated abilities to read higher order conceptual and cultural connections emerge. This reveals possibilities not present in frameworks that show an ability or a failure to meet singular, mainstream norms.

Several scholars (e.g., Baker, 1992; Du Bois, 1990; Lomawaima, 1994) suggest these higher order reading competencies on the part of students of color come directly from contingencies posed by the need to resist assimilationist requirements of the mainstream. African Americans, Latinos, and Native Americans have not been afforded the privilege of singular acceptance of their cultural perceptions. They have had to cross borders, jump trains, seek out the Lord, Spirits, and Ancestors to make conceptual sense of this "American" experience. Culturally diverse perceptions have necessarily comprised a web of layers, movements, and connections. This article has attempted to demonstrate that culturally diverse learning contexts are uniquely equipped to engage in these kinds of higher order conceptual processes. Perhaps it is time to allow ourselves to inquire with respect to

higher order conceptual practice, is it the aspiration for singular culture that truly constitutes a deficit?

Notes

7. To avoid confusion on the part of those unfamiliar with Vygotsky's writing, this article adopts a "schooled" conceptual domain, Tharp and Gallimore's (1989) re-articulation of Vygotsky's use of "scientific."
8. I use the phrase "maintaining the integrity of those ideas" to differentiate the connections made in jazz improvisation from the appropriation of culture for profit prominent in the corporate world.

References

Allington, R., & Woodside-Jiron, H. (1999). The politics of literacy teaching: How "research" shaped educational policy. *Educational Researcher, 28* (8), 4-13.

Au, K.H. (1980). Participation structures in a reading lesson with Hawaiian children: Analysis of a culturally appropriate instructional event. *Anthropology and Education Quarterly, 11,* 91-115.

Au, K.H. (1995). Multicultural perspectives on literacy research. *Journal of Reading Behavior, 27* (1), 85-100.

Au, K.H., & Raphael, T.E. (2000). Equity and literacy in the next millennium. *Reading Research Quarterly, 35* (1), 170-188.

Baker, H.A. (1992). *Workings of the spirit: The poetics of Afro-American women's writing.* Chicago: The University of Chicago Press.

Du Bois, W.E.B. (1990). *The souls of black folk.* New York: Dell Books.

Gallimore, R., & Tharp, R. (1990). Teaching mind in society: Teaching, schooling and literate discourse. In L. Moll (Ed.), *Vygotsky and education: Instructional implications and applications of socio-historical psychology* (pp. 175-205). New York: Cambridge University Press.

Garcia, E.E. (1994). Educating Mexican American students. In J.A. Banks & C.A.M. Banks (Eds.), *Handbook on multicultural education* (pp. 372-387). New York: Simon & Schuster.

Gates, H.L. (1985). Editor's introduction: Writing "race" and the difference it makes. *Critical Inquiry, 12,* 1-20.

Gee, J. (1999). New literacy studies and the social turn. Retrieved May 29, 2001 from the World Wide Web: http://www.schools.ash.org.au/litweb/page300.html.

Grant, C.A. (1994). Challenging the myths of multicultural education. *Multicultural Education, 2,* 4-9.

Heath, S.B. (1983). *Ways with words: Language, life, and work in communities and classrooms.* Cambridge, UK: Cambridge University Press.

Kozulin, A. (1986). Vygotsky in context. In A. Kozulin (Ed.), *Thought and language* (pp. xi-vi). Cambridge: Massachusetts Institute of Technology Press.

Lee, C.D. (1995). A culturally based cognitive apprenticeship: Teaching African American high school students skills in literary interpretation. *Reading Research Quarterly, 30,* 608-630.

Lee C.D., & Slaughter-Defoe, D. (1994). African American research in education. In J.A. Banks & C.A.M. Banks (Eds.), *Handbook on multicultural education* (pp. 348-365). New York: Simon & Schuster.

Lomawaima, K.T. (1994). Educating Native Americans. In J.A. Banks & C.A.M. Banks (Eds.), *Handbook on multicultural education* (pp. 331-342). New York: Simon & Schuster.

Marable, M. (1995). *Beyond Black and White: Transforming African American politics.* New York: Verso.

Moll, L.C., & Greenberg, J.B. (1990). Creating zones of possibilities: Combining social contexts for instruction. In L. Moll

(Ed.), *Vygotsky and education: Instructional implications and applications of socio-historical psychology* (pp. 319-347). New York: Cambridge University Press.

Murray, A. (1996). *The blue devils of nada: A contemporary American approach to aesthetic statement.* New York: Pantheon Books.

Porter, R.P. (1998). The case against bilingual education. *The Atlantic, 81* (5), 28-39.

Schrag, P. (2000). Education and the election. *The NationOnline.* Retrieved May 29, 2001 from the World Wide Web: http://past.thenation.com/2000/000306.shtml

Shannon, P. (1989). *Broken promises: Reading instruction in twentieth century America.* New York: Bergin & Harvey.

Slapin, B., & Seale, D. (Eds.). (1992). *Through Indian eyes: The Native experience in books for children.* Philadelphia: New Society Publishers.

Speare, E.G. (1983). *Sign of the beaver.* New York: Dell Books.

Thompson, R.F. (1984). *Flash of the spirit: African & Afro-American art and philosophy.* New York: Random House.

Vygotsky, L. (1986). *Thought and language.* Cambridge: Massachusetts Institute of Technology Press.

West, C. (1993). *Keeping faith: Philosophy and race in America.* New York: Routledge.

Willinsky, J. (1990). Matthew Arnold's legacy: The powers of literature. *Research in the Teaching of English, 24,* 343-361.

Willis, A.I., & Harris, V.J. (2000). Political acts: Literacy learning and teaching. *Reading Research Quarterly, 35,* 72-88.

Wilson, W.J. (1999). *The bridge over the racial divide: Rising inequality and coalition politics.* Berkeley: University of California Press.

Shuaib J. Meacham is assistant professor of education at the University of Delaware.

Early Literacy Practices as Predictors of Reading Related Outcomes: Test Scores, Test Passing Rates, Retention, and Special Education Referral

Genevieve Manset-Williamson
Department of Curriculum—Indiana University

Edward St. John
Indiana Education Policy Center—Indiana University

Shouping Hu
College of Education and Human Services—Seton Hall University

David Gordon
Department of Curriculum and Instruction—Indiana University

Recent focus on the reading skills of primary school children has led to the increase of funding for early literacy programs targeting students at risk for reading failure. In this study, self-reports of the frequency of currently advocated early literacy practices in Grades 1 through 3 were entered into regression models in an effort to predict mean language arts scores and passing rates on a 3rd-grade state examination, grade level retention, and referral for special education assessment. Regression models were also compared to models predicting rates of special education referral and retention. Findings indicate that the effect of early literacy practice on school-level outcomes depends on the measure used as an indicator of improvement. Explicit skill instruction was a significant predictor of higher passing rates on a state examination, as well as lower rates of referrals for special education assessment.

However, explicit skills instruction was also a predictor of higher rates of grade retention. Holistic focus was associated with higher rates of referral for special education assessment, as well as lower retention rates. Programs that included a parent–child reading feature were associated with both lower rates of referral and grade retention. Findings are discussed in light of research in classroom environments and school reform.

School reforms targeting a reduction in reading failure have become a focus of state and federal policy in recent years. These reforms have been fueled by low reading scores on the National Assessment of Educational Progress and a call for balanced, empirically supported reading instruction and interventions from the National Research Council (Snow, Burns, & Griffin, 1998). Two federal grant programs, the Reading Excellence Act, an amendment to the Elementary and Secondary Education Act (U.S. Department of Education, 1999), and the Comprehensive School Reform (PL 105–78; U.S. Department of Education, 1997) are examples of legislation that are driving school reform in these areas. The broad efforts to improve reading in schools shifts the focus from the efficacy of a single instructional methodology to interventions that affect whole school curriculum and environment. In addition, educators are pressured to not only improve actual student achievement, but to demonstrate progress on school-level indicators such as state achievement tests (Linn, 2000).

EARLY LITERACY INTERVENTION

As noted earlier, early literacy intervention programs combine a collection of either empirically proven or theoretically sound practices. Interventions such as Reading Recovery (Clay, 1993), Four Blocks Method (Cunningham & Allington, 1999; Cunningham, Moore, Cunningham, & Moore, 2000), and Success for All (Slavin, 1992) share similar features. These interventions are also embedded in the context of the day-to-day reading instruction that occurs in the classroom. The overlap in features and complexity of school environments makes direct program-to-program comparisons difficult. To simplify the process of evaluating the relation between early literacy interventions and outcomes for this study, an analytic framework to describe literacy programs was developed after an extensive review of early literacy programs (St. John & Bardzell, 1999; Figure

1). This framework provides a metastructure for assessing the linkages between the features of literacy interventions to specific literacy outcomes. These features are the specific components of literacy interventions that are thought to influence reading-related outcomes. They are categorized as those relating to the theory of philosophy of the program (not addressed in this study), professional development, parent involvement, and classroom structural–organizational and instructional features. Using this framework, the complexity of early literacy programs can be described, compared, and in this case, examined for their link to the school-level, literacy-related outcomes of test scores, test passing rates, rates of referral for special education assessment, and grade retention.

Currently, there is much discussion about the ideal qualities of an effective instructional environment. Theory and research suggests that characteristics of school environments that are effective for students at risk for reading failure include, (a) a balance between holistic, literature rich and explicit, direct skill instruction; (b) adaptability; (c) high student engagement; and (d) an enriched communicative environment (Greenwood, 1996; Mann, 1986;

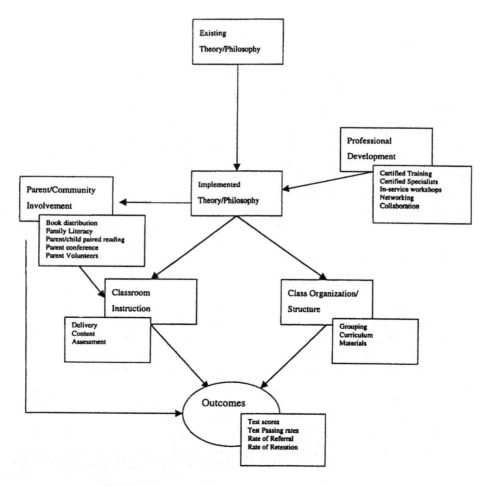

FIGURE 1 Framework for evaluating early literacy programs.

Manset & Rogers, 1998; Slavin, 1996; Snow, Burns, & Griffin, 1998; Speece & Keogh, 1996). Combinations of the key features of literacy programs serve to create these environmental characteristics. Although students in general can learn to read under a variety of differing instructional approaches, for instance, students at risk for reading failure will lack the adaptive capability of their higher achieving peers (Manset & Rogers, 1998; Sayre, 1996). Following this logic, for these students to do well, the environment must be able to adapt to their needs. Adaptability may include offering a variety of means of learning to read (i.e., balanced instruction); using small groups, tutorial, or the added expertise contributed by collaborating with specialists. It is these same organizational features that contribute to high student engagement. Students who are engaged in high rates of academic responding are more likely to make progress in basic skills (Greenwood, 1996). In addition, students at risk for reading failure often have deficits in language ability such as phonological processing, semantic, and syntactic skills (Mann, 1986). Although this may not be as necessary for students in general, students at risk may particularly benefit from environments that offer an opportunity to practice expressive language skills, as well as to link reading to oral language activities such with drama.

Vygotsky (1993) wrote that it was not the primary defect that was handicapping, but rather the distortion in social interaction that results in being locked out of higher forms of cognitive development because of that primary defect. The same may be said of the student who is at risk for reading failure. Extreme deficits in basic skills such as word attack can result in a disproportional attention to lower order skills, often during pullout or tutorial sessions when students are being exposed to holistic literacy activities. Such activities may include listening to the teacher reading aloud, paired reading with peers, individual reading of authentic literature, narrative and expository writing, or cooperative activities involving collective problem solving. These activities are associated with greater reading fluency, comprehension, and metacognitive skills.

Participating in activities that can be characterized as holistic does not preclude the fact that students at risk for school failure are in greater need for direct, explicit instruction in lower order skills (i.e., phonics, grammar). For students at risk for reading failure, the extreme deficits in lower order skills can render it impossible for them to meaningfully participate in many holistic literacy activities.

School-Level Literacy Outcomes

Many of the features of early literacy interventions outlined previously have been found to improve reading skills of students at risk (Snow et al., 1998). As a result, they have been incorporated into whole school reform models in various degrees and combinations (St. John & Bardzell, 1999). Like all efforts for change in schools, these

reforms are not occurring in a policy vacuum. Once the interventions enter the school environment, the literacy outcomes that are considered valid or a priority are defined by the current zeitgeist. Certainly a dominant reform effort that is related to the pressure to increase standards is the use of high-stakes tests (Linn, 2000). Because of these tests, educators are under increasing pressure not only to improve reading skills, but to improve scores on state-mandated tests. Reading skills and scores on high-stakes exams, however, are not necessarily synonymous. It is possible that interventions demonstrated to be effective with students will not translate into school-wide improvements on state-mandated achievement tests. To make a difference in test scores, schools must reach a high percentage of their students, and align outcomes targeted in their curriculum with those on the standardized tests. Programs must not only include effective instructional features, but be structured in such a way as to maximize the effect of that intervention in classrooms with 30 or more students. This may be particularly problematic when there is a higher percentage of students delayed in language and other skills because of an impoverished background. In addition, because test scores can be improved simply by practicing in the testing format, they may represent teaching to the test rather than actual achievement differences (Linn, 2000). Interventions that improve reading, but do not address test taking skills, may not reflect gains in state test scores.

Related School-Level Literacy Outcomes

The central concerns of two related reform efforts are the overidentification of students as having a disability and the growing movement to prevent social promotion. Students in Grades 1 through 3 who are identified for grade retention or high-incidence disabilities, primarily learning disabilities, are most often identified because of deficits in reading. Because of variability in school reading programs, student background and inconsistency in identification procedures, schools may differ greatly in the number of and characteristics of students identified or retained. Many of the early literacy programs evaluated here are designed to assist students at risk for reading failure so that they will not be retained or require special education. These programs have the potential for either directly addressing the deficits of students at risk for reading failure or in modifying the classroom environment in such a way so that teachers feel secure that their lowest achieving students are receiving the appropriate instruction. Grade retention and special education referrals serve, therefore, as indicators of the overall effectiveness of an early literacy intervention program. Because of the high costs of retention and special education, any reduction has financial benefits. A potential, positive outcome that may be expected from these early literacy programs is a reduction in grade retention and special education referral rates.

Whether a student is referred for special education assessment or is retained reflects both the student's skills, most often reading, as well as the characteristic of the classroom environment. That is, unlike achievement test scores, retention and referral are both "soft" indicators of the reading achievement of the lowest achieving students in a school. Referral and retention reflect the interaction of students skill level with the environment. In environments that are more highly tolerant (Gerber, 1988; Gerber & Semmel, 1984, 1985) of heterogeneity in student ability, educators are better able to educate the lowest achieving students in the mainstream at the appropriate grade level without labels.

This study addresses the question of which features of model early literacy programs are associated with improvement in school-level indicators of language arts outcomes. In addition, these predictors are compared to those that predict other key indicators of effective literacy instruction for primary students at risk: the rate of referrals for special education assessment and grade level retention.

METHOD

Survey Instrument

The Early Literacy Intervention Survey (St. John, Manset, & Michael, 1999) was developed specifically for this project. Surveys contained 62 closed items, including 19 questions requesting the frequency of use (i.e., never, occasionally, everyday) of program features in the early literacy programs for Grades K through 3, as well as the number of referrals for special education assessment and grade retention. Responses for only Grades 1 through 3 were combined by calculating a mean value and used for this study (sample questions can be found in the Appendix). The feature list was developed after analyzing the program along the framework described earlier. Features of early literacy intervention programs that have either a substantial research base or have been developed from a critical–empirical perspective were included. The 19 instructional features represent common practices in what is associated with either whole language, phonics-based, or balanced approaches. Different options in classroom structures were also included. Features included independent reading, one-to-one tutorial, "pullout" instruction, small groups, systematic formative evaluation, trade books, Big Books, cooperative learning, student-paired reading, direct instruction in phonics, emergent spelling, and worksheets and books. These features were reduced to factors using a principal component analysis. In addition to instructional features, the survey contained items related to parent involvement, professional development, enrollment, and number of referrals for special education assessment and grade retention.

An advisory committee of experts in early literacy and school reform provided feedback on the survey. The survey was then piloted by elementary principals. Principals provided verbal and written comments that were incorporated in the final draft of the survey. Surveys were mailed to 613 elementary schools. After 2 weeks, principals were mailed a postcard reminding them to respond. After 3 weeks, a second survey was mailed to principals, and they were also called on the phone. Participants representing 349 schools (57%) returned the survey. Of those respondents, 283 (46%) completed every item on the survey, and were therefore included in this analysis. A small number of respondents ($N = 26$) completed a second survey after approximately 5 months. When the items related to program features were compared between participants completing both a first and second survey, a standardized item alpha of .92 was calculated. Although limited by the small number of repeated surveys, the strength of the coefficient provides some evidence of the reliability of the instrument.

Respondents and nonrespondents were compared by the poverty rate (percentage of students receiving free or reduced fee lunch) of the school, generally a significant predictor of school-level outcomes. In this case, there was a statistically significant difference, $t(568) = -2.532$, $p = .012$) between the poverty rate of nonrespondent schools (32% receiving free or reduced fee lunch) and respondent schools (27% receiving free or reduced fee lunch). The poverty rate of respondent schools were more comparable to that of elementary schools in the state as a whole, which averaged 29% of students receiving free or reduced fee lunch. Therefore, the sample of schools can be said to be moderately representative of elementary schools in the state, with sample schools overall having lower poverty rates than nonresponding schools and those in the state as a whole. Interpretations of the results should be made with these differences in mind.

Predictor Variables

Contextual variables and program features were included as predictor variables in the regression analysis. Contextual variables included poverty rate as defined by the percentage of students who receive free or reduced fee lunch, percentage of students from ethnic minority groups, and school location (urban, rural). Program variables included professional development features (certified training for reading instructors, certified specialist visits the schools, in-service workshops, between school networking, opportunity for collaboration), parent involvement features (book distribution programs, family literacy instruction, parent–child-paired reading, parent conferences, parent volunteer features), and classroom environmental features created from reducing the 19 instructional features reported on the survey.

Outcome Variables

Four indicators of the impact of program features were identified for this study. The first two relate to reading and language arts achievement as measured by the state's third-grade achievement test. This high-stakes examination is taken by every public school student in the state in the early fall of the third-grade year. Reading raw scores are combined with other literacy measures to create the language arts score used in this study.[1] The correlations between the reading scores and the derived measures used here are above .9. Scale scores were created for the total in language arts scores, and a minimum score on the language arts tasks was determined by the state as a cut-off for minimum proficiency in literacy skills. Whereas mean scores represent overall achievement, passing the minimum scores represent attainment (i.e., the ability for students who are academically at the lowest margin to attain a minimum level of literacy).

Rates of referral for special education assessment and grade retention were determined through dividing the number of referrals and retention as reported by principals for Grades 1 through 3 by the number of students in those grades.

RESULTS

Data Reduction

The 19 instructional features in the Early Literacy Intervention Grant Program survey were reduced into six factors using a principal components analysis with varimax rotation. To aid interpretation, a conservative component loading of a minimum of .50 was used. Missing items were replaced with mean values (see Table 1). The first factor, holistic skills, reflects a focus in instruction on whole texts and higher order cognitive skills, such as supporting early writing through emergent spelling activities or comprehension and reading fluency with paired reading, and teachers reading aloud to students. Cooperative learning involves group problem solving and active metacognition, which can be characterized as higher order cognitive skills. Systematic formative evaluation within literacy instruction most often involves some performance task, whether it is to write for a portfolio or read a passage for an informal reading inventory. These performance tasks again are examples of activities that focus on holistic and higher order cognitive skills. The frequency of the evaluation, however, adds another dimension to this factor.

The second factor, explicit skill instruction, reflects those tasks related to decontextualized components of literacy, such as phonemic awareness, grammar, and spelling. These skills require more automaticity than complex problem solving, hence their characterization as lower order cognitive tasks. The systematic presentation of items and the practice necessary to gain automaticity in these

TABLE 1

Loadings for Early Literacy Factors

Factors	Loadings
Holistic skills focus	
Paired reading	.696
Emergent spelling	.689
Cooperative learning	.591
Systematic formative evaluation	.525
Reading aloud	.509
Explicit skills focus	
Basal readers	.619
Phonics instruction	.572
Reading drills	.786
Worksheets and books	.773
Small group–tutorial	
One–one tutoring	.679
Small group	.661
Trade books	.533
Childcentered–expressive	
Child-initiated learning center	.624
Big books	.645
Drama	.654
Ability grouping	
Ability grouping	.746
Pullout instruction	
Pullout instruction	.823

tasks are incorporated in the format of basal readers, worksheets and books, and reading drills. Phonics instruction indicates a focus on the basic sound–symbol associations in reading.

The third factor, small group–tutorial, best reflects the two highest loading components, one-to-one tutoring and small group instruction. Trade books may load on this factor because they are oftentimes used in the small literacy groups. Classrooms may have a set of trade books for a small group that can be rotated throughout the year rather than one whole class set.

The fourth factor, child centered–expressive, reflects opportunities for students to direct their instruction through learning centers, and oral language expression through the use of drama and reading aloud while using Big Books. Drama allows for an interpretation of text that can deepen comprehension as well as practice communicating orally. Big Books is an activity that involves the use of an oversized Big Book (generally, a picture book) by a teacher, and corresponding small books by students. Beginning readers can read along with the teacher, practice reading aloud, and work with words as presented by the teacher.

Factors five and six, ability grouping and pullout instruction, are single component factors. Ability grouping reflects the grouping of students into skill levels when they are divided into small groups. *Pullout Instruction* refers to early literacy interventions that require the pulling

TABLE 2

Summary of Standard Multiple Regression Model for Variables Predicting School
Mean for Language Arts Scale Score

Variable	B	$SE\ B$	β
Free lunch	−76.099%	9.609%	−.530%***
Minority	−7.828%	7.440%	−.070%
City	−2.969	3.564	−.042
Rural	4.995	2.466	.100*
Professional development			
Certified training	−4.649	2.692	−.086
Certified specialist	2.595	2.641	.047
In-service workshop	−1.038	2.801	−.019
Networking	0.536	2.410	.011
Collaboration	−2.484	2.541	−.050
Parent involvement			
Book distribution	1.020	2.310	.022
Family literacy	−4.294	2.631	−.077
Paired reading	10253.	20587.0	.024
Parent conferences	12.986	7.433	.084
Parent volunteers	0.788	2.412	.016
Classroom features			
Holistic skills focus	−0.139	1.128	−.006
Explicit skills focus	2.097	1.100	.090
Small group–tutorial	−1.205	1.229	−.048
Childcentered–expressive	1.396	1.156	.060
Ability grouping	−0.766	1.162	−.031
Pullout instruction	−0.296	1.117	−.012

Note. $N = 283$; $R = .687$***; $R^2 = .471$; Adj. $R^2 = .432$.
*$p < .05$. **$p < .001$.

out of students from their mainstream classroom to receive the instruction.

Multiple Regression Analysis

Predictor variables were entered into four separate standard multiple regression equations to predict the four outcomes of language arts scores, passing rates on the language arts exam, rates of referral for special education assessment, and rates of grade retention. Significance levels were determined at $p < .05$, .01, and .001. The combination of predictor variables significantly contributed to approximately 47% (adjusted 43%) of the variance in the first outcome variable, the language arts scale score ($R^2 = .471$, Adj. $R^2 = .432$, $p < .001$; see Table 2). The language arts scale score was significantly predicted negatively by the percentage of free lunch and positively related to a rural location. None of the program features predicted mean language arts scale score.

The predictor variables significantly contributed to 48% (adjusted 44%) of the variance in passing rates in English–language arts percentage ($R^2 = .481$, Adj. $R^2 = .442$, $p < .001$; see Table 3). Free lunch negatively predicted passing rates on achievement test scores as well. In addition, the use of

certified training and family literacy programs was negatively associated with passing rates. Explicit skill instruction was also positively associated with passing rates.

The combination of variables contributed to 15% (adjusted 9%) of the variance in the rate of referrals for special education assessment ($R^2 = .155$, Adj. $R^2 = .092$, $p < .001$). Program features were also found to predict referral rates for special education assessment (see Table 4). Programs with parent–child-paired reading and explicit skills are related to lower rates of referrals. On the other hand, a reported greater frequency of holistic skills and ability grouping were both related to greater rates of referral.

Finally, a different pattern was found for the reduction of retention than referrals or test scores (Table 4). Variables significantly contributed to 26% (adjusted 21%) of the variance in the rate of grade retention ($R^2 = .259$, Adj. $R^2 = .204$, $p < .001$). Percentage of free lunch, and percentage of ethnic minority are both significantly and positively related to greater rates of grade retention. The frequency of explicit skills practices is also related to higher rates in grade retention, which contradicts the patterns for passing rates and special education referral. Practices related to opportunity for collaboration, parent–child-paired reading, and holistic skills focus are all three negatively related to grade retention.

TABLE 3

Summary of Standard Multiple Regression Model for Variables
Predicting School Passing Rates in Language Arts

Variable	B	SE B	β
Free lunch	−.405%	.055%	−.492%***
Minority	−.075%	.042%	−.117%
City	−.007	.020	−.018
Rural	.020	.014	.086
Professional development			
Certified training	−.030	.015	−.106*
Certified specialist	.008	.015	.028
In-service workshop	−.012	.016	−.041
Networking	−.003	.014	−.011
Collaboration	−.012	.014	−.043
Parent involvement			
Book distribution	.020	.013	.083
Family literacy	−.003	.015	−.104*
Paired reading	.010	.015	.034
Parent conferences	.043	.042	.049
Parent volunteers	.020	.014	.072
Classroom features			
Holistic skills focus	.000	.006	.007
Explicit skills focus	.012	.006	.093*
Small group–tutorial	−.011	.007	−.084
Childcentered–expressive	.007	.007	.051
Ability grouping	−.004	.007	−.026
Pullout instruction	−.000	.006	−.006

Note. $N = 283$; $R = .687***$; $R^2 = .471$; Adj. $R^2 = .432$.

*$p < .05$. **$p < .01$; ***$p < .001$.

TABLE 4

Summary of Standard Multiple Regression Model for Variables
Predicting Rate of Referral for Special Education Assessment

Variable	B	SE B	β
Reading total raw score	−.002	.001	−.187*
Free lunch	.02	.016	.170
Minority	−.02	.011	−.142
City	.003	.005	.047
Rural	−.003	.004	−.060
Professional development			
Certified training	.004	.004	.064
Certified specialist	−.003	.004	−.046
In-service workshop	−.002	.004	−.040
Networking	.003	.004	.102
Collaboration	−.001	.004	−.021
Parent involvement			
Book distribution	−.001	.003	−.022
Family literacy	−.005	.004	−.079
Paired reading	−.008	.004	−.137*
Parent conferences	.005	.011	.031
Parent volunteers	.000	.004	.004
Classroom instruction			
Holistic skills focus	.004	.002	.151*
Explicit skills focus	−.003	.002	−.125*
Small group–tutorial	.000	.002	−.032
Childcentered–expressive	.002	.002	.063
Ability grouping	.003	.002	.128*
Pullout instruction	.002	.002	.071

Note. $N = 283$; $R = .393***$; $R^2 = .155$; adj. $R^2 = .092$.

*$p < .05$. **$p < .001$.

DISCUSSION

In this article, contextual features and reported practices in literacy programs were used to predict school-level outcomes on statewide achievement tests. These models were also compared to those predicting two other achievement-related outcomes: rates of special education referral and grade retention. Findings suggest that whether early literacy practices are considered effective on a school level depends on the outcome used as an indicator of progress (i.e., practices that predict achievement test scores are not necessarily those that are related to other important related outcomes such as rates of special education referral or grade retention). A summary of key findings can be found in Table 6 and are discussed here.

Poverty Rates as a Predictor of Literacy Outcomes

Indicators of socioeconomic status have been found to be consistent predictors of achievement outcomes. Students who attend schools with a higher percentage of students living in poverty score lower on state achievement tests (Linn, 2000). This was confirmed in this study as well. A greater proportion of students in high-poverty schools

are not meeting minimum literacy standards as defined by achievement tests. They are also more likely to be retained, which is in itself not considered an effective intervention (Jimerson, 1999; McCoy & Reynolds, 1999). These results underscore the continued need to address particularly early literacy instruction in high poverty.

Literacy Program Features and School-Level Achievement Test Scores

Once poverty rate was accounted for, few of the reported early literacy practices made a difference in school averages on state language test scores. This also suggests that at least with these self-reported variables, practices that have been found to be effective with students do not translate into overall language arts scores for third grade. This suggests that the latest research-based reform practices may have little influence on average test scores on standardized tests for schools overall.

A few variables did, however, predict passing rates on this same test, which suggests that the lowest achieving students may be more sensitive to the characteristics of programs than students in general. A little less than one

TABLE 5

Summary of Standard Multiple Regression Model for Variables
Predicting Rate of Grade Retention

Variable	B	SE B	β
Reading total raw score	.002	.001	.156*
Free lunch	.040%	.013%	.293%**
Minority	.032%	.009%	.299%***
City	−.000	.004	−.012
Rural	.005	.003	.125*
Professional development			
Certified training	−.019	.003	−.037
Certified specialist	−.002	.003	−.041
In-service workshop	.003	.003	.060
Networking	−.003	.003	−.069
Collaboration	−.006	.003	−.127*
Parent involvement			
Book distribution	.004	.003	.094
Family literacy	−.003	.003	−.054
Paired reading	−.006	.003	−.121*
Parent conferences	.003	.008	.024
Parent volunteers	.003	.003	.065
Classroom instruction			
Holistic skills focus	−.004	.001	−.191**
Explicit skills focus	.003	.001	.162**
Small group–tutorial	−.002	.001	−.094
Childcentered–expressive	−.000	.001	−.019
Ability grouping	−.001	.001	−.049
Pullout instruction	−.000	−.001	−.011

Note. $N = 283$; $R = .509$***; $R^2 = .259$; Adj. $R^2 = .204$.

*$p < .05$, **$p < .01$, ***$p < .001$.

half of the variance in passing rates was related at a statistically significant level to four predictors. School buildings with higher poverty rates tend to exhibit lower passing rates on the state exam. Likewise, school buildings reporting higher rates of certified training and more family literacy activity also tend to have lower passing rates. Closer examination of the data will likely show that this counterintuitive result is attributable to a recent onset of family literacy programs and certified training in some of the lowest scoring schools. The factor, explicit skill instruction, as defined by the use of basal readers and workbooks, direct instruction in phonics, and reading drills, positively predicted passing rates on that state language arts examination. This can be interpreted to mean that these explicit, highly structured methods are effective for the lowest achieving students, as well as that these activities and curriculum may be closely aligned with the paper-and-pencil test format.

Literacy Program Features as Predictors of Referral and Retention Rates

Rates of referral for special education assessment and grade retention appeared to be more sensitive to differences in the literacy program features than achievement tests scores. The models that predict these outcome variables, however, look very different. For both referral and retention rates, the reported parent–child-paired reading program is related to fewer referrals and retention. This is consistent with previous research that supports the provision of training and information to parents so that they may supplement classroom reading instruction with reading at home (Dolly & Page, 1983; Hewison & Tizard, 1980; Tizard, Schofield, & Hewison, 1982). Besides extending the time in which students may spend working on particularly holistic literacy skills such as comprehension and fluency, students have an opportunity to expand on their language skills, particularly if parents have instruction in maximizing their exchange with their children as they read. Having a parent act as a reading tutor for his or her child also extends the adaptablity of a program by providing individualized instruction. This feature alone, if structured well, extends adaptability, access to holistic skills, and enriched communication of an early literacy program. This may be why it is related to the lower rates of both referral and grade retention.

A reported focus on explicit skills, although related to higher passing rates on the state examination, is also related to lower rates of referral. This is consistent with research that suggests the need for students at risk to receive explicit instruction in lower order skills such as decoding in a structured way (Foorman, 1997; Foorman, Francis, Fletcher, & Schatschneider, 1998; Mann, 1986; Snow et al., 1998). Fewer students may be failing at reading in these programs that include explicit skills. This is confirmed by the fact that explicit skills predict higher passing rates on the language arts test. Teachers in programs that include explicit features may not feel the need to refer students out for special education services, which traditionally provide more explicit instruction in a resource room setting. Conversely, explicit skill instruction is positively associated with retention rates (i.e., there is greater retention in those programs where there is a reported greater use of reading drills, phonics instruction, and basal readers). This contradicts the model for referrals for special education. The structure imposed by the features of the explicit skills instruction, although associated with test score gains, may create a less adaptable environment. In other words, teachers have difficulty meeting the needs of the lowest achieving students within such a structured environment, and students are held back to complete with younger students.

The opposite relation was found for a holistic skill focus. The greater the focus on holistic skills, the higher the rate of referral and the lower the rate of retention. Again, in these early years, an overemphasis on activities to improve comprehension or problem solving may limit the time spent on more explicit, structured instruction. In addition, using the reasoning outlined earlier, if there is a high emphasis on holistic skills in a mainstream class-

TABLE 6

Summary of Significant Variables Predicting Outcomes

Predictor Variables	Outcome Variables
Percentage of free lunch (–)[a] Rural (+)	Language arts scale score
Percentage of free lunch (–) Certified training (–) Family literacy (–) Explicit skills (+)	Passing rates, language arts
Reading Raw Scores 1997 (–) Paired reading (parent–child) (–) Holistic skills focus (+) Explicit skills focus (–) Ability grouping (+)	Rate of referral for special education assessment
Reading raw scores 1997 (–) Percentage of free lunch (+) Percentage of minority (+) Rural (+) Opportunity for collaboration (–) Paired reading (parent–child) (–) Holistic skills focus (–) Explicit skills focus (+)	Rate of grade retention

[a]Indicates direction of relation between predictor and outcome variables.

room program, explicit skill instruction for the lowest achieving students may only occur in the special classes. On the other hand, the lower rate of retention related to this variable suggests that less structured activities that make up the holistic skills focus may again be associated with a more adaptable environment, where teachers may educate a wider range of students with their same age peers in one classroom.

Opportunity for collaboration was also found related to lower rates of retention. The shared expertise and resources that are associated with collaborative teaching add to the adaptability of a classroom program and is a key component of programs striving to support highly heterogeneous classrooms (Chalfant, Pysh, & Moultrie, 1979; Hayek, 1987; Manset & Semmel, 1997). Collaboration contributes to the adaptability in a classroom, which again can be associated with lower rates of retention.

Ability grouping was found to be positively associated with referrals for special education assessment. Despite the advantages of teaching small, homogeneous groups of students in targeting skills at an appropriate level, ability groups have been found to be ineffective means of the teaching of reading. There are exceptions to this, specifically when groups have been designed across grade levels (Slavin, 1996). Perhaps, students who are at risk for being identified for a learning disability do not benefit from the modeling provided by higher achieving students, and suffer as a result of the low expectations associated with being in a remedial group. In addition, the

actual process of designing ability groups may lead to earlier identification of those students with the most extreme skill deficits. Clearly, these findings relating ability grouping and referral warrant further examination.

This study is limited by the dependence on principals' reports on general practice across a school program as opposed to direct observation of actual practice. The program features described in the surveys may reflect only the perception or a desire of the principal, rather than the reality at each school. The methods in this study also do not allow for the differences between teaching practices, but rather forces the respondent to describe what they see as general practice. Another shortcoming is the fact that data originated from only one state. States differ in curricular emphasis, referral and retention practices, and in the content of state tests. Findings, therefore, may be very different depending on the region of the country. In addition, key limitations is that only 46% of the total sample returned completed surveys, and they represented lower poverty schools than those that did not respond. Findings may also differ if a sample that were more representative of schools in the state were included. Each of these limitations prevent the drawing of conclusive findings.

Still, given these limitations, the results provide direction for future, more direct inquiry related to practice and outcomes. A key finding is the difference between the variables that predict each of the four outcomes. Given the importance of each of the three reform movements, it is disconcerting to note that an emphasis in one area—

practices that will lead to an increase in test scores—may also create an environment that encourages more grade retention. In addition, the relation between high-stakes test scores and explicit skill instruction may drive schools to increase their emphasis on drill, practice, and workbooks over the practices that lead to other also valid literacy outcomes, some of which are not addressed in this study. Rather than emphasizing explicit versus holistic skill instruction, perhaps early literacy programs should increase the frequency of activities in each of these areas, particularly in high-poverty schools. Finally, the unexpected contradiction between what predicts referral and retention rates, given they are both dependent to a great degree on both student characteristics and a tolerant environment, warrants further research.

REFERENCES

Chalfant, J. C. , Pysh, M., & Moultrie, R. (1979). Teacher assistance teams: A model for within-building problem solving. *Learning Disabilities Quarterly, 2*, 85–96.

Clay, M. M. (1993). *Reading recovery: A guidebook for teachers in training*. Portsmouth, NH: Heineman.

Cunningham, P. M., & Allington, R. L. (1999). *Classrooms that work: They can all read and write*. New York: Addison-Wesley.

Cunningham, P. M., Moore, S. A., Cunningham, J. W., & Moore, D. W. (2000). *Reading & writing in the elementary classrooms: Strategies and observations* (4th ed). New York: Longman.

Dolly, J. P., & Page, D. P. (1983). An attempt to increase parental involvement in rural schools. *Phi Delta Kappan, 64*, 512.

Foorman, B. R. (1997). Early interventions for children with reading problems: Study designs and preliminary findings. *Learning Disabilities: A Multidisciplinary Journal, 8*, 63–71.

Foorman, B. R., Francis, D. J., Fletcher, J. M., & Schatschneider, C. (1998). The role of instruction in learning to read: Preventing reading failure in at-risk children. *Journal of Educational Psychology, 90*, 37–55.

Gerber, M. M. (1988). Tolerance and technology of instruction: Implications for special education reform. *Exceptional Children, 54*, 309–314.

Gerber, M. M., & Semmel, M. I. (1984). Teacher as imperfect test: Reconceptualizing the referral process. *Educational Psychologist, 19*, 137–148.

Gerber, M. M., & Semmel, M. I. (1985). The microeconomics of referral and reintegration: A paradigm for evaluation of special education. *Studies in Educational Evaluation, 11*, 13–29.

Greenwood, C. R. (1996). Research on the practices and behavior of effective teachers at the Juniper Gardens Children's Project: Implications for the education of diverse learners. In D. Speece & B. Keogh (Eds.), *Research on classroom ecologies: Implications for the inclusion of children with learning disabilities* (pp. 36–67). Hillsdale, NJ: Lawrence Erlbaum Associates, Inc.

Hayek, R. A. (1987). The teacher assistance team: A prereferral support system. *Focus on Exceptional Children, 20*, 1–7.

Hewison, N. S., & Tizard, J. (1980). Parental involvement and reading achievement. *British Journal of Educational Psychology, 50*, 209–215.

Jimerson, S. (1999). On the failure of failure: Examining the association between early grade retention and education and employment outcomes during late adolescence. *Journal of School Psychology, 37*, 243–272.

Linn, R. L. (2000). Assessments and accountability. *Educational Researcher, 29*(2), 4–16.

Mann, V. (1986). Why some children encounter reading problems: The contribution of difficulties with language processing and phonological sophistication to early reading disability. In J. Torgeson & B. Wong (Eds.), *Psychological and educational perspectives on learning disabilities* (pp. 133–159) Orlando, FL: Academic.

Manset, G., & Rogers, D. (1998, April) *Evaluating inclusive school programs for primary students with language and learning disabilities: Reconceptualizing our approach*. Paper presented at the annual meeting of the American Educational Research Association, San Diego, CA.

Manset, G., & Semmel, M. I. (1997). Are inclusive programs for students with mild disabilities effective? A comparative review of model programs. *Journal of Special Education, 31*, 155–180.

McCoy, A., & Reynolds, A. (1999). Grade retention and school performance: An extended investigation. *Journal of School Psychology, 37*, 273–298.

Sayre, J. E. (1996). The view from a Montessori classroom: A response to Carroll and Greenwood. In D. L. Speece & B. K. Keogh (Eds.), *Research on classroom ecologies: Implications for inclusion of students with learning disabilities* (pp. 69–79) Mahwah, NJ: Lawrence Erlbaum Associates, Inc.

Slavin, R. (1992). *Success for all: A relentless approach to prevention and early intervention in elementary schools*. Arlington, VA: Educational Research Service.

Slavin, R. (1996). *Education for all: Contexts of learning*. Exton, PA: Swets & Zeitlinger.

Snow, C. E., Burns, M. S., & Griffin, P. (Eds.). (1998). *Preventing reading difficulties in young children*. Washington, DC: National Academy of Sciences, National Research Council.

Speece, D. L., & Keogh, B. K. (1996). *Research on classroom ecologies: Implications for inclusion of children with learning disabilities*. Mahwah, NJ: Lawrence Erlbaum Associates, Inc.

St. John, E. P., & Bardzell, J. S. (Eds.). (1999). *Improving early reading and literacy: A guide for developing research-based programs*. Bloomington: Indiana Education Policy Center.

St. John, E. P. , Manset, G., & Michael, R. (1999). Early literacy intervention survey. In E. P. St. John & J. S. Bardzell (Eds.), *Improving early reading and literacy: A guide for developing research based programs* (pp. A1–A6). Bloomington: Indiana Education Policy Center.

Tizard, J., Schofield, W. N., & Hewison, J. (1982). Collaboration between teachers and parents in assisting children's reading. *British Journal of Educational Psychology, 52*, 1–15.

U.S. Department of Education. (1997). *Comprehensive School Reform Act*. Washington, DC: Author. Retrieved December 19, 2001, from the World Wide Web: http//www.ed.gov/offices/OESE/compreform

U.S. Department of Education. (1999). *Reading Excellence Act*. Washington, DC: Author. Retrieved December 19, 2001, from the World Wide Web: http://www.ed.gov/offices/OESE/REA/

Vygotsky, L. S. (1993). The fundamentals of defectology. In R. W. Reiber & A. S. Carton (Eds.), *The collected works of L. S. Vygotsky* (Vol. 2, pp. 29–64). New York: Plenum.

APPENDIX

Sample Survey Items

Instructions: Please indicate the extent to which the following features were used as part of the early literacy program in your school during the following years.

Structural–Organizational Features

Program Feature	1997-1998 Extent of Use					Description of Feature
	Never	Rarely	Occasionall	Often	Every day	
1. Ability Grouping						Students assigned to groups based on ability.
Kindergarten						
1st Grade						
2nd Grade						
3rd Grade						
2. Basal Readers						Series of graded readers.
Kindergarten						
1st Grade						
2nd Grade						
3rd Grade						

Parent Involvement

Instructions: Please indicate which of the following features were used as part of the early literacy program in

Program Feature	1997-1998				Description of Feature
	Kindergarte	1st Grade	2nd Grade	3rd Grade	
1. Book Distribution					Distributes books to households that may have limited reading materials.
2. Family Literacy					Literacy instruction provided to parents.
3. Paired Reading					Parents help children with reading.

Note

9. The total language arts score was used as opposed to the reading score because the state uses the language arts total score as the basis for determining their minimum proficiency cutoff.

Requests for reprints should be sent to Genevieve Manset-Williamson, Indiana University, ED 3220, Bloomington, IN 47405. E-mail: gmwill@indiana.edu

Using African American Children's Literature to Support Literacy Development

Sally McClellan and M. Evelyn Fields

A great disparity still exists in our schools as reflected in the achievement gap between African American and European American children. Among the reasons for this gap are the large number of African American children living in poverty and the high number of children from single-parent homes (Annie E. Casey Foundation 2003). The disparity is evident in children's test scores, in the resources available to them, and in the experience of their teachers (Darling-Hammond 1997).

Educators' ideas vary on how best to address this disparity. Haycock (2001) recommends that schools provide greater challenges to minority students, offer extra help for those who need it, and hire teachers who have the training needed to teach their assigned subjects. Ladson-Billings (1994) indicates that minority students are capable, but need meaningful curriculum to enable them to be successful in school. Hale (1991) suggests that the solution to the achievement gap is to make schools more culturally appropriate.

Children's experience should be a part of the curriculum (Ladson-Billings 1994). Books are a powerful means of providing positive images and interesting material to young children (Banfield 1998). Because stories and images make a lasting impression, children's literature can have a strong impact on young children.

Barriers to literacy

Reading is an essential skill. For young children, this skill can chart a course for school success. Without this ability, children are likely to be unsuccessful and drop out of school. According to the National Research Council publication *Preventing Reading Difficulties,* African American children are at a greater risk for reading difficulties than European American children (Snow, Burns, & Griffin 1998). The reading achievement gap widens as children go through school (Bransford, Brown, & Cocking 2000).

Minority populations may speak a nonstandard variety of English, which "can impede the easy acquisition of English literacy by introducing greater deviations in the representations of sounds, making it hard to develop sound-symbol links" (Snow, Burns, & Griffin 1998, 27-28). Children who speak a Black dialect may get confused when trying to understand the relationship between spelling and sounds. Children who are read to or have already learned to read in the dialect may have an advantage when broadening their scope to Standard English. A good example of use of dialect is found in the book *Goin' Someplace Special,* by Patricia McKissack and Jerry Pinkney.

Two additional factors associated with reading difficulties include a lack of motivation to read and an inability to see the rewards of reading. Children who live in poverty also often have fewer literacy resources in their homes and frequently find a similar situation in their classrooms (Kozol 1991).

Using African American children's literature can ensure that reading material is interesting, meaningful, and culturally appropriate. Books having these qualities can motivate children to learn to read and to want to read more. The absence of such resources can have the opposite effect.

The importance of authenticity in children's literature

The curriculum in our schools will be more inclusive and more effective when the experiences of African American children are reflected in the materials used (Delpit 1995). When children are engaged by a topic, they learn language more effectively (Bowman, Donovan, & Burns 2001). Authentic African American children's literature successfully engages children and reflects their experiences. In an authentic work, the illustrations and text are free of stereotypes and misrepresentations (Mikkelsen 1998). Authenticity includes the extent to which the children's literature

African American Children's Books

Best, C. 1995. *Red light, green light, Mama and me.* New York: Orchard.

Bunting, E. 1994. *Flower garden.* San Diego: Harcourt Brace, Jovanovich.

Caines, J. 1982. *Just us women.* New York: Scholastic.

Cowen-Fletcher, J. 1993. *It takes a village.* New York: Scholastic.

Crews, D. 1991. *Bigmama's.* New York: Scholastic.

Crews, N. 1995. *One hot summer day.* New York: Greenwillow.

Duncan, A. F. 1995. *Willie Jerome.* New York: Macmillan.

Falwell, C. 1993. *Feast for 10.* New York: Scholastic.

Flournoy, V. 1985. *The patchwork quilt.* New York: Scholastic.

Greenfield, E. 1999. *Water, water.* New York: Harper Festival.

Havill, J. 1989. *Jamaica tag-along.* New York: Scholastic (There is a series of books featuring the character Jamaica.)

hooks, b. 2002. *Be boy buzz.* New York: Hyperion.

hooks, b. 2002. *Homemade love.* New York: Hyperion.

Howard, E. 1991. *Aunt Flossie's hats (and crab cakes later).* New York: Scholastic.

Hudson, C., and B. Ford. 1990. *Bright eyes, brown skin.* New York: Scholastic.

Johnson, A. 1989. *Tell me a story, Mama.* New York: Scholastic.

Johnson, A. 1999. *The wedding.* New York: Orchard.

Johnson, D. 1999. *Sunday week.* New York: Henry Holt.

McKissack, P., and J. Pinkney. 2001. *Goin' someplace special.* New York: Antheneum Books for Young Readers.

Mitchell, M. 1993. *Uncle Jed's barbershop.* New York: Scholastic

Mitchell, R. 2001. *The talking cloth.* New York: Orchard.

Onyefulu, I. 1997. *Chidi only likes blue: An African book of colors.* New York: Cobblehill.

Smalls, I. 1999. *Kevin and his dad.* New York: Little, Brown.

Steptoe, Javaka. 1997. *In Daddy's arms I am tall: African Americans celebrating fathers.* New York: Lee & Low.

Steptoe, John. 1987. *Mufaro's Beautiful Daughters.* New York: Amistad.

Strickland, M.R. 2001. *Haircuts at Sleepy Sam's.* Honesdale, PA: Boyds Mill.

Tarpley, N.A. 1998. *I love my hair.* New York: Little, Brown.

Williams, K.L. 1990. *Galimoto.* New York: Lothrop, Lee & Shepard.

addresses the values and beliefs of African American culture rather than just attending to surface issues (Mikkelsen 1998).

Children's books that authentically reflect the experiences of African American children and are free of stereotypical messages or illustrations are available. Books such as *Mufaro's Beautiful Daughters* by John Steptoe and *The Patchwork Quilt* by Valerie Flournoy can certainly be used for instruction. One resource to consult is the NAEYC brochure *Books to Grow On*, which features an annotated bibliography of African American children's literature (Brown & Oates 2001). (See "African American Children's Books" and "Resources for Early Childhood Educators," for more ideas.) Unfortunately, although the availability of resources that provide positive images and instruction continues to increase, many more are needed. According to the Cooperative Children's Book Center at the University of Wisconsin–Madison, of 5,000 children's books published in 2002 and available for sale to public schools, only 69 were by African Americans or Africans and only 166 were about them (CCBC 2003).

There is concern about the authenticity of some books that include African American children (Mikkelsen 1998). Questions that can help teachers determine the authenticity of the books include the following:

- Do the books actually depict the real experience of African Americans, or are the stories only about European Americans with the characters colored black?

- Are the illustrations subtly stereotypical? For example, the drawings of African American children should depict recognizably unique individuals and not children who all have the same stereotypical Negroid features (Roethler 1998).

Mikkelsen (1998) and Roethler (1998) suggest examining children's literature with these questions in mind.

Mikkelsen (1998) gives preference to African American children's literature written by African American authors because he believes they can more realistically capture the experience of African Americans. Mikkelsen also notes that although African American illustrators would be sensitive to subtly stereotypical images, publishers often reject their work.

The benefits of authentic children's literature

Johnson (1990) and Hale (1982) indicate that the culture of African American children is linked to Africa, and Johnson suggests that it is difficult to understand African American literature without a study of African civilization and the history of African American people not as slaves, but as an enslaved people. Authentic African American children's literature can bring that rich history into the lives of all young children.

Teachers can also learn from books that share African American culture. When teachers understand the culture, they have a better understanding of the African American children that they teach. Literature that reflects the cultural richness of African and African American history and the dialect of African American children is beneficial to all children.

Davis (1998) notes that African American children's literature can enable children not only to learn to read language but also to read the world. Through books, children learn more about their own and other families' history and cultural heritage. Comer and Poussaint (1992) and Hale (1991) point out that an understanding of Black history can strengthen African American children's self-identity as well as help them to battle the racism they encounter. Biographies are particularly important in providing good role models for African American children (Osa 1995).

African American children's literature may take the place of family gatherings at which much of this instruction about cultural heritage used to occur (Osa 1995). Providing children with both a historical perspective and a realistic depiction of their lives has a direct impact on their future (Feelings 1995). Many European Americans can also profit from such an educational awareness to counteract the negative messages they may receive regarding African Americans. Reading authentic African American children's literature provides positive images, cultural understanding, and an appreciation for Black English. All children benefit from coming to understand African American culture (Bernd 1995).

Authentic African American children's literature helps children to better bridge the gap between their experiences at home and at school. Bransford, Brown, and Cocking (2000) propose that failure in school may be the result of the mismatch between

Resources for Early Childhood Educators
Literary Awards and Annual Events

Black Books Galore! Contest, sponsored by the Black Caucus of the American Library Association (BCALA) and John Wiley & Sons, is awarded to public and school library programs that raise awareness of and interest in African American children's literature through story time, parent/teacher workshops, and other programs. www.blackbooksgalore.com/contest_03.html

2002 first place winner: Enoch Pratt Free Library, Baltimore, MD, Melanie Townsend, Librarian

Coretta Scott King Award, established in 1970, is awarded to authors and illustrators of African descent whose work encourages a greater understanding of the "American Dream." The awards are presented annually by the Coretta Scott King. Task Force of the American Library Association's Ethnic Multicultural Information Exchange Round Table (EMIERT). www.ala.org/ala/srrt/corettascottking/corettascott.htm

2004 award winners: Author—Angela Johnson for *The First Part Last;* Illustrator—Ashley Bryan for *Beautiful Blackbird*

The National African American Read-In, sponsored by the Black Caucus of the National Council of Teachers of English (NCTE) and by NCTE, is endorsed by the International Reading Association. Every year, schools, community centers, and libraries host read-ins that feature African American authors. The African American Read-In packet includes a host invitation, news release, and recommended booklists. It can be downloaded at www.ncte.org/prog/readin/107901.htm.

John Steptoe Award for New Talent, first awarded in 1995, is presented annually by the Coretta Scott King Task Force to an African American author or illustrator who is relatively new to the field in order to bring more visibility to his or her work. The eligibility criteria specify that works celebrate the African American experience and that entrants have no more than three published works. www.ala.org/ala/srrt/corettascottking/winners/newtalentaward/newtalentaward.htm

2004 award winners: Author—Anita Smith for *The Way A Door Closes;* Illustrator—Elbrite Brown for *My Family Plays Music*

Kids Cultural Books (KCB) is a nonprofit organization created by Toni Trent Parker, the president and co-founder of the children's book service, Black Books Galore! KCB strives to connect African American children, educators, and parents with culturally appropriate literature through corporate-sponsored African American book festivals across the nation. The Web site includes information on the upcoming 6th Annual African-American Children's Book Festival. www.kidsculturalbooks.org/index.html

home and school. Many teachers do not recognize this mismatch because they lack an understanding of the cultural background of the African American family, the language differences that are part of that culture, and, in instances of poverty, children's lack of exposure to high-quality, contextually based, realistic, nonstereotypical children's literature.

Without cultural understanding, teachers frequently make a negative value judgment about Black dialect and fail to see that there is artistic value in any language. Good literature uses the language the character speaks. Classrooms that include African American children's literature provide a familiar context for children while they are in school.

Efforts to remove books that contain negative images of African Americans from the shelves of our schools and libraries are also necessary. Such negative images may depict African Americans as ignorant, inferior, oppressed, and impoverished people. Positive images depict African Americans as educated, capable, and hardworking people.

A total lack of images can be a factor of concern as well. Roethler (1998) raises the

Web sites

Cooperative Children's Book Center (CCBC), a part of the University of Wisconsin–Madison's School of Education, provides and reviews bibliographies of multicultural) books and links to publishers of books for African American children. www.soemadison.wisc.edu/ccbc

de Grummond Children's Literature Collection shares a resource bibliography for African American children's literature. The bibliography includes resources on evaluating books portraying African American children, as well as a reading list. www.lib.usm.edu/~degrum/html/collectionh1/ch-afroamericanbib.shtml

The Black Caucus of the American Library Association, Inc., provides online forums, news updates on conferences, and links to other library organizations. www.bcala.org

Schomburg Center for Research in Black Culture, a research library division within the New York Public Library, offers links to several databases of African American literature, biographies, and resources. www.nypl.org/research/sc/sc.html

question of how African American children feel when none of the books they are exposed to include African American children. This absence of images with which to identify may leave these children feeling invisible. And if European American children see no African American images in the materials in school, they may conclude that only White people are really important (Larrick 1995). Boutte (1999) and Roethler (1998) warn that to not see images of themselves harms children. Tolson (1998) notes that African American children's literature can help children to feel positive about themselves and others and to be proud of their heritage and respectful of others'.

Conclusion

Authentic African American children's literature can support literacy development, bridge the gap between home and school experiences, share positive images, and provide a historical context for African American children. Even though the focus of this article is African American children, *all* children benefit from a variety of books in their classrooms that are respect-

Books and articles

Bishop, R.S. 2000. *Free within ourselves: The development of African American children's literature.* New York: Heinemannl

Bowman, B., ed. 2002. *Love to read: Essays in developing and enhancing early literacy skills of African American children.* Washington, DC: National Black Child Development Institute.

Brock, D.R., & E. Dodd. 1994. A family lending library: Promoting early literacy development. *Young Children* 49 (3): 16-21.

Givens, A. 1998. *Spirited minds: African American books for our sons and our brothers.* New York: Norton.

Givens, A. 1998. *Strong souls singing: African American books for our daughters and our sisters.* New York: Norton.

Kirkland-Mullins, W 1997. Celebrate a people! American children's literature, Vol. 2. New Haven, CT: Yale-New Haven Teachers Institute. Online: www.yale.edu/ ynhti/curriculum/units/1997/ 2/97.02.08.x.html

Murphy, B.T. 1999. *Black authors and illustrators of books for children and young adults.* 3rd ed. New York: Garland.

Quintero, E., & M.C. Velarde. 1990. Intergenerational literacy: A developmental, bilingual approach. *Young Children* 45 (4): 10-15.

Rand, D., & T.T. Parker. 2000. *Black books galore! Guide to great African American Children's books about boys.* New York: John Wiley & Sons.

Rand, D., & T.T. Parker. 2000. *Black books galore! Guide to great African American children s books about girls.* New York: John Wiley & Sons.

Rand, D., & T.T. Parker. 2001. *Black books galore! A guide to more great African American children's books.* New York; John Wiley & Sons.

Toussaint, P. 1999. *Great books for African American children* New York: Plume/Penguin.

---

ful of culture and free from stereotypes. Such books encourage children to develop a sense of their own value and to maintain an interest in reading.

References

Annie E. Casey Foundation. 2003. *Kids Count pocket guide. African-American children: State-level measures of child well-being from the 2000 census.* Brochure. Baltimore, MD: Author. Online: www.aecf.org/kidscount/ african_american_pocketguide .pdf .

Banfield, B. 1998. Commitment to change: The Council on Interracial Books for Children and the world of children's books. *African American Review* 32 (1): 17-22.

Bernd, L. 1995. The Coretta Scott King Award. In *The all-White world of children's books and African American children's literature,* ed. O. Osa. Trenton, NJ: Africa World Press.

Boutte, G. 1999. *Multicultural education.* Belmont, CA: Wadsworth.

Bowman, B., M. Donovan, & M. Burns, eds. 2001. *Eager to learn: Educating our preschoolers.* A report of the National Research Council. Washington, DC: National Academy Press

Bransford, J., A. Brown, & R. Cocking, eds. 2000. *How people learn: Brain, mind, experience, and school.* A report of the National Research Council. Washington, DC: National Academy Press.

Brown, J.C., & L. Oates. *Books to grow on: African American literature for young children.* Brochure. Washington, DC: NAEYC.

CCBC (Cooperative Children's Book Center). 2003. Children's books by and about people of color published in the United States. Online: www. soemadison.wisc.edu/ccbc/ pcstats.htm.

Comer, J., & A. Poussaint. 1992. *Raising black children.* New York: Plume Book.

Darling-Hammond, L. 1997. *The right to learn.* San Francisco: Jossey-Bass.

Davis, O. 1998. The rhetoric of quilts: Creating identity in African-American children's literature. *African American Review* 32 (1): 67-76.

Delpit, L. 1995. *Other people's children.* New York: New Press.

Feelings, T. 1995. Illustration is my form, the Black experience, my story and my content. In *The all-White world of children's books and African American children's literature,* ed. O. Osa. Trenton, NJ: Africa World Press.

Hale, J. 1982. *Black children: Their roots, culture and learning styles.* Baltimore, MD: John Hopkins University Press.

Hale, J. 1991. The transmission of cultural values to young African American children. *Young Children* 46 (5): 7-15.

Haycock, K. 2001. Closing the achievement gap. *Educational Leadership* 58 (6): 6-11.

Johnson, D. 1990. *Telling tales: The pedagogy and promise of African American literature for youth.* New York: Greenwood.

Kozol, J. 1996. *Savage inequalities: Children in America's schools.* New York: Crown.

Ladson-Billings, G. 1994. *The dreamkeepers.* San Francisco: Jossey-Bass.

Larrick, N. 1995. The all-White world of children's books. In *The all-White world of children's books and African American children's literature,* ed. O. Osa. Trenton, NJ: Africa World Press.

Mikkelsen, N. 1998. Insiders, outsiders, and the question of authenticity: Who shall write for African American children? *African American Review* 32 (1): 33-49.

Osa, O. 1995. *African children's and youth literature.* New York: Twayne.

Roethler, J. 1998. Reading in color: Children's book illustrations and identity formation for Black children in the United States. *African American Review* 32 (1): 95-104.

Snow, C., M. Burns, & P. Griffin, eds. 1998. *Preventing reading difficulties in young children.* A report of the National Research Council. Washington, DC: National Academy Press.

Tolson, N. 1998. Making books available: The role of early libraries, librarians, and booksellers in the promotion of African American children's literature. *African American Review* 32 (1): 9-16.

Sally McClellan, PhD, is an associate professor of early childhood education at the University of South Carolina Aiken. Sally is also the director of the USCA Children's Center, the campus child care program.

M. Evelyn Fields, PhD, is an assistant professor of child development and director of the Head Start education program at South Carolina State University in Orangeburg. Evelyn focuses her research on the academic achievement of African American boys.

Effects of Running Records Assessment on Early Literacy Achievement

ABSTRACT Recent research on effective schools (e.g., Pressley et al., 2001) identified consistent associations between students' literacy achievement and teacher practice. In this study, the author extended those correlational findings by conducting a controlled experiment to test the claims about 1 practice recommended by recent effective schools research, systematic classroom assessment, represented here as the use of running records for planning instruction. Students in schools assigned to the running records treatment outperformed students in schools assigned to a near-treatment condition (action research). After controlling for prior school achievement and collective teacher efficacy, the running records intervention accounted for 12% of the between-school variance in reading and 7% in writing, confirming the correlational finding from effective schools research.

By John A. Ross
University of Toronto

Research on effective schools and teachers, which was in its heyday in the 1970s and 1980s, is resurging, particularly in the field of early literacy. The rich generalizations emerging from these correlational studies suggest a variety of instructional improvements that might plausibly contribute to higher student achievement. In this study, I examined the student achievement effects of one of the improvements, that is, the finding that teachers in effective schools are more likely than teachers in ordinary schools to use classroom assessments like running records to diagnose student needs and monitor progress. The intervention was assessed in a controlled experiment that involved all the schools with Grade 3 students in one school district.

Schools and Teachers With Effective Literacy Programs

In the 1970s and 1980s, researchers identified a cluster of practices (e.g., frequent monitoring of student progress) that consistently predicted higher levels of student literacy. That research described correlations between student achievement and school practices without providing any clues as to how effective schools became this way. It was not clear what consumers of the research should do with the results. Agents of school improvement overgeneralized the findings, transforming moderately positive correlations into one-on-one correspondences of teaching strategies with student outcomes. Training programs

that used transmission strategies to implement the findings (e.g., Hunter, 1982) produced mixed results at best (e.g., Azumi & Mitchel, 1989; Corbitt, 1989). Interest in the correlates of achievement tended to fade, although Doyle (1987) argued that lists of effective teaching techniques have value in that they act as stimulants for teacher reflection and as topics in teachers' professional discourses.

In the 1990s, researchers returned to the process–product paradigm with important changes in their approach: (a) Qualitative procedures involving relatively small samples of high-achieving and ordinary schools replaced large-scale quantitative studies; (b) data were interpreted within constructivist perspectives; (c) researchers described instructional practices in much greater detail and clustered these practices within broad models of teaching, drawing especially on balanced literacy models that combine skills development (e.g., decoding strategies) with authentic, integrated reading and writing activities. For example, Pressley et al. (2001) identified 103 behaviors that distinguished exemplary from average reading teachers in 15 paired comparisons of Grade 1 teachers. Pressley and colleagues further distinguished seven categories of action that distinguished the five best from the five poorest teachers.

Both the earlier era of effective schools research (reviewed in Hoffman, 1991) and the more recent instances highlight assessment practices as contributors to student achievement in reading and writing. In those studies, the key element is classroom assessment as opposed to external assessments. Pressley and colleagues (2001) found that the most effective teachers constructed running records (as described in Reading Recovery) during one-on-one reading. Taylor, Pearson, Clark, and Walpole (2000) found that of 14 schools studied, the moderately effective schools operated classroom-based assessment systems to monitor individual student progress and to shape instruction. Classroom-level performance results were shared with the principal and other teachers. The most effective schools reported in Taylor et al. shared assessment system data three to five times per year. Frequent classroom assessment also is a key feature in the effective literacy schools studied by the Maine Department of Education Center for Inquiry on Literacy (2000), Matsumura, Patthey-Chavez, Valdes, and Garnier (2002), Wharton-McDonald et al. (1997), and Wray, Medwell, Fox, and Poulson (2000).

Running Records

Among the many approaches to classroom assessment, running records are of particular interest. A *running record* is a literacy assessment technique that is formative; that is, it provides information that can be used to improve students' reading. When the teacher administers a running record, the student sits or stands beside him or her so that both can see the text. As the child reads, the teacher codes each word, reporting the percentage of words correctly read; the self-correction ratio (the ratio of errors + self-corrections divided by the number of self-corrections); and the categories of errors made (meaning, visual, or structure). After the reading, the student retells the story and answers questions about the story's meaning. A running record is successfully completed when the student has responded correctly to the questions about meaning and has read at 90–94% accuracy. The level of the passage read and the types of errors made by the student guide subsequent instruction (Clay, 1993).

Although running records are frequently used in research, there is little psychometric data available about the procedure. Evidence about reliability is mixed. For example, substantial discrepancies have been reported between the book levels measured by Reading Recovery teachers and those levels subsequently calculated for the same students by their regular classroom teachers using the same procedures (Chapman, Tunmer, & Prochnow, 2001: Glynn, Crooks, Bethune, Ballard, & Smith, 1989). Other researchers reported adequate test-retest reliability (Clay, 1993) or acceptable internal consistency (e.g., Pinnell, Lyons, DeFord, Bryk, & Seltzer, 1994). Validity evidence is abundant: running records correlate with other early literacy measures and discriminate among treatment conditions (e.g., Pinnell et al.). The consequential validity of running records (e.g., the extent to which the assessment procedure contributes to higher achievement) has not been addressed because the effects of the assessment have not been disentangled from the instructional treatments (such as reading recovery) in which the assessment is embedded.

Running records assessment is recommended by national curriculum authorities (e.g., in New Zealand; Limbrick, 1999) and is the method of choice of many specialist teachers. (Bean,

Cassidy, Grumet, Shelton, and Wallis [2002] found that 62% of the members of the International Reading Association who identified themselves as reading teachers used running records assessment.) Given the consistent evidence that the use of formative classroom assessment like running records distinguishes exemplary from ordinary teachers, can one assume that promotion of the technique will improve student achievement? Taylor and colleagues (2000) suggested caution, as follows:

> When all is said and done, we are examining natural correlations between program and teaching factors on the one hand and student performance on the other. These correlations … cannot be used to identify causes for improvements (or decrements) in student achievement. For that, more systematic experimentation is needed, including control groups, randomization, and careful analyses of growth over time. (p. 160)

The purpose of this study was to conduct a controlled experiment in which a sample of schools implemented running records as a strategy for aligning literacy instruction with students' need. I compared the provincial test scores of the running records schools to schools that implemented an alternative school improvement strategy (action research).

Nature of the Running Records Intervention

The running records treatment had two key components: teacher in-service and principal support. Teacher in-service consisted of six 60-min after-school workshops on ways for teachers to administer running records and use the information to focus instruction on individual student needs. Sessions were held at each school by literacy teachers (i.e., regular classroom teachers seconded for the in-service role). Procedures were demonstrated with videotapes of typical children and teachers practicing the running records procedure and comparing their assessments to those of the in-service leaders and teachers.

Previous research on attempts to change assessment practices (e.g., Briscoe, 1993) indicates that even highly motivated teachers provided with ample information on new assessment methods have difficulty implementing the change and may revert to their previous procedures (Briscoe). Black and Wiliam (1998), in a review of 250 studies of teachers' assessment practices published since 1988, found that teachers' use of assessment for formative purposes (i.e., to obtain information to modify instruction) was much less frequent than assessment for other purposes, most notably accountability. Changing assessment practices is difficult because assessment is tightly bound to deep-seated teacher beliefs about evidence, student motivation, and instructional effectiveness. To support teachers' use of running records, I worked with principals to create a collaborative culture of literacy assessment.

The in-service sessions for principals (3 sessions × 0.5 days) provided them with specific knowledge on literacy assessment (a demonstration of how to conduct a running record with opportunities to practice the technique) and information on how to support teacher change on the basis of a conception of transformational leadership (Bass, 1985; Bass & Avolio, 1994; Podsakoff, MacKenzie, Moorman, & Fetter, 1990). I defined *transformational leadership* as dedication to fostering the growth of organizational members and enhancing their commitment by elevating their goals (Burns, 1978). I followed the research reported by Leithwood, Jantzi, and Steinbach (1999) by recommending six dimensions of transformational leadership relevant to schools:

1. Symbolize good professional practice.
2. Provide individualized support.
3. Provide intellectual stimulation.
4. Hold high performance expectations.
5. Foster a vision.
6. Collaborate on decision making.

The in-service identified specific ways in which principals could apply each of these dimensions to the running records intervention. I adopted a transformational approach to leadership because the district was committed to the approach and because of evidence of the effects of transformational leadership on student achievement (Verona & Young, 2001) and on organizational learning, effectiveness, and culture (Leithwood et al.; Ross & Gray, 2003). Organizational theorists attribute these effects to social identification, which enables followers to transcend their self-interests for the good of the group (Bass, 1985; Bass & Avolio, 1994; Leithwood, 1993; Walumbwa, Wang, & Lawler, 2003).

The specific actions taken by principals in the project were to identify at least two teachers who would contribute classroom data for the project, secure resources (e.g., purchase leveled reading materials), facilitate teacher access to the in-service, coordinate the data collection in the school (two rounds of running records), and reflect on the results. Principals were encouraged to devise their own strategies for sampling their teachers, for example, selecting teachers who provided leadership in literacy teaching in their school or teachers who might particularly benefit from close interaction with the principal on literacy teaching.

Each teacher selected a sample of students (usually 5) for whom running records data would be submitted. Teachers used two broad selection strategies: a representative sample of students in the class or the 5 neediest children who did not qualify for the district's early literacy intervention. Principals were encouraged to involve all their teachers in the project, and virtually all teachers in all schools attended the in-service activities. Teachers administered running records to the student sample on two occasions, before and after the focused reading intervention. The assessments were 6–8 weeks apart. Principals collected summaries of the running records administered by teachers in the sample and submitted them to university faculty to analyze the data on behalf of the district. Each school received a report from the faculty, which was confidential to the school, and which summarized each school's results and outlined the pre-/postdifferences across the district. There was no school ranking, and the reports urged schools not to compare their results to the district as a whole because the sampling procedure was not standardized. Principals discussed the results with their teachers and with other principals in their family of school groups.

Research Hypothesis

I predicted that schools assigned to the running records treatment would have higher student achievement in reading and writing than would schools assigned to an alternative treatment. I designed a controlled experiment in which schools were assigned randomly to two school improvement strategies. To ensure a fair comparison, I used scores from the mandated provincial assessment as the dependent variables and included in the comparison prior school achievement and a school variable, collective teacher efficacy, which is a powerful predictor of achievement. I also tested the credibility of the claim that the running records intervention had an achievement effect by examining an alternative explanation for any differences that might appear.

Method

Sample

Supervisory officers in a single Ontario, Canada, school district randomly assigned schools in their areas to two treatments: running records and action research. Violations of randomness occurred when a few principals persuaded their supervisor to place them in a different treatment condition than the one to which they had been assigned. Schools were included in this study if (a) they submitted a summary of their project to the collection of action research reports published in June, 2002 (Hannay, Telford, & Bray, 2002) or submitted running records data to the running records treatment database compiled at the same time (Ross & Hogaboam, 2002), (b) they had students who wrote the Grade 3 reading and writing assessments in May 2002, and (c) their teachers completed a survey measuring collective teacher efficacy in May 2002. Seventy-three of the 75 K–6/8 schools in the district met the criteria, which produced a sample consisting of 39 running records schools and 34 action research schools. Of the 2,800 students in the study, 3% were classified as English-as-a-second-language students, 20% were receiving special education support, and 6% were exempted from the provincial assessment. The mean family income of the district was $35,040. No data were available on racial distribution.

Sources of Data

Student achievement consisted of school scores for Grade 3 reading, writing, and mathematics collected in May 2001 (prior achievement, a covariate) and 2002 (achievement, the dependent variable). The assessment was administered by teachers who followed directions from an independent testing organization for 2 hr per day for 5 days. Reported for each school were the percentages of students who met the provincial standard of Level 3 or 4 on the basis of the global score for Method I (all students included). The global score was calculated by the testing agency that combined the raw scores for the performance assessment and the multiple-choice items with a correction factor to equate scores from 1 year to the next (Education Quality and Accountability Office, n.d.).

Collective teacher efficacy (i.e., teachers' belief that the teachers in their school constitute an effective instructional team) was included as an additional covariate because it is a strong predictor of school achievement (Bandura, 1993; Goddard, 2001, 2002; Goddard & Goddard, 2001; Goddard, Hoy, & Hoy, 2000; Goddard, Hoy, & LoGerfo, 2003). It consisted of 14 items that reflected two dimensions of collective teacher efficacy: the seven items with the highest loading on the perceptions of the task factor (e.g., "Drug and alcohol abuse in the community make learning difficult for students here") and the seven items with the highest loading on the perceptions of teaching competence factor (e.g., "Teachers in this school really believe every child can learn"), reported by Goddard et al. (2000). Although the two-factor structure of the variable was maintained for face validity reasons, the two factors were highly correlated and, as in previous research, I combined the items into single scale. The items were in a 6-point, Likert-type scale anchored by *strongly disagree* and *strongly agree*.

Experimental Conditions

The running records treatment was as described in the previous paragraphs. In the action research treatment, principals, in collaboration with a team of teachers, identified a professional issue related to early literacy to work on, devised improvement activities, implemented the action plans, and reflected on and reported the results. There were four in-service sessions for principals (1 full day and 3 half days) in the action research treatment. In each session, principals met with peers from the same family of schools, except that in the third session they attended with three to four teachers who were on their school improvement team. The in-service worked through a multiphase process that consisted of (a) identifying a measurable goal, (b) designing action plans, (c) collecting and analyzing data on the effects of the intervention, and (d) reflecting on the results. Teachers in the action research treatment had access to the same set of teacher in-service sessions as the teachers in the running records schools and had the same budget for purchasing early literacy resources.

The specific projects undertaken in the action research schools varied across sites. For example, one school developed the action research question, "How can we use response journals to improve the communication strand of literacy?" Teachers implemented response journals along with the 3 R's strategy (retell, relate, reflect). A systematic sample (every 5th student) was drawn from each K–3 class for the school's data collection. Teachers used the rubric of the provincial testing organization and provincial exemplars to assess one piece of student writing at the beginning of the project and a second piece produced 6 weeks later. Other schools concentrated on questions less directly focused on early literacy, for example, "Are students transferring their knowledge about writing to mathematics?" The school improvement strategy consisted of holding mathematics workshops for all teachers and providing a collection of readings. Teachers were asked to select and try out a strategy and report the results to a staff meeting. Teachers also identified 1 student in each class at each of four levels of performance and had those students complete a mathematics performance assessment that was marked by the principal and

vice-principal who used the provincial mathematics rubric (which contained a dimension referring to communication of mathematical ideas).

Analysis Procedures

We used the General Linear Model program of SPSS to conduct a multivariate analysis of covariance. The dependent variables were the percentages of students in each school who met the provincial standard (Level 3 or better) in reading and writing in 2002. Two predictors of achievement, prior achievement and collective teacher efficacy, were included as covariates. The independent variable was assignment to the action research or running records treatment. The unit of analysis was the school. As a further test of our hypothesis, I also examined whether there were any treatment differences in 2002 mathematics achievement, controlling for prior mathematics achievement and collective teacher efficacy. If I were to find achievement differences in mathematics as well as in literacy, that might suggest that some factor other than the running records treatment was contributing to the differences between the two groups of schools.

Results

Table 1 shows the means and standard deviations for both groups of schools for each of the 2 years for all three subjects. Despite the violations to randomization during the sample assignment procedure, there were no significant differences between the two groups of schools in prior achievement in reading, $t(71) = .934$, $p = .354$, writing, $t(71) = -.027$, $p = .978$, or mathematics, $t(71) = 1.796$, $p = .077$. There also were no differences in collective teacher efficacy, $t(71) = -.821$, $p = .415$.

Reading and writing scores were correlated highly within years ($r = .79$. $N = 73$, $p < .01$ in 2001 and $r = .74$ in 2002), suggesting that a multivariate analysis was more appropriate than was analyzing the effects of treatment assignment separately for each subject. The correlations were lower within subjects between years: $r = .48$ for reading and $r = .56$ for writing but were statistically significant, suggesting that 2001 scores should be used as covariates in the analysis. (The correlation matrix for all the variables in the study is shown in Table 2.)

Because 2001 reading and 2001 writing were highly correlated ($r = .79$), I anticipated that only one of these variables would be a significant predictor of 2002 scores. The correlations of 2001 writing with 2002 achievement were slightly stronger than the correlations of 2001 reading with 2002 achievement, therefore, I anticipated that 2001 writing would enter the equation first and take all the variance shared by the two covariates. Preliminary analysis (not reported) indicated that this was the case: 2001 writing but not 2001 reading was a significant predictor of 2002 reading and writing achievement. I used only 2001 writing as a covariate in the analysis to avoid wasting a degree of freedom.

The multivariate test with reading and writing combined explained 56.5% of the variance in achievement. Student achievement in 2002 was influenced significantly by prior achievement in writing, $F(2, 68) = 15.05$, $p < .001$, $\eta^2 = .307$, by collective

TABLE 1. Percentage of Students Meeting the Provincial Early Literacy Standard by Subject, Condition, and Year

	2001		2002	
Variable/condition	M	SD	M	SD
Reading				
Assessment	48.44	16.37	52.70	17.73
Action research	45.03	14.56	42.60	18.55
Writing				
Assessment	48.67	16.56	53.48	15.83
Action research	48.76	14.00	47.66	12.98
Mathematics				
Assessment	61.03	16.50	48.85	20.50
Action research	53.38	19.85	58.95	20.64
Collective teacher efficacy				
Assessment	NA	NA	4.63	.34
Action research	NA	NA	4.70	.38

Note. Assessment condition is $n = 39$; action research condition is $n = 34$.

TABLE 2. Correlation Matrix of Study Variables ($N = 73$ Schools)

Variable/year	Reading (2001)	Reading (2002)	Writing (2001)	Writing (2002)	Mathematics (2001)	Mathematics (2002)
Reading (2001)	—					
Reading (2002)	.48***	—				
Writing (2001)	.79***	.51***	—			
Writing (2002)	.47**	.74***	.56***	—		
Mathematics (2001)	.89***	.52***	.75***	.45***	—	
Mathematics (2002)	.47***	.87***	.51***	.67***	.52***	—
CTE	.08	.33*	.27*	.36**	.17	.30*

Note. CTE = Collective teacher efficacy.
* $p < .05$.   ** $p < .01$.   *** $p < .001$.

teacher efficacy, $F(2, 68) = 3.75$, $p = .028$, $\eta^2 = .099$, and by treatment, $F(2, 68) = 4.827$. $p = .011$, $\eta^2 = .124$.

Table 3 shows the univariate effects. The results were virtually the same for reading and writing. Collective teacher efficacy and prior achievement were each significant predictors of 2002 achievement. Table 3 shows that after the effects of the covariates were removed, treatment had a significant effect on 2002 student achievement. Students from schools participating in the running records treatment outperformed students from schools participating in action research. There was a large effect for reading (12% of the variance) and a medium effect for writing (7% of the variance), with Cohen's (1988) rules for interpreting effect sizes.

I examined the effects of treatment on mathematics achievement because, if I found treatment differences in achievement for another subject, that would suggest that there was something other than or in addition to the literacy activities contributing to the changes in reading and writing scores. I found that 2002 mathematics achievement was influenced significantly by mathematics, $F(1, 69) = 19.540$, $p < .001$, $\eta^2 = .22$, and by col-

lective teacher efficacy, $F(1, 69) = 5.563$, $p = .021$, $\eta^2 = .075$, but there were no treatment effects, $F(1, 69) = 2.864$, p = .095, $\eta^2 = .040$. A further test of alternative explanations would be to examine changes in school processes, but I had only 1 year of data. I determined that there were no significant differences between the groups of schools in collective teacher efficacy in 2002, $t(71) = -.821$, $p = .415$, but I had no way of knowing whether the two groups were equivalent prior to the assignment.

The results indicated that participation in the running records treatment had a greater positive effect on achievement in reading and writing than did participation in the action research condition. Table 4 shows the district-province achievement gap. The achievement gap was obtained by subtracting the percentage of district students at the provincial standard from the percentage of district students who reached that standard in the province as a whole. The provincial average for 2002 (50% in reading and 56% in writing) was used for both years to facilitate comparisons. The table shows that the 39 schools that were in the running records treatment were below the provincial average in 2001 in reading and writing. In 2002, the same schools

TABLE 3. Effects of Condition Assignment on Grade 3 Reading and Writing, Controlling for Prior Achievement and Collective Teacher Efficacy: Univariate Effects

Source	Subject	Significance test	Partial η^2
Corrected model	Reading	$F(3, 69) = 14.222, p < .001$	.382
	Writing	$F(3, 69) = 16.009, p < .001$	.410
Intercept	Reading	$F(1, 72) = 2.490, p = .119$	.035
	Writing	$F(1, 72) = 1.168, p = .284$	.017
Collective teacher efficacy	Reading	$F(1, 72) = 5.598, p = .021$	.075
	Writing	$F(1, 72) = 6.398, p = .014$	.085
Writing 2001	Reading	$F(1, 72) = 20.786, p < .001$	.232
	Writing	$F(1, 72) = 26.915, p < .001$	.281
Experimental condition	Reading	$F(1, 72) = 7.163, p = .009$	.092
	Writing	$F(1, 72) = 4.314, p = .041$	.057

TABLE 4. District–Province Achievement Gap in Percentages, by Treatment Condition and Year

	Achievement gap	
Subject/condition	2001	2002
Reading		
Assessment	−2.17	+2.7
Action research	−4.94	−7.40
Writing		
Assessment	−8.10	−2.52
Action research	−6.97	−8.34

Note. Assessment condition is $n = 39$: action research condition is $n = 34$.

exceeded the provincial average in reading and had reduced the gap in writing by two thirds. The 34 action research schools also were below the provincial average in both subjects in 2001. However, those schools fell further behind the province in reading and writing in 2002.

Discussion

The main contribution of this study is that it confirmed, in a controlled experiment, a key correlational finding from recent qualitative research that compared high-achieving literacy sites to ordinary schools. The effective schools studies consistently reported positive associations between high student literacy and engagement in systematic classroom assessment procedures, particularly running records (Maine Department of Education Center for Inquiry on Literacy, 2000; Matsumura et al., 2002: Pressley et al., 2001; Taylor et al., 2000; Wharton-McDonald et al., 1997; Wray et al., 2000). In a correlational study, causality cannot be demonstrated. Researchers have no way of knowing whether (a) particular assessment practices lead to achievement, (b) achievement encourages certain kinds of assessment, (c) achievement and assessment are the products of some other factor, or (d) assessment and achievement are substantively related. In this study, schools that were assigned to the running

records treatment improved their reading and writing achievement and outperformed schools from the same district assigned to a near-treatment condition. Because I manipulated the conditions to which schools were assigned, the controlled experimentation greatly strengthened the credibility of the claim that schools that implement systematic classroom assessment will have higher literacy achievement.

The validity of the causal argument is enhanced by methodological features of the study: (a) demonstration that schools were equivalent on relevant variables prior to the intervention, (b) selection of the school as the unit of analysis, (c) use of appropriate covariates identified in previous research as predictors of achievement, (d) use of multivariate procedures to avoid inflating Type I error, (e) search for disconfirming evidence by testing for effects on mathematics, (f) use of a near-treatment alternative rather than a no-treatment control as the comparison group, (g) 6-week duration of the study, and (h) use of an external assessment for the criterion variables. The study met all of Slavin's (1987) requirements for inclusion of a study in a best-evidence synthesis.

All of the action research projects gave explicit attention to the measurement of the effects of project activities, and several action research projects contained substantial student assessment elements that appeared to be similar to measurement in the running records treatment. For example, in many of the action research projects, teachers applied provincial assessment rubrics to student writing. But those rubrics simply classified student writing—they did not provide specific strategies for moving students from one level to another. In contrast, the running records treatment met the four criteria identified by Black and Wiliam (1998) for an effective feedback system: Running records provided (a) data on the actual level of a measurable attribute (book level accurately read), (b) reference level of the attribute (there were 30 book levels), (c) mechanisms for comparing actual performance to a meaningful scale and generating information about the nature of the gap (First Steps continuum; Department of Education, Commonwealth of Australia, 2003) related running records data to specific reading competencies, and (d) mechanism by which the information could be used to alter the gap (identification of appropriate books for the child to read and specific reading skills to be learned).

The plans of the running records schools were focused on a relatively narrow set of assessment and instructional activities. The narrow focus contrasts with the content of Ontario school improvement plans reviewed by Nagy (2000). Plans for improving scores on provincial assessments were required of all schools. Nagy found that large-scale assessments provide general indicators of success that result in generalized action plans, which could easily be developed without reference to assessment data. At the other end of the scale, Mintrop and MacLellan (2002), in a review of Maryland schools placed on probation, found that school improvement plans were overwhelmed by minutiae—the average school listed 50 activities for the year. Most of the planned activities were incremental adjustments to existing school practices that skirted substantive change. The running records treatment avoided the overly general and excessively particular school practices. It focused teacher attention on a specific assessment procedure that accessed an elaborate but feasible approach to literacy instruction.

Limitations

In this study, the running records intervention was well aligned with the actions of other agents. The goal of improving literacy matched the priorities of the province, the provincial assessment agency, the district, and the teachers. Of particular importance was the leadership role of the principal in coordinating assessment activities in the school, including the data that the school submitted to the district. The effective schools literature of the 1970s and 1980s highlighted the role of the principal in setting high expectations and holding staff accountable for meeting them; that is, it promoted transactional leadership practices. In this study, principals were encouraged to adopt a transformational style—they attempted to develop the capacity of their staff, transforming the culture of the school. In this study, I did not measure variations in principal actions, so I could not determine how much of the impact of the running records treatment was dependent on principal actions. The amount of the impact could have been considerable because in previous research I found that transformational leadership contributed to collective teacher efficacy and to teacher commitment to professional norms (Ross & Gray, 2003), factors that were likely to have increased student achievement.

Another limitation of this study is that randomization procedures were violated in some cases by principals who petitioned their superintendent to place them in a different condition than the one to which they were assigned. I believe that these violations were few in number; I demonstrated that the groups were equivalent on two measures (prior achievement and collective teacher efficacy) that predict achievement; and I included both measures as covariates in the analysis.

Conclusions

The school effectiveness literature of the 1970s and 1980s identified correlates of achievement that were robust across

subjects, neighborhoods, and levels of schooling (see e.g., Reynolds & Teddlie, 2000). The production of this knowledge did not lead to improved schools because the research did not translate the correlates into feasible interventions and did not address the conditions that needed to be in place for instructional improvement to occur. This study suggests that the new wave of school effectiveness research is likely to be more useful because it identifies through qualitative investigations specific behaviors occurring in naturalistic settings. This specificity enables school improvement researchers to construct ecologically valid interventions to test the external validity of particular findings. In this study, implementation of running records, a classroom assessment system, contributed to higher achievement in reading and writing, as predicted by effective schools research. An essential element of the intervention was a support system for teachers developed in collaboration with principals working from a transformational leadership stance and coordination of their actions with other change agents. Because of the results of this study, I am optimistic that weaving the findings of school effectiveness research into viable change processes will lead to those kinds of improvements in achievement that motivated effective schools researchers, funding agencies, and practitioners.

NOTES

This research was funded by the Social Sciences and Humanities Research Council of Canada and the Ontario Ministry of Education and Training. The views expressed in the report do not necessarily agree with those of the council or ministry.

Peter Gray contributed to the data analysis.

An earlier version of this article was presented at the annual meeting of the American Educational Research Association, April 2004, in San Diego, California.

REFERENCES

Azumi, J., & Mitchel, L. (1989, April). *The impact of a district-wide staff development project on the attitudes and behaviors of teachers.* Paper presented at the annual meeting of the American Educational Research Association, San Francisco, CA.

Bandura, A. (1993). Perceived self-efficacy in cognitive development and functioning. *Educational Psychologist, 28*(2), 117-148.

Bass, B. (1985). *Leadership and performance beyond expectations.* New York: The Free Press.

Bass, B. M., & Avolio, B. J. (1994). *Improving organizational effectiveness through transformational leadership.* Thousand Oaks. CA: Sage.

Bean, R. M., Cassidy, J., Grumet, J. E., Shelton. D. S., & Wallis. S. R. (2002). What do reading specialists do? Results from a national survey. *The Reading Teacher. 55*(8), 736-744.

Black, P., & Wiliam, D. (1998). Assessment and classroom learning. *Assessment in Education, Principles, Policies & Practices, 5*(1), 7-74.

Briscoe, C. (1993). Using cognitive referents in making sense of teaching: A chemistry teacher's struggle to change assessment practices. *Journal of Research in Science Teaching, 30*(8), 971-987.

Burns, J. M. (1978). *Leadership.* New York: Harper & Row.

Chapman. J. W., Tunmer, W. E., & Prochnow, J. E. (2001). Does success in the Reading Recovery program depend on developing proficiency in phonological-processing skills? A longitudinal study in a whole language instructional context. *Scientific Studies of Reading, 5*(2), 141-176.

Clay, M. M. (1993). *An observation survey of early literacy achievement*. Auckland. New Zealand: Heinemann.

Cohen, J. (1988). *Statistical power analysis for the behavioral sciences* (2nd ed.). Hillsdale, NJ: Erlbaum.

Corbitt, E. (1989, April). *The three R's of staff development: Reality, relevance, and relationships*. Paper presented at the annual convention of the Council for Exceptional Children. San Francisco, CA.

Department of Education, Commonwealth of Australia. (2003). *First Steps Reading Developmental Continuum*. Retrieved June 26, 2003, from http://www.myread.org/monitoring-first.htm

Doyle, W. (1987). Research on teaching effects as a resource for improving instruction. In M. Wideen & I. Andrews (Eds.), *Staff development for school improvement: A focus on the teacher*. New York: Falmer.

Education Quality and Accountability Office. (n.d.). *Explanatory paper: Grades 3 and 6 assessment of reading, writing, and mathematics, 1999-2000*. Retrieved June 18, 2003, from http://wwv.eqao.com/eqao/home_page/pdf_e/00/00P063e.pdf

Glynn, T., Crooks. T., Bethune, N., Ballard, K., & Smith, J. (1989). *Reading recovery in context*. Wellington: New Zealand Department of Education.

Goddard, R. D. (2001). Collective efficacy: A neglected construct in the study of schools and student achievement. *Journal of Educational Psychology 93*(3), 467-476.

Goddard, R. D. (2002). A theoretical and empirical analysis of the measurement of collective efficacy: The development of a short form. *Educational and Psychological Measurement, 62*(1), 97-110.

Goddard, R. D., & Goddard, Y. L. (2001). A multilevel analysis of the relationship between teacher and collective efficacy in urban schools. *Teaching and Teacher Education, 17*, 807-818.

Goddard, R. D., Hoy, W. K., & Hoy, A. W. (2000). Collective teacher efficacy: Its meaning, measure, and impact on student achievement. *American Education Research Journal, 37*(2), 479-507.

Goddard, R. D., Hoy, W. K., & LoGerfo, L. (2003, April). *Collective teacher efficacy and student achievement in public high schools: A path analysis*. Paper presented at the annual meeting of the American Educational Research Association, Chicago.

Hannay, L., Telford, C., & Bray, C. (2002). *Aligning school-district actions to promote school improvement and accountability*. Kitchener, Ontario, Canada: OISE/UT Trent Valley Centre.

Hoffman, J. V. (1991). Teacher and school effects in learning to read. In R. Barr, M. L. Kamil, P. B. Mosenthal, & P. D. Pearson (Eds.), *Handbook of reading research* (Vol. 2, pp. 911-950). New York: Longman.

Hunter, M. (1982). *Mastery teaching*. El Segundo. CA: TIP Publications.

Leithwood, K. A. (1993, October). *Contributions of transformational leadership to school restructuring*. Paper presented at the Convention of the University Council for Educational Administration, Houston, TX.

Leithwood, K. A., Jantzi, D., & Steinbach, R. (1999). *Changing leadership for changing times*. Buckingham, England: Open University Press.

Limbrick, L. (1999, September). *The literacy debates: What are the issues in New Zealand?* Paper presented at the British Educational Research Association, Brighton, UK.

Maine Department of Education Center for Inquiry on Literacy. (2000). *A solid foundation: Supportive contexts for early literacy programs in Maine schools*. Augusta, ME: Author. (ERIC Document Reproduction Services No. ED458537)

Matsumura, L. C., Patthey-Chavez, G. G., Valdes, R., & Garnier, H. (2002). Teacher feedback, writing assignment quality, and third-grade students' revision in lower- and higher-achieving urban schools. *Elementary School Journal, 103*(1), 3-26.

Mintrop, H., & MacLellan, A. M. (2002). School improvement plans in elementary and middle schools on probation. *Elementary School Journal, 102*(4), 275-300.

Nagy, P. (2000). The three roles of assessment: Gate keeping, accountability, and instructional diagnosis. *Canadian Journal of Education, 25*(4), 262-279.

Pinnell, G. S., Lyons. C. A., DeFord, D. E., Bryk, A. S., & Seltzer, M. (19941). Comparing instructional models for the literacy education of high-risk first graders. *Reading Research Quarterly 29*(1), 9-39.

Podsakoff, P., MacKenzie, S., Moorman, R., & Fetter, R. (1990). Transformational leaders' behaviors and their effects on followers' trust in leader, satisfaction, and organizational citizenship behaviors. *Leadership Quarterly 1*(2), 107-142.

Pressley, M., Wharton-McDonald, R., Allington, R., Block, C. C., Morrow, L., Tracey, D. et al. (2001). A study of effective first-grade literacy instruction. *Scientific Studies of Reading, 5*(1), 35-58.

Reynolds, D., & Teddlie, C. (2000). The future agenda for school effectiveness research. In C. Teddlie & D. Reynolds (Eds.), *The international handbook of school effectiveness research* (pp. 322-343). London: Falmer.

Ross, J. A., & Gray, P.(2003) *Transformational leadership and teacher commitment to organizational values: The mediating effects of collective teacher efficacy*. Peterborough, Ontario, Canada: OISE/UT Trent Valley Centre.

Ross, J. A., & Hogaboam-Gray, A. (2002). *School improvement capacity building in Kawartha Pine Ridge DSB: 2002 quantitative report*. Peterborough, Ontario, Canada: OISE/UTT Trent Valley Centre.

Slavin, R. E. (1987). Best-evidence synthesis: Why less is more. *Educational Researcher 16*(4), 15-16.

Taylor, B. M., Pearson, P. D., Clark, K., & Walpole, S. (2000). Effective schools and accomplished teachers: Lessons about primary-grade reading instruction in low-income schools. *Elementary School Journal, 101*(2), 121-166.

Verona, G. S., & Young, J. W. (2001, April). *The influence of principal transformational leadership style on High School Proficiency Test results in New Jersey comprehensive and vocational-technical high schools*. Paper presented at the annual meeting of the American Educational Research Association. Seattle, WA.

Walumbwa, F. O., Wang, P., & Lawler, J. J. (2003) *Exploring new frontiers: The role of collective efficacy in the relations between transformational leadership and work-related attitudes*. Retrieved May 6, 2003, from http://cobacourses.creighton.edu//MAM/2003/papers/walumba.doc

Wharton-McDonald, R., Pressley, M., Rankin, J., Mistretta, J., Yokoi, L., & Ettenberger, S. (1997). Effective primary-grades literacy instruction = Balanced literacy instruction. *The Reading Teacher 50*(6), 518-521.

Wray, D., Medwell. J., Fox, R., & Poulson, L. (2000). The teaching practices of effective teachers of literacy. *Educational Review, 52*(1), 75-84.

Address correspondence to John A. Ross, OISE/UT Trent Valley Centre, Box 719, Peterborough, ON K9J 7A1. (E-mail: jross@oise.utoronto.ca)

From *Journal of Educational Research*, March/April 2004, pp. 186-194. Reprinted by permission of the Helen Dwight Reid Educational Foundation. Published by Heldref Publications, 1319, Eighteenth St., NW, Washington, DC 20036-1802. Copyright © 2004.

Index

Index

Test Your Knowledge Form

We encourage you to photocopy and use this page as a tool to assess how the articles in *Annual Editions* expand on the information in your textbook. By reflecting on the articles you will gain enhanced text information. You can also access this useful form on a product's book support Web site at *http://www.dushkin.com/online/*.

NAME: DATE:

_____

TITLE AND NUMBER OF ARTICLE:

_____

BRIEFLY STATE THE MAIN IDEA OF THIS ARTICLE:

_____

LIST THREE IMPORTANT FACTS THAT THE AUTHOR USES TO SUPPORT THE MAIN IDEA:

_____

WHAT INFORMATION OR IDEAS DISCUSSED IN THIS ARTICLE ARE ALSO DISCUSSED IN YOUR TEXTBOOK OR OTHER READINGS THAT YOU HAVE DONE? LIST THE TEXTBOOK CHAPTERS AND PAGE NUMBERS:

_____

LIST ANY EXAMPLES OF BIAS OR FAULTY REASONING THAT YOU FOUND IN THE ARTICLE:

_____

LIST ANY NEW TERMS/CONCEPTS THAT WERE DISCUSSED IN THE ARTICLE, AND WRITE A SHORT DEFINITION:

We Want Your Advice

ANNUAL EDITIONS revisions depend on two major opinion sources: one is our Advisory Board, listed in the front of this volume, which works with us in scanning the thousands of articles published in the public press each year; the other is you—the person actually using the book. Please help us and the users of the next edition by completing the prepaid article rating form on this page and returning it to us. Thank you for your help!

ANNUAL EDITIONS: Early Childhood and Elementary Literacy 05/06

ARTICLE RATING FORM

Here is an opportunity for you to have direct input into the next revision of this volume.
We would like you to rate each of the articles listed below, using the following scale:

1. **Excellent: should definitely be retained**
2. **Above average: should probably be retained**
3. **Below average: should probably be deleted**
4. **Poor: should definitely be deleted**

Your ratings will play a vital part in the next revision.
Please mail this prepaid form to us as soon as possible.
Thanks for your help!

RATING	ARTICLE	RATING	ARTICLE
	1. Learning to Read and Write: Developmentally Appropriate Practices for Young Children		22. Using Centers to Engage Children During Guided Reading Time: Intensifying Learning Experiences Away From the Teacher
	2. Early Literacy Instruction in the Climate of No Child Left Behind		23. Digging Up the Past, Building the Future: Using Book Authoring to Discover and Showcase a Community's History
	3. Literacy, Learning, and Libraries: Common Issues and Common Concerns		24. Teaching Expository Text Structures Through Information Trade Book Retellings
	4. Public Libraries and Early Literacy: Raising a Reader		25. Mathematics Trade Books: Establishing Their Value and Assessing Their Quality
	5. "The Best Way is Always Through the Children": The Impact of Family Reading		26. It's As Easy As A-B-C and Do-Re-Mi: Music, Rhythm, and Rhyme Enhance Children's Literacy Skills
	6. Enhancing Phonological Awareness, Print Awareness, and Oral Language Skills in Preschool Children		27. Reggio Emilia: New Ways to Think About Schooling
	7. Parent Involvement in Children's Acquisition of Reading		28. Promoting Creativity for Life Using Open-Ended Materials
	8. Beyond Shared Book Reading: Dimensions of Home Literacy and Low-Income African American Preschoolers' Skills		29. Young Children Try, Try Again: Using Wood, Glue, and Words to Enhance Learning
	9. Family Literacy: Perspective and Practices		30. Responding to Linguistic and Cultural Diversity Recommendations for Effective Early Childhood Education
	10. The Role of Child Development and Social Interaction in the Selection of Children's Literature to Promote Literacy Acquisition		31. Not Made for Defeat
	11. The Many Rewards of a Literacy-Rich Classroom		32. Vygotsky and the Blues: Re-Reading Cultural Connections and Conceptual Development
	12. Building Walls of Words		33. Early Literacy Practices as Predictors of Reading Related Outcomes: Test Scores, Test Passing Rates, Retention, and Special Education Referral
	13. Phonemic Awareness: A Crucial Bridge to Reading		
	14. False Claims About Literacy Development		34. Using African American Children's Literature to Support Literacy Development
	15. Matching Texts and Readers: Leveling Early Reading Materials For Assessment and Instruction		35. Effects of Running Records Assessment on Early Literacy Achievement
	16. Guided Reading: Who is in the Driver's Seat?		
	17. The Essentials of Early Literacy Instruction		
	18. Just Think of the Possibilities: Formats for Reading Instruction in the Elementary Classroom		
	19. Our Students are Ready For This: Comprehension Instruction in the Elementary School		
	20. A Comprehension Checklist: What if it Doesn't Make Sense?		
	21. How Do You Know? A Strategy to Help Emergent Readers Make Inferences		

(Continued on next page)

ANNUAL EDITIONS: EARLY CHILDHOOD AND
ELEMENTARY LITERACY 05/06

ABOUT YOU

Name   Date

Are you a teacher? ☐   A student? ☐
Your school's name

Department

Address   City   State   Zip

School telephone #

YOUR COMMENTS ARE IMPORTANT TO US!

Please fill in the following information:
For which course did you use this book?

Did you use a text with this ANNUAL EDITION? ☐ yes ☐ no
What was the title of the text?

What are your general reactions to the *Annual Editions* concept?

Have you read any pertinent articles recently that you think should be included in the next edition? Explain.

Are there any articles that you feel should be replaced in the next edition? Why?

Are there any World Wide Web sites that you feel should be included in the next edition? Please annotate.

May we contact you for editorial input? ☐ yes ☐ no
May we quote your comments? ☐ yes ☐ no